Composing the World

Critical Conjunctures in

Music & Sound

Series Editors Jairo Moreno and Gavin Steingo

Composing the World: Harmony in the Medieval Platonic Cosmos, Andrew Hicks

Composing the World

Harmony in the Medieval Platonic Cosmos

ANDREW HICKS

OXFORD
UNIVERSITY PRESS

OXFORD
UNIVERSITY PRESS

Oxford University Press is a department of the University of Oxford. It furthers the University's objective of excellence in research, scholarship, and education by publishing worldwide. Oxford is a registered trade mark of Oxford University Press in the UK and certain other countries.

Published in the United States of America by Oxford University Press
198 Madison Avenue, New York, NY 10016, United States of America.

Library of Congress Cataloging-in-Publication Data
Names: Hicks, Andrew J. (Andrew James), 1978–
Title: Composing the world: harmony in the Medieval Platonic cosmos/
Andrew Hicks.
Description: New York, NY: Oxford University Press, [2017] |
Includes bibliographical references and index.
Identifiers: LCCN 2016028438 | ISBN 9780190658205 (hardcover: alk. paper) |
ISBN 9780190658229 (epub)
Subjects: LCSH: Music—Philosophy and aesthetics—History—500-1400. |
Harmony of the spheres.
Classification: LCC ML172.H53 2017 | DDC 780/.0113?dc23 LC record available at
https://lccn.loc.gov/2016028438

1 3 5 7 9 8 6 4 2

Printed by Sheridan Books, Inc., United States of America

Meo magistro et amico, Eduardo Jeauneau, seni Carnotensi et opulentissimo grammatico post Guillelmum de Conchis.

CONTENTS

SERIES EDITORS' FOREWORD

Critical Conjunctures in Music and Sound offers a space from which to engage urgent questions currently animating the humanities from the perspectives of music, sound, and listening. Tied together by a common epistemological attitude, the books in this series reconstitute the place of scholarship in response to a world rapidly transforming under economic and technological integration, on the one hand, and political and social disintegration, on the other. Authors articulate new musical and sonic relations to the composition of the political, the social, and the economic, while developing new ways to analyze music's ever-shifting associations with aurality, human/nonhuman divides, materiality, nature, and ontology. These relations and associations in turn provoke new questions about the past, and a reassessment of our historical and ethnographic priorities—both empirical and speculative. The series urges philosophical and theoretical critique to mediate and question the relationship of music studies to other forms of knowledge production. What it proposes, therefore, is a form of conjunctural analysis that does not foreclose in advance how sound, music, and other forces are or have been articulated together. "Conjuncture" captures the immediate and mobile sets of circumstances determining the present, which authors engage by challenging theoretical categories and forms from a variety of disciplinary, historical, or geographical homes.

Jairo Moreno and Gavin Steingo

ACKNOWLEDGMENTS

Many *demiourgoi* had a hand in the creation of this world of words, whose cosmogony spanned three institutions. At the Eastman School of Music, where its first seeds were sown, I thank in the first instance Gabriela Currie (now at the University of Minnesota), who has seen this project through every stage of its development, as well as Patrick Macey, Martin Scherzinger, and Roger Freitas, who accepted and fostered my peculiar brand of musicology. At the Centre for Medieval Studies, University of Toronto, I thank John Magee and Peter King, who expertly advised the doctoral work that grew into the larger project that fills these pages; A. G. Rigg, who patiently read with me many of the Latin texts that populate its pages; Brad Inwood, who generously accepted me as an interloper in the Collaborative Programme in Ancient and Medieval Philosophy, whose Greek and Latin reading groups and seminars exemplified the patient analysis of ancient and medieval texts; and Fr. Édouard Jeauneau, whose mentorship, guidance, and friendship has made this book possible. Over the past five years, my colleagues at Cornell University (the Department of Music, Program in Medieval Studies, and the Department of Classics) have provided an engaging environment for the project's final stages. In particular, I thank Andy Galloway, Judith Peraino, Charles Brittain, Scott MacDonald, Roger Moseley, and Pete Wetherbee, all of whom provided valuable feedback on early drafts of some (or all) of its chapters, as well as the graduate students (and colleagues) in my seminars on the history of music theory, Latin philosophical commentaries, and medieval cosmologies (co-taught with Benjamin Anderson).

Manuscript research in many European libraries was made all the more fruitful by the generosity of my hosts John Marenbon (Trinity College, Cambridge), Irène Caiazzo (Centre national de la recherche scientifique, Paris), Michael Winterbottom (Corpus Christi College, Oxford), Martin Haltrich (Stiftsbibliothek Zwettl), Fr. Hyacinthe Destivelle and Jean-Laurent Pinard (Centre d'Études Istina and La Bibliothèque du Saulchoir), and many librarians (too many, with apologies, to list here) at the Bibliothèque nationale de France, the Institut de recherche et d'histoire des textes, the British Library, the Bodleian Library, Cambridge University Library, the Parker Library, St. John's College Library, the Biblioteca Nazionale Centrale di Firenze, the Biblioteca Medicea Laurenziana, and Leiden Universiteitsbibliotheek.

Many of these ideas were first floated in colloquia and public seminars, and I thank in particular my many interlocutors at the History of Philosophy Seminar, Trinity College (John Marenbon), the Séminaire "Histoire des sciences au Moyen Âge," École Pratique des Hautes Études (Irène Caiazzo and Danielle Jacquart), the workshop on Medieval Music Theory in Context (Christian Leitmeir), the Medieval Studies Colloquium at the University of Minnesota (Andrew Scheil), Katholieke Universiteit Leuven's Musicology Colloquium (David Burn), Yale University's History of Theory Seminar (Nathan Martin) and Medieval Song Lab (Anna Zayaruznaya and Ardis Butterfield), and colloquia at Cornell's Department of Music and Department of Classics.

Scattered components of its argument have been published elsewhere: "Pythagoras and Pythagoreanism in Late Antiquity and the Middle Ages," in *A History of Pythagoreanism*, ed. Carl Huffman, 416–434 (Cambridge: Cambridge University Press, 2014), with permission from Cambridge University Press; "Martianus Capella and the Liberal Arts," in *The Oxford Handbook of Medieval Latin Literature*, ed. David Townsend and Ralph Hexter, 307–334 (Oxford: Oxford University Press, 2012), with permission from Oxford University Press; and "*Musica speculativa* in the Cambridge Commentary on Martianus Capella's *De nuptiis*," *Journal of Medieval Latin* 18 (2008), 292–305, with permission from Brepols Publishers. Dialogue from *The Late Show with Stephen Colbert* is courtesy of the Late Show Inc. For permission to reproduce images, I thank the Walters Art Museum; the Master and Fellows of Trinity College, Cambridge; Corpus Christi College Library, Oxford; and Lennart Lannerbäck.

At Oxford University Press, I thank Suzanne Ryan, who has steered this project with an expert hand (and provided astonishingly quick replies to importune e-mails); Jairo Moreno and Gavin Steingo, who gave this undisciplined project a ready home in their new series; and my readers, who improved the book in countless ways.

Finally and first of all is my unpayable debt of gratitude to Kelli Carr, whose unflagging support and unflinching criticisms have not only made this book possible but have made it better.

ABBREVIATIONS

Abelardus, *Dial.*	L. M. De Rijk, *Petrus Abaelardus. Dialectica: First Complete Edition of the Parisian Manuscript* (Assen: Van Gorcum, 1956; rev. ed. 1970).
Abelardus, *Exp. Hex.*	M. Romig, D. E. Luscombe, and C. Burnett, eds., *Expositio in Hexameron*, Corpus Christianorum. Continuatio Mediaevalis 15 (Turnhout: Brepols, 2004).
Abelardus, *LI1*	Bernhard Geyer, ed., *Peter Abaelards Philosophische Schriften. I. Die Logica 'Ingredientibus'. 1. Die Glossen zu Porphyrius*, Beiträge zur Geschichte der Philosophie und Theologie des Mittelalters 21.1 (Münster: Aschendorff, 1919).
Abelardus, *LI2*	Bernhard Geyer, ed., *Peter Abaelards Philosophische Schriften. I. Die Logica 'Ingredientibus'. 2. Die Glossen zu den Kategorien*, Beiträge zur Geschichte der Philosophie und Theologie des Mittelalters 21.2 (Münster: Aschendorff, 1921).
Abelardus, *TChr*	*Theologia Christiana* in E. M. Buytaert, ed., *Petri Abaelardi Opera theologica II*, Corpus Christianorum. Continuatio Mediaevalis 12 (Turnhout: Brepols, 1969).
Abelardus, *TSch*	*Theologia 'Scholarium'* in E. M. Buytaert and C. J. Mews, eds., *Petri Abaelardi Opera theologica III*, Corpus Christianorum. Continuatio Mediaevalis 13 (Turnhout: Brepols, 1987), 313–549.
Abelardus, *TSum*	*Theologia 'Summi boni'* in Buytaert and Mews, *Petri Abaelardi Opera theologica III*, 85–201.

Adelardus, *De eod. et diu.*	*De eodem et diuerso* in Charles Burnett, ed. and trans., *Adelard of Bath, Conversations with His Nephew: On the Same and the Different, Questions on Natural Science and On Birds* (Cambridge: Cambridge University Press, 1998), 1–79.
Adelardus, *Quaest. nat.*	*Quaestiones naturales* in Burnett, *Conversations*, 81–235.
Alanus de Insulis, *Anticl.*	Robert Bossuat, ed., *Alain de Lille. Anticlaudianus: Texte critique, avec une introduction et des tables* (Paris: J. Vrin, 1955).
Alanus de Insulis, *De pl. nat.*	Nikolaus M. Häring, "Alan of Lille, *De planctu Naturae*," *Studi medievali* 19 (1978), 797–879.
Alcinous, *Didask.*	John Whittaker, ed., *Alcinoos. Enseignement des doctrines de Platon*, trans. Pierre Louis (Paris: Belles lettres, 1990).
Ammonius, *In Isag.*	Adolf Busse, ed., *Ammonii In Porphyrii Isagogen sive V voces*, Commentaria in Aristotelem Graeca 4.3 (Berlin: Reimer, 1981).
Anonymus, *Exp. in Mart.*	*Expositio super librum Martiani Capelle de nuptiis phylologie* iuxta Florence, Bib. Naz. Centrale, Conv. Soppr. I.1.28, ff. 49r–64v, et Zwettl, Stiftsbibliothek 313, ff. 142v–179v.
Anonymus, *Glos. Colonienses sup. Macr.*	Irène Caiazzo, *Lectures médiévales de Macrobe. Les* Glosae Colonienses super Macrobium, Études de philosophie médiévale 83 (Paris: J. Vrin, 2002).
Anonymus, *In inst. mus.*	Alexander Rausch, "Der Boethius-Kommentar in der Handschrift St. Florian XI 282," *Studien zur Musikwissenschaft: Beihefte der Denkmäler der Tonkunst in Österreich* 48 (2002), 7–83.
Aristoxenus, *El. harm.*	Rosetta Da Rios, ed., *Aristoxeni Elementa Harmonica*, Scriptores Graeci et Latini consilio Academiae Lynceorum editi (Rome: Typis publicae officinae polygraphicae, 1954).
Augustinus, *Trin.*	W. J. Mountain, *Sancti Aurelii Augustini De trinitate libri XV*, Corpus christianorum. Series Latina, 50–50A (Turnhout: Brepols, 1968).
Bernardus Carnotensis, *Bernardi Glos. sup. Tim.*	Paul Edward Dutton, ed., *The* Glosae super Platonem *of Bernard of Chartres*, Studies and Texts 107 (Toronto: Pontifical Institute of Mediaeval Studies, 1991).

Bernardus Silvestris, *Comm. in Mart.* — Haijo Jan Westra, ed., *The Commentary on Martianus Capella's* De nuptiis Philologiae et Mercurii *Attributed to Bernardus Silvestris*, Studies and Texts 80 (Toronto: Pontifical Institute of Mediaeval Studies, 1986).

Bernardus Silvestris, *Cos.* — Peter Dronke, ed., *Bernardus Silvestris. Cosmographia* (Leiden: Brill, 1978).

Boethius, *Cons. phil.* — Claudi Moreschini, ed., *Boethius. De consolatione philosophiae. Opuscula theologica*, Bibliotheca scriptorum Graecorum et Romanorum Teubneriana (Munich and Leipzig: K. G. Saur, 2005), 1–162.

Boethius, *De trin.* — Moreschini, *Boethius. De consolatione philosophiae. Opuscula theologica*, 165–181.

Boethius, *In Isag.* — Samuel Brandt, ed., *Anicii Manlii Severini Boethii In Isagogen Porphyrii commenta*, Corpus Scriptorum Ecclesiasticorum Latinorum 48 (Vienna: F. Tempsky, 1906).

Boethius, *In Perih.* — Carol Meiser, ed., *Anicii Manlii Severini Boetii commentarii in librum Aristotelis* ΠΕΡΙ ΕΡΜΗΝΕΙΑΣ (Leipzig: B. G. Teubner, 1877 and 1880).

Boethius, *Inst. ar.* — Henry Oosthout and Iohannes Schilling, eds., *Anicii Manlii Severini Boethii De arithmetica*, Corpus Christianorum. Series Latina, 94A (Turnhout: Brepols, 1999).

Boethius, *Inst. mus.* — Gottfried Friedlein, ed., *Anicii Manlii Torquati Severini Boetii De institutione arithmetica, libri duo. De institutione musica, libri quinque*, Bibliotheca scriptorum Graecorum et Romanorum Teubneriana (Leipzig: B. G. Teubner, 1867).

Calcidius, *In Tim.* — J. H. Waszink, ed., *Timaeus a Calcidio translatus commentarioque instructus*, 2nd ed., Plato Latinus 4 (London: The Warburg Institute, 1975).

Cassiodorus, *Inst.* — R. A. B. Mynors, ed., *Cassiodori Senatoris Institutiones divinarum et saecularium litterarum*, 2nd ed. (Oxford: Clarendon Press, 1961); PL 70, 1105–1220.

Eriugena, *De imag.* — Maïeul Cappuyns, "Le 'De imagine' de Grégoire de Nysse traduit par Jean Scot Érigène," *Recherches de théologie ancienne et médiévale* 32 (1965), 205–262.

Gregory of Nyssa, *De hom. op.* — *S. Gregorii Nysseni De hominis opificio*, PG 44, 123D–255C.

Guillelmus a Sancto Theodorico, *De nat. corp. et an.*	Michel Lemoine, ed., *Guillelmus de Sancto Theodorico, De natura corporis et animae*, Auteurs Latins du Moyen Âge (Paris: Belles lettres, 1988), 93–146.
Guillelmus de Conchis, *Drag.*	Italo Ronca, ed., *Guillelmi de Conchis Dragmaticon philosophiae*, Corpus Christianorum. Continuatio Mediaevalis 152 (Turnhout: Brepols, 1997).
Guillelmus de Conchis, *Glos. sup. Macr.*	*Glosae super Macrobium*, transc. Helen Rodnite Lemay (forthcoming in the *Guillelmi de Conchis Opera omnia*, Corpus Christianorum, Continuatio Mediaevalis)—Rodnite Lemay's transcriptions have been checked and corrected against the manuscripts when necessary.
Guillelmus de Conchis, *Glos. sup. Boet.*	Lodi Nauta, ed., *Guillelmi de Conchis Glosae super Boetium*, Corpus Christianorum. Continuatio Mediaevalis 158 (Turnhout: Brepols, 1999).
Guillelmus de Conchis, *Glosulae sup. Prisc.*	*Glosulae super Priscianum*, Florence, Biblioteca Laurenziana, San Marco 310 (*uersio prior*); Paris, Bibliothèque nationale, lat. 15130 (*uersio altera*).
Guillelmus de Conchis, *Guillelmi Glos. sup. Tim.*	Édouard Jeauneau, ed., *Guillelmi de Conchis Glosae super Platonem*, Corpus Christianorum. Continuatio Mediaevalis 203 (Turnhout: Brepols, 2006).
Guillelmus de Conchis, *Phil.*	PL 172, 39–102; corrected against Gregor Maurach, ed., *Wilhelm von Conches. Philosophia* (Pretoria: University of South Africa, 1980).
Ps.-Guillelmus de Conchis, *Moralium*	John Holmberg, ed., *Das Moralium dogma philosophorum des Guillaume de Conches* (Uppsala: Almqvist & Wiksell, 1929).
Hisdosus, *De anima mundi Platonica*	Paris, Bibliothèque nationale, lat. 8624, 17r–22r.
Honorius Augustodunensis, *Imago mundi*	Valerie Flint, "Honorius Augustodunensis. *Imago mundi*," *Archives d'histoire doctrinale et littéraire du Moyen Âge* 49 (1982), 7–153.
Hugo de S. Victore, *Did.*	Charles Henry Buttimer, ed., *Hugonis de Sancto Victore Didascalicon de studio legendi: A Critical Text*, Studies in Medieval and Renaissance Latin 10 (Washington, DC: Catholic University Press, 1939).
Iamblichus, *De comm. math. sc.*	Nicolaus Festa and Ulrich Klein, eds., *Iamblichi De communi mathematica scientia liber* (Stuttgart: Teubner, 1975).

Isaac de Stella, *Ep. de an.*	Caterina Tarlazzi, "L'*Epistola de anima* di Isacco di Stella: studio della tradizione ed edizione del testo," *Medioevo: Rivista di storia della filosofia medievale* 36 (2011), 167–278.
Isidorus, *Etym.*	W. M. Lindsay, ed., *Isidori Hispalensis Episcopi Etymologiarum siue Originum libri xx* (Oxford: Clarendon Press, 1911).
Macrobius, *In Som. Scip.*	James Willis, ed., *Ambrosii Theodosii Macrobii Commentarii in Somnium Scipionis*, Bibliotheca scriptorum Graecorum et Romanorum Teubneriana (Leipzig: B. G. Teubner, 1963).
Martianus, *De nuptiis*	James Willis, ed., *Martianus Capella, De nuptiis Philologiae et Mercurii*, Bibliotheca scriptorum Graecorum et Romanorum Teubneriana (Leipzig: B. G. Teubner, 1983).
Nemesius, *Prem. phys.*	Karl Burkhard, ed., *Nemesii episcopi Premnon physicon a N. Alfano archiepiscopo Salerni in Latinum translatus*, Bibliotheca scriptorum Graecorum et Romanorum Teubneriana (Leipzig: B. G. Teubner, 1917).
Nicomachus, *Harm.*	*Harmonicon enchiridion* in Karl von Jan, ed., *Musici scriptores graeci. Aristoteles, Euclides, Nicomachus, Bacchius, Gaudentius, Alypius, et melodiarum ueterum quidquid exstat* (Leipzig: B. G. Teubner, 1895), 235–265.
Nicomachus, *Intr. ar.*	Richard Hoche, ed., *Nicomachi Geraseni Pythagorei Introductionis arithmeticae libri duo*, Bibliotheca scriptorum Graecorum et Romanorum Teubneriana (Leipzig: B. G. Teubner, 1866).
Philoponus, *In de An.*	Michael Hayduck, ed., *Ioannis Philoponi in Aristotelis de anima libros commentaria*, Commentaria in Aristotelem Graeca 15 (Berlin: Reimer, 1897).
Plato, *Lach., Alc. 1, Crat., Theaet., Prot., Phaedo, Tim., Sym., Phaedrus, Leg., Rep.*	John Burnet, ed., *Platonis Opera*, Scriptorum classicorum bibliotheca Oxoniensis (Oxford: Clarendon Press, 1900–1907).
Porphyrius, *In Ptolemaei Harm.*	Ingemar Düring, *Porphyrios Kommentar zur Harmonielehre des Ptolemaios*, Göteborgs Högskolas Årsskrift 38 (Göteborg: Elanders Boktryckeri, 1932).

Proclus, *In Remp.*	Wilhelm Kroll, ed., *Procli Diadochi in Platonis Rem publicam commentarii*, 2 vols., Bibliotheca Scriptorum Graecorum et Romanorum Teubneriana (Leipzig: B. G. Teubner, 1899–1901).
Proclus, *In Tim.*	Ernst Diehls, ed., *Procli Diadochi in Platonis Timaeum commentaria*, 3 vols., Bibliotheca scriptorum Graecorum et Romanorum Teubneriana (Liepzig: B. G. Teubner, 1903–1906).
Ps.-Euclid, *Sec. can.*	André Barbera, *The Euclidean Division of the Canon: Greek and Latin Sources*, Greek and Latin Music Theory 8 (Lincoln: University of Nebraska Press, 1991), 114–184.
Ptolemaeus, *Harm.*	Ingemar Düring, *Die Harmonielehre des Klaudios Ptolemaios*, Göteborgs Högskolas Årsskrift 36 (Göteborg: Elanders Boktryckeri, 1930).
Theon Smyrnaeus, *Exp.*	Eduard Hiller, ed., *Theonis Smyrnaei philosophi Platonici Expositio rerum mathematicarum ad legendum Platonem utilium*, Bibliotheca scriptorum Graecorum et Romanorum Teubneriana (Leipzig: B. G. Teubner, 1878).

ABOUT THE COMPANION WEBSITE

www.oup.com/us/composingtheworld

Oxford has created a website to accompany *Composing the World*. There readers will find downloadable English translations of the Latin texts edited in the Appendices (excerpts from William of Conches's *Glosulae de Magno Prisciano* and Hisdosus's *De anima mundi Platonica*).

Composing the World

Prelude

Listening to the Universe

Mundus diligit concordiam.
—William of Conches, *Glosae super Platonem*, 39

"We can hear the universe!" This was the triumphant proclamation at a February 2016 press conference announcing that the Laser Interferometer Gravity Observatory (LIGO) had detected a "transient gravitational-wave signal." What LIGO heard in the morning hours of September 14, 2015, was the "sound" of cosmic forces of mind-boggling power diffused through a cosmic medium of mind-boggling expansiveness.[1] Einstein's general theory of relativity predicted that when massive stellar bodies explode or collide, the very fabric of space-time would register the reverberations of the forces unleashed, and undulating vibrations of space-time—gravitational waves—would propagate through the fabric of the universe like ripples on the surface of a pond.[2] The signal detected by LIGO was a perceptible confirmation of Einstein's equations: the transient ripple of two black holes colliding more than a billion years ago, "their orbital inspiral and merger, and subsequent final black hole ringdown."[3] The event was unseen and in

[1] "Mind-boggling" was the term used to describe the event by David Reitze, executive director of the LIGO Laboratory, in the press conference announcing the detection: "That's what we saw here. It's mind-boggling," "LIGO detects gravitational waves—announcement at press conference (part 1)." YouTube video uploaded by the National Science Foundation, at 8:28, https://youtu.be/aEPIwEJmZyE (accessed March 24, 2016).

[2] See Marcia Bartusiak, *Einstein's Unfinished Symphony: Listening to the Sounds of Space-Time* (Washington, DC: Joseph Henry Press, 2000), who anticipated the musical response to the 2015 discovery: "Firm discovery of these waves will at last complete the final movement of Einstein's unfinished symphony" (9). The mathematical model of the black hole ringdown—as yet undetected when Bartusiak was writing—is discussed in a chapter entitled, "The Music of the Spheres" (188–206, with the black hole collision at 195–196).

[3] B. P. Abbott et al., "Observation of Gravitational Waves from a Binary Black Hole Merger," *Physical Review Letters* 116 0611202 (2016), 2.

fact otherwise entirely undetectable save by the minutely tuned interferometers located in Livingston, Louisiana, and Hanford, Washington. The interferometers deployed in the ongoing experiment are most sensitive to waves between one hundred and three hundred hertz, well within the range of human hearing, could our ears hear in the medium of gravity.[4] Scientists associated with the project describe the detection of the signal as an act of listening. "We can hear gravitation waves. We can hear the universe," LIGO Scientific Collaboration Spokeswoman Gabriela Gonzalez explained in the press conference. "That's one of the beautiful things about this," she continued. "We are not only going to be seeing the universe; we are going to be listening to it."[5] David Reitze, Executive Director of the LIGO Laboratory, used similar language: "Up until now we've been deaf to gravitational waves, but today we are able to hear them."[6] Columbia University astrophysicist Szabolcs Marka made the inevitable comparison to music: "Until this moment, we had our eyes on the sky and we couldn't hear the music. The skies will never be the same."[7]

The sound of gravitational waves immediately caught the public imagination. Various computer modelings, "recordings," and remixes circulated widely on the internet.[8] Brian Greene, a physicist from Columbia University, capitalized on the attention and, in an appearance on *The Late Show with Stephen Colbert* (on February 24, 2016), explained just what we hear when we "hear" gravitational waves:

GREENE: You can actually in some sense hear the gravitational waves; they vibrate at a frequency that, if you turn it into sound, the human ear can hear, and these sounds . . .

COLBERT [interrupting]: These waves can be turned into sound?

G: They can, and these are the most spectacular sounds from the standpoint of—they herald a revolution in our understanding of the universe.

C: Okay, so I understand you brought one of these sounds with you.

G: Yeah, yeah I did.

C: And this is the sound of what? What are we listening to?

G: This is the sound of two black holes colliding.

C: Actually? This is actually a computer rendering of the gravitational waves into sound.

4 The recorded wave sweeps from 35 to 250 hertz.

5 "LIGO detects gravitational waves," at 18:43.

6 Ibid., at 10:54.

7 Sandi Doughton, "Hearing the Music of the Universe: Hanford Helps Find Einstein's Gravitational Waves," *The Seattle Times* (February 11, 2016). http://www.seattletimes.com/seattle-news/science/scientists-including-hanford-team-confirm-einsteins-theory-of-gravitational-waves/ [accessed March 23, 2016].

8 E.g., Arthur Jeffes, a London-based composer and producer, collaborated with astrophysicist Smaya Nissanke (Radboud University) to construct a "musical narrative . . . which both demonstrates the new data and responds to it artistically" (http://www.epcmusic.com/space).

G: This is a simulation, but the data agrees with the simulation . . .

C: And this is what it would sound like?

G: This is what it would sound like.

C: So, drum roll please. [Drum roll . . . a sound plays, which strikes the ears as an electric slide-whistle punctuated by a final blip. The audience laughs.]

C: Is God Bugs Bunny? What is that?

G: Big things come in little packages. Those sounds are really telling us things about the universe that we have no other way of discerning. Those kinds of sounds are the future of studying the cosmos.[9]

I want to highlight three aspects of this exchange that are directly related to the themes and arguments developed in this book. First, the human ability to hear the cosmos is predicated upon the transduction of an extrasonic signal—a signal that always exceeds or outstrips the physical, embodied limitations of the ear—into a sonic representation accommodated to human sensory realities. As Greene notes, we can "in some sense hear" gravitational waves, but only to the extent that the signal transmitted via the medium of gravity is transduced into a sonic signal that the ears can register. Put another way, only Pythagoras could hear the music of the spheres (and as Isaac Newton is reported to have claimed: "I thought Pythagoras's Musick of the spheres was intended to typify gravity").[10]

Second, these sounds are "spectacular" and "herald a revolution in our understanding of the universe." The import of these sounds is epistemological. The sounds qua spectacular (in the etymological sense of *spectaculum* as an act of seeing) allow us insight into the unseen and invisible forces of nature; as transduced sonic objects, they encode information about their sound producers and "[tell] us things about the universe that we have no other way of discerning." Put another way, to hear the cosmos is to experience the world through a cosmic acoustemology (acoustic epistemology) that privileges the experience of sound as a special kind of relational knowledge, a "knowing-with and knowing-through the audible."[11]

9 "Gravitation Waves Hit the Late Show," 6:48–8:00, http://www.cbs.com/shows/the-late-show-with-stephen-colbert/video/F42ED0EC-2452-577E-F107-1614438B56F2/gravitational-waves-hit-the-late-show/ (accessed March 25, 2016). Dialogue courtesy of Late Show Inc.

10 Peter Pesic, *Music and the Making of Modern Science* (Cambridge, MA: MIT Press, 2014), 131. The quotation is recorded by John Conduitt (husband of Newton's niece and co-resident with Newton at Cranbury) in notes gathered for a (never realized) life of Newton: Cambridge, King's College, Keynes MS 130.07, 5r. The continuation of this claim clarifies Newton's intention: "& as he makes the sounds & notes to depend on the size of the strings, so gravity depends on the density of matter." See J. E. McGuire and P. M. Rattansi, "Newton and the 'Pipes of Pan,'" *Notes and Records of the Royal Society of London* 21 (1966), 108–143; but also note the important corrective provided by Paolo Casini, "Newton: The Classical Scholia," *History of Science* 22 (1984), 1–58.

11 Stephen Feld, "Acoustemology," in *Keywords in Sound*, ed. David Novak and Matt Sakakeeny (Durham and London: Duke University Press, 2015), 12.

Third, as the comedic force of Colbert's memorable punchline—"Is God Bugs Bunny?"—suggests, there is a fundamental disjunction between sound and source. The original sonic transduction of the (at the time of this writing) only gravitational wave recorded evokes the thump of a sampled bass drum, while a frequency-adjusted version, shifted by 400Hz to accommodate human hearing better, sounds more akin to the drip of a leaky faucet in the dead of night. The still more cleaned-up simulation that was played on *The Late Show*, which optimizes the "signal-to-noise ratio," sounds even more disconnected, its blippy, sliding chirp profoundly disproportionate to the gravity of its source—less an awe-inspiring, black-hole-collision-worthy sound and more a Bugs Bunny slapstick: "boooiiing." Just as extrasonic cosmic signals always outstrip our ability to hear them, so too our desire to actually hear such sounds always outstrips the monumentality of their sonic transduction. Put another way, the sounds of the cosmos are more likely to present themselves through the ping of hammers in a humble blacksmith's forge, as in the famous account of Pythagoras's discovery of music, than as the thunderous, unmediated sound of a divine maker.

These sounds (transduced, cosmo-acoustemological, and nonetheless comically disproportionate to their cosmic origin) may well be the future of studying the cosmos, as Brian Greene predicts. This book argues, however, that sound—and, in particular, the harmonious coordination of sounds, sources, and listeners—has always been an integral part of the *history* of studying the cosmos. It seeks to document the wagers that humanity has made on the knowledge of the world's composition, and our place within its harmonious aggregate, based on aurality—our ability to hear the world and ourselves in all of its and our harmonious particularities. *Composing the World* provides evidence for a series of related claims:

1. that this harmony is grounded in material interactions and intermaterial relations;[12]
2. that harmony can be the optimistic site of a "unified theory of cosmology," which can account for the many resonances between macrocosm and microcosm, soul and body, immaterial and material worlds, even between God and humanity;
3. that harmony serves not just as the foregrounded subject of discourse about the world but even as the unarticulated ground for thinking and theorizing the world at all;
4. and, finally, that the aesthetic and affective power of phenomenal harmony as sound can be deliberately and consciously exploited to explain and instill a sense of *cosmic* affect—the sense of wonder, love, and desire to *hear* the harmony of the world.

[12] I borrow the term "intermaterial" from Nina Sun Eidsheim, *Sensing Sound: Singing and Listening as Vibrational Practice* (Durham: Duke University Press, 2015).

It is my hope that these broad claims will resonate with a wide variety of readers in the fields of music studies, sound studies, medieval studies, and the history of (natural) philosophy and science. The specific historical terrain of my argument is more circumscribed, however; it focuses upon the music-theoretical, philosophical, and philological specificity of these broader claims in the world of twelfth-century music theory and philosophy. It offers a new intellectual history of the role of harmony in medieval cosmological discourse, focused primarily on the twelfth-century reception and development of ancient and late-ancient Platonism, as transmitted by Calcidius, Macrobius, Martianus Capella, and Boethius. Its central argument—which synthesizes material from domains usually treated separately, including philosophy, logic, cosmology, music theory, and literature—affirms music theory's foundational and often normative role within the development of medieval cosmological models, at both micro- and macrocosmic levels: the microcosmic harmonies that govern the moral, physical, and psychic equilibrium of the human and the macrocosmic harmonies that ensure cosmological perfection.

Historical Motivations: "Where are the writers on music?"

The renowned twelfth-century magister Thierry of Chartres tantalizingly promised that his hexameral commentary, the *Treatise on the Works of the Six Days* (*Tractatus de sex dierum operibus*), would offer four kinds of arguments (*probationes*) to bring his readers to knowledge of their creator: "the proofs of arithmetic and music, geometry and astronomy."[13] The *probatio musicalis*, however, remains an empty promise, for the extant *Tractatus* trails off, mid-argument, before even the first arithmetical proof has proved its point. Regrettably, the twelfth century is littered with such broken promises—teasing references to works that perhaps were never written, perhaps have slipped through the fickle fingers of Fortuna and are lost forever, or perhaps still lie undisturbed and undiscovered, maybe even in plain sight, just waiting for the right reader. Examples are numerous. A commentator on Martianus Capella's *On the Marriage of Philology and Mercury* begs off a serious discussion of the soul's "vital spirit" (*uitalis spiritus*) and directs the reader elsewhere: "Enough about the vital spirit, for we have pursued this subject in more detail in our commentary on the *Timaeus*."[14] The anonymous author of a now fragmentary commentary on Boethius's *Consolation of Philosophy* makes a similar promise in his quick remarks on *hyle* or primordial matter: "What *hyle* is will not be discussed here, but in (a commentary on) Plato's *Timaeus*."[15] Likewise,

[13] Nikolaus M. Häring, ed., *Commentaries on Boethius by Thierry of Chartres and His School* (Toronto: Pontifical Institute of Mediaeval Studies, 1971), *Tractatus de sex dierum operibus*, 56.

[14] *Comm. in Mart.* 8.1043–1044: Hec de uitali spiritu. Super Platonem enim hec latius executi sumus.

[15] Biblioteca Apostolica Vaticana, Codex Vaticanus latinus 919, 198va: Quid sit yle non hic dicetur, sed in Platonis Thimeo.

an unpublished twelfth-century commentator on Plato's *Timaeus*, distinguishable from that most prolific of medieval authors, Anonymus, only because he happens to tell us that his name is Hisdosus, proudly refers his readers to his own refutation of mathematicians who claim that a disjunct harmonic proportion is impossible, "whom we plainly refute in (a commentary on Boethius's) *Arithmetic*."[16] If any of these commentaries were completed, they have not yet been found. Each new discovery seems to create as many gaps as it fills—or, to borrow a metaphor from Boethius, with every uncertainty that we pare away, innumerable others, like Hydra-heads, spring up in its place (*Cons. phil.* 4.p6.3).

Our knowledge of the twelfth-century Platonic commentary tradition is thus necessarily imperfect, and as new texts come to light, our assessment of its terrain will continue to change and, we hope, improve. But despite the gaps (both known and unknown), the extant tradition still allows us to respond to an even more fundamental question posed, now upwards of forty years ago, by Lawrence Gushee. In his magisterial survey of medieval musical writings, Gushee famously called attention to an "extremely odd facet" of the twelfth century and posed the question bluntly: "Where are the writers on music?"[17]

Gushee is not alone in posing the question. It is a common belief that the twelfth century offers a meagre harvest in the field of music theory. Despite the remarkable effort expended upon the post-twelfth-century adoption, expansion, and critique of Aristotelian thought in musical discourse,[18] the period immediately preceding the full integration of Aristotelian vocabulary has not received as much attention. In part, this inattention stems from a perceived lack of texts; there are no "Neoplatonic" musical treatises from the twelfth century comparable in scope to the "Aristotelian" veneer of, say, the thirteenth-century *Ars musicae* of Magister Lambertus or the several fourteenth-century scholastic *Quaestiones de musica* that have figured prominently in recent scholarship.[19] But the apparent dearth of twelfth-century "writers on music" lamented by Gushee does not reflect the evidence of surviving texts; rather, it is a product of modern disciplinary

[16] Paris, Bibliothèque nationale, lat. 8624, 20r: quos in Arismetica euidentissime confutamus.

[17] Lawrence Gushee, "Questions of Genre in Medieval Treatises on Music," in *Gattungen der Musik in Einzeldarstellungen: Gedenkschrift Leo Schrade*, ed. Wulf Arlt, Ernst Lichtenhahn, and Hans Oesch (Munich: Francke Verlag, 1973), 410.

[18] See, for instance, Dorit Tanay, *Noting Music, Marking Culture: The Intellectual Context of Rhythmic Notation, 1250–1400*, Musicological Studies and Documents 46 ([s.l.]: American Institute of Musicology, 1999); Frank Hentschel, *Sinnlichkeit und Vernunft in der mittelalterlichen Musiktheorie: Strategien der Konsonanzwertung und der Gegenstand der musica sonora um 1300*, Beiheft zum Archiv für Musikwissenschaft 47 (Stuttgart: Franz Steiner Verlag, 2000).

[19] E.g., Cecilia Panti, "The First 'Questio' of ms Paris, B.N. lat. 7372: 'Utrum musica sit scientia,'" *Studi medievali* 33 (1992), 265–313; Frank Hentschel and Martin Pickavé, "'Quaestiones mathematicales': Eine Textgattung der Pariser Artistenfakultät in frühen 14. Jahrhundert," in *Nach der Verurteilung von 1277: Philosophie und Theologie an der Universität von Paris im letzten Viertel des 13. Jahrhunderts*, ed. Jan A. Aertsen, Kent Emery Jr., and Andreas Speer (Berlin: Walter de Gruyter, 2001), 618–634; Hentschel, *Sinnlichkeit und Vernunft*, 281–313.

divisions and musicological expectations. As a result of this inattention, some scholars have even gone so far as to claim that the twelfth century witnessed the near complete withdrawal of music from quadrivial studies. The new "autonomy" of music, confirmed for historian of science Guy Beaujouan by a detachment from generalized studies, led (Beaujouan claims) to the "eclipse" of Boethius: "Not until the fourteenth century, with the *ars nova*, did music once more become a specialization of masters of arts interested in mathematics. . . . [Then,] the *De musica* of Boethius was studied with renewed interest."[20]

As many modern histories would have it, musical treatises in the late eleventh and early twelfth centuries began to shy away from the mathematical and cosmological concerns that had bound music to the quadrivium.[21] Following a late-eleventh-century flurry of activity in South German monasteries, capped at the turn of the century by Johannes Affligemensis's *De musica*,[22] music-theoretical discourse seems to exhibit a decisive change in register. Save for the midcentury treatises clustered around Cistercian chant reform,[23] most twelfth-century writings on music (and there aren't all that many) share a common theme: codifying the rules and precepts of the quickly developing polyphonic practices. The rules set forth in *Ad organum faciendum* (*On composing organum*) in the early twelfth century or the so-called "Vatican Organum Treatise" (at least some of whose teachings stem from the late twelfth century), for instance, arose not from armchair speculation but from repeated and tested practical verification.[24] Although such organum tracts are not entirely devoid of philosophical interest, scholars are right to observe that testimony to a thriving tradition of speculative music theory they are not.

So where are the writers on music? Exploring this question and its implications for the history of music theory led Gushee to the doorstep of the so-called

[20] Guy Beaujouan, "The Transformation of the Quadrivium," in *Renaissance and Renewal in the Twelfth Century*, ed. Robert L. Benson and Giles Constable (Cambridge, MA: Harvard University Press, 1982), 467.

[21] Hans Heinrich Eggebrecht, "Die Mehrstimmigkeitslehre von ihren Anfängen bis zum 12. Jahrhundert," in *Die mittelalterliche Lehre von der Mehrstimmigkeit*, Geschichte der Musiktheorie 5 (Darmstadt: Wissenschaftliche Buchgesellschaft, 1984), 9–87; Sarah Fuller, "Early Polyphony," in *The New Oxford History of Music*, Vol. 2: *The Early Middle Ages to 1300*, 2nd ed., ed. Richard Crocker and David Hiley (Oxford: Oxford University Press, 1990), 485–556; in Guy Beaujouan's discussion of twelfth-century quadrivial studies, the section about music is entitled "The secession of music" ("The Transformation of the Quadrivium," 465–467)

[22] *Iohannes Affligemensis, De musica cum tonario*, ed. Joseph Smits van Waesberghe ([Rome]: American Institute of Musicology, 1950); English translation in *Hucbald, Guido, and John on Music: Three Medieval Treatises*, ed. Claude V. Palisca, trans. Warren Babb (New Haven and London: Yale University Press, 1978), 85–198.

[23] Claire Maître has re-edited the most important of these treatises, the *Regule de arte musica*, with a substantial discussion of its role in the reform; see *La réforme cistercienne du plain-chant: Étude d'un traité théorique* (Brecht: Commentarii Cistercienses, 1995).

[24] See, Eggebrecht, "Die Mehrstimmigkeitslehre," 86–87.

"School of Chartres," but he did not enter, warded off perhaps by its intimidating philosophical bent, noting that "while music's position in the liberal arts was strong [at Chartres], the texts used may rarely have had relevance to the practical concerns of standard plain-chant. The notorious (neo) Platonism of the intellectuals of Chartres must have something to do with this."[25] On one level Gushee was absolutely correct: the often speculative and generally non-practical deployment of music theory in the writings of many twelfth-century authors—especially, but not only, those commonly associated with the "School of Chartres"—had everything to do with the "notorious (neo) Platonism" that characterizes much (though certainly not all) of twelfth-century thought. But I must caution that if we neglect as extramusical or as somehow less relevant to musicology medieval musical writings that do not directly bear on the "practical concerns of standard plain-chant" (and Gushee is right that these twelfth-century authors have little to say on such matters), then we have done ourselves and the discipline of musicology a grand disservice. For although Bernard of Chartres, William of Conches, Thierry of Chartres, and the host of other commentators and thinkers who populate the pages to come may not—or at least not in any strong sense—be *musici* (roughly, "music theorists") in the same way that many were praised by their contemporaries as *philosophi* ("philosophers") and *grammatici* ("grammarians"), their thoughts on music can and do, as I will argue, offer us a window onto a world of musical speculation, and musical speculation on the world, that has been little mapped by musicologists, one that offers sometimes surprising correctives to the "standard history" of medieval music theory as viewed from the standpoint of the "technical tradition."

If my focus on twelfth-century traditions may come as a surprise for historians of music theory, it will not surprise intellectual historians. Since Charles Homer Haskins single-handedly turned the attention of generations of scholars to the "Renaissance of the twelfth century" in his 1927 book of the same title, this period has been pinpointed as the originary locus for various regulative concepts, including medieval humanism, as both a renewed study of Latin literary classics and a new emphasis on human dignity, virtue, and agency;[26] individual subjectivity and quasi-Foucauldian "technologies of the self," born of both an introspective turn toward the inner life and the outer textualization of the self (thought to be exemplified in Abelard's *Historia calamitatum*);[27] standardized educational structures and curricula, which pushed education beyond the traditional monastic schools and into cathedral schools, independent schools, and princely courts

[25] Gushee, "Questions of Genre," 423.

[26] R. W. Southern, *Medieval Humanism and Other Studies* (Oxford: Blackwell, 1970); *Scholastic Humanism and the Unification of Europe*, Vol. 1: *Foundations* (Oxford: Blackwell, 1995). Willemien Otten, *From Paradise to Paradigm: A Study of Twelfth-Century Humanism* (Leiden: Brill, 2004).

[27] Colin Morris, *The Discovery of the Individual 1050–1200* (New York: Harper, 1972); Bridget K. Balint, *Ordering Chaos: The Self and the Cosmos in Twelfth-Century Latin Prosimetrum* (Leiden: Brill, 2009);

across Europe;[28] and the (re)discovery of nature, no longer conceptualized as the simple manifestation of God's will but "as the object of a study aiming to know the *legitima causa et ratio* ["lawful cause and reason"] of every natural event."[29]

This last "innovation" is most immediately associated with a network of like-minded but fiercely independent scholars including Bernard of Chartres (a master and subsequently chancellor at the cathedral school at Chartres) and his students William of Conches and Thierry of Chartres (also chancellor at Chartres), as well as the English scholar Adelard of Bath (who studied at Tours and taught at Laon) and Bernard Silvestris (probably working at Tours), both of whom have literary and intellectual ties to Thierry: Adelard's mathematical translations were included in Thierry's *Heptateuchon* (a compilation of texts on the liberal arts), and Bernard dedicated his most successful work, the *Cosmographia*, to Thierry. Many of these scholars have, at one time or another, been associated with the so-called "School of Chartres," whose pride of place was first anchored by the 1895 doctoral thesis of the Chartrian scholar and canon, Alexandre Clerval;[30] thereafter, it quickly became "received wisdom" in the publications of Baeumker, Flatten, and Parent.[31] Richard Southern's repeated challenges to the reified conception of a "School of Chartres" (as either historical reality or intellectual disposition) has rightly introduced a more sober, cautionary tone, and the basic point of Southern's criticism remains valid—that medieval scholars narrowly associated with Chartres deserve consideration as part of a broader scholastic context.[32] Indeed they do, and this book is part of that project.[33] Nevertheless, against Southern's arguments, Édouard Jeauneau has defended the importance of Chartres,[34] and following his

Caroline Walker Bynum, "Did the Twelfth Century Discover the Individual?" *Journal of Ecclesiastical History* 31 (1980), 1–17.

28 C. Stephen Jaeger, *The Envy of Angels: Cathedral Schools and Social Ideals in Medieval Europe, 950–1200* (Philadelphia: University of Pennsylvania Press, 1994); Stephen Ferruolo, *The Origins of the University: The Schools of Paris and Their Critics, 1100–1215* (Stanford: Stanford University Press, 1985).

29 Tullio Gregory, "La nouvelle idée de nature et de savoir scientifique au XIIe siècle," in *The Cultural Context of Medieval Learning*, ed. J. E. Murdoch and E. D. Sylla (Dordrecht and Boston: D. Reidel, 1975), 195–196. Andreas Speer, *Die entdeckte Natur: Untersuchungen zu Begründungsversuchen einer 'scientia naturalis' im 12. Jahrhundert* (Leiden: Brill, 1995).

30 Alexandre Clerval, *Les écoles de Chartres au Moyen Âge* (Paris: A. Picard et fils, 1895).

31 Clemens Baeumker, *Der Platonismus im Mittelalter* (Munich: Verlag der K. B. Akademie der Wissenschaften, 1916); Heinrich Flatten, *Die Philosophie des Wilhelms von Conches* (Koblenz: Görres-Druckerei, 1929); Joseph-Marie Parent, *La doctrine de la création dans l'École de Chartres* (Paris: J. Vrin, 1938).

32 Southern, *Medieval Humanism*, 61–85; *Platonism, Scholastic Method and the School of Chartres, The Stenton Lecture 1978* (Reading: University of Reading Press, 1979).

33 Hence, following Winthrop Wetherbee's lead ("Philosophy, Cosmology, and the Twelfth-Century Renaissance," in *A History of Twelfth-Century Western Philosophy*, ed. P. Dronke [Cambridge: Cambridge University Press, 1988], 21–53), I will collectively refer to masters such as Adelard of Bath, Bernard and Thierry of Chartres, William of Conches, and Bernard Silvestris as "cosmologists," not "Chartrians."

34 See, for instance, Jeauneau, *Rethinking the School of Chartres*, trans. Claude Paul Desmarais (Toronto: University of Toronto Press, 2009).

lead Winthrop Wetherbee maintains that there remain "important and widely influential common elements in the thought of those masters whose names have been most frequently associated with Chartres."[35] Most characteristic of these commonalities are, first and foremost, (1) an avowed sympathy for Platonism, specifically the *Timaeus* in Calcidius's incomplete translation (through 53c), (2) the promotion of reason over authority, and (3) a conception of nature as the (proximate) efficient cause of material creation.

The twelfth-century cosmologists who are the primary subject of this book—that is, scholars interested in nature and natural processes—developed and articulated their doctrines in dialogue with Platonic texts, primarily by way of commentary on Plato's *Timaeus* (via Calcidius's fourth-century Latin translation and commentary), Macrobius's *Commentary on the Dream of Scipio* (beginning of the fifth century), Martianus Capella's *On the Marriage of Philology and Mercury* from the late fifth century, and three primary works in Boethius's oeuvre, the *Fundamentals of Arithmetic,* the *Fundamentals of Music,* and the *Consolation of Philosophy* (all from the first few decades of the sixth century). These were the four late-ancient authors who offered related yet distinct points of entry into a single, overarching fascination with the secrets of nature. Modern scholarship has generally examined these commentary traditions individually on a diachronic axis. While this sort of inquiry usefully highlights the seams and joints in the reception history of the textual traditions singly, it nevertheless obscures the profoundly synchronic relationship among these four texts in the twelfth century. The works of Plato and his late-ancient proponents were not approached as autonomous, self-contained tracts; rather, they were seen to complement each other in fundamental ways. The *Timaeus* and Calcidius's commentary provided a basic cosmological framework and the three metaphysical principles, God, Ideas (or Exemplars), and the "Receptacle," which was conflated with Aristotelian prime matter (*hyle* or, in Latin, *silva*); Macrobius equipped them with a hermeneutic model of fictitious but heuristic fables and allegories through which they could harmonize classical myth and philosophy with Christian theology; Martianus afforded a sweeping allegorical structure for such an inquiry; and, finally, Boethius showed the way along the fourfold mathematical path (the quadrivium) that led to the proper end, the ascent to "the Good" (the *summum bonum*), which was the final cause of all cosmological inquiry: the ascent through creatures to the creator (*per creaturas ad creatorem*).

Not only did these late-antique texts themselves model this ascent; the very disciplinary structure of the music-theoretical tradition they transmitted provided an often explicit "methodology" for thinking through and listening to the interconnected stages of this ascent. The second part of this monograph (Chapters 3 through 5) attempts to exemplify and mobilize the intricate scheme of cross-cosmic correspondences that animate the medieval cosmos and its inhabitants

35 "Philosophy, Cosmology, and the Twelfth-Century Renaissance," 21.

(human and nonhuman). These chapters collectively trace this material, intellectual, and anagogic ascent *per creaturas ad creatorem* in the same musical terms employed by the twelfth-century cosmologists: from the microcosmic harmonies of the *human* (Chapter 3), via the material harmonies of sonorous *instruments and voices* (Chapter 4), to the macrocosmic harmonies of the *universe* (Chapter 5). Readers with even a passing familiarity with the history of music theory will recognize this anagogic trajectory as roughly corresponding to Boethius's influential tripartition of music into *musica instrumentalis, musica humana,* and *musica mundana*, set forth in the prooemium to his *Fundamentals of Music*.[36] Cosmic music (*musica mundana*) arises from the harmonic structures and periods of the celestial bodies, from the delicate balance of the four elements, and from the cyclical succession of the seasons;[37] human music (*musica humana*) comprises the harmonic structures governing the human soul, the human body, and the relations between soul and body;[38] and instrumental music (*musica instrumentalis*) encompasses the sonorous sounds arising from instruments and voices, which are the servants of song.[39] Each level is an analogue of the others (at the material, anthropological, or cosmic level, mutatis mutandis), and collectively they actualize the continuous proportionality that ensures the continuity and integrity of the worldly machine (*machina mundi*).

Contemporary Motivations: The Afterlives of a Dead Metaphor

One of my secondary aims is to bring the less familiar discourse of medieval musical cosmology to the attention of scholars working in more familiar areas of musical and philosophical inquiry, medieval and modern. What might it mean to situate and reassess the harmonic and semiotic perspectives of medieval cosmology in the context of recent developments in biosemiotics and critical theory, in particular the *Umwelt* theory of Jakob von Uexküll (1864–1944), an early-twentieth-century theoretical biologist, whose work has been taken up by such recent theorists as Maurice Merleau-Ponty, Gilles Deleuze, and Félix Guattari?[40]

36 *Inst. mus.* 1.2 (187.18–23): Principio igitur de musica disserenti illud interim dicendum uidetur, quot musicae genera ab eius studiosis conprehensa esse nouerimus. Sunt autem tria. Et prima quidem mundana est, secunda uero humana, tertia, quae in quibusdam constituta est instrumentis, ut in cithara uel tibiis ceterisque, quae cantilenae famulantur. Since a full explication of this division and its influence on subsequent music-theoretical and philosophical traditions forms the heart of this study, I here sketch only a brief outline of the division.

37 *Inst. mus.* 1.2 (187.23–188.26).

38 *Inst. mus.* 1.2 (188.26–189.5).

39 *Inst. mus.* 1.2 (189.5–12).

40 Brett Buchanan, *Onto-Ethologies: The Animal Environments of Uexküll, Heidegger, Merleau-Ponty, and Deleuze* (Albany: SUNY Press, 2008).

To be clear, I do not encourage the construction of concrete genealogical connections between the harmonicizing traditions of medieval Platonism and Deleuze and Guattari's "cosmic refrain of the sound machine,"[41] nor the anachronistic collapse of semantic differences between, say, Badiou's famous declaration that "mathematics = ontology"[42] and Thierry of Chartres's claim that "the creation of numbers is the creation of reality" (*creatio numerorum rerum est creatio*).[43] Instead, by framing the medieval in light of the modern, if only briefly in this prologue and again in the postlude, I seek to help us better hear the sympathetic resonances that emanate from both sides of such a juxtaposition; these resonances, in turn, can attune our ears to both the strikingly "modern" (if decidedly unmodish) concerns of medieval intellectuals and the hidden "intellectual medievalisms" embedded within the condition and critique of modernity itself. Although the central chapters of this book are unabashedly and unapologetically historical in focus, the broader impetus for the project (and, I hope, its utility) gains force from a more contemporary set of concerns that have shaped the current trajectory of humanistic disciplines, music studies included. The continued and indeed resurgent recourse to musical metaphors, analogies, and expressive modalities in contemporary philosophy, especially after the so-called "speculative turn" and its return to an overturned Platonism,[44] makes a more robust account, *on its own terms*, of the premodern but postclassical history of such modalities all the more pressing. We cannot think the present without understanding the past.

In the early twentieth century, Jakob von Uexküll revived the long-dormant music of the spheres. From the distant echoes of its ancient harmonies, Uexküll constructed what he called a *Kompositionslehre der Natur* ("composition theory of nature"), to which my title obliquely alludes. In a series of monographs spread across the first half of the twentieth century—including *Umwelt und Innenwelt der Tiere* (1909), *Theoretische Biologie* (1920), and *Bedeutungslehre* (1940)—Uexküll attempted to situate humankind within a broader, biologically and materially constituted semiotic nexus that encompasses the human and the nonhuman, the organic and inorganic, whose *harmonic* interrelations Uexküll deemed the "musical laws of nature" or a "theory of the music of life." Uexküll explicitly frames his semiotic project as an antimodern (specifically anti-Darwinian) critique of a mechanistic objectivism that would reduce the living organism to a functionalist "physico-chemical machine."[45] Uexküll's universe, much to the contrary, is perceptually alive, its semiotic web woven from a "functional cycle" (*Funktionskreis*)

41 Gilles Deleuze and Félix Guattari, *A Thousand Plateaus: Capitalism and Schizophrenia*, trans. Brian Massumi (Minneapolis: University of Minnesota Press, 1987), 349.

42 Alain Badiou, *Being and Event*, trans. Oliver Feltham (London: Continuum, 2005), 6.

43 Nikolaus M. Häring ed. *Commentaries on Boethius*, 570.

44 Iain Hamilton Grant, *Philosophies of Nature After Schelling* (London: Continuum, 2006), 6–14.

45 Jakob von Uexküll, *Theoretische Biologie* (Berlin: Verlag von Gebrüder Paetel, 1920), xiii.

of *Merkzeichen* and *Wirkzeichen*, "perception signs" and "operation signs," whose reintegration provided the means of rehabilitating a modern biology gone wrong. According to Uexküll, the modern split of the subjectively constituted perceptual universe from the objectively constituted functional universe can be dated with surprising accuracy. "It lies between Kepler and Newton":[46]

> Astronomy was originally a science of the perceptual side (*Merkseite*); it was a matter of finding the design behind the bewildering multitude of stars, a design ordained by God that made it possible for them to move in perfect harmony: on his search for the harmony Kepler found the laws governing the planetary motions. Newton on the other hand we find completely immersed in the operational side (*Wirkseite*) of the starry sky, as he formulates the laws of gravity. Kepler was looking for a design—Newton was looking for a cause for the same phenomenon.

Here, Kepler and Newton are mere historical foils for the real target of the severance of *Merkseite* from *Wirkseite*: Darwin's meaningless, mechanized universe, the inevitable result of the astronomical swerve from the perceptual to the operational.[47]

> First, the starry sky became a meaningless mechanical thing that turned around without accomplishing anything. As long as God was listening to the music of the celestial spheres, the sky did have a purpose, a divine performance. Without reaching the ear of God it dissolved into nothing and became a mechanical movement. . . .
>
> Ever since Darwin, the biologists were ardently trying to spirit away the perceptual side of living things (*die Merkseite der Lebewesen*) and only to pay attention to the operational side (*ihre Wirkseite*). Finally Man himself became an accidental product with purely mechanical, aimlessly functioning physical processes.

Uexküll's nostalgia, if I may call it that, for a premodern phenomenal world of appearances retroactively posits a premodern *arche* as its antimodern *telos*. His view of this magical unity of perception and activity that had declined into soulless, inhuman mechanical operations relies on an analogy of the difference between simply calculating the functions of this worldly mechanism and actually perceiving the result of its ongoing activity. But this is more than an analogy. When function supplanted perception, he proposes, "scientists began to deal

[46] Uexküll, "The New Concept of *Umwelt:* A Link between Science and the Humanities," trans. Gösta Brunow, *Semiotica* 134 (2001), 114.

[47] Ibid.

with the world in the way a deaf person deals with a street organ. The turning of the roller, the vibration of the tongues and the aerial waves, these things he can establish—but the tune stays hidden from him."[48] On the one hand, harmony is the result of a mechanistic worldview, but it is also an irreducible supplement to that mechanism; to know only the mechanics as a dull and lifeless thing, without the transcendental harmony that it produces, would be to remain deaf to the broader phenomenological and semiological perspectives that the worldly mechanism affords. "The countless environments [*Umwelten*] represent . . . the keyboard upon which Nature plays her symphony of meaning, beyond time and space. In our lifetime, and in our *Umwelt*, we are given the task of constructing a key in this gigantic keyboard, over which an invisible hand glides, playing."[49]

I begin with Uexküll—to whom, joined by Merleau-Ponty, Deleuze, Guattari, and Steven Shaviro, we will return in the postlude—not as an exercise in reception history, but precisely because his celestial harmony seems so distant from the classical accounts of cosmic concord. His is not a noetic harmony grounded in the abstract dance of mathematical structures. Quite the contrary, his is a perceptually, materially grounded harmony that seems antithetical to the Pythagorean emphasis on number. The most common story told about cosmic harmony, and about the harmony of the spheres specifically, is a story of "disenchantment," which usually entails a rather abstract account of "the ancients" and the magical grip that number and music had upon their minds, blinding them to their own presuppositions. As a token of this type, consider Daniel Chua's claim: "Tuning, for the ancients, was a magical formula; its numbers ordered the cosmos. . . . This enabled the inaudible sounds of the heavens to vibrate within the earthly soul, and conversely, for the audible tones of human music to reflect the celestial spheres, so that heaven and earth could be harmonized within the unity of a well-tuned scale."[50] Uexküll, however, can remind us that the concept of cosmic harmony is not to be understood as a pointedly historicized "fact" about the natural world that was eventually (finally) discredited and abandoned in an epistemic rupture or paradigm shift of a Foucauldian or Kuhnian sort. "To disenchant the world," Chua writes, "modernity had to sever the umbilical link of the monochord, disconnecting itself from the celestial realms in order to remove music as an explanation

48 Ibid.

49 Uexküll, *Bedeutungslehre*, Bios, Abhandlungen zur theoretischen Biologie und ihrer Geschichte sowie zur Philosophie der organischen Naturwissenschaften, Bd. 10 (Leipzig: Verlag von J. A. Barth, 1940), 159: "All die zahllosen Umwelten liefern . . . die Klaviatur, auf der die Natur ihre überzeitliche und überräumliche Bedeutungssymphonie spielt. Uns ist während unseres Lebens die Aufgabe zugewiesen, mit unserer Umwelt eine Taste in der riesenhaften Klaviatur zu bilden, über die eine unsichtbare Hand spielend hinübergleitet." On this passage, and the media-archeological history of its keyboard analogy, see Roger Moseley, "Digital Analogies: The Keyboard as Field of Musical Play," *Journal of the American Musicological Society* 68 (2015), 151–228 (at 206–207).

50 Daniel Chua, "Vincenzo Galilei, Modernity and the Division of Nature," in *Music Theory and Natural Order from the Renaissance to the Early Twentieth Century*, ed. Suzannah Clark and Alexander Rehding (Cambridge: Cambridge University Press, 2001), 21.

of the world."[51] Uexküll points us in a different direction and encourages us to consider this harmony as a site for the construction of materially constituted meaning.

In this, I join voice with Bruce Holsinger in decrying any claim on a "resolutely anticorporeal ontology" of medieval music, but I do so for a very different reason. Holsinger maintains, for instance, that "the platonist worldview adumbrated by Boethius and reiterated so often in medieval musical theory demands that the body stand precisely for the material remainder, for that which 'stains' and thus can never be fully assimilated to the universal order inherent in celestial *harmonia*."[52] There is no shortage of evidence for the line taken by Holsinger, or for the very real worries about the body voiced by medieval writers on music, some of it clearly in view in the passages discussed later in this book. But the material "stain" invoked by Holsinger—an echo of the lament in the ninth-century *Scholica enchiriadis* that sounding number is always "stained by the corporeal matter of voices and movements" (*corporea uocum et motuum materia decolorantur*)—conflates two different kinds of bodies that were carefully disentangled in many medieval accounts of (musical) sound and perception. Holsinger targets *sounding bodies*, that is, the bodily causes of sounds, "the fleshly instruments, constructed from the distended viscera of animals, the intestines and sinews of sheep and oxen that resonate whenever a stringed instrument is plucked or strummed";[53] I target (real and imagined) *sonic bodies*, the material effect of some action (deliberate or mechanical) upon a potentially resonant body (natural or artificial), which can be, and often was, considered separately from the bodily source of the sound. This move, of course, does not eliminate or even alleviate the "material stain"; if anything, it sharpens the problem and focuses our attention on the materiality of sound as the result of intermaterial relations. The materialistic harmonies of the micro- and macrocosms are not "material remainders" that can "never be fully assimilated to the universal order"; they are in fact the material condition for the human knowledge of, and on some accounts the very existence of, the objects constituted by and through harmonically organized intermaterial relations.

In this, I follow Brian Kane's "simple law": "Every sonic effect is the result of the interaction of a source and a cause."[54] Holsinger targets this passage from the *Scholica enchiriadis* precisely because it seems a clear instance of what Kane has deemed the "ontological separation of sound from source."[55] Stated more strongly: the *Scholica enchiriadis* uncannily anticipates the "phantasmagoric

[51] Ibid., 22–23.

[52] Bruce Holsinger, *Music, Body, and Desire in Medieval Culture: Hildegard of Bingen to Chaucer* (Stanford: Stanford University Press, 2001), 12, 6.

[53] Ibid., 9.

[54] Brian Kane, *Sound Unseen: Acousmatic Sound in Theory and Practice* (Oxford: Oxford University Press, 2014), 134.

[55] Ibid., 137.

separation of musical sound from the conditions of production," which is both the product and producer of the "history and rise of the autonomous musical work in the nineteenth century."[56] Roger Scruton might as well be describing the musical listener that the *Enchiriadis* tradition seems to presuppose when he argues:[57]

> The person who listens to sounds, and hears them as music . . ., is hearing the sounds *apart* from the material world. They are detached in his perception, and understood in terms of their experienced order. . . . What we understand, in understanding music, is not the material world, but the intentional object: the organization that can be heard in the experience.

Replace Scruton's "order" with the moniker preferred by the *Scholica enchiriadis*, "number," and the claim rings surprisingly similar (Schmid 113–114):

> Igitur quicquid in modulatione suave est, numerus operatur per ratas dimensiones vocum, quicquid rithmi delectabile prestant sive in modulationibus seu in quibuslibet rithmicis motibus, totum numerus efficit. Et voces quidem celeriter transeunt, numeri autem, qui corporea vocum et motuum materia decolorantur, manent.
>
> Whatever is pleasing in measured melody (*modulatio*) is brought about by number through fixed quantitative relations among musical sounds (*per ratas dimensiones uocum*). Whatever delight rhythms afford, whether in melodies or any rhythmic motions, is entirely the result of number. Musical sounds (*uoces*) pass away quickly, but numbers, though stained by the corporeal matter of musical sounds and motions, remain.

Sound by its very nature is always already embodied. Moreover, like the relation of smoke to fire, it indexes the bodily interactions that occur within the material world. But it also indexes the organization and structure of such interactions and thereby reveals through its very material presence the immaterial (numerical) relations instantiated between and among the indexed bodies. This is why twelfth-century philosophers, for instance, can insist upon hearing the human voice (*uox*) as an index of creative nature itself (*artifex natura*), as will be described in Chapter 4. Humanly generated sound is the result of an entirely natural, and entirely necessary, set of processes that ensure the balance (*temperamentum*),

[56] Ibid., 136–137.

[57] Roger Scruton, *The Aesthetics of Music* (New York: Oxford University Press, 1997), 221; qtd. in Kane, *Sound Unseen*, 137.

continuity, stability, and integrity of the human body. For the twelfth-century cosmologists, as for Uexküll, *Merkseite* and *Wirkseite*, perception and function, must go hand in hand. Not only does God listen to the divine performance of the celestial harmony, the cosmos itself is a listener that loves its own concord.

Mundus diligit concordiam

William of Conches puts it bluntly in his commentary on Plato's *Timaeus*: "The world loves concord."[58] There are three striking features of William's deceptively simple statement: agency, affect, and vulnerability. First, agency. For William could easily have ducked the issue and written that the "world has a kind of harmony," "is harmonious," or "is harmonized." Or he could have followed a well-established line of reasoning and granted explicit divine agency to that harmony, as does a contemporary commentator on the *Timaeus*, the otherwise unknown Hisdosus, who claims that harmony is the creator's eternal love, "by which he created all and harmoniously rules his creation with concord."[59] But William of Conches does neither. Rather, he allows that the world exercises an agency of its own and actively loves (the principle of) concord. Hence, even in this succinct formulation, the world is granted striking autonomy as a self-sustaining order. The world loves and actively seeks its own principle, thereby becoming a kind of Lucretian *machina mundi* (albeit without all the chancy, willy-nilly metaphysics that the original expression might still conjure). William's many appeals to the *machina mundi* do crucial and often explicitly anti-occasionalist philosophical work: divine power, he would say, is *too* powerful when dealing with the mundane details of natural philosophy. With customary acerbic wit, he writes in his *Philosophia*: "God can make a cow out of a tree trunk, but has he ever done so? Therefore, show some reason or purpose for why a thing is so, or cease to hold that it is so."[60] The devil is in the details, or rather God is *not* in the details; appeals to divine power merely duck the question and leave in William's mouth the bitter taste of "folk religion." To subsume the mechanisms of the "How?" under the omnipotence of the "Who?" is "to believe like peasants" (*credere ut rusticos*).[61]

The world does not merely seek harmony, maintain harmony, or engender harmony; it *loves* harmony, which brings up the second point I want to highlight:

[58] *Guillelmi Glos. sup. Tim.* 39.23–25.

[59] Paris, Bibliothèque nationale, lat. 8624, 17r: amor aeternus quo cuncta creauit et creata concorditer regit ea concordia.

[60] *Phil.* 2.3 (58C): Ut autem verbis rustici utar: "Potens est deus de trunco facere vitulum": Fecitne umquam? Vel igitur ostendant rationem, quare; vel utilitatem, ad quam hoc sit; vel sic esse iudicare desinant.

[61] *Phil.* 1.23 (56B): Sed quoniam ipsi nesciunt vires naturae, ut ignorantiae suae omnes socios habeant, nolunt eos aliquid inquirire, sed ut rusticos nos credere nec rationem quaerere. . . . Nos autem dicimus, in omnibus rationem esse quaerendam.

affect. William's cosmic love suggests an affective dimension to the worldly concord that (deliberately, no doubt) recalls Boethius's hymn to cosmic love at the end of book 2 of the *Consolatio philosophiae* (2.m8.13–15):

hanc rerum seriem ligat
terras ac pelagus regens
et caelo imperitans amor.

What binds all things in order,
Governing earth and sea and sky,
Is love.

In this poem, delivered by Lady Philosophy, Boethius exalts the cosmic love that binds the opposing forces of sensual reality and exhorts the realm of human interrelations to heed its harmonies, concluding, "O happy would be the human race, if the love that rules the heavens would also rule in your hearts!"[62] Its placement in the larger sweep of Boethius's argument, however, suggests a subtle but important distinction between Boethius's and William's affective evocations. In the *Consolation of Philosophy*, this poem is the linchpin in an argument intended to undermine the inconstant conceit, articulated by "Boethius" (as a character in the work), that the world is always at odds, that the order of the heavens contrasts with the tyranny of human experience. William of Conches shifts this cosmic love from a static unitary principle to a dynamic, autonomic affect exercised by the world itself. The world's balance and order, its proportionate structures, are loved because they are beautiful, and the recognition of that beauty puts the lover and loved in relation, in proportion, in concord, and the cycle starts all over again. Love, on the cosmic scale imagined by William's simple statement, is ultimately a self-love (not divine love) that blurs subject and object into a mutually affective entailment.

But love is fickle, and therein lies the rub, the negative logic of the cosmological affect and the third issue I want to tease out: vulnerability. If concord makes the world go round, then its converse, discord, is a continual, if hypothetical, threat to the maintenance of that world order. For discord would break the bonds of love. This becomes clear in the continuation of William's claim: "The world loves concord. And if the elements were to become discordant, the world would also dissolve" (*Mundus diligit concordiam. Et, si fieret discordia elementorum, dissolueretur et mundus*).[63] So too Boethius (2.m8.16–21):

Hic si frena remiserit,
quicquid nunc amat invicem

[62] *Cons. phil.* 2.m8.28–30: O felix hominum genus, / si vestros animos amor / quo caelum regitur regat! Cf. *Cons. phil.* 4.m6.

[63] *Guillelmi Glos. sup. Tim.* 39.23–25.

bellum continuo geret
et quam nunc socia fide
pulchris motibus incitant
certent solvere machinam.

If love's rein slackened
All things now held by mutual love
At once would fall to warring with each other
Striving to wreck that engine (*machina*) of the world.
Which now they drive
In mutual trust with motion beautiful.

Love, itself a kind of concord, thus imposes order that, if lacking, would leave the *machina mundi* vulnerable to dissolution. Comfortingly, the macrocosm comes with a divine warranty equally assured by both biblical and Platonic promises, for instance the Noahic covenant sealed by a rainbow in Genesis 9 and Timaeus's claim that amity, the *philia* of the cosmos, is "indissoluble by any agent other than Him who had bound it together" (32c). The microcosm, however, comes with no such money-back guarantee, and its vulnerability is an all too real, not at all hypothetical threat.

Finally, there is the concord itself. In many twelfth-century cosmological accounts, the mutual love that created entities share, understood as a concord among them, is a "real" feature of the world, a feature in fact that makes the world a unified whole and guards against the (potential) vulnerability of the aggregate. This concord is grounded in proportionally related quantitative structures actually present in the world around us (for instance, in the elements, the movements of the planets, the seasonal round, and the bodies of animals and plants, as well as, of course, in vibrating strings and other resonant musical instruments). This view presents us with an ontologically flattened world, wherein the lowest order of things (the elements) have the power, the agency, to be the very undoing of the entire cosmic structure. The world's cosmological affect, its love of concord, would extend equally to both the most elemental harmony, the concordant relations among and between earth, air, fire, and water, and the most transcendental harmony among the highest of the celestial beings, the harmony of the spheres. Concord is ontologically indifferent and is loved equally, whatever and wherever its manifestation. It is in this sense that William of Conches can claim, in a striking reversal of the usual ontological hierarchy, that the soul loves the body (as we will see in Chapter 3). Macrocosmic concord maps onto the microcosmic realm, where the vulnerability of human corporeality, of human frailty, is yet the very condition of possibility for the soul's agency and affect.

But there is another way to understand talk of cosmological concord. In this second view it is not a "real" feature of certain worldly phenomena but an epistemological avenue toward the understanding of worldly realities through the anagogic function of analogy. The language of concord and harmony would offer ways of talking about different kinds of natural relations, even if the phenomena themselves are not, *stricto sensu*, quantitative and subject to "real" arithmetic and harmonic, much less material, interrelations. Qua analogy, it presupposes some sort of fundamental difference between the way we talk about natural phenomena and the ontology of the natural phenomena themselves.[64] This way of thinking about the harmony of the world was particularly employed in the case of the psychological harmonies of both individual human souls (Chapter 3) and the world soul (Chapter 5). Here an ontological hierarchy is strictly maintained, in that lower-level analogies, which themselves may yet embody a necessary ontological relation between cause and effect, provide an anagogic tool for understanding a higher ontological reality.

The two ways of approaching cosmological concord, then, are (1) as a mode of *being* in the world, and (2) as a mode of *knowing* beings in the world. Moreover, the harmonic and sonic structures and analogies that can explain both how things exist and how they are known in turn engender a mode of articulation, a resonant semiotic system, that is at once communicative and affective, rational and aesthetic. For, in positing the cosmos as a well-ordered and harmonized collection of interconnected created entities, the theory itself mimetically captures that order; the theory itself marshals a kind of aesthetic attractiveness that allures, seduces, incites, and demands an affective response from the knower. It provokes and instills the understanding for which it argues.

The Harmony of the Spheres: Material and Affect

Even Aristotle recognized the aesthetic allure of the Pythagorean music of the spheres, the doctrine that the celestial bodies in their eternal revolutions make a sweet harmony. In an otherwise devastating critique of this cosmic harmony in his *De caelo* (290b30ff.), Aristotle describes the doctrine as one that has been formulated "melodiously and musically" (ἐμμελῶς καὶ μουσικῶς). Although the adverbs could be a mere rhetorical charm of Aristotle's own, a punning play on the musical theory that he targets, Stephen Halliwell has argued that they "can hardly be ironic." Rather, "they acknowledge a certain attractiveness of language and perhaps a poetic imaginativeness in the terms in which the doctrine is couched."[65]

[64] Cf. Reviel Netz's claim about Pythagorean proportional statements: "This is proportion: the most basic way of saying, in a literal way, that two separate domains are, in some defined way, the same. They are different; and yet they embody the same relations. Thus proportion-statements are the most natural route to be taken by the Pythagoreans. Their project was to offer an intellectually systematic correlate of a mystery practice" ("The Pythagoreans," in *Mathematics and the Divine: A Historical Study*, ed. T. Koetsier and L. Bergmans [Amsterdam: Elsevier, 2004], 94).

[65] Stephen Halliwell, "An Aristotelian Perspective on Plato's Dialogues," in *New Essays on Plato*, ed., F.-G. Herrmann (Swansea: Classical Press of Wales, 2006), 193.

But Aristotle's literalization of the harmony of the spheres, or the literalized version of the theory that he takes as exemplary, materializes the harmony of the spheres in such a way that the very materialization, the sounding reality, becomes "disproportional" to the cosmos that would give rise to such a sonic experience. Aristotle claims that if the celestial bodies produced sound, then the tremendous sounds that they made would be immensely destructive, cataclysmic, world-shattering. The aesthetic allure of the theory belies the deaestheticized, disproportionate reality. Aristotle's anti-Pythagorean argument, however, culminates in a remarkably Pythagorean conclusion: "It is as though nature had foreseen the result, that if their movement were other than it is, nothing on this earth could maintain its character."[66] Aristotle beats the Pythagoreans at their own game and reinscribes the well-ordered unfolding of Nature's plan by destroying the literalization of celestial music while simultaneously underscoring its analogical logic. In other words, nature maintains its own harmonious stability, maintains the delicate equilibrium of all things here on earth, by providentially ensuring the *silence* of the heavens. Whatever harmony there might be, it must remain unsounded; the very excessiveness of its literal, material realization would be the cosmos's own undoing.[67]

Nearly a millennium later, amidst a set of strenuous arguments in support of the very *musica mundi* that Aristotle had so vociferously decried, Boethius used an argument surprisingly analogous to the Aristotelian claim that it is as if nature had foreseen what is necessary for its own stability. In his *De institutione musica*, the foundational text for music's universal scope, Boethius similarly argued that nothing can exist whose excessiveness could destroy anything else.[68]

> Et sicut in gravibus chordis is vocis est modus, ut non ad taciturnitatem gravitas usque descendat, atque in acutis ille custoditur acuminis modus, ne nervi nimium tensi vocis tenuitate rumpantur, sed totum sibi sit consentaneum atque conveniens: ita etiam in mundi musica pervidemus nihil ita esse nimium posse, ut alterum propria nimietae dissolvat.

> For just as there is a proper measure of pitch in the lower strings, so that the lowness does not descend all the way to silence, and likewise the proper measure of pitch in the higher strings is carefully maintained, so that the strings, when stretched too taut, are not

[66] *De caelo* 2.9, 291a24–26: ὥσπερ τὸ μέλλον ἔσεσθαι προνοούσης τῆς φύσεως, ὅτι μὴ τοῦτον τὸν τρόπον ἐχούσης τῆς κινήσεως οὐθὲν ἂν ἦν τῶν περὶ τὸν δεῦρο τόπον ὁμοίως ἔχον.

[67] Cf. Reviel Netz's observation on this passage: "The music of the harmony of the spheres is taken literally, and so a strange, absurd world comes into being—an ever-present, never-heard soundtrack to accompany the universe. Aristotle's Pythagoreans listen to the inaudible" ("The Pythagoreans," 84).

[68] *Inst. mus.* 1.2 (188.15–21).

> broken by the tenuity of the pitch, but the whole is consistent and harmonious with itself: so too in the music of the world we discern that nothing is able to exist which would dissolve anything else by its excessiveness.

What is most surprising about this statement is not its conclusion but the analogical ground of its argument. What it shares with Aristotle's denial is the "refus[al] to treat the theory as a more abstract metaphysical statement—e.g., that the true account of the motions of the stars is that they manifest the mathematical *structure* of musical harmony."[69] For Boethius they doubtless do. And yet Boethius's description here of the *musica mundana* relies not on the concept of number but on the *physical* (not metaphysical) equilibrium that the manifold bodies of and in the cosmos maintain. I will have more to say about this in Chapter 5. For now, I highlight only the aspects of Boethius's presentation that are relevant to my claim that this cosmic harmony is not (only) a matter of abstracted, noetic, numerical precision but is predicated upon material interactions and intermaterial relations. Boethius's harmony of the celestial mechanics (*machina caeli*) is described in terms of spatial location and orbital speed of the celestial bodies; of the elements, in terms of their various and contrary powers; and of the seasons, in terms of the periodic patterning of generation and corruption, the fruits that are destroyed or brought to harvest as the seasonal round rings it cyclical changes. All are likened to the *physical*—not numerical—equilibrium of well-tuned strings: the low strings not so slack as to descend into silence; the high strings not so taut as to snap. Strings, sound, and silence—not number—are the operative principles. Aristotle calls it nature, Boethius calls it harmony, but both, if from opposing philosophical camps, are talking about the same thing: the physical world of appearances (τὰ φαινόμενα).

The seasons, according to Boethius, embody this principle: "Whatever exists either brings forth its own fruits or assists others in bringing forth their own. For what winter constrains, spring loosens, summer heats, and autumn ripens, and the seasons in their turn either bring forth their own fruits or contribute to the fruitfulness of the other seasons."[70] The phenomenological approach taken here comes into sharper focus when we compare Boethius's account of the seasonal

[69] Netz, "The Pythagoreans," 84. Aristotle demonstrably knew the metaphysical structure that undergirds the Pythagorean enterprise; e.g., *Met.* 985b31–986a3: "Moreover, because they [the "so-called" Pythagoreans] saw that the attributes and ratios of musical scales consisted in numbers—well, since other things seemed to be modeled [ἀφωμοιῶσθαι] on numbers in their nature in its entirety, and numbers seemed to be primary of all nature, they began to assume that the elements of numbers were the elements of things that are and that the whole of heaven was musical scale [ἁρμονία] and number [ἀριθμός]."

[70] *Ins. mus.* 1.2 (188.21–25): Verum quicquid illud est, aut suos affert fructus aut aliis auxiliatur ut afferant. Nam quod constringit hiems, ver laxat, torret aestas, maturat autumnus, temporaque vicissim vel ipsa suos afferunt fructus vel aliis ut afferant subministrant.

round against other "Pythagorean" *testimonia* to the harmony of the seasons. For instance, Aristides Quintilianus (a Greek music theorist of the late third or early fourth century) presents a seasonal harmony directly correlated with an elemental harmony derived from the Platonic elemental solids (*Tim.* 55d–56b): fire = pyramid = summer = 4; earth = cube = autumn = 6; air = octahedron = spring = 8; and water = icosahedron = winter = 12. "Thus," Aristides concludes, "as Pythagoras is reported to have said, spring stands to autumn in the ratio of the fourth, to winter in that of the fifth, and to summer in that of the octave. . . . Their proportionality is thus musical, completing the duple ratio in various ways from epitritic and hemiolic, and the other way round."[71] Plutarch (ca. 46–120), while discussing the sun's solstices and equinoxes with an ear to the harmony of the spheres, ascribes a slightly different theory to the Chaldeans, i.e., mathematical astronomers, but the result is the same: the harmony of seasons instantiates (somehow) the octave.[72] The "Pythagorean" *musica mundana* proffered by Aristides and Plutarch is more concerned with an abstract set of correspondences between specific numbers—correlated to the elements, and thereby the quality of the seasons in which those elements dominated—than with their physico-temporal unfolding as a *lived* reality for humans within the cosmos. This differs *toto caelo* from the materially and temporally extended analogy of the Boethian evocation of the balance of the seasons. Aristides and Plutarch present us with a static, if symmetrical, proportioning of the seasons based on the divisions of the octave. Boethius's musical analogy for the seasonal round, however, makes no reference to the numerically proportionate structure(s) of his strings. Instead, he invites us to consider the very materiality of the strings themselves, a materiality which imposes a limit upon the otherwise unlimited slackness or tautness at either extreme of their sounding. Excess in either direction would destroy their harmony.

In fact, the disharmony of "excess" and the harmony of "moderation" are the primary themes of Boethius's *De institutione musica*, whose prooemium stands as an elegant encomium of music's great moderating force. With a rhetorical technique that we may aptly deem "shock and awe," Boethius marshals an astonishing array of ancient *testimonia* to music's affective materiality, well before he has grounded such effects in the numerical principles that it embodies. The arcane

[71] Aristides Quintilianus, *De musica* 3.19 (119.15–18); trans. Andrew Barker, *Greek Musical Writings II: Harmonic and Acoustic Theory*, Cambridge Readings in the Literature of Music (Cambridge: Cambridge University Press, 1989), 519.

[72] Plutarch, *De anim. procr.* 1028f; ed., and trans. Harold Cherniss, *Plutarch: Moralia, XII.1*, Loeb Classical Library (Cambridge, MA: Harvard University Press), 329–331: "The Chaldaeans assert that spring turns out to be related to autumn in the ratio of the fourth and to winter in that of the fifth and to summer in that of the octave." If Euripides is to be believed, Plutarch continues (citing frag. 990), "it is in the ratio of an octave that the seasons change." Cherniss (ad loc.) reports the view of Otto Neugebauer that "the ratios were derived from twelve, nine, eight, and six, taken to be the number of days by which spring, summer, winter, and autumn respectively exceed a common measure."

Lacedaemonian decree, in whose impenetrable (even for Boethius!) Spartan dialect the rabble-rouser Timotheus was censured for introducing immoderate and excessive "chromatic" melodies that threatened the very moderation of virtue (*uirtutis modestia*); the mythic tales of ancient sages, such as Pythagoras and Empedocles, calming many a frenzied youth; the wondrous healing power of melody exploited by Terpander, Ismenias the Theban, and Democritus over bodily ills exacerbated by disturbed states of mind: all of these attest to the unique sway that music has over both soul and body. Hence Boethius's most famous claim: "Whence it is that, since there are four mathematical disciplines, the other three share with music the task of searching for truth; but music is associated not only with speculation but with morality as well."[73] The prooemium, then, is more than an encomium; it is also a powerful argument for the reality of the harmonic composition of cosmos, body, and soul. The many mythic, even anecdotal examples of music's affective power (both therapeutic and corruptive) are wrapped in arguments that frame this musical ethics in terms of the *musica mundana* and *musica humana*. Near the beginning of the prooemium, immediately following an approving glance at the *Timaeus* and its harmonious construction of the "world soul" (on which see Chapter 5),[74] Boethius suggests (entirely in line with *Tim.* 47d2) that the harmonies in sound are akin to the harmonies in us. When we hear melodies and are delighted by them, we can recognize that we too are composed in the same likeness.[75] Thus, with it established as a basic principle that "likeness attracts, whereas unlikeness disgusts and repels,"[76] Boethius launches into his many examples, finally circling back again at the end of the prooemium to remind us what his various stories prove in toto:[77]

> Sed quorsum istaec? Quia non potest dubitari, quin nostrae animae et corporis status eisdem quodammodo proportionibus videatur esse compositus, quibus armonicas modulationes posterior disputatio coniungi copularique monstrabit.
>
> But to what purpose are all these? So that there can be no doubt that the state of our soul and body seems to be composed, somehow, by the

[73] *Inst. mus.* 1.1 (179.20–23): Unde fit ut, cum sint quattuor matheseos disciplinae, ceterae quidem in investigatione veritatis laborent, musica vero non modo speculationi verum etiam moralitati coniuncta sit.

[74] *Inst. mus.* 1.1 (180.3–5): Hinc etiam internosci potest, quod non frustra a Platone dictum sit, mundi animam musica convenientia fuisse coniunctam.

[75] *Inst. mus.* 1.1 (180.5–9): Cum enim eo, quod in nobis est iunctum convenienterque coaptatum, illud excipimus, quod in sonis apte convenienterque coniunctum est, eoque delectamur, nos quoque ipsos eadem similitudine compactos esse cognoscimus.

[76] *Inst. mus.* 1.1 (180.9–10): amica est enim similitudo, dissimilitudo odiosa atque contraria.

[77] *Inst. mus.* 1.1 (186.8–187.10).

> very same proportions that, as subsequent demonstrations will prove, join and unite harmonic melodies (*armonicas modulationes*).

Following Aristotle's lead nearly a millennium after Boethius, however, the fourteenth-century music theorist Johannes de Grocheio dismissed the Boethian *musica mundana* and *musica humana* as mere figments of the Pythagorean imagination: "Those who posit such divisions either make them up, wish to obey Pythagoras (or others) rather than the truth, or are ignorant of nature and logic."[78] As if in direct response to Boethius's rhetorical question—"What else [but *musica humana*] could blend together the elements of the body or hold its parts together in a calculated harmony (*rata coaptatio*)?—Grocheio posed his own rhetorical question: "Who ever heard a complexion make a sound?"[79] Twelfth-century readers, however, were not so literal-minded, and by synthesizing Boethius with Plato, Calcidius, Macrobius, and Martianus, they conceived a remarkable variety of solutions to explain and exploit for its full philosophical and affective powers the various (material, sonorous, natural-philosophical, and metaphysical) modalities of *musica*. The solutions they offered, and the questions they posed, are the subject of this book.

[78] Ernst Rohloff, ed., *Der Musiktraktat des Johannes de Grocheo nach den Quellen neu herausgegeben mit Übersetzung ins Deutsche und Revisionsbericht* (Leipzig: Komissionsverlag Gebrüder Reinecke, 1943), 46.35–37: Qui vero sic dividunt, aut dictum suum fingunt, aut volunt Pythagoricis vel aliis magis quam veritati oboedire, aut sunt naturam et logicam ignorantes. For more on the survival and denial of the traditional Boethian tripartition in the thirteenth and early fourteenth centuries, see Gilles Rico, "Music in the Arts Faculty of Paris in Thirteenth and Early Fourteenth Centuries" (PhD diss., Oxford University, 2005).

[79] Rohloff, *Der Musiktraktat des Johannes de Grocheo*, 46.42–43: Quis enim audivit complexionem sonare?

PART I

THE FRAMEWORK

1

Harmonizing the World

Natural Philosophy and Order

Et est mundus ordinata collectio creaturarum.
—William of Conches, *Glosae super Platonem*, 36

"Imagine a large hall like a theatre." So begins the final fantasy of Lewis Fry Richardson's 1922 landmark publication in modern meteorology, *Weather Prediction by Numerical Process*.[1] Consciously or not, the maverick English mathematician and statistician here follows in a long and prestigious tradition of theater metaphors that were popular throughout antiquity and late antiquity—metaphors that sought to capture the unfolding drama of providence and fate through talk of the world as "akin to a theater" (*quemadmodum theatrum*, as in Cicero, for instance).[2] But Richardson's meteorological fantasy has a twist and his metaphor is mixed. His theatrical world is a symphony in the round (see figure 1.1):

> After so much hard reasoning, may one play with a fantasy? Imagine a large hall like a theatre, except that the circles and galleries go right round through the space usually occupied by the stage. The walls of this chamber are painted to form a map of the globe. The ceiling represents the north polar regions, England is in the gallery, the tropics in the upper circle, Australia on the dress circle and the antarctic in the pit. A myriad computers [i.e., workers who compute] are at work upon the weather of the part of the map where each sits, but each computer attends only to one equation or part of an equation. . . . From the floor of the pit a tall pillar rises to half the height of the hall. It carries a large pulpit on its top. In this sits the man in charge of the whole theatre; he

[1] Lewis Fry Richardson, *Weather Prediction by Numerical Process* (Cambridge: Cambridge University Press, 1922), 219.

[2] *De finibus* 3.67.

Figure 1.1 Lewis Fry Richardson's "symphonic" weather-calculating theatre (Alf Lannerbäck), reproduced from *Dagens Nyheter* (September 22, 1984). Courtesy of Lennart Lannerbäck.

> is surrounded by several assistants and messengers. One of his duties is to maintain a uniform speed of progress in all parts of the globe. In this respect he is like the conductor of an orchestra in which the instruments are slide-rules and calculating machines.

For many readers, Richardson's whimsical fantasy of a fully computistical world has proven surprisingly prescient. It has often been pointed out that the architecture of his forecasting theater has a striking resemblance to the architecture of a modern massively parallel processor.[3] But even more striking than the computational structure of Richardson's fantasy are the mixed metaphors in which it is couched. The world is at once machine, theater, church, and orchestra—the mechanistic play of drama, theology, and music. In this respect, its closest analogues are not presciently modern but decidedly premodern, namely the many medieval wind and season diagrams that "give insight not only into conceptions of the structure and the functioning of the sublunary and corporeal part of the world but also into its relation to divinity"[4] (e.g., Figure 1.2).

[3] See Peter Lynch, *The Emergence of Numerical Weather Prediction: Richardson's Dream* (Cambridge: Cambridge University Press, 2014), 247; also, Frederik Nebeker, *Calculating the Weather: Meteorology in the 20th Century* (San Diego: Academic Press, 1995), 58ff.

[4] Barbara Obrist, "Wind Diagrams and Medieval Cosmology," *Speculum* 72 (1997), 33–84, at 84.

Figure 1.2 Twelfth-century wind diagram (*rota*), accompanying Isidore, *Etym.* 13.11.1–14. Walters Art Museum, MS W 73, f. 1v. Courtesy of the Walters Art Museum.

Richardson's fantasy is a reimagining of cosmic harmony, what Boethius had called *musica mundana*, albeit composed not through Boethius's simple whole number ratios but in minute and complex differential equations that, when properly orchestrated, recompose the cosmic performance of the weather. At stake in his symphonic calculating machine is the *predictability* of nature, and thereby our ability to reverse engineer its underlying structure in order to forecast future states and events. Moreover, the determination of this regularity and predictability requires calculated effort. In a jaunty mnemonic couplet that would have pleased medieval readers, Richardson summarized one object of his calculations, namely turbulence: "big whirls have little whirls that feed on their velocity, and little whirls have lesser whirls and so on to viscosity."[5]

Twelfth-century natural philosophers set themselves to a similar task, if both more universal in scope and more limited in the specificity of its claims. In this chapter, I seek to demonstrate the irreducibly relational and intermaterial composition of the natural world, according to the cosmologists, and the concomitant idea of nature as a carefully ordered and harmonized set of principles governing the created world. The intent is partly polemical. By all classical accounts, I'm looking for harmony in all the wrong places: not in the mathematical structures of the quadrivium but in the material realm of natural philosophy, known (then and now) as physics (*physica*). In the second chapter of this first part I will present evidence for the disciplinary configurations, the divisions of philosophy, which enabled this approach to the world. And rest assured that in part 2 of this book (Chapters 3 through 5) we will drill down, deep down, into the mathematical substructures that nature embodies. I want to start, however, by thinking more holistically about nature as a superstructural phenomenon, understood as the sum total of the various and sundry created entities that crowd, jostle, and compete within its capacious embrace.

One popular twelfth-century definition of the world neatly captures this holistic perspective: "the world is an ordered collection of all created entities" (*mundus est ordinata collectio omnium creaturarum*).[6] The crux of this definition turns on the precise meaning of "ordered" (*ordinata*). While there is nothing about the

5 Richardson, *Weather Prediction*, 66.

6 William of Conches, *Glos. sup. Tim.* 36.3; *Glos. sup. Boet.*, 2.m8.13 et 3.m9.26–27; *Glos. sup. Macr.*, comment. ad 1.3.4 and 1.14.2. Cf. the *Florilegium Rothomagense* (ed. Édouard Jeauneau, *"Lectio philosophorum." Recherches sur l'École de Chartres* [Amsterdam: A. M. Hakkert, 1973], 107) and the *Compilacio Monacensis* (ed. Martin Grabmann, *Handschriftliche Forschungen und Mitteilungen zum Schrifttum des Wilhelm von Conches* [Munich: Verlag der Bayrischen Akademie der Wissenschafter, 1935], 52); Hisdosus, *De anima mundi Platonica* (Paris, BnF, lat. 8624, f. 17r—see Appendix 2); Anon., *Glosae super Trismegistum* 54 (ed. Paolo Lucentini, "*Glosæ super Trismegistum*: Un commento medievale all'*Asclepius* ermetico," *Archives d'histoire doctrinale et littéraire du Moyen Âge* 62 [1995], 251). The phrase ultimately derives from Apuleius, *De mundo*, cap. 1: Mundus est ornata ordinatio.

definition itself that presupposes any musical context, any musical analogy, or even any mathematical formula (save for a sequence of events and entities that could presumably be numerable and enumerated), twelfth-century cosmologists frequently explain this cosmically ordered structure in musical, proportional, and often affective terms as a way of confirming the self-sustaining cosmic order set in motion by divine power at the moment of creation. In the Apuleian phrase (*De mundo* 1 [289]) whence this definition derives, this order is "an ornamented ordering" (*mundus est ornata ordinatio*). Apuleius's *De mundo* attempts here to accommodate in Latin the elegant word play of the Greek, pseudo-Aristotelian *On the World* (Περὶ κόσμου, 391b9) that Apuleius himself was adapting for Latin readers. The play of κόσμος ("universe, order") and διακόσμησις ("ordering, arrangement") becomes the play of *ornata* ("arranged, ornamented") and *ordinatio* ("ordering, regulating").

I trace the brief history of this definition partly as a cautionary tale: the idea of a well-ordered and harmonized nature is not new to the twelfth century, and it has a long and complicated history, which I could (but won't) trace through early Pythagoreans such as Philolaus[7] and Archytas,[8] through to later Greek commentators on Plato such as Proclus.[9] But the comparison of this version, "the world is an ordered collection of all created entities," against its ancient analogues can also reveal something new about twelfth-century inquiries into nature: namely, their focus on the multiplicity and universality of the natural world. It is not just an ordered arrangement *simpliciter*; it is an ordered aggregate of all the singular parts of that whole. Their task was bigger and, in a way, harder: like Richardson's ambitious attempt to forecast the weather, they began from the turbulent and bewildering multiplicity of the world around us and sought to reverse engineer the natural laws that held the aggregate in order. William of Conches didn't mince words about the immensity of the efforts involved: *soli ueritati insudabimus!* ("We will sweat only for the truth!").

[7] Fr. 6 (= Stobaeus, *Eclogae* 1.21.7d): it is necessary that such things [sc. unlike and unrelated things] be bonded together by *harmonia*, if they are going to be held in an order (ἐν κόσμῳ). On Philolaus's conception of nature and harmony, see Carl Huffman, *Philolaus of Croton, Pythagorean and Presocratic: A Commentary on the Fragments and Testimonia with Interpretive Essays* (Cambridge: Cambridge University Press, 1993), 123–145; Phillip Sidney Horky, *Plato and the Pythagoreanism* (Oxford: Oxford University Press), 144–149.

[8] Fr. A19c (= ps.-Plutarch, *On Music* 1147a): For Pythagoras, Archytas, Plato and their associates as well as the rest of the ancient philosophers used to say that the motion of the universe and the movement of the stars did not arise and become organized without music. For they say that all things were arranged by god in accordance with harmony. On which, see Carl Huffman, *Archytas of Tarentum: Pythagorean, Philosopher and Mathematician King* (Cambridge: Cambridge University Press, 2005), 481–482.

[9] Marije Martijn, *Proclus on Nature: Philosophy of Nature and Its Methods in Proclus' Commentary on Plato's* Timaeus (Leiden: Brill, 2010).

In Search of Nature

Twelfth-century cosmologists were not without late-ancient support in this quest. As was so often the case, Boethius (himself indebted to the second-century Pythagorean, Nicomachus of Gerasa) provided them a key, a most profound teaching (*profundissima disciplina*), that he promised would unlock the entire force of nature and the integrity of its constituent parts (*quae ad omnem naturae vim rerumque integritatem maxima ratione pertineat*):[10]

> bonitas definita et sub scientiam cadens animoque semper imitabilis et perceptibilis prima natura est et suae substantiae decore perpetua, infinitum vero malitiae dedecus est, nullis propriis principiis nixum, sed natura semper errans a boni definitione principii tamquam aliquo signo optimae figurae impressa componitur et ex illo erroris fluctu retinetur. Nam nimiam cupiditatem iraeque immodicam effrenationem quasi quidam rector animus pura intelligentia roboratus adstringit, et has quodammodo inaequalitatis formas temperata bonitate constituit.
>
> Goodness, [being] limited, tractable to knowledge, and forever imitable and perceptible to the soul, is by nature first and perpetual in the beauty of a substance all its own, whereas the baseness of evil, being unlimited and resting on no principles of its own but by nature forever wandering, acquires composure from the limited nature of the principle associated with the Good by having impressed upon it, as it were, a kind of seal of the noblest form and finds respite from its fluctuating wandering. For, like a kind of ruler, the soul, strengthened by pure intelligence, curbs excessive cupidity and immoderate, unbridled irascibility and, in a way, reduces these forms of inequality to a tempered goodness.

At stake here is the ultimate reducibility of inequality to equality. According to Boethius, inequality is an "ugly" (*dedecus*) privation of the knowable and beautiful (*decus*) limit of "the Good," and it must thereby be tempered, we might say "harmonized" or "tuned" (*temperata*), by the "limited nature of the principle associated with the Good."[11] Boethius returns to this idea again and again in his quadrivial works on arithmetic and music. Equality is the "mother" and "root" (*mater*

[10] *Inst. ar.* 1.32 (66.8–15).

[11] The view articulated here is additionally embedded within a psychological context, specifically the Platonic tripartition of the soul into its "limited" rational aspect (λογιστικόν) and its "unlimited" irrational appetite, *cupiditas* (ἐπιθυμία), and spiritedness, *iracundia* (θυμός). The ethical implications of this psychological reformulation of Pythagorean doctrines can't detain us here, but we will return to it at the end of this chapter.

and *radix*) from which the multitudinous forms of inequalities grow and degenerate, and by which it has set a limit (*margo*) for their otherwise unbounded contrariety.[12] Thierry of Chartres, in his commentary on the *De institutione arithmetica*, recognized the precise utility of this "most profound teaching": it pertained to the "penetration and understanding of physics, i.e., natural philosophy."[13] In twelfth-century cosmology, the much-touted "rediscovery" of this harmonized nature, the reduction of inequality to equality, was a crucial component in understanding and articulating the establishment and maintenance of the world-order, the cosmos.

"Nature," however, is an equivocal term. This simple fact was not lost on twelfth-century thinkers. Perhaps finding solace in Cicero's own admission that "nature itself is difficult to define" (*De inuent.* 1.34), Gilbert of Poitiers, a student of Bernard of Chartres and chancellor at Chartres, lingers briefly on the ambiguity of the concept in his commentary on Boethius's *Opuscula sacra*: "Nature is such an equivocal term (*multiplex nomen*) that it is said of various kinds of things in the various disciplines not only in different ways but even with different meanings (*significationes*). For philosophers, ethicists, logicians, and theologians employ this term in most disparate ways."[14] In his *Didascalicon*, Hugh of St. Victor concurs and, for the benefit of his readers, distills (*conicere*) the prolixity of the ancient authorities on the subject into three general definitions: nature is (1) the archetypal exemplar, within the divine mind, for all creation, (2) the property or unique individuator (*proprium* or *propria differentia*) of each thing individually, and (3) a creative fire (*artifex ignis*).[15] Alan de Lille, nearer the end of the century, makes no such concession to his readers' patience. His theological dictionary, the *Distinctiones*, lists no less than eleven distinct definitions of *natura*, which run the gamut from Boethian metaphysics to Salernian physiology.[16] Confronted with this proliferation of definitions and no less confronted with the brute multiplicity of the natural world, twelfth-century intellectuals sought to carve out some kind of order—or rather, to unmask the order already latent within the world, for, in

[12] *Inst. ar.* 1.32 (66.20–22): ut ipsa quodammodo aequalitas matris et radicis obtinens vim ipsa omnes inaequalitatis species ordinesque profundat. *Inst. ar.* 2.1 (77.15–18): Ita igitur, quoniam ex aequalitatis margine cunctas inaequalitatis species proficisi videmus, omnis a nobis inaequalitas ad aequalitatem velut ad quoddam elementum proprii generis resolvatur.

[13] Irène Caiazzo, ed., *Thierry of Chartres, The Commentary on the De arithmetica of Boethius* (Toronto: Pontifical Institute of Mediaeval Studies, 2015), 145.

[14] *CEut.* 1.2: Natura enim multiplex nomen est adeo quod non solum multis modis uerum etiam multis significationibus de rebus diuersorum in diuersis etiam facultatibus generum dicitur. Nam et philosophi et ethici et logici et theologici usu plurimo ponunt hoc nomen (Nikolaus Häring, ed., *The Commentaries on Boethius by Gilbert of Poitiers* [Toronto: Pontifical Institute of Mediaeval Studies, 1966], 243).

[15] *Did.* 1.10: plura veteres de natura dixisse inveniuntur, sed nihil ita ut non aliquid restare videatur. quantum tamen ego ex eorum dictis conicere possum, tribus maxime modis huius vocabuli significatione uti solebant, singulis suam definitionem assignando.

[16] *Dist.* s.v. *natura*, PL 210, 871.

the already cited Apuleian phrase, which becomes a constant refrain in the twelfth century, *est mundus ordinata collectio creaturarum* ("the world is an ordered collection of created entities").

While Boethius provided one key to unlocking the secrets of nature, Plato himself, through the medium of his fourth-century translator and commentator Calcidius, provided the rationale for the quest in the first place. Plato's dictum, in *Timaeus* 28a, that "nothing can come to be without a cause" (παντὶ γὰρ ἀδύνατον χωρὶς αἰτίου γένεσιν σχεῖν) was silently elaborated by Calcidius, who expanded this foundational principle to read: "nothing can come into being, whose rise is not preceded by a lawful cause and reason (*legitima causa et ratio*)."[17] While we might first assume that *causa et ratio* is an innocent hendiadys for Plato's αἰτία ("cause"), an assumption that would well suit Calcidius's usual translation strategy,[18] and that *legitima* ("lawful") is likewise a rather innocuous expansion upon Plato's parsimonious principle, there is more at work here, which will prove foundational in the twelfth-century quest for a science of nature.

In the opening of his commentary, Calcidius explains the textual strategy of the *Timaeus* itself in strikingly similar terms: "Since this book treats of the constitution (*status*) of the universe and provides a causal explanation (*causa et ratio*) of all those things the cosmos comprises, it was inevitable that many and varied questions would arise."[19] As Christina Hoenig has observed, the same phrase *causa et ratio* appears again in Calcidius's rendering of the famous passage (29b2–d3) in which Timaeus reflects upon his own methodology and describes his account as but an εἰκὼς λόγος (a "likely account"), constrained as it is by the "likeliness" of its target, the created world, itself a copy or likeness of its uncreated model.[20] What is at stake, for Calcidius and Timaeus alike, is the (metaphysical) status of the *causa et ratio*, here translating λόγος, that can be proffered when dealing with the differential metaphysical status of copy and model: "the explanatory account (*causa et ratio*) of an abiding kind and stable nature, discernible to intellect and wisdom, is itself constant, discernible, and unimpeachable, but the explanatory account of

[17] *Tim.* 28a5–6. *Translatio Calcidii* 20.21–22: Nihil enim fit, cuius ortum non legitima causa et ratio praecedat.

[18] E.g., in the passage analyzed below (47c4–e2, pp. 53–56) we find: συγγενεῖς = cognatas et uelut consanguineas; ἀνάρμοστον = discrepantes et inconsonantes; ἄμετρον = *numerorum et modorum nesciam*, etc.

[19] *In Tim.* 2 (58.1–3): In hoc porro libro cum de statu agatur uniuersae rei omniumque eorum quae mundus complectitur causa et ratio praestetur, necesse fuit multas et uarias existere questiones. Recently, Christina Hoenig ("Εἰκὼς λόγος: Plato in Translation(s)," *Methodos* 13 [2013], 29) has suggested that the *causa et ratio* here reflects Calcidius's own exegetical strategy, translating, "In this work, since it treats of the nature of the universe of all those things the cosmos comprises, let an explanatory account be provided." While I cannot agree with her translation and maintain that the *causa et ratio* discussed here is Plato's, not Calcidius's, her discussion of this and other passages in Calcidius's translation and commentary have been helpful in clarifying the exegetical connections between the translation and commentary.

[20] See Hoenig, "Εἰκὼς λόγος," 27–37.

that which is generated (*facta*) as a similitude of what is constant and perpetual, seeing as it is an image of an image and a simulacrum of reason, can acquire but a fleeting likeness (*perfunctoriam similitudinem*)."[21] Calcidius's expansion of Plato's αἰτία in the dictum at 28a with his go-to phrase *causa et ratio* suggests that here, too, it is not merely an ontological principle but a reflection upon Plato's (and his commentator's) methodological and exegetical strategies. It is a hermeneutic invitation to find and explain the chain of causes within the created realm.

Calcidius's additional specification that this "cause and reason" must be "lawful" or "legitimate" (*legitima*) strengthens this line of interpretation. Calcidius, from the very beginning of his preface, is insistent that every valid account or proof *must* belong to the same domain as the object or question it seeks to elucidate; "individual matters (*singulae res*) must be explained by methods of reasoning that are akin and of the same domain (*domesticis et consanguineis rationibus*)."[22] Of course, it is the exegete's prerogative and privilege to define the domain in which the individual *causa et ratio* at stake is most "at home." *Legitima* may also have another valence, however. In chapter 23 of his commentary, which returns indirectly to the question of an uncreated atemporal model versus a created, time-bound copy, Calcidius reformulates the issue as a tripartition of works: "Everything that exists is a work of god, nature, or man acting as an artisan in imitation of nature."[23] He continues (*In Tim.* 23 [73.12–74.12]):

> Operum naturalium origo et initium semina sunt, quae facta conprehenduntur uel terrae uisceribus ad frugis arboreae cerealisue prouentum, uel genitalium membrorum fecunditate conceptum animalium germen adolentium. Quorum omnium ortus in tempore; par enim et aequaeuum natale naturae ac temporis. Ita naturae opera, quia ortum habent ex eo quo esse coeperunt tempore, finem quoque et occasum intra seriem continuationemque eius sortita sunt, at uero dei operum origo et initium inconprehensibile; nulla est enim certa nota, nullum indicium temporis ex quo esse coeperunt, sola, si forte, causa—et haec ipsa uix intellegitur—cur eorum quid quamue ob causam existat, certum est siquidem nihil a deo factum esse sine causa. Ut igitur illis quae lege naturae procreantur fundamenta sunt semina, ita eorum quae deus instituit fundamenta sunt causae, quae sunt perspicuae diuinae prouidentiae.

[21] *Translatio Calcidii* 22.3–7: ita constantis quidem generis stabilisque naturae intellectui prudentiaeque perspicuae rei causa et ratio constans perspicuaque et inexpugnabilis reperitur, at uero eius quae ad similitudinem constantis perpetuaeque rei facta est ratio, utpote imaginis imaginaria simulacrumque rationis, perfunctoriam similitudinem mutuatur.

[22] *In Tim.* 2 (58.7–8).

[23] *In Tim.* 23 (73.10–12): Omnia enim quae sunt uel dei opera sunt uel naturae uel naturam imitantis hominis artificis.

> The origin and beginning of natural works are seeds which, once formed, are received either in the bowels of the earth for the production of fruit and grain or in the fertility of the genital organs [for] the conception and germination of living beings endowed with the power of growth. Of all such things the beginning occurs in time, for the birth of nature is the same as and coeval with that of time. Thus the works of nature, since they have their beginning from the time when they begin to exist, are also allotted their end and death within the continuous concatenation of time, whereas the origin or beginning of the works of god is incomprehensible, for there is no fixed mark, no indication of the time from which they began to exist; perhaps only the cause—and even that is scarcely intelligible—why or wherefore any of them exists is certain, since nothing is created by god without cause. Well then, as seeds are the foundation for all that is procreated according to the law of nature, so the causes foreseen by divine providence are the foundation for all that god establishes.

Read in light of this passage, *legitima* would capture, in addition to the disciplinary specificity suggested above, the *metaphysical* specificity of the *causa et ratio* in question, whether it is a temporal cause subject to the law of nature (*lex naturae*), with all the concomitant temporal limitations of birth and death, or an eternal cause known only to divine providence, subject to no law of time. Both of these Calcidian claims—that "nothing can come into being, whose rise is not preceded by a lawful cause and reason" and that "everything that exists is a work of god, nature, or man acting as an artisan in imitation of nature"—issued a challenge to his twelfth-century readers, and they responded in kind.

The Secularization of Nature

The first claim, as Andreas Speer has taught us, became the dominant leitmotif of twelfth-century cosmology.[24] In twelfth-century talk of the creation and governance of the world, the questions "Who?" and "How?" were sharply differentiated: "who" inquired after matters of God and faith—the province of theology; "how" issued forth a new theoretical view of nature and the natural world—this was the province of the developing "natural science" (*scientia naturalis*).[25] To conflate these

24 Andreas Speer, *Die entdeckte Natur*, 290: "Die Suche nach der 'legitima causa et ratio' wird zum Programm einer 'philosophia mundi.'"

25 M.-D. Chenu, "Découverte de la nature et philosophie de l'homme à l'École de Chartres au XIIe siècle," *Cahiers d'histoire mondiale* 2 (1954), 313–325; Tullio Gregory, "L'idea della natura nella scuola di Chartres," *Giornale critico della filosofia italiana* 4 (1952), 433–442; Tullio Gregory, *Anima mundi: La filosofia di Guglielmo di Conches e la scuola di Chartres*, Pubblicazioni dell'Istituto di Filosofia dell'Università di Roma 3 (Florence: Sansoni, 1955), 175–246; Speer, *Die entdeckte Natur*; Andreas Speer, "The Discovery

questions and subsume the mechanisms of the "How?" under the omnipotence of the "Who?" was to take the easy path, "to believe like peasants," as William of Conches complained;[26] to painstakingly track down and account for the causes and effects at work in the natural world demanded "a little more sweat."[27] To be sure, the cosmologists did not see their task as antithetical to theology (however vehemently the theologians might disagree with them); they were, after all, merely entering the Divine Mansion through the side door and rummaging through the garage to find the hidden screws and nails (Calcidius's *invisibiles gomphi, Tim.* 43a) with which it was constructed. The stark simplicity of the creation story in Genesis, the obvious starting point for such an inquiry, was perhaps too simplistic; the biblical account offered a narrative blueprint for creation, but it was too imprecise in its handling of the particulars. Instead, the cosmologists found in the *Timaeus*, supported by Calcidius's commentary, the more nuts-and-bolts approach they sought. Together, the two texts furnished twelfth-century authors with precious physical details on primordial matter (*hyle*), the elements, the movement of heavenly spheres, and the like.

Calcidius's tripartition of divine, natural, and human works likewise provided a crucial distinction for understanding nature's role in the maintenance of the world order. This tripartition allowed twelfth-century authorities to establish a new foothold in the ancient debate about nature: they reconfigured nature as the *efficient cause of material creation*. God alone performed the original creative act and remained the final link in the chain of efficient causes, but after the creation *ex nihilo*, the active, sustaining force of *natura operans* (or *natura naturans*) took over and followed a customary course that could be traced through a sequence of lawful (*legitima*) rational causes. Nature became, so to speak, God's subcontractor and went about the business of managing and building the causes and effects in the material world as He had supremely willed it. Even the talk of "subcontractor" is not all that fanciful. A certain Magister Gilbertus described the relationship between God and Nature in just this way: although we customarily say that a rich man has built many a building, it was in fact the carpenter who completed the task under the authority and command of his master.[28] These natural relations, structures, and causes became the proper objects of a philosophy of nature.

of Nature: The Contributions of the Chartrians to Twelfth-Century Attempts to Found a *scientia naturalis*," *Traditio* 52 (1997), 135–151.

[26] *credere ut rusticos*, this being William of Conches's cranky reply to his critics. See *Phil.* 1.23 (56B): Sed quoniam ipsi nesciunt vires naturae, ut ignorantiae suae omnes socios habeant, nolunt eos aliquid inquirire, sed ut rusticos nos credere nec rationem quaerere.... Nos autem dicimus, in omnibus rationem esse quaerendam.

[27] To cite Chenu's paraphrase of William of Conches's rallying cry, *Phil.* 2.praef. (57B): soli veritati insudabimus. M.-D. Chenu, *Nature, Man, and Society in the Twelfth Century: Essays on New Theological Perspectives in the Latin West*, trans. Jerome Taylor and Lester K. Little (Chicago: University of Chicago Press, 1968), 12.

[28] *Notae super Johannem secundum magistrum Gilbertum*, MS London Lambeth Palace 360, f. 32rb; quoted in Chenu, *Nature, Man, and Society*, 40: Similiter usualiter dici solet de aliquo diuite quod multa

This conception of the scope of nature, now recast as a kind of *tertium quid* between God and Man, went against the received wisdom of past authorities on the subject. In the ninth century, *natura* was an umbrella term that cast a much broader shadow. Eriugena's vast dialogue on the subject, the *Periphyseon*, proposes a working definition of nature that encompasses all things, existent and nonexistent, human and divine.[29] In contrast to the "heady" talk of intelligible and perceptible nature in the ninth century, in the twelfth century nature became a more materialized affair—that is to say, nature was increasingly limited to the matter of the world. Thierry of Chartres is perhaps most succinct on this point: to inquire after the nature and status of things in the manner of a *physicus* (i.e., as a natural philosopher or, if you like, a physicist) is to grasp the forms and status of things in matter.[30] As Paul Dutton has argued, for all the talk of the discovery of nature in the twelfth century, "it would be more accurate to speak of a shift in the perception of nature . . ., one that led from the totalization to the materialization of nature."[31]

But twelfth-century cosmologists did not materialize nature itself or hypostatize it as a rational substance with "real" existence in the world, despite the many personifications of Lady Nature that populate twelfth-century literature. Nor were they engaged in a reductive project of materialism or physicalism; on the contrary, they remained committed to the metaphysical import of Platonic forms and the participation of matter in an immaterial archetypal reality. Following Dutton's lead but tempering it with the Platonic commitments that would contradict a radical "materialization of nature," I suggest that twelfth-century natural philosophy amounts to an *enmattered vitalism*, whereby nature is not merely reducible to inert matter itself, or even to the form that matter embodies, but it has in addition a dynamic and animating impetus of its own, "a generative power to produce, organize, and enliven matter."[32] On the one hand, nature is immanent

fecit edificia, quae eadem singulariter fecit et carpentarius, sed alter auctoritate sola et iussu, alter ministerio.

29 *Periphyseon* I, prol. (441A): Est igitur natura generale nomen, ut diximus, omnium quae sunt et quae non sunt. Eriugena's definition is broader still than that of Boethius, who defined nature as that which could be said *de omnibus rebus quae quocumque modo esse dicuntur* (*Contra Eutychen*, I). On Eriugena and Boethius's thoughts on nature, see Dominic O'Meara, "The Concept of Nature in John Scottus Eriugena," *Vivarium* 19 (1981), 126–145.

30 *Lectiones in Boethii librum de Trinitate* 2.21 (ed. Häring, *Commentaries on Boethius*, 161): Est igitur una pars speculatiue NATVRALIS IN MOTV INABSTRACTA ut expositum est . . . INABSTRACTA dicitur i.e. inseparabilis eo quod forme quas considerat inabstracte uel inseparabiles sunt a materia i.e. non possunt esse nisi in materia. On Thierry's conception of *naturalis scientia*, see Speer, "Discovery of Nature," 139–142.

31 Paul E. Dutton, "The Materialization of Nature and of Quaternary Man in the Early Twelfth Century," in *Man and Nature in the Middle Ages*, edited by S. J. Ridyard and R. G. Benson (Sewanee, TN: University of the South Press, 1995), 137–156, here at 140.

32 Jane Bennett, *Vibrant Matter: A Political Ecology of Things* (Durham, NC: Duke University Press, 2010), 80.

insofar as it is inextricably bound up in bodies. It is always enmattered. Without bodies, there is no physics, only metaphysics. Moreover, its immanence also entails that any part of the micro- or macrocosm can be taken as an entry point to grasping the totality of the whole. This is why the twelfth-century project to build nature from the bottom up could succeed at all.

On the other hand, nature is vitally transcendent, insofar as it is causally prior to any enmattered realization. Without its differentially distributed vitality, there are no natural bodies, no natural kinds, which could, by force of its vitality, strive for their own natural replication. Nature as enmattered vitalism, on this reading, productively resonates with but does not fully replicate Jane Bennett's "vital materiality" or "vibrant matter," which she (partially) locates in "one of the many historical senses of the word *nature*." It comes then as no surprise that the historicized senses of *natura* proffered by Bennett, e.g., Spinoza's distinction between *natura naturata* and *natura naturans* ("*Natura naturata* is passive matter organized into an eternal order of Creation; *natura naturans* is the uncaused causality that ceaselessly generates new forms"),[33] are themselves the direct descendants of twelfth-century natural philosophy, which in addition to *natura naturata* and *natura naturans* made good use of the closely related phrases *natura elementans* ("elementing nature") and *elementata* ("elemented substances").[34]

Twelfth-century cosmologists, moreover, had a name (one of many) for the vitalistic principle: the Platonic "world soul" (*anima mundi*), whose manifold harmonies we will explore in the fifth chapter of this study. United by its harmonious principles, nature itself finds harmony and forestalls the vulnerability of its otherwise imbalanced aggregate. Hisdosus, a twelfth-century commentator on the *Timaeus*, identifies the *anima mundi* as a manifestation of "the creator's eternal love, by which he created all and harmoniously rules his creation with a concord

[33] Ibid., 117–118.

[34] E.g., Bernard Silvestris, *Cos.* Megacosmos, 4.7: Precedit Yle, Natura subsequitur elementans; elementanti Natura elementa, elementis elementata conveniunt ("*Hyle* [primordial matter] comes first; there follows *elementing Nature*; the elements arise from the elementing nature, and elemented substances from the elements"). Bernard goes on to identify this "elementing nature" with the creative power of the firmament and the wandering stars, "which arouse the elements to their inborn activities," and concludes: "Thus their cosmic bonds do not grow weary, nor are they broken, for they universally derive from one cardinal principle which binds them indissolubly together" (Est igitur elementans Natura celum stelleque signifero pervagantes, quod elementa conveniant ad ingenitas acciones. Sua igitur in mundo non fatiscunt ligamina, nec solvuntur, quod universa a cardine nexu sibi continuo deducuntur). On *elementata*, see Theodore Silverstein, "*Elementatum*: Its Appearance Among the Twelfth-Century Cosmogonists," *Mediaeval Studies* 16 (1954), 156–162; Ralph McKeon, "Medicine and Philosophy in the Eleventh and Twelfth Centuries: The Problem of Elements," *The Thomist* 24 (1961), 211–256; Dorothy Elford, "William of Conches," in *A History of Twelfth-Century Western Philosophy*, ed. Peter Dronke (Cambridge: Cambridge University Press, 1988), 308–27; and most recently, Irène Caiazzo, "The Four Elements in the Work of William of Conches," in *Guillaume de Conches: Philosophie et science au XIIe siècle* (Florence: SISMEL Edizioni del Galluzzo, 2011), 10–14. See also below, Chapter 5.

that cannot cease without immediately dissolving the *machina mundi*."[35] So too William of Conches, glossing Boethius's cosmic hymn, *O qui perpetua mundum*, avers that if the elements were not joined by proportional relations and were not properly disposed in their spatial coordination (earth at the bottom, fire at the top), then they would rend the fabric of the world and dissolve the worldly machine (*dissolverent machinam mundi*).[36] A mid-twelfth-century commentary on Boethius's *De institutione musica* makes an identical point with nearly identical language: if each elemental quality did not have its proper contrary, by which it is tempered, then the "whole *mundana machina* would be dissolved."[37] This theme finds poetic articulation in Bernard Silvestris's *Cosmographia* through Natura's intervention on behalf of Silva, or primordial matter, who is first characterized in Bernard's opening words as a "formless mass" (*congeries informis*). Natura pleads on Silva's behalf: "and desiring to depart from its ancient state of tumult, [Silva] demands the creative number and musical linkages" (*et a ueteri cupiens exire tumultu / artifices numeros et musica uincla requirit*).[38] In this way, the principles of *concordia, harmonia*, and *proportio* become the formal but vitalistic, life-giving cause of an enmattered musical aesthetics of creation.

Just as importantly, human knowledge of nature can be demarcated (though not necessarily divorced) from the knowledge of its creator. The twelfth-century English scientist Adelard of Bath is repeatedly questioned by his pesky and conservative nephew in his *Quaestiones naturales*: "To what else can you attribute this save to the marvelous effect of the marvelous divine will?" Adelard firmly replies that, without detracting from God, his creation, the discretion of nature "does not exist confusedly and without arrangement, which human knowledge *must listen to*, insofar as it can." Only when human understanding utterly fails should we have recourse to direct divine causality.[39] As already quoted in the Prelude to this study, William of Conches in his *Philosophia* expresses the same but more bluntly: "God can make a cow out of a tree trunk, but has he ever done so?"[40]

[35] Paris, BnF, lat. 8624, f. 17r: Anima igitur mundi est ille creatoris amor aeternus quo cuncta creauit et creata concorditer regit ea concordia quae, si deficiat, statim mundi machinam dissoluat.

[36] *Glos. sup. Boet.* 3.m9.463–466: Si enim aliquid esset supra ignem uel aliquid inferius terra, semper illud superius peteret, illud inferius, et ita dissoluerent machinam mundi.

[37] *In Inst. mus.* 36: similiter deficiente terra vel aqua, quia remanebunt duo calida, peribit incendio; item deficiente igne remanebunt unum solum calidum s. aer et duo frigida: duo frigida adversus unum solum calidum prevalebunt, et ita necessario cum igne peribit et aer, et remanebunt terra et aqua, sed cum illa duo contrariis participent qualitatibus s. frigiditate, quae nullum haberet contrarium, quo temperaretur, necessario fieret infinita frigiditas, ut sic etiam tota mundana machina dissolveretur.

[38] *Cos.* Megacosmos 1.21–22.

[39] Adelard of Bath, *Quaest. nat.* 4 (96–97): Deo non detraho. Quicquid enim est, ab ipso et per ipsum est. Id ipsum tamen confuse et absque discretione non est. Que quantum scientia humana procedit audienda est; in quo vero universaliter, ad Deum res referenda est.

[40] *Phil.* 2.3 (58C): Ut autem verbis rustici utar: "Potens est deus de trunco facere vitulum": Fecitne umquam?

For both authors, as for twelfth-century natural philosophy generally, nature is both the product and the mirror of divine stability, but it is also autonomous, predictable, and (to just that extent) knowable.[41]

Enmattered vitalism can productively account for *natura* when it is conceived as the creative, active totality of the forces and their interrelationships within material creation. This is the force of nature captured by the active participial constructions *natura naturans* or *natura elementans* ("naturing nature" or "elementing nature"). But there is also a second broad conception of nature at work in the twelfth century, *natura* as the created essence or particularity of a particular thing or kind of thing, captured by the passive participial construction *natura naturata* or *natura elementata* ("natured nature" or "elemented nature"). This more Aristotelian, metaphysical nature was clearly what Hugh of St. Victor, for instance, had in mind in the second of his three definitions quoted above: "the property or unique individuator (*proprium* or *propria differentia*) of each thing individually."[42] Andreas Speer is willing to believe that William of Conches countenances both views of nature, but the only examples he can adduce—e.g., the "nature" of primordial material or the specific properties of the elements, which are *naturaliter* heavy or light—retain the strong flavor of their cosmological ingredients and are in no way metaphysically robust.[43]

In fact, rarely do we find in the writings of the cosmologists anything like a "common nature," "generic nature," or "specific nature" (*communis, generalis uel specialis natura*), concepts which most clearly indicate that a developing metaphysical concept of nature is at work. Ludger Honnefelder suggests that the medieval reception and re-creation of the metaphysical and cosmological conceptions of nature "does not happen all at once": the twelfth century gets cosmology; the thirteenth century gets metaphysics.[44] This seems unsatisfactory, for there is a writer contemporary with the cosmologists who articulates a distinctly metaphysical conception of nature(s). Peter Abelard, the staunch nominalist of the twelfth century, scatters the term *natura* throughout his metaphysics (including *communis, generalis et specialis natura*), employing it, for instance, as the explanatory ground for both the extension of universal terms and the truth value of modal propositions. In his own hexameral commentary, however, Abelard also

[41] David Albertson, *Mathematical Theologies: Nicholas of Cusa and the Legacy of Thierry of Chartres* (Oxford: Oxford University Press, 2014), 98–99.

[42] See p. 35 above.

[43] "Discovery of Nature," 143–144.

[44] Ludger Honnefelder, "The Concept of Nature in Medieval Metaphysics," in *Nature in Medieval Thought*, edited by C. Koyama (Leiden: Brill, 2000), 75–93, here at 76: "The early discussions about nature as essence in the theological treatises of Boethius is followed in the twelfth century by a discussion of the (cosmological) concept of nature as *nature* in the context of the creation problem; finally, the thirteenth-century reception of Aristotle and his Arabic interpreters focuses on the question about nature as created in the context of grace and—notably through Ibn Sina—about nature as *essence* in the context of metaphysics."

offers a definition of nature entirely in line with the enmattered, vitalistic account I have argued for above. Nature, Abelard explains, is "a certain power conferred on things during their creation, whereby they thenceforth were capable of reproducing themselves or bringing about whatever effects were to proceed from or be engendered by them."[45] And like the cosmologists, Calcidius's tripartition of works (divine, natural, and human) underlies many of Abelard's arguments. To account for this, in the next two sections I argue for the harmony of the cosmological and metaphysical *natura* in the thought of Abelard. Under his pen, *natura* becomes the nexus of physics and metaphysics, insofar as both "the way things are" (the *natura* of natural philosophy) and "the way we talk about the way things are" (the *natura* of metaphysics) are functions of natural processes, or, if you prefer, natural history. In short, it is possible to read Abelard as a strong naturalist. The lessons he learned from the cosmologists offered him satisfactory explanatory ground for problems he faced in his metaphysics.

Musically minded readers of this book should be forewarned: this discussion will take us far afield from the usual stomping grounds of music theory. But that is precisely the point, in a way, for in this I seek to demonstrate just how deep the commitment to a well-ordered, harmoniously regulated nature ran in the twelfth century. It was not solely the prerogative of the Platonists but in fact bled into the thought of one of the foremost Aristotelians of the twelfth century, the peripatetic of Pallet, Peter Abelard. The first task will be to consider *natura*'s force and employment in the things of the world: its function in the creation and governance of the world, its role in substantial generation, and its relation to causality. In this respect, Abelard is of a piece with the idea of *natura* promulgated by the "Platonic" natural philosophers. With this discussion firmly in mind, I will turn briefly to Abelard's use of *natura* in metaphysical contexts, namely, the common cause of the imposition of universal terms, the terrain of nominalism for which Abelard is most famous. As I will argue, the very ability of language to refer successfully to "natural kinds" (rocks, cantaloupes, peacocks, humans, etc.) is dependent upon the proper maintenance of this very same natural order. By keeping the cosmological, creative force of nature in play, it will become apparent how Abelard solves metaphysical problems with cosmological solutions.

Abelard on Nature and Natures

In Genesis, 1:6. God declares: "Let there be a firmament made amidst the waters and let it divide the waters from the waters." For scholars interested in naturalized

[45] *Exp. Hex.* 151: hoc est uis quaedam conferebatur illis rebus quae tunc fiebant, unde ipsae postmodum ad multiplicationem sui sufficerent uel ad quoscumque effectus inde processuros uel tamquam nascituros. Cf. Ibid., 121–123.

cosmology, this proved a particularly thorny passage: how can water be suspended above the firmament, and why?[46] For Abelard, it occasioned his clearest explanation of nature and natural powers and their relationship to divine power. To the hypothetical *aliquis* wondering what natural force (*ui naturae*) might sustain the supracelestial waters, Abelard responds:[47]

> Ad quod primum respondeo nullatenus nos modo, cum in aliquibus rerum effectis uim naturae uel causas naturales requirimus uel assignamus, id nos facere secundum illam priorem dei operationem in constitutione mundi, ubi sola dei uoluntas naturae efficiciam habuit in illis tunc creandis uel disponendis; sed tantum ab illa operatione dei VI diebus illis completa. Deinceps uim naturae pensare solemus, tunc uidelicit rebus ipsis iam ita preparatis, ut ad quaelibet sine miraculis facienda illa eorum constitutio uel preparatio sufficeret.... Naturam itaque dicimus uim rerum ex illa prima preparatione illis collatam, ad aliquid inde nascendum, hoc est efficiendum, sufficientem.
>
> To this I respond first that although we now seek out or assign a natural power or natural causes in the effecting of some things, we in no way can do this with respect to that prior work of God in the constitution of the world. For then (*tunc*) God's will alone had the efficacy of nature in creating or arranging things. [We can seek or assign natural causes] only after those things had been completed in six days by God's doing. From that time onward (*deinceps*), we customarily think about the force of nature, namely after these things have already been arranged in such a way that, without any miraculous intervention, their constitution and preparation suffices for doing things.... Therefore, we call nature the power of things conferred upon them during the initial preparation [of creation] so that they should suffice for bringing something into being, that is, causing something.

Abelard is clear about nature's role, and it hinges on "then" and "thereafter."[48] Then (*tunc*), during the first six days, God went about his business of creating supernaturally, and part of that business was to prepare creation for a more autonomous existence. Thereafter (*deinceps*) nature operated and will continue to operate on its own and in its own mundane fashion, without any miraculous

[46] On the exegetical history of this passage, see Helen Rodnite Lemay, "Science and Theology at Chartres: The Case of the Supracelestial Waters," *British Journal for the History of Science* 10 (1977), 226–236.

[47] *Exp. Hex.* 120–123.

[48] Richard C. Dales, "A Twelfth-Century Concept of Natural Order," *Viator* 9 (1978), 179–192, here at 182–183.

intervention (*sine miraculis*). The natural world owes its existence to God's direct efficacious will, but God saw to it that natural substances would have sufficient natural power (*uis naturae*) to carry on the divine plan after the creative deed was done. For after God rested, nature ensured per se the continuation and multiplication of each species.[49] Nature continues in "real time" what God directly effected during primordial time. Nor is it necessary for God to intervene directly in the established natural order, for Abelard agreed with Plato that the order of the world is the best possible order:[50]

> Apparet itaque maxime ex ipsa mundanae fabricae uniuersitate tam mirabiliter facta, tam decenter ornata, quantae potentiae, quantae sapientiae, quantae bonitatis eius artifex sit qui tantum et tale opus de nihilo facere potuit et uoluit et tam sollerter et rationabiliter cuncta temperauit, ita ut in singulis nihil plus aut minus quam oportuerit actum sit. Vnde et Plato ipse cum de genitura mundi ageret, in tantum diuinae potentiae ac sapientiae bonitatem extulit, ut adstrueret Deum nullatenus potuisse mundum meliorem facere quam fecerit.

> Thus it is maximally apparent from the whole universe of the worldly fabric, so miraculously made and so beautifully adorned, what power, wisdom, and goodness belonged to its creator, who both could and would make such and so great a creation from nothing, who so skillfully and rationally tempered all things that in every case only what is necessary is actually done—no more, no less. Hence Plato too, when he discussed the generation of the world, extolled the goodness of divine power and wisdom to demonstrate that God could not have made a world better than the world he made.

Abelard's nature, like his ontology, is parsimonious yet comprehensive. But what might it mean to bestow a natural power upon things so as to establish a natural world sufficient for an autonomous, self-propagating existence? Abelard's theory of a two-stage creation (*prima/secunda creatio*), articulated elsewhere in his philosophical works, offers a model that can help us bring philosophical sense to this cosmological shoptalk. Abelard's double account of creation maps a twofold process onto the distinction between creation and formation. It was the job of primary creation to bring matter into being from the well of nothingness. This is, first and foremost, the creation of substance *ex nihilo*, the event described in

[49] *Exp. Hex.* 332: Nulla quippe de speciebus illis postmodum peritura erat, ut ad eam reparandam non sufficeret per se natura iam preparata, sicut et ad indiuidua specierum multiplicanda. Etsi enim ponamus phoenicem speciem esse, uel aliquas species herbarum uel florum quandoque deperire, iam tamen ita natura ex primordialibus causis est praeparata ut ad haec restauranda sufficiat.

[50] *Comm. Rom.* (ad 1:20).

the opening lines of Genesis: the creation of "heaven and earth" encompasses the generation of the four elements;[51] "the face of the abyss" signals their undifferentiated mass (*confusam necdum distinctam elementorum congeriem*), which poets and philosophers are wont to call "chaos."[52] Secondary creation is the carving of this primordial lump of undifferentiated matter into different and properly differentiated natural kinds (cantaloupes, peacocks, humans, and so on) through the application of substantial forms (*substantiales formae*), which turn undifferentiated stuff into natural objects: corporeal substance becomes animate through "being alive" (*animatio*), becomes an animal through "capacity for sense perception" (*sensualitas*), or "through other forms becomes a member of one or another species—an ass or a man."[53]

Combining these two creation narratives, we can suppose that the *uis naturae* is nothing other than these supervenient substantial forms that differentiate the natural kinds. Particular combinations of substantial forms confer particular natural powers, or particular *natures*, which in turn determine not only what sort of thing it is but the capabilities that sort of thing has. We can talk about these capabilities in two ways: generically (all animals have the ability to perceive) or specifically (all men have the ability to reason or laugh). This way of thinking about *natura* as the bestowal of particular substantial differentiae seems to be confirmed by Abelard's general account of what first and second creation effected. In these creations, "substances were arranged into generic or specific natures.... Whence such *differentiae* are called substantial, which, supervening on substance, both make substances discrete and unite them in a common nature; nor can we include anything within generic or a specific nature save those things that divine operation unites *by the nature of their substance*."[54]

[51] *Exp. Hex.* 15: IN PRINCIPIO CREAVIT DEVS CELVM ET TERRAM. Celi et terre nomine hoc loco quatuor elementa comprehendi arbitror, ex quibus tamquam materiali primordio cetera omnia corpora constat esse composita.

[52] *Exp. Hex.* 25: ET TENEBRE ERANT SVPER FACIEM HABISSI. Habissum, id est profunditatem, uocat totam illam confusam necdum distinctam, sicut postmodum fuit, elementorum congeriem. Quam quidem confusionem nonnulli philosophorum seu poetarum chaos dixerunt, quod enim profundum est minus apparet et uisui patet.

[53] *LI2* 298.6–10: eas uero creationes secundum quas materiam iam praeparatam per formas superuenientes in species diuersas natura redigit, posteriores appellamus, ueluti cum corpoream substantiam aut per animationem facit animatam aut per sensualitatem animal aut per alias formas in quascumque species uariaret, ut in ⟨asinum⟩ uel hominem. *Dial.* 419.13–15: Secundae vero creationes sunt, cum iam creatam materiam per adiunctionem substantialis formae novum facit ingredi esse, veluti cum de limo terrae hominem Deus creavit. See Peter King, "Metaphysics," in *The Cambridge Companion to Abelard*, edited by J. E. Brower and K. Guilfoy (Cambridge: Cambridge University Press, 2004), 65–125, here at 75–76, and John Marenbon, *The Philosophy of Peter Abelard* (Cambridge: Cambridge University Press, 1997), 125–126.

[54] *Dial.* 420.30–421.8: In quibus quidem naturae creationibus generales ac speciales constitutae sunt substantiae.... Unde etiam substantiales sunt appellatae huiusmodi differentiae, quae in substantiam venientes et discretionem substantiae faciunt et unionem communis naturae; neque enim alia in speciali aut generali natura concludimus nisi ea quae natura substantiae diuina univit operatio.

Abelard's account of primary and secondary creation is part of a more general discussion of substantial generation. His primary intention is to prove that substantial generation is the province of God alone. Human actions lack all power of generation; we mortals can only shuffle around existing matter by joining or reshaping it into artificial kinds, such as houses, swords, ping-pong balls, and the like.[55] As an example of our inability to generate substance, Abelard offers glassmaking as a particularly tricky case that would prove the more straightforward examples as a matter of course.[56] When creating glass, we ready the materials (gather ash, put it in a kiln, and turn on the heat), but our role and even our understanding of the process ends there. "Even when we are ignorant of the physics, God himself by some unknown means works on the nature of the substances that we have readied and turns it into a new substance."[57] But Abelard is speaking loosely here, and he tightens his description of the process in other passages treating the same subject. Strictly speaking, it is *natura* (deputized by the Divine Will) that enables the transformative process. God could turn baked ash into anything he likes; he is in no way bound to making glass alone. The omnipotence of God is more power than glassmaking requires. *Natura*, however, because of the "nature" of the substances involved, can only make glass, consistently and identically every time. This is how Abelard describes the process elsewhere:[58]

> Nota etiam quod solius Dei est generare, id est operatione sua in substantiam promouere, quod est creare. Nam etsi ex coitu patris quaedam portio separata sit quae formetur in hominem, patre tamen defuncto non minus natura opifex operatur in uisceribus matris de infuso semine, ipsum scilicet formando et uiuificando in hominem. Vnde puer ipse non hominis opus est sed naturae, id est Dei, hominum autem operatio alterare tantum materiam uidetur secundum accidentia, ueluti dum domum componit uel gladium, non etiam in substantiam generare. Neque enim uitrum, quod species metalli dicitur, hominis est opus sed naturae, quia praeparatis ab homine quae necessaria sunt ad creationem uitri in materia praeparata a nobis sola natura operator eam in uitrum conuertens, nobis quoque physicam ignorantibus. Si quis autem dicat aues quoque creare pullos, dum, calefaciendo oua propria, ea uiuificant, ideoque pullos opera auium uocet, fallitur. Non enim opera dicenda sunt nisi eius qui ex deliberatione et ex discretione facit nec opifex recte dicitur nisi rationalis substantia. Ex affectu uero quem

[55] *Dial.* 420.7: Nulla itaque generatio nostris actibus est permissa.

[56] *Dial.* 419.37–420.6.

[57] *Dial.* 420.2–4: sed ipse Deus nobis etiam phisicam ignorantibus in natura eorum quae preparavimus, occulte operatur ac novam perficit substantiam.

[58] *LI2* 298.28–299.5.

natura mittit, non ex discretione rationis uiuificat auis calefaciendo oua, ignara penitus futuri effectus, quem per eam natura operatur.

Note that the power of generation is God's alone, that is to bring things into substance (i.e., to create) by his operation. For although in the sexual act a certain part (*portio*) of the father is separated and formed into a man, even with the father out of the picture, creative nature (*natura opifex*) no less works on the seed within the mother's womb by forming and vivifying it into a man. Whence a child is not the work of man but the work of nature (i.e., of God). The works of man seem only to alter the accidents of the material, such as when he builds a house or makes a sword; man does not generate substance. Nor is glass, which is a species of metal, a work of man, but a work of nature. When man has prepared the materials necessary for glassmaking, nature alone works on the prepared materials, turning them into glass even if we do not understand the physics. But if someone were to say that hens create chicks because they bring their eggs to life by warming them, and hence were to call the chicks the work of the hen, he is mistaken. For works can only be ascribed to someone who acts according to deliberation and discretion. Nothing can be called an artisan (*opifex*) unless it be a rational substance. It is because of the affect bestowed by nature and not any rational discernment that a bird brings an egg to life by warming it, for the bird is entirely unaware of its future effect, which nature brings about through the bird.

Given God's direct creation of nature, Abelard can speak of natural means as divine means without introducing unnecessary confusion. At the same time, given the division of labor set forth in the *Expositio de Hexameron*, it is clear that he thought that the actions of *natura*, though in a way identical to divine actions, are nevertheless distinct.

But does this line of reasoning force us to conclude, as David Luscombe has argued, that Abelard hypostasized nature?[59] Clearly it does not. The argument (another reply to that pesky *aliquis*) turns on *opera*, not *substantia*, and runs as follows: (1) Hens seem to create chicks and hence are creators of works. (2) Creation requires rational discernment of the creative act's result (i.e., intention). (3) Hens have no rational intent to vivify their eggs and blindly act in accordance with their nature. (4) Hence hens are not creators. The argument extends no farther. The accidental syllogism (*Natura est opifex. Opifex est rationalis substantia. Natura est rationalis substantia*) requires the conflation of two related but distinct arguments.

[59] David Luscombe, "Nature in the Thought of Peter Abelard," in *La filosofia della natura nel medioevo* (Milan: Società editrice Vita e pensiero, 1966), 316: "Abelard seems even to say . . . that nature is itself a rational substance."

We might complain that Abelard did not realize the wider implications of the juxtaposition, but the more limited scope of his intent is clear from the context.

This much is clear about Abelard's view of nature's role in the creative, cosmological context: (1) *Natura* is a power created by God and conferred on natural substances at the time of their creation, a power sufficient to continue, per se, the work God had begun. (2) This was effected through the bestowal of supervenient substantial forms, which both divided up the world into different natural kinds and united members of the same natural kind in a common nature. (3) Depending on how we attend to them, natures can be more or less similar, either generic or specific. (4) Nature is the efficient cause of the propagation of each species; natural kinds naturally (*operatione naturae*) propagate themselves (*ad multiplicandum sui*), which ensures that all members of a natural kind are naturally similar. It remains to be seen how Abelard puts these cosmological conceptions of nature to work when confronted with a particular metaphysical problem: the common cause (*communis causa*) of the imposition of universal terms.

Abelard on Nature and Names

According to Abelard, the truth value of predication is a function of the "nature of things" (*natura rerum*). The fool who asserts that "Man is a stone" does not deserve a slap on the wrist for any grammatical foul but for asserting something that is clearly nonsensical *in natura rerum*.[60] Used in this way, the "nature of things" seems an obvious and transparent turn of phrase, meaning simply "the way the world is." In order for linguistic systems to be useful tools of communication, our assertions must have some basis in or correspondence to "reality." *Grammatica* must be supplemented by *physica*. Though we may remain generally ignorant about the real nature of things in all their complexities and subtleties, we nevertheless need some inkling, faint though it may be, of how the world works (e.g., that stone is not predicable of man) in order to create assertions that match the world in a meaningful way. But this generalized "way of the world" is hardly enough to ground language *in* the world. It offers no account of just how we bridge the gulf between words and things, which is precisely what we need in order to explain how the sentence "Socrates is a man" is somehow more true, or at least more meaningful, than "Toves are slithy." In short, Abelard needs to have an account of how the noun "man" can pick out or refer to (*nominare*) things in the world.

60 *LI1* 17.21–27: Si quis ita dicat *Homo est lapis*, non hominis uel lapidis congruam fecit constructionem ad sensum quem uoluit demonstrare, nec ullum uitium fuit grammaticae et licet quantum ad uim enuntiationis lapis hic praedicatur de homine, cui scilicet tamquam praedicatum construitur, secundum quod falsae quoque categoricae praedicatum terminum habent, in natura tamen rerum praedicabile de eo non est.

This is where the *natura rerum* gains traction. Abelard grounds language in reality by arguing that the *extension* of universal terms—the ability of words such as "human," "stone," and "peacock" to refer to all and only individual humans, stones, and peacocks—is determined by nature.[61] But words attach to particular things on account of human ingenuity. In his commentary on Genesis (2:19), Abelard confers on Adam the original act of imposition (i.e., the constitutive declaration that "tree" will henceforth refer to these particularly configured natural substances, "peacock" those natural substances, and so on). Adam achieved this by first inspecting the *naturae* of things, then choosing words apt for designating them.[62] In his logical writings, Abelard describes imposition in similar terms, as a name conferred according to "natures or properties" (even if the original impositor was not entirely certain what that nature was).[63] Though the Supreme Artificer entrusted to men the imposition of names, God left the nature of things, and hence the extension of the names thus imposed, to his own arrangement.[64]

As we have seen, the world is divided into natural kinds, and particular substances belong to particular natural kinds solely on the basis of natural similarity: a natural term is common to many things for the reason that they are mutually similar (*multorum commune est secundum hoc quod sibi inuicem similia sunt*).[65] Again, this natural similarity is a brute, unalterable fact about the world. The name of a species refers (*nominare*) to particular individual substances (its extension) because of a similarity (*conuenientia*) that arises from the "creation of nature" (*ex creatione naturae*), which retains its strongly cosmological overtones.[66] Division

61 *LI1* 16.25–28: Est autem uniuersale uocabulum quod de pluribus singillatim habile est ex inuentione sua praedicari, ut hoc nomen 'homo,' quod particularibus nominibus hominum coniungibile est secundum subiectarum rerum naturam quibus est impositum. *Sent.* §17: Unde hoc nomen quod est 'homo' natura dicimus, quod ex una ipsius impositione commune est naturaliter multis rebus secundum hoc quod inuicem sibi naturaliter sunt similes (in eo scilicet quod unaqueque eorum sit animal rationale mortale).

62 *Exp. Hex.* 473: VT VIDERET, scilicet prius inspiciendo naturas eorum, ad quas designanda postmodum aptaret uocabula. The original context of this bestowal, buried as it is in an almost exclusively cosmological context, is significant. The terms *natura* and *naturae* in Abelard's commentary on Genesis always retain a cosmological spin (the adjective *naturalis*, for instance, generally appearing with *ordo*, *causa*, and *facultas*).

63 *LI1* 23.22–24: secundum aliquas rerum naturas uel proprietates inuentor ea [sc. nomina] imponere intendit, etsi nec ipse bene excogitare sciret rei naturam aut proprietatem.

64 *Dial.* 576.35–37: Vocum enim impositionem Summus Artifex nobis commisit, rerum autem naturam propriae Suae dispositioni reseruauit.

65 *Sent.* §18: Et hanc interrogationem "Quid est homo?" naturae dicimus, istam autem "Quis est iste?" uel "Quae est ista?" dicimus esse personae; unde, ad illud, uocabulum naturae seu similitudinis respondemus (quod uidelicet multorum commune est secundum hoc quod sibi inuicem similia sunt), ut "homo," "animal"; ad istud uero, uocabulum personae seu discretionis (quod uidelicet unam rem determinate ac discrete significat), ut "Petrus," "Marcha."

66 Abelard, *Logica "Nostrorum petitioni sociorum"* (ed. Bernhard Geyer, *Peter Abaelards Philosophische Schriften*) 553.29–31: SPECIES EST COLLECTIVVM MVLTORVM IN VNAM NATVRAM (Por. *Isag.* §3 12.15–17), id est speciale uocabulum res subiectas nominat secundum hoc quod conueniunt ex creatione

into natural kinds may be a "shallow fact" about the world,[67] but it nevertheless has deep roots. The real similarity among individual members of the same natural kind is, deep down where it matters, a function of the creative force of nature. By dint of the powers invested in it, nature (and natures) can do nothing but generate similar things: man from man, ass from ass, grass from grass. Deputized by the Supreme Opifex, that's simply what *opifex natura* did, does, and will do, *in saecula saeculorum*.

Commentators on Platonic texts and the creation story of Genesis alike bear witness to this new tendency to view nature as a particular configuration of material creation that suffices, through that configuration, to continue to "bring about" the stuff of the world. Bernard of Chartres's commentary on the *Timaeus* defines nature as "the force and cause of generation."[68] William of Conches concurs but is more precise: "Nature is the power invested in things for producing like from like."[69] Nature holds a similar explanatory power in contemporary hexameral literature. Thierry of Chartres, reflecting the Stoic conception of spermatic *logoi* (likely transmitted through Augustinian channels[70]) describes the *ordo naturalis* as the interplay of the *causae seminales* dwelling within the elements.[71] Unsurprisingly, his disciple Clarembald of Arras thinks of nature in an analogous way: "the force invested in the elements (*uis insita elementis*) or in those things which are made from the elements is called the "natural aptitude," . . . for the aptitude, which is the seminal reason, is the seed though which certain things produce other similar things."[72] All these conceptions of nature as an innate, efficacious force within things share in an enmattered vitalistic account of nature: *enmattered* because it focuses on the cosmological conception of nature in the context of material creation; *vitalistic* because it seeks to trace the (natural) *causae rerum* that underlie the material world back to the common animating final cause that defines the world as an ordered whole, a *cosmos*, an *ordinata collectio omnium creaturarum*.[73]

From *auditus* to *res intelligibilis*

The harmony of nature's well-ordered whole, however, is not just the solipsistic means by which nature forestalls the destruction of its own mechanism. As the

naturae. In the parallel passage from *LI1* (57.27–29), Abelard is more laconic (using a phrasing closer to *Sent.* §17): id est speciale uocabulum res subiectas nominat secundum id quod conueniunt et sibi similes sunt.

67 Peter King, "Metaphysics," 84.

68 *Bernardi Glos. sup. Tim.* 4.33–34: Natura quidem est uis et ratio gignendi.

69 *Guillelmi Glos. sup. Tim.* 37.8–9: Est natura uis rebus insita similia de similibus operans.

70 Cf. *Trin.* 3.8.13; *De Genesi ad litteram* 4.33.51.

71 *Tractatus de sex dierum operibus*, 10.

72 *Tractatulus super librum Genesis*, 27.

73 See Speer, "Discovery of Nature," 148–151 (6. A Unified Theory of Nature).

cosmologists learned from the *Timaeus* and Calcidius's commentary, nature also affords *help* to its mortal inhabitants through its own modeling of the eternal paradigm, i.e., the model according to which the Demiurge has made "this All."[74] Cosmology, in this instance, assumes a pointedly *philosophical* import, insofar as the perceptible, ordered motions of the natural world express, mimetically, the intelligence (νοῦς) of its maker and the intelligible status (νοητός) of the paradigm the maker followed. Accordingly, when our perceptions are properly deployed for the realization of the divine intelligent cause for which they have been granted, the philosophical insight they provide "leads us to enquire about the whole universe and brings well-being to our rational soul. For the contemplation of the 'revolutions of Intelligence in the heavens' [47b7] is our kindred soul's mimesis of the cosmic one. This mimesis steadies the revolutions in us into their proper courses."[75]

Plato's primary example is vision (46e7–47c4), whose primary utility and greatest good is the acquisition of philosophy, but hearing, too, is properly directed toward the intelligible. For the movements of harmony are akin to the motions of soul; this claim is the essential connective tissue within the first reference to music (μουσική) in the *Timaeus*, namely the commendation of hearing, particularly musical hearing, as a helpmate (σύμμαχος) to the soul (47c4–e2). I quote here the passage in full, both Plato's Greek and Calcidius's Latin, followed by a synthetic English translation that combines both and indicates Calcidius's expansions and omissions with italic type and brackets respectively.

> φωνῆς τε δὴ καὶ ἀκοῆς πέρι πάλιν ὁ αὐτὸς λόγος, ἐπὶ ταὐτὰ τῶν αὐτῶν ἕνεκα παρὰ θεῶν δεδωρῆσθαι. λόγος τε γὰρ ἐπ' αὐτὰ ταῦτα τέτακται, τὴν μεγίστην συμβαλλόμενος εἰς αὐτὰ μοῖραν, ὅσον τ' αὖ μουσικῆς φωνῇ χρήσιμον πρὸς ἀκοὴν ἕνεκα ἁρμονίας ἐστὶ δοθέν. ἡ δὲ ἁρμονία, συγγενεῖς ἔχουσα φορὰς ταῖς ἐν ἡμῖν τῆς ψυχῆς περιόδοις, τῷ μετὰ νοῦ προσχρωμένῳ Μούσαις οὐκ ἐφ' ἡδονὴν ἄλογον καθάπερ νῦν εἶναι δοκεῖ χρήσιμος, ἀλλ' ἐπὶ τὴν γεγονυῖαν ἐν ἡμῖν ἀνάρμοστον ψυχῆς περίοδον εἰς κατακόσμησιν καὶ συμφωνίαν ἑαυτῇ σύμμαχος ὑπὸ Μουσῶν δέδοται· καὶ ῥυθμὸς αὖ διὰ τὴν ἄμετρον ἐν ἡμῖν καὶ χαρίτων ἐπιδεᾶ γιγνομένην ἐν τοῖς πλείστοις ἕξιν ἐπίκουρος ἐπὶ ταὐτὰ ὑπὸ τῶν αὐτῶν ἐδόθη (47c4–e2).

> Eadem uocis quoque et auditus ratio est ad eosdem usus atque ad plenam uitae hominum instructionem datorum, siquidem propterea sermonis est ordinata communicatio, ut praesto forent mutuae uoluntatis indicia; quantumque per uocem utilitatis capitur ex musica, totum hoc constat hominum generi propter harmoniam tributum. Harmonia

[74] *Tim.* 28c5–29a5.

[75] Sarah Broadie, *Nature and Divinity in Plato's* Timaeus (Cambridge: Cambridge University Press, 2011), 174.

> uero, id est modulatio, utpote intentio modificata, cognatas et uelut consanguineas habens commotiones animae nostrae circuitionibus, prudenter utentibus Musarum munere temperantiaeque causa potius quam oblectationis satis est commoda, quippe quae discrepantes et inconsonantes animae commotiones ad concentum exornationemque concordiae Musis auxiliantibus reuocet; rhythmus autem datus est ut medela contra illepidam numerorumque et modorum nesciam gratiaeque expertem in plerisque naturam (44.23–45.8).
>
> The same account applies also to voice and hearing, which have been bestowed [by the gods] for the same [end and] purposes, *namely the full instruction of human life*, seeing as the *communication of* speech was ordained for just this end [to which it makes an outstanding contribution], *in order that we might indicate our inclinations to each other*; [that part of music which can be deployed] *however much utility is garnered from music* by the voice [through hearing] has clearly been given *to the human race* entirely for the sake of harmony. And harmony, *that is, harmonious measuring, namely a measured tension*, which has motions akin *and, as it were, related* to the revolutions of the soul within us, is useful to anyone who treats the *gift of the* Muses intelligently, not for the sake of [irrational] pleasure [—as is nowadays generally supposed—] *but for the sake of temperance* [but as having been given by the Muses as an ally in the attempt to bring] *seeing as, with the aid of the Muses, it recalls* the [revolution] *movements* of our soul, which [has become] *are discordant and* ill-attuned, into *the* [proper] order and concord [with itself] *of harmony*. Rhythm, moreover, was given [us from the same heavenly source to help us in the same way because] *as a remedy for our nature* generally [our condition is] *charmless*, ignorant of *number and* measure, and lacking in grace.

As we have come to expect, differences are immediately apparent, although some are more cosmetic, others more substantive. For instance, by allowing the bestowal of harmony (*datorum* = παρὰ θεῶν δεδωρῆσθαι and *datus* = ὑπὸ τῶν αὐτῶν ἐδόθη) to stand alone without an agent, Calcidius effectively silenced Plato's specification that it was the gods who bestowed harmony and rhythm,[76] a sin of omission calculated to appease his (presumably) Christian patron, Osius.[77] This also appeased

[76] Music as a divine gift is a consistent theme in the Platonic dialogues; cf. the similar language at *Rep.* 411e, as well as the parallels (*Leg.* 653c–654a, 665a, 672d, 796e; *Sym.* 197ab; *Crat.* 404e–406a) noted in Francesco Pelosi, *Plato on Music, Soul and Body*, trans. Sophie Henderson (Cambridge: Cambridge University Press, 2010), 68, n. 1.

[77] The precise identity of this Osius has been a matter of considerable dispute. The twelfth-century manuscript tradition generally identifies him as *Osius Episcopus* (Bishop Osius), presumed to be the bishop of Cordoba (in which account Calcidius becomes his *archidiaconus*, his archdeacon), on which

twelfth-century commentators, who were quick to supply the assumed (and of course singular) agent: bestowed "by God" (*a Deo*).[78] Likewise, Calcidius alters Plato's brief commendation of the spoken word (*ordinata communicatio sermonis* = λόγος, 47c6). Where, in Plato's text, speech "makes the greatest contribution to the same [reason]" (τὴν μεγίστην συμβαλλόμενος εἰς αὐτὰ μοῖραν), Calcidius substitutes a more concrete rationale, which has no parallel in the Greek: "in order that we might indicate our inclinations to each other" (*ut praesto forent mutuae uoluntatis indicia*).

At Plato's first mention of music, he does not leave the term (which had extraordinarily large compass) unqualified but incorporates it into the more precise, if still ambiguous, construction ὅσον ταὖ μουσικῆς φωνῇ χρήσιμον πρὸς ἀκοὴν (47c7–d1). Plato's intent here has been the subject of some debate, and it will require some philological unpacking. Some commentators, such as Cornford, have supposed that ἀκοὴν is the complement of χρήσιμον πρὸς and read φωνῆς for φωνῇ (against the majority of the manuscripts), thus construing the phrase: "all that part of music that is serviceable with respect to the hearing of sound."[79] Andrew Barker, however, takes φωνῇ as complement to χρήσιμον and construes πρὸς ἀκοὴν independently, translating "so much of μουσική as is adapted to sound in relation to the hearing" and elsewhere, "that part of music which can be deployed by the voice and directed to the hearing."[80] Calcidius, however, construes ὅσον not with the partitive genitive μουσικῆς (as all modern translators assume) but with χρήσιμον (*quantum utilitatis*), and he streamlines the syntax by suppressing πρὸς ἀκοὴν altogether: "however much utility is garnered from music by the voice" (*quantumque per uocem utilitatis capitur ex musica*). Calcidius's translation,

see Paul Edward Dutton, "Medieval Approaches to Calcidius" in *Plato's "Timaeus" as Cultural Icon*, ed. Gretchen Reydams-Schils (Notre Dame, IN: University of Notre Dame Press, 2003), 185–188. Many modern scholars have followed suit: Johann Wrobel, ed. *Platonis "Timaeus" intreprete Chalcidio cum eiusdem commentario* (Leipzig: B. G. Teubner, 1876); B. Wladislaus Switalski, *Des Chalcidius Kommentar zu Plato's Timaeus: Eine historisch-kritische Untersuchung* (Münster: Aschendorff, 1902); J. C. M. van Winden, *Calcidius on Matter: His Doctrines and Sources: A Chapter in the History of Platonism* (Leiden: Brill, 1959). Recently, Bakhouche, following the lead of an earlier suggestion by Pierre Courcelle ("Ambroise de Milan et Calcidius," in *Romanitas et Christianitas*, ed. W. den Boer, P. G. van der Nat, et al. [Amsterdam: North-Holland, 1973], 45–53), has linked Calcidius's Osius to a high-ranking Christian official in late-fourth-century Milan, an Osius who held senior fiscal offices. See Béatrice Bakhouche, *Calcidius: Commentaire au* Timée *de Platon* (Paris: J. Vrin, 2011), 8–13.

78 E.g., *Guillelmi Glos. sup. Tim.* 152.20–21: EADEM RATIO EST VOCIS ET AVDITVS quae et uisus, DATORVM homini a Deo AD EOSDEM VSVS.

79 Francis MacDonald Cornford, *Plato's Cosmology: The* Timaeus *of Plato, Translated with a Running Commentary* (London: Routledge, 1977), 158. Cornford offers the following justification in a footnote: "reading φωνῆς χρήσιμον πρὸς ἀκοὴν, φωνῆς being governed by ἀκοὴν. . . . φωνῇ χρήσιμον can hardly mean 'vocal'; and why should instrumental music be excluded? Nor can it mean 'expressed in sound'; and 'useful to the voice' is irrelevant."

80 Andrew Barker, "Timaeus on Music and the Liver," in *Reason and Necessity: Essays on Plato's* Timaeus, ed. M. R. Wright (London: Duckworth and the Classical Press of Wales, 2000), 85; *The Science of Harmonics in Classical Greece* (Cambridge: Cambridge University Press, 2007), 325.

as against modern interpretations, focuses squarely on music's *utility*, not just its domain (*per uocem*), anticipating and strengthening the cognate expressions to follow: that music is *useful* (*commoda* = χρήσιμος) to those who *use* it wisely (*prudenter utentibus* = τῷ μετὰ νοῦ προσχρωμένῳ).[81]

Calcidius, moreover, thought it necessary to intervene at 47d2 and gloss Plato's invocation of harmony (ἁρμονία), a term used only once before in the *Timaeus*, at 36e6–37a1, where Plato noted that soul "participates in reason and harmony" (λογισμοῦ δὲ μετέχουσα καὶ ἁρμονίας ψυχή). There, Calcidius handled ἁρμονίας with the Latin term *modulaminis*: "partaking of reason as well as harmony" (*rationis tamen et item modulaminis compos*, 29.7–8). Here, however, at its second occurrence, he deploys the loan word *harmonia* and offers a translator's gloss that itself is nearly impossible to translate. Its spirit can be captured with something like "that is, harmonious measuring, namely a measured tension" (*id est modulatio, utpote intentio modificata*).[82] The linguistic play of *modulatio* and *modificatus*, both cognate with *modulamen* at 37d1 and all three derived from the root concept *modus* ("measure," "mode," and "melody"), stresses that this *harmonia* is a measured, mathematical, and not (merely) phenomenological concept.

The inclusion of *intensio*, however, pulls in another direction: the precise identification of a musical "note." The ancient music theorist, Aristoxenus, had defined a musical note (φθόγγος) as the "incidence of the voice on one tension/pitch" (φωνῆς πτῶσις ἐπὶ μίαν τάσιν),[83] which quickly became the standard definition and was imported (often without attribution) into Pythagorean musical treatises as well. Boethius, too, for instance (presumably following his Greek source text by Nicomachus of Gerasa), defines a note (*phthongus*) as "an incidence of the voice . . . on one tension/pitch" (*uocis casus . . . in unam intensionem*).[84] Calcidius's *modificata intensio* may reflect this same tradition, and if so, the gloss he supplies for *harmonia* pulls in two different directions simultaneously, toward the domains of noumenal mathematics and phenomenal sound both.

The tension and interplay of the intelligible and the sensible are precisely targeted by Calcidius in his commentary on this passage (*In Tim.* 167 [272.3–273.6]):

> Transit deinde ad alterius sensus examinationem. Ait enim: Eadem uocis quoque et auditus ratio est ad eosdem usus atque ad plenam uitae hominum instructionem datorum. Sunt igitur principales duo sensus uisus et auditus, utique philosophiam adiuuantes; quorum alter

[81] Cf. Pelosi, *Plato on Music*, 71.

[82] The nominal form of the relatively rare *modificatus* reappears in a similar sense in Martianus Capella's description of Apollo's musical grove (*De nuptiis* 1.11 [7.5–6]): Nec mirum quod Apollinis silva ita rata modificatione congrueret, cum caeli quoque orbes idem Delius moduletur in Sole.

[83] Rosetta Da Rios, ed., *Aristoxeni Elementa Harmonica* (Rome: Typis publicae officinae polygraphicae, 1954), 1.15.14–24 (20:15–19).

[84] *Inst. mus.* 1.8 (195.2–3).

quidem euidentior, utpote qui res ipsas acie sua comprehendat, alter latior, ideo quod etiam de rebus absentibus instruat, modulatus siquidem aer articulatae uoci factusque uox et intellegibilis oratio pergit ad intimos sensus audientis intellectui nuntians tam praesentia quam absentia. Idem auditus quod intellectum quoque adiuuet, sic probat: *Quantumque per uocem utilitatis capitur ex musica, totum hoc constat hominum generi propter harmoniam tributum*, quia iuxta rationem harmonicam animam in superioribus aedificauerat naturalemque eius actum rhythmis modisque constare dixerat, sed haec exolescere animae ob consortium corporis necessario obtinente obliuione proptereaque immodulatas fore animas plurimorum. Medelam huius uitii dicit esse in musica postiam, non in ea qua uulgus delectatur quaeque ad uoluptatem facta excitat uitia non numquam, sed in illa diuina, quae numquam a ratione atque intellegentia separetur; hanc enim censet exorbitantes animas a uia recta reuocare demum ad symphoniam ueterem. Optima porro symphonia est in moribus nostris iustitia, uirtutum omnium principalis, per quam ceterae quoque uirtutes suum munus atque opus exequuntur, ut ratio quidem dux sit, uigor uero intimus, qui est iracundiae similis, auxiliatorem se rationi uolens praebeat; porro haec prouenire sine modulatione non possunt, modulatio demum sine symphonia nulla sit, ipsa symphonia sequitur musica. Procul dubio musica exornat animam rationabiliter ad antiquam naturam reuocans et efficiens talem demum qualem initio deus opifex eam fecerat. Tota porro musica in uoce et auditu et sonis posita est. Utilis ergo etiam iste sensus est philosophiae totius assecutioni ad notationem intellegibilis rei.

[Plato] then transitions to an examination of another sense, saying "the same account [as given for vision] applies also to voice and hearing, which have been bestowed for the same purposes [as vision], namely the full instruction of human life." Hence, there are two principal senses, vision and hearing; each is conducive to philosophy—the former more evidently, insofar as it comprehends things in themselves with the keenness of its glance; the latter more broadly, insofar as it also offers instruction about things absent, since air, when measured in harmony with an articulate voice and made into a voice and an intelligible enunciation, reaches the inmost senses of the listener and announces to the intellect things that are present as well as absent. That hearing is also a helpmate to the intellect, Plato proves by saying, "however much utility is garnered from music by the voice has clearly been given to the human race entirely for the sake of harmony." For earlier Plato had constructed the soul in accord with harmonic ratios and had claimed that its natural actions are comprised of rhythm and measure. But because of the forgetfulness that, of

> necessity, occurs when the soul is joined to the body, these harmonies fade away; hence the souls of many are rendered out of tune. Plato says that the cure for this ill is held within music—not within the music that delights the common crowd, since such music, created for pleasure, often stirs up more faults, but within the divine music that can never be separated from reason (*ratio*) and intelligence. For Plato is of the opinion that this music can, at long last, recall souls that are wandering astray from the right path to their former harmony. Moreover, the greatest consonance (*symphonia*) of our character is justice, the chief of all virtues; through it, all the others acquire their right goal and end, provided that reason take its place as leader and that inner vigor, similar to irascibility, willingly offer itself as an aid to reason. Furthermore, none of this can occur without harmonious measuring (*modulatio*), but there can be no harmonious measuring without consonance (*symphonia*), and consonance is a consequence of music. Without a doubt, then, music rationally adorns the soul; it recalls it to its pristine nature and renders it such as it was when god the creator had made it in the very beginning. But music is entirely comprised of voice, hearing, and sound. Whence this sense too is useful for the pursuit of all philosophy, for the understanding of intelligible reality.

The essential claim highlighted above—that *harmonia* has movements cognate to the revolutions of soul within us—is passed over in silence. Calcidius says nothing explicit or concrete about the affinity or similarity between music and soul, but only vaguely directs us to earlier passages (*in superioribus*), presumably to the construction of the human soul at 41d and its mathematical structure analogous to the world soul at 35bff.[85] On the more difficult question of what Plato precisely means by ἁρμονία in this passage, Calcidius again says nothing (save for the gloss in his translation, discussed above). Instead, he chooses to focus on the very point that his translation highlighted: the therapeutic *utility* of music—its ability, through a kind of soul therapy, to restore the soul to its

[85] In a chapter on the ontology of the soul (*In Tim.* 228 [243.13–244.10]), Calcidius tries to defend Plato against commentators who accuse him of inconsistency, as the *Phaedrus* proposes a simple soul but the *Timaeus* a seemingly composite soul: hoc loco calumniari solent homines quibus ueri indagandi cura nulla est. Dicunt enim Platonem in Phaedro quidem asserere animam esse sine ulla compositione proptereaque indissolubilem (cf. *Phaedrus* 245c5–246a2, translated by Calcidius at 82–83, [104.18–105.18]), in Timaeo tamen compositam rem confiteri, siquidem faciat eam constare ex indiuidua diuiduaque substantia et ita diuersa eademque natura. Against those impugning Plato's self-contradiction, Calcidius replies that the Timaean composite soul is not actually composite but has a *ratio compositionis*, a system or ratio of composition, as in a musical concord like the diatessaron: quiddam uero, quod compositum quidem non sit, habeat tamen rationem compositionis, ut in musica symphonia, quae diatessaron uocatur.

former harmony.[86] This is surprising. Plato here gives us no account for the disharmony of the soul such that it would require music's restorative powers; we are only told that music is an ally (σύμμαχος) in the reharmonization of the disharmonious revolution of soul within us (ἐπὶ τὴν γεγονυῖαν ἐν ἡμῖν ἀνάρμοστον ψυχῆς περίοδον). Calcidius, however, explicitly names the source of this disharmony. The culprit is the body, through conjunction with which the soul is necessarily cast into a state of oblivion: "when the soul is joined to the body, these harmonies fade away."[87] Hence, through the corporeal contagion of union with the body, the soul *forgets* its former harmony (*antiqua harmonia*) and becomes an out-of-tune, pale echo of the perfection that obtained at the moment of its creation.

At the same time, however, music is presented as a cure, a means of restoring the soul to its pristine harmony. Calcidius's specification of the proper soul therapy as "the divine music that can never be separated from reason (*ratio*) and intelligence" recalls Plato's account of musical harmony at *Tim.* 80ab. There Plato observes that the proper blending of low and high tones (arising, respectively, from slower and faster motions) produces a single sensation (μίαν ἐξ ὀξείας καὶ βαρείας συνεκεράσαντο πάθην, 80b4–5) that is a source of (bodily) pleasure (δονή) to the unintelligent but a source of (intellectual) delight (εὐφροσύνη) to the intelligent,[88] insofar as they recognize in it "an imitation of *divine harmony*" (τὴν τῆς θείας ἁρμονίας μίμησιν, 80b6–7). The all-important participation of the intellect, present in both 80b and 47d, is further stressed by Calcidius: only divine music, never divorced from reason and intellect, can go beyond mere irrational, bodily

[86] Music as a form of soul therapy or, conversely, moral character as a kind of musical modality is manifest in Plato's early ethical dialogues as well: cf. *Laches* 188d, 193de. It is worth observing the repeated mention of Damon (180d, 197d, 200ab; cf. *Rep.* 400b2), who is introduced in the *Laches* as a music teacher (180d). The connection between Damon and the training of character through music is attested also in fragment B7 (= Aristides Quintilianus, *De musica*, 2.14). On this fragment, and on music as soul therapy in general, see Frédérique Woerther, "Music and the Education of the Soul in Plato and Aristotle: Homoeopathy and the Formation of Character," *Classical Quarterly* 58 (2008), 89–103; Pelosi, *Plato on Music*, 29–67.

[87] Although Calcidius has no account of the (late Platonic) descent of the soul, such as we find in Macrobius (on which see M. A. Elferink, *La descente de l'âme d'après Macrobe* [Leiden: Brill, 1968]), his language here (*exolescere, obtinente obliuione*) obliquely recalls *Phaedrus* 248c and anticipates, if only faintly, Macrobius *In Som. Scip.* 1.12.7–8 (49.6–16): anima ergo cum trahitur ad corpus, in hac prima sui productione siluestrem tumultum id est ὕλην influentem sibi incipit experiri . . . unde et comes ebrietatis *obliuio* illic animis incipit iam latenter obrepere. There is, however, no hint in Calcidius of the soul's "intoxication" as in the *Phaedrus* and Macrobius.

[88] Cf. *Prot.* 337c1–4, which presents an identical contrast between εὐφραίνεσθαι, to feel intellectual delight through intellectual activity alone (αὐτῇ τῇ διανοίᾳ), and ἥδεσθαι, to feel bodily pleasure through the body alone (αὐτῷ τῷ σώματι): εὐφραίνεσθαι μὲν γὰρ ἔστιν μανθάνοντά τι καὶ φρονήσεως μεταλαμβάνοντα αὐτῇ τῇ διανοίᾳ, ἥδεσθαι δὲ ἐσθίοντά τι ἢ ἄλλο ἡδὺ πάσχοντα αὐτῷ τῷ σώματι—pace Pelosi, *Plato on Music*, 97, who notes the parallel but opines that "it is highly improbable that one can read the contrast to be found at *Tim.* 80b5–8 in analogous terms. In particular, not only is it difficult

pleasure (the ἡδονὴν ἄλογον of 47d4) to provide a psychological cure. Insofar as the *diuina harmonia* is manifest through mortal motions (ἐν θνηταῖς . . . φοραῖς, 80b7), the musical cure is only effective provided the soul is united to a body, to that "mighty river" of sensations (αἰσθήσεις, 43a6–c7), which allows music to work through the body upon the soul. For Calcidius, the body is simultaneously the destroyer and restorer of harmony: it is the (source of the) illness; it is the (conduit for the) cure.

The final theme developed in Calcidius's comments on *Tim.* 47ce is the harmony of the virtues, justice (*iustitia*) in particular, a theme that cements music's utility to the pursuit of philosophy and the understanding of intelligible reality. Justice is not only the chief of the virtues, but it is also the *optima symphonia*, the "best consonance," a phrase that obliquely suggests the octave, which, according to many Greek harmonic theorists, was the chief of the consonances and the closest to equality.[89] Calcidius locates the harmony of justice within the proper relationship between the ruling power of reason (*ratio*) and the ruled inner vital force (*intimus uigor*).[90] Without signaling the transition, Calcidius here has slid into a discussion of Platonic psychology and articulates a view similar to the Boethian passage quoted at the outset of this chapter (p. 34 above).[91] When reason, the soul's immortal, rational aspect, is the leader (*dux* = *rector* in Boethius) and the mortal and quasi-irrational inner vital force (*intimus uigor* = *cupiditas* and *effrenatio* in Boethius) is willingly reason's servant, then justice, the concord (*symphonia*)

to understand the *hēdonē* in *Tim.* 80b5 as a pleasure of the body, but there is also doubt that it is a pleasure that can be traced to the sphere of sensibility, i.e., of the senses and the mortal soul."

89 It is worth recalling that Plato, at *Rep.* 430e3–4, relates temperance to a συμφωνίᾳ τινὶ καὶ ἁρμονίᾳ προσέοικεν μᾶλλον ἢ τὰ πρότερον. Proclus, in his commentary on the *Republic*, identifies this συμφωνία with the octave (*In Remp.* I 213.28–29: ταῦτα μὲν οὖν παρεξέβημεν ἐνδεικνύμενοι, πῶς ἁρμονίαν διὰ πασῶν ὁ Σωκράτης εἶπεν τὴν σωφροσύνην). On Proclus's discussion, see O'Meara, "The Music of Philosophy in Late Antiquity," in *Philosophy and the Sciences in Antiquity*, ed. R. W. Sharples (Aldershot: Ashgate, 2005), 143–144, and the note by Winnington-Ingram on Proclus, *In Remp.* I 212.26ff. in André-Jean Festugière, trans., *Proclus: Commentaire sur le République* (Paris: J. Vrin, 1970), II.194–195. Cf. Aristotle, *Top.* 4.123a33–37, who observes that such a usage of συμφωνία is strictly metaphorical (οὐ κυρίως ἀλλὰ μεταφορᾷ· πᾶσα γὰρ συμφωνία ἐν φθόγγοις). On the octave as the first and best consonance, see the Ps.-Aristotelian *Problemata* 19.35 and 39; Ptolemy, *Harm.* 1.5 (11.22ff.), 1.7 (15.2ff.); Aristides Quintilianus, *De musica* 2.12 (77.16ff.); Boethius, *Inst. mus.* 2.18 (249.22–29), 2.20 (251.16–20).

90 Cf. *Rep.* 441e4-6: οὐκοῦν τῷ μὲν λογιστικῷ ἄρχειν προσήκει, σοφῷ ὄντι καὶ ἔχοντι τὴν ὑπὲρ ἁπάσης τῆς ψυχῆς προμήθειαν, τῷ δὲ θυμοειδεῖ ὑπηκόῳ εἶναι καὶ συμμάχῳ τούτου; on this passage and Plato's psychology of justice in general, see John M. Cooper, "The Psychology of Justice in Plato," *American Philosophical Quarterly* 14 (1977), 151–157.

91 Care must be taken when dealing with Calcidius's psychology, for his levels of division within the soul change depending on the needs of any given passage. Sometime he employs, as here, a bipartition into the immortal rational part (λογιστικόν) and a mortal irrational part, which comes into being precisely to deal with the conditions of embodiment (appetite, movement, etc.); cf. *In Tim.* 230 (244.21–245.1). On the Platonic bipartition generally, see D. A. Rees, "Bipartition of the Soul in the Early Academy," *Journal of Hellenic Studies* 77 (1957), 112–118; Dillon, *Alcinous: The Handbook of*

between leader and follower, obtains within the soul.[92] Calcidius, at last, brings his argument to a close by drawing an inferential chain that links the harmony of justice and the virtues in general, what he calls "intelligible reality" (*res intelligibilis*), to the "reality" of sounding music. Justice supposes balanced measure (*modulatio*), balanced measure supposes concord (*symphonia*), and concord supposes music (*musica*). If this is the case, then voice, sound, and *hearing* can inaugurate the sequential chain that runs from music to psychological virtue and back again. Hearing is thus one pathway to intelligible reality. The twelfth-century cosmologists were ready to listen.

Microcosmic Lessons in Macrocosmic Principles

For both Bernard of Chartres and William of Conches, Plato's *Timaeus* (more accurately, as we have discovered, the Calcidian *Timaeus*) was a deeply moral text; it was a handbook in macrocosmic ethics, known as "natural justice" (*iustitia naturalis*), which arises from the rational order of the cosmos and in turn is reflected on a microcosmic scale in "positive justice" (*iustitia positiua*), the laws, customs, and ethics of human society.[93] Accordingly, both these Timaean commentators interpret the gifts of sight and hearing (*Tim.* 47ae) in a moral light, and Calcidius's *utilitas* becomes an almost exclusively moral utility. Both sight and hearing are essential for human morality and proper conduct: sight, so that we can see and

Platonism (Oxford: Clarendon Press, 1993), 149–150. Although Calcidius seems generally to favor the late Platonic bipartition, he does assign the traditional *iracundia* (θύμος) and *cupiditas* (ἐπιθυμία) as the parts of the appetitive aspect of the soul (*In Tim* 201 [221.2–3]). For a brief synopsis of Calcidius's division(s) of the soul, see Stephen Gersh, *Middle Platonism and Neoplatonism: The Latin Tradition* (Notre Dame, IN: University of Notre Dame Press, 1986), 486–488.

92 It is possible that Calcidius here is reliant on an intermediary, as a similar but more developed theory of virtues as consonances reemerges in the thought of Iamblichus, Proclus, and Damascius. They too associated the virtues with the perfection of number and harmony, and Proclus in particular seems to have associated temperance and justice with the octave; justice, in these contexts, is described in similar terms as the harmony of ruler to ruled; e.g., Damascius, *In Phaedonem* II.55 (reporting the teaching of Proclus): "Justice is discriminating concord, whereas moderation is integrating concord; justice seeks its own in such a way as to keep each thing distinct, yet common to all. Moderation, then, is concord between the controlling and the controlled, justice between the rulers and the ruled" (quoted and translated in O'Meara, "The Music of Philosophy in Late Antiquity," 144). For a fuller discussion of ethical arithmetic and harmonics, see ibid., 143–145; O'Meara, *Pythagoras Revived: Mathematics and Philosophy in Late Antiquity*, 70–76; and A. A. Long, "The Harmonics of Stoic Virtue," in *Stoic Studies* (Berkeley: University of California Press, 2001), 202–223.

93 *Bernardi Glos. sup. Tim.* 1.11–14, 20–22, 32–36; *Guillelmi Glos. sup. Tim.* 3.1–14; for a transcription and discussion of other examples of the political mirror of the cosmos in Timaean *accessus*, see Tullio Gregory, *Platonismo medievale: Studi e ricerche* (Rome: Istituto storico italiano per il Medio Evo, 1958), 59–73; for a detailed study of one aspect of this tradition, see Paul Edward Dutton, "*Illustre ciuitatis et populi exemplum*: Plato's *Timaeus* and the Transmission from Calcidius to the End of the Twelfth Century of a Tripartite Scheme of Society," *Mediaeval Studies* 45 (1983), 79–119.

imitate the harmony that the universe maintains between the heavens' motions, one rational (the fixed stars), the other irrational (the planets);[94] hearing, so that we can compose within our morals and conduct the same sort of harmony that we hear between pitches in proper proportion.

Both commentators are initially interested in the classification and typology of the "voices" (*uoces*) that populate Calcidius's translation. Bernard begins his comments on this passage by observing that there are three kinds of *uoces* that have utility in their hearing. These are intellectual (*intellectae*), melodious (*modulatae*), and rhythmical (*numeratae*) voices, corresponding to the spoken word, heard music, and metrical prosody respectively.[95] An extended gloss exclusive to a Vatican manuscript of William's *Glosae super Platonem* (Urbinas latinus 1389) connects the "voices" of *Tim.* 47ce to an adaptation of the Ptolemaic division of the "sounds suitable for harmony" (*uoces armoniae aptae*) at *De institutione musica*, 5.6. The spoken *uox* is "continuous" and thus *exmelica* (sc. ἐκμελής) or unmelodious; the musical *uox* is "discontinuous" (*discreta*) and thus *emelica* (sc. ἐμμελής) or melodious.[96] According to both commentators, it is the musical and rhythmical *uoces* that prove their moral worth. Thus, for Bernard of Chartres, the greatest utility of what he calls "exterior music" (*musica exterior*) is to our moral compass:[97]

> Docet quomodo auditus ualeat ad philosophiam: quia ualet ad correctionem morum. Auditis [*scripsi*, auditus *Dutton*] enim consonantiis

[94] *Bernardi Glos. sup. Tim.* 7.389–394: Ad quae uisus est necessarius, quia per uisum notamus rationabilem motum aplanos, qui et se ipsum mouet sine errore et planetarum erraticos motus contemperat. Quod notantes debemus aplanon nostrae mentis ita instituere, ut se ipsum sine errore moueat et erroneos motus uitiorum refrenet, quae morum correctio ualet in publicis et priuatis rebus. *Guillelmi Glos. sup. Tim.* 151.19–23: Dedit ergo Deus oculos homini ut, cum perciperet homo duos esse motus in caelestibus et similies in se, quemadmodum diuina ratio facit erraticum motum sequi rationabilem motum firmamenti ita erraticos motus carnis subdere rationabili motui spiritus.

[95] *Bernardi Glos. sup. Tim.* 7.452–458: Nota uoces per auditum prodesse nobis tribus modis: Intellectae, id est sola significatione, nobis prosunt ad mutuam uoluntantem intimandam. Modulatae etiam absque significatione prosunt ad concentum, scilicet morum, qui in cantu notatur. Numeratae quoque prosunt ad parilitatem et conuenientiam, quae alteri ab altero exhibenda est, quod in rithmo consideratur. Rithmus enim interpretatur numerus.

[96] *Guillelmi Glos. sup. Tim.* 153.6 cum apparatu critico: Ita habemus quod uox alia est continua ut usualis sermo, quod dicitur 'exmelica' [*scripsi*, ex melica *cod.*], id est extra melodiam, alia est discreta que uocatur e[t]melica [*scripsi*, et melica *cod.*], id est cum melodia, ut est musica que consistit in elleuatione et depressione. Sed dictum de continua. Modo dicit de discreta, scilicet de musica. Sed de musica quedam est melica, id est cum melodiis ut instrumentis et cantilenis; quedam est rithmica, que constitit in equali numero; similiter quedam est metrica ut in numero pedum. Sed prius ostendit utilitatem melice musice, uocans eam armoniam, id est modulatam quia ex intensione cordarum habet fieri. Postea aget de duabus aliis simul, ostendens scilicet quod sicut ibi obseruatur numerus et modus, ita natura hominis reducatur ad modum, ad numerus, ita scilicet quod nichil extra modum uel numerum faciat [*scripsi*, fatiat *cod.*]. Cf. *Inst. mus.* 5.6 (356.26–357.11) et *Guillelmi Glos. sup. Tim.* 152.23–25: Ostensurus quae utilitas sit in uoce, prius hoc ostendit circa *uocem continuam*, id est sine modulatione, quae dicitur sermo communis.

[97] *Bernardi Glos. sup. Tim.* 7.437–443.

> musicis, debemus in moribus nostris uirtutum consonantia reformari. Licet enim anima secundum consonantias sit compacta, tamen ipsae consonantiae ex corporum coniunctione dissonae fiunt et reformandae sunt per exteriorem musicam. Et hoc est: tota musica data est hominibus non ad delectationem, sed ad morum compositionem.[98]
>
> [Plato] teaches how hearing is of value to philosophy: because it has value for the correction of morals. For when we hear musical consonances, we should be reformed in our morals by the consonance of the virtues. For although the soul is joined together according to the musical consonances, nevertheless, those consonances are knocked out of tune (*dissonae fiunt*) by conjunction with the body, and so ought to be reformed through external music. And this is what Plato means when he says: All music was given to men not for the sake of pleasure, but for the composition of their morals.

So too, for William of Conches, the utility of melody consists in its ability to "shape within one's morals the same sort of concord one perceives in sounds."[99] Both, moreover, explicitly *externalize* the musical cure and understand Calcidius's gloss on *harmonia* as a signpost for sounding music. For Bernard, the *intensio modificata* obtains "either between two strings, or between weights, or between voices" (*uel inter duas cordas, uel inter pondera, uel inter uoces*).[100] William breaks the terms into two separate but related glosses. *Intensio* indicates that one voice or pitch is higher than another, but since dissonant pitches are not yet excluded by such a definition, *modificata* makes the necessary specification that it is an *intensio* made according to measure or proportion, "for consonance is the concordant diversity of sounds."[101]

There is one significant difference between Bernard and William. Bernard, as he often does, silently follows Calcidius's commentary and identifies the body as the root cause of the soul's disharmony.[102] For William, however, this disharmony

[98] Cf. *Bernardi Glos. sup. Tim.* 3.64–68: ita nutriendi sunt tutores patriae, ut prompti ad laborem et affabiles sint obedientibus. Quod prompti sint per exercitium, scilicet cursum, uenatum, et ludos gymnasii; quod mites et affabiles, per delinimenta praeparatur musicae, quae per sonorum conuenientiam morum docet concordiam.

[99] *Guillelmi Glos. sup. Tim.* 153.1–4: Ostenso quae utilitas sit in communi sermone, ostendit quae utilitas sit in melodiis, haec scilicet ut qualem concordiam in sonis homo perciperet, eandem in moribus conformaret.

[100] *Bernardi Glos. sup. Tim.* 7.444–445.

[101] *Guillelmi Glos. sup. Tim.* 153.7–11: Et quid est armonia? ARMONIA VERO ID EST MODVLATIO. Et quare modulatio? VTPOTE id est sicut INTENSIO, quia una uox est altior altera. Sed quia hoc totum habet dissonantia, addit: MODIFICATA, id est in modo et proportione facta—est enim consonantia diuersitas sonorum concors. Cf. Bernard Silvestris, *Comm. in Mart.* 8.330–331: RATA MODIFICATIONE, certa proportione, que dicitur modificatio, quia facit modos, scilicet simphonias.

[102] *Bernardi Glos. sup. Tim.* 7.439–441: Licet enim anima secundum consonantias sit compacta, tamen ipsae consonantiae ex corporum coniunctione dissonae fiunt.

is explained on psychological grounds, namely the "opposing and disharmonious commotions of the soul," which include *ira* (anger) and *turbulentia* (agitation).[103] But William has not left the bodily realm entirely: these psychological "commotions" equate to the mortal parts of the soul that exist to deal with the conditions of embodiment.[104] William's explanation of the union of body and soul (as we will see in Chapter 4) in fact requires the body to have a harmony of its own, and thus cannot, or at least not directly, be the sole agent of the soul's disharmony.

Bernard's "consonance of the virtues" and William's "concord in morals" are not unique in the twelfth century; on the contrary, the topos of music's ethical domain and dominion approaches ubiquity. Adelard of Bath, noting music's great power over souls, remarks that in the wisdom of old age a listener is not only delighted by harmonious voices (*uocum concordiam*) but strives to bring his character and all his deeds into ethical consonance (*ethicam consonantiam*).[105] In Honorius of Autun's *On the Exile and Homeland of the Soul* (*De animae exilio et patria*), soul-travelers are cast into interior exile (the body) on account of their ignorance and thus journey through ten cities (the liberal arts, physics, mechanics, and economics) in their return to wisdom. In the fifth city, the "city of music" (*ciuitas musica*), they are taught that they must pass through the melody of morals (*per modulamen morum*) on their way to the celestial concord (*concentum caelorum*).[106] In Alan de Lille's *De planctu naturae* (from the 1160s), personified Natura laments that within her dominion, man alone has scorned the "cithara of my moderation and is deluded by the lyre of a delirious Orpheus."[107] It can be no mere coincidence, then, that in Alan's *Anticlaudianus*, an epic poem on the creation of a "perfect man" who will lead the Virtues to victory, it is Discord and her minions, the avowed enemies of Concord, that mount the Vices' first charge in the elaborate *psychomachia* at the poem's end.[108] Finally, the compiler of the *Teachings of Moral Philosophy* (*Moralium dogma philosophorum*), a twelfth-century ethical florilegium sometimes ascribed to William of Conches,[109] saw fit to bring the text to a rousing conclusion with an

[103] *Guillelmi Glos. sup. Tim.* 153.18–19.

[104] *ira* = *iracundia* (θυμός) and *turbulentia* = *cupiditas* (ἐπιθυμία).

[105] *De eod. et diu.* 52: In senectute vero tantam hoc decus efficatiam obtinet ut non solum vocum concordiam hec etas exposcat, verum et mores et facta universa in ethicam consonantiam redigere et gaudeat et nitatur. Unde et, hac intentione firmiter constituta, a quampluribus sapientibus hec etas "gravis" appellatur.

[106] PL 172, 1244C: In hac urbe docentur viantes per modulamen morum transire ad concentum coelorum.

[107] *De pl. nat.* VIII.2: Solus homo, mee moderationis citharam aspernatus, sub delirantis Orphei lira delirat.

[108] *Anticl.* 8.221–223: prima sitit bellum Discordia, prima tumultus / appetit et primi preludia Martis inire / preparat. . . . Ibid., 9.9–10: prima viro movet assultus Discordia, primum / aggreditur Martem, primo casura tumultu.

[109] For a review of the scholarship, see John R. Williams, "The Quest for the Author of the *Moralium dogma philosophorum*, 1931–1956," *Speculum* 32 (1957), 736–747.

extended musical analogy based on a passage from Cicero, which returns us to the centrality of listening:[110]

> Vt enim in fidibus aut tibiis quamuis paulum discrepent, tamen id ab artifice animaduerti solet, sic nobis ducenda est uita, ne forte quid discrepet, uel etiam multo magis in quantum melior est actionum quam sonorum concentus. Itaque ut in fidibus musicorum aures uel minima sentiunt, sic nos, si uolumus esse acres uitiorum animaduersores, magna sepe intelligemus ex paruis: ex occulorum obtutu, ex remissis aut contractis superciliis, ex mesticia, ex hilaritate, ex risu, ex locutione, ex contentione uocis, ex summissione, ex ceteris similibus facile iudicabimus, quid eorum apte fiat quidue ab officio discrepet.
>
> Just as in strings or flutes, even if they are only slightly out of tune, this is nevertheless usually detected by their creator, so too ought we to lead our life, lest anything happen to be out of tune, or rather we should do so all the more, insofar as a harmony of actions is greater than a harmony of sounds. Thus, just as the ears of musicians perceive the slightest variation in strings, so too we, if we want to be keen observers of moral flaws, will often understand things of great importance in the smallest of matters: from a glance of the eyes or a raising or furrowing of the brows, from sorrow, joyfulness, laughter, or speech, from a high or low tone of a voice, or the like, we will easily judge what would be right to do, or what would be out of tune with our purpose.

The act of listening—of close, intense listening—is the aspirational goal of a humanity attuned to the world around it, even when, or especially when, this means straining to hear the inaudible: the intermaterial, ordered aggregate that is the *mundus*. As Adelard of Bath reminds us, nature's *discretio* must be heard (*audienda est*), and must be given a hearing by human reason.[111] The twelfth-century

110 *Moralium*, Conclusio operis. Cf. Cicero, *De officiis* 1.146. It is worth observing, however, that in the *Moralium* the virtue of *Concordia* is presented as a subspecies of justice and thus as a public, political virtue, not a private, moral one: Concordia est uirtus conciues et compatriotas in eodem iure et cohabitacione spontanee uinciens (*Moralium* I.B.2.bII.ζ). This too concords with Cicero, *De officiis* 2.20.78, where *concordia* (alongside *aequitas*) is deemed one of the *fundamenta rei publicae*. In Alan de Lille's *Anticlaudianus*, Concordia, the first of Nature's sisters and counselors, is likewise first described in civic terms; her garment (described at 2.178–199) depicts famed biblical and classical friendships (David and Jonathan, Theseus and Pirithous, Tydeus and Polynices, Nisus and Euryalus, etc.), and she is introduced as holding in her right hand an olive branch (2.205–207: virginis in dextra, foliorum crine comatus, / flore tumens, fructus expectans, ramus olive / pubescit); finally, her initial words lament provocations of civil strife, including those of Crassus, Pompey, Caesar, and Anthony (2.213–241). At this point, the description of Concordia turns from political concord to cosmological concord.

111 Adelard of Bath, *Quaest. nat.* 4 (cited above, p. 42, n. 39).

concepts of natural order that I have surveyed in this chapter range from the analogical musicality of the inner life of the human and the sounding reality of "exterior music" (*musica exterior*) to the sometimes implicit, sometimes explicit harmonization of the entire natural world. This harmonized world, moreover, was understood not as the continual divine presence within human lived experience but as a consistent and autonomous aggregate of all created entities, humans included, ordered in accordance with a regular and predictable pattern of natural causation, which I have called enmattered vitalism. The musical analogies, metaphors, and modalities of nature proposed by twelfth-century philosophers articulate a reciprocity that bridges seemingly unbridgeable ontological divides, but also provide a vibrant ontology that embeds humanity within a musically animated natural world with which it must harmonize, with which it sings, and from which it can learn to harmonize itself. Who said the book of nature can only be read?

2

Knowing the World

Music, Mathematics, and Physics

Musica est scientia perpendendi proportiones ad cognitionem concordie et discordie rerum.

—Paris, BnF, ms lat. 8624, 23v

The previous chapter approached the twelfth-century conception of the world as an "ordered collection of all created entities" from the material vantage point of "enmattered vitalism," the creative (*naturans*) and created (*naturata*) totality of natural forces and their interrelationships immanent within material creation and coordinated according to a musical logic. This view was born of the twelfth-century encounter with the world, the brute multiplicity of things that are the purview of the *physici*. It is buttressed, however, by a textual, discursively constituted world of words, which is the central target of this chapter. Here I take as a point of departure, but not as axiomatic truth, the Foucauldian claim (which he intended *as* axiomatic) that in the Renaissance, or more broadly in the "premodern" episteme, "the great metaphor of the book that one opens, that one pores over and reads in order to know nature, is merely the reverse and visible side of another transference, and a much deeper one, which forces language to reside in the world, among the plants, the herbs, the stones, and the animals."[1]

In this chapter, I argue that the order of the world rematerializes as text(s) in and of the libraries constituted through late-ancient and early-medieval encyclopedic organizations of knowledge. From this perspective, the world is subject to variously configured disciplinary regulations and is ordered (in this instance) through the *division of philosophy*, the textualized and discursive aggregate of

[1] Michel Foucault, *The Order of Things: An Archaeology of the Human Sciences* (London and New York: Routledge Classics, 2002), 39. For a critique of Foucault's "two fundamental distortions: a myopic explanation of the texts' exegetical nature and the refusal to entertain the possibility of discursive heterogeneity," see Mary Franklin-Brown, *Reading the World: Encyclopedic Writing in the Scholastic Age* (Chicago: University of Chicago Press, 2012), 87–92, which has been helpful in formulating my own (brief) response to Foucault.

the known and the knowable. Furthermore, the universality of that textualized order, however aspirational, is nonetheless always subject to constraints, contingencies, and inconsistencies. Indeed, the divisions of philosophy analyzed herein confirm Mary Franklin-Brown's conclusion to her survey of scholastic orderings of knowledge: each is and can only be a "partial solution."[2] But such fissures and gaps, disjunctions and interstices, are the very condition of possibility for the discursive rewriting of the world. For Foucault, the world-as-book metaphor condemns the "Renaissance episteme" to the eternal return of the same: a "non-distinction between what is seen and what is read, between observation and relation, which results in the constitution of a single, unbroken surface in which observation and language intersect to infinity."[3] I argue in this chapter for a strong non-identity between what is seen and what is read, or rather, that what is read (and what is written) constitutes the continual re-creation of what is seen (or heard). The cosmographic project, the writing of the world, is cosmogonic: a world-creating act.[4]

Musica played a crucial role in this knowing, writing, and (re)creation of the world's discursive order. At issue are the placement, order, and scope of *musica* in the constitution of the knowable world through the division of philosophy, specifically the intercalation of music between physics (the study of the natural world) and mathematics (the study of number). A fully comprehensive account of late-ancient and twelfth-century *divisiones philosophiae* would be more than a single chapter could manage.[5] Instead, I sketch in broad strokes the expansive (and indeed expanding) conception of *musica* within quadrivial and natural-philosophical contexts through a limited subset of texts: first, the late-ancient divisions available in the twelfth century, and second, a select group of twelfth-century commentators (primarily Bernard of Chartres, William of Conches, and

2 Franklin-Brown, *Reading the World*, 82.

3 Foucault, *The Order of Things*, 43.

4 Linda Lomperis describes the writing of Bernard Silvestris's *Cosmographia* (mid-twelfth century) in precisely these terms: "What we witness in the *Cosmographia*, then, is nothing less than a subtle process of poetic transformation: poetry undergoes a transformation from that which functions as the medium of vehicle of God's creativity to that which operates as itself a creative agent, the usurper, if you will, of God's role" ("From God's Book to the Play of the Text in the *Cosmographia*," *Medievalia et Humanistica* 16 [1988], 57).

5 The literature is extensive. Several classic studies can still be consulted with profit: Pierre Hadot, "Die Einteilung der Philosophie im Altertum," *Zeitschrift für Philosophische Forschung* 36 (1982), 422–444; J. Mariétan, *Problème de la classification des sciences d'Aristote à St-Thomas* (St-Maurice and Paris: Felix Alcan, 1901); Ludwig Baur, *Dominicus Gundissalinus: De divisione philosophiae*, Beiträge zur Geschichte der Philosophie des Mittelalters, 4.2–3 (Münster: Aschendorff, 1903); Martin Grabmann, *Die Scholastische Methode von ihren ersten Anfängen in der Väterliteratur bis zum Beginn des 12. Jahrhunderts*, vol. 1 of *Die Geschichte der Scholastischen Methode* (Freiburg im Breisgau: Herdersche Verlagshandlung, 1909). On the twelfth century, see Franco Alessio, "La filosofia e le *artes mechanicae* nel secolo XII," *Studi medievali* 6 (1965), 71–161; Gilbert Dahan, "Les classifications du savoir aux XIIe et XIIIe siècles," *L'enseignement philosophique* 40 (1990), 5–27.

Bernard Silvestris) whose texts offer testimony to the continued viability and utility of what would later be deemed "speculative music theory" (*musica speculativa*). I also outline the basic philosophical conditions by which *musica* as a disciplinary practice both regulated its objects and was itself regulated.

Put simply: *musica* in the twelfth century was a liberal art embracing both a mathematically grounded science of musicology, so to speak, and a metaphysical science of nature. These distinct but related domains of activity have often been cast in terms of a division between *musica activa* (the practical side of musical knowledge) and *musica speculativa* (the theoretical side of musical knowledge), which has long been an organizing principle in discussions of medieval musical thought.[6] This division is largely fictitious. In musical discourse, theory and practice emerge not as neatly distinct epistemological categories but as messy, overlapping tendencies, ever in flux with changing intellectual contexts. Moreover, the terminological distinction was not articulated until the middle of the twelfth century (in the Latin adaptations and translations of al-Farabi's *Classification of the Sciences*)[7] and did not stabilize until the mid-thirteenth century. In the twelfth-century commentary tradition, *musica* is employed without qualification as the music of the medieval schoolroom. It takes its place in the quadrivium alongside arithmetic, geometry, and astronomy, and it encompasses two interrelated conceptual realms: (1) the elucidation of the definitions, first principles, and divisions that form the foundations of the science (and practice) of music, and (2) the extension of more abstract, metaphysical musical concepts (such as

[6] E.g., Gerhard Pietzsch, *Die Klassifikation der Musik von Boethius bis Ugolino von Orvieto* (Halle: M. Niemeyer, 1929); Nan Cooke Carpenter, *Music in the Medieval and Renaissance Universities* (Norman: University of Oklahoma Press, 1958); cf. Leo Schrade, "Das propädeutische Ethos in der Musikanschauung des Boethius," *Zeitschrift für Geschichte der Erziehung und des Unterrichts* 20 (1930), 179–215. Lawrence Gushee's "Questions of Genre in Medieval Treatises on Music," though employing more fluid criteria that take into account "intellectual style," "the goals and methods of certain institutions," and "the special problems inherent in a given musical style" (365–367), nevertheless appeals to an underlying speculative/practical distinction. The most comprehensive discussion of *musica speculatiua* remains Albrecht Riethmüller, "Probleme der spekulativen Musiktheorie im Mittelalter," in *Rezeption des antiken Fachs im Mittelalter*, ed. Frieder Zaminer, Geschichte der Musiktheorie 3 (Darmstadt: Wissenschaftliche Buchgesellschaft, 1990), 163–201.

[7] Primarily the *De diuisione philosophiae* of Dominicus Gundissalinus, the tenth chapter of which classifies music in terms of *theorica* and *practica*. The literal translations of Al-Farabi's treatise by Gundissalinus and Gerard of Cremona promulgated the *speculativa/practica* terminology. See Don Michael Randel, "Al-Farabi and the Role of Arabic Music Theory in the Latin Middle Ages," *Journal of the American Musicological Society* 29 (1976), 173–188; Henry George Farmer, *Al-Farabi's Arabic-Latin Writings on Music* (New York: Hinrichsen Edition, 1965); Muhsin Mahdi, "Science, Philosophy, and Religion in Alfarabi's Enumeration of the Sciences," in *The Cultural Context of Medieval Learning: Proceedings of the First International Colloquium on Philosophy, Science, and Theology in the Middle Ages—September 1973*, ed. John Emery Murdoch and Edith Dudley Sylla (Boston: D. Reidel, 1975), 113–147. On the *theorica/practica* distinction in general, see Guy Beaujouan, "Réflexions sur les rapports entre théorie et pratique au Moyen Âge," in *The Cultural Context of Medieval Learning*, 437–484.

proportio, harmonia, concentus) beyond the sensual, corporeal realm of sounding music. *Musica* offers neither pedagogical nor practical introduction for the musician (in the modern sense of the term), but a road (one of four, of course) to the study of philosophy.

Foundational Divisions: Boethius

The division of philosophy attributed to Boethius has often been synthesized and schematized as in figure 2.1.[8] Though the schematic remains correct in its outline, the details of this division are not as neatly presented in Boethius's own writing as the schematic might suggest. Its various subdivisions are scattered throughout Boethius's work, and the various sources do not always easily cohere. Since Boethius is the primary source, directly or indirectly, of most divisions of philosophy articulated in the twelfth century, it will be necessary to work through, in some detail, the divergent and scattered accounts on which this division rests.

Boethius knows two divisions of philosophy: (1) a bipartite division into theory and practice (*theoretica–practica*), allied with the Peripatetic tradition, and (2) a tripartite division into logic, ethics, and physics (*logica–ethica–physica*), associated with the Stoic and Academic traditions.[9] To the latter Boethius alludes only three times: twice as a heuristic approach to the Aristotelian corpus,[10] once in the course of presenting the Stoic case for logic as a part of philosophy.[11] When, however, Boethius has the division of philosophy proper in his sights (e.g., *In Isag.* I.8.1ff., *In Isag.* II.140.18–19; cf. *Cons. phil.* 1.p1.4), he is unambiguous. There are two species of

[8] E.g. John Magee, "Boethius," in *Cambridge History of Philosophy in Late Antiquity*, ed. Lloyd P. Gerson (Cambridge: Cambridge University Press, 2010), 797; Joseph Dyer, "The Place of *Musica* in Medieval Classifications of Knowledge," *Journal of Musicology* 24 (2007), 3–71; James A. Weisheipl, "The Nature, Scope, and Classification of the Sciences," in *Science in the Middle Ages*, ed. David C. Lindberg (Chicago: University of Chicago Press, 1978), 461–482.

[9] Both Cicero (*Acad.* 1.5.19) and Augustine (*De ciu. Dei* 8.4) attribute this tripartite division to Plato, an attribution that likely stems from Antiochus of Ascalon. Aristotle seems already to have suggested a similar division at *Top.* 1.14 (105b20ff.). On the sources for Augustine's presentation, see Frank Regen, "Zu Augustins Darstellung des Platonismus am Anfang des 8. Buches der *Ciuitas Dei*," in *Platonismus und Christentum. Festschrift für Heinrich Dörrie*, ed. Horst-Dieter Blume and Friedhelm Mann (Münster: Verlag Aschendorff, 1983), 217–218.

[10] *In Cat.* 161b: Haec quoque nobis de decem praedicamentis inspectio, et in physica Aristotelis doctrina, et in moralis philosophiae cognitione perutilis est. *In Perih.* II.79.18–20: ut si quid ex logicae artis subtilitate, ex moralis gravitate peritiae, ex naturalis acumine veritatis ab Aristotele conscriptum sit. The inconsistent ordering ([logic]–physics–ethics, logic–ethics–physics) may be symptomatic of Boethius's less than systematic employ of this division; hence, "heuristic."

[11] *In Isag.* II.140.18–141.19: iam uero inquiunt: cum in his tribus philosophia uersetur cumque actiuam et speculatiuam considerationem subiecta discernant, quod illa de rerum naturis, haec de moribus quaerit, non dubium est quin logica disciplina a naturali atque morali suae materiae proprietate distincta sit (at II.141.7–12). Cf. Augustine, *De ciu. Dei* 8.4 (cited above).

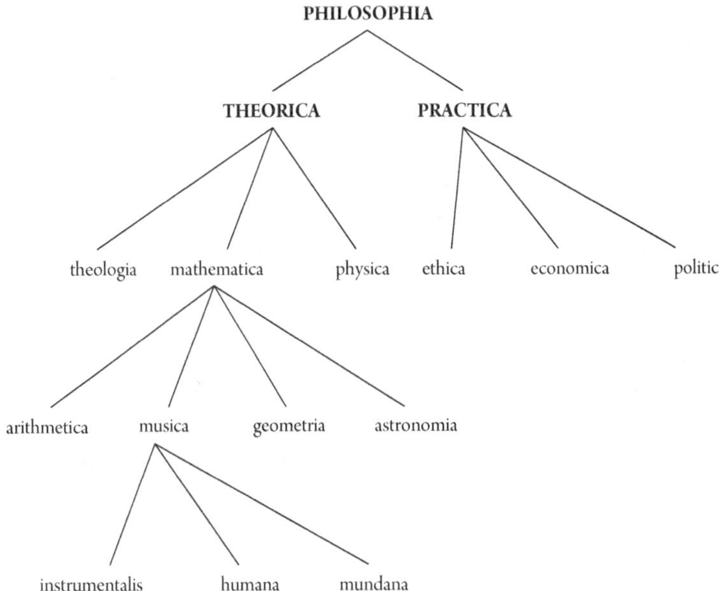

Figure 2.1 Division of philosophy according to Boethius (synthesizing *In Isag* I.8–9, *De trin.* 2, *Inst. ar.* 1.1, and *Inst. mus.* 1.2).

philosophy: theoretical and practical.[12] Although the Stoic tripartition is not without utility, it is not Boethius's preferred position, for his primary allegiance, alongside that of Ammonius (e.g., Ammon. *In Isag.* 11.6ff.),[13] lies with the Peripatetic bipartition. But in the prolegomena to his first *Isagoge* commentary, Boethius's first and only full explication of the theoretical–practical divide is idiosyncratic in many of its details. Where Ammonius's initial accounting of practical philosophy (ethics, economics, politics) is concise and direct, Boethius's is periphrastic and oddly ordered (ethics–politics–economics, nowhere named as such and without

[12] *In Isag.* I.8.1–2: est enim philosophia genus, species uero duae, una quae theoretica dicitur, altera quae practica, id est speculatiua et actiua.

[13] I cannot, however, agree with James A. Weisheipl, "Classification of the Sciences in Medieval Thought," *Mediaeval Studies* 27 (1965), 59 (doubtless under the sway of Courcelle, *Late Latin Writers*) that Boethius was "following Ammonius' commentary on the same work [sc. Porphyry's *Isagoge*]." What evidence there is points away from Ammonius. The theoretical–practical division alone is too general to prove reliance, and the numerous points of divergence between Ammonius's and Boethius's subdivisions cloud attempts to read Boethius's as a crib of Ammonius. John Magee, *Anicii Manlii Severini Boethii De divisione liber*, Philosophia Antiqua 77 (Leiden: Brill, 1998), xxxvii, fn. 8 cautiously notes that, "given the quadripartition of mathematical sciences at *Inst. ar.* I 1.4 (cf. *In Isag.* I.9.21f.), the system resembles Ammonius, *In Isag.* 11.6ff." Since *Inst. ar.* 1.1.4 follows Nicomachus, *Intr. ar.* 1.3 (6.1–7), which Ammonius undoubtedly knew as well, the mathematical division thus can shed little to no light on Boethius's knowledge of Ammonius. Resemblance is the most we can claim, and that is not claiming very much.

further comment).[14] Likewise Ammonius's primary subdivision of theoretical philosophy into theology, mathematics, and physics is equally concise and closely parallels *Met.* 1026a13–16.[15] But Boethius, after observing that the three branches of theoretical philosophy answer to three levels of being,[16] slides from epistemology to ontology.[17] The objects of theoretical philosophy thus comprise, in order of ontological priority: (1) intellectibles (*intellectibilia = theologia*),[18] (2) intelligibles (*intellegibilia* = ?),[19] (3) natural entities (*naturalia = physiologia*).[20] The difficulty here lies in the specification of the second rung. If the parallel with Ammonius were to hold, it should be mathematics or Neoplatonic "mathematicals," and if Boethius were to have countenanced the separate subsistence of mathematicals, we would expect to find them here. But he makes no such identification. Intelligibles hover between lower and higher realities: through corporeal contagion (*corporum tactu*: cf. *Cons. phil.* 3.p12.1) and association with natural bodies, they degenerate from the intellectibles to become a lower reality; through their own contemplation of intellectibles, they become "more blessed" (*beatiora: In Isag.* I.9.2–6). And

14 Ammon. *In Isag.* 15.2f.: διαιρεῖται τοίνυν τὸ πρακτικὸν εἴς τε τὸ ἠθικὸν καὶ οἰκονομικὸν καὶ πολιτικόν. Boet. *In Isag.* I.9.13–21: est enim prima [= ethics] quae sui curam gerens cunctis sese erigit, exornat augetque uirtutibus, nihil in uita admittens quo non gaudeat, nihil faciens paenitendum. secunda [= politics] uero est quae rei publicae curam suscipiens cunctorum saluti suae prouidentiae sollertia et institutiae libra et fortitudinis stabilitate et temperantiae patientia medetur; (3) tertia [= economics] uero, quae familiaris rei officium mediocri componens dispositione distribuit. Ammonius's subdivision of each into legislative and judicial (Ammon. *In Isag.* 15.11–16.4) is passed over by Boethius at *In Isag.* I.9.21f.: sunt harum etiam aliae subdiuisiones, quas nunc persequi supersedendum est. This is the only division of practical philosophy in Boethius's entire corpus.

15 Ammon. *In Isag.* 11.22f.: πάλιν τὸ θεωρητικὸν διαιρεῖται εἰς θεολογικὸν μαθηματικὸν καὶ φυσιολογικόν.

16 Boet. *In Isag.* I.8.3–5: erunt autem et tot speculatiuae philosophiae species quot sunt res in quibus iustae speculatio considerationis habetur—a direct echo of *Met.* 1004a2.

17 Cf. Magee, "Boethius," 806: "[Boethius] in effect converts a traditional Peripatetic classification into an ontological hierarchy that reflects a late Platonism of some kind. . . . His analysis targets a hierarchy of things and the mind's (soul's) descent into the world of matter rather than the sciences as such."

18 *In Isag.* I.8.13–19: est enim intellectibile quod unum atque idem per se in propria semper diuinitate consistens nullis umquam sensibus, sed sola tantum mente intellectuque capitur. quae res ad speculationem dei atque ad animi incorporalitatem considerationemque uerae philosophiae indagatione componitur: quam partem Graeci θεολογίαν nominant.

19 *In Isag.* I.8.19–9.6: secunda uero est pars intellegibilis, quae primam intellectibiliem cogitatione atque intellegentia comprehendit. que est omnium caelestium supernae diuinitatis operum et quicquid sub lunari globo beatiore animo atque puriore substantia ualet et postremo humanarum animarum. quae omnia cum prioris illius intellectibilis substantiae fuissent, corporum tactu ab intellectibilibus ad intellegibilia degenerarunt, ut non magis ipsa intellegantur quam intellegant et intellegentiae puritate tunc beatiora sint, quotiens sese intellectibilibus applicarint.

20 *In Isag.* I.9.6–8: tertia theoretices species est que circa corpora atque eorum scientiam cognitionemque uersatur: quae est physiologia, quae naturas corporum passionesque declarat. Pace Dyer, "The Place of *Musica* in Medieval Classifications of Knowledge," 10–11, these subdivisions do not, as he claims, "correspond to three degrees of abstraction, an Aristotelian principle encountered also in *De trinitate*."

Boethius concludes by noting that the substance of the intelligibles rightly holds the medial position, since it has the dual role of animating bodies and contemplating the intellectibles.[21] It seems unavoidable that the second rung is more psychology than mathematics, even if it is, in the final analysis, neither.

In *De trin*. 2, where Boethius presents a second division of theoretical philosophy, Neoplatonic ontology gives way to a more sober Aristotelian epistemology (cf. *Met*. 1026a13–16) that evinces no direct correlation between objects of knowledge and levels of being. The object of physics is in motion (i.e., mutable) and unabstracted (i.e., dependent);[22] that of mathematics, motionless and unabstracted;[23] that of theology, motionless, abstract, and separable.[24] Where the first *Isagoge* commentary presented a Platonic ontic descent, *De trin*. 2 offers an Aristotelian epistemic ascent. Where the first division left the middle rung unspecified and verging on psychology, the second clearly identifies it with mathematics. And finally, where the *Isagoge* commentary stated that the middle rung (the intelligibles) degenerated from the highest ontic category (the intellectibles) through contact with bodies, thereby implying the underlying bipartition (1) *intellectibilis/intelligibilis* (2) *naturalis, De trin*. 2 links the middle rung (mathematics) with the lowest epistemic category (physics), thus suggesting the underlying bipartition (1) *theologica* (2) *mathematica/naturalis*. The tension between the two divisions appears irreducible.[25]

This second division, however, even if it is more Aristotelian in its outline, better accords with Boethius's outlook elsewhere. For instance, when Boethius notes that the different sciences offer differing accounts of one and the same reality,[26] one of his two examples suggests, in accord with Aristotle (*Phys*. 193b21–34; *Met*. 1061a28–b3), that the physicist and mathematician study the same objects but in different ways.[27] It seems, then, that in his logical and theological writings Boethius espouses an abstractionist approach to mathematics: mathematical

[21] *In Isag*. I.9.10–12.

[22] *De trin*. 2: naturalis, in motu inabstracta, ἀνυπεξαίρετος (considerat enim corporum formas cum materia, quae a corporibus actu separari non possunt, quae corpora in motu sunt, ut cum terra deorsum ignis sursum fertur, habetque motum forma materiae coniuncta); cf. ἡ μὲν γὰρ φυσικὴ περὶ χωριστὰ μὲν ἀλλ' οὐκ ἀκίνητα, *Met*. 1026a13–14.

[23] *De trin*. 2: mathematica, sine motu inabstracta (haec enim formas corporum speculatur sine materia ac per hoc sine motu, quae formae cum in materia sint, ab his separari non possunt); cf. τῆς δὲ μαθηματικῆς ἔνια περὶ ἀκίνητα μὲν οὐ χωριστὰ δὲ ἴσως ἀλλ' ὡς ἐν ὕλῃ, *Met*. 1026a15.

[24] *De trin*. 2: theologica, sine motu abstracta atque separabilis (nam Dei substantia et materia et motu caret); cf. ἡ δὲ πρώτη καὶ περὶ χωριστὰ καὶ ἀκίνητα, *Met*. 1026a16.

[25] Cf. Magee, "Boethius," 806.

[26] *Intr. syll. cat*. 762c: non enim una atque eadem diuersarum ratio disciplinarum, cum sit diuersissimis disciplinis una atque eadem substantia materies.

[27] Ibid.: nec eodem modo lineam uel superficiem mathematicus ac physicus tractant. Cf. *Inst. mus*. 1.1 (179.12–14): Rursus cum quis triangulum respicit vel quadratum, facile id quod oculis intuetur agnoscit, sed quaenam quadrati vel trianguli sit natura, a mathematico necesse est petat.

objects are considered as separate from matter and motion, but they are not separate subsistents over and above sensible bodies.[28] Does Boethius hold this same position in his mathematical works?

The "first fruits" of Boethius's intellectual labors (*laboris mei primitiae*), the *De institutione arithmetica*, is a loose translation of Nicomachus of Gerasa's *Introductio arithmetica*, which Boethius seems to have undertaken early in his career, likely during the same period as the first *Isagoge* commentary.[29] Following Nicomachus, and obliquely echoing his first *Isagoge* commentary, Boethius begins his *De institutione arithmetica* with an account of philosophical knowledge from the standpoint of ontology. He declares that the objects of philosophy (*sapientia*) are "what exist and have been allotted their own immutable substance," which are not subject to quantitative, qualitative, or substantial change. These then are: "qualities, quantities, forms, greatnesses (*magnitudines*), smallnesses (*paruitates*), equalities (*aequalitates*), habitudes, acts, dispositions, places, times, as well as anything that is found in some way united to bodies."[30] While they themselves are incorporeal and immutable, through their participation in bodies and the contagion of changeable things they necessarily share in bodily, material flux. Boethius's abridgment of this passage in the *De institutione musica* makes explicit what is only implied in his first handling of this Nicomachean material: that this is a fundamentally Pythagorean ontology, which serves as a prelude to a Pythagorean division of mathematics.[31] The similarity of this language to the description of the second ontic category in the first *Isagoge* commentary is striking: both are intermediaries "degraded" by *tactu corporum* (*In Isag.*) or *tactu uariabilis rei* (*Inst. ar.*); though themselves incorporeal, they are incorporated; and qua intermediary, they are a conduit from the lower to the higher, for as Boethius concludes later in the prooemium, the mathematic disciplines are (famously) a quadrivium,

[28] Cf. *In Isag.* II.160.23: duae quippe incorporeorum formae sunt, ut alia praeter corpora esse possint et separata a corporibus in sua incorporalitate perdurent, ut deus, mens, anima, alia uero cum sint incorporea, tamen praeter corpora esse non possint, ut linea uel superficies uel numerus uel singulae qualitates quas tametsi incorporeas esse pronuntiamus, quod tribus spatiis minime distendantur, tamen ita in corporibus sunt, ut ab his diuelli nequeant aut separari aut, si a corporibus separata sint, nullo modo permaneant.

[29] See Magee, "Boethius," 790–796 for a concise summary of scholarship on the dating of Boethius's works.

[30] *Inst. ar.* 1.1 (7.26–8.11). Cf. *Intr. ar.* 1.1.3 (2.21–3.3): ποιότητες, ποσότητες, σχηματισμοί, μεγέθη, μικρότητες, ἰσότητες, σχέσεις, ἐνέργειαι, διαθέσεις, τόποι, χρόνοι, πάντα ἁπλῶς, οἷς περιέχεται τὰ ἐν ἑκάστῳ σώματι. See Dominic J. O'Meara, *Pythagoras Revived: Mathematics and Philosophy in Late Antiquity* (Oxford: Clarendon Press, 1989), 16–18.

[31] *Inst. mus.* 2.2 (227.20–228.2): primus omnium Pythagoras sapientiae studium philosophiam nuncupauit, quam scilicet eius rei notitiam ac disciplinam ponebat, quae proprie uereque esse diceretur. Esse autem illa putabat, quae nec intentione crescerent, nec deminutione decrescerent nec ullis accidentibus mutarentur. Haec autem esse formas magnitudines qualitates habitudines ceteraque quae per se speculata inmutabilia sunt, iuncta uero corporibus permutantur et multimodis variationibus mutabilis rei cognatione vertuntur. Cf. Proclus, *In Euc.* 35.16ff.

a "fourfold road that must be traversed by those whom a more excellent soul leads away from the senses inborn within us to the greater certainties of understanding (*quadruuium, quo his uiandum sit, quibus excellentior animus a nobiscum procreatis sensibus ad intellegentiae certiora perducitur*).[32] Hence, in its ontic focus in general, and its Platonic ontology in particular, *Inst. ar.* 1.1 seems closer to the first *Isagoge* commentary than it does to *De trin.* 2.

Boethius then divides the objects of mathematics into discrete quantity (*multitudo*, τὸ ποσόν) and continuous quantity (*magnitudo*, τὸ πηλίκον).[33] Each of these has a second bipartition: multitude into those known "by themselves" (*per se*, καθ' ἑαυτό) = arithmetic, and those known "in relation to another" (*ad aliquid*, πρὸς ἄλλο) = music; magnitude into the "immobile" (*immobilis*, ἐν μονῇ καὶ στάσει) = geometry, and the "mobile" (*mobilis*, ἐν κινήσει καὶ περιφορᾷ) = astronomy.[34] Hence, arithmetic is the science of multitudes by themselves, whereas music is the science of multitudes in relation to each other; geometry is the science of immobile magnitudes, but astronomy the science of magnitudes in motion. The order is not arbitrary, as the four mathematical sciences are not, strictly speaking, coordinate. Rather, they demonstrate a clear order of priority, and this priority takes the tidy form of two parallel priorities—the absolute (arithmetic) is prior to the relative (music) just as stasis (geometry) is prior to motion (astronomy)—nested within the single overarching priority of arithmetic to the other mathematical sciences.[35]

In the prooemium to the *De institutione musica*, the second of his mathematical works and likewise an interpolated translation of a (no longer extant) musical treatise by Nicomachus, Boethius sets out a further tripartite division of music, which has already been introduced in the prelude to this book (p. 11): *musica mundana, humana,* and *instrumentalis*.[36] It remains uncertain whether Boethius found this division already articulated in Nicomachus or whether it is of his own devising. What little evidence there is suggests the latter, for despite the wide influence

[32] *Inst. ar.* 1.1 (9.28–10.2).

[33] τὸ ποσόν is a finite multitude, as opposed to the infinite πλῆθος; likewise, τὸ πηλίκον is a finite magnitude, as opposed to the infinite μέγεθος: *Intr. ar.* 1.2.5 (4.20–5.12); cf. Iamblichus, *De comm. math. sc.* 7 (29.22–30.7). Boethius does not (and perhaps could not) make the terminological distinction; *multitudo* and *magnitudo* are the only terms he employs. He compensates, however, by displacing until after the full mathematical division the discussion of finite versus infinite quantity, excused as a brief addendum (9.13–26: Illud quoque addendum arbitror, etc.).

[34] *Inst. ar.* 1.1 (9.1–5) = *Intr. ar.* 1.3.1–2 (6.1–7).

[35] *Inst. ar.* 1.1 (10.8–12.12) = *Intr. ar.* 1.4–5 (9.5–11.23); cf. Dominic J. O'Meara, "The Music of Philosophy in Late Antiquity," in *Philosophy and the Sciences in Antiquity*, ed. R. W. Sharples, Keeling Series in Ancient Philosophy (Aldershot: Ashgate, 2005), 134–135.

[36] *Inst. mus.* 1.2 (187.18–23): Principio igitur de musica disserenti illud interim dicendum uidetur, quot musicae genera ab eius studiosis conprehensa esse nouerimus. Sunt autem tria. Et prima quidem mundana est, secunda uero humana, tertia, quae in quibusdam constituta est instrumentis, ut in cithara uel tibiis ceterisque, quae cantilenae famulantur.

of Nicomachus's mathematical works on the commentaries and treatises of the (Greek) Neoplatonists (especially Iamblichus and Proclus), there exists no direct Greek parallel to Boethius's division.[37] Moreover, already at *Inst. ar.* 1.2, Boethius had listed three numerically based realities in support of the assertion that number was the primary exemplar (*principale exemplar*) in the mind of the world's creator: the balanced cycles of the elements, seasons, and heavenly motions.[38] While this list strongly anticipates the parts of cosmic music enumerated at *Inst. mus.* 1.2, significantly it has no literal analogue in Nicomachus, for the parallel passage (*Intr. ar.* 1.6.1 [12.11–12]) offers the longer and more generic list "time, motion, the heavens, the stars, and all sorts or revolutions" (χρόνος, κίνησις, οὐρανός, ἄστρα, ἐξελιγμοὶ παντοῖοι).

Such are the divisions and subdivisions scattered throughout Boethius's work, and they are not without problems and contradictions in their synthesis, some of which have already been noted. On one hand, the mathematical divisions cannot easily be subsumed into the theoretical division of the first *Isagoge* commentary, since mathematics has no explicit role in the division. On the other hand, while the mathematical discussions may seem, prima facie, to accord with the division of *De trin.* 2 (whose second category is mathematics), there are several attendant contradictions. First, if the theoretical mathematics of *De trin.* considers its objects *sine motu*, how can astronomy as defined in the *Inst. ar.* (*mobilis magnitudo*) be a mathematical, as opposed to physical, science?[39] Second, and more significantly, the prefaces to the mathematical works project a "seamless continuum between the mathematical sciences and philosophy in all of its other manifestations."[40] In fact, Nicomachus presents the division of mathematics as a division of philosophy, insofar as Pythagoras (in Nicomachus's account) first properly defined *sophia* (wisdom) as the science of "true being," i.e., "those things which always continue uniformly and the same in the universe and never depart even briefly from their existence" (ὄντα δὲ τὰ κατὰ τὰ αὐτὰ καὶ ὡσαύτως ἀεὶ διατελοῦντα ἐν τῷ κόσμῳ καὶ οὐδέποτε τοῦ εἶναι ἐξιστάμενα οὐδὲ ἐπὶ βραχύ: *Intr. ar.* 2.10–13), and in support of this claim he musters the testimony of *Timaeus* 27d6–28a4: "What is that which always is, and has no birth, and what is that which is always becoming but never is? The one is apprehended by the mental processes, with reasoning, and is ever the same; the other can be guessed at by opinion in company with unreasoning

[37] Cf. Calvin Bower, "Boethius and Nicomachus: An Essay Concerning the Sources of *De institutione musica*," *Vivarium* 16 (1978), 44–45.

[38] *Inst. ar.* 1.2 (12.17–19): hinc enim quattuor elementorum multitudo mutuata est, hinc temporum uices, hinc motus astrorum caelique conuersio.

[39] One solution would be that astronomy is merely an exception, especially since its motions are eternal and unchanging and thus of a different order than the motion (= change) considered by physics; cf. Ammon. *In Isag.* 14.8–10, who draws the distinction between γνῶσις ποσοῦ συνεχοῦς ἀκινήτου (geometry) and γνῶσις ποσοῦ συνεχοῦς ἀεικινήτου (astronomy).

[40] Magee, "Boethius," 798.

sense, a thing which becomes and passes away, but never really is."[41] Boethius, in distilling Nicomachus's first few chapters into his own prooemium, tones down the broader claims and suppresses the Timaean citation, but mathematics clearly still holds a paradigmatic role, and Boethius maintains the strongly Pythagorean commitment to the numerical basis of reality. This latter view rubs uncomfortably against the abstractionist mathematics of the later logical and theological works. Thus the sources do not easily cohere on the division of philosophy: the first *Isagoge* commentary casts a Peripatetic division in distinctly Platonic terms but conspicuously avoids any engagement with the mathematical or numerical realities that might underpin such a worldview; *De trin.* 2, by contrast, maintains a strict Aristotelian division in which mathematical objects are fundamentally *inabstracta*, even if they are considered "without [their] material and, consequently, as unchanging" (*sine materia ac per hoc sine motu*). Hence, from an ontological standpoint, the mathematical works concord with the first *Isagoge* commentary, where mathematics is missing, but they are not easily subsumed within the Aristotelian epistemology of *De trin.* 2, where mathematics is explicitly included.

Whether or not Boethius intended for the scattered pieces to be assembled into a coherent, multilevel division, his readers took up the project for themselves. In the twelfth century, scholars used various strategies to bring the pieces into harmony, from selective citation and strategic omission to subtle terminological shifts and bold emendations. Boethius's division, however, was not the only division of philosophy in circulation; the philosophical commentaries by Calcidius and Macrobius, as well as the encyclopedic compendia of Martianus, Cassiodorus, and Isidore were brought to bear on the problem as well.

The Division of Philosophy as Exegetical Strategy: Calcidius and Macrobius

Calcidius (fourth century) bears the considerable honor and the heavy burden of being the first and only Latin commentator on the *Timaeus* from the ancient world. And much effort has been spent trying to determine precisely what he had read and on whom he relied. The influence or absence of Porphyry has been central to the debate. J. H. Waszink, in the magisterial *apparatus fontium* to his critical edition, is at pains to adduce a great number of *comparanda* in Porphyry's oeuvre; Angelo Sodano's collection of the surviving fragments of Porphyry's lost *Commentary on the Timaeus* followed suit.[42] But there is little reason to assume Calcidius's use of Porphyry's commentary, regardless of whether he may have

[41] This citation was clearly standard within the tradition; cf. Numerius fr. 7; O'Meara, *Pythagoras Revived*, 10–16.

[42] Angelo Raffaele Sodano, ed., *Porphyrii In Platonis Timaeum commentariorum fragmenta* (Naples: s. n., 1964). Andrew Smith's *Porphyrii philosophi Fragmenta* (Stuttgart: Teubner, 1993) does not consider

known it.[43] First, at the very level of the *diuisio textus*, Calcidius parts ways with Proclus, who ostensibly followed Porphyry's division. And when we direct our attention to 35bff., the division of the world soul, whether or not Calcidius knew of Porphyry's commentary, he certainly does not follow his lead, but turns instead to the (now lost) Timaean commentary by Adrastus of Aphrodisias, a second-century Peripatetic philosopher, as can be deduced by triangulating parallel citations in Theon of Smyrna and Macrobius. It is from Adrastus, for instance, that Calcidius adopts his diagrammatic representations of the division of the world soul, the so-called "lambda diagram," of which Calcidius uses three successive versions (each with different numbers representing different stages in the division); this diagrammatic tradition extends, according to Plutarch, back to Krantor.[44] This alone separates Calcidius sharply from Porphyry, who in his commentary followed the tradition of a linear diagram, along with Theodorus, Severus, Macrobius, and Proclus. Even the Greek text that Calcidius translated, insofar as we can see through his often oblique translation, suggests a close alliance to a Middle Platonic text, a recension which is no longer witnessed by the direct manuscript tradition,[45] but which is occasionally hinted at by Middle Platonic handbooks (such as Alcinous's *Didascalicon*).[46]

the Commentary on the Timaeus. See also the brief remarks by Gretchen Reydams-Schils, "Calcidius," in *The Cambridge History of Philosophy in Late Antiquity*, ed. Lloyd P. Gerson (Cambridge: Cambridge University Press, 2010), 507–508, where she notes that even at moments where Porphyry's influence seems strongest, the threads of influence remain complex and inconclusive.

43 On this point, see John Dillon, *The Middle Platonists: 80 B.C. to A.D. 220*, rev. ed. (Ithaca: Cornell University, 1996), 403 "But to the unprejudiced eye there is nothing in Calcidius that requires us to postulate his acquaintance with any distinctively Neoplatonic doctrine, and much to suggest that he knew nothing of Porphyry's *Commentary*."

44 On Calcidius's diagrams, see Michel Huglo, "Recherches sur la tradition des diagrammes de Calcidius," *Scriptorium* 62 (2008), 185–230.

45 Or at least not in Burnet's *apparatus criticus* to the OCT edition of the *Timaeus*.

46 For example, at 38d2 Alcinous knows Venus not by the Timaean term ἑωσφόρος ("dawn-bringer") but rather as φώσφορος ("light-bringer"). This variant is not attested in the extant manuscripts of the *Timaeus*, but it does appear as *Lucifer* in Calcidius (31.1) and in Cicero's Latin *Timaeus* as well (9.29 [204.5]); see John Dillon, trans. *Alcinous: The Handbook of Platonism* (Oxford: Clarendon Press, 1993), 131. Likewise, Alcinous, when quoting 40c1–2, a passage that describes the earth as φύλακα καὶ δημιουργὸν νυκτός τε καὶ ἡμέρας ("guardian and creator of night and day"), omits καὶ δημιουργὸν, an omission shared by Calcidius (*diei noctisque custodem*: 33.21) but not by Cicero (*diei noctisque effectricem eandemque custodem*: 10.27 [210.13–14]), which John Dillon suggests is an "ideological emendation" explained by an "unease in Middle Platonic circles" to allow the "august term δημιουργός to characterize anything other than Cosmic Intellect," the second of the three divine entities of Middle Platonism (ibid., 135). Finally, there is the famous question of a second ἀεί (*semper*, always) at 27d6–28a1: "What is it that always exists (τί τὸ ὂν ἀεὶ), having no generation, and what is it that is always coming to be (τί τὸ γιγνόμενον μὲν ἀεί), never having existence." Calcidius omits the second ἀεί (20.15–16: quid item quod gignitur), which is a common (and perhaps the original) reading, found in Cicero as well (2.3 [178.3–4]: et quod gignatur); nonetheless, it is worth noting that it is also the reading overwhelmingly preferred among the early exegetes, including Nicomachus, Numenius, Alexander of Aphrodisias, and Sextus

Calcidius knows both the Stoic and Peripatetic divisions, alluding to the former in his discussion of fate (*In Tim.* 148 [185.4–5]: *quippe de hoc* [sc. *fato*] *plurimae disceptationes habentur morales naturales logicae*) and presenting the latter, rendered as *consideratio* (= *theoretica*) and *actus* (= *practica*), in his discussion of vision (*In Tim.* 264 [269.23–27.14]). But here too the status of mathematics and number within the Peripatetic division is only articulated circuitously:[47]

> Duplex namque totius philosophiae spectatur officium, consideratio et item actus, consideratio quidem ob assiduam contemplationem rerum diuinarum et immortalium nominata, actus uero, qui iuxta rationabilis animae deliberationem progreditur in tuendis conseruandisque rebus mortalibus. Utrique autem officiorum generi uisus est necessarius, ac primum considerationi. Diuiditur porro haec trifariam, in theologiam et item naturae sciscitationem praestandaeque etiam rationis scientiam. Neque enim quisquam deum quaereret aut ad pietatem aspiraret, quod est theologiae proprium, nec uero id ipsum quod nunc agimus agendum putaret nisi prius caelo sideribusque uisis et amore nutrito sciendi rerum causas, eorum etiam, quae ortum habent temporarium, exordia; haec quippe demum ad naturalem pertinent quaestionem. Quid quod dierum et noctium uice considerata menses et anni et horarum curricula dinumerata sunt numerique ortus et genitura dimensionis intro data? Quod ad tertiam partem philosophiae pertinere perspicuum est.
>
> The whole of philosophy has a twofold occupation: consideration and action. Consideration is so named because of the continuous contemplation of divine and immortal matters; action, on the other hand, is so named because, in accord with the deliberation of the rational soul, it proceeds in overseeing and observing human affairs. Sight, though necessary for both, has particular import for consideration, which is divided three ways: into (1) theology, (2) the inquiry into nature, and (3) the science of offering an account (*praestandae rationis scientiam*). No one would ever seek God or aspire to piety (a matter proper to theology), nor would he even think to do what we are now doing, unless he should first begin by observing the heavens and stars and by nourishing a love for investigating the causes of things, even those things which have a temporal origin (for precisely these matters pertain to natural questions). And what about the fact that months, years, and the progression of hours are reckoned by considering the alternation

Empiricus, on which see John Dillon, "Tampering with the Timaeus: Ideological Emendations in Plato, with Special Reference to the Timaeus," *American Journal of Philology* 110 (1989), 60.

[47] *In Tim.* 264 (269.23–270.14).

of day and night, and that this has given rise to number and measure? This clearly pertains to the third part of philosophy.

Because Calcidius here has his eye squarely on the "praise of vision" (*laus uidendi*)[48] and is primarily concerned with the priority of vision as a conduit to philosophy in all of its manifestations, the descriptions of the three subdivisions of theoretical philosophy closely adhere to the logic of *Tim.* 46e6ff., and the clarity of the passage qua a coherent division of philosophy suffers as a consequence.[49] Thus the description of mathematics, nowhere named as such but only the periphrastic *scientia rationis praebendae*,[50] deliberately recalls Plato's assertion of mathematics' natural origin (*Tim.* 47a4–6): ἡμέρα τε καὶ νὺξ ὀφθεῖσαι μῆνές τε καὶ ἐνιαυτῶν περίοδοι καὶ ἰσημερίαι καὶ τροπαὶ μεμηχάνηνται μὲν ἀριθμόν ("the sight of day and night, months and cycling years, equinoxes and solstices has created number").[51] Because of its oblique presentation, Calcidius's third subdivision, the *scientia rationis praebendae*, engendered more than a little confusion about its proper domain and objects.

Note, too, the peculiar ordering—theology, physics, mathematics—as against the usual Aristotelian order of theology, mathematics, physics.[52] This is not a local aberration but a programmatic feature of Calcidius's approach to Platonism; Calcidius's division of philosophy, oblique though it may be, neatly maps his systematization of the Platonic corpus as a whole, the *Timaeus* included. As Gretchen Reydams-Schils has convincingly argued, "Calcidius uses the *Timaeus* as a vehicle

48 As the contents list deems this chapter: *In Tim.* 7 (60.5–618).

49 So much so that it is difficult to pinpoint Calcidius's source here; Waszink cautiously notes Albinus's *Epitome*, 3 (aka Alcinous's *Didaskalikos*). Indeed something like Alcinous's διττοῦ δ' ὄντος τοῦ Βίου, τοῦ μὲν θεωρητικοῦ, τοῦ δὲ πρακτικοῦ (*Didask.* 2 [152.30–31]) may underlie Calcidius's *consideratio–actus* distinction; e.g., compare *Didask.* 2 (153.3–5), ἔστι τοίνυν ἡ θεωρία ἐνέργεια τοῦ νοῦ νοοῦντος τὰ νοητά, ἡ δὲ πρᾶξις ψυχῆς λογικῆς ἐνέργεια διὰ σώματος γινομένη, against Calcidius's parallel claim (*In Tim.* 264 [270.2–4]): consideratio quidem ob assiduam contemplationem rerum diuinarum et immortalium nominata, actus uero, qui iuxta rationabilis animae deliberationem progreditur in tuendis conseruandisque rebus mortalibus. Gretchen Reydams-Schils follows Waszink in tracing Calcidius's division back to Alcinous; see "Meta-Discourse: Plato's *Timaeus* According to Calcidius," *Phronesis* 52 (2007), 315.

50 Cf. the similar terminology for the mathematical sciences found elsewhere in the commentary: *artificiosa ratio* (*In Tim.* 1 [57.3]; 119 [164.6–7]; 185 [211.19–20]) and *artificialia remedia* (*In Tim.* 2 [58.6]), as rightly noted in Reydams-Schils, "Calcidius," 499. Claudio Moreschini translates this third branch of consideratio as "dialettica" ("Questa si divide poi in tre parti, teologia, fisica e dialettica") and notes Arist. *Met.* 1025b3ff. as a parallel (Claudio Moreschini, trans., *Calcidio: Commentario al "Timeo" di Platone; Testo latino a fronte*, Bompiani Il Pensiero Occidentale [Milan: Bompiani, 2003], 547).

51 Calcidius's translation of this passage (which he knew without καὶ ἰσημερία καὶ τροπαὶ) confirms the intended reference: At nunc diei noctisque insinuata nobis alterna uice menses annorumque obitus et anfractus nati sunt eorumque ipsorum dinumeratio et ex dinumeratione perfectus et absolutus extitit numerus (44.7–9).

52 Cf. the similar order theology–physics–mathematics in Alcinous (*Didask.* 3 [153.45–154.5]) as against the Aristotelian order; see Dillon, *Alcinous: The Handbook of Platonism*, 53–60.

for a comprehensive and step by step overview of what he calls theoretical philosophy."[53] The structure of theoretical philosophy, she points out, is implicit in the broader architecture of Calcidius's commentary, which begins with mathematics (arithmetic and geometry [chapters 8–39], music [40–55], astronomy [61–118]), proceeds through physics (119–267), and culminates in theology (268–355). Moreover, it recapitulates within a single dialogue the metastructure of the Platonic corpus, which, at least since the first century C.E., had been likened to the initiation into a sacred mystery. According to Theon of Smyrna's *Mathematics Useful for Reading Plato* (later echoed by Albinus and Alcinous), the philosophical rite of initiation proceeds in five stages: (1) purification (καθαρμός), (2) the transmission (παράδοσις) of doctrine, (3) the visionary revelation (ἐποπτεία), (4) teaching new initiates, and finally (5) assimilation to god (ὁμοίωσις θεῷ).[54] Theon's primary concern is with the initial purificatory stage, which, on the authority of Plato (presumably the seventh book of the *Republic*, 527d), he equates with mathematics, the subject of his own book: "For Plato, this purification is derived from the five mathematical disciplines: arithmetic, geometry, stereometry, music, and astronomy." The *epopteia*, on the other hand, is the "study of intelligibiles and of Real Being, that is to say, the Platonic ideas."[55] For Calcidius, as for Moderatus and other Neopythagoreans before him, this meant the *Parmenides*,[56] a dialogue he explicitly describes as offering an "epoptic discussion" (*epoptica disputatio*) "in that it flows from the fountainhead of the purest knowledge of reality," higher than that of the *Timaeus*, which he identifies with a "physical discussion" (*naturalis disputatio*), "a somewhat wavering image that is limited to the level of stability associated with verisimilitude."[57]

Macrobius, writing perhaps a century after Calcidius,[58] brings his *Commentarii in Somnium Scipionis* to the rousing conclusion that there is "nothing more complete than this work" (*nihil hoc opere perfectius*), meaning of course Cicero's *Dream of Scipio* (2.17.17). The truth of this claim rests upon Macrobius's affirmation that his exegetical target encapsulates the whole of philosophy (*quo universa philosophiae continentur*), a move that equally secures the pedagogical and curricular value of Macrobius's commentary, which *eo ipso* also traverses the whole of philosophy. That totality, however, is not theoretical philosophy in its "Aristotelian" tripartition, as in Calcidius, but the Stoic tripartition into ethics, physics, and logic (2.17.15). This division, in its basic formulation, allows no obvious way of

53 Reydams-Schils, "Meta-Discourse," 314–319 (quotation at 319).

54 *Exp.* 14.17–16.2; cf. Alcinous, *Didask.* 28 (182.2–14).

55 *Exp.* 15.11–18.

56 See Harold Tarrant, *Thrasyllan Platonism* (Ithaca: Cornell University Press, 1993), 150–161.

57 *In Tim.* 272 (277.5–8): Haec [sc. the *Timaeus*] quippe naturalis, illa [sc. the *Parminides*] epoptica disputatio est, naturalis quidem, ut imago nutans aliquatenus et in uerisimili quadam stabilitate contenta, epoptica uero, quae ex sincerissimae rerum scientiae fonte manat.

58 See Alan Cameron, "The Date and Identity of Macrobius," *Journal of Roman Studies* 56 (1966), 25–38.

integrating mathematics or metaphysics, but the Platonic tradition had long accommodated the division to its own curriculum (to the point of attributing the division, erroneously, to Plato). Physics, for Macrobius, encompasses the discussion of "divine bodies" (*de divinis corporibus disputat*), including celestial bodies; hence it is to this category that Macrobius explicitly assigns, *inter alia*, the task of "revealing the secret of celestial harmony" (*cum . . . harmoniae superum pandit arcanum, physicae secreta commemorat*), a position which opened the door for the incorporation of physics and mathematics, and which many twelfth-century commentators will echo. But Macrobius's definition of "rational philosophy" will find few adherents. Eschewing the traditional (Stoic) definition of rational philosophy in terms of dialectic and rhetoric and following the expansion already evidenced by Origen (who substitutes *epoptica* in the place of logic),[59] Macrobius assimilates his *rationalis philosophia* with Platonic ontology. It thereby includes "the motion and immortality of the soul, in which there is clearly nothing corporeal, and whose being not sense perception but only reason can comprehend" (2.17.16).[60] In the twelfth century, however, most commentators (even commentators on Macrobius himself) will assign questions of the soul and other incorporeals to the realm of theology, the highest theoretical science in the Aristotelian bipartition.

The Encyclopedic Tradition: Martianus, Cassiodorus, and Isidore

Much remains uncertain about Martianus Minneius Felix Capella's allegorical encyclopedia. Dates proposed for its composition have swung between the fifth century's early and late decades;[61] we know next to nothing about its author save for the work's possible autobiographical glimmers, e.g., *De nuptiis* 1.2 (2.6–7), 6.577 (203.8–11), 9.999–1000 (385.11–386.4); and its original intent and audience remain shrouded in obscurity. One thing can be said with absolute certainty: it is a difficult

[59] *In Cant. cant.*, prol. ch. 3.1: Generales disciplinae, quibus ad rerum scientiam perventiur, tres sunt, quas Graeci ethicam, physicam, epopticen appellarunt. Ibid., 3.3: inspectiva [i.e., epoptice] dicitur, qua supergressi visibilia de divinis aliquid et caelestia contemplamur, eaque mente sola intuemur, quoniam corporum supergrediuntur adspectum.

[60] *Comm. in Som. Scip.* 2.17.16: at cum de motu et immortalitate animae disputat, cui nihil constat inesse corporeum, cuiusque essentiam nullus sensus sed sola ratio deprehendit, illic ad altitudinem philosophiae rationalis ascendit.

[61] 410–439 remains the *communis opinio*, most recently defended in Jean-Yves Guillaumin, ed. and trans., *Les noces de Philologie et de Mercure: Livre VII; L'arithmétique* (Paris: Belles lettres, 2003); 470s or 480s is argued in Danuta Shanzer, *A Philosophical and Literary Commentary on Martianus Capella's* De Nuptiis Philologiae et Mercurii *Book 1* (Berkeley: University of California, 1986) and Samuel I. B. Barnish, "Martianus Capella and Rome in the Late Fifth Century," *Hermes* 114 (1986), 98–111; as late as 496–523 according to Sabine Grebe, "Gedanken zur Datierung von De nuptiis Philologiae et Mercurii des Martianus Capella," *Hermes* 128 (2000), 353–368.

text. Replete with recondite syntax and hapax legomena, it has taxed generations of editors, medieval and modern alike. As early as 534, its first editor, a certain Securus Melior Felix, lamented the corrupt state of the manuscripts,[62] and any emendations that Felix might have provided seem still insufficient, for the proliferation of medieval copies stem from a single Merovingian archetype that itself was of suspect authority.[63] The complaints of the medieval commentators—*locus iste corruptus scriptorum vitio*, noted Remigius[64]—still echo as *locum pro desperato reliqui* in the apparatus of J. Willis's Teubner edition, and even more passages not obelized by Willis may drive readers to despair.[65] The syntactical and lexical difficulty of the *De nuptiis* is not merely a matter of historical curiosity; it is central to one of its most puzzling aspects: how and why did such a formidable text seize the medieval literary imagination and establish itself as one of the most important medieval school texts, surviving in no less than 244 copies? On one level, as Mariken Teeuwen observes, the "intricate Latin was seen as a good test case for one's knowledge of the language (on an 'expert level'), and a good opportunity to expand one's vocabulary and grammatical skills."[66] Indeed, there are abundant examples of scholars mining the *De nuptiis* for its lexographical riches; the annotations of Rather of Verona (890–974) are one such instance.[67] But Martianus's text was more than just a whetstone for sharpening linguistic competence, and it was as much the allegorical form of the *De nuptiis* as its scholastic content that recommended it to its medieval readers.

The *De nuptiis Philologiae et Mercurii* consists of two parts: the first and second books establish a framing allegory, the eponymous marriage of Philology and Mercury, and the seven subsequent books comprise short treatises on the seven liberal arts, diegetically framed as Mercury's wedding gifts presented as a procession of seven learned *dotales virgines*. Martianus's liberal arts, however, are not the *sobriae disciplinae*, stripped of fictitious embellishments, promised in the last metrum of book two (2.220 [58.3]), for Martianus's muse protests: "let the arts

62 See Alan Cameron, "Martianus and His First Editor," *Classical Philology* 81 (1986), 320–328; Jean Préaux, "Securus Melior Felix, l'ultime Orator Urbis Romae," in *Miscellanea patristica, historica et liturgica Eligio Dekkers O.S.B. XII lustra complenti oblata*, 2 vols. (Bruges: Sint-Pietersabdij, 1975), 2, 101–121.

63 Willis, *Martianus Capella*, vi; Danuta Shanzer, "Felix Capella: *Minus sensus quam nominis pecudalis*," *Classical Philology* 81 (1986), 62–81.

64 Cora E. Lutz, ed., *Remigii Autissiodorensis Commentum in Martianum Capellam*, 2 vols. (Leiden: Brill, 1962–1965), 195.17–18.

65 See the list in Shanzer, "Felix Capella: *Minus sensus quam nominis pecudalis*," 78–79.

66 Mariken Teeuwen, "The Study of Martianus Capella's *De nuptiis* in the Ninth Century," in *Learned Antiquity: Scholarship and Society in the Near East, the Greco-Roman World, and the Early Medieval West*, ed. Alasdair A. MacDonald, Michael W. Twomey, and Gerrit J. Reinik (Leuven: Peeters, 2003), 186.

67 See Claudio Leonardi, "Raterio e Marziano Capella," *Italia Medioevale e Umanistica* 2 (1959), 73–102; Claudio Leonardi, ed., *Notae et glossae autographicae Ratherii Veronensis* (Turnhout: Brepols, 1984); Mariken Teeuwen, "The Vocabulary of Martianus Capella Commentators of the Ninth Century: Some Observations," *Archivum Latinitatis Medii Aevi* 63 (2005), 71–81.

be clothed!" (*vestiantur Artes*: 3.222 [59.7]). The muse has her way, and far from sober, Martianus's arts are loud, boisterous, even comic personifications[68] whose nuptial offerings to the bride take the form of seven orations on the liberal arts, declaimed in the order: grammar, dialectic, rhetoric (later the trivium), geometry, arithmetic, astronomy, and music (later the quadrivium). Accounting for the number and order of Martianus's arts is tricky business, especially since it seems likely that any preexistent system was modified to suit Martianus's literary purposes; e.g., music comes last to occasion Hymenaeus's epithalamium (9.902–903).[69] But let the classicists worry about Martianus's antecedents. Whether Martianus had before him Varro's lost *Disciplinarum libri*[70] or a later, Porphyrian, Neoplatonic source[71] is immaterial for the later medieval commentators. And regardless of whether Martianus's summary dismissal of medicine and architecture as "having nothing in common with heaven or the gods" (9.891 [339.5–6]) departs deliberately from Varro's ninefold scheme[72] or reflects a Middle Platonic unease with their propaedeutic value,[73] the dismissal highlights one important theme that strongly recommended the *De nuptiis* throughout its long reception history: the ascent from the corporeal to the incorporeal, from the terrestrial to the celestial.[74]

This (Neoplatonic) *reditus* is allegorized by Philology's apotheosis in book two, and it remains discernible within the ascent through the individual *disciplinae* of the seven subsequent books, the quadrivium in particular. The first of the quadrivial maidens, Geometria, whose (notably Grecian) sandals are worn thin from her globetrotting (6.581), offers primarily a compendium of terrestrial geography. Geometry's closest sister, the second maiden, Arithmetica, introduces herself to the assembly by requesting that Jupiter himself acknowledge her as the "source of his own unique and originary nature" (7.730 [262.7–8]), as indeed the mother of the entire celestial throng. The third maiden, Astronomia, appears enclosed in a globe of ethereal light (9.810), and her numinous presence startles the lesser deities of the aerial, terrestrial, marine, and subterranean realms. Finally, Harmonia, the last maiden, enters the celestial senate to the melodious strains of the *musica caelestis*, and all stand in reverence and awe of the extramundane

[68] Lucio Cristante, "*Spectaculo detinemur cum scripta intellegimus aut probamus*: Per un riesame della rappresentazione delle *Artes* in Marziano Capella," *Incontri triestini di filologia classica* 4 (2005), 375–390.

[69] Ilsetraut Hadot, *Arts libéraux et philosophie dans la pensée antique: Contribution à l'histoire de l'éducation et de la culture dans l'Antiquité*, 2nd ed. (Paris: J. Vrin, 2005), 149.

[70] The traditional opinion, upheld most recently by Shanzer, *A Philosophical and Literary Commentary*; Danuta Shanzer, "Augustine's Disciplines: *Silent diutius Musae Varronis*?" in *Augustine and the Disciplines: From Cassiciacum to Confessions*, ed. Karla Pollman and Mark Vessey (Oxford: Oxford University Press, 2005), 69–112; and Muriel Bovey, *Disciplinae cyclicae: L'organisation du savoir dans l'oeuvre de Martianus Capella* (Trieste: Edizioni Università di Trieste, 2003).

[71] As maintained by Hadot, *Arts libéraux et philosophie*.

[72] Shanzer, *A Philosophical and Literary Commentary*, 15.

[73] Hadot, *Arts libéraux et philosophie*, 150.

[74] Cf. Aug., *De ord.* 2.5.14, 2.14.39–15.43; *Retr.* 1.6.

intelligence (9.910, cf. 2.202), a gesture of respect accorded Harmonia alone. The Christianization of this avowedly pagan, Neoplatonic ascent, and its implications for the arrangement and purpose of the liberal arts, remained a primary theme throughout the commentary tradition.[75]

In striking contradistinction, M. Aurelius Cassiodorus, former *magister officiorum* under Theodoric (r. 475–526) and then Amalasuntha's regency (526–534), prepackages the liberal arts and the whole of philosophy for a markedly Christian audience (James J. O'Donnell paints an idyllic scene: "One elderly politician, out of office for many years and exiled, had returned home to a monastery he had founded, to settle down to collecting books").[76] Cassiodorus's *Institutiones* is essentially an analytic bibliography or annotated library catalogue for the books he had brought to Vivarium, the monastery he had founded in the 550s (or earlier). The second of its two books is devoted to the liberal arts, which are dealt with in the order: grammar, rhetoric, dialectic, arithmetic, music, geometry, and astronomy. Cassiodorus knew of the *De nuptiis* but had failed to procure a copy (*Inst.* 2.3.20, cf. 2.2.17).[77] At the beginning of his chapter "On Dialectic," Cassiodorus remarks that it is traditional to include a division of philosophy among the prolegomena to an exposition of Porphyry's *Isagoge* (2.3.3).[78] Though he doubtless knew Boethius's *Isagoge* translation and commentaries (2.3.18),[79] the terminology and structure of Cassiodorus's division suggest a closer connection to Ammonius's Porphyry commentary (or, more likely, another commentary within the same tradition),[80] although the Peripatetic scheme is lightly recast within the Neoplatonic framework of Origen's commentary on the Song of Songs. Philosophy divides into *inspectiua* (= theoretical philosophy) and *actualis* (= practical philosophy); these divide respectively into *naturalis–doctrinalis–diuina* and *moralis–dispensatiua–ciuilis.* Of the three theoretical sciences, *doctrinalis* (a literal rendering of μαθηματική) bears the expected subdivision into *arithmetica–musica–geometria–astronomia*, enumerated in their Nicomachean order and with similar criteria for division (*quantitas secundum se, numerus ad aliquid, magnitudo immobilis*); only astronomy lacks the Nicomachean specification of *magnitudo mobilis* and is described periphrastically

75 On which, see Hicks, "Martianus Capella and the Liberal Arts," in *The Oxford Handbook of Medieval Latin Literature*, ed. David Townsend and Ralph Hexter (Oxford: Oxford University Press, 2012), 307–334.

76 James J. O'Donnell, *Cassiodorus* (Berkeley: University of California Press, 1979), 178.

77 The interpolations from Martianus in the Φ recension, subsequently expunged from the Δ recension, have nothing to do with Cassiodorus; see Danuta Shanzer, "Tatwine: An Independent Witness to the Text of Martianus Capella's *De Grammatica*?" *Rivista di filologia e d'istruzione classica* 112 (1984), 299–301.

78 PL 70, 1168B: Consuetudo itaque est doctoribus philosophiae, antequam ad Isagogen veniant exponendam, divisionem philosophiae paucis attingere: quam nos quoque servantes, praesenti tempore non immerito credimus intimandam.

79 Cf. PL 70, 1202D-1203A: Isagogen transtulit patricius Boetius, commenta eius gemina derelinquens.

80 Cf. Courcelle, *Late Latin Writers*, 341–344; Hadot, *Arts libéraux et philosophie*, 199–202).

as the "discipline which contemplates all the course of the heavens and the patterns of the stars" (*disciplina quae cursus coelestium siderumque figuras contemplatur omnes*).[81]

There are two notable points of contrast between Cassiodorus's and Boethius's accounts of the mathematical sciences, music in particular. First, whereas Boethius, presumably following Aristotle, had defined mathematics as dealing with things "motionless and unabstracted," Cassiodorus specifies that mathematics deals with "abstracted quantity" (*abstracta quantitas*), which has been mentally separated from matter or from other accidents.[82] Second, and in direct tension and antagonism with the first, Cassiodorus's thrice repeated definition of *musica* (1168D, 1203C, 1209B) construes the *ad aliquid* specification differently than did Boethius (and Nicomachus). For Boethius, as we have seen, "in relation to another" targeted the proportional, number to number, basis of musical knowledge. Cassiodorus twists this formulation and construes *ad aliquid* as a cross-domain relation: music is the discipline that deals not with numbers "in relation to other numbers" *simpliciter* but with numbers "in relation to those [numbers] which are found in sounds" (*disciplina quae de numeris loquitur, qui ad aliquid sunt his qui inueniuntur in sonis*),[83] a claim that accords with the similarly restricted definition in his *Expositio Psalmorum* (97.219–21): "music is the discipline which scrutinizes the differences and harmonies of things that are congruent with each other, that is, sounds" (*musica est disciplina quae rerum sibi congruentium id est sonorum differentias et conuenientias perscrutatur*). This restriction of *musica* to number insofar as it relates to sounds seems to be Cassiodorus's own intervention upon his source(s). Finally, while Cassiodorus situates music squarely among the mathematical sciences and his chapter on music begins with a discussion that echoes Boethius's categories of *musica humana* (e.g., musical rhythms govern the "inward

81 PL 70, 1168D–1169A (2.3.6): Arithmetica est disciplina quantitatis numerabilis secundum se. Musica est disciplina quae de numeris loquitur, qui ad aliquid sunt his qui inueniuntur in sonis. Geometrica est disciplina magnitudinis immobilis et formarum. Astronomia est disciplina quae cursus coelestium siderumque figuras contemplatur omnes, et habitudines stellarum circa se et circa terram indagabili ratione percurrit. Here Cassiodorus departs from Ammonius, who explains the four mathematical sciences in the order geometry–astronomy–arithmetic–astronomy (*In Isag.* 14.8–22). Cassiodorus knew of two translations of Nicomachus's *Intr. ar.*, the translation by Boethius and a (now lost) translation by Apuleius. PL 70, 1208B (2.3.7): arithmetica disciplina, quam apud Graecos Nicomachus diligenter exposuit. Hunc primum Madaurensis Apuleius, deinde magnificus uir Boetius Latino sermone translatum Romanis contulit lectitandum.

82 PL 70, 1168D (2.3.21): Doctrinalis dicitur scientia, quae abstractam considerat quantitatem. Abstracta enim quantitas dicitur, quam intellectu a materia separantes vel ab aliis accidentibus, ut est, par, impar vel alia huiuscemodi, in sola ratiocinatione tractamus.

83 It cannot, however, mean "the discipline which treats of numbers in relation to those *things* which are found in sounds" (which would require *qui ad aliquid sunt his* **quae** *inueniuntur in sonis*), as translated by William Strunk Jr. and Oliver Strunk (and revised by James McKinnon) in *Source Readings in Music History*, rev. ed. (New York: W. W. Norton, 1998), 144.

pulse of our veins")[84] and *mundana* (e.g., "heaven and earth, even everything that happens within them from divine dispensation, are not without the discipline of music"),[85] his subsequent technical exposition knows nothing of Boethius's *De institutione musica*,[86] and in fact owes more to the Aristoxenian tradition than it does to Pythagorean mathematics. Two of Cassiodorus's sources, Gaudentius (via the now lost translation by an otherwise unknown Mutianus) and Alypius, bear marked affinities with the Aristoxenian tradition, and Cassiodorus's primary division of music into harmonics, rhythmics, and metrics[87] is ultimately Aristoxenian in origin.[88]

A few decades later, in the early seventh century, the titan of taxonomy,[89] Isidore of Seville, put before the readers of his mammoth *Etymologiae* all these classificatory systems in all their contradictory glory: both divisions of philosophy and at least three classificatory schemes for parsing the discipline of music. John Henderson has aptly described Isidore's project with playful Isidorian language: "his writing models the belief system it subtends, as the monumental text morphs through its taxonomers' paradise of totalization through system, dramatizing power *as* power over knowledge."[90] *In nuce*: "The more you know . . .," as NBC's long-running PSA taught generations of viewers. Isidore's totalization of "metaknowledge," his taxonomy of taxonomies, however, threatens fragmentation. Isidore, as did Cassiodorus before him and Boethius before *him*, prefaces his compendium of dialectic (which starts predictably with Porphyry's *Isagoge*) with the definition and division of philosophy (2.24), according to *both* the Stoic tripartition[91] (via Augustine) *and*, a few sections later, the Peripatetic bipartition (via Cassiodorus, specifically,

84 PL 70, 1209A: quidquid enim loquimur, uel intrinsecus uenarum pulsibus commouemur, per musicos rhythmos harmoniae uirtutibus probatur esse sociatum. Musica quippe est scientia bene modulandi; quod si nos bona conuersatione tractemus, tali disciplinae probamur semper esse sociati.

85 Ibid.: coelum quoque terram, uel omnia quae in eis dispensatione superna peraguntur, non sunt sine musica disciplina, cum Pythagoras hunc mundum per musicam conditum et gubernari posse testetur.

86 Cassiodorus certainly knew that Boethius was an authority on musical matters (cf. *Variae* 2.41, 2.46), but the *Inst. mus.* is not cited in the *Institutiones*, and there is no direct evidence that would place the work in Cassiodorus's library, either in Rome or at Vivarium.

87 Cf. *Exp. Ps.* 80.97–102: Est enim disciplinae ipsius magna uis delectabilisque cognitio, quam doctores saecularium litterarum . . . fecerunt doctrinabili lectione cognosci, quam in rerum natura prius tenebantur abscondita. Prima ergo huius disciplinae partitio est harmonica, rhythmica, metrica.

88 Cf. Aristoxenus, *El. harm.* 32.7; Alypius, *Introd. mus.* 364.7; Aristides Quintilianus, *De mus.* 1.5.

89 Cf. John Henderson, *The Medieval World of Isidore of Seville: Truth from Words* (Cambridge: Cambridge University Press, 2007), 5.

90 Ibid., 7.

91 *Etym.* 2.24.3: Philosophiae species tripertita est: una naturalis, quae Graece physica appellatur, in qua de naturae inquisitione disseritur; altera moralis, quae Graece ethica dicitur, in qua de moribus agitur; tertia rationalis, quae Graeco uocabulo logica appellatur, in qua disputatur quemadmodum in rerum causis uel uitae moribus ueritas ipsa quaeratur.

an abbreviated recension of the *Institutiones*).[92] Within the Stoic classification, Isidore makes explicit what was already hinted at in Macrobius: the subdivision of physics into the mathematical sciences, which Isidore attributes to Plato and lists in the distinctive order: arithmetic, geometry, music, astronomy.[93] The Peripatetic division (2.24.10–14) closely follows Cassiodorus (though again music is generally presented as the third of the mathematic sciences), as does the definition of music at the outset of book three (3.1: "music is the discipline which speaks of numbers that are discovered in sounds," *musica est disciplina quae de numeris loquitur qui inueniuntur in sonis*) and the subsequent tripartition of music into harmonics, rhythmics, and metrics (3.18). Isidore follows this, however, with a second threefold division, perhaps Varronian in origin, derived from Augustine:[94] "it is agreed that for every sound that forms the material for songs, there is a threefold nature" (*ad omnem autem sonum quae materies cantilenarum est triformem constat esse naturam*). This "material" division encompasses *harmonica* (vocal music or *uox*), *organica* (music from wind instruments or *flatus*), and *metrica* (music from plucked or struck instruments or *pulsus*)—that is to say, music as one of the beaux arts and not as a reflection of a number-based metaphysics. The final section of the chapter (3.23), "On musical numbers," abruptly returns in force to a fundamentally Pythagorean view that neatly encapsulates a third tripartition echoing (indirectly) the Boethian categories of *musica mundana, humana*, and *instrumentalis* (3.23.2):

> Sed haec ratio quemadmodum in mundo est ex uolubilitate circulorum, ita et in microcosmo in tantum praeter uocem ualet, ut sine ipsius perfectione etiam homo symphoniis carens non consistat. Eiusdem musicae perfectione etiam metra consistunt in arsi et thesi, id est eleuatione et positione.
>
> But just as this same arrangement[95] [sc. the harmonic proportion] exists in the universe from the revolutions of the planetary spheres,

[92] See Louis Holtz, "Quelques aspects de la tradition et de la diffusion des *Institutiones*," in *Atti della settimana di studi su Flavio Magno Aurelio Cassiodoro (Cosenza-Squillace, 19–24 settembre 1983)*, ed. Sandro Leanza (Soveria Mannelli: Rubbettino, 1986), 281–312.

[93] This follows the order of Cassiodorus's first presentation (2.*praef.*4), which everywhere else in the *Inst.* is discussed in the order arithmetic, geometry, music, astronomy. On which, see Jean-Yves Guillaumin and Giovanni Gasparotto, eds. and trans., *Isidor: Étymologies, livre 3 (la mathématique)* (Paris: Belles lettres, 2009), xvi–xviii.

[94] *De doct. christ.* 2.17.27: facile erat animadvertere omnem sonum, quae materies cantilenarum est, triformem esse natura (this division, moreover, is embedded within an explicitly Varronian context, namely, Varro's tale of the origin of the nine muses). Cf. *In psalm.* 150.7; *De ord.* 2.14.39; see Jacques Fontaine, *Isidore de Séville et la culture classique dans l'Espagne wisigothique*, 2 vols. (Paris: Études augustiniennes, 1959), 426ff.

[95] *haec ratio* = *numeri secundum musicam*, meaning "harmonic numbers," sc. the "harmonic proportion," which Isidore has just derived with the example 12:8:6 in a manner that closely approximates the method and language of Theon of Smyrna (*Exp.* 1.61), as noted by Guillaumin and Gasparotto in their note to this passage. The geometric proportion is described (3.13) with identical language, *numeri*

> so also it has so much force (beyond just voices) in the microcosm that without its completive power (*sine ipsius perfectione*) no man who lacks such harmonies could exist. Meters too exist from the perfection of this same musical [proportion] in *arsis* and *thesis*, that is, in the elevation and depression [of the voice].

Isidore adds texture to the oft-quoted claim with which he had begun (3.17.1): "without music no discipline can be complete, for without it there is nothing" (*itaque sine musica nulla disciplina potest esse perfect, nihil enim sine illa*). Henderson's exegetical glee is unrestrained on this point: "Furthermore, 'Music harmonizes the universe into a composition': take a bow, first of many to come, *mundus* and *caelum*. For Music makes the world 'go round' . . . Sing Isidore's hymn to harmony."[96] As a compilation, however, that blithely leaps centuries in a single bound and flattens voluminous schools of thought into a smooth surface that belies the depths that lie beneath, Isidore's etymological song book is spiced with unresolved discursive dissonance.[97] *Musica* is *both* a physical science that investigates the (Platonic) causes of the world *and* a mathematical, "doctrinal" science, one of four that mediate between their theoretical companions, physics (below) and theology (above). *Musica* is *both* inextricably intertwined with the material of song, born of bodily motions and organic matter (throats, reeds, sinews, skins, etc.), *and* inseparable from the universe itself, whose macro- and microcosmic volubility can only speak through the completive power of its harmonic numbers.

The twelfth-century readers of the *divisiones philosophiae* sketched above reveled in these dissonances. Resolving, recombining, and refashioning the mosaics of citations and taxonomies they found in Boethius, Calcidius, Macrobius, Martianus, Cassiodorus, and Isidore, they created new universalizing totalities, new worlds of words.

Hugh of St. Victor and Related Texts: Boethius Redivivus

Exemplary of this synthetic approach, firmly grounded in Boethius's *Isagoge* commentary but supplemented continually by his mathematical treatises as well as by Cassiodorus, Isidore, and Macrobius, is Hugh of St. Victor's *Didascalicon* (composed in the 1120s). Hugh's fourfold classification of the sciences—theoretical,

secundum geometriam. Hence *haec ratio* may mean "this proportion" (conflating *ratio* and *analogia*); at 3.8.1 (the outline of three proportions) Isidore's language is more precise, and the arithmetic proportion is deemed (properly) the *analogicum arithmeticae*.

96 Henderson, *The Medieval World of Isidore of Seville*, 56.

97 Jean-Yves Guillaumin, "Boethius's *De institutione arithmetica* and its Influence on Posterity," in *A Companion to Boethius in the Middle Ages*, ed. Noel H. Kaylor and Philip E. Phillips (Leiden: Brill, 2012), 157.

practical, mechanical, and logical—has been exhaustively studied, and the many details do not need to be repeated here.[98] Hugh is the first (in a long tradition) to ground the division of theoretical philosophy in Boethius's *Isagoge* commentary.[99] Despite Hugh's clear Boethian affinities, there is a common misunderstanding that Hugh's division (in the words of James Weisheipl, who is often cited on this point) "is a successful combination of the Boethian and Stoic divisions of 'science.' . . . The basic division of scientific knowledge is *that of the Stoics*. In this case 'physics' is taken to be equivalent to 'theoretical' and coextensive with Boethius' tripartite classification of speculative 'philosophy.'"[100] Numerous scholars have followed suit.[101] Hugh is clear, however, that the Stoic division is not in his sights, and he addresses it directly at 2.16 (*De physica*). After describing the (preferred) Boethian perspective (*Physis natura interpretatur, unde etiam in superiori divisione theoricae physicam naturalem Boethius nominavit*), he notes that "sometimes (*aliquando*) physics is broadly construed as equivalent to theoretical philosophy," and that "some scholars (*quidam*, an odd usage if he counted himself among them) divide philosophy into three parts: physics, ethics, and logic."[102] This is not a distinction without a difference, for it directly bears on the status and object of the mathematical sciences. They are not *subsumed* under the broader heading of physics, as in the expanded Stoic classification encountered in Isidore, but *mediate* theology and physics in a specifically Boethian manner. Hugh reconciles the middle theoretical category of Boethius's *Isagoge* (intelligibles) with Cassiodorus's definition of mathematics (abstract quantity), even to the point of providing (in *Did.* 2.4) an arithmetical account of the soul's procession and return (*processio et regressio*). The soul descends (1) from simple essence (the monad) to (3^1) a "virtual" triad (the tripartite Platonic soul), to (3^2) the regulation of the music of the human body (*ad regendam humani corporis musicam*) in the number nine (the orifices that provide the primary interface between the body and the external world, and through which influx and efflux maintain the body's natural balance), to (3^3) full bodily extension

[98] See the studies listed above in note 5 (p. 68).

[99] *Did.* 2.1: theorica dividitur in theologiam, mathematicam et physicam. hanc divisionem Boethius facit aliis verbis, theoricen secans in intellectibilem et intelligibilem et naturalem, per intellectibilem significans theologiam, per intelligibilem, mathematicam, per naturalem, physicam.

[100] Weisheipl, "The Nature, Scope, and Classification of the Sciences," 473–474; Weisheipl, "Classification of the Sciences in Medieval Thought," 65–66 [my emphasis].

[101] E.g., Elspeth Whitney, *Paradise Restored: The Mechanical Arts from Antiquity through the Thirteenth Century* (Philadelphia: American Philosophical Society, 1990), 84; Jeremiah Hackett, "Roger Bacon on the Classification of the Sciences," in *Roger Bacon and the Sciences: Commemorative Essays*, ed. Jeremiah Hackett (Leiden: Brill, 1997), 54; Dyer, "The Place of *Musica* in Medieval Classifications of Knowledge," 21; etc.

[102] *Did.* 2.16: haec etiam physiologia dicitur, id est, sermo de naturis disserens, quod ad eandem causam spectat. physica aliquando large accipitur aequipollens theoricae, secundum quam acceptionem philosophiam quidam in tres partes dividunt, id est, physicam, ethicam, logicam, in qua divisione mechanica non continetur, sed restringitur philosophia circa physicam, ethicam, logicam.

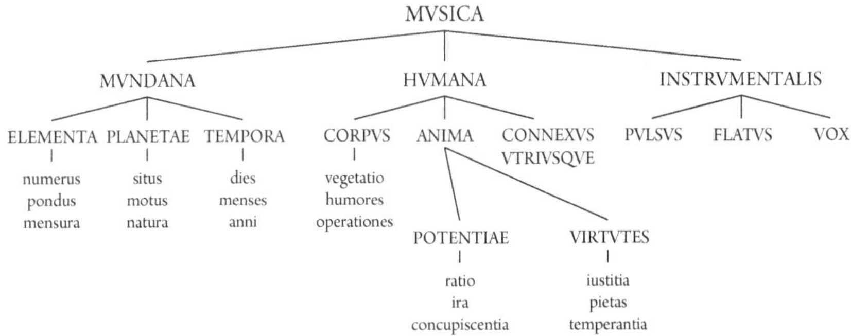

Figure 2.2 Division of *musica* according to Hugh of St. Victor (*Did.* 2.12).

and sensual diffusion in twenty-seven (the first cubic number), at which point the *progressio* becomes a *regressio* to monadic simplicity in final multiplication to (3^4) eighty-*one* (the reappearance of "one" designating the return to unity, while "eighty" designates the natural measure of human life).[103]

It is no surprise, then, that Hugh's Boethian musical division at 2.12, the most extensive of all the quadrivial subdivisions in the *Didascalicon* (see figure 2.2),[104] pays closest attention to *musica humana* in all its triadic (trinitarian?) substructures: the virtual triad of the soul's tripartition of powers (*ratio, ira*, and *concupiscentia*), its triplet of virtues (*iustitia, pietas*, and *temperantia*, purchased at the cost of suppressing the usual *four* cardinal virtues), and the threefold realities of bodily existence (its vegetative powers, its humors, and its operations). The subdivisions of *musica mundana* echo *Inst. mus.* 1.2 (187.23–188.26), but the subdivision of *musica instrumentalis* is Isidorian (*uox, flatus*, and *pulsus*).

The influence of Hugh's quadripartite reckoning of philosophy is widespread and can be detected throughout the twelfth century; his subdivision of music, however, is particularly central to a short mid-twelfth-century treatise on the division of philosophy, generically known as the *Tractatus quidam de philosophia et partibus eius*.[105] The greater part of this *divisio philosophiae* is occupied by an exhaustive *divisio musicae* (see figure 2.3). Though obviously modeled on Hugh's

103 *Did.* 2.5 then provides a parallel account for the *quaternarium corporis*, taking the first even (and thus divisible) number, 2, as the base for the calculation of its subsequent powers (2, 4, 8, 16, 32); the return of "two" in its fourth power indicates "that everything composed of divisibles is itself also divisible" (*in quo intelligi datur omne quod a solubilibus compositionem accipit ipsum quoque esse dissolubile*).

104 Arithmetic is described in 46 words (2.11), geometry in 96 words (2.13), and astronomy (2.14) in 101 words. The chapter on music (2.12) is longer than all three combined: 268 words.

105 The treatise was edited by Gilbert Dahan in 1982 from Paris, BnF, lat. 6750, 57r–59r, the only copy known to him: "Une introduction à la philosophie au XIIe siècle: Le *Tractatus quidam de philosophia et partibus eius*," *Archives d'histoire doctrinale et littéraire du Moyen Âge* 49 (1982), 155–193. A better copy of this same text is found in Paris, BnF, lat. 8624, 23v–24r, immediately following a commentary on Plato's *Timaeus* (Hisdosus, *De anima mundi Platonica*). This latter commentary is discussed in Chapter 5.

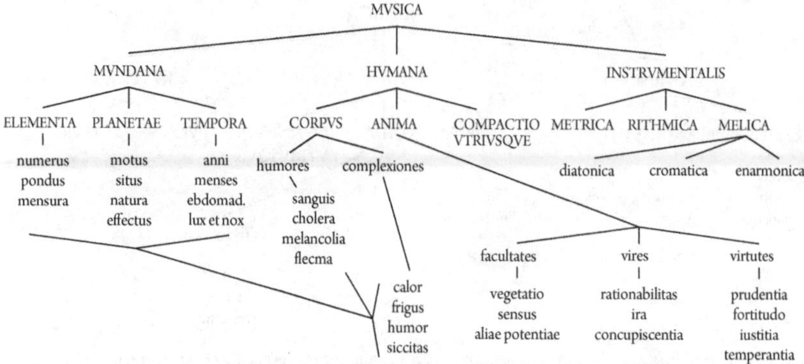

Figure 2.3 Division of *musica* according to the *Tractatus quidam* (ed. Gilbert Dahan, with emendations from Paris, BnF, lat. 8624, ff. 23v–24r).

Didascalicon, the general definition of music in this treatise betrays a strong cosmological and natural philosophical affiliation: *musica* is the "science of comprehending proportions in order to understand the concord and discord of *things*."[106] This definition explicitly grants *musica* a broad mandate to investigate the nature of things in the world. The more restricted examination of sonorous consonance and dissonance belongs only to music's third part, *instrumentalis*.[107] The ensuing scholastic divisions of *musica mundana* and *humana* further expand music's scope in the study of the *natura rerum*. The basic outline draws again upon Boethius's *De institutione musica*, 1.2, and Hugh's *Didascalicon*, but the categories are further expanded to encompass developments in twelfth-century natural philosophy, most notably humoral physiology and elemental theory, both of which had been well served by texts newly translated from Arabic (particularly the *Isagoge ad artem Galeni* and the *Liber Pantegni* of Constantinus Africanus).[108]

The *Tractatus de philosophia* also offers insight into the relationships among the quadrivial arts. The author notes that each liberal art has its own *elementum* by which the questions proper to each discipline are addressed: arithmetic and music deal with axioms (*axiomata*); that is to say, they provide the foundational, rationally demonstrable principles of the mathematical arts. Geometry and astronomy, on the other hand, handle theorems (*theoremata*), insofar as their investigations are based on theoretical, visual models such as the diagrams of planetary movements and the geometrical figures central to the translations of

106 BnF, lat. 8624, 23v: musica est scientia perpendendi proportiones ad cognitionem concordie et discordie rerum.

107 Ibid.: Secundum uero tertiam partem, id est instrumentalem, sic describitur: Musica est scientia perpendendi proportiones ad cognitionem consonantie et dissonantie.

108 Humoral physiology and elemental theory are taken up in Chapters 3 and 5 respectively.

Euclid's *Elements*.[109] These axioms and theoretical models form the foundation for *philosophia*.

Further support for this view is provided by a curious division of philosophy found in a small tract (awkwardly known as *Ut testatur Ergaphalau*, its incipit) that prefaces Adelard of Bath's *De opere astrolapsus*. It presents an idiosyncratic, astrologically grounded model of philosophy, but its description of the parts of *sapientia* reinforces the view of music as foundational to natural philosophy. This text divides *sapientia* into ministering (*ministrans*) and ministered (*ministrata*) parts: arithmetic and music, the sciences of number *simpliciter* and *ad aliquid* (as in Boethius), again lead to knowledge of natural things. And they (together with geometry) are the *ministrantes scientiae* propaedeutic to the *ministrata scientia* of physics, defined as the study of the movements of natural things, both macrocosmic and microcosmic.[110] Andreas Speer connects this passage to the later thirteenth-century conception of the subaltern sciences,[111] but even if we can read subalternation into the language of *ministrans* and *ministrata*, the subalternation suggested by this passage would be at odds with the Aristotelian system developed in the thirteenth and fourteenth centuries. Whereas the theory of *subalternatio* generally subsumed music to mathematics, or less commonly to natural

[109] BnF, lat. 8624, 24v: et artes liberales habent propria [prima *Dahan*] elementa quibus dubia uniuscuiusque fidem habeant: grammatica, rationes; dialectica, per se nota et maximas propositiones; rethorica, locos communes et generales; arismetica et musica, anxiomata [antexiomata Dahan]; geometria et astronomia, theoremata [thoreumata *Dahan*]. See Hentschel, *Sinnlichkeit und Vernunft*, 251–253 for a brief discussion of the terms *axiomata* and *theoremata*. Cf., *Anticl*. Prologus (wrongly punctuated by Bossuat [56]): Quoniam igitur in hoc opere resultat grammatice syntaseos regula, dialectice lexeos maxima, oratorie reseos communis sententia, arismetice matheseos paradoxa, musice melos anxioma, geometrie gramatis theorema, astronomice ebdomadis excellentia, theophanie celestis emblema. The phrase *musice melos anxioma*, however, remains a *locus nondum sanatus* (hence Boussat's punctuation: musice melos, anxioma geometrie, gramatis theorema). I think it likely that the uncommon Greek genitive *meleos* (parallel with *syntaseos, lexeos*, etc.) has been flattened into the more familiar but grammatically incorrect *melos* (whose genitive is usually *huius meli*). Emend thus: *musice meleos anxioma, geometrie gramatis theorema*. Cf. Alexander Neckam's *Sacerdos ad altere*: Sic a regulis grammatice transeat quis ad maximas dialetice, dehinc ad communes locos rhetorice, postmodum ad aporismata arismetice, postea ad axiomata musice, deinde ad theoremata geometrie . . ., deinde ad canones Tholomei accedat. Dyer, "The Place of *Musica* in Medieval Classifications of Knowledge," 5, misconstrues *axiomata* in Neckam's work, suggesting that it is "possibly a reference to Book 19 of the pseudo-Aristotelian *Problemata* whose subject is music."

[110] Charles Burnett, "Adelard, Ergaphalau, and the Science of the Stars," in *Magic and Divination in the Middle Ages: Texts and Techniques in the Islamic and Christian Worlds* (Aldershot: Ashgate, 1996), 143: Ministrans est sapientia ut musica et arismetica, que [per] numerorum absolutionem, simpliciter et ad aliquid, ad scientiam vel ad noticiam naturalium introducunt. Ministrata est velut geometria et physica quarum altera tantum alteri ministrat. . . . Est igitur sola phisica ministrata que naturales immutationes rerum secundum transitum et moras continenter absolvit. Que duplex reperitur. Alia enim dicitur microcosmica, alia megacosmica.

[111] Andreas Speer, "*Scientia quadruvii: Musica* in den 'Timaios'-Kommentaren des 12. Jahrhunderts," in *Musik – und die Geschichte der Philosophie und Naturwissenschaften im Mittelalter*, 105.

philosophy, here it is *physica* itself that requires musical, specifically proportional conclusions with which to explain the visible and invisible world.

Bernard of Chartres and the *Glosae Colonienses super Macrobium*

In the accessus to his *Glosae super Platonem*,[112] Bernard considers the part(s) of philosophy to which the *Timaeus* properly belongs. From the various guises in which Plato presents his primary subject matter (*naturalis iustitia*), Bernard surmises that the dialogue, not surprisingly, encompasses all three parts of philosophy: ethics, logic, and physics.[113] That is to say, Bernard subscribes to the Academic-Stoic tripartition (cf. 6.165–66).[114] This division, as is clear from its discussion above, is commonplace enough, but Bernard may have consciously chosen to employ it because of Augustine's (and Isidore's) insistence that the division was genuinely Platonic in origin.[115] Later in the *Glosae* (at 7.377–838, commenting upon *Tim.* 47a), Bernard deploys the idiosyncratic Calcidian version of the Peripatetic bipartition, *consideratio* and *actus*. There Bernard seems to divide theoretical philosophy into theology, physics, and logic (*consideratio in tria diuiditur, in theologiam, phisicam, logicam*), and his editor, Paul Dutton, takes him at his word.[116] Bernard is clearly grasping here for a term with which to define Calcidius's nebulous third category, and *logica* (presumably intended to encapsulate Calcidius's periphrastic *scientia rationis praebendae*) seems a poor fit, as the burden of Bernard's *logica* is the consideration of the "rational ordering of both other [arguments?] and time" (*de rationabili ordinatione tum aliorum, tum temporum*: 7.382–383). This is further

112 Bernard's authorship, as argued by Paul Edward Dutton, "The Uncovering of the *Glosae super Platonem* of Bernard of Chartres," *Mediaeval Studies* 46 (1984), 192–221 and Dutton, *The Glosae super Platonem of Bernard of Chartres*, has faced serious challenges from Peter Dronke, "Introduction," in *A History of Twelfth-Century Western Philosophy*, ed. Peter Dronke (Cambridge: Cambridge University Press, 1988), 14–17; Sten Ebbesen, "Review of Dutton, *The Glosae super Platonem of Bernard of Chartres*," *Speculum* 71 (1996), 123–125; Caiazzo, *Glosae Colonienses super Macrobium*, 132– 141; and most recently Dronke, *The Spell of Calcidius: Platonic Concepts and Images in the Medieval West*. Although these arguments usefully highlight moments in the text where Bernard is less original than Dutton had supposed, they do not decisively disprove authorship. Even Dronke's suggestion that the glosses "reflect pre-twelfth-century Platonic discussions," for which he offers no evidence, does not necessarily deny Bernard's authorship as a consequence. William of Conches's *Glosae super Priscianum* likewise reflects pre-twelfth-century grammatical discussions.

113 *Bernardi Glos. sup. Tim.* 1.56–60: Supponitur uero ethicae, secundum quod de naturali iusticia uel de ordinatione rei publicae agit. Respicit logicam, cum per aliorum sententias suas firmat rationem. Ad phisicam tendit, cum de planis figuris et solidis corporibus, de incorporatione animae mundi et aliarum earumque motu perpetuo, de stellarum discursibus ratis et errantibus loquitur.

114 Bernard is followed in this by his students, Gilbert of Poitiers and John of Salisbury.

115 As noted by Dutton, *The Glosae super Platonem of Bernard of Chartres*, 63.

116 Dutton, *The Glosae super Platonem of Bernard of Chartres*, 63.

fleshed out, though by no means clarified, when Bernard comments on the letter of the text:[117]

> AC DIEI. Hic docet quod uisus ualeat ad rationem ordinationis, quae est in logica. Et hoc est: DIEI ET NOCTIS INSINVATA NOBIS, per uisus, ALTERNA VICE NATI SVNT MENSES, et alia tempora, et existit nobis DINVMERATIO EORVM temporum per uisum, ET EX DINVMERATIONE PERFECTVS NVMERVS, ut annus mundanus et similia.
>
> AND OF DAY. Here [Plato] teaches that sight is useful for the system of organization, which consists in logic. This is what Plato says: WITH THE MUTUAL ALTERNATION OF DAY AND NIGHT REVEALED TO US through sight, MONTHS ARISE, as well as other measurements of time, and we gain a MEASUREMENT OF THESE times through sight, AND OUT OF THIS MEASUREMENT [ARISES] PERFECT NUMBER, such as the cosmic year and the like.

How this system of ordering (*ratio ordinationis*) relates to *logica* in its standard formulation[118] remains oblique (to say the least). Bernard here is simply following Calcidius's lead: the *laus uidendi* once again trumps the *diuisio philosophiae*. The passage, in short, is too single-minded to provide support for interpreting this division as an intentional, novel hybrid of the Stoic and Peripatetic division, as argued by Andreas Speer, who goes so far as to deem the division "a mixed model characteristic of the twelfth century."[119] Far from being "characteristic," this ad hoc division is unique enough to pinpoint Bernard as the source for all its other attestations, including its appearance in several glossed copies of the *Timaeus*.[120] By far the most interesting use of this division arises not in a Timaean commentary but in an early-twelfth-century commentary on Macrobius's *Commentarii in Somnium Scipionis*, the *Glosae Colonienses super Macrobium*.

This anonymous commentator, commenting upon 1.1.4, saw in Macrobius's claim that Plato "thoroughly inspect[ed] the nature of all things and actions" (*rerum omnium Plato et actuum naturam penitus inspiciens*) an oblique reference to the division of philosophy: the nature of things implies *contemplatio*, and the nature of actions implies *ethica*. While William of Conches in his *Glosae super Macrobium*

117 *Bernardi Glos. sup. Tim.* 7.402–6.

118 It even strains Bernard's own description of the Timaean employ of logic (at 1.57–58): Respicit [sc. liber Platonis] logicam, cum per aliorum sententias suas firmat rationes.

119 Speer, "*Scientia quadruvii*," 11.

120 E.g., Leipzig, Universitätsbibliothek, Lat. 1258, f. 6vb (lemmatic commentary) (Dutton, *The Glosae super Platonem of Bernard of Chartres*, 257, Appendix 3.1); El Escorial, Biblioteca del real monasterio de San Lorenzo, S. III.5, f. 138r (as noted in Caiazzo, *Glosae Colonienses super Macrobium*, 118); London, British Library, Royal 12.B.XXII, f. 39r (Dutton, *The Glosae super Platonem of Bernard of Chartres*, 276, Appendix 3.6); and Vienna, Österreichische Nationalbibliothek, 278, f. 68 (ibid., 295, Appendix 3.14–15).

connects this passage to the standard Peripatetic division,[121] the author of *the Glosae Colonienses* turns instead to Calcidius and parses the division of contemplation into theology, physics, and logic.[122] As Irène Caiazzo observes,[123] the commentator's version of the Calcidian division is very close to Bernard's—close enough in fact to suggest (direct?) dependence; e.g., logic is here defined as the *ordinabilis dispositio temporum*.[124] The oddity of this definition seems to have necessitated some special pleading on the part of the commentator, who parenthetically notes that "they have taken (*acceperunt*) logic very strictly" (the anonymous *acceperunt* further supports dependence on an external source).[125] Since, however, the *Glosae Colonienses* directly attributes this division to Calcidius, whereas Bernard gave no indication of his source, the author of the *Glosae Colonienses* either had both Calcidius and Bernard before him, or knew the division from a version of Bernard's gloss that correctly identified its source.

Since Bernard's presentation of the Stoic tripartition offers no subdivisions and his version of the Peripatetic bipartition omits mathematics, the question arises: does music have any substantial role in Bernard's commentary? First, its presence as part of the quadrivial subdivision of physics (as in Isidore) seems to be assumed as a matter of course. When discussing the division of the world soul (a subject explicitly included under *physica* in the accessus), Bernard comments:[126]

> Et per haec omnia scientia quadruuii intelligitur, in quo est perfectio scientiae: per numeros, arithmetica; per hoc quod lineares superficiales cubici sunt numeri, geometria; per consonantias proportionaliter notatas, musica et astronomia, in qua de musico concentu sperarum agitur.

> And throughout this passage understand the knowledge of the quadrivium, in which consists the perfection of knowledge: through numbers, understand arithmetic; through the fact that there are linear, square, and cubic numbers, understand geometry; through the consonances that are proportionally marked out, understand music as well

[121] *Glos. sup. Macr.*, comment. ad 1.1.4: NATVRAM OMNIVM RERVM ET ACTVVM. Commendat Platonem, dicendo ipsum praecellentem aliis in omni philosophiae specie qua philosophi utuntur, id est in practica et theorica quae in suas species sic diuiduntur. Practica, ut diximus, in tres species: ethicam, economicam, politicam. Similiter theorica in tres, quas supra assignauimus. Dicit ergo Platonem inspicere NATVRAM OMNIVM RERVM, quantum ad theoricam . . . ET ACTVVM, quantum ad practicam.

[122] *Glos. Colonienses sup. Macr.*, comment. ad 1.1.4 (169.9–170.1): Calcidius sic dividit philosophiam. Philosophia dividitur in contemplationem et actionem. Contemplatio III habet partes: theologiam, phisicam, loicam [*sic*].

[123] Caiazzo, *Glosae Colonienses super Macrobium*, 117–118.

[124] *Glos. Colonienses sup. Macr.*, comment. ad 1.1.4 (170.1–3): Theologia est scientia de divinis, ut de togaton, de mente et anima; phisica de corporeis essentiis tam divinis quam caducis; loica ordinabilis dispositio temporum.

[125] *Glos. Colonienses sup. Macr.*, comment. ad 1.1.4 (170.3–4): stricte multum acceperunt loicam.

[126] *Bernardi Glos. sup. Tim.* 5.143–147.

as astronomy, which deals with the musical harmony of the celestial spheres.[127]

Musica, for Bernard, is subsumed within *physica*, though it does not receive explicit attention per se (no further subdivision, no independent definitions, etc.). Although Bernard may not be as generous in his attention to music as were later authors in the commentary tradition, he nonetheless laid the important groundwork for these later developments by codifying mathematics, the concept of proportion in particular, as the primary epistemological ground for *physica* in the context of Timaean cosmology.[128] In his comments on the concluding sentence of Calcidius's translation (53c), Bernard asserts that the arithmetic, geometric, and harmonic proportions are the "steps of philosophy" *gradus philosophiae*.[129] In Calcidius's conclusion, however, these "steps" are not the proportions but the disciplines themselves—geometry, music, arithmetic, and astronomy.[130] Thus, in Bernard's slight but significant modification, it is the explanatory power of proportion, whose highest *gradus* is the *harmonica proportio*, that allows us to unravel the secrets of the visible world and its invisible bonds.

William of Conches and the Proportion of Things

A similar emphasis on *proportio* opens William of Conches's *Glosae super Platonem*. After setting out a lightly modified Boethian *divisio philosophiae*, William points out that "something of all these parts of philosophy is contained [in the *Timaeus*]." The entirety of the quadrivium, however, is summed as follows: "Where [Plato discusses] number and proportion, there [he deals with] mathematics."[131] *Musica*, of course, was the mathematical science best suited for this sort of work, insofar as

127 I quote this passage in full partly because neither Dutton's original punctuation (Dutton, *The Glosae super Platonem of Bernard of Chartres*, 178–179) nor Schrimpf's "corrected" punctuation (Gangolf Schrimpf, "Bernhard von Chartres, die Rezeption des 'Timaios' und die neue Sicht der Natur," in *Aufbruch—Wandel—Erneuerung: Beiträge zur "Renaissance" des 12. Jahrhunderts*, ed. Georg Wieland [Stuttgart-Bad Cannstatt: Frommann-Holzboog, 1995], 207), later adopted by Speer, "*Scientia quadrubii*," 109, is correct, and the misunderstanding obscures the proper division of the quadrivial sciences.

128 Speer, "Discovery of Nature," 149–150.

129 *Bernardi Glos. sup. Tim.* 8.444–448: DEMONSTRARI CONVENIT NOVO GENERE, scilicet per quasdam proportiones arithmeticas, geometricas, armonicas, qui sunt gradus philosophiae.

130 *In Tim.* 355 (346.5–6): a pueris aetas illa ueluti principiis altioris doctrinae et tamquam gradibus imbuebatur: geometrica musica arithmetica astronomia.

131 *Guillelmi Glos. sup. Tim.* 6.1–6: De omnibus igitur partibus philosophiae aliquid in hoc opere continetur: de practica in recapitulatione positiuae iustitiae, de theologia ubi de efficiente et formali et finali causa mundi et de anima loquitur. Vbi uero de numeris et proportionibus, de mathematica; ubi uero de quatuor elementis et creatione animalium et de primordiali materia, de phisica.

it alone properly concerned *multitudo relata*. And among the quadrivial sciences, only music received multiple levels of subdivision within his broad *divisio scientiae*.

Throughout his works, William maintains a remarkably consistent division that attests, along with Hugh of St. Victor, to the twelfth-century rehabilitation of the Boethian perspective (though William does not directly cite Boethius and may have known the division as transmitted by Isidore).[132] William, however, subsumes Boethius's division within an expanded *divisio scientiae*, which includes the Peripatetic bipartition as one of two branches (see figure 2.4). *Scientia* has two species, *sapientia* and *eloquentia*. Although the broad *sapientia–eloquentia* division may have originally been inspired by Cicero's *De inventione* (1.1.1),[133] its twelfth-century proliferation was more indebted to Martianus's allegorized marriage of Mercury and Philology. In the prologue to his *Philosophia*, William directly connects this Ciceronian passage to the marriage of Mercury and Philology. To divorce *eloquentia* and *sapientia*, he claims, "is tantamount to nullifying the marriage of Mercury and Philology, sought with such great effort by Virtue and Apollo and approved by the full assembly of the gods."[134] Eloquence, which is propaedeutic to wisdom, encompasses the trivium (*grammatica, dialectica, rethorica*), and although it is a branch of knowledge, it is not a branch of philosophy; only wisdom is identical with philosophy, "the true comprehension of visible and invisible being,"[135] which is coextensive with Boethius's Peripatetic bipartition.

In his *Accessus ad Platonem*, William divides music into the Boethian tripartite scheme discussed above, but reorders it without further comment: *instrumentalis, mundana, humana* (an ordering attested also in the diagram of William's division in BL, Add. 22815, f. 53v). *Instrumentalis* further divides into the Cassiodorian (and Isidorian) tripartition: *melica, metrica*, and *rithmica*, of which the first divides finally into *diatonica, enarmonica*, and *cromatica* (the three melodic genera discussed in Boethius's *De institutione musica*). Although here William closely adheres to Boethius's order of the theoretical sciences (*theologia, mathematica*, and *physica*), when he discusses the sciences from the standpoint of an epistemological ascent (i.e., the *ordo philosophiae*), he strikingly reverses the order of mathematics and

[132] Dyer, "The Place of *Musica* in Medieval Classifications of Knowledge," 20 inexplicably claims that "[William's] classification is based on a pedagogical model ('ordo vero discendi') that corresponds to the Platonic-Stoic scheme: dialectic, ethics, and physics."

[133] *Inv.* 1.1.1: eloquentiam sine sapientia multum obesse, sapientiam sine eloquentia parum prodesse. For its employ as a division of philosophy, see the tenth-century diagrammatic colophon in Leiden, Bibliotheek der Rijksuniversiteit, Voss. Lat. Q. 33, fol. 56r; on which see Michael Evans, "The *Ysagoge in Theologiam* and the Commentaries Attributed to Bernard Silvestris," *Journal of the Warburg and Courtauld Institutes* 54 (1991), 8.

[134] *Phil.* 1.prol.1: Nam idque agere est Mercurii et Philologiae coniugium tanta cura Virtutis et Apollinis quaesitum, omni conventu deorum approbatum, solvere.

[135] *Glos. sup. Boet.* 1.pr1.281–284: Sapientia et philosophia idem sunt. Vnde potest dici quod eloquentia nec aliqua pars eius de philosophia est. *Glos. sup. Macr.*, accessus: Sapientia et philosophia idem sunt. Unde potest videri quod nec eloquentia nec aliqua eius pars de philosophia est. *Guillelmi Glos. sup. Tim.* 5.1–2: Philosophia igitur est eorum quae sunt et non uidentur et eorum quae sunt et uidentur uera comprehensio. Cf. *Phil.* 1.1 (43B).

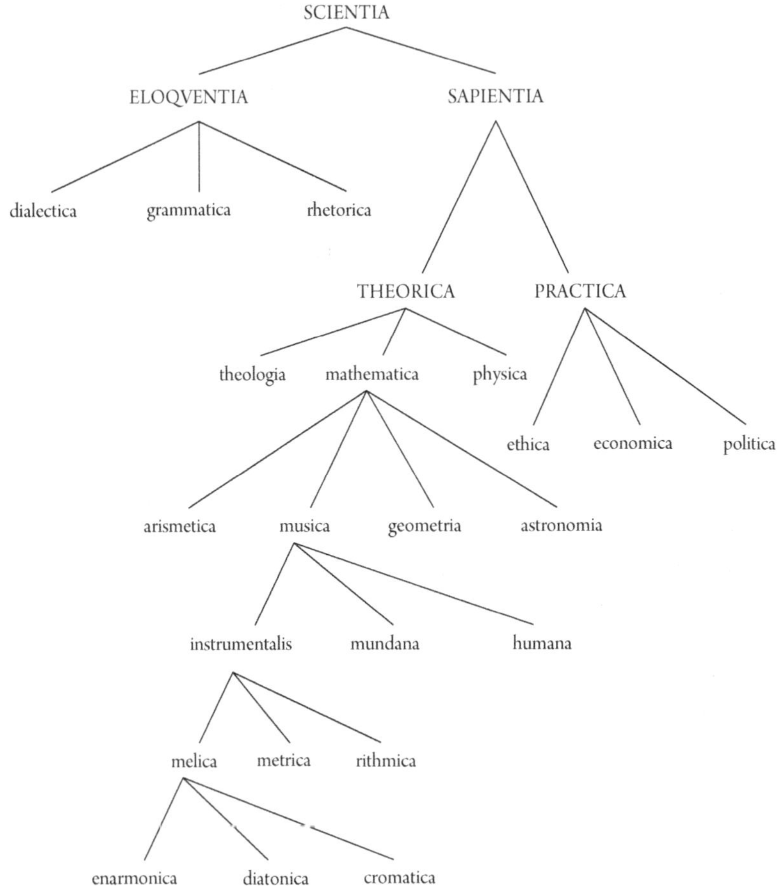

Figure 2.4 Division of *scientia* according to William of Conches.

physics—again without any further comment.[136] This subtle reordering accords well with William's synthesis of the Peripatetic and Stoic division found in the *Glosae super Macrobium*. Encountering Macrobius's tripartition at the end of the *Commentarii in Somnium Scipionis*, William quickly brings the Stoic tripartition into the Peripatetic fold. Macrobius's *moralis* is equated with ethics (i.e., *practica*) and *rationalis* is equated with *omnis theorica*. *Naturalis*, however, encompasses the quadrivium.[137] The apparent duplication of the quadrivium (under both *naturalis* and *rationalis*) must not obscure the larger point: the mathematical, quadrivial sciences serve the study of nature throughout William's oeuvre, despite their coordinate

[136] *Glos. sup. Boet.* 1.pr1.343–356: Notandum quod dicit ad hoc gradus illos esse ut ab inferiori ad superius ascendatur, non de superiori descendatur ad inferius, quia de practica ascendendum est ad theoricam. . . . Deinde cum istis [sc. moribus] est perfecte exercitatus, debet transire ad contemplationem eorum quae sunt circa corpora, per mathematicam et phisicam, usque ad caelestia; deinde ad contemplationem incorporeorum usque ad creatorem per theologicam. Et hic est ordo philosophiae.

[137] *Glos. sup. Macr.*, comment. ad 2.17.15: MORALIS, ethica. NATVRALIS, sub ista specie continetur totum quadriuium. RATIONALIS, haec tertia species continet omnem theoricam.

presentation in his *divisio philosophiae*. In particular, the harmonic language of proportion, as in Bernard of Chartres, holds considerable explanatory value, for as William defines it, proportion is not solely the property of numbers—it is the "relationship of thing to thing" (*habitudo rei ad rem*).[138]

William's engagement with Boethius and the broader music-theoretical tradition went well beyond the occasional glance to the *De institutione musica* to help illuminate the more technical music-theoretical moments in Macrobius or to explain the propagation of the *uox* in Priscian. Most striking for historians of music theory is William's knowledge of the work of Guido of Arezzo. William's musical authorities in his *Glosae super Macrobium* include both the *musica Boethii* and the *musica Guidonis*, which he cites on three points:

1. "Guidonian" letter notation:

   Nam in primis instrumentis non erant nisi octo chordae et resonabat prima usque ad octauam ⟨diapason⟩. Vnde erat altior et magis in altum extendebatur diapason quam ceterae consonantiae. Inde Guido tali modo composuit suam musicam quod plus quam octo uoces uoluit contineri in aliqua consonantia et illas in solo diapason, et a prima uoce conscripsit unam litteram, 'a' scilicet, et ab octaua aliam 'a'.

   For the first instruments had only eight strings and the first to the eighth sounded the diapason. Whence the eighth was higher [than the rest] and the diapason extended higher than the other consonances. Then Guido composed his music in a way that required more than eight *uoces* to be included within a given consonance, more even then those within a single diapason. The first *uox* he wrote as one letter, namely A, and the eighth, another a.[139]
2. the identification of consonances larger than the octave as the replication of consonances rather than consonances *simpliciter*:

   Postea super illas octo uoces nulla erat consonantia, sed semper replicatio consonantiarum. . . . QVAE DICITVR DIAPASON KAI DIAPENTE. "Kai" in Graeco "et" dicitur in Latino. Vnde "diapason et diapente." Et numeratur pro una sola consonantia secundum Musicam Boetii, non secundum Musicam Guidonis, quia Guido non uolebat esse simpliciter consonantias, sed replicationes.

   After these eight *uoces* there were no consonances, but always the replication of consonances. . . . WHICH IS CALLED THE DIAPASON KAI DIAPENTE. "Kai" in Greek means "and" in Latin, so [the phrase means] "an octave and a fifth." This counts

[138] *Guillelmi Glos. sup. Tim.* 82.1.

[139] *Glos. sup. Macr.*, comment. ad 2.1.17. Cf. Joseph Smits van Waesberghe, ed., *Guidonis Aretini Micrologus* ([Rome]: American Institute of Musicology, 1955), 2.4–5 (93–94): Sequuntur septem alphabeti litterae graves ideoque maioribus litteris insignitae hoc modo: .A.B.C.D.E.F.G. Post has eaedem septem litterae acutae repetuntur, sed minoribus litteris describuntur. Cf. ibid., 5.2–8 (107): Diapason autem est in qua diatessaron et diapente iunguntur; cum enim ab .A. in .D. sit diatessaron, et ab eadem .D. in .a. acutam sit diapente, ab .A. in alteram .a. diapason existit. . . . Nam sicut finitis septem diebus eosdem repetimus, ut semper primum et octavum eundem dicamus, ita primas et octavas semper voces easdem figuramus et dicimus. Cf. *Glos. Colonienses sup. Macr.*, comment. ad 2.1.3 (254.10–12): VII sunt discrimina vocum simplicium, que signabantur per alfabetum in monocordo, quarum duae semper unam consonantiam faciunt.

as only one consonance according to the *Musica* of Boethius, but not according to the *Musica* of Guido, because Guido did not want [such consonances] to be consonances *simpliciter*, but rather replications [of consonances].[140]

3. the parallels between grammatical units (letters, syllables, and words) and musical units:

   QVID IN SONIS PRO LITTERA. In musica Boethii non habemus aliquod pro nomine integro, uel pro syllaba, uel pro littera. In musica tamen Guidonis pro integro nomine habetur consonantia, pro syllaba sonus, pro littera ptongus, id est imperfectus sonus.

   WHAT AMONG SOUNDS [IS EQUIVALENT] TO THE LETTER. The *Musica* of Boethius does not give us a musical equivalency for the integral name, the syllable, or the letter. The *Musica* of Guido, however, holds that the consonance is equivalent to the integral name, a sound to a syllable, and a musical note to the letter.[141]

This last citation is representative of William's rather free and loose use of Guido. William ascribes to Guido the following grammatical parallels: *littera–phthongus, syllaba–sonus, nomen–consonantia*. These do not, however, match Guido's own parallels as given in the fifteenth chapter of the *Micrologus*.[142] The misrepresentation may stem from the fact that William has attempted to bring Guido in line with the terms set by Macrobius, who says that it is none of his business to detail *quid in sonis pro littera, quid pro syllaba, quid pro integro nomine accipiatur*.[143] Guido's discussion does not easily map onto Macrobius's terms, for Guido says nothing of

140 *Glos. sup. Macr.*, comment. ad 2.1.17–18. Guido in fact does not take up consonances beyond the octave. He does, however, several times stress that anything beyond the *septem discrimina vocum* (*Aeneid.* 6.646) is a matter of repetition, not addition: quia etsi plures fiant, non est aliarum adiectio sed earundum renovatio et repetitio (Waesberghe, *Guidonis Aretini Micrologus*, 5.17–19 [112]). Clearly, however, this position was, at some point, attributed to Guido. The attestation in William of Conches is the earliest that I know; later examples include Amerus's *Practica artis musicae* (1271): Non autem dico perfectio cantus quod non possit ultra octavam vel duplam cantari, sed quia infra octavam possunt fieri omnes symphonie, scilicet: dyatessaron, dyapente et dyapason, et ultra octavam nulla est symphonia sed replicatio symphoniarum secundum musicam Guidonis, secundum autem musicam Boecii replicationes symphonie sunt (Cesarino Ruini, ed., *Ameri Practica artis musice* [Neuhausen-Stuttgart: American Institute of Musicology, 1977], 20.13 [83–84]); and Engelbertus Admontensis, *De musica* 2.13: Est enim tripla proportio istarum vocum ad invicem; videlicet sicut est a C.fa.ut usque ad g.sol.re.ut supremum, quam Guido dicit non esse consonantiam, cum transcendat unum diapason: sed dicit illas voces ultra diapason esse solas replicationes inferiorum (Martin Gerbert, *Scriptores ecclesiastici de musica* [St. Blaise, 1784], 2.308–309).

141 *Glos. sup. Macr.*, comment. ad 2.4.11.

142 Waesberghe, *Guidonis Aretini Micrologus*, 15.2–5 (162–163): Igitur quemadmodum in metris sunt litterae et syllabae, partes et pedes ac versus, ita in harmonia sunt phtongi, id est soni, quorum unus, duo vel tres aptantur in syllabas; ipsaeque solae vel duplicatae neumam, id est partem constituunt cantilenae; et pars una vel plures distinctionem faciunt, id est congruum respirationis locum. See Karen Desmond, "*Sicut in grammatica*: Analogical Discourse in Chapter 15 of Guido's *Micrologus*," *Journal of Musicology* 16 (1998), 467–493.

143 *In Som. Scip.* 2.4.11 (109.5–9): nam netas et hypatas aliarumque fidium uocabula percurrere et tonorum uel limmatum minuta subtilia et quid in sonis pro littera, quid pro syllaba, quid pro integro nomine accipiatur adserere ostentantis est, non docentis.

the *nomen* and employs the term *syllaba* in both a grammatical and musical sense. This latter is a melodic gesture composed of one, two, or three *phthongi, id est soni*, and that, perhaps, is the origin of William's identification of *sonus* with *syllaba*.

The most striking example of Guidonian theory, however, occurs without any direct reference to Guido: the systematic use of the solmization syllables. As Stefano Mengozzi has noted in his recent study of the Guidonian hexachord in Medieval and Renaissance music theory, "Until the mid-thirteenth century, the music masters displayed no interest in developing a hexachordal terminology, much less in organizing the six syllables into a fully fledged system."[144] William's *Glosae super Macrobium* and Bernard's *Commentum in Martianum*, however, suggest that the syllables were already a fully systematized pedagogical standard by the early twelfth century. The context of their remarks—the etymology of *diatessaron* (fourth), *diapente* (fifth), and *diapason* (octave)—is entirely conventional, but their explanations of the etymologies are, to my knowledge, without precedent:

Glos. super Macr., comment. ad 2.1.15–17: Vnde [sc. diatessaron] dicitur quasi 'de quatuor' quia continet quatuor uoces coniunctas, has scilicet ut re mi fa.

Whence [the diatessaron] means "from four" because it contains four conjunct pitches, namely these: *ut re mi fa*.

Ideo [sc. diapente] ergo 'de quinque' dicitur quia efficitur in quinque uocibus, quae sunt hae ut re mi fa sol.

Thus [the diapente] means "from five" because it is produced in five pitches, which are these: *ut re mi fa sol*

Et dicitur diapason quasi 'de octo' uel 'de omnibus' quia continet infra se octo uoces, has scilicet: ut re mi fa sol la-re mi fa.[a]

And the diapente means "from eight" or "from all" because it contains within it eight pitches, namely these: *ut re mi fa sol la-re mi fa*.

[a] *post* fa *exp.* sol Bern, Burgerbibl. 266, f. 14v. København, Kgl. Bibliotek, Gl. Kgl. S. 1910 4°, f. 105r *sic distinguit*: ut.re.mi.fa.sol.lare.mi.fa

Comm. in Mart. 8.277–284: Dicitur autem diatessaron, id est 'de quatuor' quia in quarta corda reperitur, veluti ut–fa, re–sol.

This is called a diatessaron, meaning "from four" because it is found on the fourth string, e.g., *ut* to *fa, re* to *sol.*

Dicitur autem diapente, id est 'de quinque' quia in quinta corda invenitur, veluti re–la vel ut–sol.

This is called a diapente, meaning "from five" because it is discovered on the fifth string, e.g., *re* to *la, ut* to *sol.*

Et dicitur diapason 'de octo' quia in octava corda occurrit, veluti si c-fa-ut[a] ascendas ad c-sol- fa-ut.[b]

And the diapason means "from eight" because it occurs at the eighth string, e.g., if you ascend from C-*fa-ut* to C *sol-fa-ut*.

[a] cefaut *cod.*, re-fa-ut *scripsit Westra*
[b] cesolfaut *cod.*, re-fa-ut *scripsit Westra*

[144] Stefano Mengozzi, *The Renaissance Reform of Medieval Music Theory: Guido of Arezzo between Myth and History* (Cambridge: Cambridge University Press, 2010), 45.

These two texts present slightly different stages in the reception and expansion of the basic Guidonian hexachord. William's usage presupposes at least a double hexachord system, with *ut* transposed to both C and G. When explaining the primary musical consonances, William enumerates their steps with the solmization syllables: the diatessaron (*'de quatuor' uocibus*) and diapente (*'de quinque' uocibus*) are easily explained within a single hexachord: *ut–fa* and *ut–sol* respectively. The diapason (*'de octo' uocibus*), however, requires mutation, and William's explanation of the eight *uoces* in the octave accordingly uses two hexachords; the diapason is *ut re mi fa sol la-re mi fa*. The point of mutation from one hexachord to the next is indicated by the doubled syllable *la-re*. The Martianus commentary ascribed to Bernard Silvestris—in a passage clearly related to William's own discussion—utilizes a full tri-hexachordal system. The diapason, the commentator explains, is the ascent from C-*fa-ut* to C-*sol-fa-ut*. The appearance of the *littera* + *uox* nomenclature here is striking, and it is surprisingly early testimony (ca. 1150 at the latest) to a full tri-hexachordal nomenclature. Even more telling is the ease with which the syllables are bandied about within both commentaries. Clearly, neither commentator felt a need to explain the meaning of the syllables to their readers and simply assumed that readers would be well aware how (in William's version, for instance) nine syllables could explain *de octo*.

William's knowledge of Boethius may also have extended to the point of writing a commentary on the work. Macrobius, at the close of his self-described *tractatus de musica* (*In Som. Scip.* 2.1–4), explicitly excuses himself from a longer discussion of matters musical by claiming that to do so would be more ostentation than edification, and he rounds out his musical discussion with a *praeteritio*, listing the technicalities of which he will not speak.[145] William of Conches, in his commentary on Macrobius, follows suit.[146] But William, in his own *praeteritio*, does not excuse himself entirely, but says that he will leave the discussion of such matters for a more appropriate context, a commentary on Boethius's *De institutione musica*: "we will say enough about this in [a commentary on Boethius's] *Musica*."[147]

If William ever completed such a commentary, it has not yet been found or identified. Nonetheless, there does exist a mid-twelfth-century lemmatized commentary on Boethius's *De institutione musica* that has many suggestive connections

[145] *In Som. Scip.* 2.4.10–12 (109.3–12): ad inluminandam ut aestimo obscuritatem verborum Ciceronis de musica tractatus succinctus a nobis qua licuit brevitate sufficiet. nam netas et hypatas aliarumque fidium vocabula percurrere et tonorum vel limmatum minuta subtilia, et quid in sonis pro littera, quid pro syllaba, quid pro integro nomine accipiatur adserere ostentantis est, non docentis.

[146] *Glos. sup. Macr.*, comment. ad 1.4.11: Vere iste tractatus de musica habitus sufficit. Nam multa sunt in musica quae ad hunc tractatum non pertinent.

[147] *Glos. sup. Macr.*, comment. ad 1.4.11: ALIARVMQVE FIDIVM, quarum quaedam mese uocantur, quaedam hyperboleos. Nam apud antiquos in instrumento erat tetrachordum, fides cuius tetrachordi uocabantur hypatae, id est principales fides; fides secundi tetrachordi mesae, quasi mediae, aliae scilicet altiores netae, id est excellentes dicebantur; ultimae hyperboleae, id est supra excellentes. Similiter

to the thought of William of Conches, one in which Macrobius and Calcidius predominate and the approach is overtly "philosophical," with no (direct) concern for contemporaneous practice—an anonymous commentary copied in a manuscript from St. Florian around the turn of the fourteenth century. Max Haas, who first brought the St. Florian commentary to light, offered a single footnote's argument that the commentary was perhaps from the twelfth century, but its subsequent editor, Alexander Rausch, claimed, without any clear line of argumentation, that the text arose (hypothetically, he cautions) from the first half of the thirteenth century.[148] Other scholars have seemed content to split the difference and place it somewhere around the turn of the thirteenth century.[149] The accessus format employed by the commentator, however, seems to affiliate the commentary with a specifically twelfth-century tradition and thus strengthens Haas's argument for a twelfth-century origin against Rausch's later dating. The commentator begins by dutifully listing the ten *didascalica* to be treated: "First we must see what music is, what its genus is, its material, its function, its parts, its species, its instrument, its practitioner, why it is so named, and in what order it should be taught and learned."[150] This is not a customary thirteenth-century list, when the scheme was often reorganized to align with the four Aristotelian causes (*causa materialis*, *efficiens*, *formalis*, and *finalis*), but it exactly accords with a mid-twelfth-century accessus format.[151] This elaborate accessus format seems to have developed during the second quarter of the twelfth century in the writings of William of Conches, Petrus Helias, Thierry of Chartres, and Gundissalinus, and while there is often overlap between twelfth-and thirteenth-century accessus structures, it would have been odd for a thirteenth-century commentator

etiam singulis fidibus tetrachordarum imposita sunt uocabula in musica, quod quaedam uocantur hypatae, quaedam parhypatae, de quibus satis dicemus in Musica.

148 Max Haas, "Studien zur mittelalterlichen Musiklehre I: Eine Übersicht über die Musiklehre im Kontext der Philosophie des 13. und frühen 14. Jahrhunderts," in *Aktuelle Fragen der musikbezogenen Mittelalterforschung: Texte zu einem Basler Kolloquiumdes Jahres 1975*, ed. Hans Oesch and Wulf Arlt (Winterthur: Amadeus, 1982), 338: "ihre Entstehung dürfte ins 12. Jahrhundert anzusetzen sein." Rausch, "Der Boethius-Kommentar," 11–12: "Demnach läßt sich die Entstehung des Kommentars hypothetisch auf die erste Hälfte des 13. Jahrhunderts ansetzen."

149 Hochadel, *Commentum Oxoniense in musicam Boethii: Eine Quelle zur Musiktheorie an der spätmittelalterlichen Universität*, 30: "dem vermutlich um die Wende zum 13. Jahrhundert entstandenen Kommentar im Codex St. Florian. . . ."

150 *In inst. mus.* 19: ⟨P⟩rimo uidendum est, quid sit musica, quod genus est, quae materia, quod officium, quae partes, quae species, quod instrumentum, quis artifex, quare sic dicatur, quo ordine docenda sit et discenda.

151 Consider, for instance, William of Conches's accessus to his second, midcentury redaction of the *Glosulae super Priscianum*, which treats the following: quid sit ars ipsa, quod nomen ipsius, quae causa nominis, quod genus, quod officium, quis finis, quae materia, quae partes, quod instrumentum, quis artifex, quis auctor [*scripsi*, doctor *cod.*], quae auctoris intentio (Paris, Bibliothèque nationale, lat. 15130, 1ra). Petrus Helias's *Summa super Priscianum*, also midcentury and largely based on William's first redaction, offers an even stronger parallel to the St. Florian commentary: Ad maiorem artis gramatice cognitionem primo videndum est quid sit gramatica, quod genus eius, que materia, quod

to have employed what would have been by then a quite recherché list of ten (or eleven) *didascalica*.[152]

The St. Florian commentary's twelfth-century sympathies run deeper than mere structural parallels. Consider the second sentence of the accessus, his definition of music that fulfills the first promised *didascalicon*:[153]

> Musica igitur est scientia multitudinis relate virtutes proportionum considerans ad concordias rerum, quia sicut arithmetica est scientia multitudinis per se, ita musica est scientia multitudinis relate, et sicut arithmetica virtutes numerorum considerat, sic musica virtutes proportionum, et sicut arithmetica virtutes numerorum ad declarationem nature rerum, sic ista ad declarationem concordiarum.
>
> Music therefore is the science of related multitudes that considers the value of proportions for the concordance of things (*rerum*). For just as arithmetic is the science of multitudes per se, so music is the science of multitudes in relation to each other; just as arithmetic considers the value of numbers, so music [considers] the value of ratios; just as arithmetic [considers] the value of numbers to explain the nature of things, so music [considers the value of numbers] to explain the nature of concordances.

The commentator immediately underscores and emphasizes the broad sweep of his definition, reiterating the importance of the *concordia rerum* within the scope of *musica*: "Rightly do I say 'of things,' because it must not be thought that music considers only the concordance of sounds, but also [the concordance] of the four elements, the four seasons, and the motions of the planets (both among themselves and with the firmament) as well as their effects."[154] This broad-scope

officium, quis finis, que partes, que species, quod instrumentum, quis artifex, quare gramatica dicatur, quo ordine etiam docenda sit et discenda (Leo A. Reilly, ed., *Petrus Helias, Summa super Priscianum* [Toronto: Pontifical Institute of Mediaeval Studies, 1993], 61.2–5). In fact, the St. Florian accessus is actually closer in structure to Petrus Helias's than his opening list may suggest, for although St. Florian omits *quis finis* in his initial enumeration of the *didascalica*, he nonetheless sneaks it into the accessus at its proper place, that is, between *officium* and *partes* (*In inst. mus.* 22: Officium est congruus actus artificis secundum artem, id est, virtutes proportionum contemplati. Finis est, ut propter quod fit officium, id est, invenisse concordias rerum. Partes artis sunt ea . . .).

[152] See Nikolaus M. Häring, "Thierry of Chartres and Dominicus Gundissalinus," *Mediaeval Studies* 26 (1964), 271–286; Richard W. Hunt, "The Introductions to the 'artes' in the Twelfth Century," in *The History of Grammar in the Middle Ages: Collected Papers*, ed. G. L. Bursill-Hall (Amsterdam: John Benjamins, 1980), 117–144; Alexander Fidora, *Die Wissenschaftstheorie des Dominicus Gundissalinus: Voraussetzungen und Konsequenzen des zweiten Anfangs der aristotelischen Philosophie im 12. Jahrhundert* (Berlin: Akademie Verlag, 2003), 67–72.

[153] *In inst. mus.* 19.

[154] *In inst. mus.* 19: bene dico 'rerum,' quia non est intelligendum quod musica tantum consideret sonorum concordias, sed etiam quatuor elementorum et quatuor temporum et planetarum motuum, tum inter se tum ad firmamentum, et eorundem effectuum.

definition echoes the similarly material and physically grounded definitions of music employed elsewhere in twelfth-century accounts of *musica*.[155]

Bernard Silvestris and the elevation of *musica humana*

The division of the sciences in Bernard Silvestris's *Commentum in Martianum*[156] follows William in the Boethian bipartite division. *Scientia*, the "knowledge of all things comprehensible" (*agnitio rerum comprehensibilium*) is a genus with four species: *sapientia, eloquentia, poesis*, and *mecania*.[157] The first two map William's Boethian *divisio*, but with explicit and epistemologically motivated discrepancies, already hinted at (but not fleshed out) in William's works. Bernard enumerates the order of the theoretical sciences differently than did Boethius, for whom (as already noted) mathematics held the medial position between theology and physics. Bernard, however, rates theology and physics as theoretical sciences "higher" than mathematics. His rationale synthesizes Boethius's ontological and epistemological approaches: the three theoretical sciences, from an ontological standpoint, descend from theology (invisible substances) through physics (invisible causes of the visible world) to mathematics (visible forms of the visible world); from an epistemological standpoint (deemed by Bernard the *ordo discendi*), human knowledge must ascend from the visible to the invisible. Bernard buttresses this reordering with the language of Boethius's *De institutione arithmetica*, reminding us that the mathematical sciences of the quadrivium both lead the mind from sense perception to "the greater certainties of understanding"—by which (according to Bernard) Boethius intends theology—and reilluminate the eye of the mind.[158] Thus all theoretical knowledge has as its starting point the *sapientia* (Philologia) of the quadrivium, the bride of *eloquentia* (Mercurius). Martianus and Boethius are brought into harmony.

155 Recall, for instance, the *Tractatus quidem de philosophia: musica* is the *scientia perpendendi proportiones ad cognitionem concordie et discordie rerum*; or William of Conches's definition of *proportio*: the *habitudo rei ad rem*.

156 *Comm. in Mart.* 3.889–1018. Bernard's authorship of the commentary has been disputed. See Stephen Gersh, "(Pseudo?-) Bernard Silvestris and the Revival of Neo-Platonic Virgilian Exegesis," in *Sophiēs maiētores: Chercheurs de sagesse; Hommage à J. Pépin*, ed. Marie-Odile Goulet-Gazé, Goulven Madec, and Denis O'Brien (Paris: Institut d'Études augustiniennes, 1992), 573–593; Michael Evans, "The *Ysagoge in theologiam*"; Julian Ward Jones, "The So-Called Silvestris Commentary on the *Aeneid* and Two Other Interpretations," *Speculum* 64 (1989), 835–848; E. R. Smits, "New Evidence for the Authorship of the Commentary on the First Six Books of Virgil's *Aeneid* Commonly Attributed to Bernardus Silvestris," in *Non nova, sed nove: Mélanges de civilisation médiévale dédiés à Willem Noomen*, ed. Martin Gosman and Jaap Van Os (Groningen, 1984), 239–246. Haijo Westra and I will take up this question again in our jointly edited revised edition of the commentary for CCCM.

157 See the diagram reproduced in Westra, *The Comm. on Martianus Capella*, 81.

158 *Comm. in Mart.* 1.14–23; cf. Wetherbee, *Platonism and Poetry*, 112–113.

Although by the twelfth century the interest in Martianus's technical treatises on the arts (i.e., books three through nine) had waned, this narrowed focus nevertheless did not dissuade commentators from reading music theory into the text. If anything, it gave them further license to exploit music-theoretical arguments in overtly philosophical and cosmological contexts. Far from being a sequestered, technical discourse relegated to the end of an exhausting nine books, music theory was an ever-present theme, a counterpoint, as it were, to Martianus's mythological text. Bernard, in this way, harmonizes his own music-theoretical interpolations with his larger interpretive aims. This twelfth-century reader interprets Martianus's work as a Virgilian and Boethian ascent *ad summum bonum*. Through different narrative trajectories, these three authors nevertheless express one and the same transcendental quest for the realm of true philosophy.[159] And the musical implications of this ascent are nowhere better displayed than in Bernard's extensive gloss on Martianus's opening *metrum* (1.1 [1.4–2.4]: *Tu quem psallentem*).

This cosmic hymn invokes Hymenaeus as the sacred union of the gods, one who binds together the warring elements with secret chains, nurtures discordant alliances, unites body and soul, reconciles the sexes, and fosters the faith of love. Bernard, like modern scholars,[160] found this song of cosmic harmony and love concordant with meters from Boethius's *Consolatio philosophiae* (2.m8: *Quod mundus stabili fide*, and 3.m9: *O qui perpetua mundum*). But he also noted another Boethian resonance, that other famous discussion of harmony—the *De institutione musica*. His comments on the invocation to Hymenaeus begin thus:[161]

> Himeneus vero et large sumitur pro qualibet concordia et stricte pro nupciis. Unde legis quia illius dei officium est in nuptiis sedes distribuere, quia concordie est unicuique rei locum in rerum coniunctione dare. Himeneus itaque, qui preest nuptiis, sit concordia, causa tocius coniunctionis. Namque Himeneus confederationis Grece interpretatio est. Hec autem universalis musica plures habet efficatias, quas huius dei officia intelligimus, quasque versus isti exprimunt. . . . Dividitur autem musica in mundanam et humanam et instrumentalem. Mundana quidem est in elementis, in temporibus, in astris; humana in humoribus corporis, in potenciis anime, in coniunctione anime et corporis. Instrumentalis autem est in metris, in rithmis, in melis. Tria ergo sunt Himinei [sic] officia.

159 *Comm. in Mart.* 2.114–9: Auctoris [sc. Martiani] vero imitatio est, quia Maronem emulatur. Sicut enim apud illum ducitur Eneas per inferos comite Sibilla usque ad Anchisem, ita et hic Mercurius per mundi regione Virtute comite ad Iovem. Ita quoque et in libro De Consolatione scandit Boetius per falsa bona ad summum bonum duce Philosophia. Que quidem tres figure fere idem exprimunt.

160 *Comm. in Mart.* 3.23–34, 362–3. Cf. Christopher J. McDonough, "The Verse of Martianus Capella: Text, Translation, and Commentary on the Poetry in Books 1–5" (PhD diss., University of Toronto, 1968), 210–211; Stock, *Myth and Science in the Twelfth Century: A Study of Bernard Silvester*, 33.

161 *Comm. in Mart.* 3.16–40.

> Hymenaeus is construed both broadly as any sort of concord and narrowly as marriage. Whence you read that it is the function of this god to set out the foundations in marriage, as it is concord's job to give each and every thing a place in the union of things. Hence let Hymenaeus, who presides over marriages, be concord, the cause of every union. For in Greek, Hymenaeus means "confederation." This universal music is influential in many aspects, which we understand as the functions of this god and which these verses express. . . . For music is divided into *mundana*, *humana*, and *instrumentalis*. *Mundana* consists in the elements, the seasons, and the stars; *humana* in the bodily humors, in the powers of the soul, and in the union of soul and body. *Instrumentalis*, however, consists in meters, rhythms, and melodies. These then are the three functions of Hymenaeus.

Boethius's *De institutione musica* 1.2, of course, is the source for this threefold division, but what follows is not just a tissue of literal quotations and cribs. Nor is it simply a passing mention, a mere demonstration that the commentator had dutifully read his Boethius. Rather, the division generates the interpretive framework for the metrum and provides an epistemological rationale. Just as music has three parts, so too there are three mental judgments (*iudicia animi*): *sensus, ratio*, and *intelligentia. Sensus* and *ratio* judge *instrumentalis, ratio* alone deduces *mundana*, and *ratio* and *intelligentia* together determine *humana—ratio* the body and *intelligentia* the soul. Because we ascend from sense perception through reason to understanding, "*instrumentalis* is first, *mundana* second, and *humana* last." The commentator then proceeds to read this pedagogical and epistemological order back into the *De institutione musica*: "Boethius, attending to this order, since he took pains to discuss the totality of music, began with *instrumentalis*, then spoke of *mundana*, and finally *humana*. For teaching must follow the order of understanding, not the order of reality."[162] To my knowledge, the link Bernard

[162] *Comm. in Mart.* 3.42–63: Instrumentalis quidem partim iudicium habet sensum, partim rationem. Auditus namque gravitatem et acumen capit in vocibus, ratio vero intervallum et proportionem et numerum. Mundane autem iudicium est ratio, at humane ratio quantum ad corpus, intelligentia quantum ad animam. Et quia familiarior est sensus ratione humanitati, ratio quoque intelligencia, que solius Dei est et paucorum admodumque lectorum hominum, ideo doctrina et agnitione instrumentalis prima est, secunda mundana, novissima humana. Sicut enim homo maior est mundo, qui propter eum factus est, et musica humana maior mundana. Secundum animam quidem attenditur ista maioritas. Quantum ad corpus enim dicitur homo microcosmus. Sola vero anime concupiscentia, que quasi eius portio est, maior est mundo, unde eo repleri non potest. Prefatum ordinem attendens Boetius, cum de tota musica disserere curam suscepisset, ab instrumentali orsus est, succendentur dicturus de mundana, tandem humana. Doctrina enim eligit ordinem agnitionis non nature in rebus. Unde tractatus de creaturis ubique tractatum de creatore precedit. . . . Et eundem ordinem observans Martianus primo instrumentalis indicat efficatiam, dicens: Tu quem psallentem, et cetera; deinde mundane his verbis: semina qui archanis, et cetera; novissime humane.

forges between the *iudicia animi* and the tripartite division of music is original. Far from slavishly following his sources, Bernard strives to use his own music-theoretical interpolation to create a loose hermeneutic framework—albeit one showing the strains of ad hoc assembly[163]—that will support his interpretation of this metrum as an ascent "through creation to the creator" (*per creaturas ad creatorem*): from *sensus (musica instrumentalis)*, via *ratio* (*musica mundana*), to the level of true *intelligentia (musica humana)*.

This is a strategic, powerful, and (one assumes) purposeful misreading of Boethius, for *De institutione musica* 1.2 (as we have already seen) clearly draws the epistemological continuum from *instrumentalis* to *mundana; humana* was the intermediary, not the summit.[164] The reordering, however, harmonizes the Boethian division of music with twelfth-century Timaean cosmology. Calcidius divided the translated portion of the *Timaeus* into two parts: the first, through 39e, covers the causes and creation of the world; the second, 40a to 53c, concerns the creation of animate beings, including man. The twelfth-century readers of the *Timaeus* structured both their commentaries and their understanding of Plato's *ordo discendi* accordingly: *mundana* precedes *humana* (consider, for instance, Bernard's *Cosmographia: megacosmos* precedes *microcosmos*). Hence, by reversing the mundane and the humane in the *De institutione musica*, Bernard sought to make Boethius a better (twelfth-century) Platonist; late-ancient music theory now serves twelfth-century humanism.

The second part of this book follows this line of argumentation deep into its particulars: *musica humana* as the ideal harmonized goal to which *humanitas* aspires (Chapter 3), mediated by the materialized harmonies of *musica instrumentalis* realized in voices and instruments (Chapter 4), themselves modeled upon the idealized but no less material *musica mundana* instantiated by the cosmic elements, the material horizon for the continual cycle of generation and corruption, and the celestial harmony of the planetary choreography (Chapter 5). We have spent long enough in the worlds of words. It is time for the particulars.

163 On account of this framework, the commentator is occasionally obliged to backtrack or excuse off-topic asides. For instance, his gloss on Calliopea (*Comm. in Mart.* 3.76–84), included within the opening *musica instrumentalis* division for grammatical reasons, briefly touches on the *armonia celestis.* Hence, as he begins his subsequent discussion of *musica mundana*, he is forced to comment (*Comm. in Mart.* 3.288–90): Hactenus de instrumentali. Quod enim de Calliopea dixit non ad mundanam referendum est, set potius ad instrumentalem.

164 As the anonymous author of an *Epistola cum tractatu de musica instrumentali humanaque ac mundana* formulates it: Mundana musica longe supereminet omnibus scientiis. Haec enim est diliciosa scientia. Haec philosophorum gloria. Haec facit familiarem et conscium divini consilii (J. Smits van Waesberghe, ed., *Adalboldi Episcopi Ultraiectensis Epistola cum tractatu de musica instrumentali humanaque ac mundana* [Buren: Knuf, 1981]).

PART II

THE PARTICULARS

3

Composing the Human

Harmonies of the Microcosm

Quid est enim quod illam incorpoream rationis vivacitatem corpori misceat, nisi quaedam coaptatio et veluti gravium leviumque vocum quasi unam consonantiam efficiens temperatio?

—Boethius, *De institutione musica*, 1.2

In 1633, the same year that Galileo Galilei was denounced by the Catholic Church for his heretically heliocentric eccentricities (the last gasp of the geocentric macrocosm within which this book wholly resides), another thinker strayed into delirium in his radical decentering of the microcosm. It was René Descartes in *L'homme* or, to be more anatomically precise, it was Descartes's account of the human eardrum, the tympanum, that did away, "in one bold stroke, with the Renaissance *episteme* of semblance and the logic of representation."[1] So Veit Erlmann, "with a precision rare in cultural history," locates the first intertwining of the twinned trajectories of reason and resonance.[2] His argument, as this quotation would suggest, tracks Foucault's account of the "classical" break with the Renaissance *episteme*, with its "single, unbroken surface in which observation and language intersect to infinity" (and with which my previous chapter began). Echoing Foucault's semantic web of resemblance across the four figures of *convenientia, aemulatio, analogy*, and *sympathy* (with its twin, *antipathy*), Erlmann locates the *minor mundus*, the human "microcosmic replica of the macrocosm," in the "ability of each and every element to be affected by and in turn to influence all the other elements by similitude, adjacency, antipathy, and sympathy."[3] It is only within such a sympathetically resonant world that Descartes could have claimed, just fifteen years earlier in his *Compendium musicae* of 1618, that "the human voice seems most pleasing to us because it, more than anything else, conforms to our spirits," seeing as such

1 Veit Erlmann, *Reason and Resonance: A History of Modern Aurality* (New York: Zone Books, 2014), 64.

2 Ibid., 12–13.

3 Ibid., 49.

pleasure arises from the sympathy and apathy of the affections (*sympathia et dispathia affectuum*), and is proven, finally, by the silence of a sheepskin drum in the acoustic presence of a resonating drum from a wolf's pelt.[4] What changed in the intervening fifteen years?

To summarize Erlmann's nuanced argument: it was the result of both Descartes's unhinging of *sensation* from the external object that caused it—itself the result of the eardrum's withdrawal from the *episteme* of semblance—and the concomitant elevation of the auditory nerve (occupying a "somewhat more liminal position between physiology and psychology") as an "epistemic thing" in Descartes's continued quest for "reasonance" (reason combined with a "theory of hearing couched entirely in terms of resonance")[5] Erlmann's terminology is telling. Resonant theories of hearing aside, the very idea of "sensation" as a way of talking about "phenomenal content independent of its (external) cause (if any)" is a relatively modern concept, as Peter King has observed in his study of the medieval mind-body non-problem.[6] But even if twelfth-century philosophers (much less their ancient sources) didn't have the language with which to articulate the "raw feels" (*qualia* in modern terms) that motivate contemporary accounts of Cartesian substance dualism, that doesn't mean they did not have to deal with some version of a mind-body or (more appropriately) soul-body problem. After all, the philosophical terrain of this book is primarily Platonic, focused as it is on the twelfth century, before the widespread rediscovery of the Aristotelian hylomorphic compound of soul and body. And among the ancients, Plato stands out as the loudest proponent of a strong version of soul-body dualism, in which the human soul and the human body are distinct substances, and sensing belongs to the soul rather than to the body, which, as King points out, is all that is needed for the problem to arise.[7] But it did not, or at least not in Cartesian terms. This non-problem, or rather the problem of a non-Cartesian dualism, is the central focus of this chapter, and it amounts to a prehistory of Erlmann's "twinned trajectories of reason and resonance" within the human microcosm.

4 René Descartes, *Compendium musicae*, in *Oeuvres de Descartes*, ed. Charles Adam and Paul Tanery, vol. 10 (Paris: Librairie Philosophique J. Vrin, 1973–1978), 90.1–7: Id tantum videtur vocem humanam nobis gratissimam reddere, quia omnium maxime conformis est nostris spiritibus. Ita forte etiam amicissimi gratior est, quam inimici, ex sympathia et dispathia affectuum: eadem ratione qua aiunt ovis pellem tensam in tympano obmutescere, si feriatur, lupina in alio tympano resonante.

5 Ibid., 65–66.

6 Peter King, "Why Isn't the Mind-Body Problem Medieval?" in *Forming the Mind*, ed. Henrik Lagerlund (Dordrecht: Springer Verlag, 2007), 189. The Latin root of the modern term, *sensatio*, is a "surprisingly late coinage," which only first appears in the early thirteenth century and only starts to articulate a Cartesian-flavored mind-body problem (as an absurd position proving its opposite) in the fourteenth century.

7 King, "Why Isn't the Mind-Body Problem Medieval?" 200.

Suzanne Cusick once suggested that music "is the exact site of an actual solution to the mind/body problem."[8] Although Cusick pursues this claim in very different terms, remapping the mind-body opposition as the (historically) oppositional relation between composer/analyst (mind) and performer (body), this chapter seeks to historicize and, in a limited way, substantiate this claim across the terrain of natural philosophical accounts of the "harmonic" relation(s) both between soul and body and within individual bodies and souls singly. There is, I suggest, something sound in Cusick's suggestion, insofar as the construal of the relation between body and soul as a *musical* relation, in both a proportional and performative sense, avoids, indeed negates and neutralizes, Cartesian dualism from the very outset. Despite the fact that some twelfth-century accounts verge on "instrumentalism," the thesis that the soul *uses* the body (which seems unavoidably intertwined with dualism), the implicit musicality of the bodily "instrument" (literalized by thinkers such as William of St. Thierry and Isaac of Stella) led to the strong integration of body and soul via the triad (first broached in the prelude to this study) of vulnerability, agency, and affect.[9] But first we need to articulate an important distinction, that between soul's *being* a harmony and *having* a harmony. And we begin with the most famous and influential *denied* argument in the history of Platonic philosophy.

Soul: Being Harmony, Having Harmony

At the earliest appearance of the argument that soul is harmony—more precisely, a harmony resulting from a particular arrangement of bodily elements (hereafter the Harmony Thesis)—it is emphatically denied οὐκ ἄρα, ὦ ἄριστε, ἡμῖν οὐδαμῇ καλῶς ἔχει ψυχὴν ἁρμονίαν τινὰ φάναι εἶναι ("in no way at all then, my friend, do we approve of the thesis that soul is a kind of harmony"). In these words from Plato's *Phaedo* (94e8–95a1), Socrates dismisses the thesis first articulated by his interlocutor, Simmias. The Harmony Thesis, however, was doomed from the start by the very dialectical structure of Plato's larger argument: it is proposed not as a positive thesis but as a potent challenge to the immortality of the soul. Hence

[8] Suzanne Cusick, "Feminist Theory, Music Theory, and the Mind/Body Problem," *Perspectives of New Music* 32 (1994), 18.

[9] Historicizing this affective "solution" to the mind-body problem is all the more timely because recent philosophical and musicological critiques of Cartesian dualism have returned to musical solutions, if not as "the exact site of an actual solution" then at least as part of a broader dialogue between music and philosophy: e.g., Amy Cimini, "Vibrating Colors and Silent Bodies: Music, Sound and Silence in Maurice Merleau-Ponty's Critique of Dualism," *Contemporary Music Review* 31 (2012), 353–370; Holly Watkins and Melina Esse, "Down with Disembodiment; or, Musicology and the Material Turn," *Women and Music* 19 (2015), 160–168.

Plato was obliged to refute it.[10] Simmias proposes the Harmony Thesis as a counterargument to Socrates's affinity argument for the soul's immortality. Socrates had concluded (78b–80a) that since the soul's being is closer to the sort of being possessed by the Forms (the Equal, the Beautiful, and the like) than it is to the homonymous being (πάντων τῶν ἐκείνοις ὁμωνύμων) possessed by individual instantiations of the Forms (equal sticks and stones, beautiful men or horses, etc.), we could expect that the soul shares with the Forms the property of immortality. In response, Simmias offers an affinity argument of his own: since "the harmony of a lyre and its strings is something invisible and incorporeal and very lovely and divine in the harmonized lyre, while the lyre itself and its strings are corporeal bodies and composite and earthy and akin to the mortal" (85e3–86a3), then perhaps in an analogous manner "our body is kept in tension, as it were, and held together by hot and cold, dry and wet, and the like, and our soul is a blending and harmony of these same things, when they are blended with each other in due proportion" (86b7–c1). Against Socrates's immortal soul, Simmias's countermove proposes a soul that necessarily perishes with the body. Just as the harmony immanent "in the harmonized lyre" (ἐν τῇ ἡρμοσμένῃ λύρᾳ, 86a1) ceases to exist when the lyre is smashed, so too the soul (according to the Harmony Thesis) dies with the body. The defining features of the Harmony Thesis as proposed by Simmias, then, are that it is about the essence of the soul, that it claims that the soul is metaphysically posterior to the body, and that it proposes the soul to be either the mixture of bodily elements or the ratio of their mixture.

There is no need here to delve into the many details of Plato's sustained refutation of the Harmony Thesis, a refutation which (as numerous commentators have observed) exploits and oscillates between multiple senses of the word ἁρμονία.[11] These various senses are carefully distinguished in the second appearance and subsequent refutation of the Harmony Thesis, Aristotle's *De anima* (407b27–408a28).[12]

[10] On the strength of the Harmony Thesis as a challenge to the affinity argument, see Ellen Wagner, "Supervenience and the Thesis that the Soul Is a *Harmonia*," in *Essays on Plato's Psychology*, ed. Ellen Wagner (Lanham: Lexington Books, 2001), 69–88.

[11] The two basic arguments that Plato employs are (1) a nobility argument: soul has dominion over and can oppose body feelings; harmony, however, always depends on the state and arrangement of its components; hence, a harmony cannot act upon its components, and thus the soul cannot be the harmony of the body (this is the argument employed by Plotinus to refute the same at *Enn.* 4.7.8); and (2) a reductio ad absurdum: no harmony can be more or less harmonious; hence the Harmony Thesis cannot account for both good and bad souls, as it leads to the absurdity that either a bad soul cannot exist (false) or that no soul is more virtuous than any other soul (equally false). See David Gallop, *Plato: Phaedo* (Oxford: Clarendon Press, 1975), 156–167; C. C. W. Taylor, "The Arguments in the *Phaedo* Concerning the Thesis that the Soul is a *Harmonia*," in *Essays on Plato's Psychology*, ed. Ellen Wagner (Lanham: Lexington Books, 2001), 51–67.

[12] On which see Ronald M. Polansky, *Aristotle's* De anima (Cambridge: Cambridge University Press, 2007), 104–122; William Charlton, "Aristotle and the *Harmonia* Theory," in *Aristotle on Nature and Living Things: Philosophical and Historical Studies Presented to David M. Balme on his Seventieth Birthday*, ed. Allan Gotthelf (Pittsburgh: Mathesis, 1985), 131–150; and Rae Langton, "The Musical, the Magical,

According to Aristotle, soul as harmony admits of two interpretations: harmony is identified either with the combination (σύνθεσις) of magnitudes or the ratio (λόγος) that governs the combination thereof (408a5–9). In Aristotle's estimation, however, neither of these produces a coherent view of the soul.[13] Moreover, the Harmony Thesis fails to account for a basic psychic faculty, namely locomotion. Hence, for Aristotle, too, the soul cannot be harmony.

At *Politics* 1340b16–18, when discussing the educational benefits of music, Aristotle pushes a further distinction: καί τις ἔοικε συγγένεια ταῖς ἁρμονίαις καὶ τοῖς ῥυθμοῖς εἶναι· διὸ πολλοί φασι τῶν σοφῶν οἱ μὲν ἁρμονίαν εἶναι τὴν ψυχήν, οἱ δ' ἔχειν ἁρμονίαν. ("There seems to be in us a sort of affinity to harmonies and rhythms. Wherefore many of the wise say, some that the soul is harmony, others that it has harmony"). The distinction between εἶναι ἁρμονίαν and ἔχειν ἁρμονίαν, between the soul's *being* harmony and its *having* harmony, is crucial. In a recent study of music's role in Plato's thought, Francesco Pelosi argues, apropos the *Phaedo*'s Harmony Thesis, for Plato's "recovery and re-employment of this notion [of soul as harmony] in other dialogues."[14] To make such a claim, however, flattens out important differences in Plato's deployment of psychological harmonies. None of Plato's other dialogues in any way rehabilitates, much less "re-employs," the specific argument of the Harmony Thesis. The *Republic* and the *Timaeus* do envisage a harmonic psychology, but on very different terms—different enough that they in no way undermine or revise the rejection of the Harmony Thesis in the *Phaedo*. Pelosi's own statements reveal this transformation without admitting it openly. In the later dialogues, Pelosi argues, "Plato will be moved to reconsider the possibility of seeing harmony *in* the soul."[15] To posit harmony *in the soul*, however, is not the same as positing the soul *as harmony*. Plato's "mythic" speculations on the harmonic structures *in* the soul, most fully articulated in the Timaean psychogony, should not and do not, as Pelosi claims, "ring out as a response to Simmias' objection."[16] Although Pelosi is correct that the "harmonic representation of the soul can cohabit with the conviction of the immortality of the soul,"[17] the soul's "harmonic representation" in the *Timaeus* has little in common with Simmias's Harmony Thesis, as is evident from the simple fact that the Timaean (human) psychogony (*Tim.* 41d4–e2) occurs—at the mythic level—*prior* to the creation of the human body (44d3ff.); this, of course, does not demand any sort of real temporal priority, but the ontological

and the Mathematical Soul," in *History of the Mind-Body Problem*, ed. Tim Crane and Sarah A. Patterson (London: Routledge, 2000), 13–33.

13 *De anima* 408a9–15: That the soul is a harmony in the sense of the combination of the parts of the body is a view easily refutable. . . . It is equally absurd to identify the soul with the ratio of the mixture.

14 Pelosi, *Plato on Music*, 181.

15 Ibid., 183, my emphasis.

16 Ibid.

17 Ibid.

priority (cf. 34b10–35a1) suggested by the creation "myth" is largely incompatible with Simmias's Harmony Thesis.[18] Moreover, far from being the source or cause of harmony, body in the *Timaeus* is in fact the cause of the soul's disharmony (43d4–e4). Thus, with Aristotle, we should make a careful distinction between the Harmony Thesis and the harmonic structure of the soul, between those who claim that the soul *is* harmony and those who claim that it *has* harmony. Plato cannot be counted among the adherents to the former, but he does countenance the latter, the harmonic structure of the soul itself. Soul is not the harmony of the body, but it has a harmony of its own.

It is almost exclusively the latter harmonic strain of thought—that the soul has a harmony independent of the body it animates—that animates twelfth-century discussions of *musica humana*. One reason for the near exclusion of the Harmony Thesis in the twelfth century is the simple fact of the availability of texts: twelfth-century philosophers did not have direct access to the thesis as presented in either the *Phaedo* or the *De anima*. Although Henricus Aristippus, archdeacon of Catania, translated the *Phaedo* into Latin in 1156, this translation did not have impact and influence until the thirteenth century, and even then only faintly, never approaching the ubiquity of the *Timaeus*.[19] Aristotle's *De anima*, available by at least the mid-twelfth century in the Latin translation of James of Venice, was not incorporated into the standard philosophical curriculum until the very end of the twelfth and beginning of the thirteenth centuries.[20] Thus, the Harmony Thesis in its classical form was largely unavailable and generally unknown until the thirteenth century.

There were, however, at least four other preeminent authorities—Cicero, Augustine, Nemesius of Emesa, and Macrobius—who transmitted a version of the Harmony Thesis. While these authorities certainly were known, cited, and debated, their presentations of the thesis would hardly have recommended it as a viable position; each discusses (and dismisses) the view within a doxographical context, enumerating it among the errors of his philosophical predecessors (the fact that none agrees as to who held this view serves well to highlight the

[18] Cf. Leonardo Tarán, "The Creation Myth in Plato's *Timaeus*," in *Collected Papers (1962–1999)* (Leiden: Brill, 2001), 306–309.

[19] See Raymond Klibansky, *The Continuity of the Platonic Tradition During the Middle Ages: Outlines of a Corpus Platonicum Medii Aevi* (London: The Warburg Institute, 1939), 27–28; Raymond Klibansky, ed., *Phaedo interprete Henrico Aristippo* (London: The Warburg Institute, 1950).

[20] There are occasional echoes of the *De anima* in the later twelfth century in Hermann of Carinthia's *De essentiis*, Costa ben Luca's *De differentia animae et spiritus liber* (translated by John of Spain), and Dominicus Gundissalinus's *De anima*. Such citations, however, are usually secondhand, indebted not to James of Venice's translation but to the brief citations of the *De anima* in Calcidius (*In Tim.* 222 [235.8–9]: at uero Aristoteles animam definit hactenus: anima est prima perfectio corporis naturalis organici possibilitate uitam habentis = *De anima* 412a27f.) and Nemesius (*Prem. phys.* 2.4: Aristoteles vero eam [sc. animam] dicit esse explementum primum corporis naturalis officialisque, potestate vitam habentis).

complexity of the tradition).[21] More pointedly, however, each presents it as entailing the soul's mortality.

Cicero's summary of views on the soul in *Tusculanae disputationes* 1.10.19 (= Aristoxenus fr. 120a) begins with the "last of the ancients" and attributes to Aristoxenus, "the musician and philosopher," the view that the soul is "a kind of tension in the body, as if in song or strings, which is called harmony (ἁρμονία)."[22] Thus, upon the death of the body, the soul too will dissolve.[23] Augustine's *De immortalitate animae* twice floats (without ascription) the theory that the soul is the "harmony of the body" (*harmonia corporis*: 2.2) or "some proportioning of the body" (*aliqua temperatio corporis*: 10.17),[24] but he denies the thesis, since it would force the soul to be, like shape or color, inseparably present in the body,[25] and thus the soul would be as mutable as the body (2.2) and could not withdraw from the body to perceive intelligible things (10.17).[26] The *De natura hominis* by Nemesius of Emesa, a fourth-century Greek theologian, a work translated into Latin in the eleventh century by Alfanus of Salerno as the *Premnon physicon*, lists the view of a certain "Dinarchus"[27] who claimed that the soul is the "harmony of

[21] The root of this doxographical tradition may well be Aëtius's *Placita philosophorum*; see Jaap Mansfeld, "Doxography and Dialectic: The *Sitz im Leben* of the 'Placita,'" *Aufstieg und Niedergang der Römischen Welt* II 36.4 (1990), 3056–3229. Although Calcidius's treatise on the soul (*In Tim.* 213–235 [228.14–248.14]) is clearly indebted to the same doxographical tradition, the Harmony Thesis is nowhere mentioned or discussed explicitly. On Calcidius's "doxographical pattern," see Gretchen Reydams-Schils, "Calcidius on the Human and the World Soul and Middle-Platonist Psychology," *Apeiron* 39 (2006), 178–192.

[22] *Tusc.* 1.10.19: Aristoxenus musicus idemque philosophus ipsius corporis intentionem quandam, velut in cantu et fidibus quae ἁρμονία dicitur: sic ex corporis totius natura et figura varios motus cieri tamquam in cantu sonos.

[23] *Tusc.* 1.11.24: si [anima] est Aristoxeni harmonia, dissoluetur. For a brief discussion of how this view would cohere with Aristoxenus's music theory in general, see Gioia Maria Rispoli, "La musica e le forme," in *La Musa dimenticata: Aspetti dell'esperienza musicale greca in età ellenistica; Convengo di studio Pisa, Scuola Normale Superiore 21–23 settembre 2006*, ed. Maria Chiara Martinelli, Francesco Pelosi, and Carlo Pernigotti (Pisa: Edizioni della Normale, 2009), 135–136.

[24] Cf. *Trin.* 10.9 (on the corporeality and the incorporeality, the mortality and immortality of the soul): sed ipsam temperationem corporis nostri uel compagem primordiorum, quibus ista caro tamquam connectitur, esse opinati sunt. eoque hi omnes eam mortalem esse senserunt, quia siue corpus esset siue aliqua compositio corporis, non posset utique immortaliter permanere.

[25] *De immor. an.* 2.2: quaecumque harmonia corporis est, in subiecto corpore sit necesse est inseparabiliter. Ibid., 10.17: sed in subiecto corpore tamquam color et forma inseparabiliter inesset.

[26] *De immor. an.* 2.2: Mutabile est autem corpus humanum, et immutabilis ratio. Mutabile est enim omne quod semper eodem modo non est.... Nullo modo autem potest, mutato subiecto, id quod in eo est inseparabiliter non mutari. Non est igitur harmonia corporis animus. Nec mors potest accidere immutabilibus rebus. Ibid., 10.17: non ullo modo se ab eodem corpore ad intellegibilia percipienda conaretur avertere. On the ambiguity of Augustine's *temperatio*, see Robert J. O'Connell, *St. Augustine's Early Theory of Man, A.D. 386–391* (Cambridge, MA: The Belknap Press of Harvard University Press, 1968), 140–142.

[27] Δείναρχος = Δικαίαρχος, a pupil of Aristotle; see David C. Mirhady, "Dicaearchus of Messana: The Sources, Text and Translation," in *Dicaearchus of Messana: Text, Translation, and Discussion*, ed.

the four elements" (*harmonia quattuor elementorum*), which Nemesius (as translated by Alfanus) glosses as "the blending and concord of the elements, not a concordant balance arising from sounds but of the hot, cold, wet, and dry in the body" (*temperantiam et concordiam elementorum, non constantem ex vocibus, sed in corpore calidorum et frigidorum et humidorum et siccorum concordem temperiem*: 2.4). The arguments Nemesius mounts against "Dinarchus" are those given by Socrates against Simmias in the *Phaedo*.[28] Thus, even if the *Phaedo* itself was not widely available in the twelfth century, the *Premnon physicon*—which was known and cited by William of Conches, William of St. Thierry, and John of Salisbury, among many others[29]—provided an (albeit not entirely accurate) summary of its primary arguments against the Harmony Thesis; however, it seems not to have been utilized on this score.[30] Finally, within this same tradition, Macrobius's *Commentarii in Somnium Scipionis* 1.14.19 offers a similar doxographic compendium.[31] The fourth of his nineteen views on the nature of the soul is that of "Pythagoras and Philolaus" (an attribution not attested in Aëtius), who, according to Macrobius, held the view that "soul is harmony."[32] Embedded, as it is, within a doxographical

W. W. Fortenbaugh and E. Schütrumpf (New Brunswick, NJ: Transaction, 2001), frs. 13–32. On the organization and sources of Nemesius's doxography generally see Heinrich Dörrie, *Porphyrios' "Symmikta Zetemata": Ihre Stellung in System und Geschichte des Neuplatonismus nebst einem Kommentar zu den Fragmenten* (Munich: C. H. Beck, 1959), 111–151; Mansfeld, "Doxography and Dialectic," 3076–3082.

[28] *Prem. phys.* 2.32: Quia vero Dinarchus harmoniam esse diffinivit animam,—contra dicens enim Socrati animam harmoniam dixit esse, dicens imitari animam harmoniam, corpus vero lyram—exponendum igitur huius solutiones, quae sunt in Phaedone Platonis. The summary of Socrates's arguments in the *Phaedo* continues through 2.38.

[29] E.g., *Guillelmi Glos. sup. Tim.* 68.6–7; William of St. Thierry, *De nat. corp. et an.* 1.3–6, 10 (70–77, 80–81); John of Salisbury, *Metalogicon*, 4.20; Charles Burnett's claim—in "The Chapter on the Spirits in the *Pantegni* of Constantine the African," in *Constantine the African and ʿAlī ibn al-ʿAbbās al-Maǧūsī: The* Pantegni *and Related Texts*, ed. Charles Burnett and Danielle Jacquart (Leiden: Brill, 1994), 112–113—that Adelard of Bath "certainly knew Alfanus's translation of Nemesius, from which he takes Xenocrates's definition of the soul as a 'harmony' in an earlier section of *De eodem et diuerso*," is inconclusive: Adelard's reference to Xenocrates's definition of soul as *numerus se mouens* (*De eo. et diu.* 46) more closely corresponds to Macrobius, *In Som. Scip.* 1.14.19 (58.31–32), *Xenocrates [dixit animam] numerum se mouentem* than it does to Nemesius, *Prem. phys.* 2.71: Pythagoras ... diffinivit et animam esse numerum se ipsum moventem, quod et Xenocrates imitatus exponit. Burnett maintains Nemesius as the source in Burnett, *Conversations*, 78.

[30] The first citation and use of Nemesius *contra* the Harmony Thesis (that I know of) is Albert the Great's *De homine* I, q.4, a.5, as noted by Stephen Gersh, "Ancient Philosophy Becomes Medieval Philosophy," in *Cambridge History of Philosophy in Late Antiquity*, ed. Lloyd P. Gerson (Cambridge: Cambridge University Press, 2010), 913.

[31] For a concise survey of modern views on the source(s) for Macrobius, see Mansfeld, "Doxography and Dialectic," 3073, n. 49.

[32] *In Som. Scip.* 1.14.19 (58.320–59.1). In his extensive study of the Philolaean fragments, Huffman argues that Macrobius's attribution of this view to Philolaus may stem more from an "overreading of the *Phaedo*" (namely, ascribing the view to Philolaus on the grounds that Simmias "heard" Philolaus at Thebes) than from any direct knowledge of Philolaus's writings or teachings. Nonetheless (Huffman continues), on the basis of the other surviving fragments, "it might appear that Philolaus was almost

summary, Macrobius does not expand on the subject here. Earlier in the text, however, within a long digression on the nature of the numbers seven and eight (which when multiplied generate 56, the age of Scipio), he described the harmony of the soul in terms of the numbers three and four, which when combined generate seven. Here, too, the view is first connected to the Pythagoreans:[33]

> nec solum explicandis corporibus hi duo numeri [sc. ternarius et quaternarius] conlativum praestant favorem, sed quaternarium quidem Pythagorei quem τετρακτύν vocant, adeo quasi ad perfectionem animae pertinentem inter arcana venerantur, ut ex eo et iuris iurandi religionem sibi fecerint:
>
> οὐ μὰ τὸν ἁμετέρᾳ ψυχᾷ παραδόντα τετρακτύν.
> per qui nostrae animae numerum dedit ipse quaternum.
>
> ternarius vero adsignat animam tribus suis partibus absolutam, quarum prima est ratio quam λογιστικόν appellant, secunda animositas quam θυμικόν vocant, tertia cupiditas quae ἐπιθυμητκόν nuncupatur. item nullus sapientum animam ex symphoniis quoque musicis constitisse dubitavit. inter has non parvae potentiae est quae dicitur διὰ πασῶν. haec constat ex duabus, id est διὰ τεσσάρων et διὰ πέντε, fit autem διὰ πέντε ex hemiolio et fit διὰ τεσσάρων ex epitrito, et est primus hemiolius tria et primus epitritus quattuor. quod quale sit suo loco planius exsequemur. ergo ex his duobus numeris constat διὰ τεσσάρων et διὰ πέντε. ex quibus διὰ πασῶν symphonia generatur, unde Vergilius nullius disciplinae expers plene et per omnia beatos exprimere volens ait, "o terque quaterque beati."
>
> Not only do these two numbers [sc., three and four] offer a common disposition to form bodies, but the Pythagoreans call the quaternary the *tetraktys*, and so revere it among their secrets as pertaining to the perfection of the soul that they have made a religious oath from it: "By him who gave the quaternary number to our soul." The number three, indeed, designates that the soul is comprised of its three parts, the first being reason (*logistikon*), the second irascibility (*thymikon*), and the

trivially committed to the view that the soul is a *harmonia* or attunement" (Carl A. Huffman, *Philolaus of Croton*, 327–328). See also David Sedley, "The Dramatis Personae of Plato's *Phaedo*," in *Philosophical Dialogues: Plato, Hume, Wittgenstein*, ed. Timothy J. Smiley (Oxford: Oxford University Press, 1995), 22–26; and in Carl A. Huffman, "The Pythagorean Conception of the Soul from Pythagoras to Philolaus," in *Body and Soul in Ancient Philosophy*, ed. Dorothea Frede and Burkhard Reis (Berlin: Walter de Gruyter, 2009), 21–43.

[33] *In Som. Scip.* 1.6.41 (25.24–26.15); William Harris Stahl, trans., *Macrobius: Commentary on the Dream of Scipio* (New York: Columbia University Press, 1952), 107–108 (lightly modified).

> third cupidity (*epithymetikon*). Moreover, all wise men do not doubt that the soul consists in musical concords. Among these an important one is the *diapason*, which consists of two others, the *diatessaron* and the *diapente*. The *diapente* arises from the hemiolic ratio and the *diatessaron* from the epitritic ratio; the first hemiolic number is three, and the first epitritic number is four; this we shall discuss more fully in its proper place. Suffice it to say that the *diatessaron* and *diapente* consist in these numbers, and from them the concord of the *diapason* arises. Whence Virgil, schooled in all the arts, when he wished to express that men were fully blessed in all respects, called them "O thrice and four times blest!"

The soul is somehow, someway connected to harmony. After all, the Pythagoreans swore by it, wise men have never doubted it, and the omniscient Virgil of course knew it too. Hence, twelfth-century philosophers and commentators could hardly ignore the thesis. But what did they make of it?

Twelfth-Century Psychological Harmonies *per similitudinem*

When medieval commentators encountered Macrobius's claims about the harmony of the soul, many were hesitant to follow them literally and turned instead to an analogy of psychic powers and the suitability of the body to receive a soul (with its own incorporeal ontology). Occasionally, the metaphysical claims were suppressed entirely. For instance, the anonymous author of the *Glosae Colonienses super Macrobium* explains Macrobius's Pythagorean and Philolaean definition of the soul ("the soul is harmony") as merely an indication that "whosoever has a soul is captured by musical sweetness" (*quicumque habent animam capiuntur musica dulcedine*);[34] while such a claim may presuppose a "harmonic soul," the larger metaphysical implications seem to have been lost in the compression of Macrobius's doxographical presentation. William of Conches reads more into the definition, but he too understands the identification of *anima* with *harmonia* more as a matter of metaphor than metaphysics. Properly speaking, *harmonia* is a "concord of sound" (*concordia uocis*), and thus its application to *anima* can only be understood as a kind of metaphor (*quadam translatione*):[35]

> Anima ergo dicitur harmonia quadam translatione, quia harmonice et concorditer corpus uegetat et ex concordia quattuor elementorum

[34] *Glos. Colonienses sup. Macr.*, comment. ad 1.14.19 (223.16).

[35] *Glos. sup. Macr.*, comment. ad 1.14.19. Cf. *Guillelmi Glos. sup. Tim.* 78.28–30: Vt igitur animam corpus concorditer mouere significaret, numeros concordes in eius compositione posuit. Ibid. 92.9–12: Quamuis anima est coniuncta corpori, quod ex sui natura caret ratione, tamen ipsa est COMPOS RATIONIS, id est potens uti ratione; ET ITEM est compos MODVLAMINIS, id est potens modulandi et regendi corpora.

> habet existere in corpore. Et sunt huiusmodi diffinitiones ut praediximus datae per causam.
>
> The soul is called a harmony in a metaphorical sense, because it harmonically and concordantly animates the body and because it derives its existence in the body from the harmony of the four elements. Definitions of this sort, as we have already explained, are causal definitions.

We will return to the corporeal, even psychosomatic, implications of this gloss below. First, however, we turn to another commentator who likewise construed the *harmonia animae* as a manner of speaking *per similitudinem*, the anonymous author of the St. Florian commentary on Boethius's *De institutione musica*.

The St. Florian commentator's fullest discussion of "psychological harmony" is prompted not by Boethius's brief résumé of *musica humana* but by his claim that music is conjoined to morality. The commentator summarizes the logic of Boethius's argument as follows:[36]

> Quod musica moralitati est coniuncta, quod remittitur dulcibus sonis et offenditur contrariis, inde potest cognosci Platonem non sine causa dixisse animam esse compactam ex musicis consonantiis, cum enim delectetur dulcibus; omnis autem delectatio ex similitudine fit, sicut offensio ex dissimilitudine. Probat enim in se illius habere similitudinem quo ipsa delectatur, et ideo anima ex musicis consonanciis, quoniam in eis delectatur, est compacta.
>
> From the fact that music is connected to morality, that we are soothed by sweet sounds and offended by their opposite, it can be understood that Plato with good reason said that the soul is constructed from musical consonances, since it is delighted by sweet [sounds]; every delight, however, arises from similitude, just as offense arises from dissimilitude. It is proven, then, that the soul has within itself the similitude of that by which it is delighted, and thus the soul is constructed from musical consonances, because it takes delight in them.

Music's connection to morality is predicated upon its ability to affect the soul,[37] and its ability to affect the soul is, in turn, predicated upon some sort of similarity (*similitudo*) obtaining between musical structure and psychological structure. Hence the structure of the soul is, in a manner of speaking, harmonic.

36 *In inst. mus.* 27.

37 *In inst. mus.* 26: Omnis enim quae animorum est commotiva moralitati est coniuncta, et musica maxime. Ipsa enim lascivioribus sonis animum reddit dissolutum, asperioribus austerum, quarum uterque mores invertit, mediocribus temperatum, quod ad mores pertinet informandos.

The commentator is at pains, however, to demonstrate that neither Boethius nor Plato before him "really" thinks that the soul is or has any kind of "real" harmonic structure, as such a position would undermine the soul's simplicity. We would be wrong to suppose from talk of the "harmony of the soul" that the soul is a composite entity (as is, necessarily, any concord) or that the soul is a quantity with quantitative parts. To the contrary, the soul is entirely *simplex*, and the soul's musical and thus numerical structure is only a similitude, and this on several levels. First, by describing the soul in numerical terms, Plato intended to highlight the soul's perfection, because number is *perfectissimus* and the first perfection after God (*prima enim perfectio in numeris post deum*).[38] The commentator's wording recalls the language of Macrobius, who similarly noted that "as thought moves from ourselves to the divine realm, the first perfection of incorporeality occurs in numbers" (*cogitationi a nobis ad superos meanti occurrit prima perfectio incorporalitatis in numeris*).[39] The logic of the argument, however, is fully in line with William of Conches, who, when explaining the numerical construction of the *anima mundi* in Plato's *Timaeus*, made the very same claim: Plato turned to numbers in order to reveal the perfection of the soul, since there is nothing else, after God, that is as perfect as number.[40] Second, even if soul is *simplex*, the commentator continues, we can yet speak of the soul's "parts" *per similitudinem*. Such parts are not parts proper, but rather are potential or virtual parts (*potentiales siue uirtuales*); that is, they are parts in the sense of the soul's powers: the *uis rationabilis, concupiscibilis*, and *irascibilis*.[41] In a properly functioning soul, these virtual parts are joined, *sola similitudine*, so that they produce the same concord and proportion as

[38] *In inst. mus.* 27: Notandum est igitur quod Plato animam dixit esse ex numeris compactam et eam etiam esse ex musicis consonanciis compactam, non quia una res sit compacta, immo simplex est, sed ut notaretur esse quiddam perfectissimum, sicut numerus perfectissimus est; prima enim perfectio in numeris post deum reperitur.

[39] *In Som. Scip.* 1.5.4 (15.10–11); cf. 1.5.13 (17.17–18): prima est igitur perfectio incoporalitatis in numeris.

[40] *Guillelmi Glos. sup. Tim.* 77.9–12: Numeros ergo apposuit ut perfectionem animae insinuaret. Vt enim in principio huius operis diximus, nichil post Deum tam perfectum est quam perfectus est numerus. Cf. ibid. 12.18–21: Plato igitur, ut pitagoricus, sciens maximam perfectionem in numeris esse, quippe cum nulla creatura sine numero possit existere, numerus tamen sine qualibet potest existere, ut perfectionem sui operis ostendere, a perfectis scilicet numeris incepit. Cf. Bernard Silvestris, *Comm. in Mart.* 5.53–59: Numerus perfeccionis indicium et concordie causa est. Nulla enim res est tante perfectionis, cum nichil fit quod absque numero possit esse, cum, quicquid est, vel proportiones vel potencias vel etates in numero habeat. Nulla autem res est sine qua numerus esse non possit. Si enim ternarius non esset in his tribus rebus, in aliis esset. Unde Macroibus: "Cogitationi," inquam, "a nobis ad superos meanti prima perfectio occurrit in numeris."

[41] *In inst. mus.* 27: Partes autem, ut prenotavimus, non proprie signantur in anima, sed tantum per similitudinem, et dicuntur partes potentiales sive virtuales, quae et naturam partium virtualium et naturam servant partium integralium. Nam et animae subiciunt⟨ur⟩ [*scripsi*] cum dicitur: "anima irascibilis est" et "concupiscibilis est anima" et "rationabilis est anima," et etiam ista tria quasi unam animae iungunt substantiam. Unde apparet hec [*scripsi*, hoc *Rausch*] non proprie dici partes, quoniam

do concordant *uoces*.[42] How, then, do these virtual parts harmonize? The answer is not particularly sophisticated. The commentator envisages two possibilities: they harmonize either among themselves or with their principle (*uel ipsae inter se vel ipsae ad suum principium*). When the soul's virtual parts do what they should do—e.g., when the *rationabilis uis* discerns the good from the bad, the *concupiscibilis uis* pursues the good, and the *irascibilis uis* flees the bad—then the parts harmonize among themselves and with their principle, which is the *bonum* to which the soul returns (*redit enim sic ad suum principium, scilicet, ad bonum*); when, however, the parts decline to do what they should—the *irascibilis uis* flees the good and the *concupiscibilis uis* chooses the bad—then the soul produces dissonance, and it only stretches toward its principle, without attaining it.[43] When the St. Florian commentator reaches Boethius's discussion of *musica humana* proper, he subsumes this virtual tripartition of the soul within the "Aristotelian" bipartition alluded to by Boethius, that the soul is the conjunction of its rational and irrational aspects (*ex rationabili inrationabilique coniuncta est*). The soul's irrational aspect includes *concupiscibilitas* and *irascibilitas*; each of these is, in a manner of speaking,

nec in isto genere nec in illo proprie poni possunt. Cf. Boethius, *De div.* 40.24–27: Sed non est anima horum genus sed totum, partes enim hae animae sunt, sed non ut in quantitate, sed ut in aliqua potestate atque uirtute, ex his enim potentiis substantia animae iungitur. Cf. *Guillelmi Glos. sup. Tim.* 79.5–9: est enim anima totum quoddam non uniuersale nec integrum sed uirtuale, quia scilicet plures habet potentias et uirtutes—RVRSVSQVE HOC VNVM, id est unam et eandem animam mundi, DIVISIT IN PARTES non integrales sed in potentias. *Glos. Colonienses sup. Macr.*, comment. ad 1.6.5 (190.12–16): Non credo quod aliquis philosophorum animam constare ex numeris vel habuisse principium [dixerit]; sed cum vellent potentias eius describere, nullum eius exemplar tantae evidentiae in rebus invenerunt quam praedictos numeros, id est duplares, qui numeri lucide vires animae ostendunt. *Glos. Colonienses sup. Macr.*, comment. ad 1.6.3 (190.10–11): philosophi non poterunt vires et potentiam animae expressius pronuntiare vel exemplificare quam per proportiones numerourm, que omnia constare faciunt. Hugh of St. Victor, *Did.* 2.4 (27.28–28.5): prima igitur progressio animae est qua de simplici essentia sua, quae monade figuratur, in virtualem ternarium se extendit, ubi iam per concupiscentiam aliud appetat, aliud per iram contemnat, per rationem inter utrumque discernat. . . . neque enim vel rationem solam vel iram solam vel concupiscentiam solam tertiam partem animae dicere possumus, cum nec aliud, nec minus sit in substantia ratio quam anima, nec aliud, nec minus ira quam anima, nec aliud, nec minus concupiscentia quam anima, sed una eademque substantia secundum diversas potentias suas diversa sortitur vocabula.

42 *In inst. mus.* 27: Ex musicis autem consonanciis dixit eam esse compactam sola similitudine, quia scilicet partes anime ita sibi sunt concatenate, ut eandem reddant concordiam et proportionem, vel ipse inter se vel ipse ad suum principium, quam concordiam et proportionem faciunt voces ad reddendam musicam consonantiam.

43 *In inst. mus.* 27–28: Qualiter ergo iste tres partes vel inter se vel ad suum principium musicas reddant consonantias, videamus. Secundum vim rationabilem anima bonum a malo discernit, secundum vim concupiscibilem bonum eligit, secundum vim irascibilem malum fugit, et cum hoc, quod facit anima secundum suas partes, tunc partes animae et inter se servant musicas consonancias et ad suum principium; redit enim sic ad suum principium, scilicet ad bonum, redituque suo singula gaudiorum, sed quando secundum has potencias non ita operatur, secundum immo vim irascibilem bonum fugit et secundum concupiscibilem malum eligit, tunc facit dissonantias, et inter suas potencias et ad suum principium, quia tunc tendit ad suum principium.

unlimited (*infinitum*) unless it be well tempered by *rationabilitas*, the soul's *bonus rector*:[44]

> irrationabilitas autem comprehendit **concupiscibilitatem et irascibilitatem**, quae duo quasi vicia quedam sunt, naturaliter enim utcumque est **infinitum**, nisi quodam **bono rectore**, scilicet rationabilitate moderatione **quadam temperante**.
>
> Irrationality, however, comprises concupiscence and irascibility, both of which are, as it were, vices. For each of them is somehow unlimited, unless [it be limited] by a certain good ruler, namely rationality, which tempers through a kind of moderation.

Hence, the rational soul provides a limit, a well-tempered moderation, to the soul's nonrational drives. Reason harmonizes nonreason, and this is what it means for the soul to have harmony. The language of this passage (especially the terms printed in bold), however, betrays its Boethian origins—not from the *De institutione musica*, but rather from its arithmetical companion, the *De institutione arithmetica*. The St. Florian commentator here draws on the description of the harmony within the soul at *De institutione arithmetica* 1.32, wherein Boethius, following Nicomachus, reveals how the primacy of *aequalitas* to *inaequalitas* pertains not just to numerical calculations[45] but also, at a more fundamental level, to the nature of the universe (*omnem naturae uim rerumque integritatem* = τῶν ὅλων φυσιολογίαν) and the soul in particular:[46]

> bonitas definita et sub scientiam cadens animoque semper imitabilis et perceptibilis prima natura est et suae substantiae decore perpetua, **infinitum** vero malitiae dedecus est, nullis propriis principiis nixum, sed natura semper errans a boni definitione principii tamquam aliquo signo optimae figurae impressa componitur et ex illo erroris fluctu retinetur. Nam nimiam **cupiditatem iraeque** immodicam effrenationem quasi quidam **rector animus** pura intelligentia roboratus adstringit, et has quodammodo inaequalitatis formas **temperata bonitate** constituit.
>
> Goodness, [being] limited, tractable to knowledge (*scientia*), and forever imitable and perceptible to the soul (*animus*), is by nature first and perpetual in the beauty of a substance all its own, whereas the

[44] *In inst. mus.* 37.

[45] I.e., the primary subject of the chapter at hand. The method of reducing inequality to equality described by Nicomachus and Boethius can be traced, through Theon of Smyrna (*Exp.* 107.15–25ff.), to Adrastus and Eratosthenes.

[46] *Inst. ar.* 1.32 (66.8–15); cf. *Intr. ar.* 1.23.4–5 (65.1–13).

> baseness of evil, being unlimited and resting on no principles of its own but by nature forever wandering, acquires composure from the limited nature of the principle associated with the Good by having impressed upon it, as it were, a kind of seal of the noblest form and finds respite from its fluctuating wandering. For, like a kind of ruler, the soul (*animus*), strengthened by pure intelligence, curbs excessive cupidity and immoderate, unbridled irascibility and, in a way, reduces these forms of inequality to a temperate goodness.

As Jean-Yves Guillaumin has commented, this passage betrays "a Neoplatonic philosophical substrate: in the world as in the domain of number, equality, which pertains to the Same, is a principle prior to inequality, which pertains to the Different. Hence, all can be reduced to the equality, even inequality."[47] Whether by accident or by design, by reading against the grain of the Aristotelian veneer (*ut Aristoteli placet*) of Boethius's psychological division and turning instead to the *De institutione arithmetica*, the St. Florian commentator has paved a way to harmonizing Plato and Aristotle. According to the St. Florian commentator, Aristotle's position amounts to the same thing as Plato, even if it uses a different philosophical lexicon: "that the soul consists in the nature of the Same and the Different" (*est idem quod Plato aliis verbis dixit, quod anima constat ex eadem et diversa natura*).[48]

In a similar analogical fashion, the *Glosae Colonienses super Macrobium* neutralizes the metaphysical implications of Macrobius's Pythagorean oath by interpreting the "quaternary" that grants being to the soul as the four cardinal virtues (prudence, courage, justice, and temperance) or the four stages of understanding (sense perception, imagination, reason, and intellect). The claim that "wise men do not doubt that the soul consists in musical concords," furthermore, is taken not as a statement about the human soul but as an observation about the harmonious effect of the world soul: "That that SOUL CONSISTS IN MUSIC CONCORDS means that the firmament and the spheres below it, as the world soul moves them, make musical sounds."[49] Finally, the Virgilian *terque quaterque beati* encapsulates the three psychological powers (reason, cupidity, and irascibility) and the four bodily humors (*melancolia, colera, sanguis, flegma*).[50] These various triads and

[47] Jean-Yves Guillaumin, ed. and trans., *Boèce: Institution arithmétique* (Paris: Belles lettres, 1995), 67, fn. 201: "le substrat philosophique néoplatonicien: dans le monde comme dans le domaine du nombre, l'égalité, qui relève du Même, est plus principielle que l'inégalité, qui relève de l'Autre. Tout peut donc se ramener à l'égalité, même l'inégalité."

[48] *In inst. mus.* 37. There is a second (and less developed) level to the St. Florian commentator's analysis of the harmony within the soul. The commentator briefly suggests that the microcosmic movements of soul parallel the macrocosmic movements in the heavens. This theory will be dealt with in chapter 5.

[49] *Glos. Colonienses sup. Macr.*, comment. ad 1.6.41–43 (197.15–27): nichil aliud est ANIMAM CONSTARE EX SIMPHONIIS quam quod firmamentum et subiectae sperae, mundana anima inpellente, musicos sonos faciant.

[50] *Glos. Colonienses sup. Macr.*, comment. ad 1.6.44 (197.28–30).

tetrads, however, are left unresolved and unrelated, with no explicit connection to the *symphoniae* discussed by Macrobius. In his comments on the number seven, however, the author of the *Glosae Colonienses* does briefly allude to a theory similar to that expounded by the St. Florian commentator, but it too is applied only to the world soul. The numbers utilized by Plato (and discussed by Macrobius) in the construction of soul are not employed in a way that would permit the soul to be constituted from parts or divided into parts, for the soul itself remains *simplicissima*. Thus the number seven refers either to the harmony of the seven spheres (as above) or to the seven principal powers of the world soul, by which it "embraces, completes, and penetrates all things."[51]

William of Conches briefly dwells on the three powers, and his discussion parallels that given by the St. Florian commentator, but he too neglects to comment explicitly on the connection between the powers of the soul and the harmony of the soul.[52] The *quaternarius*, as in the *Glosae Colonienses*, accords with the four cardinal virtues but also the four elements: "the quaternary granted being to the soul, because of the four elements; for if there were not four elements, then bodies would not exist; and if there were no bodies, then the soul could not have its being within bodies."[53] "That the soul consists in musical concords" merely prompts William to delve into an etymological discussion of the term *symphonia* and the various ratios mentioned by Macrobius. The metaphysical implications, again, are completely glossed over.[54] William does, however, grant that the soul

[51] *Glos. Colonienses sup. Macr.*, comment. ad 1.6.2 (189.29–190.5): Hae proportiones numerorum non ideo assignantur animae, ut ipsa vel constituatur ex aliquibus partibus vel dividatur in partes, sed ideo quia omnia proportionaliter constare faciunt ad similitudinem numerorum. Ipsa enim anima simplicissima est, licet in rebus sit partes habentibus. Vel aliter, scilicet per assignatas proprotiones ostenditur mundana anima caelestem concentum facere in VII speris, quod fit proportionaliter ad similitudinem numerorum per VII discrimina vocum, quae per VII limites possunt notari. Vel aliter, per diversas proportiones et VII limites non notatur aliquas esse partes animae, sed diversae et principales VII eius potestates, scilicet vivificatio, rationalitas, sensualitas, vegetatio, generatio, corruptio et omnium existentia; his enim VII potestatibus omnia ambit, omnia complet, omnia penetret.

[52] *Glos. sup. Macr.*, comment. ad 1.6.42: TRIBVS PARTIBVS, non quod habeat partes ex quibus constat, sed partes uocat in hoc loco animae proprietates. QVARVM PRIMA EST RATIO. Modo uideamus qua necessitate Deus contulit animae has tres potentias. Vidit Deus quaedam homini esse nociua et mala, quaedam minime. Vt ergo homo mala a bonis discernere sciret, animae Deus contulit rationem, id est discretionem mali et boni. Item, quia parum uel nihil prodesset homini discretio nisi appetitum boni haberet et sciret fugere malum, animae eiusdem Deus contulit concupiscentiam de eis quae placent, irascibilitatem de eis quae displicent.

[53] *Glos. sup. Macr.*, comment. ad 1.6.41: Vel aliter: quaternarius dedit esse animae, quia sunt quattuor elementa, et si non essent, nec corpora; et si non corpora, nec anima haberet esse in corporibus.

[54] *Glos. sup. Macr.*, comment. ad 1.6.43: ITEM NVLLVS SAPIENTVM. Aliam dignitatem praedictorum numerorum in musicis consonantiis ostendit. EX SYMPHONIIS, id est consonantiis, quia "sin" con uel simul interpretatur, "phone" sonus. FIT AVTEM DIAPENTE EX HEMIOLO. "Hemi" dimidium dicitur, "olon" totum, inde hemiolius dicitur numerus qui continet alium totum et eius dimidietatem, ut III ad II. Sed ex tali proportione fit diapente, quia duae uoces non possunt facere diapente nisi una contineat alteram et eius dimidietatem. EX EPITRITO. "Epi" supra, "tritos" tertium. Quid sint istae consonantiae in sequenti uolumine explicabimus.

may consist in such proportions. Glossing the Virgilian *terque quaterque beati*, he explains the passage with respect to the (human) soul, "which consists from the proportion which is found in these numbers."[55] But how does soul consist in such proportions? He does not specify. Even if William was less inclined to speculate on the harmony of the human soul per se and was generally content to refer such psychological harmony to its harmonious regulation of the body or its parallels with the *anima mundi*,[56] he found the language of concord, proportion, and harmony a fruitful way of thinking about the construction of the human body and the conjunction of soul with the body.

Somatic Harmonies: The *corpus organicum*

The Timaean Demiurge—in his famous address to the "gods of gods" (θεοὶ θεῶν at 41a7ff.)—delegated (inter alia) the construction of human bodies and their union with souls to the created gods. They took up the august task (at 42e) with due reverence, and, imitating their own creator (μιμούμενοι τὸν σφέτερον δημιουργόν), they fashioned human bodies from borrowed portions of the cosmic elements: earth, air, fire, and water. These four they joined together with close-packed and invisible (but still corporeal) fastenings (πυκνοῖς γόμφοις, 43a3). Although nothing in Plato's highly compressed account suggested any harmonic aspect to the creation of bodies,[57] Bernard of Chartres hints at an underlying proportionality in his gloss on this passage:[58]

> Et EA QVAE ACCEPERANT, id est elementa, CONGLVTINABANT, id est coniungebant, sed NON tam firmis NEXIBVS, sicut sua corpora, SED ALIIS GOMPHIS INVISIBILIBVS, non quia corpora non sit, sed OB INCOMPREHENSIBILEM BREVITATEM. Gomphi proprie dicuntur quaedam instrumenta ferrea, quibus adhaeret ostium, recurua ut hami. Hic uero dicit gomphos quaedam colligamenta partium corporis, scilicet

55 *Glos. sup. Macr.*, comment. ad 1.6.44: quantum ad animam, quae constat ex proportione quae in istis numeris reperitur.

56 *Guillelmi Glos. sup. Tim.* 118.1–11: HAEC DIXIT. Sed quia non est Creatoris promittere et non exequi, ostendit Plato qualiter executus sit promissum, id est creationem humanae animae, more suo deseruiens integumento, huic scilicet quod reliquias illius mixturae ex qua animam mundi commiscuerat in eodem uase posuit et inde animam fecit. Cuius haec est ueritas: anima hominis ex reliquiis mundanae animae est facta quia ut illa ex diuidua substantia et indiuidua et ex eadem natura et diuersa facta est et ut illa mixtura in septem partes proportionaliter est diuisa et ut interualla binis medietatibus sunt fulcita, sic et anima hominis. Sic ergo ut ea ibi exposuimus circa animam mundi, hic exponantur circa animam hominis.

57 Suggestively, πυκνόν is also a technical music-theoretical term referring to two "close-packed" intervals in the chromatic and enharmonic tetrachords. Plato was doubtless familiar with the usage (cf. *Rep.* 531a: πυκνώματ' ἄττα), but I don't think any music-theoretical wordplay was intended in this passage.

58 *Bernardi Glos. sup. Tim.* 7.5–11.

> coaceruationem minorum corpusculorum proportionaliter in corporibus dispositam.
>
> And WHAT THEY TOOK, that is the elements, THEY GLUED TOGETHER, i.e., they joined together, but NOT WITH BONDS so firm as those that held together their own bodies, BUT WITH OTHER GOMPHI, WHICH WERE INVISIBLE not because they were incorporeal but BECAUSE OF THEIR IMPERCEPTIBLE SMALLNESS. The term "gomphi" properly refers to certain iron implements, bent like hooks, that hold doors closed. Here, however, he intends by "gomphi" certain ligaments that join the body's parts, namely an aggregate of small bodily particles proportionally disposed within bodies.

Bernard drew his primary explanation of the *gomphi*—"an aggregate of small bodily particles" (*coaceruationem minorum corpusculorum*)—from Calcidius's commentary,[59] but the specification that the bodily aggregate was arranged *proportionally* seems to be Bernard's own contribution. He leaves it at that, however, and gives no clear indication as to what sort of proportions between what sorts of things were necessary in the constitution of the human body. By the end of the twelfth century, the "musicality" of these *invisibiles gomphi* were assumed as a matter of course—so much so, in fact, that this obscure Timaean word, now accepted as a technical Latin term, *gomphus*, may well have been sung aloud at the magnificent cathedral of Notre Dame de Paris in a monophonic conductus preserved in the famous repertoire book for the cathedral's polyphony and monophony (Florence, Biblioteca Medicea Laurenziana, Pluteus 29.1). This conductus, in the manuscript's tenth fascicle, sets Alan de Lille's *Rhythmus de incarnatione Domini*, where these *gomphi* take their place among other musical terms in the fifth strophe on *musica*:[60]

> Dum Factoris et facture
> Mira fit coniunctio,

[59] *In Tim.* 203 (222.10–17): Inuisibiles porro coniunctiones gomphos appellat, uel min⟨im⟩orum corpusculorum coaceruationem, ut Diodorus, uel eorundem similium inter se conglobationem formabilem, ut Anaxagoras, uel supra dictorum multiformem implicationem, ut Democritus et Leucippus, uel interdum concretionem interdum discretionem, ut Empedocles, concretionem quidem amicitiam, discretionem porro et separationem inimicitiam uocans, uel, ut Stoici, corporum diuersorum usque quaque concretionem.

[60] On which see Marie-Thérèse d'Alverny, "Alain de Lille et la *Theologia*," in *L'homme devant Dieu: Mélanges offerts au Père Henri de Lubac*, vol. 2 ([Paris]: Aubier, 1964), 123–125, with an edition at 126–128. These same *gomphi* are deployed in the union of body and soul effected by Concord in *Anticl.* (7.56–61): Postquam materiem Naturae dextra beavit / vultibus humanis, animam Concordia carni / foederat et stabili connectit dissona nexu. / Iunctura tenui, gunfis subtilibus aptat / composito simplex, hebeti subtile, ligatque / foedere complacito, carni divina maritat.

Quis sit modus ligature
  Quis ordo, que ratio,
Que sint vincla, que iuncture,
  Qui gumphi, que unio,
Stupet sui fracto iure
  Musica proportio.

When the miraculous joining of creator and creation takes place, what would be the mode of their ligature? What would be the order? What would be the ratio? What would be the links? What would be the junctures? What would be the bonds? What would be the union? Musical proportion is astonished when her rule is broken.

The thread that connects the vague *proportionaliter disposita* of Bernard's *gomphi* to the explicit, perhaps even sung, musicality of Alan's use of the term is a theory of a humoral and elemental concord: the harmonic constitution of the body through the harmonious union of the humors, themselves a microcosmic mirror of the cosmic elements. This developed in dialogue with two traditions: Platonic philosophy and Galenic physiology. The first tradition, the philosophical strain, is deeply connected to the classical Harmony Thesis, or at least to Nemesius's extended refutation of it. After listing the Platonic arguments against Simmias's proposition, Nemesius continues by engaging and refuting the second tradition that fueled twelfth-century talk of bodily harmony, the "Galenic" version of the Harmony Thesis, namely that the soul is the *crasis* or *temperantia* of the body.[61] Nemesius musters five discrete arguments against this view;[62] it is the fifth and final argument that concerns us here:[63]

corporis et spiritus cum dispositione carnium et nervorum aliorumque bona temperantia est fortitudo, et calidorum et frigidorum et siccorum et humidorum bona temperantia salus est, et moderatio membrorum cum bono colore pulchritudinem efficit corporis. Si igitur harmonia hoc est concordia salutis et fortitudinis atque pulchritudinis anima est, necesse esset hominem viventem nec infirmari nec debilitari nec

[61] *Prem. phys.* 2.39: Galenus autem testari videtur in demonstrativis sermonibus, tamquam nihil de anima appareat loquens; sed est videre ex his, quae dicit, ut magis velit crasin id est temperantiam esse animam (hanc enim consequuntur morum differentiae), ex dictis Hippocratis confirmans rationem.

[62] The first four arguments are: (1) Si igitur corporis crasis est anima, nullum erit inanimatum (2.41); (2) si anima crasis est, cum crases permutentur secundum aetates, et tempora et diaetas et anima permutabitur (2.44); (3) crasis non repugnat desideriis corporis, sed cooperatur (2.45); (4) si crasis est anima, cum crasis sit qualitas, qualitas vero et adsit et absit praeter subiecti corruptionem, et anima separabitur absque subiecti corruptione (2.46).

[63] *Prem. phys.* 2.49.

> deturpari. Sed frequenter evenit non unam solum, sed has tres simul eucrasias deperdi et vivere hominem.
>
> Strength is a good blending of the body and spirit, along with the arrangement of the flesh, nerves, and other bodily parts; health is the good blending of hot and cold, dry and wet; and the beauty of the body arises from the regularity of the bodily limbs, together with a good complexion. If, therefore, the harmony, i.e., the concord, of health, strength, and beauty is the soul, then it would be necessary that man, for as long as he lives, be neither ill, weak, or disfigured. It frequently happens, however, that not only is one, but even all three of these good temperaments (*eucrasias*) are lost at the same time, yet man still lives.

The harmony of the bodily elements, the body's *eucrasia*, is not equivalent to the soul, but it is a necessary condition for bodily strength, health, and beauty (*fortitudo, salus*, and *pulchritudo*). Galen's theory of *crasis* was available in two other closely related texts: the *Pantegni*, a vast compendium of Greek and Arabic medical science translated from Arabic in the eleventh century by Constantinus Africanus, and the *Isagoge ad artem Galieni*, also translated from Arabic in the eleventh century by a scholar closely connected to Constantinus, if not Constantinus himself.[64] As Danielle Jacquart has highlighted, the *Ysagoge* and *Pantegni* handle Galen's *crasis* differently; the *Ysagoge* uses *commixtio*, whereas the *Pantegni* employs, "perhaps for the first time in medical terminology," *complexio*.[65] Alfanus, Nemesius's translator, opted for a third solution (seen in the passage quoted above), *temperantia*. The twelfth-century medical tradition, in particular the commentaries on the *Articella*, a corpus of medical texts that formed the basic medical curriculum, developed a rich and complex conceptual vocabulary for conceiving this bodily temperament in both physiological and therapeutic terms.[66] And this medically inspired bodily harmony appears in the writings of William of St. Thierry and William of Conches. Despite the famous scuffle between these two authors over the boundaries of (natural) philosophy and theology, their use of the medical tradition is, in many ways, quite similar.[67]

64 On both, see Danielle Jacquart, "Aristotelian Thought in Salerno," in *A History of Twelfth-Century Western Philosophy*, ed. Peter Dronke (Cambridge: Cambridge University Press, 1988), 411–416, with the bibliography cited there, as well as Charles Burnett and Danielle Jacquart, eds., *Constantine the African and 'Alī ibn al-'Abbās al-Maǧūsī: The* Pantegni *and Related Texts* (Leiden: Brill, 1994).

65 Jacquart, "Aristotelian Thought in Salerno," 415.

66 See Danielle Jacquart and Agostino Paravicini Bagliani, eds., *La scuola medica Salernitana: Gli autori e i testi* (Florence: SISMEL, Edizioni del Galluzzo, 2007).

67 See Paul Edward Dutton, *The Mystery of the Missing Heresy Trial of William of Conches* (Toronto: Pontifical Institute of Mediaeval Studies, 2006).

According to William of Conches, the human body is created from the elements, which give rise to the four humors. These in turn constitute the *homiomira* (the parts of the body that share the same essence, such as bones, flesh, nerves, etc.), which themselves constitute the *organica* (the bodily limbs, such as the hand, the foot, etc.). William, following Constantinus, describes this as a process of both composition and (mental) division.[68] The elements, moreover, must be properly and proportionally disposed, as William explains in his gloss on the Timaean *gomphi*:[69]

> Ostenso ex quibus humanum corpus sit excogitatum, subiungit et qualiter dicens: CONGLVTINABANT id est proportionaliter coniungebant EA QVAE ACCEPERANT id est quatuor elementa—aliter enim satisfacere uitae non posset—sed NON TAMEN EISDEM NEXIBVS QVIBVS ILLI sunt conglutinati: hoc quantum ad stellas. Non est enim indissolubilis proportio elementorum in homine ut est in stellis. SED ALIIS GVMPHIS: gumphus est latens coniuctio duarum gantarum in rota. Per gumphum igitur intellexit proportiones elementorum in humano corpore. INVISIBILIBVS quia a paucis intelliguntur; et hoc OB INCOMPREHENSIBILEM BREVITATEM id est subtilitatem.

> Having demonstrated from what the human body was constituted, he adds how it was so constituted, saying: THEY GLUED TOGETHER, i.e., they joined together proportionally WHAT THEY TOOK, i.e., the four elements—for otherwise it would be insufficient to confer life—but

[68] Composition, e.g., *Guillelmi Glos. sup. Tim.* 127.18–23: Et nota quod non dicit ex qualitatibus elementorum humanum corpus constare ut quidam gartiones confingunt, garrientes quod si ex igne constaret homo, haberet ignem in barba et sic exureretur, ignorantes qualiter elementa transeant in humores, humores spissati in homiomira, homiomira in organica. *Phil.* 1.21 (49A): Voluit autem iste Constantinus ex quatuor elementis constare humores, ex humoribus spissatis partes tam omiomiras, id est consimiles ut est caro et ossa, quam organicas, id est officiales, ut manus, pedes et similia. Division, e.g., *Guillelmi Glos. sup. Tim.* 59.3–8: Diuiditur enim humanum corpus in organica scilicet in manus, etc., organica in homiomira, homiomira in humores, humores in elementa. Cuius diuisionis pars actu, pars sola cogitatione et ratione fieri potest quia, ut ait Boetius, "uis est intellectus coniuncta disiungere et disiuncta coniungere" (*In Isag.* II.165.3–4). Cf. *Phil.* 1.21 (49BC): Dividitur enim, ut figuraliter dicatur, humanum corpus in organica, scilicet in manus etc., organica vero in omiomira, i.e. consimilia, videlicet in particulas carnis et ossis etc., omiomira autem in humores, melancholiam etc., et humores in elementa, id est in simplas et minimas particulas. Cf. Constantinus, *Pantegni*, Theorica, I, 2 (3): Dissolutio est res in mente conceptas usque ad partes deducere ignotas, uerbi gratia, corpus humanum in membra officialis. . . . Compositio dissolutorum ab inferiori ad superiora reductio, ut elementorum in cibum, cibi in humores. . . . The terminology of *homiomira* and *organica* is drawn from Nemesius, *Prem. phys.* 4.9–13; see Theodore Silverstein, "Guillaume de Conches and the Elements: *Homiomeria* and *Organica*," *Mediaeval Studies* 26 (1964), 363–367. Cf. Bernard Silvestris, *Comm. in Mart.* 3.391–397.

[69] *Guillelmi Glos. sup. Tim.* 127.27–36.

> NOT WITH THE SAME BONDS BY WHICH THEY were glued together. Understand this with respect to the stars. For humans do not have the same indissoluble proportion of elements as stars do. BUT WITH OTHER GOMPHI: a "gomphus" is the hidden conjunction of two rims on a wheel. Therefore, by "gomphus" understand the proportions of the elements in a human body. INVISIBLE, because they are understood by very few, and this ON ACCOUNT OF THEIR IMPERCEPTIBLE SMALLNESS, i.e., subtlety.

The Timaean *gomphi* have thus become the proportions of the elements that constitute the human body, and William closely adheres to Plato in attributing the initial forging and continual maintenance of these elemental proportions to the *Dii Deorum*. Plato deems the "created stars and spirits" the "Gods of Gods," William explains, because they have dominion over the four elements.[70] To those who would charge him with heresy for believing the stars and planets to have such wide dominion over the human body, William replies:[71]

> Si enim uerum est quod planetae calorem et siccitatem, frigus et humiditatem conferunt terris, si uitam herbis et arboribus, si temperiem uel distemperiem humanis corporibus, quid mirum si in conceptione, in utero, in natiuitate, in uita, corpora contrahunt temperiem qualitatum ad diu uiuendum et ad animam conseruandam, uel distemperiem ad contrarium?

> For if it is true that the planets confer heat and dryness, cold and moisture on the land, life on plants and trees, temper or distemper on human bodies, why should it be surprising if, in their conception, gestation, birth, and life, bodies contract either the temper of [elemental] qualities in order to sustain life and preserve the soul, or the distemper [of the elemental qualities], which has the opposite effect?

William saw the creation of the human body as part of a more generalized cosmogonic process of species differentiation brought about by the heat of the newly created stars. The stars heated the water, causing it to evaporate and reveal the mud

[70] *Guillelmi Glos. sup. Tim.* 113.1–7: Finito tractatu de creatione caelestis animalis tam uisibilis quam inuisibilis, transit ad creationem ceterorum animalium, more suo ad integumentum se transferens quod tale est quod, creatis stellis et spiritibus, conuocauit eos Deus in uno conuentu habitaque oratione iniunxit eis officium formandi corpora ceterorum animalium, et maxime hominis, coniungendique animam corpori et conseruandi eam cum corpore, dandi cibi incrementa et dissoluendi. 113.24–26: Dicit ergo: O DII DEORVM. Stellae et spiritus dii deorum sunt quia dominantur quatuor elementis quae, ut supra expositum est, dii reputantur. For a longer discussion of William's interpretation of the Platonic injunction to the *dii deorum*, see Dronke, *The Spell of Calcidius: Platonic Concepts and Images in the Medieval West*, 129–133.

[71] *Guillelmi Glos. sup. Tim.* 119.25–30.

of the newly formed earth; this muddy earth, itself now boiling from the heat, bubbled up lumps of this primordial earth, which subsequently became different animals depending on the differing elemental (im)balances of the lumps that bubbled forth: those that had more elemental fire became lions; earthy lumps, asses; watery lumps, pigs; and so on. Only an equally proportioned elemental lump can create man (*ex quadam uero parte in qua elementa conueniunt aequaliter, humanum corpus factum est*).[72] William thinks that this natural process can even account for the fact that only a single member of the human species was created in this way, for, according to the authority of Boethius, the *inaequalitas* of the imbalanced lumps that generate the *melancolica, flegmatica*, and *colerica animalia* is "numerous and multiple" (*numerosa et multiplex*), whereas the *aequalitas* of the balanced elemental lump that is man is "few and finite" (*pauca et finita*).[73] Human exceptionalism is reduced to statistical probability. This general account of the differentiation of species, which remains largely consistent across William's oeuvre,[74] led him, in his *Philosophia*, to develop a metaphorical take on the creation of woman from the "rib" of Adam. William argues that Eve's creation from Adam's rib must be a metaphorical (*non ad litteram*) expression for the earth just around Adam. William sums up the silliness of taking the text at its word by coining a silly word to describe it—surely God would not de-rib (*excostare*) the first man.[75]

72 *Guillelmi Glos. sup. Tim.* 52.1–23: Sed cum terra ex praecedenti humore esset lutosa, ex calore bulliens, diuersa genera animalium creauit. Et, si in aliqua parte illius plus fuit de igne, nata sunt colerica animalia ut leo; si de terra, melancolica ut asinus; si de aqua, flegmatica ut porcus. Ex quadam uero parte, in qua elementa conueniunt equaliter, humanum corpus factum est. Et hoc est quod diuina pagina dicit Deum hominem ex limo terrae fecisse.

73 *Guillelmi Glos. sup. Tim.* 52.27–30: Vnde, cum diuersa melancolica facta sint animalia et infinita flegmatica et colerica, unus solus homo formatus est quia, ut ait Boetius in *Arismetica*: "Omnis aequalitas pauca est et finita, inaequalitas uero numerosa et multiplex." Cf. *Inst. ar.* 1.21–22 (*ad sensum*).

74 Cf. *Phil.* 1.23 (55D); *Glos. sup. Boet.* 3.m9.289–301; *Drag.* 3.4.1–5.

75 *Phil.* 1.23 (56A): ex uicino limo terrae corpus mulieris esse creatum uerisimile est . . . et hoc est quod diuina pagina dicit, deum fecisse mulierem ex latere Adae. Non enim ad litteram credendum est deum excostasse primum hominem.' Cf. the later retraction of this theory in *Drag.* 3.4.5.40–45: Sed ut esset adiutorium simile illi, inmisso in illo sopore, tulit unam ex eius costis, ex qua mulierem plasmauit. Quod non penuria materiae fecit, sed ut mulierem uiro coniunctam et subditam esse debere significaret et sacrum coniugii confirmaret et ecclesiam, quae ex latere eius in sacramentis profluxit, praefiguraret. Note that William's revised view closely adheres to the criticisms levied by William of St. Thierry in *De erroribus Guillelmi de Conchis* (ed. P. Verdeyen, CCCM 89A [Turnhout: Brepols, 2007]), 9.315–328: In creatione uero mulieris palam omnibus legentibus est, quam stulte, quam superbe irridet historiam diuinae auctoritatis, scilicet excostasse Deum primum hominem ad faciendam de costa eius mulierem. Et physico illud sensu interpretans, nimis arroganter ueritati historiae suum praefert inuentum, paruipendens magnum illud sacramentum de quo Apostolus dicit: "Hoc nunc os ex ossibus meis, et caro de carne mea. Ego autem dico in Christo et in ecclesia." Augustinus: "Adam, qui erat forma futuri, rerum imaginem et magnum indicium sacramenti nobis praebuit, immo Deus in illo. Nam et dormiens meruit accipere uxorem, quae de costa eius facta est, quoniam de Christo in cruce dormiente futura erat ecclesia de latere eius dormientis, quia de latere in crucis pendentis lancea perfosso sacramenta ecclesiae profluxerunt."

In one of William's last works, the *Dragmaticon*, he retracts his *non ad litteram* interpretation of the Genesis account, but he does not temper the naturalistic impulse behind it. Rather, he transfers it from the creation account to that of the Fall. The first man, he claims, was perfectly balanced in his four qualities (*primus enim homo inter quatuor qualitates fuit temperatus*), but:[76]

> postquam amoenitate paradisi expulsus in ualle lacrimarum et miseriae in labore manuum suarum coepit uesci pane, suo labore uigiliis ieiuniis cepit desiccari atque naturalis calor extingui. Similiter ex intemperie aeris, ex qualitate cibi et potus. Omnes igitiur ex eo nati, utpote ex corrupto, sunt corrupti, neque postea perfecta sanitas in homine fuit inuenta. Est enim perfecte sanum quod est in homoeomeriis eucraticum et in organicis aequale.
>
> after he had been expelled from the beauty of paradise and began to eat bread by the labor of his hands in the valley of tears and misery, he began to dry out from his labor as well as the deprivations of food and sleep, and his natural heat began to fade. Similarly, he was affected by the intemperate weather and the quality of his food and drink. His descendants, therefore, born as they were from a corrupt ancestor, have all been corrupted, and never afterward has perfect health been found in humans. For that is perfectly healthy which is well tempered in its homeomeric parts and uniform in its organic parts.

However, the lack of *perfecta sanitas* is not yet a full bodily *discordia*, for as we will see in the final section of this chapter, it is the harmony of the body (even if an imperfect harmony) that is the *conditio sine qua non* for the soul's union with the body.

William of St. Thierry, William of Conches's staunchest and loudest critic, cried heresy at the natural-philosophical meaning (*physicus sensus*) that his opponent so arrogantly asserted in the realm of divine history: "how foolishly, how hubristically he mocks the [creation] account vouched for by divine authority!" (*quam stulte, quam superbe irridet historiam divinae auctoritatis*!).[77] Nonetheless, William of St. Thierry was not opposed to the proper application of the very same medical and philosophical principles that motivated William of Conches's boldest

[76] *Drag.* 6.13.11–19; Italo Ronca and Matthew Curr, trans., *William of Conches: A Dialogue on Natural Philosophy* (Notre Dame, IN: University of Notre Dame Press, 1997), 147 (translation lightly modified). On the "hidden moral recesses of *natura operans*" at work in this passage, see Willemien Otten, "Nature, Body and Text in Early Medieval Theology: From Eriugena to Chartres," in *Divine Creation in Ancient, Medieval, and Early Modern Thought: Essays Presented to the Rev'd Dr. Robert D. Crouse*, ed. Michael Treschow, Willemien Otten, and Walter Hannam (Leiden: Brill, 2007), 252–255.

[77] *De erroribus Guillelmi de Conchis* 9.315–317.

interpretations. The first half of St. Thierry's *De natura corporis et animae* opens with a theory of the constitution of the body that similarly bespeaks the influence of both Constantinus and Nemesius in its alternation between *complexio* (the language of Constantinus's *Pantegni*) and *temperantia* (the language of Nemesius as translated by Alfanus):[78]

> Itaque in corpore animali sua propria est complexio prima et naturalis in ipso elementorum coniunctio, quae si aequalis est et bene composita, ut contraria non impugnentur uel destruantur a contrariis, sed calida temperentur a frigidis, frigida a calidis, sicque de reliquis, bona fit complexio, et consentiente natura fit eucrasia, bona scilicet temperantia quatuor qualitatum. Rebus enim naturalibus in temperamento manentibus, impossibile est humanum corpus ab aliquo morbo infestari, si est, ut dictum est, eucraticum, id est bonae complexionis. His autem distemperatis, necesse est alterari corpus.
>
> Thus in an animal's body, its own first and natural complexion is the conjunction of elements within it. If this conjunction is balanced and well composed so that contraries are not assailed and destroyed by contraries, but hot is tempered by cold and cold in turn by hot (and so on), then there is a good complexion and, with nature consenting, good temperament (*eucrasia*) obtains. For when the natural things remain in balance (*in temperamento*), it is impossible for the human body to be assailed by any disease, if it is, as it was said, well tempered, that is, of a good complexion. When, however, these things are distempered, then it is necessary for the body to be altered.

Eucrasia, a term that William of St. Thierry seems to have taken from Nemesius, occurs *consentiente natura*—it is, in other words, the result of natural processes. At the beginning of the second section, namely the *De natura animae*, William reiterates the natural quality of the human body in order to draw the distinction between the natural body and the divine soul. The power of life (*ad uiuendum uirtus*) does not, William claims, arise from any single part of the body:[79]

> sed auctrice anima a Deo data, plurimis particulis natura ad uitae constitutionem suas occasiones et efficientias inspirans, necessariam

[78] *De nat. corp. et an.* 1.5 (73–75).

[79] *De nat. corp. et an.* 2.53 (133). In numerous other passages William grants *natura* (often *natura prouida*) a creative power: e.g., 1.28 (101): . . . et per poros quos in eis *prouida creauit natura* . . .; 1.30 (113): *Natura* enim *prouida* septem paria neruorum in ipso cerebro fundauit . . .; 2.52 (131): Nam caetera omnia adiectio quaedam sunt bonorum, quae propter bene uiuere *natura* contulit homini . . .; 2.53 (133): Sunt uero quaedam ex eis *a natura* uitae constitutionibus adiecta, et uitae officinis subseruientia, sine quorum adminiculo suum illae officium implere non possunt, sicut sunt uenter et pulmo et caetera nonnulla.

> quandam et mirabilem et pene inscrutabilem ex omnibus in unum uiuendi facit collationem.
>
> but with the God-granted soul as its source, nature, breathing into the many parts the causes and capacities for the constitution of life, makes the necessary, wondrous, and nearly incomprehensible collection of all the parts into one living being.

This *mirabilis et pene inscrutabilis collatio* that we call the human body is, as William emphasizes elsewhere in the same work, a harmony that mirrors at the microcosmic level (in bodily humors) macrocosmic harmonies (in the cosmological elements): just as the elements of the world are concordant in their diversity, so too are the bodily humors.[80]

The body, then, is a well-harmonized whole—and it came to be likened to an instrument, a *corpus organicum*, whose potential harmony is realized by a soul-musician. The instrumentalized body, in both the musical and nonmusical senses of the term, is a metaphor that, as Harold Cherniss has pointed out, extends back to Plato's *Alcibiades I* 130A.[81] The primary source for twelfth-century discussions of the instrumental body, however, is Gregory of Nyssa's *De opificio hominis*, as translated by Eriugena.[82] Gregory is the source, for instance, of William of St. Thierry's claim that the body is an instrument (*organum*) and the soul its musician. Moreover, the proper "harmonic" quality of the body is a necessary (but not fully sufficient) condition for beautiful body music; it also depends in part on the skill of the musician, that is, the quality of the soul that plays upon the body. William's focus, however, is the body:[83]

> Et sicut in organo musico modulari scientes, aptum artis suae instrumentum inuenientes, sollemniter artis ipsius officium exercent, si

[80] *De nat. corp. et an.* 1.11 (81–83): Eodem enim modo elementa operantur in mundo maiori quo operantur quatuor humores in mundo minori qui est homo, id est microcosmos, ut supra dictum est, ex sua sibi diuersitate concordantia et per concordem diuersitatem facientia pulcherrimam ordinis sui unitatem. Cf. Alan de Lille, *De pl. nat.* 6.6: Ego sum illa, que ad exemplarem mundane machine similitudinem hominis exemplavi naturam, ut in eo velut in speculo ipsius mundi scripta natura compareat. Sicut enim quatuor elementorum concors discordia, unica pluralitas, consonantia dissonans, consensus dissentiens, mundialis regie structuram conciliat, sic quatuor complexionum compar disparitas, inequalis equalitas, difformis conformitas, diversa idemptitas, edificium corporis humani compaginat. Et que qualitates inter elementa mediatrices conveniunt, eedem inter quatuor humores pacis sanciunt firmitatem. Cf. *Exp. in Mart.* 50r: nam ex seminis particulis proportionaliter sibi commixtis hominis corpus producitur, et quatuor elementa (sicut in mundi constitutione, quoniam microcosmus est) proportionaliter aptantur.

[81] Harold Cherniss, *The Platonism of Gregory of Nyssa* (Berkeley: University of California Press, 1934), 72, n. 67. Plato's examples are the shoemaker and his tools, the harpist and the harp.

[82] On which, see (with care) Bruce W. Holsinger, *Music, Body, and Desire in Medieval Culture: Hildegard of Bingen to Chaucer* (Stanford, CA: Stanford University Press, 2001), 46–53.

[83] *De nat. corp. et an.* 2.66 (149) (= *De imag.* 12 [223.44–224.5]). Gregory's thought here is Plotinian, e.g., *Enn.* 1.4, which concludes with a body = cithara analogy. Cf. *Prem. phys.* 2.51: Corpus namque organum

> uero carie uel uetustate fuerit attritum uel quolibet euentu turbatum, artifex quidem de arte nil perdit, organum uero inactuosum manet et absonum, sic et animus totum corporis organum obtinens, et intellectualibus operationibus singulas partes sicut consueuit tangens, in his quidem quae [*scripsi*, qui *Lemoine*; cf. *De imag.* 12 (224.3)] secundum naturam disponuntur quod suum est operatur, in his uero quae infirmantur artificialem sui motum pigrum habet et inactuosum. Vnde et natura organum corporis usui rationis per omnia componit et coaptat.

> Just as those who know how to make music on a musical instrument, upon finding an instrument suited to their art, well exercise the office of their art, but if the instrument is worn by rot or age or damaged by some accident, although the artist loses nothing of his art, the instrument still remains unresponsive or silent; so too the intellectual soul takes possession of the whole instrument of the body, and touching each part singly in its intellectual operations as is its wont, in those parts which are naturally disposed, it accomplishes its own operations, but in those which are weakened, its operation is sluggish and inactive. Whence nature prepares and adapts the instrument of the body to the use of reason in everything.

William continues, still following Gregory, by enumerating the various parts of the body and the ways in which they contribute to its instrumentality: without hands, for instance, man would have been like beasts on all fours and his mouth would have thus had a canine roughness; thus without hands, man could never have had an *articulata uox*. William's soul-musician is an excellent example of what Stephen Gersh has queried as a possible interpretation of Boethius's *musica humana*: "is it something . . . like the process whereby the soul's silent inner thoughts achieve external expression in sound?"[84] This is precisely how William explains the relationship between soul and body. *Musica humana* (though it is never deemed as such in William's treatise) is the soul's expression, which finds voice through the instrument of the body:[85]

> ut plectri instar, dum [sc. animus] oris particulas uoci coaptatas tangit, per talem sonorum formationem interiorem suum loquendo

id est instrumentum existens animae, si quidem congrue adaptetur, cooperatur animae ipsumque convenienter habet; si vero incongrue, obstat et tunc usus rerum animae oppugnatur ab incongruitate organi; et si nimis repugnaverit, ad illud quoque convertitur, quemadmodum musicus simul peccat cum distortione lyrae, nisi prius eam bene correxerit. Ideo igitur usus animae est ex congruitate corporis, ut componat illud organum sibi congruum. Hoc autem facit ratione et moribus, haec quidem intendendo, illa vero remittendo, velut in harmonia, ut ipsa sibi congruum illud componat eoque tamquam organo convenienter utatur, sin autem, ipsa convertetur ad illud; quod saepe contingit.

84 Stephen Gersh, *Concord in Discourse: Harmonics and Semiotics in Late Classical and Early Medieval Platonism* (Berlin and New York: Mouton de Gruyter, 1996), 44.

85 *De nat. corp. et an.* 2.68–69 (151–153) (= *De imag.* 9 [219.9–18]).

> interpretetur motum, ueluti si quis musicae peritus existens, propriam ex passione aliqua non habens uocem, uolens autem manifestam facere musicam alienis uocibus modulatur, per tibias siue lyras artem publicans. Sic animus diuersorum intellectuum inuentor cum ipse incorporeus corporeas dictiones per se non habeat, intelligentiae impetus per corporales sensus sufficit ostendere.
>
> When the intellectual soul touches, like a plectrum, the parts of the mouth adapted for voice, through such a formation of sounds it expresses in speech its own interior motion, as if it were a skillful musician, who, by some affliction, has no voice of his own but still desires to make music, does so through voices not his own, revealing his art through tibiae or lyres. Since the intellectual soul, the author of diverse thoughts, being itself incorporeal does not have, on its own, corporeal words, it elects to reveal the impetus of its intelligence through the corporeal senses.

In this striking reversal of the usual ontological hierarchy, the soul is cast as a disabled musician, whose body becomes a prosthetic supplement for the soul's otherwise voiceless existence, an instrument for the soul's exterior musical agency in the world. Metaphors of prosthesis often invoke and provoke the inherent vulnerability, variability, and incompleteness of bodies, bodies that refuse to "conform to the mind's desire for order and rationality,"[86] but here it is the body, qua prosthesis, that reveals the incompleteness of the disembodied soul.

Psychosomatic Harmonies: The Union of Body and Soul

Despite the uniform stance of the classical and late-ancient authorities against the Harmony Thesis, there is one twelfth-century author who approached (independently, it seems, of any of these sources) a similarly "harmonic" conception of the relation between soul and body. It is Isaac of Stella, who, in his *Epistola de anima* (written later, probably sometime in the 1160),[87] invokes a harmony metaphor in order to affirm what the Harmony Thesis (in all of its varieties) uniformly denied: the immortality of the soul. Isaac describes the body in a manner reminiscent of William of St. Thierry: it is a well-tuned and harmonized instrument that is suited

[86] As noted by David Mitchell and Sharon Snyder, *Narrative Prosthesis: Disability and the Dependencies of Discourse* (Ann Arbor: University of Michigan Press, 2000), 48.

[87] I cite the *Ep. de an.* according to the edition of Caterina Tarlazzi, "L'*Epistola de anima* di Isacco di Stella: Studio della tradizione ed edizione del testo," *Medioevo: Rivista di storia della filosofia medievale* 36 (2011), 167–278; for ease of reference, however, I key the citations to the *Patrologia Latina* column numbers (PL 194), included in Tarlazzi's edition.

to be played by the rational soul.[88] The soul receives the body gladly, as if it were the instrument of its operation and delight, and upon receiving it, exults with the joy of "lyrists waxing lyrical upon their lyres" (*citharedorum citharizantium in citharis suis*, Apoc. 14.2).[89] Isaac then characterizes the union between body and soul as a harmony (*conuenientia*) realized through two harmonized means (*per duas medietates conuenientissimas*): the *sensualitas carnis* (perception) and the *phantasticum spiritus* (imagination), both of which are of a fiery nature and thus what Virgil had in mind when, speaking of souls, he wrote: "Fiery is their power and divine their origin" (*Aeneid.* 6.792: *igneus est illis uigor, et coelestis origio*).[90] Isaac raises the following hypothetical objection: if the soul is present to the body via the medium of *sensualitas*, which is a bodily spirit, then why does the body not live through that spirit after the departure of the soul?[91]

To this, Isaac replies that as long as the *sensualitas* has *integritas* and *temperantia*, the soul does not recede from the body, but when it becomes *distemperata* and *disrupta*, the soul unwillingly departs, taking with it all its powers (*sensus, imaginatio, ratio*, etc.).[92] Isaac then expounds upon the harmonic tinge already implied

88 *Ep. de an.* 1882A: rationali tamen anime compositione sui humani corporis habitaculum mage congruit, quasi rationabilibus et armonicis eius motibus seu numeris summi cithariste plectro obtemperatum et consonum.

89 *Ep. de an.* 1882B: quasi instrumentum operationis et delectationis illud anima et libenter suscipiat et sollicita custodiat et inuita dimittat et dimissum desiderabunda expectet et in recepto gratulabunda exultet, sicut est apud Iohannem "citharedorum citharizantium in citharis suis."

90 *Ep. de an.* 1882C: Per duas etenim medietates conuenientissimas facile et firmae duae dissidentes extremitates necti possunt: quod in magni, ut quidam dicunt, animalis, id est mundi huius fabrica cernere facile est. Conuenientissima autem media sunt animae et carnis, iuxta quod dictum est, et multiplicius assignari possent, sensualitas carnis, quae maxime ignis, et phantasticum spiritus, quod igneus uigor dicitur. Quidam de animabus loquens, ait: Igneus est illis uigor et coelestis origo. Cf. Bernard Silvestris, who similarly links body and soul with a (single) *spiritus* midway between the two. *Comm. in Mart.* 3.707–731: Hunc spiritum animalem *auram* dicit. Hic plus habet se ad animam quam corpus, quia insensibilis est. Sensus namque non capit ipsos sensus. Plus item se habet ad corpus quam ad anima; est enim ex elementis. Hic animalis spiritus est et dissolubilis. Et quia plus convenit illis quam illa ad invicem, ideo medio interveniente iunguntur in homine. . . . Tria hec ergo habet in se homo: corpus et animam divinam, quam hic "mentem" dicit—de qua alias disputabitur—et habet animalem spiritum, quo medio duo illa conveniunt. Atque hoc est quod dicit: TV, Musica, SOCIAS AVRAM, id est spiritum animalem corporibus, que aura est MENTIS, id est divine anime, quasi famula domine. Superior enim natura, que est mens, inferiorem hanc sensualitatem cohibere debet, quasi diceret: corpori iungis AURAM et hac media mentem. Cf. *Phil.* 4.33 (98D): Tunc enim naturalis virtus per membra discurrere incipit, sine qua vita non potest esse nec anima in corpore.

91 *Ep. de an.* 1882C: Hic fortasse dicet aliquis: si per sensualitatem illam, que spiritus corporeus est, inest anima corpori, quare post ipsius discessum eo spiritu, qui utique uita est, non uiuit corpus?

92 *Ep. de an.* 1882D: Ad quod dicimus: dum illius sensualitatis integritas et temperantia congruens uiuificationi manserit, numquam recedere animam; cum autem distemperata et dirupta, inuitam recedere, secum omnia sua ferre, sensum uidelicet et imaginationem rationem intellectum intelligentiam concupiscibilitatem irascibilitatem, et ex his secundum merita affici ad delectationem siue ad dolorem.

in the terms *temperantia* and *distemperata*, explaining the relation between soul and body with an extended metaphor that echoes the Harmony Thesis:[93]

> corpus autem tamquam organum, quod prius integrum contemperatum et dispositum, ut melos musicum in se contineret et tactum resonaret, nunc confractum et inutile e regione iacere; perisse quidem organum sed non perisse melos siue cantum, nisi tantum sonum cantum putaueris. Neque enim anima, que corpus non est, localis esse potest nec localiter accedere inhabitare uel recedere, sed sicut in organo musico seu antiphonario folio cantus inest siue melos musicum dum corde seu notule congrue disposite sunt, cum autem disponuntur accedit, cum confunduntur discedit, ita et anime est ratio cum suo corpore. Et si queris ubi sit anima post corpus, quero ubi sit cantus post folium aut post sonum . . .
>
> The body, as if an instrument, which had previously been whole, well tuned, and arranged so that it might contain within itself a musical melody and resound when touched, now, on the contrary, lies broken and useless. The instrument, yes, has perished, but the melody or song has not, unless you suppose that the song is only the sound. For the soul, which is not a body, cannot be located anywhere, nor can it approach, reside within, or depart from anywhere. But just as a song or musical melody is present within a musical instrument or the page of an antiphoner, provided the strings or the notes are congruently arranged, when these are so arranged, music approaches, when they are torn asunder, music departs; so too is the relationship (*ratio*) of the soul with its body. And if you ask me "Where is the soul after the

[93] *Ep. de an.* 1882D–1883A. This argument was incorporated into the Pseudo-Augustinian *De spiritu et anima* (PL 40, 791) and was later picked up by, among others, Thomas of Cantimpré in his thirteenth-century encyclopedia *Liber de natura rerum*, where it appears in a corrupt but still recognizable form: Corpus autem quod prius integrum tanquam organum contemperatum et dispositum, ut melos musicum in se concineret et tractum [*sic*] resonaret, nunc confractum et inutile e regione iacet (Helmut Boese, ed., *Thomas Cantimpratensis: Liber de natura rerum* [Berlin: Walter de Gruyter, 1973], 2.11.40–42). Bruce Holsinger, not realizing the origin of this phrase, assumed that it was an encapsulation of William of St. Thierry's arguments and offered the following (mis)translation: "For the body, because it is first created well-tempered and ordered, is like a musical instrument, for sweet music harmonized in it and, drawn out, resonates, and when finished is expelled from the unused region" (Holsinger, *Music, Body, and Desire in Medieval Culture*, 221). It also appears, explicitly attributed to Augustine, in the *Commentum Oxoniense in musicam Boethii*: Etenim quandiu equalitas, concordia et proporcio humorum per alimentum corporis viguerit, manet anima regens corpus integrum et quasi organum unum contemperatum et dispositum, ut in se melos musicos contineret, secundum Augustinum De spiritu et anima 2°; sed cum omnis dissolucio ex discordia et inequalitate contingat . . ., post receussum anime corpus quasi confractum et inutile iacet sine regimine (Hochadel, *Commentum Oxoniense in musicam Boethii*, 78.30–37).

> body?" I ask you, "Where is a song after you turn the page or after the sound falls silent?"

Despite the apparent echo of the Harmony Thesis, Isaac's metaphor drifts away from its classical formulation at several crucial points. Firstly and most obviously, Isaac speaks nowhere of harmony. Rather, his language is that of *melos musicum* and *cantus*, musical melody and song, a change that wreaks philosophical havoc on the Harmony Thesis—primarily because these are audible phenomena and thus directly accessible by the senses, which the soul, as an entirely incorporeal entity, is not.[94]

Isaac, however, addresses this in his central premise, which turns the Harmony Thesis on its head: "when the instrument has perished, the melody or song *does not* perish along with it, unless you suppose that the song is only the sound." For Isaac, *cantus* and *melos* are clearly something over and above *sonus*; presumably that something would be the transcendental harmonic structures, the musical proportions that give rise to the harmonious sounds and continue to exist even when the immanent sound has fallen silent. Thus, his second departure from the Harmony Thesis. Isaac, in effect, pulls the harmony out of the body and posits it as a transcendental that is not solely dependent upon the body but is present within or absent from the body, depending on the body's state. Isaac's argument partly turns on a thought of central importance to Gregory of Nyssa: the soul cannot be localized within the body, as an incorporeal cannot be contained by a body (*neque enim anima, que corpus non est, localis esse potest nec localiter accedere inhabitare uel recedere*).[95] Isaac's argument, therefore, denies one crucial premise of the Harmony Thesis: that the harmony is somehow localized "in the tuned lyre" (ἐν τῇ ἡρμοσμένῃ λύρᾳ, *Phaedo* 86a1). Isaac's metaphorically musical soul cannot be explained through epiphenomenalism, supervenient dualism, or any sort of functionalism *avant la lettre* (to list a few modern theories often floated in discussions

[94] Such an interpretation of the theory was proposed by A. E. Taylor, who suggested that "'mind' is the tune given out by the 'strings' of the body, the music made by the body," and compared it with the epiphenomenalism of T. H. Huxley (A. E. Taylor, *Plato: The Man and his Work*, 3rd ed., revised and expanded [London: Methuen, 1929], 194).

[95] For this claim, cf. *De hom. op.* 178BC = *De imag.* 16231.26–35; cf. *Periphyseon* IV, 2108–2120: Sed quia non in parte quadam eorum quae in nobis sunt animus comprehenditur, sed aequaliter in omnibus et per omnia est, . . . neque intus existens (non enim in corpore incorporale tenetur)—neque extra comprehendens (non enim circumprenditur in corporale), sed secundum quendam modum superrationabilem et inintelligibilem appropinquat animus naturae, et coaptatus in ipsa et circa ipsam consideratur, neque intus positus, neque circumplexus. The importance of this claim for Gregory is highlighted and discussed by Cherniss, *The Platonism of Gregory of Nyssa*, 24. Cf. William of St. Thierry, *De nat. corp. et an.* 2.64 (147): Auctor enim naturae intellectualis substantiae ad corporalem societatem et contactum quendam uoluit esse ineffabilem et inintelligibilem, scilicet ut neque intus existat, neque enim in corpore incorporale tenetur, neque comprehenditur a corpore, neque exterius inueniatur eadem naturae lege.

of the Harmony Thesis). This point is highlighted by a subtle shift in the metaphor. No longer does Isaac speak only in terms of a musical instrument, something that can be tuned, but he adds a quite different sort of analogy: the notes on the page of an antiphoner. When the strings of an instrument or the notes on the page of an antiphoner are properly arranged (*corde seu notule congrue disposite*), melody approaches (*accedit*); when they are in disarray, melody departs (*discedit*).

This shift, from instrument to notation (which will eventually give way to sound itself), reveals the real burden of Isaac's metaphor. He seeks neither to give a robust ontology of the soul nor to explain the soul in terms of any bodily constitution or arrangement; rather, he seeks to illuminate, via a metaphor that would be familiar and accessible to his readers, just how a permanent incorporeal substance can be present to and depart from a transitory corporeal body. And the "presence" of eternal incorporeal music within a perishable corporeal instrument is only one way of conveying the concept, for Isaac eventually abandons the body-as-instrument metaphor altogether. Asking where the soul is "after the body" is like asking where the song is after the page is turned or the sound falls silent. The body as a well-tuned instrument is no longer needed to make his point, and Isaac concludes by listing other comparisons that extend well beyond the musical metaphor with which he began:[96]

> Et si queris ubi sit anima post corpus, quero ubi sit cantus post folium aut post sonum, ubi sit sensus post uerbum, ubi sententia post uersum, ubi numerus post numeratum. Pone quatuor lapillos et tres, et sunt septem. Aufer illos: nonne tria et quatuor sunt septem? Numerabilia ergo uel numerata, si placet, quasi quoddam corpus sunt numeri, et sententie uersus, sensus uero sermo, et cantilene modulatio uocis. Quibus omnibus quasi corporibus tenentur incorporea, interdum autem accedunt, nonnumquam uero recedunt.

> And if you ask me "Where is the soul after the body?" I ask you, "Where is a song after you turn the page or after the sound falls silent? Where is the meaning after the word is spoken? Where is the number when you have finished counting?" Lay out four pebbles and then three more: they make seven. Take away the pebbles, and are not three and four still seven? Hence, countable or counted things, if you will, are a kind of body for number, a sentence is a body for sense, speech a body for meaning, and the harmony of the voice a body for song. Incorporeals are held, so to speak, by all of these corporeals: sometimes they draw close, sometime they pull away.

Bernard McGinn has argued that Isaac identifies the *spiritus corporeus*, rather than the soul, with the harmony of the body and that "Isaac has used an originally

[96] *Ep. de an.* 1883A.

Pythagorean doctrine condemned by Plato to defend the Platonic doctrine of the soul's spirituality and immortal nature."[97] The shifting terms of Isaac's metaphor, however, which range across concepts as varied as *organum, notulae, sonus,* and *modulatio uocis*, make any such strict identification nearly impossible. *Pace* McGinn, the *spiritus corporeus* is not the harmony of the body, but then again, neither is the soul. Rather, the soul is present to the body in a manner similar to the presence of music in an instrument, notation, sound, or vocal melody, for music does not perish when the instrument is broken, when the antiphoner is shut, when the sound is silenced, or when the voice ceases to sing. McGinn concludes that Isaac's explanation of the harmonious union between body and soul "cannot be described as a philosophical triumph,"[98] but it is more subtle than McGinn allows. Classicists may in fact recognize the argument, as it approaches an independent reconstruction of Porphyry's position articulated in the *Sententiae* 18, in which the inseparable (immanent) harmony of the body is the instrument of the rational soul's separable (transcendent) harmonies, which the soul plays via perception and imagination (i.e., nonrational powers) mediated by pneumatic vehicles (= *igneus vigor, spiritus*).[99]

Isaac's Harmony Metaphor, as we might call it, also closely recalls a more naturalistic explanation of the union of body and soul that is found in twelfth-century commentaries on Plato, Macrobius, and Martianus. The commentators knew from Calcidius that the union of body and soul is not to be construed as an attachment, admixture, or concretion (*applicatio, permixtio*, or *concretio*).[100] Instead, it is a conjunction (*coniunctio*).[101] But the question remains, what is that *coniunctio* between *corpus* and *anima*? When William of Conches is pushed to give a *physica*

97 Bernard McGinn, *The Golden Chain: A Study in the Theological Anthropology of Isaac of Stella* (Washington, DC: Cistercian Publications, 1972), 167.

98 Ibid., 160.

99 Porphyry, *Sent.* 18: ὅταν γὰρ τὸ ζῷον αἰσθάνηται, ἔοικεν ἡ μὲν ψυχὴ ἁρμονίᾳ χωριστῇ ἐξ ἑαυτῆς τὰς χορδὰς κινούσῃ ἡρμοσμένας ἁρμονίᾳ ἀχωρίστῳ, τὸ δὲ αἴτιον τοῦ κινῆσαι, τὸ ζῷον, διὰ τὸ εἶναι ἔμψυχον ἀνάλογον τῷ μουσικῷ διὰ τὸ εἶναι ἐναρμόνιον, τὰ δὲ πληγέντα σώματα διὰ πάθος αἰσθητικὸν ταῖς ἡρμοσμέναις χορδαῖς (ed. Luc Brisson, *Porphyre: Sentences* [Paris: Librairie Philosophique J. Vrin, 2005], vol. 1, 316.8–14; see also the commentary in vol. 2, 485–496).

100 *In Tim.* 221 (234.6–235.7): Societas porro uel ex applicatione fit uel ex permixitione uel ex concretione. Si applicita sint corpus et anima, quid ex applicatione compositum horum duum, quatenus totum erit uiuum? . . . Si uero permixta sunt, anima unum aliquid non erit, sed permixta multa. . . . Superest, ut ex concretione manent; ergo et per se inuicem transeunt duo corpora et locus unus quo corpus continetur duobus corporibus praebebit capacitatem, cum uas quod aquam recipit uinum et aquam simul sapere non possit. Neque igitur ex applicatione neque permixtione neque uero concretione corpus et anima sociantur. As Gersh observes (Gersh, *Middle Platonism and Neoplatonism: The Latin Tradition*, 483–484), these three correspond to Stoic theories of mixture: παράθεσις, μῖξις, and σύγχυσις.

101 Cf. Bernard Silvestris, *Comm. in Mart.* 3.607–615: Solet queri utrum anima sit apposita corpori vel concreta vel commixta vel coniuncta. Si apposita esset, cum omne appositum aliter extra illud sit, et ipsa extra corpus esset. Non ergo equaliter illud moveret. Omne enim appositum in proximo magis

ratio, one that would go beyond the simple, obvious answer that God joins soul and body, he has recourse to the language of music:[102]

> Quod uero quaeris, quid eam illi coniungit, quid eam illud amare facit, etsi possem dicere Deus, quia tamen physicam quaeris, accipe. Omni animae amor proportionis et concordiae tantus a Deo est datus, ut etiam in sonis, qui extra ipsam sunt, penitus illam diligat. Et hoc est quod Plato significare uoluit, cum Deum animam ex musicis consonantiis constituisse commemorauit. Corpora uero humana ex quatuor elementis proportionaliter et concorditer coniunctis sunt constituta. Haec proportio et concordia animam allicit et corpori coniungit et in corpore retinet. Et si uere et proprie uelimus loqui, dicemus animam non corpus, non eius qualitates, sed proportionem et concordiam, quibus partes corporis sunt coniunctae, diligere. Vnde ea quae illam proportionem conseruant appetit et quae illam destruunt fugit. Sed ex quo incipiunt elementa discordare, abhorret anima corpus et ab eo separatur.

> As regards your question on what joins the soul to the body, or what makes it love the body, even if I could say, "It is God," since you ask for a physical explanation, here it is. To every soul such a love of proportion and concord has been given by God that even in sounds, which are outside it, the soul deeply appreciates proportion and concord. And this is what Plato meant to say by mentioning that God constituted the soul from musical consonances. Now, human bodies are constituted from

viget, ut ignis linee materie appositus. Si concreta esset, ex sua in corporis substantiam transiret, ut ⟨aqua⟩ in lapidem per frigus vel in salem per ebullitionem. Si commixta esset, neutrum eorum esse suum retineret, ut dum aurum et argentum in electrum miscentur. Coniucta ergo sunt corpus et anima. *Drag.* 6.25.1: Cum et corpus et anima in constitutione sunt hominis, uel anima est apposita corpori uel commixta uel concreta uel coniuncta. Sed si apposita illi est, extra ipsum est. Iterum omne quod est appositum alicui fortius exercet uires suas in exteriori parte illius quam in interiori. Ignis enim appositus michi plus me accendit extra quam intus; aqua apposita plus humectat. Sed anima magis exercet uiras suas in nostris interioribus quam exterioribus. Non est igitur corpori apposita. Si iterum corpori mixta esset, ex illis duobus unum fieret, neutro remanente quod prius erat, ut cum aurum et argentum in constitutione electri miscentur. Cum igitur utrumque in homine esse suum retineat, non est mixta corpori. Si corpori concreta est, tunc in qualitatem corporis est uersa, ut aqua in qualitatem salis, quod minime est uerum. Si est illi coniuncta, cum proprius locus spirituum caelum sit, et omnis res quod suum est appetit atque suum contrarium fugit, quid est quod illam tam immundo uasi coniungit? Quid est quod tam immundum quid amare eam facit? Cf. *Phil.* 4.32 (98AB).

[102] *Drag.* 6.25.3–4. Cf. *Glos. sup. Macr.*, comment. ad 1.13.11: Vere mors est naturalis cum corpus animam deserit, quia quaedam numerorum ratio, id est proportio illa numerorum, et quaedam qualitatum complexio conuincit animam corpori. Quae quamdiu permanserit, non potest fieri naturalis dissolutio. Sed ex quo dissoluitur proportio illa numerorum, naturali dissolutione dissoluitur anima a corpore. Et tunc anima corpus non relinquit, sed corpus illam animam, cum illa proportione dissoluta, non est aptum animari.

> the four elements linked together proportionally and concordantly. This proportion and harmony attracts the soul, joins it to the body, and retains it in the body. And if we were to speak truly and properly, we should say that the soul loves not the body, not its qualities, but proportion and concord by which the parts of the body are joined together. So the soul seeks whatever preserves that proportion and shuns whatever destroys it. But as soon as the elements begin to be in discord with one another, the soul shuns the body and separates itself from it.

The harmony of the body is, therefore, the *conditio sine qua non* for the soul's existence in the body.[103] The soul, in a manner of speaking, is an aesthete that takes pleasure in the well-tempered, eucratic beauty of its body. The body's concord seduces (*allicit*) the soul and keeps it enmattered, incorporated; the soul's affect and the body's agency together forestall the vulnerability of this fragile *coniunctio*, the life of the organism.

In his commentary on Martianus, Bernard Silvestris connects this bodily harmony to the influence of the celestial spheres and the cosmic elements (in a manner more explicit than what we find in William of Conches). Commenting on *De nuptiis* 1.7, wherein Martianus describes Psyche as the daughter of the Sun and Endelechia,[104] Bernard seizes on the opportunity to discuss the diversity of views about the generation of the soul (*de natiuitate animae diuersae . . . sententiae*). Among those discussed is Plato's account of the creation of souls and the allotment of each soul to its own star (*Tim.* 41de). Although Bernard insists that, if properly understood, Plato says nothing that would contradict Catholic doctrine,[105] his interpretation of Plato's text goes so far as to claim that the *anima* qua *anima* ceases to exist upon the dissolution of the bodily harmony, and his remarks come very close to a quasi-functionalist account of the soul:[106]

> Set numerum stellarum dixit proportionem quam effectu suo dant stelle corpori, id est concordiam caloris et frigoris, humoris et siccitatis,

103 Cf. *Glos. Colonienses sup. Macr.*, comment. ad 13.11 (218.1–6): Constat enim corpus ex quatuor elementis proportionaliter collatis ad habilitatem animandi. Vel habet humores IIII item proportionaliter sibi collatos, qui crescunt in diversis temporibus, regnant in diversis etatibus. Cumque ipsa elementa vel ipsi humores in corpore suas servant proportiones, nec deficiunt, nec superhabundant, habile est corpus animari. Deficientibus autem his vel superhabundantibus, corpus negat posse animari.

104 *De nuptiis* 1.7 (4.10–12)

105 *Comm. in Mart.* 6.526–527: Set in his verbis non habetur omnes animas simul creatas nec aliquid quod Catholicorum sententie sit obvium.

106 *Comm. in Mart.* 6.530–542. Cf. the more innocuous formulation of William of Conches's *Philosophia* (which he had nonetheless backed away from in the *Dragmaticon* passage cited above), *Phil.* 4.32 (98C): Unde Plato, omnium philosophorum doctissimus, dicit deum creatorem stellis creatis a se et spiritibus curam formandi hominem injecisse, ipsum vero animam fecisse, et illis tradidisse, quia ministerio spirituum et effectu stellarum corpora humana existunt et crescunt, sed sua voluntate creatoris anima existit.

ponderis et levitatis, quam nullus dubitat a stellis et aliis speris haberi. Unde enim alium esset frigus nisi a terra, aqua, luna, Mercurio, Saturno, cum alia mundana frigus naturale non habeant? Vel unde calor nisi a Iove, igne, aere, Marte, sole et Venere? Huic proportioni compar est anima. Ex quo enim adest corpori horum concordia, incipit anima esse: soluta autem eadem, desinit anima esse, non quia substantia illa immortalis desinat esse, set quia ulterius ipsa substantia, licet semper vivat anima, non est anima. Anima enim nomen est officii. Ideoque, completo spatio animationis ipsius, non est ulterius anima.

But he [sc. Plato] called the number of stars the proportion that the stars grant to the body through their effect, i.e., the concord of hot and cold, wet and dry, heavy and light, which no one doubts is had from the stars and the other spheres. From where else could cold come but the earth, water, the Moon, Mercury, and Saturn, given that other worldly things do not have natural heat? Or from where could heat come save from Jupiter, fire, air, Mars, the Sun, and Venus? The soul is equivalent to this proportion. When the concord of these is present in the body, the soul begins to exist, but when that concord is dissolved, the soul ceases to exist, not because that immortal substance itself ceases to exist, but that substance—although the soul always lives—is no longer a soul. For the soul is the name of a function. And thus, when the duration of its animation is completed, it is no longer a soul.

On this view, soul qua soul is necessarily embodied, for the soul is the animating function (*officium*) that it exercises throughout the duration of its embodiment. In an anonymous, late-twelfth-century commentary on Martianus (which will be discussed more fully in Chapter 5), glossing the same passage of the *De nuptiis* (1.7), all the threads that we have been tracing—the body as an elemental harmony, the influence of the stars upon the body, and the soul's bodily existence as a consequence of the body's harmony—are interwoven with a theory of celestial harmony.[107]

Planetarum igitur filia dicetur anima similiter, non secundum creationem sed secundum incorporationem. Planetarum enim beneficio ex calido et humido coniungitur corpus. Et ex quatuor elementis

[107] *Exp. in Mart.* (*F* = Florence, Bib. Naz. Centrale, Conv. Soppr. I.1.28, ff. 57v–58r; *Z* = Zwettl, Stiftsbibliothek 313, ff. 145va–b). Cf. Macrobius, *In Som. Scip.* 1.12.13–14 (50.11–24). On this commentary, and its connections to the thought of William of Conches, see Hicks, "Martianus Capella and the Liberal Arts," 322–24; Hicks, "Editing Medieval Commentaries on Martianus Capella," in *The Arts of Editing Medieval Greek and Latin: A Casebook*, ed. Elisabet Göransson, Gunilla Iversen, et al. (Toronto: Pontifical Institute for Mediaeval Studies, 2016), 138–159.

temperatur ut uiuificandum aptum sit animae domicilium. Operantibus etenim eisdem [eis *F*] habet anima manere in corpore. Ex his enim calorem et humorem et alimenta accipit corpus humanum, sine quibus in eo anima perseuerare non potest. Quoniam igitur supradicta anima motum planetis prestat, [quoniam—prestat *om. F*] motus uero planetarum uitam hominis dispensat, bene endelichiae ac solis filia perhibetur, presertim cum a singulis planetarum diuersas ipsa contrahat proprietates, quas in humano corpore retinet. Per quas dii ad eius conuiuium corrogati dicuntur [*De nuptiis* 1.7], quia ad eius coniunctionem cum corpore [cum corpore *om. F*] omnes planetae conueniunt, ut singuli singulos in ea ostendant effectus. A Saturno enim tristiciam, a Ioue moderationem, a Marte animositatem, a Venere cupiditatem, a Mercurio interpretandi possibilitatem, a sole calorem ⟨et aestheticon⟩ [*scripsi cum Macrobio*, quieticam *F*, quieticon *Z*], id est sentiendi uis dicitur, a luna phyticam accipit, quod appelatur incrementum. Vnde etiam Macrobius testatur: per hos circulos descendens, in quibus celestis armoniae concinentia [continentia *F*] consistit, quasdam musicas ad humanum corpus secum trahit consonantias [ad humanum—consonantias *om. F*], quibus illi aptatur, quas aliquando audiens [ardens *F*] in instrumentis, quasi celestis armoniae dulcedinis memor delectatur.

The soul, therefore, will similarly be called the daughter of the planets, not with regard to its creation but with regard to its incorporation. With the support of the planets, the body is joined together from the hot and the wet, and it is tempered from the four elements in order that it may be home for the soul, a home well suited to be vivified. For as long as these are in effect, the soul is able to remain in the body. From the planets the human body receives heat, moisture, and nourishment, without which the soul cannot perdure in the body. Because the aforementioned soul [the world soul] grants motion to the planets, but the motions of the planets dispense the life of man, rightly [the soul] is said to be the daughter of Endelechia and Sun, especially since from each of the planets the soul contracts its various properties, which it retains within the human body. Because of these [planetary] properties, the gods are said to be summoned to the soul's [birthday] banquet, because all the planets convene for the soul's conjunction with the body, as each shows its own effect upon the soul. From Saturn the soul accepts sadness, from Jupiter moderation, from Mars animosity, from Venus cupidity, from Mercury the possibility of interpreting, from the Sun heat and *aestheticon*, i.e., the power of sensation, from the Moon *phyticon*, which means growth. Whence Macrobius attests that, as [the soul] descends through these [celestial] spheres, in which consists the concord of celestial harmony, it pulls along with it certain

> musical consonances to the human body, by which it is suited to the body. When it sometimes hears these harmonies in instruments, it is delighted, as if reminded of the sweetness of the celestial harmony.

Reason and resonance are fully intertwined. The microcosmic body, like the macrocosm itself, is written in the alphabet of the elements, in the harmonic language of the celestial bodies and their terrestrial influences. Its harmonies—whether we call them Plato's *gomphi*, Nemesius's *eucrasia*, or Constantinus Africanus's *complexio*—entice the soul and allow for its temporal, embodied perdurance. But the soul, as we have seen, has harmonies of its own, and thus the desire is a mutually affective entailment. The anonymous Martianus commentator, however, adds a new dimension to this mind-body/*anima-corpus* entailment, one that seems to draw the attention of this fragile *coniunctio*, the life of the human organism, away from its own interior psychosomatic harmonies to the delight and the affective attraction it might find in the audible world around it: the pleasures of exterior music (to recall Bernard of Chartres's phrase) realized in musical instruments. What, then, is the role of hearing in the constitution and understanding of both micro- and macrocosmic harmonies? To answer this question, it is necessary to understand what is not so obviously "harmonized" among body, soul, and sense perception—a problem that had a long if somewhat subterranean set of fault lines in the philosophical tradition of musical theory, natural philosophy, and grammar. This will be the subject of the next chapter.

4

Hearing the World

Sonic Materialisms

Nam si nullus esset auditus, nulla omnino disputatio de vocibus extitisset.

—Boethius, *De institutione musica*, 1.9

William of Conches's *Glosulae super Priscianum*, a commentary on Priscian's monumental sixth-century grammar, the *Institutiones grammaticae*, begins in an odd place for a grammatical work. After a quick nod to some preliminary considerations (the basic structure of Priscian's initial argument), William zooms out with dizzying speed from the local to the universal. With only a resumptive *igitur* ("now then") to hold on to by way of transition, we are immediately confronted with the cosmological, creative force of *artifex natura*.[1] From here, this highest vantage point, William gradually zooms back in to the subject at hand via a remarkable mechanistic causal chain that connects nature's artfully creative force to the contingent inevitability of its sonic expression in voice, a *uox*, the proper object of the sense of hearing (Appendix 1, 264.9–20):

> Now then, creative nature has here established that nothing is able to live unless heat dominates the other qualities. (For even if some men are said to be cold, this is not because they do not have more heat than cold but because they have more cold than men's natural complexion would require.) Whence nature has established in the midst of the human body three very hot members—namely the heart, liver, and gallbladder. But because it is a property of heat to consume itself

[1] William's gloss to *Inst. gramm.* 1.1.1–2 has been partially transcribed in Irène Rosier-Catach, "Le commentaire des *Glosulae* et des *Glosae* de Guillaume de Conches sur le chapitre *De voce* des *Institutiones grammaticae* de Priscien," *Cahiers de l'Institut du Moyen-Âge grec et latin* 63 (1993), 135–144, but the usefulness of her transcription is vitiated by frequent transcription and construal errors. All citations of William's *Glosulae de Magno Prisciano (Versio altera)* are drawn from my own edition of the text (printed below as Appendix I), which has been fully collated with Rosier-Catach's transcription.

> and other things unless they have some means of tempering the heat, nature has granted a remedy to this danger through the intake of cold air, and it has deputized this task to the members best suited to it, namely the lungs and windpipe. But because no one is able to take in as much air as this tempering would require, and likewise [because] the air, once taken in, quickly heats up, it was necessary that that air be expelled and more cold air be taken in. Hence, when the lung opens, air is drawn in, but when it compresses, air is expelled. In this way the process of breathing and respiration is completed. But it often happens that air, as it is expelled, is struck by the natural instruments in the mouth and is formed into different shapes. The air so formed, as it is expelled from the mouth and touches the air adjacent to the mouth, informs that [nearby] air with a similar form, and so [the process] continues from that initial impetus until air, formed in this way, strikes the ears of those standing nearby.

There is a striking instrumentality and an unequivocal materiality to the functioning of William's vocal apparatus, as both process and product. Stated most simply, *uox* is the byproduct of a natural thermodynamic system. The lungs and windpipe, primarily the cooling mechanisms for the vital if potentially destructive heat of the central hot organs, are also (if incidentally) a kind of bellows that provide the exhalation of air necessary for the production of vocal sound. The mouth, in turn, provides the natural "instruments"—the lips, tongue, palate, and teeth[2]—by which the passing air is given shape (literally *figura*: form, shape, figure). This informed air thus inaugurates a secondary mechanistic chain: contiguous particles of air, the *medium*, propagate this form, or "information," to nearby hearers, whose ears interpret this airy information as the perceptible form proper to them, namely *sound*. At this point, William turns from the natural generation and propagation of sound to the perception of that sound by those standing within earshot (Appendix 1, 264.23–27):

> The soul, roused by this percussion, emits a certain airy substance, deputized for this very purpose, through certain nerves to the ears. This airy substance, when it touches the exterior air, is impressed with a similar form, and it returns to the soul with this form, in which the soul comprehends the intention of the speaker.

[2] On the functioning of the "natural instruments" as an indication of *quanta opera machinata natura sit*, cf. Cicero's *De natura deorum* 2.59.149: Primum enim a pulmonibus arteria usque ad os intimum pertinet, per quam vox principium a mente ducens percipitur et funditur. Deinde in ore sita lingua est finita dentibus; ea vocem inmoderate profusam fingit et terminat atque sonos vocis distinctos et pressos efficit cum et dentes et alias partes pellit oris. Itaque plectri similem linguam nostri solent dicere, chordarum dentes, nares cornibus iis qui ad nervos resonant in cantibus.

The imagined journey of the human *uox* is thus cyclical, from the natural interiority of the corporeal life-process (physiology), through the medial conduit of the exterior world (physics), and back into the body via the ear (physiology again) and onward to the soul (psychology).[3] The *uox*, however, is not merely an objective, material entity that conforms to natural law. It is also a subjective, meaning-bearing entity that connects the intention of the speaker (*uoluntas loquentis*) to the perception of the perceiving soul. That perception, however, is grounded in a relationship of *similitudo* (similarity) between the form of the air thus struck and the form assumed by the airy substance (*aeria substantia*) that the soul deputizes as its external *medium*, the point of transition between the *external* material *res* (thing) and the *internal* immaterial perception, on the part of the soul, of a will or intention. The movement from external to internal is guaranteed not just by the similarity of form (*similis forma*) but by the similarity of *media* involved: the *similis forma* is transferred from the external *aer* to the internal *aeria substantia*. There is thus a double homology between external and internal: both the *media* of perceptual exchange and the *form* of the "information" in that media (and medial) transfer.

The only explicit authority to whom William turns, however, in his natural philosophical account of the *uox* is Boethius, specifically *De institutione musica* 1.14, where the natural propagation of a *uox* in air is likened to circular ripples in a still pond disturbed by a stone (Appendix 1, 264.27–30):

> Thus Boethius, in his book on music, demonstrates the formation of a *uox* through the example of a stone cast into a pool of standing water. The stone makes a very small circle, and this circle, by striking the nearby water, makes a broader circle that in turn makes another circle (and so on) until it reaches the bank. Air, therefore, which has been struck in the way I've described, once formed by that striking, is a *uox*.

There is nothing particularly novel about this citation in William's *Glosulae super Priscianum*; it is a commonplace in grammatical and philosophical discussions of the *uox*. In fact, through a repeated pattern of (mis)citation, Boethius's *De*

3 Compare this with the "imagined journey of the tone itself" in Hugo Riemann's "The Nature of Harmony": "The natural science of music extends immediately to the investigation of the nature of sounding bodies and is then part of physics, and specifically acoustics; if it pursues tone farther on its path into the human ear and examines the tone sensations excited by it, then it is part of physiology; if it concerns itself finally with the nature of tone representations and their combination, then it enters the area of psychology." Benjamin Steege comments, "the path Riemann maps out from a bird's-eye view exactly coincides with the imagined journey of the tone itself: from the exterior world (physics), to the human body in its full corporeality (physiology), and "beyond" to the human imagination itself (psychology)" (Steege, "'The Nature of Harmony': A Translation and Commentary," in *The Oxford Handbook of Neo-Riemannian Music Theories*, ed. Edward Gollin and Alexander Rehding [Oxford University Press, 2011], 57).

institutione musica became a cornerstone in twelfth-century grammatical and natural philosophical accounts of sound and hearing. In what follows, I will try to show why this is the case and to detail its *materialistic* implications for the epistemological foundations of hearing and the ontological status granted to the "objects" of hearing, both sound in general and (when possible) musical sounds in particular. To do so, I will follow the journey of the *uox* as imagined by William of Conches, tracing both its migrations across the domains of physiology, physics, and psychology and its textual permutations across the disciplines of music theory, grammar, and natural philosophy, in late antiquity and the twelfth century. In my story, the intellectualization of *musica* qua number is not in direct, binary opposition to the sense-perceptible manifestation of *musica* qua sound. Rather, already in Boethius and continuing through the twelfth century, these two approaches existed simultaneously, and both find sophisticated expressions and detailed accounts that require us to reconsider the oppositional relation between incorporeal, "bodiless" number and corporeal, embodied sounds that has been constructed and promulgated in modern scholarship. It is not a binary either-or but a dialectical both-and.

I am not the first to resist and rewrite this oppositional history; part of this story has already been told. In *Sung Birds*, Elizabeth Eva Leach has compellingly demonstrated how "the precepts of grammatical teaching, which was closely allied with the teaching of singing in medieval schools, offered a useful model for music theory."[4] The first chapter of Leach's book documents the various ways in which the grammatical tradition of the *uox*, specifically the four species adumbrated by Priscian, provided a vocabulary for the articulation of an "ontology of music." Her laudable goal is "to turn on its head the modern dismissal of *musica mundana* and *musica humana* from the domain of music" and "instead to puzzle the question from the opposite starting point: given that the medieval ontological reality of music was a matter of rational measurement, how did medieval theorists manage to bring the actual practice of song and dance into its fold?"[5] I here follow Leach's lead in offering a topsy-turvy account of the modern puzzle over *musica mundana* and *musica humana*, but I take a slightly different tack. My account emphasizes not rationality as the denominator common to all three categories, but rather the very materiality upon which, even more counterintuitively, all three—*mundana, humana,* and *instrumentalis*—rely. In other words, I want to push back against the claim that the ontological reality of medieval music is a "matter of rational measurement" to argue that it would be better to say "matter *and* rational measurement." This is why for William of Conches, the *uox* can be an index of *artifex natura*. Humanly generated sound is the result of an entirely natural, and entirely

[4] Leach, *Sung Birds: Music, Nature, and Poetry in the Later Middle Ages* (Ithaca: Cornell University Press, 2007), 24.

[5] Ibid., 14.

necessary, set of tempering (*temperamentum*) processes that ensure the continuity, stability, and integrity of the human body. Without *artifex natura* there would be no bodily integrity, and without bodily integrity there would be no *uox*. There are clear lines of connection between the external laws of physical and mathematical acoustics and the internal world of experience—connections between the laws of nature and laws of perception.

It is my contention that even though vision remained the paradigm of sensation in the Middle Ages (as it had been for antiquity), particular privilege is nonetheless granted to hearing as the perceptual modality that most embodies knowledge, that evinces the most direct connection between the physical and the mental. The sonorous, material systems of the human voice and of (musical) sounds generally are not merely conditioned by or in conformity with natural law; they are in effect (and in their affect) the very perceptible embodiment of *artifex natura* itself. Hence it is that William of Conches colonizes Priscian's grammatical *Institutiones* and proudly plants there the flag of the natural philosopher: "the definition of a *uox* is not the purview of the grammarians but belongs to the natural philosophers" (*non enim pertinet ad grammaticos sed ad phisicos uocem diffinire*). We will return to William's remarks on Priscian at the end of the chapter. First, however, let me be clear. To claim that sounds are the embodiment of *natura* is not to claim that perception is or was thought to be infallible (for it can be quite fallible), or that it is a transparent medium guaranteeing the perfect homology of external and internal (for it can be quite opaque), or that hearable and heard sounds cannot lie (for they can be dangerously mendacious). Boethius knew this well, and, worrying explicitly about the *fallacia sensuum* (the "deceit of the senses") in *De institutione musica* 1.9, he cautions that we "must not give all judgment to the senses, but must more trust reason" (*non omne iudicium dandum esse sensibus, sed amplius rationi esse credendum*). Nonetheless, he continues, "the whole origin of this discipline [sc. *musica*] is taken from the sense of hearing" (*quamquam a sensu aurium huiusce artis sumatur omne principium*). This is precisely where Boethius's story begins.

The *uox* at Journey's End: Epistemology and Perception

Boethius opens his *De institutione musica* with a claim that pretends to a simple observation of an obvious truth:[6]

> Omnium quidem perceptio sensuum ita sponte ac naturaliter quibusdam viventibus adest, ut sine his animal non possit intellegi. Sed

[6] *Inst. mus.* 1.1 (178.24–179.2); here I quote Calvin Bower's translation (Bower, trans., *Anicius Manlius Severinus Boethius: Fundamentals of Music*, ed. Claude V. Palisca [New Haven: Yale University Press, 1989], 1).

> non aeque eorundem cognitio ac firma perceptio animi investigatione colligitur.
>
> Perception through all the senses is so spontaneously and naturally present in certain living creatures that an animal without them cannot be conceived. But knowledge and clear perception of the senses themselves are not so immediately acquired through inquiry with the mind.

The assured certainty of Boethius's claim about the self-evident nature of the senses, however, is quietly undermined by the ambiguity of its expression. Semantics is partly to blame—namely, the variable interpretation of the several terms (*perceptio, cognitio, intellegere, colligere*) that crowd and compound the central equivocality of *sensus*, which in Boethius's lexicon can encompass the activity of sensation (sense perception), the content or product of that activity (sense data), or the faculties that enable such activity (the five senses themselves).[7] Syntax does not help matters. Is *ac* in the second sentence a simple coordinating conjunction ("knowledge and firm perception"), as all modern translators have heretofore assumed;[8] is it epexegetical and thus glossing *cognitio* with *firma perceptio* ("knowledge, that is a firm perception"); or, possible but unlikely, is it correlative with *non aeque* and thus comparative in force ("It is not so much knowledge of the senses as it is a firm perception that is adduced by mental investigation")?[9] Moreover, is *eorundem* a subjective or objective genitive? That is, does it specify the *cognitio* furnished by the senses (subjective), or is the *cognitio* of—that is, about—the senses themselves (objective)? And, compounding matters, is this genitive distributive across *ac*, as all translators have supposed? If so, why should the meaning of *perceptio sensuum* in the first sentence (which Calvin Bower, for instance, translates as "perception *through* all the senses") be distinguished from its occurrence in the second sentence (which Bower renders as "perception *of* the senses")?[10] When magnified by the philologist's microscope, Boethius's simple observation turns out to be anything but a simple matter. As we will see, at least one twelfth-century commentator focuses on these grammatical ambiguities as a

[7] See John Magee, *Boethius on Signification and Mind* (Leiden: Brill, 1989), 98–100.

[8] Bower translates: "But knowledge and clear perception of the senses themselves are not so immediately acquired through inquiry with the mind" (Bower, *Fundamentals of Music*, 1); Strunk (rev. McKinnon) likewise translates, "Yet an inquiry by the mind will not provide to the same degree a knowledge and clear understanding of the senses themselves" (Oliver Strunk, ed., *Source Readings in Music History*, rev. ed. [New York: W. W. Norton, 1998], 137). Meyer partially follows suit: "Or la connaissance et la perception sûre qu'ils procurent" (Christian Meyer, trans., *Boèce: Traité de la musique* [Turnhout: Brepols, 2004], 21).

[9] Reading this way, the second sentence would translate: "But it is not so much knowledge of the senses as it is a firm perception that is adduced by mental investigation."

[10] Strunk/McKinnon skirts the problem by translating *perceptio* differently in each case: *perceptio omnium sensuum* = "the perceptive power of all the senses," but *firma perceptio (eorundem)* = "firm understanding of the senses themselves" (Strunk, *Source Readings in Music History*, 137). Meyer opts

deliberate, performative expression of the difficulties in understanding the activities entailed by *perceptio* and *cognitio*.

Boethius's continuation helps to clarify these ambiguities. He has three things in his sights: (1) that the perception of sensibles by means of sensation is an effortless activity (*inlaboratum est enim quod sensum percipiendis sensibilibus rebus adhibemus*), but that it is not obvious, and is in fact a matter for serious philosophical study, to understand both (2) the nature of the senses themselves (*quae vero sit ipsorum sensuum, secundum quos agimus, natura*) and (3) the nature of the objects they grasp (*quae rerum sensibilium proprietas*).[11] Reading backwards, then, allows us to best construe Boethius's opening gambit:

> Perception, which is furnished by all [five] senses, is so spontaneously and naturally present in certain living creatures that an animal without them cannot be conceived. But knowledge of the senses themselves and a firm perception [of sensibles] are not so readily adduced by mental investigation.

Hence, at the outset of the *De institutione musica*, it is precisely the ambiguity of perception—at both an epistemological and ontological level—that Boethius forces to the fore. Qua activity, Boethius's example of the problem is not hearing but sight, which remained for Boethius, as it was for the entire ancient tradition, the paradigmatic sense.[12] Boethius seeks not to explain the mechanics of sight but only to gloss cursorily two standard but opposing theories, Epicurean intromission and Stoic/Academic extramisson,[13] as proof positive that even the learned are in disagreement over the nature of *sensus*.[14] Qua content, the visual paradigm

for the subjective genitive but likewise ducks the repetition of *perceptio*: *perceptio omnium sensuum* = "la faculté de percevoir par tous les sens," but *perceptio eorundem* = "la perception sûre qu'ils procurent" (Meyer, *Boèce: Traité de la musique*, 21).

11 *Inst. mus.* 1.1 (179.2–8).

12 Alan Towey's claim (in "Aristotle and Alexander on Hearing and Instantaneous Change: A Dilemma in Aristotle's Account of Hearing," in *The Second Sense: Studies in Hearing and Musical Judgement from Antiquity to the Seventeenth Century*, ed. Charles Burnett, Michael Fend, and Penelope Gouk [London: The Warburg Institute, 1991], 9) that Aristotle "tak[es] hearing as the paradigm of sensation" rests upon a series of obscure and difficult arguments that are discussed in depth by Andrew Barker, "Aristotle on Perception and Ratios," *Phronesis* 26 (1981), 248–266. Aristotle, however, does not mince words at *De sensu* 437a4–6: vision, regarded as a supply for the primary wants of life, is in its own right the superior sense, but for developing thought, hearing incidentally (κατὰ συμβεβηκὸς) takes precedence.

13 A twelfth-century gloss in Vat. Reg. lat. 1005 properly identifies these theories; see Michael Bernhard and Calvin Bower, eds., *Glossa maior in Institutionem musicam Boethii* (Munich: Bayerische Akademie der Wissenschaften, 1993–2011), nos. 82 and 83, I: 13.

14 *Inst. mus.* 1.1 (179.8–11): Adest enim cunctis mortalibus visus, qui utrum venientibus ad visum figuris, an ad sensibilia radiis emissis efficiatur, inter doctos quidem dubitabile est, vulgum vero ipsa quoque dubitatio praeterit.

remains dominant: whosoever looks at (*respicere*) a triangle or square recognizes (*agnoscere*) what he sees with his eyes (*id quod oculis intuetur*), but only a mathematician knows the true nature of the mathematical forms. But again, how the mathematician moves from the vagaries of *sensus* to the certainty of *intellectus* is nowhere explained. Boethius then generalizes the epistemological and ontological problems inherent in *uisus* to all sense-perceptible objects (*idem quoque de ceteris sensibilibus dici potest*). But the stakes are apparently higher with regard to the judgment of the ears (*arbitrium aurium*), for "the faculty of hearing (*uis aurium*) strives to comprehend sounds (*sonos captat*) in such a way that it not only forms judgments about them and recognizes differences between them, but even more often it is delighted if their measure be sweet and well joined, or it is distressed if they strike the sense as ill arranged and unconnected."[15] Although sight may offer the paradigm of sensation, hearing is yet the most valuable (if vulnerable) sense, insofar as it offers the most direct route to instruction or knowledge (*nulla enim magis ad animum disciplinis via quam auribus patet*), a claim analogous to the Aristotelian stance on the superiority of hearing for the acquisition of knowledge.[16]

Hearing, moreover, is the very origin of (at least central aspects of) the discipline of music.[17] But if hearing is a necessary first principle,[18] it alone is not sufficient. Perception serves rather as a kind of exhortation or admonition (*quasi admonitio*) to the reasoning faculty to flesh out the occasionally confused and specious perceptions of the ears. The sustained argument of 1.9 makes this point clear: the judgment of the ears is blunt (*obtusa*); without the support of *ratio*, it has no sure judgment (*nullum iudicium certum*), no comprehension of truth (*nulla veri est conprehensio*). But Boethius stops short of denying aural criteria, the "judgment of the ears" (*iudicium aurium*), any role whatsoever within Pythagorean harmonics. In fact, the very phrase *iudicium aurium* allows for the perceptual judgment of *sensibilia* within the domain of perception (which thus cannot be entirely passive).[19] Boethius's worries about perception, as articulated at 1.9, are not Platonic worries of the sort articulated in the *Theaetetus*—wherein perception, since its objects are not unchangingly "real" but always bound within the realm of

[15] *Inst. mus.* 1.1 (179.16–20): quarum vis ita sonos captat, ut non modo de his iudicium capiat differentiasque cognoscat, verum etiam delectetur saepius, si dulces coaptatique modi sint, angatur vero, si dissipati atque incohaerentes feriant sensum.

[16] *De sensu* 437a10.

[17] *Inst. mus.* 1.9 (195.18–19); cf. *De anima* 432a7–8.

[18] *Inst. mus.* 1.9 (195.17–18).

[19] E.g., *Inst. mus.* 1.33 (223.24–25): omnia . . . et numerorum ratione et aurium iudicio comprobabo; 1.28 (220.2–3): Consonantiam vero licet aurium quoque sensus diiudicet, tamen ratio perpendit; etc. On these and other passages regarding *sensus* and *ratio*, see Klaus-Jürgen Sachs, "Boethius and the Judgement of the Ears: A Hidden Challenge in Medieval and Renaissance Music Theory," in *The Second Sense: Studies in Hearing and Musical Judgement from Antiquity to the Seventeenth Century*, ed. Charles Burnett, Michael Fend, and Penelope Gouk (London: The Warburg Institute, 1991), 169–198.

becoming, is sharply distinguished from knowledge[20]—but rather are Aristotelian worries about the epistemological accuracy of perception. Consider, for instance, the claim at 1.9 that:[21]

> Ipse enim sensus aeque maximis minimisque corrumpitur. Nam neque minima sentire propter ipsorum sensibilium parvitatem potest, et maioribus saepe confunditur, ut in vocibus, quas si minimae sint, difficilius captat auditus, si sint maximae, ipsius sonitus intentione surdescit.
>
> Sense perception itself is equally destroyed by the great and the small. For it cannot sense the smallest things on account of the smallness of such sensibles, and it is often destroyed by greater things, as happens in pitches which, if they are very quiet, the hearing captures only with difficulty, but if they are very loud, the hearing is deafened by the intensity of the sound.

This largely recapitulates Aristotle's argument that "the excess of either high or low pitch destroys the hearing," a claim which is generalized to all the senses: "and in the same way in the case of flavors, excess destroys the sense of taste, in the case of colors also the too bright or dark destroys sight, and in the case of smell, a strong odor, either sweet or bitter, is destructive."[22] It is worth reiterating the point: Boethius's concern here is not with the deceptive nature of the object out there in the world, but rather with the limitations of the organ (or process) that is to perceive the object. In other words, Boethius still allows that, provided sense perception occurs in the proper way by the proper perceiver under the proper circumstances, perception can and indeed does provide a foundation for rational activity. Without hearing, there is no study of music—a very non-Platonic position, insofar as Plato's criteria for a proper science of harmonics (as in *Republic* 531c) demand that sense data be rejected from consideration. We do not, Plato writes, need to stretch out our ears as if eager eavesdroppers.[23] Why? Because the objects of perception are not and cannot be the objects of knowledge. It is not a matter of epistemological uncertainty—it is rather a question of an unbridgeable ontological divide between the always fluctuating world of becoming and the immutable realm of Real Being.

[20] *Theaet.* 184–186.

[21] *Inst. mus.* 1.9 (196.10–15).

[22] *De anima* 426a30–426b2: καὶ διὰ τοῦτο καὶ φθείρει ἕκαστον ὑπερβάλλον, καὶ τὸ ὀξὺ καὶ τὸ βαρύ, τὴν ἀκοήν· ὁμοίως δὲ καὶ ἐν χυμοῖς τὴν γεῦσιν, καὶ ἐν χρώμασι τὴν ὄψιν τὸ σφόδρα λαμπρὸν ἢ ζοφερόν, καὶ ἐν ὀσφρήσει ἡ ἰσχυρὰ ὀσμή, καὶ γλυκεῖα καὶ πικρά. On this passage, see Barker, "Aristotle on Perception and Ratios"; Deborah K. Modrak, *Aristotle: The Power of Perception* (Chicago and London: University of Chicago Press, 1987), 56–32.

[23] *Resp.* 531a: οἷον ἐκ γειτόνων φωνὴν θηρευόμενοι.

Despite the wash of Pythagorean skepticism regarding the veridicality of perception, Boethius ultimately subscribes to an Aristotelian and Stoic optimism regarding the move from sense perception to knowledge. A crucial passage that points in this direction—a passage that momentarily bridges the seemingly unbridgeable gap between perception and knowledge—occurs at 2.18, wherein Boethius (*secundum Nicomachum*) ranks the consonances on the basis of merit and measure. The diapason graces the top of the list, but the argument for its excellence is grounded in sensation, and strikingly so. In a passage that has puzzled modern translators, Boethius writes:[24]

> Haec enim ponenda est maxime esse prima suavisque consonantia, cuius proprietatem sensus apertior conprehendit. Quale est enim unumquodque per semet ipsum, tale etiam deprehenditur sensu. Si igitur cunctis notior est ea consonantia, quae in duplicitate consistit, non est dubium, primam esse omnium diapason consonantiam meritoque excellere, quoniam cognitione praecedat.
>
> The consonance whose property sense perception (*sensus*) apprehends more readily ought to be classified as the primary and most pleasant (*prima suavisque*) consonance. For everything is apprehended through sense perception to be such as it is in itself (*quale est enim unumquodque per semet ipsum, tale etiam deprehenditur sensu*). If, therefore, the consonance that consists in the duple ratio is better known to everyone (*cunctis*), then there can be no doubt that the octave is the first of all consonances and is surpassing in merit, because it comes first in cognition.

This crucial passage seems *prima facie* to break ranks with the Pythagoreans. So to keep Boethius from marching out of step, Bower translates both instances of *sensus* as "critical faculty."[25] "Boethius, or his Pythagorean source," Bower argues, "is obviously not arguing that 'as every single thing is in itself, so it is perceived by the sense'; to do so would blatantly contradict the basic tenet of Pythagorean thought that the senses are unreliable."[26] Bower's worry is justified,[27] but the trajectory of Boethius's argument is perhaps less obvious than Bower suggests. Would Boethius have deployed *sensus* in such a loaded context if he did not actually intend

[24] *Inst. mus.* 2.18 (249.22–29). Surprisingly, Sachs omits this passage from his synopsis of the "most important quotations from the *De institutione musica* concerning the criteria" (Sachs, "Boethius and the Judgement of the Ears," 171–175).

[25] Bower, *Fundamentals of Music*, 72–73.

[26] Ibid., 73.

[27] E.g., in Book 5, an (incomplete) paraphrase of Ptolemy's *Harmonics*, Boethius is more careful: "sense observes (*advertit*) a thing as indistinct (*confusum*) and nearly to be such as is the object it senses" (5.2 [352.7–8]).

to bring sense perception into play? Nor does the supposition of an unspecified "critical faculty" clarify matters much. What is this critical faculty? And on what grounds and with what sort of data does it facilitate critique? The usual suspects—the Aristotelian *sensus communis*, the Stoic ἡγεμονικόν, or even the Augustinian *sensus interior*—seem unlikely; such perceptual faculties responsible for perceptual judgments or discriminations held little interest for Boethius, and they are not employed in any of his other writings. This critical faculty is also, presumably, not yet fully cognitive, since Boethius had a perfectly good set of terms (*cognitio, intellectus*, etc.) had he intended to make such a claim. So this critical faculty, as postulated in Bower's translation, must somehow fall vaguely between sense perception and cognition, and it unduly complicates the stages in the intellectual process. While the translation "critical faculty" deftly sidesteps any seemingly "blatant contradiction" with Pythagorean orthodoxy, it fails to offer a cogent alternative.

There are two hints—one lexical, the other contextual—that Boethius here intends *sensus* as sense perception. Lexically, Boethius's use of the adjective "pleasant" (*suauis*) is neither innocent nor otiose; rather, it deliberately evokes his definition of consonance, which is consistently couched in aesthetic terms that trade on an irreducibly sense-perceptible property: "pleasantness" (*suauitas*).[28] At 1.8, a consonance is defined as a "mixture of high and low sound sweetly (*suauiter*) and uniformly falling upon the ears" (*consonantia est actui soni gravisque mixtura suaviter uniformiterque auribus accidens*).[29] Likewise at 4.1: "those sounds are consonant that, when struck at the same time, sound pleasant (*suauem*) and intermingled with each other" (*consonae quidem sunt, quae simul pulsae suavem permixtumque inter se coniungunt sonum*).[30] Hence the pleasantness of a consonance is first and foremost a feature of its *perception*, the domain of *sensus*.

Contextually, this passage functions explicitly[31] as a transition from the fundamentally arithmetical concerns of 2.1–17, the theory of ratios (*proportiones*) and means (*medietates*), to the fundamentally musical concerns of 2.18–30, the connection between ratios and consonances, namely which ratios correspond to which musical intervals. This chapter thus inaugurates a discussion of "how the Pythagoreans proved that the musical consonances are associated with the ratios discussed above," and this transition thus seeks to bridge the gap between Boethius's definition of consonance, which is dependent upon sense perception, and arithmetical ratios, which are understood through the application of reason.[32] The octave, the sense-perceptible manifestation of the ratio 2:1,

28 The remarks of Hentschel are helpful: "... läßt sich schließen, daß er keine Differenz zwischen der Qualität eines Klangs selbst und der Qualität seiner Wahrnehmung annimmt, die aus der sinnlichen Wahrnehmung resultiert, so daß mögliche Ursachen wie Gewöhnung oder Konvention nicht ins Blickfeld rücken" (Hentschel, *Sinnlichkeit und Vernunft*, 25).

29 *Inst. mus.* 1.8 (195.6–8).

30 *Inst. mus.* 4.1 (302.2–4).

31 Note its opening words: *sed de his hactenus* ("but enough about this").

32 cf. Hentschel, *Sinnlichkeit und Vernunft*, 29–32.

is not just the simplest mathematical ratio; it is also, in a more basic way, readily apprehended to be such through perception. The point is simple: who would deny that the octave sounds consonant? It is as easily recognized as such by any reasonable listener as a shape is recognized by a reasonable observer to be a square or a triangle (cf. *Inst. mus.* 1.1). Notably, Augustine makes an identical point at *De trinitate* 4.2, observing that even untrained listeners (*imperiti*) recognize the "consonance of one to two." Boethius is not, however, claiming that a listener would know from perception alone the real nature of consonance, any more than a casual glance would reveal the mathematical nature of a triangle or square. Rather, perception captures some distinguishing feature (*proprietas*), and it is in this limited sense that we should read Boethius's (overstated) claim that "everything is apprehended through sense perception to be such as it is in itself."[33]

Nor is this claim as radically contradictory to (Boethius's presentation of) Pythagorean thought as it might seem. It well concords with Boethius's earlier claim that the Pythagoreans "investigate certain things only by the ear," which include, he continues, the measuring of consonances, although the precise calculations of how the consonances differ among themselves is entrusted only to *ratio*, the judge and ruler over subservient *sensus*.[34] Similarly, early commentators on Pythagorean harmonics emphasize the foundational role of perception in establishing the basic nature of consonance, even if reason ultimately plays a trump card in some special cases (e.g., the eleventh).[35] For instance, Ptolemais's *Eisagoge* claims that "Pythagoras and his successors . . . wish to accept perception as a guide for reason at the outset, to provide reason with a spark, as it were; but they treat reason, when it has set out from these beginnings, as working on its own in separation from perception."[36] The passage in Boethius provides precisely this sort of spark; it presents an attempt to fan the spark of sensation into the fire of rational knowledge.

Still, despite the optimistic (from the Pythagorean perspective) bridge that Boethius builds between perception and knowledge at 2.18, we are given here no account of the movement across the bridge. The closest Boethius comes to such an account in the whole of the *De institutione musica* is late in the game, after he

[33] Alternatively, might we read more into this claim than the minimalist interpretation that I've offered? The senses, as mere receptors, simply take in and report what's offered to them. Hence, the senses don't deceive, insofar as the appeal to how things *seem* to me is invulnerable to critique (the wall in front of me may not be white, but no one can dispute that it *appears* white to me, even if that apparent whiteness is actually the result of a white light hitting a grey wall in just the right way, etc.). Understood in this way, the senses only deceive if I go on to *believe* that the wall is white solely on the basis of the sensory report. This line of interpretation (which has solid Stoic and Augustinian precedent), however, seems to run afoul of Boethius's additional stipulation that the report of the senses accurately reflects a thing *per semet ipsum* ("such as it is in itself").

[34] *Inst. mus.* 1.9 (196.1–7).

[35] André Barbera, "The Consonant Eleventh and the Expansion of the Musical Tetraktys: A Study of Ancient Pythagoreanism," *Journal of Music Theory* 28 (1984), 191–223.

[36] ap. Porphyry, *In Ptolemaei Harm.* 25.25–30; trans. Barker, *Greek Musical Writings II*, 242.

has put down his first and primary Greek source (Nicomachus) and picked up his second (Ptolemy). At 5.2, near the beginning of the apparently incomplete project to continue his translation of Nicomachus with a (full?) translation of Ptolemy's *Harmonica*, Boethius returns (*secundum Ptolemaeum*) to the relation between *sensus* and *ratio* and offers a claim similar to, but slightly (and crucially) modified from, its first appearance at 2.18. The perceptible and the perception are no longer in a direct relation of *tale* . . . *quale* ("such . . . as"), but rather a qualified relation, *proxime tale* . . . *quale* ("nearly such . . . as"): "sense perception attends to something indistinctly and *nearly such as* is the object it senses" (*sensus namque confusum quiddam ac proxime tale, quale est illud, quod sentit, advertit*).[37] This important qualification, the approximate nature of perception, is repeated twice more in quick succession: "sense perception in fact finds things to be indistinct and approximate to the truth" (*sensus invenit quidem confusa ac proxima veritati*);[38] "sense perception does not conceive anything in its fullness, but attains only to the proximate" (*sensus nihil concipit integritatis, sed usque ad proximum venit*).[39] It is reason (*ratio*) that supervenes upon the approximate and imprecise discriminations of sense perception and draws them toward *integritas* and *veritas*.

The role of sense perception in the *De institutione musica* thus echoes (if in a simplistic, streamlined fashion) the more robustly philosophical approach articulated in his *De interpretatione* commentaries. There, *sensus* (along with imagination, *imaginatio*, which has no comparable role in the *De institutione musica*) provides the initial outlines (*primae figurae*) upon which, as upon a foundation, the supervening intellect rests. Boethius offers an analogy: just as painters are wont to sketch a preliminary outline (*designare lineatim corpus*) which serves as a substrate for the likeness they seek to color, so too sense perception and mental images (*imaginatio*) are natural substrates for the soul's perception. For when some sensible object falls under perception or thought, first it is necessary for a certain mental image of it to arise, and then the more robust intellect supervenes and fleshes out in intellective, cognitive terms what had been indistinctly presumed by the mental image.[40] In short, sense perception is the origin of thought, the *origo intellectus*.[41]

37 *Inst. mus.* 5.2 (352.7–8). This translation, which attempts to preserve the modified *tale quale* relation, is admittedly awkward. I can do no better without recourse to paraphrase, e.g., Bower's translation (*Fundamentals of Music*, 163): "The sense perceives a thing as indistinct, yet approximate to that which it is."

38 *Inst. mus.* 5.2 (352.9–10).

39 *Inst. mus.* 5.2 (352.13–14).

40 *In Perih.* II.28.28–29.10: sensus enim atque imaginatio quaedam primae figurae sunt, supra quas velut fundamento quodam superveniens intellegentia nitatur. nam sicut pictores solent designare lineatim corpus atque substernere ubi coloribus cuiuslibet exprimant vultum, sic sensus atque imaginatio naturaliter in animae perceptione substernitur. nam cum res aliqua sub sensum vel sub cogitationem cadit, prius eius quaedam necesse est imaginatio nascatur, post vero plenior superveniat intellectus cunctas eius explicans partes quae confuse fuerant imaginatione praesumptae.

41 *In Perih.* II.24.15.

For Ptolemy too, as for Boethius, *ratio* requires *sensus*, as *ratio* on its own has no independent access to external reality. Ptolemy formulates it thus in his *On the Criterion*: "Mind could not begin to think of anything without a transmission from sense perception."[42] Again, we are reminded of Boethius: *Nam si nullus esset auditus, nulla omnino disputatio de vocibus extitisset* ("For if there was no hearing, we wouldn't think at all about pitches").[43] Why then is sense perception, though necessary, inferior? The answer is found in sense perception's close connection to matter: whereas the mind is "simple and unmixed," sense perception is bound up in matter.[44] But Ptolemy does not go so far as Plato's *Theaetetus* in sharpening the divide between matter and mind. Boethius, moreover, seems to have gone beyond Ptolemy in fleshing out this relation (and it again is worth remarking the predominantly visual orientation of the passage—*peruidere, intueri*):[45]

> Hoc vero idcirco est, quoniam sensus circa materiam vertitur, speciesque in ea conprehendit, quae ita sunt fluvidae atque inperfectae nec determinatae atque ad unguem expolitae, sicut est ipsa materia. Quare sensum quoque confusio sequitur, mentem vero atque rationem quoniam materia non moratur, species, quas pervidet, praeter subiecti communionem intuetur, atque ideo eam integritas comitatur ac veritas, potiusque, quod in sensu aut peccatur aut minus est, aut emendat aut conplet.

> This [sc. that sense is sometimes mistaken] occurs for the following reason: because sense perception is caught up in matter and apprehends forms (*species*) in it (*in ea*), forms which are as fluid, imperfect, indeterminate, and imprecise as matter is itself.[46] This is why indistinctness (*confusio*) characterizes sense perception, but because matter does not hinder mental reasoning,[47] reason beholds the forms that it considers free from their inherence in a subject; hence, wholeness and

[42] 13.18–20; cited and trans. in Andrew Barker, *Scientific Method in Ptolemy's Harmonics* (Cambridge: Cambridge University Press, 2000), 19.

[43] *Inst. mus.* 1.9 (195.18–19).

[44] See Barker's discussion in *Scientific Method in Ptolemy's Harmonics*, 19–20.

[45] *Inst. mus.* 5.2 (352.17–26).

[46] Bower translates (Bower, *Fundamentals of Music*, 163) "and it [sense] grasps species in those things that are in flux and imperfect and that are not delimited and refined to an exact measurement, just like matter itself is." The antecedent of *quae*, however, must be the feminine plural *species* and not *ea*, which Bower seems to take as neuter plural ("those things"). Boethius's point is that the forms (*species*), before they are mentally abstracted from matter, are subject to the same material flux.

[47] The expression *mentem atque rationem* is best understood as a hendiadys, hence my translation "mental reasoning."

> truth characterize reason, and it either emends or completes what is apprehended wrongly or less completely through sense perception.

The term *species* ("form") is Boethius's handling of Ptolemy's εἶδος, but the precise movement of this argument seems to be Boethius's own intervention upon his source (doubtless *Harm.* 1.1). Bower's claim, however, that "these sentences linking the sense with matter and affirming the independence of mind and reason from matter do not appear in Ptolemy's argument" is true only to a point.[48] For Ptolemy makes both links explicit.[49] What does not appear in Ptolemy's argument, the real burden of Bower's observation, is the recombination of these connections into a new form that has no direct Ptolemaic parallel. For Ptolemy, the realms of perception and reason are (in a way) distinct and divided: hearing is concerned with matter and quality, reason with form and cause.[50] For Boethius, however, perception and reason are concerned with the same thing in different ways: the object remains identical, and it is the mode of comprehension that changes.[51] The repeated description of perception's apprehensions as indistinct[52] strongly recalls the indistinct mental images (*imaginationes*)—the direct result (impression?) of sense perceptions—and perceptions found repeatedly in his logical commentaries.[53] Boethius here transforms Ptolemy into an abstractionist of a surprisingly Aristotelian cast.

48 Bower, *Fundamentals of Music*, 163.

49 The independence of reason from matter = *Harm.* 1.1.16: τὸν μὲν λόγον συμβέβηκεν ἁπλοῦν τε εἶναι καὶ ἀμιγῆ; the close connection of sense to matter = *Harm.* 1.1.17: τὴν δὲ αἴσθησιν μεθ' ὕλης πάντοτε πολυμιγοῦς τε καὶ ῥευστῆς.

50 Ptolemaeus, *Harm.* 1.1.4–6: κριτήρια μὲν ἁρμονίας ἀκοὴ καὶ λόγος, οὐ κατὰ τὸν αὐτὸν δὲ τρόπον ἀλλ' ἡ μὲν ἀκοὴ παρὰ τὴν ὕλην καὶ τὸ πάθος, ὁ δὲ λόγος παρὰ τὸ εἶδος καὶ τὸ αἴτιον. It must be admitted, with Barker, that to read this claim as a resolution of the "conflict between reason and perception . . . by dividing up the territory between them, distinguishing different parts of it as the proper concern of each to the exclusion of the other" is "altogether too simplistic. The operations of the two faculties, and the matters on which they are competent to pronounce, [are] interwoven in complex ways" (Barker, *Scientific Method in Ptolemy's Harmonics*, 16).

51 Cf. *Cons. phil.* 5.p4.26–30: eandem corporis rotunditatem aliter visus, aliter tactus agnoscit; ille eminus manens totum simul iactis radiis intuetur, hic vero cohaerens orbi atque coniunctus circa ipsum motus ambitum rotunditatem partibus comprehendit. Ipsum quoque hominem aliter sensus, aliter imaginatio, aliter ratio, aliter intellegentia contuetur. Sensus enim figuram in subiecta materia constitutam, imaginatio vero solam sine materia iudicat figuram. Ratio vero hanc quoque transcendit speciemque ipsam, quae singularibus inest, universali consideratione perpendit. Intellegentiae vero celsio oculus exsistit; supergressa namque universitatis ambitum ipsam illam simplicem formam pura mentis acie contuetur.

52 *Inst. mus.* 5.2, 352.7–8: sensus namque *confusum* quiddam . . . advertit; 352.9–10: sensus invenit quidem *confusa* ac proxima veritati; 352.12–13: [ratio] accipit [sc. a sensu] vero *confusam* ac proximam veri similitudinem; 352.21: quare sensum quoque *confusio* sequitur; 352.26–27: quod sensus non integre sed *confuse* atque a veritate minus . . . agnoscit, etc.

53 *In Perih.* II.29.8–10: post uero plenior superueniat intellectus cunctas eius explicans partes quae *confuse* fuerant imaginatione praesumptae; *In Isag.* II.136.22–23: sed eas *imaginationes confusas* atque

The *uox* at Journey's Beginning: The Production and Propagation of Sound

What then are these sonic objects? The answer belongs to the science of acoustics and remains preliminary to the science of harmonics proper.[54] Accordingly, the acoustical knowledge deemed necessary for an account of harmonics is summarized by Boethius in the first book of the *De institutione musica* at 1.3, i.e., the beginning of the treatise proper after the prooemium of chapters 1 and 2.[55] Thus we can assume that Nicomachus began his *Eisagoge* with a discussion of acoustics—a traditional starting point attested as early as Archytas.[56] In this opening chapter, Boethius defines sound as movement, produced by a blow, that is transferred to and transmitted through the air to the ears, and he quantifies this movement to establish a correspondence between number and pitch. In chapter 14, he then describes the diffusion of sound via the Stoic example of waves in water.

First, chapter 3. Boethius ultimately subscribes to a Peripatetic view of sound production and transmission.[57] For Aristotle, the striking of a (potentially) resonant object produces a movement within the medium (generally air, but water

---

inevidentes sumunt; *In Isag.* II.164.21–165.7: sed animus cum *confusas res permixtasque* in se a sensibus cepit, eas propria ui et cogitatione distinguit. . . . at uero animus, cui potestas est et disiuncta componere et composita resoluere, quae *a sensibus confusa* et corporibus coniuncta traduntur, ita distinguit, ut incorpoream naturam per se ac sine corporibus in quibus est concreta, speculetur et uideat.

[54] A history of ancient acoustical theory remains a scholarly desideratum. Frederick Vinton Hunt's posthumous *Origins in Acoustics: The Science of Sound from Antiquity to the Age of Newton* (New Haven and London: Yale University Press, 1978)—the manuscript, left incomplete, was published by his student Robert Apfel—treats the Greek tradition only in survey. The article by H. B. Gottschalk, "The *De Audibilibus* and Peripatetic Acoustics," *Hermes* 96 (1968), 435–460—omitted from the bibliography in Charles Burnett, Michael Fend, and Penelope Gouk, eds., *The Second Sense: Studies in Hearing and Musical Judgement from Antiquity to the Seventeenth Century* (London: University of London, 1991)—remains fundamental. On Aristotelian acoustics (as presented in *De anima* 2.8), see Michael Wittmann, *Vox atque sonus: Studien zur Rezeption der Aristotelischen Schrift "De anima" und ihre Bedeutung für die Musiktheorie* (Pfaffenweiler: Centaurus-Verlagsgesellschaft, 1987), 19–122; see also Barker's annotated translation in *Greek Musical Writings II*, 77–80.

[55] 1.2 (189.12–13) concludes: Sed proemii satis est. Nunc de ipsis musicae elementis est disserendum.

[56] ap. Porphyry, *In Ptolemaei harm.* 56.11–12: πρᾶτον μὲν οὖν [sc. τοὶ περὶ τὰ μαθήματα] ἐσκέψαντο, ὅτι οὐ δυνατόν ἐστιν εἶμεν [*scripsi cum Huffman*, ἦμεν *Düring*] ψόφον μὴ γενηθείσας πληγᾶς τινων ποτ' ἄλλαλα, etc., on which see Carl A. Huffman, *Archytas of Tarentum*, 129–130.

[57] Michael Wittmann's brief remarks (Wittmann, *Vox atque sonus*, 128) on Boethius's account of the physics of sound are unduly optimistic regarding Boethius's own hand in shaping the discussion. First, Wittmann's opening claim that "Boethius nachweislich *De anima* gekannt [hat] und . . . sich auch in der Einleitung zu *De institutione musica* darauf [bezieht] [i.e., 1.2])" seems to misdirect Boethius's citation of Aristotle. At 1.2 (189.1–3), Boethius divides the soul into rational and irrational parts, *ut Aristoteli placet*; as Bower observes, this is probably (if a direct reference at all) a reference to the similar division mentioned approvingly in the *Nicomachean Ethics* (13.1102a26–1103a3; many other passages could be added: *EN* 11.1138b6–13; *Pol.* 1260a5–17, 1333a17–30, 1334b7–28) and not to the *De anima* (432a24–b7), where Aristotle criticizes the rational/irrational bipartition as one of the two common, but incomplete,

is allowed as well), and this movement is transmitted to the ear.[58] But it is only movement that is transmitted, not anything within the medium nor the medium itself. Thus, Aristotle would likely object[59] to the "missile" theory of sound found in Archytas (frag. 1)[60] and perhaps alluded to by Plato (*Tim.* 80a)—sound is not a body, neither air nor water (*De anima* 419b18), but a movement within a bodily medium (whether airy or watery). High and low sounds, then, are produced by (but not identified as) fast and slow movements respectively. *De anima* 420a31–33 makes this clear: "It is not the case that the sharp [i.e., high-pitched] is swift and the heavy [i.e., low-pitched] slow: rather, the movement of the one acquires its quality because of the speed, that of the other because of the slowness."[61] Aristotle thus continues to think of pitch in terms of variable speed, but the speed in question is the speed of the originating blow, not the speed of transmission, a crucial modification of the theory maintained by Archytas and Plato.[62]

Boethius begins his acoustical preliminaries: "Consonance, which rules every musical melody (*omnem musicae modulationem*), requires sound; sound cannot be caused without a blow or strike; a blow or strike cannot occur unless it is preceded by motion. If everything were immobile, nothing could strike anything else so that one thing impelled another, but if everything remained stationary and still, no sound could arise."[63] This adheres closely to the logic of the Euclidean *Sectio*

soul divisions. Wittmann may be correct that Boethius "nachweislich" knew the *De anima* (he could have pointed to, e.g., *In Perih.* II.27.25ff., though perhaps this is secondhand?), but we cannot infer from the musical treatise's prooemium that *De anima* was necessarily on Boethius's mind. Thus, it is hardly surprising that "das unmittelbar folgende Tonkapitel (*Inst. mus.* I, 3) . . . sich nicht direkt auf *De anima* II, 8 beziehen [läßt]." Wittmann likewise claims (*Vox atque sonus*, 126) that Boethius "in der Einleitung zu seinem *De interpretatione*-Kommentar . . . referiert wesentliche Gedanken aus *De anima* II, 8 [hat]," but in support of this claim he cites the full prologue (by PL column numbers) without precision. Presumably he has in mind such passages as *In Perih.* II.4.18–26: Vox est aeris per linguam percussio quae per quasdam gutturis partes, quae arteriae uocantur, ab animali profertur. Sunt enim quidam alii soni, qui eodem perficiuntur flatu, quos lingua non percutit, ut est tussis. Haec enim flatu fit quodam per arterias egrediente sed nulla linguae impressione formatur atque ideo nec ullis subiacet elementis, scribi enim nullo modo potest. Quocirca uox haec non dicitur sed tantum sonus. This simultaneously condenses and expands upon *De anima* 420b28ff. (e.g., that a *tussis* cannot be written has no parallel in Aristotle but rather accords with the grammatical tradition).

58 *De anima* 420a4ff.

59 Cf. the Peripatetic *Problemata* 899b1–7.

60 βέλη: ap. Porphyry, *In Ptolemaei harm.* 57.7–9.

61 *De anima* 420a31–33: οὐ δὴ ταχὺ τὸ ὀξύ, τὸ δὲ βαρὺ βραδύ, ἀλλὰ γίνεται τοῦ μὲν διὰ τὸ τάχος ἡ κίνησις τοιαύτη, τοῦ δὲ διὰ βραδυτῆτα.

62 See, for instance, Arist. *Sens.* 448a20–b2, as against Plato *Tim.* 80ab; cf. *Inst. mus.* 1.30 (221.12–16): Plato autem hoc modo fieri in aure consonantiam dicit. Necesse est, inquit, velociorem quidem esse acutiorem sonum. Hic igitur cum gravem praecesserit, in aurem celer ingreditur, offensaque extrema eiusdem corporis parte quasi pulsus iterato motu revertitur, etc.

63 *Inst. mus.* 1.3 (189.15–22): Consonantia, quae omnem musicae modulationem regit, praeter sonum fieri non potest, sonus vero praeter quendam pulsum percussionemque non redditur, pulsus vero atque percussio nullo modo esse potest, nisi praecesserit motus. Si enim cuncta sint inmobilia, non

canonis, a short work on Pythagorean harmonics written around 300 B.C.E.,[64] but Boethius's continuation—"hence, sound is defined as a percussion of air that is unbroken all the way to the hearing" (*idcirco definitur sonus percussio aeris indissoluta usque ad auditum*)[65]—parts ways with the *Sectio canonis* (in which it has no parallel) and reveals his (probable) Nicomachean source text; it is very nearly a literal translation of a similar claim by Nicomachus: "generally speaking, we say the sound is an impact of air that is unbroken as far as the hearing" (καθόλου γάρ φαμεν ψόφον μὲν εἶναι πλῆξιν ἀέρος ἄθρυπτον μέχρι ἀκοῆς).[66] The Latin adheres much more closely to Nicomachus than to the parallel claim in the *De anima* (420a3–4): "a thing capable of producing a sound is a thing capable of setting in movement a single [mass of] air continuous up to the hearing" ψοφητικὸν μὲν οὖν τὸ κινητικὸν ἑνὸς ἀέρος συνεχείᾳ μέχρις ἀκοῆς; e.g., Boethius's *indissoluta* is Nicomachus's ἄθρυπτον (both modifying the blow) and not Aristotle's συνεχείᾳ (which primarily characterizes the air—a crucial distinction).

In line, then, with post-Aristotelian developments in (Peripatetic) acoustical thought, Boethius quantifies pitch not in terms of the velocity of transmission, nor even (solely) in terms of the velocity of the blow,[67] but in terms of the variable rate of pulsation, which encompasses both velocity and frequency:[68]

> Idcirco enim idem nervus, si intendatur amplius, acutum sonat, si remittatur, grave. Quando enim tensior est, velociorem pulsum reddit

poterit alterum alteri concurrere, ut alterum inpellatur ab altero, sed cunctis stantibus motuque carentibus nullum fieri necesse est sonum.

64 Cf. *Sec. can.* Intro. (114.1–6): εἰ ἡσυχία εἴη καὶ ἀκινησία, σιωπὴ ἂν ἔιη· σιωπῆς δὲ οὔσης καὶ μηδε νὸς κινουμένου· οὐδὲν ἂν ἀκούοιτο· εἰ ἄρα μέλλει τι ἀκουσθήσεσθαι· πληγὴν καὶ κίνησιν πρότερον δεῖ γενέσθαι. ὥστε ἐπειδὴ πάντες οἱ φθόγγοι γίνονται πληγῆς τινος γινομένης· πληγὴν δὲ ἀμήχανον γενέσθαι μὴ οὐχὶ κινήσεως πρότερον γενομένης; and compare with the translation from *Inst. mus.* 4.1 (301.12–16): Si foret rerum omnium quies, nullus auditum sonus feriret. Id autem fieret, quoniam cessantibus motibus cunctis nullae inter se res pulsum cierent. Ut igitur sit vox, pulsu est opus. Sed ut sit pulsus, motus necesse est antecedat. Ut ergo sit vox, motum esse necesse est. See Barbera's remarks in *The Euclidean Division of the Canon* (Lincoln: University of Nebraska Press, 1991), 115 and 231. On the acoustic theories of the *Sectio canonis*, see David Creese, *The Monochord in Ancient Greek Harmonic Science* (Cambridge: Cambridge University Press, 2010), 164–171.

65 Assumed by Michael Wittmann to be Boethius's own insertion, as it has no direct parallel in the *Sectio canonis*: "Auch dies läßt sich nicht aus der *Sectio canonis* ableiten, insofern dort lediglich ein Schlag gefordert wird. . . . Daß es sich dabei um ein Einfügung von Boethius handelt, liegt nahe" (Wittmann, *Vox atque sonus*, 130).

66 *Harm.* 4 (242.20–21).

67 Cf. the *manus* example from this same chapter (189.23–190.1): Motuum vero alii sunt velociores, alii tardiores, eorundemque motuum alii rariores sunt alii spissiores. Nam si quis in continuum motum respiciat, ibi aut velocitatem aut tarditatem necesse est conprehendat, sin vero quis moveat manum frequenti eam motu movebit aut raro. Et si tardus quidem fuerit ac rarior motus, graves necesse est sonos effici ipsa tarditate et raritate pellendi. Sin vero sint motus celeres ac spissi, acutos necesse est reddi sonos.

68 *Inst. mus.* 1.3 (190.2–11). Mustering a dubious parallel in Philoponus's *De anima* commentary (*ad* 420a29; *In de An.* 373.31–34), Wittmann considers this, too, a Boethian intervention. It is clear

> celeriusque revertitur et frequentius ac spissius aerem ferit. Qui vero laxior est, solutos ac tardos pulsus effert rarosque ipsa inbecillitate feriendi, nec diutius tremit. Neque enim quoties chorda pellitur, unus edi tantum putandus est sonus aut unam in his esse percussionem, sed totiens aer fertitur, quotiens eum chorda tremebunda percusserit.
>
> For this reason, the same string, if it is stretched taut, sounds a high sound; if it is relaxed, it sounds a low sound. For when it is stretched more tightly, it reverberates with a swifter pulse, returns more quickly, and strikes the air more frequently with close-packed blows. When, however, it is relaxed, it reverberates with loose and slow pulses, which are infrequent because of the weakness of the blow, nor does it vibrate for very long. You should not suppose that when a string is struck only one sound is given forth or that there is but one blow in the sound, for every time the vibrating string percusses the air, the air is struck.

The continuation of this claim, namely that the sound produced by a vibrating string, although perceived as continuous, is actually a discrete set of pulsations, is nowhere developed in Nicomachus's extant works. Boethius's example is a spinning top:[69]

> velut si conum, quem turbinem vocant, quis diligenter extornet eique unam virgulam coloris rubri vel alterius ducat, et eum qua potest celeritate convertat, tunc totus conus rubro colore videtur infectus, non quo

from the larger context, however, that in the parallel Wittmann adduces, Philoponus is thinking primarily in terms of "velocity," not "frequency of vibration," as the pitch determinant, e.g., *In de An*. 373.21–23: οὕτως οὖν καὶ ἐπὶ τῶν ψόφων ὀξὺν μὲν λέγομεν τὸν ταχέως παραγινόμενον ἐπὶ τὴν αἴσθησιν καὶ ἐπιμένοντα, βαρὺν δὲ τὸν ἀνάλογον τῷ ἀμβλεὶ τὸν βραδέως παραγινόμενον ἐπὶ τὴν αἴσθησιν καὶ ταχέως ἀποπαυόμενον. Philoponus's point is that a tighter string, such as the *nete*, will more rapidly affect the sound-conducting medium of air (τὸ διηχὲς τοῦ ἀέρος) than does a more slack string, such as the *hypate*. A later passage (374.3–5) not mentioned by Wittmann does discuss string vibration, but the point there concerns only the duration of the sound, not its pitch. It is even more unlikely that this passage, as Wittmann claims, is a reflection of what Boethius learned about the *De anima* from Ammonius (since "Boethius, like Johannes Philiponus, was a student of Ammonius" [*Vox atque sonus*, 132–133]). There is, however, no evidence for Courcelle's thesis that Boethius studied with Ammonius in Alexandria (on which see John Magee, "On the Composition and Sources of Boethius's Second *Peri Hermeneias* Commentary," *Vivarium* 48 [2010], 7–54). It is needless to go hunting for a parallel in Philoponus, much less to suppose the hand of Ammonius. Boethius is still in full accord with Nicomachus, *Harm*. 4 (243.18–244.1): τῶν μέν γε ἐντατῶν αἱ τάσεις αἱ μείζονες καὶ εὐτονώτεραι μείζονας καὶ ὀξυτέρους φθόγγους ἀπεργάζοναι, αἱ δ' ὀλιγώτεραι νωχελεστέρους τε καὶ βαρυτέρους. μεταστήσαντος γὰρ τὰς χορδὰς τοῦ πλήκτρου, ἀπὸ τῆς οἰκείας χώρας ἀφεθεῖσαι αἱ μὲν τάχιστά τε σὺν πολλῷ τῷ κραδασμῷ καὶ πολλαχοῦ τὸν περικείμενον ἀέρα τύπτουσαι ἀποκαθίστανται ὥσπερ ἐπειγόμεναι ὑπ΄ αὐτῆς τῆς σφοδρᾶς τάσεως, αἱ δὲ ἠρέμα καὶ ἀκραδάντως κατ΄ εἰκόνα τῆς τεκτονικῆς στάθμης.

69 *Inst. mus*. 1.3 (190.15–21).

> totus ita sit, sed quod partes puras rubrae virgae velocitas conprehendat et apparere non sinat.
>
> For instance, if someone should carefully fashion a cone, called a top, draw on it a single strip of color, say red or some other color, and then spin it as fast as he could, then the whole cone seems to be dyed red, not because it is really completely red, but because the speed of the red stripe overwhelms the uncolored sections and does not allow them to be seen.

This metaphor is not original to Boethius (witness the translator's gloss: *quem turbinem uocant*), and this "particulate" perspective on sound, combined with the example of "color blurs," is found twice in Porphyry's commentary on Ptolemy's *Harmonics*: once quoting a fragment of Heraclides's *Eisagoge*,[70] and once in the extended quotation from the Peripatetic *De audibilibus*, which Porphyry attributes to Aristotle.[71] In the latter, we read that (803b) "the impacts made on the air by strings are many and separate, but because of the smallness of the time between them the ear is unable to detect the gaps, and hence the sound seems to us single and continuous."[72] The clarifying example that immediately follows (803b34ff.) is drawn from the visual domain of color: separate bits of color often seem to us to be joined together when they are moving quickly.[73] The color analogy in Boethius, however, is closer still to Heraclides: "For often when a cone is in motion, and there is on the cone one white or black spot, it appears that there is a circle on the cone of the same color as the spot. And again, if there is a single white or black line on the moving cone, the whole surface appears to be of the same colour as the line."[74] Andrew Barker has argued that these sources still operate on the assumption of pitch determination through velocity, and not through frequency of impacts or pulses (since the latter is the indirect result of the former: a swifter velocity yields more frequent impacts).[75] The *Sectio canonis*, however, argues the point directly: "of motions, there are the more dense and the more rare. The more dense produce higher notes, and the more rare, lower."[76] Boethius's presentation thus combines the pitch determination argument of the *Sectio canonis* with the top metaphor as in the *De audibilibus* and Heraclides. As Nicomachus seems

70 *In Ptolemaei Harm.* 30.1–31.21.

71 *In Ptolemaei Harm.* 67.24–77.18.

72 *Aud.* 803b34–37 (*In Ptolemaei Harm.* 75.14–17): αἱ δὲ πληγαὶ γίνονται μὲν τοῦ ἀέρος ὑπὸ τῶν χορδῶν πολλαὶ καὶ κεχωρισμέναι, διὰ δὲ σμικρότητα τοῦ μεταξὺ χρόνου τῆς ἀκοῆς οὐ δυναμένης συναισθάνεσθαι τὰς διαλείψεις, μία καὶ συνεχὴς ἡμῖν ἡ φωνὴ φαίνεται (trans. Barker, *Greek Musical Writings II*, 107).

73 See Gottschalk, "The *De Audibilibus*," 438.

74 ap. Porphyry, *In Ptolemaei Harm.* 30.28–31.2; trans. Barker, *Greek Musical Writings II*, 236.

75 Barker, *Greek Musical Writings II*, 107, n. 40 and 236, n. 110. For an opposing view, see Gottschalk, "The *De Audibilibus*."

76 *Sec. can.* Intro. (114.6–8): τῶν δὲ κινήσεων αἱ μὲν πυκνότεραί εἰσιν· αἱ δὲ ἀραιότεραι· καὶ αἱ πυκνότεραι ὀξυτέρους ποιοῦσι τοὺς φθόγγους· αἱ δὲ ἀραιότεραι βαρυτέρους.

to have modeled his discussion of sound production on the *Sectio canonis*, and since the theory presented in 1.3 is entirely consistent with the theory of consonance attributed to Nicomachus at 1.31, it seems most economical to assume that Nicomachus is responsible for shaping the material, not Boethius. Thus, any similarities with *De anima* 2.8 or the Peripatetic tradition generally is due to the Peripatetic strand of thought that entered the Greek music-theoretical tradition of acoustics and not from any direct intervention by Boethius.

This sound is conveyed to the ears through the medium of the air in the manner of a wave, as Boethius explains in *Inst. musc.* 1.14:[77]

> Tale enim quiddam fieri consuevit in vocibus, quale cum [in] paludibus vel quietis aquis iactum eminus mergitur saxum. Prius enim in parvissimum orbem undam colligit, deinde maioribus orbibus undarum globos spargit, atque eo usque dum defatigatus motus ab eliciendis fluctibus conquiescat. . . . Ita igitur cum aer pulsus fecerit sonum, pellit alium proximum et quodammodo rotundum fluctum aeris ciet, itaque diffunditur et omnium circum stantium simul ferit auditum.
>
> The same sort of thing generally happens in sounds that happens when a stone is thrown from above into a still pool of water. It first produces a wave with a very small circumference; then it disperses into circular waves with larger and larger circumferences until the motion, exhausted in the spreading waves, comes to a stop. . . . So too, therefore, when air that has been struck makes a sound, it sets in motion other air nearby and generates a kind of circular wave of air, and so it is diffused and simultaneously strikes the hearing of all who stand nearby.

Boethius's influential analogy of waves in a pool of water, probably taken directly from Nicomachus, originated in Stoic sources.[78] Just as circular waves are caused by a stone dropped into a pond, so the air when struck instigates a movement in the immediate airy medium, and this then strikes contiguous air and so on until the movement, propagated thus from its point of origin in a circle, reaches the ears. As with a wave, which weakens in proportion to the distance traveled, so too with the motion of sound, the intensity diminishes as the "wave" propagates through the air and (occasionally) encounters obstacles. This metaphor proved particularly tenacious in medieval traditions and provided the primary interface between the grammatical and musical discussions of sound. And as we ride its wave, it brings us back to the beginning of Boethius's story and his very real worries about what happens when waves of sound crash over our ears.

[77] *Inst. mus.* 1.14 (200.7–21).

[78] See the parallels cited in Gottschalk, "The *De Audibilibus*," 445, fn. 3.

Some Twelfth-Century Worries

So let us return to the opening of Boethius's *De institutione musica* and read again his simple claim about an obvious truth, now through the eyes of his twelfth-century readers. *Omnium quidem perceptio sensuum*: the anonymous St. Florian commentator immediately recognizes the ambiguity of this opening gambit. *Perceptio sensuum*, the commentator notes, can be understood in two different ways: it either signals that we possess sensation (*sensum percipimus, id est habemus*)[79] or indicates that we comprehend things by means of sensation (*percipimus sensu, id est per sensum aliqua comprehendimus*).[80] This is intentional, the commentator argues, for Boethius intends and in fact pursues both meanings.[81] The second sentence continues the ambiguity:[82]

> SED COGNITIO EORVNDEM, scilicet sensuum, AC, pro scilicet, FIRMA eorum PERCEPTIO, id est cognitio eorum, quae firma deberet dici, id est quam habent illi qui firmiter rerum naturas investigant, scilicet philosophi. Quasi dicit: cognitio naturae vel ipsius sensus vel eorum quae sensu percipiuntur, NON EQVE COLLIGITVR, id est non ab omnibus eque comprehenditur, INVESTIGATIONE ANIMI, scilicet ratione et intellectu. Vel aliter: COGNITIO EORVNDEM, scilicet sensuum, AC FIRMA PERCEPTIO eorum quae sensu percipiuntur ita: natura sensuum vel natura eorum quae sensu percipiuntur, et est eadem sententia: NON EQVE etc.

> BUT THE UNDERSTANDING OF THOSE SAME THINGS, namely the senses, AND, meaning "namely," THE FIRM PERCEPTION of them, that is the understanding of them, the sort of understanding that ought to be deemed firm, that is, the sort of understanding gained by those who firmly investigate the natures of things, that is, the philosophers. As if he should say: the understanding of the nature either of sensation itself or of things that are perceived through sensation IS NOT EQUALLY ADDUCED, that is, it is not comprehended equally by all, THROUGH THE INVESTIGATION OF THE MIND, that is, through reason or intellect. Or understand this in another way: THE UNDERSTANDING OF THOSE SAME THINGS, namely the senses, AND THE FIRM PERCEPTION of those things

[79] Cf. the paraphrase of Boethius's opening sentence in Adelard of Bath, *Quaest. nat.* 23 (136): Omnium quidem habitudo sensuum, ut Boetius in Musica testatur, omnibus animalibus presto est, set que eorumdem sit vis quisve modus, non nisi intellectui philosophantis perspicuum est. Burnett (*Conversations*, 231, fn. 39) misses the reference, suggesting that "Adelard may be recalling inaccurately Boethius, *De musica* I.1, p. 179: 'Adest enim cunctis mortalibus visus.'"

[80] *In inst. mus.* 23.

[81] *In inst. mus.* 24: Et utroque modo hic debet intelligi, quia utroque modo exequetur.

[82] Ibid.

which are perceived through sensation, meaning thus: the nature of the senses or the nature of those things that are perceived by the sensation. And the meaning remains the same, NOT EQUALLY, ETC.

The commentator thus embraces simultaneously all the options ventured by modern translators: *eorundem* is both subjective and objective; *cognitio ac perceptio* are both parallel and divergent. As to the force of *non aeque*, the commentator follows the interpretation that had long been established in the margins of the text: "not equally by all people" (*non aeque ab omnibus hominibus*).[83] When glossing *Inst. mus.* 1.9, the commentator notes that Boethius has made frequent mention of the senses throughout his various definitions of sound and consonance. Hence, the commentator worries that it may seem to some that the entire science rests upon sense perception. Thus, in this chapter, Boethius clarifies by demonstrating that while some matters are entrusted to sense perception, others are entrusted only to reason.[84] The commentator sums up the Boethian position: "[The science of music] has its beginning in sense perception but its completion in reason" (*Inicium enim est per sensum, sed per rationem consummatio*).[85] For when we hear that two sounds produce some consonance between them, we are (so to speak) admonished by the hearing to investigate the reason (*illam rationem*) why such sounds produce a consonance. When he comes to gloss Boethius's definition of *sonus*—*percussio aeris indissoluta usque ad auditum*—the commentator carefully elucidates what he understands as the incorporeal implications of Boethius's definition:[86]

> AERIS PERCUSSIO. Percussio [*scripsi*, percussam *Rausch*] dicitur, quia sonus nec est aer percussus nec eius actio aut passio, sed ex percussione facta ad aerem nascitur.
>
> PERCUSSION OF AIR. It is called a percussion, because sound is neither percussed air nor is it an action nor a passion of air; rather, it arises from a percussion made against the air.

Sound is a percussion of air, not percussed air. This is not a trivial distinction. The commentator here has entered an ancient fray about the *uox* specifically, which Aulus Gellius had already described, in the second century C.E., as an "old and perpetual point of contention among the most famous philosophers: whether the *uox* is a body or an incorporeal" (*uetus atque perpetua quaestio inter nobilissimos*

83 Bernhard and Bower, *Glossa maior* no. 40, I: 8.

84 *In inst. mus.* 46: Quia omnia ista diffinierat faciendo mentionem de sensu, videretur alicui quod haec scientia tota sensui inniteretur, ideo hoc removet docens quod quedam quidem sunt, quae sensui committenda sunt, quedam vero, quae soli rationi.

85 *In inst. mus.* 46.

86 *In inst. mus.* 38.

philosophorum . . ., corpusne sit vox an incorporeum).[87] The debate pitted the materialist Stoics (and Epicureans) against everyone else (but, according to Gellius, principally the Platonists).[88] According to the Stoics, a *uox* must be a corporeal entity, since causal interaction only obtains between bodies (though effects are incorporeal).[89] The Stoic position predominated in grammatical contexts, and it provided the point of departure for Priscian's *Institutiones grammaticae* (1.1.1): *Philosophi definiunt vocem esse aerem tenuissimum ictum* ("Philosophers define the *uox* as most subtle air that has been struck.")

The debate raged on in the twelfth century, largely in the grammatical tradition, and it is likely the grammatical tradition that the St. Florian commentator had in his sights.[90] His claim that sound is neither an action (*actio*) nor passion (*passio*) of air may in fact reply to a grammatical strand of thought that held precisely such a position. For instance, an unedited mid-twelfth-century commentary, included in a compendium of grammatical and logical texts (Vienna, Österreichische Nationalbibliothek, VPL 2486, ff. 17r–35r), offers a collection of views on the status of *uox*, among which we find a view that corresponds precisely to St. Florian's criticism:[91] "Others say that the *uox* is an action or passion, because a percussion of air is an action or passion, and a percussion of air is a *uox*. Therefore, a *uox* is an action [or passion]" (*Alii dicunt quod vox est actio vel passio, quia percussio aeris est actio vel passio et percussio aeris est vox; ergo vox est actio* ⟨*vel passio*⟩). Regrettably, the St. Florian commentator offers us little more than a negative assessment of the *uox*: it must not be conflated with its medium (air), nor

[87] *Noctes Atticae* 5.15. Gellius sizes up the combatants as follows: Sed vocem Stoici corpus esse contendunt eamque esse dicunt ictum aera; Plato autem non esse vocem corpus putat; non enim "percussus" inquit "aer," sed "plaga" ipsa atque percussio, id vox est.

[88] Cf. Adam Parvipontanus's example of a disjunctive question (*interrogatio electiua*) in the first category (the category *quid*) in his *Ars disserendi*, cxxxiii: Est ergo primi generis interrogatio electiva ut cum queritur "an vox sit corpus" ut Stoicis visum est "an non," ut Platoni (L. Minio-Paluello, *Twelfth-Century Logic: Texts and Studies I; Adam Balsamiensis Parvipontani Ars disserendi (Dialectica Alexandri)* [Rome: Edizioni di storia e letteratura, 1956], 86).

[89] E.g., Sextus Empiricus, *Aduersus mathematicos* 9.211: "The Stoics say that every cause is a body which becomes a cause to a body of something incorporeal (εἴγε Στωικοὶ μὲν πᾶν αἴτιον σῶμά φασι σώματι ἀσωμάτου τινὸς αἴτιον γίνεσθαι). For instance the scalpel, a body, becomes a cause to the flesh, a body, of the incorporeal predicate 'being cut.' And again, the fire, a body, becomes the cause to the wood, a body, of the incorporeal predicate 'being burnt'" (A. A. Long and D. N. Sedley, *The Hellenistic Philosophers* [Cambridge: Cambridge University Press, 1987], I.333 (55B), with commentary at 340–341; Greek text at II.333).

[90] Cf. the commentator's grammatical interpretation of Boethius's definition of a musical sound (*casus uocis in unam intensionem, Inst. mus.* 1.8): vocis autem casus dicitur, id est vocis inflexio, quia sicut in inflexione, id est terminatione, dictionis fere omnem eius noticiam accipimus, sic in fine vocis agnoscimus utrum sonus ad musicam consonantiam aptus vel non (*In inst. mus.* 44).

[91] Vienna, VPL 2468, f. 18r; qtd. from L. M. De Rijk, *The Origin and Early Development of the Theory of Supposition*, vol. II.1 of *Logica Modernorum: A Contribution to the History of Early Terminist Logic* (Assen: Van Gorcum, 1967), 238; for a description of the manuscript, see ibid., 89–91.

is it an *actio* or *passio* of the air. Whether the St. Florian commentator thus held that sound was a quality or quantity (the two other options discussed at length in the grammatical tradition), he does not say. But his conclusion that "sound arises from a percussion made against the air" (*percussio facta ad aerem*) corresponds to what William of Conches, in his *Glosulae de Magno Prisciano, Versio Altera*, deems a causal definition (*diffinitio data per causa*). William's example of such a definition invokes (without naming his source) Victorinus's canonical (and likewise Stoic) αἰτιολογική *definitio:* "day is the sun shining upon the earth" (*dies est sol lucens super terram*).[92] Such a definition requires that the whole *definitio* be predicated of the *definiendum*, and not just some part of it. Just as we cannot claim, on the basis of the definition *dies est sol lucens supra terras*, that *dies est sol*, so too it does not follow from *uox est aer tenuissimus ictus* that *uox est aer uel corpus*.[93]

The brief discussion and conclusion offered by the St. Florian commentator on the nature of *sonus* bears a close connection to the grammatical and logical discussions of *uox*,[94] and it indicates a cross-pollination between the grammatical tradition and the musical tradition regarding the ontological status of *sonus* and *uox*. It is thus worth examining the various grammatical and logical discussions to see what light they can shed on the ontological status of the musical *uox*. But first a word of caution: even if the traditions overlap in significant ways, we cannot assume the semantic stability of *uox* across multiple domains. The *uox*, for instance, of Boethius's *De institutione musica* is not the same thing as the *uox* of the *De interpretatione* commentaries, and to assume naively an identity relationship between them will inevitably lead to misunderstandings.[95] The point of

92 Victorinus, *Liber de definitionibus*: Quinta decima species est definitionis aitiologike, Latini secundum rei rationem vocant, ut "dies est sol supra terras," "nox sol sub terris," ut enim aut dies aut nox sit, causa est aut supra terras sol aut sub terris (Andreas Pronay, C. Marius Victorinus, *Liber de definitionibus: eine spätantike Theorie der Definition und des Definierens* [Frankfurt am Main: P. Lang, 1997], 28.13–29.2).

93 *Glosulae sup. Prisc.*: Qui tenent hanc sententiam [sc. uocem non esse aera nec corpus] aiunt hanc diffinitionem datam esse per causam, uelut ista est: "dies est sol lucens super terram." Sed diffinitionis datae per causam haec est natura quod tota simul de diffinito ponitur, non tamen partes illius. Verum est enim quod dies est sol lucens super terram, non tamen dies est sol. Similiter uox est aer tenuissimus ictus, quia talis aer est causa uocis, nec tamen inde sequitur quod uox sit aer uel corpus. Oddly, Margaret Cameron deems this line of interpretation a "modified corporealist view" (Margaret Cameron, "William of Champeaux and Early Twelfth-Century Dialectic" [PhD diss., University of Toronto, 2005], 83). The commentators, however, uniformly agree that this explanation is proffered by those who reject the corporealist view; it is a way to evade the corporealist implications of Priscian's definition.

94 E.g., compare the St. Florian commentator's remark "sonus . . . ex percussione facta ad aerem nascitur" with the *Compendium Logicae Porretanum* by a disciple of Gilbert of Poitiers: at hic sonus nec aer est neque percussio, sed ex collisione solidi ad aerem vel ad solidum nascitur (ed. Sten Ebbesen, Karin Margareta Fredborg, and Lauge Nielsen, *Cahiers de l'Institut du Moyen-Âge grec et latin* 46 [1983], 2).

95 For instance Blair Sullivan, "*Nota* and *notula*: Boethian Semantics and the Written Representation of Musical Sound in Carolingian Treatises," *Musica disciplina* 47 (1993), 71–97, constructs a unconvincing theory of "musical semantics" that assumes the stable identity of *uox* across Boethius's musical and logical writings.

contact that will be explored and exploited in the following remarks focuses on the phonetic core of the spoken *uox*—i.e., *uox* qua sense-perceptible *sonus*, regardless of its semantic force.

The Grammatical *uox*

Twelfth-century discussions of the ontology of *uoces* are deeply indebted to an earlier (late-eleventh and early-twelfth-century) tradition of glosses on Priscian, known collectively as the *Glosulae*.[96] The *Glosulae* organizes its opening discussion of *uox* according to the Aristotelian categories, each with arguments pro and contra: *uox* is (1) substance (*aer ictus*), (2) quality (*percussio aeris*), or (3) quantity (on the authority of Aristotle—*dicit enim Aristoteles in quantitate orationem esse*). A *uox*, according to the first solution, is not simply in the category of substance as a species of substance. For in answer to the question, "Is a *uox*, when defined in this way [as *aer tenuissimus ictus*], a species of air? i.e., does it signify some universal thing that would be a species in the category of substance?" the commentator replies in the negative: "We say that this is not the case."[97] *Vox* does not essentially signify air qua air, but rather accidentally, qua its having been struck by the mouth's natural instruments. Considered with respect to its significative force (*secundum significationem*), the physical attribute of the *uox* is merely accidental (*accidentale esse*), but considered as a vocal utterance (*secundum uocem*, which later grammarians would deem material supposition), the *uox*'s ontological entanglement with air is sufficient to ensure the correctness of Priscian's definition as one "derived from substance" (*a substantia sumpta*).[98] Some (*aliqui*), however, attempt to refute such a definition—namely, *uox est aer*—by supposing that "if *uox* is air, it is also a body" (*si uox est aer, et est corpus*).[99] Thus the fundamental conflict: on the authority of Augustine, "no individual body is found at one and the same time wholly in different places" (*nullum corpus individuale in eodem tempore totum in*

[96] For an introduction to the tradition and the scholarship, see Irène Rosier-Catach, "The *Glosulae in Priscianum* and Its Tradition," in *Flores grammaticae: Essays in Memory of Vivien Law* (Münster: Nodus, 2005), 81–99. The opening comments on *uox* have been edited by Rosier-Catach in "Le commentaire des Glosulae."

[97] Rosier-Catach, "Le commentaire des *Glosulae*," 120: In primis quaerendum est an vox sic diffinita species sit aeris, idest significet aliquam rem universalem quae sit species in predicamento substantiae. Quod dicimus non esse.

[98] Ibid.: Vox enim aeres in essentia sui, scilicet in hoc quod sunt aeres non significat, sed potius ex quadam accidentali causa, in hoc, scilicet, quod percussi sunt naturalibus instrumentis. Dicimus ergo hoc vocabulum "vox" accidentale esse, id est sumptum a quadam qualitate, percussione videlicet, non secundum vocem, sed secundum significationem. Non est ergo substantialis diffinitio praemissa si "vox" aerem non significat.

[99] Ibid.: Hanc diffinitionem aliqui putant se infringere hanc hypoteticam in suae rationis exordio ponentes: "si vox est aer, et est corpus."

diversis locis reperitur).[100] But on the authority of Boethius, "the same utterance [*sermo*], as an integral whole, that is, with all of its [constituent] elements, reaches the ears of different listeners at the same time, as if it is in different places" (*idem sermo totus et integer, cum omnibus scilicet suis elementis, ad aures diversorum pervenit in eodem tempore, quasi in diversis locis est*).[101] The *Glosulae* then attempts to salvage the authority of both (*salva utriusque auctoritate*) by interpreting the identity relation in Boethius's claim as a formal, not material, identity. "For it is in fact true," the *Glosulae* continues, "that a *uox*, formally and not materially identical, fills the hearing of different people at the same time." It cinches the argument by invoking the Boethian example of waves in water: "for instance, a stone cast into water makes a circular ripple (*orbis*), and that circle, when it strikes the nearby waters, makes another, and that yet another, and in this way many circles, different in matter and location but identical in form, take their form from that first circle."[102] The wave model thus provides the commentator with the primary rationale for the corporealist view:[103]

> Eodem modo aer in ore loquentis naturalibus instrumentis formatus vicinos impellit aeres et in sua afficit [*scripsi cum Burnett*, conficitur *Rosier-Catach*] forma. Ita fit ut vox eadem secundum formam sit in auribus diversorum, sed quantum ad materiam diversorum, ut ita dicam, aerum diversa. Potest igitur esse ut nullum corpus in eodem tempore totum in diversis habeatur locis, et erit vox corpus, et tamen ipsa secundum formam, id est soni similitudinem, eadem in eodem tempore in diversis auditur locis. Et hanc similitudinem de aqua ponit Boethius in prologo quem praemittit in Musica.
>
> In the same manner, air shaped in the mouth of the speaker by the natural instruments strikes the nearby air and imparts upon it its own form. In this way it happens that a *uox*, identical in respect of its form, can be in the ears of different people [at the same time], but it

[100] As Rosier-Catach points out (ibid., 120–121, fn. 22), this maxim had wide circulation under Augustine's name (according to Abelard, it is to be found in Augustine's "in Cathegoriis") but it is not found in the *Paraphrasis Themistiana* (which was attributed to Augustine); there is only a weak parallel in the *De musica* (1.1).

[101] Closely corresponding to Boethius, *In Categorias* 164D: Dicitur quoque commune quod ipsum quidem nullis diuisum partibus, totum uno tempore in singulos uenit, ut uox uel sermo ad multorum aures uno eodemque tempore totus atque integer peruenit; *De differentiis topicis* IV 1211CD: Vox uno tempore ad plurimorum aures peruenit cum suis integra partibus, id est elementis, nam eodem tempore tota causa ad diuersas species cum suis partibus transit.

[102] Rosier-Catach, "Le commentaire des *Glosulae*," 121: Est enim verum quod vox formaliter eadem et non materialiter in eodem tempore diversorum replet auditum, ut puta iacto lapide in aqua fit orbis, et orbis iste vicinas undas impellens alium orbem facit, et ille alium. Et sic multi orbes, materia quidem et loco diversi sed in forma idem [idem *scripsi*, idest *Rosier-Catach*], a primo illo orbe formantur.

[103] Ibid.

> is different in respect of its material, as the material consists of (so to speak) different airs. Therefore it can be the case that no body is found wholly in different places at the same time, and *uox* can be a body, and yet a *uox*, identical in respect of its form (i.e., a similitude of sound), is heard in different places at the same time. Boethius too posits the analogy of water in the prologue to his *Musica*.

It must be noted, however, that the author of the *Glosulae* seems to know the *De institutione musica* only secondhand, or at least was writing without directly consulting his copy of Boethius's musical treatise, for there is no reference to the waves *in prologo quem praemittit in Musica*; the analogy occurs only midway through book 1 (1.14). The *Glosulae* then quickly dispenses with the qualitative and quantitative positions in quick succession. The *sententia* that *uox* is a quality is a simple misunderstanding of Boethius's statement (*In Perih*. II.4.18) that a *uox* is a *percussio aeris*. We must not suppose that this *percussio* belongs in the category of quality; it is, rather, simply another way of expressing the *sententia* already endorsed in the *Glosulae*, namely *aer percussus*.[104] Likewise, the quantitative position, held by those who adhere to the authority of Aristotle, arises from the equivocal understanding of the term *oratio*, which the *Glosulae* claims "signifies one thing when in the category of quantity, but something quite different when it is subordinated to the *uox* in the category of substance."[105] In the end, however, the *Glosulae* leaves the question open, admitting that whichever of the *sententiae* commentators may prefer, each can offer a suitable reply to the basic question: "What does Priscian define?" when he defines a *uox* as *aer tenuissimus ictus*.[106]

The quantitative position is articulated most fully in the writings of Peter Abelard, who was compelled to think carefully about the *uox* in order to think even more carefully about the more pressing problem of universals. If Abelard were to

[104] Rosier-Catach, "Le commentaire des *Glosulae*," 123–124: Opponitur iterum praemissae diffinitioni, quae dicit vocem esse aerem, quod Boetius in secundo commento Perihermeneias dicit vocem esse aeris percussionem per linguam, quod si aeris percussio qualitati supponitur, vocem eidem supponi necesse est. Sed si quis diligenter dicta Boetii consideret, inveniet vocem qualitati non supponi. Non enim dicit vocem simpliciter esse percussionem, sed aeris percussionem, id est aerem percussum. Et est dictum ad expressionem.

[105] Ibid., 124: Alii vero Aristotelis auctoritate muniti vocem in quantitate ponunt. Dicit enim Aristoteles in quantitate orationem esse. Sed in quo praedicamento est species, ibidem esse oportet genus ipsius speciei. Huic obiectioni sic respondetur quod illi equivocatione orationis decepti nesciunt illam vocem quae est oratio, aliud significare in quantitate, aliud quando subiicitur voci in substantia. Voces enim eaedem saepe et significant substantiam quodam respectu, et quantitatem alio respectu, ut "corpus" ista vox.

[106] Ibid., 127: Si autem quaeratur in alterutra sententia quid Priscianus hic diffiniat, potest congrue responderi: haec prolatio "vox" (secundum hoc quod significat et nominat omnes aeres naturalibus ictos instrumentis) uel hic aer, seu quantitas "homo," et sic de singulis aliis per se secundum hanc proprietatem quod naturalibus percutiuntur instrumentis, uel qualitas illa a qua sumitur vox secundum hoc quod adiacet aeribus percussionem suscipientibus.

argue that universals are *uoces*, as he in fact does in his *Logica ingredientibus*, then he needs to account for the fact that, in at least one reading (a tenacious and vocal reading at that), *uoces* are things. Without addressing this line of interpretation, Abelard would end up looking much like the naive vocalists, the very objects of his withering critique. Abelard, famously, changed his terminology to clarify his position: universals are not *uoces* (vocal utterances per se), but rather *sermones* (significative words, or sounds taken along with their meaning). But even before the flight from *uoces* to *sermones*, Abelard offered a set of sophisticated arguments, motivated by Aristotle's claim in the *Categories* that *oratio* is an accident in the category of quantity, that *uoces* are quantitative entities, quantitative measurements of air suitably struck.[107]

Abelard's most developed discussion occurs in his *Dialectica*. After dispatching the *magna dissensio* over the meaning of *oratio* as a matter of mere verbal quibbling,[108] he gets down to business with a detailed and (perhaps surprisingly) often physical discussion of *oratio siue uox*:[109]

> Nunc autem attentius inspiciendum est quam aeris prolati quantitatem orationem sive vocem appellamus. Cum enim multae sint aeris quantitates ceteris rebus communes, quibus vel secundum numerum partium vel secundum tempus vel fortasse secundum lineas vel superficies vel corpora mensurantur, praeter has omnes in prolatione quamdam dimensionem ac quemdam tenorem habet, quem Priscianus spiritum vocat [*Inst. gramm.* 2.44], ex quo in prolatione tantum ac sono mensuratur, secundum hoc scilicet quod obtusum sonum vel clarum habet vel tenuem vel spissum vel humilem vel altum. Quos quidem tenores Aristoteles orationes appellat sive etiam fortasse voces, quas etiam significare voluit quando una cum aere ipso proferuntur.
>
> Now we must carefully consider just how it is that we deem a quantity of articulated air an *oratio* or a *uox*. For although air has many sorts of quantity in common with other things as well—such as to be measured by the number of its parts, by time, or perhaps even by lines, surfaces,

[107] E.g., *LI2*, 173.7–9: Est autem hoc loco oratio nomen cuiusdam mensurae aeris strepentis et sonantis, secundum quam eum auditu metimur.

[108] *Dial.* 66.23–27: sive enim tam aeres prolati quam eorum tenores voces vel orationes seu nomina vel verba vel syllabae vel litterae dicantur, seu tantum huiusmodi quantitatum commune nomen sit "oratio," nichil impedit nec quicquam nominis impositione de naturali proprietate rerum mutaverit. Cf. *LI2*, 174.11–12: Sed non est magna de controversia nominum quaestio, dummodo rei naturam teneamus.

[109] *Dial.* 66.28–67.4. Cf. *LI2*, 173.9–13: Nam praeter lineas vel superficies ceterasque mensuras, quas habet aereum corpus communes cum ceteris corporibus, habet quandam propriam, quae mensuratur, dum sonat, tenorem videlicet quandam ei adiacentem, qui modo maior, modo minor discernitur pro eo quod aer vehementius vel remissius percutitur.

and bodies—in addition to all these, air has in its articulation a certain dimension, that is, a certain tenor, which Priscian calls "spirit." This can only be measured in the articulation and the sound, according to the fact that it, for instance, has a dull or clear sound, a thin or full sound, a low or high sound. Aristotle calls these "tenors" *orationes* or perhaps even *uoces*, and he means that these are bearers of meaning when they are articulated together with the air itself.

Abelard thus makes a careful distinction between the substance of the *uox* (*aer percussus*) and an accident of this substance that he deems its tenor, which is an accident in the category of quantity. What we may perceive as the qualities of sound (that it can be dull, clear, thin, full, low, and high) are in fact reducible to the quantitative. Abelard asserts this view over and against the authority of *noster magister*, presumably William of Champeaux, who held the *sententia* that, "properly speaking, only the air is heard, sounds, and bears meaning," and the "tenors" would merely come along with the air, insofar as they are adjacent to the heard, meaningful air.[110] Abelard, however, pushes his view even further and makes a general claim that outstrips the requirements of his argument. The tenor is not just the semantic bearer of a *uox* (the minimal claim he needs for his argument to succeed), it is in fact the very thing that makes air perceptible to the senses as sound. In short, tenor is the proper form of air, and it is only qua its tenor that air is sense-perceptible (qua sound) at all, for air can convey all sorts of "forms" that do not convey any sound (or, what is more important for Abelard, do not bear any meaning):[111]

Sed iam et sic quamlibet ipsius aeris formam, ut colorem aliquem eius, audiri ac significare possemus confiteri. Nos autem ipsum proprie sonum audiri ac significare concedimus, qui, dum aer percutitur, in ipso procreatur, atque per ipsum aer quoque sensibilis auribus efficitur. Sicut enim ceteris sensibus formas ipsas substantiarum proprie discernimus atque sentimus, ut gustu ⟨sapores, odoratu⟩ [*scripsi*] odores, visu colores, tactu calores, ita quoque auditu proprie tenorem prolationis concipimus atque sentimus.

But on this view [i.e., that of *noster magister*] we could grant that any form of the air, say its color, is heard and bears the meaning. We do, however, concede that, properly speaking, sound itself is heard and

[110] *Dial.* 67.5–8: Nostri tamen, memini, sententia Magistri ipsum tantum aerem proprie audiri ac sonare ac significare volebat, qui tantum percutitur, nec aliter huiusmodi tenores vel audiri vel significare dici, nisi secundum hoc quod auditis vel significantibus aeribus adiacent.

[111] *Dial.* 67.8–15. Cf. *LI2*, 174.31–33: Et sunt nonnulli, qui solum aerem velint sonare, audiri, significare. Nos vero tenorem praecipue auditu discerni volumus et proprie significare.

> bears meaning. For sound is generated in the air when the air is struck, and air, too, is made sensible to the ears through sound. For just as, in the case of the other senses, we properly discern and perceive the forms of substances—flavors by taste, scents by smell, colors by sight, and temperature by touch—so also we properly discern and perceive the tenor of an articulation by the sense of hearing.

The tenor, defined in Abelard's glosses on the *Categories* as a *strepitus aeris* ("sound of the air") belonging to the category of quantity,[112] is thus the proper object for the sense of hearing, just as color is the proper object of vision, scent the proper object of the sense of smell, etc. But how is it, then, that the tenor is quantitative; i.e., what is it that makes it a measurable *dimensio*? Vocal sounds, in Abelard's view, are ultimately reducible beyond the seemingly smallest elements, namely letters (deemed elements by analogy with the cosmological elements), for the articulation of a single letter (*prolatio unius litterae*), viewed from the physical standpoint of a vocal sound, is not a simple entity but is in fact composed from many parts (*ex pluribus partibus coniuncta*). Abelard explains:[113]

> Cum enim cuiuslibet litterae sonum proferimus, plures aeres in minutissimas [*scripsi*, mitissimas *De Rijk*] partes lingua nostra percutimus, quae singulae quemcumque sonum habere videntur, licet per se non discernatur, sicut nec per se profertur. Oportet itaque huiusmodi sonum proprie simplicem atque indivisiblem appellari qui in indivisibili parte aeris consistit. Totam vero unius litterae prolationem non aliter indivisibilem dici nisi ad partes per se prolatas, utpote ad aliarum litterarum prolationes, quas elementa nuncupant.
>
> When we articulate the sound of any one letter, we strike the air with our tongue into many tiny pieces, and each of these individually seems to have some sort of sound, although this sound is not discerned per se, just as it is not articulated per se. It is thus necessary that this sound be properly deemed the simple and indivisible sound, which consists in indivisible particles of air. The complete articulation of a single letter can be called indivisible only with regard to those parts that are articulated per se, namely the articulations of the letters called elements.

112 *LI2*, 173.13–14: Hic autem tenor ipse est strepitus aeris, quem hoc loco Aristoteles quantitatem vocat.

113 *Dial.* 67.24–31. Cf. *LI2*, 174.14–19: Quod autem supra tetigimus, quosdam scilicet tenores indivisibiles esse secundum partes, non videtur verum. Si enim proferam "a" vel quodlibet literale elementum, quod individuam vocem Priscianus vocat, non videtur tenor vocis individuus, quippe plures simul aeris partes sicut percuti, ita etiam quantulumcumque sonum habere videntur, licet auditus eos non distinguat neque discernat.

In his glosses on the *Categories*, Abelard makes what may seem a surprising appeal to Macrobius to support his thesis that the *tenores*—quantitative entities composed of many "particles" of sound—are the proper objects of hearing, not the air.[114] I say surprising because Macrobius's discussion of sound generation centers upon the generation of a most specific (and problematic) instance of sound: the *musica caelestis*. In arguing for the "reality" of the music of the spheres in the face of all sensory evidence to the contrary (namely, that we hear nothing), Macrobius contends that the violent collision of two bodies naturally and necessarily results in the production of sound.[115] According to Abelard, the authority of Macrobius—and by extension, the normative status of the sonic *musica caelestis*—thus supports the view that sound is something other than the bodies that collide to produce it (which, in the case of a *uox*, would be *lingua* et *aera*). This "something" is Abelard's "tenor":[116]

> Macrobius etiam huic plane consentire videtur, ut ipsum tenorem sonum appellemus, non aerem, ubi videlicet de motu planetarum loquens sonum fieri dicit ex duorum corporum violenta collisione, qui diversus est a collisis corporibus. Ex quo et illud convincitur, quicquid ex collisione linguae et aeris factum sonat, diversum esse tam ab aere ipso quam a lingua. Id vero est tenor qui aerem in prolatione mensurat. Si quis tamen aerem quoque audiri dicat vel significare, fortassis concedi poterit, sicut et corpus cum colore ipso videri dicimus, sed praecipue tenorem significare.
>
> Macrobius also clearly appears to agree with this view—namely that we call sound the tenor, not the air—where, when he speaks of the motion of planets, he says that sound arises from the violent collision of bodies, which is something quite apart from the bodies that have collided. Hence it is clear that, whatever it is that sounds when there is a collision of tongue and air, it is something other than the air itself or the tongue itself. This, of course, is the "tenor," which measures the

[114] Abelard was not the first to turn to Macrobius for support. The *Glosulae* already noted Macrobius's relevance to the quantitative position: Sed primum quid vox in quantitate tantum posita significet videamus. Auctores huius sententie ex rationibus Macrobii qui de planetarum motu loquens, sonum ex duorum corporum violenta collisione fieri dicit, confirmant vocem significare quendam sonum ex aere confectum et lingua (Rosier-Catach, "Le commentaire des *Glosulae*," 125).

[115] *In Som. Scip.* 2.1.5 (95.3–96.4): ex ipso enim circumductu orbium sonum nasci necesse est, quia percussus aer ipso interventu ictus vim de se fragoris emittit, ipsa cogente natura ut in sonum desinat duorum corporum violenta conlisio. Cf. 2.4.2–3 (107.17–23): diximus numquam sonum fieri nisi aere percusso. ut autem sonus ipse aut acutior aut gravior proferatur, ictus efficit qui dum ingens et celer incidit acutum sonum praestat, si tardior lentiorve, graviorem. indicio est virga quae dum auras percutit, si impulsu cito feriat, sonum acuit, si lentiore, in gravius frangit auditum.

[116] *LI2*, 174.37–175.9.

> air in its articulation. If someone should yet claim that it is the air that is heard or that bears the meaning, perhaps that could be conceded, in the sense that we say that a body is seen together with its color, but it is still the tenor that is the primary meaning bearer.

Committing, as Abelard does, to a quantitative view of *oratio* or *uox* does not, however, remove the same problem that taxed other commentators on Priscian, namely how a single *uox* can reach the ears of different listeners at the same time.[117] Abelard gives two possible answers, and the second is a matter of physics (*physica consideratio*), namely the Boethian wave model. Yet Abelard does not interpret the transmission of the form as a straightforward "formal" identity (as in the *Glosulae*); rather, he consistently deems the form that is transmitted via the "undulation" of the air only an "entirely similar form" (*consimilis forma*). Although in the *Dialectica* (quoted below) Abelard attributes the view to unnamed thinkers, in his later logical works he adopts it as his own, claiming that such a view is the more rational option (*uidetur magis ad rationem accedere*):[118]

> Illi autem qui audiri nolunt nisi praesentia, hanc in voce physicam considerant quod quando lingua nostra aerem percutit sonique formam ipsi nostrae linguae ictus attribuit, ipse quidem aer cum ab ore nostro emittitur exterioresque invenit aeres quos percutit ac reverberat, ipsis etiam quos reverberat, consimilem soni formam attribuit illique fortasse aliis qui ad aures diversorum perveniunt. Unde etiam Boethium dicunt in libro musicae artis ad huiusmodi naturam similitudinem de lapillo misso in aquam adhibuisse. . . . Sic vocem non secundum essentiam, sed secundum consimilem formam eamdem ad aures diversorum essentialiter venire quidam contendunt.
>
> Those who think that only things present [to the ears] are heard consider this physical matter regarding the *uox*, that when our tongue strikes the air and the blow of our tongue bestows on the air a sounding

117 *Dial.* 70.15–19: At vero quomodo vel ipsa quantitas vel ipse aer in diversis locis simul esse poterit? Quae enim individua sunt, in diversis locis esse auctoritas negat atque in hoc ab universalibus separat, quae simul in pluribus reperiuntur.

118 *Dial.* 70.36–71.12. Cf. *LI2*, 176.23–35: Aer itaque oratione emissus et sonans alios aeres percutit eisque consimiles sonus confert, qui circumque diffusi ad aures diuersorum ueniunt et ita audiuntur. Unde Priscianus de uoce agens, "ipsa," inquit, "tangit aurem" et Boethius in Arte musica dicitur ad naturam uocis demonstrandam conuenientem similitudinem inducere de lapillo proiecto in aqua, qui dum aquam percutit, quam inuenit, ipsa statim aqua percussa, dum in orbem diffunditur, orbicularem formam assumit undisque aliis quas ad ripas impellit, consimilem formam attribuit, dum ipse quoque in orbem diffunditur. Sic et aer aerem impellit et consimilem sonum ei confert, qui diffusus ad aures diuersorum peruenit per partes, quae singulae consimilem sonum habent, et ita ⟨a⟩ diuersis adstantibus uox eadem, id est consimilis in sono, audiri dicitur et ad aures diuersorum peruenire.

> form, that same air, as it is emitted from our mouth, comes upon [particles of] air, which it strikes and causes to reverberate, and it too bestows on the reverberating [particles of] air an entirely similar (*consimilis*) sounding form, and those perhaps [bestow the sounding form] on still more particles, which reach the ears of different listeners. Thus they contend that a *uox*, the same not according to its being (*essentia*) but according to its entirely similar form, essentially reaches the ears of different listeners.

Abelard's *physica consideratio* thus returns us to the wave model of *De institutione musica*, which was the starting point for natural-philosophical considerations of the ontology of the *uox*.

The Natural-Philosophical *uox*

In Adelard of Bath's *Quaestiones naturales*, the full complex of arguments regarding the *uox*, which were drawn from Augustine, Boethius's logical commentaries, as well as the wave model of the *De institutione musica*, are foisted upon the *De institutione musica* alone:[119]

> Sed hec eius sententia in Musica ab eodem [sc. Boetio] sic exposita est ut cum vox aer sit, aer autem corpus, corpus vero individualiter idem et unum in diversis locis eodem tempore totum esse non conveniat, sic eadem vox in diversis auribus hominum simul esse non possit. Subdit igitur quodmodo esse possit, dicens: "Aer quidem ore loquentis formatus linguaque impulsus proximum sibi eadem forma afficit aerem, et secundum tercium, tercius quartum, itaque usque ad aures astantium. Sicque similes non eidem audiuntur aeres." Unde et idem Boetius exempli similitudinem in iactu lapidis circulorumque formatione subdit.
>
> But Boethius explains his opinion in [his book about] music in this way: since sound is made up of air, but air is a body, and one and the same body taken on its own cannot be complete in different places at the same time, thus the same sound cannot be simultaneously in the ears of different men. To explain how this can happen, he therefore has to add: "The air is formed by the mouth of the speaker and propelled by the tongue. It then shapes the air closest to itself with the same form, and the second [parcel of] air shapes the third, and the third the fourth, and so on until it reaches the ears of the bystanders. Thus they hear

[119] *Quaest. nat.* 21 (130).

> similar [parcels of] air, but not the same." Hence the same Boethius adds as an illustration the throwing of a stone into water and the formation of circles.

As Charles Burnett has convincingly demonstrated, Adelard here is, in fact, closely reliant upon the *Glosulae*, not Boethius.[120] Adelard's "Boethian" summary of the *Glosulae* was in turn picked up by William of Conches in his *Dragmaticon*.[121] But it is William's glosses on Priscian, with which this chapter began, that offer his fullest account of the physical and philosophical contexts for the *uox*. William sides with the corporealists—"therefore air, which has been struck in this way and takes form from the percussion, is a *uox*"—and only mentions in passing the competing views from the incorporealist camp. Some claim, he tells us, that sound is comparable to odor insofar as it is discerned in the air, but is not itself identifiable with the air. The incorporealists, however, disagree as to whether the *uox* is thus quality, quantity, or any one of the Aristotelian categories. William does not explain these views but tersely promises to handle them elsewhere (*sed de hoc alias dicetur*).[122]

The corporealist camp, William notes, still has to deal with the fundamental aporia. William first invokes the same (pseudo-)Augustinian maxim encountered in the *Glosulae*: "Augustine says that no body can be wholly present at one and the same time in different places." This incontrovertible position, however, uncomfortably jostles the Boethian perspective on hearing, here represented not by Boethius's *In Categorias* but by *Consolatio philosophiae* 2.p5.6: "But Boethius says of the *uox* that one *uox* equally fills the hearing of many individuals."[123] Hence the

120 Burnett, "Adelard, Music, and the Quadrivium," 175–180.

121 Cf. *Drag.* 6.21.1–2: Dicit Boetius auditum fieri sic: aer naturalibus instrumentis percussus in ore loquentis formam quandam accipit. Qui exiens particulam aeris, quam tangit, simili forma informat et illa aliam, donec ad aures, quae ad modum tympani sunt concauae, perueniat. Quo in earum concauitate resonante excitatur anima, emittit que quandam partem praedictae aereae substantiae per neruos, qui a medio cerebri hinc et inde usque ad aures extenduntur. Quae tangens aera quem in aure reperit simili forma informatur, cum qua ad animam in logistica cellula recurrit. Ibi anima figuram nostrae uocis perpendit, et fit auditus. Ad quod demonstrandum inducit idem Boetius tale exemplum: lapis proiectus in medio stagni facit breuissimum circulum, qui impellens undas facit laxiorem circulum, et ille alium; et hoc fit donec uel ad ripas peruenerit uel impetus defecerit. Diuersae igitur particulae aeris, sed simili forma informatae, sunt in auribus diuersorum. Dicitur tamen eadem uox ibi esse propter expressam similitudinem. Cf. *Guillelmi Glos. sup. Tim.* 152; *Phil.* 4.28 (PL 172, 97AB).

122 267.3–9: Sunt quidam qui propter praedictas obiectiones dicunt uocem non esse aera nec corpus, im⟨m⟩o quiddam quod in aere ipso auditu discernitur, quemadmodum quiddam quod in aere odore discernitur. Qui tamen odor aer non est, sed in aere perpenditur. Similiter quiddam est quod in ipso aere auditu discernitur, sed quid sit illud—an qualitas, an quantitas—dissentiunt. Alii enim dicunt illud esse qualitatem, alii quantitatem, tertii dicunt neutrum, nec aliquid de praedicamentalibus. Sed de hoc alias dicetur.

123 *Cons. phil.* 2.p5.6: et uox quidem tota pariter multorum replet auditum.

aporia: "if *uox* is air, and air is a body, how can it possibly stand that one and the same thing be in the ears of different individuals?"[124]

In his answer to this question, William puts his own stamp upon the tradition. William offers four responses, and each resolves the problem through differing approaches to either the ontological status of the *uox* or the perceptual process of *auditus*. William's solutions to the "*uox* problem" recapitulate *in nuce* the various solutions offered to the problem of universals—the similarities between the solutions no doubt stemming from the similarity of the root problem, namely how it is that one thing can be wholly in diverse things at one and the same time. Of William's four solutions, two of them (1 and 3) closely map positions on universals, whereas the other two (2 and 4) are closely tied to theories of perception and the way that sound travels (or does not travel) from source to ears. Here, then, are the four solutions:

1. The *consimilitudo* theory (265.4–11): the same *uoces* in the ears of different individuals are not completely identical (*non penitus eadem*) but only similar in all respects (*consimilis*), so that there is no perceptible difference between them (*ita quod nulla potest ibi perpendi differentia*). The negative formulation echoes the version of the indifference theory held by Abelard's master, William of Champeaux. One consequence of this view is that *uoces* are fundamentally "irrevocable"—every *uox* is different (if imperceptibly so in the case of tokens of the same type). Even though this view, as William admits, has the apparent endorsement of Aristotle (*Cat.* 6.5a33–35: *dictum est et non potest amplus sumi*) and Horace (*Epist.* 1.18.71: *et uolat emissum semel irreuocabile uerbum*), he seems to have held it in little regard, and he excoriates a consequence of this position with his preferred derogatory slight, *confingere*:[125] *ideoque huiusmodi confingunt sententiam*. Although the precise *sententia* that William derides has been garbled by the scribe, it seems to have gone something like this: if *uoces* are nonrepeatable, then we can only describe the *euangelium* as *consimile*. William seems resistant to the idea that the Gospel is only identifiable with the sense of the words and not the words themselves.[126]
2. The *extramissio* theory (265.12–19): *auditus* works like *uisus*, and thus the ears emit an airy substance (the *instrumentum audiendi*) that travels from the ears

[124] 265.1–4: Dicit igitur Augustinus nullum corpus uno et eodem tempore totum potest esse in diuersis locis. Sed Boethius de uoce dicit, "et uox quidem una pariter replet auditum multorum." Si igitur uox est aer, et aer corpus, quomodo poterit stare quod ipsa sit in a⟨u⟩ribus diuersorum una et eadem?

[125] Cf. *Guillelmi Glos. sup. Tim.* 127.18–20: Et nota quod non dicit ex qualitatibus elementorum humanum corpus constare, ut quidam garciones confingunt. . .; *Drag.* 3.5.1.9–11: Huius [sc. Aristotelis] sententiam super hoc [sc. super quintam essentiam] exponerem, nisi quosdam de nostris timerem, qui, coquina Aristotilis [*sic*] indigni, se esse illius filios confingunt.

[126] The questionable passage reads: Ideoque huiusmodi confingunt sententiam: neque aliquid euangelium nisi consimile. Non dicatur euangelium sensus uerborum. I have been unable to find any eleventh- or twelfth-century theory that holds that the *euangelium* is *non nisi consimile*.

to the source of the percussed air (here the *os loquentis*), assumes the form that it finds there, and upon its return reports this form to the listener's soul (*formata forma quam reperit in aere percusso in ore, reuertitur ad animam. Et sic audit anima*). William, along with Adelard of Bath,[127] allows for this theory of hearing in special cases—namely, when a sound (a hiss or whistle: *sibilus*) is produced by a sharp intake of breath through terse lips.[128]

3. The *collectio* theory (265.20–25): indefinitely many bits of air, when they share the same form (*eadem forma informati*), are said to be one and the same *uox*, although they are not the same *corpus*, just as infinite words (*infinitae dictiones*) are only one part of speech, even though they are not *una dictio*. Thus a *uox* is many bodies at once such that it is any one of them (*eadem uox est multa corpora ita quod unumquodque eorum*). William gives no indication as to whether he agrees or disagrees with this view.
4. The *circulus* theory (265.26–30): If a *uox* is transmitted like waves in a pool, then a *uox* is identifiable as the outermost circle of air in its entirety (*ille ultimus circulus aeris totus est una uox*). Part is in my ears and part in your ears. Each part, however, is coextensive with the whole, in that each part contains the entire form and meaning of the *uox*. Whether or not William agrees that the *uox* is identifiable with the *ultimus circulus*, the Boethian model of sound propagation as akin to waves in water remained a fixed feature in William's account of hearing.

In the end, William does not decide among these views, but perhaps the particularities of each matters less than the underlying feature that they all share: the irrefutable corporeality and materiality of the *uox*, indeed of sound generally. In each case, the sonic body that is the object of perception is differently configured and belongs to different stages, so to speak, of the imagined journey of the *uox* with which this chapter, and William's *Glosulae*, began. The *extramissio* theory gets us closest to the source. The soul's airy instrument, journeying forth into the external world, obviates any role for a medium and instead takes the form directly from the horse's mouth (so to speak). At the other extreme, the *circulus* theory, the corporeal *uox* becomes synonymous with the final stage of the medial transfer itself. The *uox is* the medium, and the medium is the message. These two theories, moreover, preserve the *numerical* identity of the sound heard by different perceivers through the spatiotemporal proximity of the perceiver to the perceived: the numerical identity of the form encountered at the source by the *instrumentum*

[127] *Quaest. nat.* 21 (132): Sicut enim, dum a me aerem impellendo formo, ad diversos diversi venientes sentiuntur, sic, dum ad me trahendo infra labia eum illido, a diversis per attractionem venientes ab eis a quibus veniunt sentiuntur.

[128] E.g., *Drag.* 6.21.4: dum sibilamus, stringendo labia aera attrahimus. Qui attractus uicinum sibi attrahit, et ille alium, donec illum qui est in auribus attrahat. Qui secum praedictum instrumentum usque ad os sibilantis attrahit; ibi forma accepta ad anima reuertitur, sicque sibilus auditur.

audiendi (*extramissio*) or the numerical identity of the continuously informed medium (*circulus*) taken as a whole.[129] The *consimilitudo* and *collectio* theories, on the other hand, do not explicitly locate the sonic body spatiotemporally. Instead, they invoke the criterion of *qualitative* identity to account for the simultaneous perception of *una uox* by different perceivers. Numerically different sonic bodies are either imperceptibly similar (*consimilitudo*) or formally identical (*collectio*).

The imagined journeys of sonic materialities from physiology to psychology, and from late antiquity to the twelfth century, teach us several lessons. (1) *Sonus* or *uox* is either the material result of bodily interactions in the world or the immaterial trace (qua tenor) of such interactions. (2) In either case, sound is not *merely* the remainder of those bodily interactions, whose causes it would encourage us to pursue with means over and above the physical (i.e., mental, rational consideration, to which the sounds are a *quasi admonitio*); it is also a sonic object in the world worthy of consideration in its own right. (3) Nor, however, are sounds entirely *epistemologically* divorced from the source-interaction of bodies and actions. Sounds *can* tell us meaningful things about the world, over and above any (conventional) semantic or symbolic content that the structure of human languages might have accorded those sounds. Combining these lessons can help us make sense of the "aspirational" aurality that is required to "hear" the imaginative and intellective music of the spheres, for imaginary sounds "dissolve the unity of sonic source, cause, and effect as parts of a single physical event or process, and draw an ontological line between the effect and its source or cause."[130] This is yet another way of saying that to hear the harmony of the spheres is not to deny the materiality of sonic bodies; it is, after all, the very materiality of the spheres themselves that guarantees the reality of their sonic effects.

[129] Strictly speaking, of course, two listeners do not hear numerically identical parts of the wave but numerically distinct parts that each are coextensive with the whole. However, if we, with William, construe the *uox* as the entire *ultimus circulus*, then we might say that there is a quasi-numerical identity insofar as each part experienced is coextensive with a numerically identical whole.

[130] Kane, *Sound Unseen*, 134.

5

Composing the Cosmic

Harmonies of the Macrocosm

Qui enim fieri potest, ut tam velox caeli machina tacito silentique cursu moveatur?

—Boethius, *De institutione musica*, 1.2

The argument that proves the existence of the harmony of the spheres is simple, at least as it was first presented in Aristotle's *De caelo* (2.9) as a Pythagorean truth ripe for criticism:

1. given that the motions of small earthly bodies produce modest sounds, the number, size, and rapidity of the celestial bodies must produce a sound immensely great;
2. the speeds of these celestial bodies are in the same ratios (*logoi*) as musical consonances; hence,
3. "the sound given forth by the circular movement of the stars is a harmony."

It is difficult, however, to write about the harmony of the spheres without sounding trite. That the doctrine, Aristotle's protestations notwithstanding, captivated the western imagination,[1] that it has been subject to countless variations and "reharmonizations,"[2] and that nevertheless it somehow captures a secret "harmonic master plan of Creation"[3]—all of these stories have been told elsewhere and do not need repeating, lest I continue to sing the same old unchanging cosmic

[1] S. K. Heninger Jr., *Touches of Sweet Harmony: Pythagorean Cosmology and Renaissance Poetics* (San Marino, CA: The Huntington Library, 1974); Leo Spitzer, *Classical and Christian Ideas of World Harmony: Prolegomena to an Interpretation of the Word "Stimmung"* (Baltimore: Johns Hopkins Press, 1963).

[2] James Haar, "*Musica mundana*: Variations on a Pythagorean Theme" (PhD diss., Harvard University, 1960).

[3] Jacomien Prins, *Echoes of an Invisible World: Marsilio Ficino and Francesco Patrizi on Cosmic Order and Music Theory* (Leiden: Brill, 2015), 6.

song. If anything, the "sacred mystery of the harmony of the spheres" (*harmoniae superum arcanum*, as Macrobius describes it)[4] has become the victim of its own success, suffering from a kind of media oversaturation. It has become, *in nuce*, a figure of speech, a synecdochic reduction for a vague "Pythagoreanism" (or sometimes "Neoplatonism"), for an enchanted world in which the book of nature is "written in the language of arithmetic,"[5] for a timeless ahistorical perfection that might heal the instability and fragmentation of (post)modern life.[6] (Just a few minutes of internet searching can confirm all of these and more.)

But the harmony of the spheres is also a site of anxiety. In the most famous literary accounts of the initial encounter between a mortal listener and the celestial symphony, it is an *acousmatic* sound, i.e., one of uncertain origin; it demands an explanation and a search for its cause. Scipio Africanus the Younger heard it first in the sixth book of Cicero's *De re publica*, the *Dream of Scipio*: "What is this sound, so great and delightful, that fills my ears?" (*"quid hic," inquam, "quis est qui complet aures meas tantus et tam dulcis?"*)[7] Later, Dante wondered the same as he entered Paradise: "The newness of the sound and the bright light / lit in me such keen desire to know their cause / as I had never with such sharpness felt before" (*La novità del suono e 'l grande lume / di lor cagion m'accesero un disio / mai non sentito di cotanto acume).*[8] It is not enough to wallow in the sheer acoustic presence and pleasure of the celestial harmony. The affect it instills is epistemic in its orientation. It instills the desire *to know*, "to use the knowledge . . . garnered from fellow senses to make sense of [the] auditory experience."[9] Historical, earth-bound cosmologists confront the precise opposite of the acousmatic condition of sound unseen. The music of the spheres is sight unheard. It demands an aspirational aurality that is itself the product of an anxious desire to know and to hear.

4 *In Som. Scip.* 2.17.16 (153.29–30).

5 Daniel Heller-Roazen, *The Fifth Hammer: Pythagoras and the Disharmony of the World* (New York: Zone Books, 2011), 27.

6 To give but a few examples: Guy Rosolato's idea of the "sonorous envelope" of the maternal voice as heard within the womb is "the first model of auditory pleasure"; "music finds its roots and its nostalgia in this original atmosphere, which might be called a sonorous womb, a murmuring house—or *music of the spheres*" (emphasis in original): "La voix: Entre corps et langage," *Revue française de psychanalyse* 38 (1974), 81; qtd. and trans. in Philip Brett, "Musicality, Essentialism, and the Closet," in *Queering the Pitch: The New Gay and Lesbian Musicology*, ed. Philip Brett, Elizabeth Wood, and Gary C. Thomas, 2nd ed. (New York and London: Routledge, 2006), 12. Or Frances Dyson, *The Tone of Our Times: Sound, Sense, Economy, and Ecology* (Cambridge, MA: MIT Press, 2014), 109: "From 'energy to information,' from things to signs, from the harsh sounds of physical labor with the muscles working in unison—banging out metal in the forge for instance, shaping it into the silent relations of tonal harmonies that orbit the music of the spheres."

7 Macrobius, *In Som. Scip.* 2.1.2.

8 Dante, *Par.* I.82–84; qtd. and trans. in Francesco Ciabattoni, *Dante's Journey to Polyphony* (Toronto: University of Toronto Press, 2010), 207.

9 Brian Kane, *Sound Unseen*, 224.

But "for whom would [the planets] sound?"[10] Frances Dyson has posed this question bluntly. Her answer, however, tracks the same Foucauldian *episteme* of semblance and unity that has haunted the introductions to my second and third chapters:

> As the planets required an ear to hear them, a mind to perceive them, and a reason for their co-relation, they affirmed the existence of a divine being, an infinite universe, and the sanctity of what was called "the fourfold" all at once. Yet at the same time, these neat correlations instituted one of the major flaws of unitary thinking: the impossibility of change.[11]

For Dyson, as for her primary interlocutor, Daniel Heller-Roazen, the "Pythagoreans" (employed as a blanket term for most music theorists from Greek antiquity until Nicole Oresme in the fourteenth century) were willfully blind to the many incommensurabilities, "unspeakable relations," and "uncountable remainders" on which their musical logic relied: "Ratios might be sought and found beyond all audition and all imagination. Yet something numberless continued, obstinately, still to sound."[12] So it may appear from the lofty heights of a neo-Kantian *Geistesgeschichte*. But the twelfth-century cosmologists—it should go without saying—did not aspire to hear a "regulative concept," and incommensurability is hardly the sole purview of an enlightened mentalité. The late-ancient and twelfth-century accounts of the harmony of the spheres are anything but unanimous and unchanging. They offer, in fact, a cacophonous chorus of conflicting scales and mathematical rationales, dependent entirely on the sources they followed, the arguments they tracked, and the precise end to which such harmonies might lead.

More importantly, the planetary strains are not the final end of musical speculation. They are a symptom, not a cause, of the broader commitment to a well-composed world; their harmony is expressive of an epistemic attitude, an aspirational aurality, and *not* a cosmic ontology. This chapter seeks to undo the common synecdochic reduction and to reintegrate the music of the spheres into the wider pattern of causal sequences that maintain the integrity of the cosmic body and soul. After laying out the principles of "corporeal" harmony within the world's body, which amounts to a study of elemental theory, the bulk of this chapter is dedicated to the world soul, the Platonic *anima mundi,* whose harmonious vitality was *both* perceptible (and intelligible) to humans through its harmonic regulation of the world's body *and* the condition of possibility for that perception

[10] Dyson, *The Tone of Our Times*, 27.

[11] Ibid.

[12] Heller-Roazen, *The Fifth Hammer*, 29.

in the first place. I will trace the vicissitudes of the world soul through twelfth-century commentaries and treatises, beginning with Bernard of Chartres and concluding with an unpublished twelfth-century commentary on the Timaean *psychogonia*, a commentary which amounts to a summa on the subject.

In the final section, we see the twelfth-century cosmologists begin to move away from the sonorous "reality" of the music of the spheres as a musico-astronomical concept, in sharp contrast to the extended discussions of precise musical structures generated by the planetary motions such as we find in Carolingian commentaries. In the final analysis, the cosmologists were less concerned with the harmonic structures of the *musica caelestis* than with its symbolic, anagogic, and affective employ as an epitome of (Platonic) celestial perfection and as a model for human ethics. Increasingly, they stripped away the Platonic astronomical principles (the world soul included) that underlie the mechanics of the celestial harmony, and they turned instead to a more Peripatetic view of the cosmos. But this, it must be stressed, was adopted before the widespread availability of Aristotle's *De caelo* and still in dialogue with the very same Platonic texts that had inspired the auditory quest for the *musica caelestis* in the first place. The supposed opposition, then, between the musical heavens of the Platonists and the silent heavens of the Peripatetics is revealed as a false dichotomy. In fact, the epistemic attitude it encourages can, and did, survive the gradual eclipse of the music of the sphere's materially grounded reality and its absorption into a more generic concept of nature.

Musica elementorum

"Indeed, all the natural philosophers posit opposites as starting points and establish the cosmos as arising from the harmonization of opposites."[13] Such is Proclus's starting point for his discussion of the composition of the world's body, and the claim well characterizes the basic approach to what was deemed in the twelfth century the music of the elements (*musica elementorum*).[14] In order to understand the twelfth-century accounts, we must first attend to the late-ancient conceptual framework for the theory of elemental qualities and their harmonious linkages. Most famously, Boethius evokes the harmonious balance of the elemental forces in the *Consolatio*'s great Timaean hymn, 3.m9: "You bind the elements by numbers, so that the cold convenes with the hot, / the dry with the wet, lest the more

[13] Proclus, *In Tim.* I 205.16–20: πάντες γὰρ οἱ φυσικοὶ τὰ ἐναντία ποιοῦσιν ἀρχὰς καὶ ἐκ τῶν ἐναντίων ἁρμοσθέντων τὸν κόσμον ὑφιστᾶσιν. On which Marije Martijn comments: "The sensible universe is characterized by a 'war' of contraries, and one of the main results of the activities of the Demiurge is the establishing of a regular order between those contraries, keeping them at peace with each other" (*Proclus on Nature*, 63).

[14] E.g., Bernard Silvestris, *Comm. in Mart.* 3.539.

rarefied fire / fly away or weight submerge the earth."[15] Although Boethius here employs the language of Aristotelian qualities (hot, cold, wet, and dry), the primary target is in fact Plato's *Timaeus*, 31b–32c. As Magee has remarked, this blending of Aristotelian language within a summary of Platonic metaphysics ranks as "Boethius' subtlest, and philosophically weakest, attempt to harmonize Plato and Aristotle."[16] Proclus, as Magee notes, observed the futility of reconciling the two systems,[17] while both Calcidius and Macrobius forged a way to map Aristotelian doctrine onto the Platonic system.

At *Timaeus* 31b–32c, Plato describes the generation of the sensible world from the four elements, harmonized through proportional linkages. Fire and earth, located at opposite extremes, require two intermediary elements, air and water, to bring them into continuous proportion (the *ratio continui competentis* in Calcidius's language),[18] which ensures the continuity of the cosmic body.[19] Plato's explanation follows the rule of geometric proportions: two plane or square numbers (e.g., 4 and 9) require a single mean (6) to bring them into continuous proportionality (4 : 6 : 9), whereas two solid or cubic numbers (e.g., 8 and 27) require two means (12 and 18) to effect the same contiguity (8 : 12 : 18 : 27).[20] Such is the mathematical explanation that Boethius offers at *De institutione arithmetica* 2.46 as the key to the abstruse cosmology (*cosmopoeia*) of Plato's *Timaeus*.[21] In his *Commentarii*, Macrobius's brief exposition of the four elements draws primarily on the four Aristotelian qualities in order to create a continuous proportionality (*iugabilis competentia*): earth (cold and dry) and water (cold and wet), although contrary in their dryness and wetness, are united in coldness; water (cold and wet) and air (hot and wet), although contrary in their coldness and hotness, are united in wetness, etc.[22] Macrobius concludes that the bonds of the four elements are

15 *Cons. phil.* 3.m9.10–12. Tu numeris elementa ligas, ut frigora flammis, / arida conveniant liquidis, ne purior ignis / euolet aut mersas deducant pondera terras. Cf. 4.m6.19–24: Haec concordia temperat aequis / elementa modis, ut pugnantia / vicibus cedant humida sicis / iugantque fidem frigora flammis, / pendulus ignis surgat altum / terraeque graves pondere sidant. On the carefully constructed parallels between these passages, see Magee, "Boethius' Anapestic Dimeters," 156–157 and 161–162. Cf. Martianus, *De nuptiis* 1.1 (1.7): namque elementa ligas uicibus.

16 Magee, "Boethius," 802.

17 *In Tim.* 2.37.33–38.16. Magee, "Boethius," 802.

18 *In Tim.* 18 (68.25), 21 (72.13), etc.

19 *Tim.* 32b3–c4.

20 *Tim.* 32a7–b3.

21 *Inst. ar.* 2.46 (191.1–193.30): Post haec igitur tempus est, ut expediamus nunc quiddam nimis utile in Platonica quadam disputatione, quae in Timaei cosmopoeia haud facili cuiquam vel penetrabili ratione versatur.

22 *In Som. Scip.* 1.6.25–26 (22.28–23.4): ita enim elementa inter se diversissima opifex tamen deus ordinis opportunitate conexuit, ut facile iungerentur. nam cum binae essent in singulis qualitates, talem uni cuique de duabus alteram dedit, ut in eo cui adhaereret cognatam sibi et similem reperiret. terra est sicca et frigida, aqua vero frigida et umecta est. haec duo elementa, licet sibi per siccum umectumque contraria sint, per frigidum tamen commune iunguntur. Cf. *Prem. phys.* 5.8: Sed quia contraria inuicem conuenire non possunt sine aliquo uinculo medio ordinato connectente ea, ordinauit creator infra terram et aerem

unbreakable, as two extremes are held together by two means.[23] Just as Boethius does in his *Consolatio*, Macrobius uses Aristotelian (qualitative) elemental theory to target the Platonic (quantitative) elemental bonds, though he alludes also to other qualities that could effect the same proportional bond.[24]

Calcidius's *Commentary* (21–22) had already expanded upon this latter gesture by Macrobius and presents a much richer theory that attempts to "mathematicalize" the elemental series, as has been well discussed by Stephen Gersh.[25] Calcidius carefully distinguishes, as Gersh has noted, two separate problems within Plato's account: "first, what is the precise nature of the mathematical series? And secondly, with what physical properties do the mathematical values correlate?"[26] In answer to the first question, Calcidius proves, as did Boethius, that the proportionality in question is an *analogia*, a ratio of continuous proportion (*analogia, id est ratio continui competentis*).[27] In answer to the second question, Calcidius equates the mathematical *analogia* with the six elemental qualities that are briefly mentioned in a later passage of the *Timaeus* (55d8ff., beyond where Calcidius's translation stops),[28] though he does allude to the possibility of other correlations,[29] including the four Aristotelian qualities and their cyclical interchange in the process of generation and corruption.[30] Fire is subtle, mobile, and sharp (*subtilis, mobilis*, and *acutus*), but earth is diametrically opposed in being corpulent, immobile, and dull (*corpulenta, immobilis*, and *obtunsa*).[31] Thus the proportional

contraria existentia aquam, dans ei duas qualitates, frigiditatem et humiditatem, per quas posset extremis coniuncta ea conectere. Per frigiditatem namque concordat terrae, humiditate autem coniungitur aeri.

23 *In Som. Scip.* 1.6.26 (23.14–21): haec tamen varietas vinculorum, si elementa duo forent, nihil inter ipsa firmitatis habuisset; si tria, minus quidem valido aliquo tamen nexu vincienda nodaret, inter quattuor vero insolubilis conligatio est cum duae summitates duabus interiectionibus vinciuntur, quod erit manifestius si in medio posuerimus ipsam continentiam sensus de Timaeo Platonis excerptam.

24 *In Som. Scip.* 1.6.32 (24.4–7): nam quantum interest inter aquam et aerem causa densitatis et ponderis, tantundem inter aerem et ignem est; et rursus quod interest inter aerem et aquam causa levitatis et raritatis, hoc interest inter aquam et terram, etc.

25 Gersh, *Concord in Discourse*, 128–138.

26 Ibid., 130.

27 On the general theme of *analogia* in Calcidius, see Anna Somfai, "Calcidius' *Commentary* on Plato's *Timaeus* and Its Place in the Commentary Tradition: The Concept of *Analogia* in Text and Diagrams," in *Philosophy, Science and Exegesis in Greek, Arabic and Latin Commentaries* (London: Institute of Classical Studies, University of London, 2004), 203–220.

28 See Waszink, *Timaeus a Calcidio translatus*, lxv–lxvi.

29 As noted by Gersh, *Concord in Discourse*, 132. *In Tim.* 14 (66.8–11): siquidem in illo igni plus est claritudinis, aliquanto minus moderati caloris, exiguum uero soliditatis, in terrae autem globo plus sit soliditatis, aliquantum uero humoris, perexiguum lucis, aeris et aquae duae medietates quam habeant cognationem cum supra memoratis elementis intellegamus.

30 *In Tim.* 317–318 (313.7–314.16): Etenim terra duas habet proprias qualitates, frigus et siccitatem. . . . Similiter aqua in duabus qualitatibus inuenitur, humoris uidelicet et frigoris, et est propria qualitas terrae quidem siccitas, aquae uero humor, communis uero utriusque natura frigoris. Cum igitur terra late fusa conuertetur aliquatenus in aquam, tunc siccitas quidem eius mutata erit in humorem, etc.

31 *In Tim.* 21 (72.7–17); cf. the same system, articulated through a synonymous yet different set of Latin terms in *Prem. phys.* 5.29 (*acumen, raritas* and *motus*, on the one hand, and *hebitudo, densitas*, and *statio* on the other).

transformation from one extreme to the other is effected by changing one quality at a time, thus exemplifying in tripled qualitative terms the quantitative sequence 8 (= 2×2×2) : 12 (=3×2×2) : 18 (= 3×3×2) : 27 (= 3×3×3).

In the twelfth century, the Aristotelian language of Macrobius and the Platonic language of Calcidius were united in an attempt to explain Plato's reference to single and double means within the elemental harmony, and a remarkably consistent theory coalesced around the (already existing) theory of elemental syzygies (*sinzugiae*).[32] Although the original usage of the elemental *sinzugiae* employed only the four Aristotelian qualities, twelfth-century commentators were quick to roll Calcidius's "Platonic" qualities into the theory. Thus the elemental syzygies were expanded to encompass two *sinzugiae*: a *plana sinzugia* formulated through the double Aristotelian qualities, and a *cubica sinzugia* formulated through the triple Calcidian qualities. Irène Caiazzo has usefully traced the development of this theory in the thought of William of Conches:[33] the double *sinzugiae* appear already in William's earliest work, the *Glosae super Boethium*, though he only explains the *plana sinzugia* and nowhere mentions the Calcidian qualities.[34] Similarly, the *Glosae super Macrobium* alludes to double and triple qualities but does not specify them.[35] The first definitive employ of the Calcidian elemental qualities occurs in William's *Philosophia*,[36] and thereafter the double elemental links remained one of the few stable points in his ever-changing position on the elements.

[32] As pointed out by Irène Caiazzo, the term, employed to describe the links between the elements, is found in a commentary on Boethius's *Consolatio* attributed to Remigius of Auxerre (Edmund Taite Silk, ed., *Saeculi noni auctoris in Boetii Consolationem philosophiae commentarius* [Rome: American Academy in Rome, 1935], 334–335): Nam quatuor sunt elementa quorum sex sunt coniunctiones quas Graeci sinzugias vocant. Quarum quatuor sunt inmediatae et duae mediatae. It is also employed by Eriugena in his translation of Gregory of Nyssa's *De opificio hominis* (*De imag.* 257.28). See Irène Caiazzo, "The Four Elements in the Work of William of Conches," in *Guillaume de Conches: Philosophie et science au XIIe siècle* (Florence: SISMEL Edizioni del Galluzzo, 2011), 3–66. On the theory of the elemental syzygies generally, see Peter Vossen, "Über die Elementen-Syzygien," in *Liber floridus: Mittellateinische Studien; Paul Lehmann zum 65. Geburtstag am 13. Juli 1949*, ed. Bernhard Bischoff and Suso Brechter (St. Ottilien: Eos Verlag der Erzabtei, 1950), 33–46.

[33] Caiazzo, "The Four Elements in the Work of William of Conches."

[34] *Glos. sup. Boet.* 3.m9.475–479: Quod ut apertius sit, dicatur primo de illa coniunctione quae fit uno medio, quae dicitur plana sinzugia, id est plana coniunctio; postea de illa quae fit duobus mediis, quae est cubica sinzugia, id est solida coniunctio.

[35] *Glos. sup. Macr.*, comment. ad 1.6.24: Quare si habeant duas qualitates sese dissoluentes, ut terra et aer, indigent uno solo medio, ut aqua quae est medium inter illa. Item si habeant tres qualitates agentes, indigent duobus mediis, ut terra et ignis. In coniunctione ergo unius medii ternarius habet magnam potentiam, quia ad minus oportet illa esse tria, unum medium et duo extrema. In coniunctione contrariorum duobus mediis interpositis quattuor obtinet uim uinculorum, quia ad minus oportet illa esse quattuor, duo scilicet media et duo extrema, quare id quod est partium attribuitur toto.

[36] *Phil.* 1.21 (51BC): Idcirco iecit deus quasi fundamenta ignem et terram. Sed quoniam in eis sunt contrarietates—quippe terra est corpulenta, obtusa, immobilis, ignis acutus, subtilis, mobilis—videt deus sine medio ea iungi non posse et ideo inter ea medium creavit. On the *coniunctio elementorum*, see *Phil.* 1.21 (51C–52D). Cf. *Guillelmi Glos. sup. Tim.* 63.1–39; *Drag.* 2.5.1.

The theory of the elemental syzygies enjoyed a wide circulation in twelfth-century commentaries on Boethius, Macrobius, Martianus, and Plato,[37] and the theory (though without the term *sinzugia*) is employed in the St. Florian commentary on the *De institutione musica* to explain Boethius's harmony of the elements. "Although the elements appear contrary," the St. Florian commentator writes, "some (*quidam*) join them together in musical harmony, just as contrary voices create one musical consonance."[38] This harmony, he explains, takes two forms: "sometimes according to binary qualities, sometimes according to ternary qualities," and there follows a cogent summary of the Macrobian and Calcidian positions.[39] But then, as a quick aside, he engages in brief speculation as to what these elements are. He notes the position that the elements (as some assert) are the qualities that naturally inhere in the elements, but he maintains in response that elements, because they are constitutive of bodies, must themselves be bodies.[40] The commentator's brief remarks on the ontological status of the elements align well with William of Conches's early (pre-*Philosophia*) standpoint on the elements, as articulated in his first work, the *Glosae super Boetium*. William too refutes those who say that the properties of elements are themselves the true elements, and after dismissing a few other erroneous positions, he concludes that the elements are simply what we see as separable in the sensible world: earth, water, air, and fire.[41]

[37] *Comm. in Mart.* 3.440ff. Anon., *Commentum in 'O qui perpetua mundum,'* Vat. lat. 919, 199v–200r: LIGAS ELEMENTA NVMERIS . . . Sed sciendum quod in istis alia est plana zinzugia (id est iunctura), alia est solida zinzugia. . . . Ad coniungendum illos duos [sc. quaternarium et nouenarium] sufficit senarius. Sic ad caliditatem et siccitatem ignis coniungendam cum frigiditate [frigido *ante corr. cod.*] et humiditate aquae sufficit una ligatura, aer uidelicet, qui caliditate ignis caliditati coniungatur, humiditate humiditati aquae coniungatur. Iterum ad coniugendum terram et aquam sufficit frigiditas. . . . Solida uero zinzugia in numeris colligatur duobus mediis. . . . Ad similitudinem horum fit in elementis solida zinzugia, quia, cum tres sint proprietates principales in quolibet elemento (et ignis sit leuis, acutus ⟨et⟩ mobilis; terra uero corpulentia, obtusa et immobilis), quo modo possent uno elemento colligari. On this text, see Bernhard Pabst, *Atomtheorien des lateinischen Mittelalters* (Darmstadt: Wissenschaftliche Buchgesellschaft, 1994), 195–202.

[38] *In inst. mus.* 35: Elementa enim licet contraria esse uideantur, quidam tamen musica armonia coniungunt, sicut contrarie voces unam faciunt musicam consonantiam.

[39] *In inst. mus.* 35: Sed assignatur quandoque contrarietas secundum binas qualitates, quandoque secundum ternas. Quae vero binis repugnant qualitatibus, uno medio iunguntur ad similitudinem tetragonorum, ut ignis et aqua binis repugnant qualitatibus, quia ignis est calidus et siccus, aqua vero frigida et humida, et ligantur uno solo medio interposito s. aere. . . . Assignatur etiam quandoque contrarietas ternis qualitatibus, et tunc opportet illam duobus mediis conligari, ut ignis et terra, nam ignis est subtilis, acutus, et mobilis, terra gravis, obtusa et immobilis, ideo duobus mediis conligantur ad similitudinem cuborum.

[40] *In inst. mus.* 35: CONTRARIAS EORVM POTENTIAS, i. contrarias proprietates naturaliter eis adherentes s. frigiditatem, humiditatem, caliditatem, siccitatem, quas quidam esse elementa asserunt, sed cum elementa partes sint corporum, corporis autem nihil est pars nisi corpus, constat quod melius dicuntur ipsa corpora elementa.

[41] *Glos. sup. Boet.* 3.m9.375–391: Et dicunt alii proprietates elementorum esse elementa, et ita constare omnia ex quatuor elementis, id est ex quatuor proprietatibus. . . . Sed nec istud nec illud michi placet. Immo placet michi elementa esse quae videntur a nobis separata, scilicet terra et aqua et cetera.

William would quickly change his tune, however. In the *Philosophia*, and then further elaborated in the *Glosae super Platonem*, the purest form of the elements are imperceptible and accessible to thought alone; the elements as apprehended by sense perception, "i.e., seen and perceived in an impure state, mixed with other elements," are in fact not *elementa* but *elementata* ("elemented" or "constituted from elements").[42] The effect of this shift was to remove any phenomenality from the concord of the elements; such harmonies are not perceptible, even in a metaphorical or analogical sense. They have receded more deeply into the worldly machine, and this recession anticipates the broader shift away from the mechanistic system of the harmony of the spheres to a "higher-level" abstraction, thus paving the way to more fully metaphorical ideas (and ideals) of order. But that does not make their harmony any less integral. To recall the passage from the *Glosae super Platonem* quoted in my prelude, which comes from this same "late" stage in William's elemental theory: "The world loves concord. And if the elements were to become discordant, the world would also dissolve" (*Mundus diligit concordiam. Et, si fieret discordia elementorum, dissolueretur et mundus.*)[43] In short, mechanism requires the harmony provided by a vital inner force; the *machina mundi* (at least for a time) required an *anima mundi.*

Anima mundi et harmonia: The Late-Ancient Reception

"The concord that flows through our ears and consists in soundings and strikings differs entirely from the life-giving, noetic concord."[44] So explains Proclus, as he sets forth the principles that guide his elucidation of the *anima mundi.* Soul has only a noetic harmony: it is not corporeal (even if the Demiurge manipulates it as if it were—mixing it, cutting it, shaping it); it has no dimensions (even if the Demiurge measures it and divides it as if it did); and it is not quantitative (even if the Demiurge imparts to it a distinctly quantitative structure). Phenomenal harmony, however, is all of these—corporeal, dimensional, and quantitative—and yet Plato tells us (*Tim.* 47d2): ἡ δὲ ἁρμονία, συγγενεῖς ἔχουσα φορὰς ταῖς ἐν ἡμῖν τῆς ψυχῆς περιόδοις ("harmony [has] movements that are akin to the periodic revolutions of soul within us"). The world soul's harmonic structure is thus ultimately anagogic: through the medium of a lower reality (mathematical harmonics), it offers a way to conceive of higher ontological reality (the soul). In the words, again, of Proclus: "The being of soul does not consist in mathematical numbers and ratios, but all of these ratios and numbers are representations of the real essence of soul and the creative, life-giving divisions within it."[45]

42 See Caiazzo, "The Four Elements in the Work of William of Conches" for the most recent and thorough account, with the further bibliography at 10–14.

43 *Guillelmi Glos. sup. Tim.* 39.23–25.

44 Proclus, *In Tim.* II 195.15–17: ἡ γὰρ δι' ὤτων εἰσρέουσα συμφωνία καὶ ἐν ἤχοις καὶ πληγαῖς ὑφισταμένη τῆς ζωτικῆς καὶ νοερᾶς ἐξήλλακται.

45 Proclus, *In Tim.* II 212.5–9: οὐ γὰρ ἐκ μαθηματικῶν ἀριθμῶν ἐστι καὶ λόγων ἡ οὐσία τῆς ψυχῆς, ἀλλ' οὗτοι πάντες οἱ λόγοι καὶ οἱ ἀριθμοὶ τὴν ὄντως οὐσίαν αὐτῆς ἀπεικονίζονται καὶ τὰς ἐν αὐτῇ διαιρέσεις τὰς δημιουργικάς τε καὶ ζῳογονικάς. On which see Martijn, *Proclus on Nature*, 195–201.

Here, then, are the ratios and numbers presented, perplexingly, by Plato in the Demiurge's construction of the world soul. The initial ingredient list is six, two pairs of three: Being (indivisible and divisible), Sameness (indivisible and divisible), and Difference (indivisible and divisible). In each case, he mixed the indivisible and divisible kinds together to forge a mixed medium between the two. As Francesco Pelosi explains, the indivisible and divisible mixture of each provides the Demiurge with a psychic substance "halfway between the full Existence, Sameness and Difference of the Forms and those changeable in the dimension of becoming. In this way, the soul is predisposed to participate in both dimensions: the intelligible and the sensible."[46] Then the Demiurge blended together all three intermediary mixtures (of Being, Sameness, and Difference) to form a whole whose subsequent psychic parts would be coextensive with the mixture of the psychic whole. Then he begins the harmonic division:

> ἤρχετο δὲ διαιρεῖν ὧδε. μίαν ἀφεῖλεν τὸ πρῶτον ἀπὸ παντὸς μοῖραν, μετὰ δὲ ταύτην ἀφῄρει διπλασίαν ταύτης, τὴν δ' αὖ τρίτην ἡμιολίαν μὲν τῆς δευτέρας, τριπλασίαν δὲ τῆς πρώτης, τετάρτην δὲ τῆς δευτέρας διπλῆν, πέμπτην δὲ τριπλῆν τῆς τρίτης, τὴν δ' ἕκτην τῆς πρώτης ὀκταπλασίαν, ἑβδόμην δ' ἑπτακαιεικοσιπλασίαν τῆς πρώτης· μετὰ δὲ ταῦτα συνεπληροῦτο τά τε διπλάσια καὶ τριπλάσια **διαστήματα**, μοίρας ἔτι ἐκεῖθεν ἀποτέμνων καὶ τιθεὶς εἰς τὸ μεταξὺ τούτων, ὥστε ἐν ἑκάστῳ **διαστήματι** δύο εἶναι **μεσότητας**, τὴν μὲν ταὐτῷ μέρει τῶν ἄκρων αὐτῶν ὑπερέχουσαν καὶ ὑπερεχομένην, τὴν δὲ ἴσῳ μὲν κατ' ἀριθμὸν ὑπερέχουσαν, ἴσῳ δὲ ὑπερεχομένην. ἡμιολίων δὲ **διαστάσεων** καὶ ἐπιτρίτων καὶ ἐπογδόων γενομένων ἐκ τούτων **τῶν δεσμῶν** ἐν ταῖς πρόσθεν **διαστάσεσιν**, τῷ τοῦ ἐπογδόου **διαστήματι** τὰ ἐπίτριτα πάντα συνεπληροῦτο, λείπων αὐτῶν ἑκάστου μόριον, τῆς τοῦ μορίου ταύτης **διαστάσεως** λειφθείσης ἀριθμοῦ πρὸς ἀριθμὸν ἐχούσης τοὺς ὅρους ἓξ καὶ πεντήκοντα καὶ διακοσίων πρὸς τρία καὶ τετταράκοντα καὶ διακόσια.
>
> This is how he began to divide. First he took away one part from the whole, then another, double the size of the first, then a third, one and a half times the second and three times the first, then a fourth, double the second, then a fifth, three times the third, then a sixth, eight times the first, then a seventh, twenty-seven times the first. Next he filled out the double and triple **intervals**, once again cutting off parts from the material and placing them in the intervening gaps, so that in each **interval** there were two **means**, the one [the harmonic mean] exceeding and exceeded by the same part of the extremes themselves, the other [the arithmetic mean] exceeding and exceeded by an equal number. The hemiolic, epitritic, and epogdoic **spaces** arose from these

[46] Pelosi, *Plato on Music, Soul and Body*, 191.

> links within the previous **spaces**; and he filled up all the epitritics with the epogdoic kind of **interval**, leaving a part of each of them, where the **space** of the remaining part had as its boundaries, number to number, 256 : 243.[47]

Plato's mathematical recipe for the construction of a well-tuned world soul leaves too much underdetermined for it to be construed straightforwardly as a recipe for a well-tuned musical system.[48] Commentators ancient and modern have sought repeatedly to construct its "scale,"[49] but as Andrew Barker notes, Plato does not set himself to the "task of making his construction correspond at every point to the shape of a system that could be used in practice.... There are no notes or pitches in his *harmonia*; there are only numbers."[50] But this is not quite the whole truth, for there are more than just numbers, that is, discrete quantities; there are also parts (μοῖραι), as well as intervals and spaces (διαστήματα and διαστάσεις), that is, continuous magnitudes. In fact, it could be argued that there are no discrete numbers at all, just magnitudes related to one another in determinately, numerically, specifiable ways. A quick scan of the bolded Greek terms, corresponding to bold text in the English translation, reveals a striking feature of this famous passage: spatial terms (διάστημα and διάστασις) appear where we might expect Plato to use λόγος, or "ratio," a term not used anywhere in the division (although λόγος does appear in the conclusion of his description of the world soul, where Plato observes that the circles within it move with speeds ἐν λόγῳ ["according to ratio": 36d6]). I have dealt with the music-theoretical implications of this elsewhere.[51] Here, I want to follow the cosmological implications of the world soul's harmonies.

Calcidius consistently describes the world soul in language that implies a harmonic structure: it is "analogous (*conuenire*) to number and measure," it has a "rational composition (*ratio compositionis*) akin to a musical concord (*symphonia*)," and it is "divided by numbers, comprised of analogies, close packed with

47 *Tim.* 35b4–36b3. I follow the translation, with minor modifications, of Andrew Barker, *The Science of Harmonics*, 319.

48 E.g., if we multiply the base sequence (1, 2, 3, 4, 8, 9, 27) by 6 to accommodate the harmonic and arithmetic means in whole numbers (as was standard in the exegetical tradition, e.g. Calcidius, *In Tim.* 41–42 [89.22–91.19]), the resultant sequence and its intercalated means (**6**, 8, 9, **12**, 16, **18**, **24**, 27, 32, 36, **48**, **54**, 81, 108, **162**) contains several non-epitritic ratios (32 : 27, 81 : 54, 162 : 108), whose proper subdivision is not prescribed (see Barker, *The Science of Harmonics*, 320–322).

49 The literature is extensive. Classic and recent studies include Jacques Handschin, "The 'Timaeus' Scale," *Musica Disciplina* 4 (1950), 3–42; Francis MacDonald Cornford, Plato's Cosmology: *The* Timaeus *of Plato, Translated with a Running Commentary* (London: Routledge & Kegan Paul, 1937), 66–72; Barker, *The Science of Harmonics*, 318–326; Dirk Baltzly, trans., *Proclus: Commentary on Plato's Timaeus*, Vol. 4: *Book 3, Part II: Proclus on the World Soul* (Cambridge: Cambridge University Press, 2009).

50 Barker, *The Science of Harmonics*, 322.

51 Andrew Hicks, "Re-interpreting an Arithmetical Error in Boethius's *De institutione musica*," *Music Theory & Analysis* 3 (2016), 1–26.

[numerical] means, and ordered with musical ratios."[52] Nevertheless, Calcidius nowhere goes so far as to call any soul, whether world or human, "number" or "harmony." Instead, in the words of Gretchen Reydams-Schils, he "couches his analysis systematically in terms of a kinship or a matching; the structure of the soul reflects certain relationships among numbers."[53] The implications of these numerical structure and musical ratios within the soul, in Calcidius's view, pertain more to the points of connection between the psychic and the corporeal than they do to any explicitly harmonic or musical rationale. Thus Calcidius provided medieval scholars with a model of interpreting the Platonic soul's numerical and harmonic structure as fundamentally anagogic, a mathematical expression of a higher ontological reality. For instance, the underlying numerical structure of the world soul—the series 1 2 3 4 9 8 27 and its (Adrastan) diagrammatic representation—is adduced by Calcidius as proof of the *ratio* that underlies the union of soul and body (*animae corporisque coniugium*):[54]

> Ista ergo descriptio quae partium ex quibus anima constare dicitur genituram seu coagmentationem deliniat, ostendit rationem animae corporisque coniugii. Quippe corpus animalium, quod inspiratur animae uigore, habet certe superficiem habet etiam soliditatem. Quae igitur cum uitali uigore penetratura erat tam superficiem quam soliditatem, similes soliditati, similes etiam superficiei uires habere debuit, siquidem paria paribus congregantur.
>
> Therefore, this diagram [sc. the lambda diagram], which delineates the generation or combination of the parts in which the soul is said to consist, reveals the *ratio* of the union of body and soul. Indeed, the body of living creatures, which has the uigor of soul breathed into it, assuredly has surface and also solidity. Because soul was designed to penetrate both surfaces and solids with its uital uigor, it was necessary that it possess powers akin to the solid [i.e., the cubic numbers 9 and 27] and the surface [the square numbers 4 and 8], insofar as like flocks with like.

This last claim, "insofar as like flocks with like," Calcidius elsewhere identifies as a fundamentally Pythagorean teaching (*Pythagoricum dogma*), citing the well-known formula "like is known by like" (*similia non nisi a similibus suis comprehendi*).[55] Hence, the numerical and harmonic structure within the world soul comports with the world's body, and the similitude accounts for the ability of the soul to penetrate bodies and to have knowledge of both the intelligible and the

52 *In Tim.*51 (100.3–5), 228 (244.1–2), and 102 (153.3–4).

53 Reydams-Schils, "Calcidius on the Human and World Soul," 193.

54 *In Tim.* 33 (82.9–15).

55 *In Tim.* 51 (100.8–11).

sensible world.[56] Later in the commentary, Calcidius summarizes his view on the division process, again highlighting the correlation of the psychic and the corporeal, and in the process he connects arithmetical and harmonic means within the world soul to the numerical bonds between the elements (as discussed above):[57]

> Horum numerorum interualla numeris aliis contexi uolebat, ut esset in animae textu corporis similitudo. Itaque limitibus constitutis, uno sex, altero duodecim qui est duplex, duabus medietatibus, octo et nouem sex et duodecim limitium interuallum continuauit epitrita, item sescuplari potentia, perindeque ut inter ignis limitem terraeque alterum limitem insertis aeris et aquae materiis mundi corpus continuatum est, ita numerorum potentiis insertis, ⟨ut⟩ tamquam elementis materiisque membra animae intellegibilia conecterentur essetque aliqua inter animam corporumque similitudo.
>
> He wanted the intervals of these numbers to be interwoven with other numbers, so that there might be a likeness of body woven within the soul. Thus, when he had established the limits at six and twelve (the duple of six) and the two means at eight and nine, the power of the epitritic and hemiolic united the interval between the limits six and twelve, in the same manner as the world's body has been united by inserting the substances of air and water between the limits constituted by fire and earth. These numerical potencies have been inserted such that intelligible parts of soul are joined as if by elements and substances, and that there is a kind of likeness that obtains between soul and body.

As Gersh argues, the presence of numerical relations in both the division of the soul and the conjunction of the elements allows Calcidius to posit another connection between psychic substance and worldly corporeality: "Thus, the original parts of psychic substance correlate with point, line, surface and solid in the sphere of physical bodies while—thanks to the doctrine of harmonic and arithmetical means—the original and supplementary parts of psychic substance correlate with extreme and intermediate elements in that sphere of physical bodies."[58]

The only perceptible manifestation of the harmony within the world soul is the *musica caelestis*, which is a direct consequence of the soul's numerical "structure":[59]

> Huic ergo adumbrationi, qua depinxit animam, imaginem similitudinis aemulae speciemque mundi deliniat septemque circulos instituit planetum eosdemque aduersum se distare facit interuallis musicis, ut

[56] *In Tim.* 53 (102.4–8).

[57] *In Tim.* 92 (144.19–145.4).

[58] Gersh, *Concord in Discourse*, 137.

[59] *In Tim.* 95 (148.2–11).

iuxta Pythagoram motu harmonico stellae rotatae musicos in uertigine modos edant, similiter ut in Politia Sirenas singulis insistere circulis dicens, quas rotatas cum circulis unam ciere mellifluam cantilenam atque ex imparibus octo sonis unum concordem concentum excitari.

[Plato] delineated the form of the world as an image with a likeness comparable to the sketch that he employed to depict the world soul; he established seven circles and separated them by musical intervals, so that, in accord with Pythagoras, as the stars rotate with a harmonic motion, they might produce musical modes in their rotation. Plato says something similar in his *Republic*, namely that a Siren resides in each individual sphere, and each Siren spins with its sphere, each produces a single mellifluous song. From these eight unequal sounds a single, concordant harmony arises.

This celestial harmony, moreover, allows Calcidius to forge yet another parallel between the world soul and human souls. Although the world soul does not have the irrational psychic aspects (*iracundia* and *cupiditas*) that are present in the less pure human souls, it nonetheless has a certain corollary to them in the celestial harmony produced by the world soul's animation of the cosmos. The *aplanes* (the sphere of the fixed stars) is akin to the soul's rational aspect (*ratio*), and the *planetes* (the spheres of the planets) are likened to the irrational aspects, the spirited (*iracundia*) and appetitive (*cupiditas*) parts; the harmony of these maintains the well-tuned life (*modificata uita*) of the entire universe.[60] In Calcidius's account, the world soul's harmonic structure, understood as an anagogic *analogia*, serves both ontological and epistemological ends.

In contrast, Macrobius is inclined to accept in a more literal manner the numerical and musical structure of the soul, which he readily attributes to Pythagoras's influence on Plato (*In Somn.* 2.2.1). The world soul is, in a favored Macrobian phrase, "woven from numbers" (*contexta numeris*);[61] it originated from music and thus confers a musical structure upon everything that it animates, both celestial bodies and animate bodies that move in and upon the earth, air, and water.[62] Thus the *anima mundi*, in its role as the source of harmoniously regulated life, becomes

[60] *In Tim.* 95 (148.9–11): Erit ergo animae aplanes ratio, planetes ut iracundia et cupiditas ceterique huius modi motus quorum concentu fit totius mundi uita modificata. Cf. 144 (182.16–183.1): tripertita [sc. anima mundi] in aplanem sphaeram inque eam quae putatur erratica et in sublunarem tertiam.

[61] *In Som. Scip.* 2.2.1 (99.22–24): in Timaeo suo mundi animam per istorum numerorum contextionem ineffabili providentia dei fabricatoris instituit. 2.2.14 (101.19–22): Timaeus igitur Platonis in fabricanda mundi anima consilium divinitatis enuntians ait illam per hos numeros fuisse contextam. 2.2.19 (102.30–103.2): ergo mundi anima, quae ad motum hoc quod videmus universitatis corpus impellit, contexta numeris musicam de se creantibus concinentiam. Cf. 1.6.43 (26.4–6): item nullus sapientum animam ex symphoniis quoque musicis constitisse dubitavit.

[62] *In Som. Scip.* 2.3.11 (106.1–9): inesse enim mundanae animae causas musicae quibus est intexta praediximus, ipsa autem mundi anima viventibus omnibus vitam ministrat. . . . Iure igitur musica capitur

the crucial link in the Homeric "golden chain" (*catena aurea*): "from the supreme god even to the bottommost dregs of the universe there is one tie, binding at every link and never broken."[63] In line with his Porphyrian source(s), Macrobius's "golden chain" amounts to a cosmological framework that describes a descending ontology. The highest god, "the Good and the First Cause" and "the beginning and source of all things which are and which seem to be," from the superabundance of his greatness generates a mind (*mens*, νοῦς), which in turn, when it looks downward and away from the highest god, creates the world soul; the soul in turn, when it looks downward and away from the creative mind, degenerates into bodies, even as it remains itself undivided in its harmonic animation of the material world, including the celestial spheres.[64]

Anima mundi et harmonia: The Twelfth Century

Plato's *anima mundi* is not for the faint of heart. Even in 1770, in a short exegetical article that marked the initial rise of the *Weltseele* (world soul) in German Romanticism, it is described as "eines von den dunkelsten Geheimnissen in seiner ganzen Philosophie" ("one of the most obscure mysteries in [Plato's] entire philosophy").[65] In the late eleventh century, the German master Manegold of Lautenbach claimed much the same but with deliberate polemical intent: *ipsa [sc. uerba] suae obscuritatis insolentia animum auditoris obtundunt* ("the sheer obscurity of his gibberish stupefies the mind of the reader").[66] Calcidius, thankfully, had set a more optimistic tone for his twelfth-century readers:[67]

> Even the ancients regarded Plato's *Timaeus* as a work that was difficult to understand, not because of obscurity born of awkward language—for what is more accessible than Plato?—but because his readers were unaccustomed to the technical reasoning that he used to explicate questions concerning the natures of things.

omne quod vivit, quia caelestis anima, qua animatur universitas, originem sumpsit ex musica. haec dum ad sphaeralem motum mundi corpus impellit, sonum efficit.

63 *In Som. Scip.* 1.14.14–15 (57.25–58.13): a summo deo usque ad ultimam rerum faecem una mutuis se vinculis religans et nusquam interrupta conexio.

64 This summarizes *In Som. Scip.* 1.14.6–15.

65 Anonymous [author named as "M"], "Gedanken über die Welt-Seele des Plato," in *Philologische Bibliothek*, 1770, vol. 1, 1–14; quoted in Miklós Vassányi, *Anima Mundi: The Rise of the World Soul Theory in Modern German Philosophy* (Dordrecht: Springer, 2011), 355.

66 Manegaldus, *Liber contra Wolfelmum*, 2; ed. Wilfried Hartmann, MGH Quellen zur Geistesgeschichte des Mittelalters 8 (Weimar: Hermann Böhlaus Nachfolger, 1972), 48.15–16; trans. Robert Ziomkowski, *Manegold of Lautenbach: Liber contra Wolfelmum* (Paris and Leuven: Peeters, 2002), 39.

67 *In Tim.* 1 (17.1–4): Timaeus Platonis et a ueteribus difficilis habitus atque existimatus est ad intellegendum, non ex imbecillitate sermonis obscuritate nata—quid enim illo uiro promptius?—sed quia legentes artificiosae rationis, quae operatur in explicandis rerum quaestionibus, usum non habebant.

Whatever Plato's readers made of the *anima mundi*, they agreed on one thing: it demanded hard exegetical labor. And the twelfth-century commentators were the first since Calcidius to attempt to work through both the spirit and letter of Plato's text, as much of it as Calcidius had provided them (17a–53c). These efforts produced a remarkable diversity of views, so much so that a complete discussion of the philosophical, cosmological, mythological, and theological applications of the *anima mundi* and its connections to the divine nature (most famously, as a Platonic expression of the Holy Spirit) is well beyond the scope of this book.[68] Hence I focus here solely upon the harmonic and musical implications of the world soul in the twelfth-century commentary tradition.[69]

For Bernard of Chartres, the *anima mundi* is a "vital motion for the purpose of tempering things" (*uitalis motus temperandarum rerum*), which is diffused equally through all parts of the world, but because it found some bodies more suited to its nature than others, it exercises its power more in some bodies and less in others, as exemplified in the Virgilian line "insofar as mortal bodies don't impede it" (*quantum non noxia corpora tardant: Aeneid* 6.731).[70] As we will see, this line of interpretation is taken up by nearly all twelfth-century commentators, though it will pushed farther than Bernard does here. Nor does Bernard specify exactly what sort of vital motion (*uitalis motus*) the *anima mundi* confers upon worldly bodies. Bernard in general is more interested in the components of the world soul, and his comments on the psychic substance provide a complex doxography interweaving (at least five) differing opinions on the identity of the divisible and indivisible substance, the same and different nature. About the division of the world soul, in contrast, Bernard has comparatively little to say, and his remarks are more concerned with numeric symbolism than with the harmonic calculations that generated the numerical sequence. The seven limits, for instance, indicate (as in Calcidius and Macrobius) a psychic purity comparable to Minerva, who neither

[68] See Gregory, *Anima mundi: La filosofia di Guglielmo di Conches e la scuola di Chartres*, esp. 123–174. For more recent approaches to the subject, see Irène Caiazzo, "La discussione sull'*Anima mundi* nel secolo XII," *Studi filosofici* 16 (1993), 27–62; Irène Caiazzo, "L'âme du monde: Un thème privilégié des auteurs chartrains au XIIe siècle," in *Le temps de Fulbert: Actes de l'Université d'été du 8 au 10 juillet 1996* (Chartres: Société archéologique d'Eure-et-Loir, 1996), 79–89; Frank Bezner, *Vela Veritatis: Hermeneutik, Wissen und Sprache in der Intellectual History des 12. Jahrhunderts* (Leiden: Brill, 2005), esp. 107–124, 324–337.

[69] For a longer view, see Béatrice Bakhouche, "Lectures médiévales de l'harmonie musicale de l'âme selon Platon (*Timée* 35b–36b): l'influence de Calcidius," *Revue de musicologie* 98 (2012), 339–362.

[70] *Bernardi Glos. sup. Tim.* 5.1–8: et ANIMAM IN MEDIETATE EIVS LOCAVIT, id est uitalem motum temperandarum rerum. Non quod per medium hic accipias terram uel solem, qui secundum quosdam cor mundi et medius planetarum dicitur, sed ideo dicit animam in medio locatam, ut per hoc innuat animam per omnes partes mundi diffusam aequaliter. Sed quia quaedam corpora magis idonea suae naturae inueniebat, quaedam minus, in eis magis uel minus uim suam exercet. Vnde Virgilius: 'quantum non noxia corpora tardant.' Cf. Macrobius *In Som. Scip.* 1.14.14 (57.33–58.15): utque adsereret eundem esse in anima semper vigorem, sed usum eius hebescere in animalibus corporis densitate, adiecit, quantum non noxia corpora tardant et reliqua. Cf. *Guillelmi Glos. sup. Tim.* 71.11 cum nota.

is generated nor generates.[71] The six intervals (*interualla*) amidst the seven terms indicate the perfection of the soul, as six is a perfect number.[72] Bernard only briefly remarks on the musical aspect of the world soul: "Likewise, among the seven parts all musical consonances are considered; by this it is indicated that harmony is naturally embedded (*insita*) within the soul" (*Item inter septem partes omnes musicae consonantiae considerantur, per quod armonia animae naturaliter insita denotatur*).[73] He clearly knew that he was dealing with the ratios of musical consonances but thought it unnecessary to deal with them in detail. For instance, Plato's mention of the *leimma* (the minor semitone = 256 : 243) in the division of the soul prompts Bernard to note only that "two continuous epogdoic ratios [9 : 8] do not complete an epitritic ratio [4 : 3] without the addition of the minor semitone."[74] He is correct, but why this is the case, how it could be mathematically proven, and why it is at all relevant to a discussion of the soul is not Bernard's concern.

William of Conches, in contrast, is more interested in the cosmological and harmonic implications of the world soul than he is in its philosophical role. The world soul, in William's influential formulation, is "a kind of spirit invested in things for conferring life and motion upon them" (*spiritus quidam rebus insitus motum et uitam illis conferens*).[75] It thus has a kinship to nature, which (according to William) is likewise a power embedded within things (*uis rebus insita*), but nature has a further generative force that the world soul seems to lack, namely the power of producing like from like (*similia de similibus operans*).[76] In his earliest known commentary, the *Glosae super Boetium*, William boldly identifies the *anima mundi* with the third person of the Christian Trinity, the Holy Spirit (*spiritus sanctus*):[77]

71 Bernardi *Glos. sup. Tim.* 5.136–139: Puritas etiam animae per septenarium habetur, quia septenarius a ueteribus dictus est Minerua, quia sicut illa sine matre et prole est, ita septenarius infra denarium nec gignit nec gignitur. Cf. Calcidius, *In Tim.* 36 (85.14–18, cum notis); Macrobius, *In Som. Scip.* 1.6.11 (20.15–22).

72 *Bernardi Glos. sup. Tim.* 5.140–141: Item per sex interualla septem limitum perfectio animae notatur, quia senarius perfectus est. Cf. Calcidius, *In Tim.* 38 (87.15–16); Macrobius, *In Som. Scip.* 1.6.12 (20.22–28).

73 Bernardi *Glos. sup. Tim.* 5.141–143. Cf. his comment on the opening line of the *Timaeus* (3.34–39): Si uero Socratem cum tribus consideres, quattuor sunt, in quo numero omnes musicas consonantias uel proportiones inuenies. Duo enim ad unum duplus est, scilicet diapason; tres ad duo sesquialter, id est diapente; quattuor ad tres sesquitercius, id est diatessaron; ad unum idem quattuor quadruplus, id est bis diapason. Quibus simphoniis mundi fabricam constructam esse docebit. Non sine causa ergo quartus auditor subtractus est.

74 *Bernardi Glos. sup. Tim.* 5.175–176: duo epogdoi continuati non perficiunt epitritum sine additione minoris semitonii.

75 *Guillelmi Glos. sup. Tim.* 71.8–9. For a concise comparison of William's definition(s) of the world soul with other twelfth-century sources, see Caiazzo, "La discussione sull'*Anima mundi* nel secolo XII," 59–61.

76 *Guillelmi Glos. sup. Tim.* 37.8–9. See Chapter 1 (p. 52).

77 *Glos. sup. Boet.* 3.m9.522–528.

Anima mundi est naturalis uigor quo quaedam res tantum habent moueri, quaedam crescere, quaedam sentire, quaedam discernere. Sed quid sit ille uigor naturalis quaeritur. Sed ut michi uidetur ille naturalis uigor est spiritus sanctus, id est diuina et benigna concordia, quia diuino amore et concordia habent omnia esse, moueri, uiuere, crescere, sentire, discernere.

The world soul is that natural vigor through which some things have the capacity to move, some to grow, some to perceive, and some to [rationally] discern. But it is asked what precisely is this natural vigor. As it seems to me, it is the Holy Spirit, i.e., the divine and good concord, because from this divine love and concord all things have the capacity to exist, move, live, grow, perceive, and discern.

In his later commentaries, however, including the *Glosae super Macrobium*, which seem to have been composed only shortly after the Boethius glosses, William qualifies this identification: the Macrobius glosses hold the view at arm's length and attribute it to certain (anonymous) exegetes: "according to some (*secundum quosdam*) [the world soul] is the Holy Spirit, proceeding from both, which vivifies and moves all things in the world." But as if (quietly) vouching for the orthodoxy of the view, William immediately supports the *quidam* by appealing to scripture (*Sap*. 1:7): "The Spirit of the Lord has filled the whole world" (*Spiritus enim Domini repleuit orbem terrarum*).[78] In his glosses on Plato, William foists the view upon the same *quidam* but omits the biblical reference and takes an explicitly noncommittal stance: "Some say that this spirit is the Holy Spirit, which we now neither deny nor affirm."[79] Finally, in his last work, the *Drągmaticon*, the *anima mundi* has disappeared entirely. Thus we should be careful of attributing a single doctrine of the *anima mundi* to William of Conches; clearly his view on the issue changed over time—and the change is not limited to the identification of the *anima mundi* with the *spiritus sanctus*, which has dominated modern literature on the subject. In fact, William of St. Thierry, in his letter to Bernard of Clairvaux, *De erroribus Guillelmi de Conchis*, says nothing about William's position on the world soul as Holy Spirit, perhaps because when he had attacked Abelard on the same grounds, Bernard of Clairvaux had dismissed this point as a trifle not worthy of serious rebuttal.[80]

[78] *Glos. sup. Macr.*, comment. ad 1.14.6: Ergo subiungit de anima mundi, quae secundum quosdam est spiritus sanctus ex utroque procedens, qui omnia in mundo mouet et uiuificat.

[79] *Guillelmi Glos. sup. Tim.* 71.13–14: Hunc spiritum dicunt quidam esse Spiritum Sanctum, quod nec negamus modo, nec affirmamus.

[80] PL 182, 1062BC: Omitto quod dicit . . . Spiritum sanctum esse animam mundi; mundum, juxta Platonem, tanto excellentius animal esse, quanto meliorem animam habet Spiritum sanctum. Ubi dum multum suadat, quomodo Platonem faciat christianum, se probat ethnicum. Haec, inquam, omnia aliasque istiusmodi naenias eius non paucas praetereo: venio ad graviora.

The *Glosae super Platonem* constitutes William's longest and final words on the subject of the *anima mundi*. In schematic form, his account is structured as follows:

1. chs. 72–73: how the world soul is located within the world;
2. chs. 74–76: from what the Creator contrived (*excogitare*) the world soul;
3. chs. 77–86: how the Creator contrived the world soul;
   a) why he posited numbers in its composition;
   b) why he posited *these* numbers in its composition;
   c) why he posited neither more nor fewer numbers in its composition;
   d) why [he described it] in the guise of such a figure (*quare sub tali figura*);
4. chs. 87–103: the conjunction (*coniunctio*) of the world soul and world body and the functions (*officia*) that it exercises in the world.

First, the matter of location. William glosses Plato's specification that it was located "in the middle" (*in medietate*) as meaning "in common" (*in communi*) and thereby "locates" the *anima mundi* as fully extended throughout creation. Although wholly present in all creation, however, it does not exercise equal powers in every instance: "One and the same world soul is wholly in the planets, where it exercises motion; in grasses and trees [it exercises] vegetation; in brute animals [it exercises] sense perception; in humankind [it exercises] reason. Thus it operates in each according to its nature, wholly existing within them, but not exercising all its powers."[81] Harmony enters the discussion early on, even before the harmonic division, with William finding it in the term *reconciliatio*. According to Calcidius's translation, the world's body, through the application of the world soul, suffices for its own *conciliatio*, but William's manuscript must have read *reconciliatio*.[82] What is this *reconciliatio*? William explains: "Reconciliation is the returning (*reductio*) of some things from discord to concord,"[83] and he locates this movement from discord to concord within the elements and the seasonal round (*temperies anni*):[84]

> Inter elementa uero est quasi quaedam discordia, quoniam unum de elementis aliquid de alio consumit in substantiamque sui transformat, ut calor ignis aliquid de terra et aequa et aere. Sed huius discordiae est reconciliatio quia quantum de uno elemento in uno tempore consumitur, tantum de alio in idem reformatur, ut praedictum est, quia quantum de aqua in aestate consumitur tantum in hieme restauratur.

[81] *Guillelmi Glos. sup. Tim.* 71.22–26: Vna enim et eadem anima mundi tota est in planetis sed motum ibi operans, in herbis et arboribus uegetationem, in brutis animalibus sensum, in homine rationem. Ita iuxta naturam singulorum in singulis operatur, tota in eis existens, sed non omnes potentias exercens.

[82] *Translatio Calcidii* 26.21: sufficeret conciliationi propriae nec extraordinario cuiusquam indigeret auxilio.

[83] *Guillelmi Glos. sup. Tim.* 72.15–16: Et est reconciliatio de discordia ad concordiam aliquorum reductio.

[84] *Guillelmi Glos. sup. Tim.* 72.15–23.

> For among the elements there exists a kind of discord, because one of the elements consumes something from another of the elements and transforms it into its own substance (for instance the heat of fire consumes and transforms something from earth, water, and air). But there is a reconciliation of the discord, because however much of one element in one season is consumed, an equal amount is reshaped into that same element from still another element, because, however much water is consumed in the summer, the same amount is restored in the winter.

The world is always, William continues, concordant with itself, and from that perpetual concord, the world acquires highest blessedness and divine power.[85]

Passing over William's discussion of the components of the world soul, the next question is how the world soul was forged. The first sticking point is the matter of its creation at all. William knows well that to speak of the world soul as created, if the identification of the world soul and the Holy Spirit were maintained, would be heretical: no person in the Trinity could be "created." William notes that the term used by Plato/Calcidius, *excogitare*, rightly describes the "generation" of the world soul, for it was neither made (*factus*), created (*creatus*), nor generated (*genitus*) but rather proceeds (*procedens*).[86] And he continues with an appeal to the *aurea catena*, in which the world soul is the *tertium genus*: "For the divine essence is such that it exists from nothing, divine wisdom exists from it, the world soul from both, the celestial bodies from those three, and the terrestrial bodies from the four."[87]

As to its harmonic structure, William delves far deeper than Bernard. He explains in meticulous detail the ratios that obtain between the initial limits and the interposed means,[88] appeals at length to Boethius's *De institutione arithmetica* to explain the three different kinds of proportionality,[89] and, finally, gives a full mathematical proof that the minor semitone (the Platonic *leimma*) consists in and only in the ratio 256 : 243, a proof that amounts to a short, quasi-independent treatise on the division of the tone.[90] The base text for the discussion was, of course, Boethius's *De institutione musica* 2.28–30, but William's mathematical method reveals a pedagogical distillation of Boethius's calculations. Boethius's demonstration that the minor semitone consists in the ratio 256 : 243 is not light

85 *Guillelmi Glos. sup. Tim.* 72.30–34: Deinde subiungit quid inde sequatur: AMICVMQVE SEMPER SIBI id est concordem GENVIT eum; ET IDEO quia ibi est perpetua concordia, SVMME id est perfecte BEATVM, quia ei nullum bonum deest, ET PRAEDITVM DIVINA POTENTIA, id est indissolubilitate.

86 *Guillelmi Glos. sup. Tim.* 74.3–6: Et bene dicit "excogitauit" et non "creauit" secundum quod anima dicitur Spiritus Sanctus. Non enim a Deo factus est nec creatus nec genitus sed procedens est Spiritus Sanctus.

87 *Guillelmi Glos. sup. Tim.* 74.9–12: Diuina enim essentia ita est quod a nullo, diuina uero sapientia est ab illo, anima mundi ex utroque, caelestia corpora ex illis tribus, terrestria ex quatuor.

88 *Guillelmi Glos. sup. Tim.* 80–81.

89 *Guillelmi Glos. sup. Tim.* 82–83.

90 *Guillelmi Glos. sup. Tim.* 84–86.

reading, and though he gives his readers a few basic *regulae* to grasp along the way, these rules are neither numerous nor frequent. William makes liberal use of such "shortcut" *regulae* for his calculation of the ratio. Moreover, several of these rules are either not found, or at least not formulated as such, in Boethius's mathematical texts. William, for instance, offers a *regula in musica* that determines whether two numbers are in a given superparticular ratio,[91] and likewise a rule for generating numbers that contain a specified part.[92] William concludes, however, by begging off (with a learned glance to Macrobius) from further discussion of the semitonal mathematics. Exactly why the whole tone cannot be divided into two equal parts and what the ratio of the greater semitone (the *apotome*) is, William declines to say: "for even if [Plato] here makes mention of music, it is not necessary to say *everything* that could be said about the subject" (*non enim, si facit hic mentionem de musica, sunt omnia dicenda quae de ea dici possunt*).[93]

The world soul's "semitonal" mathematics, however, was a central theme in both music theoretical and philosophical texts, as evidenced by the wide circulation of a concise but elaborate diagram on the subject, which serves well to highlight the point of connection between twelfth-century philosophical theory and explicitly music-theoretical writings. The diagram in question appears in the anonymous *Quaestiones in musica* from around the turn of the twelfth century,[94] a critical and skillful compilation of texts primarily from eleventh-century south German theorists who engaged in a reconfiguration of modal theory through critical dialogue with the authoritative Boethian tradition and the innovations of Guido and Pseudo-Odo.[95] The *Quaestiones* divides into two basic parts: the first offers a résumé of south German theory (interval species, the tetrachords, the division of the monochord, etc.); the second expounds upon the mathematical foundations of the first part's more practical theory, with frequent recourse to later sections in the Carolingian *Scholica enchiriadis*.[96] The twentieth *quaestio*, falling near the end of the second part, proposes a discussion of the three means (the arithmetic,

91 *Guillelmi Glos. sup. Tim.* 86.7–12: Est enim regula in musica quod si duo numeri dicantur esse in aliqua superparticulari proportione et uelimus probare utrum ita sit an non, multiplicemus nomen a quo proportio denominatur per differentiam; si inde fit minor numerus sunt in illa proportione, sin aliter non sunt in illa.

92 *Guillelmi Glos. sup. Tim.* 85.1–5: Est alia regula artis arismeticae. Si in aliquibus numeris in aliqua proportione constitutis quaeramus partem quam non habeant, multiplicemus illos nomine partis quam quaerimus. Qui inde fient, in eadem erunt proportione et partem quam quaerimus optinebunt.

93 *Guillelmi Glos. sup. Tim.* 86.26–34. Cf. Macrobius, *In Som. Scip.* 2.4.12 (109.9–12): nec enim quia fecit in hoc loco Cicero musicae mentione, occasione hac eundum est per universos tractatus qui possunt esse de musica.

94 Rudolf Steglich, ed., *Die Quaestiones in musica: Ein Choraltraktat des zentralen Mittelalters und ihr mutmasslicher Verfasser Rudolf von St. Trond (1070–1138)* (Leipzig: Breitkopf & Härtel, 1911).

95 On the "south German circle," see Thomas J. H. McCarthy, *Music, Scholasticism, and Reform: Salian Germany, 1024–1125* (Manchester and New York: Manchester University Press, 2009), 11–94.

96 On the *Quaestiones*, see the remarks and further literature cited in ibid., 50–52.

geometric, and harmonic) in order to determine "by what arrangement [or ratio] in a series of sounds are whole tones interwoven with semitones" (*qua ratione in sonorum serie toni cum semitoniis contexantur*).[97] In the course of the discussion, based exclusively on *Scholica enchiriadis*,[98] one of the three manuscript sources for the *Quaestiones* (Darmstadt, Universitäts- und Landesbibliothek, 1988, f. 140bisr) intercalates (from another manuscript) a diagrammatic summary, the "triple lambda diagram" drawn from the pages of the Calcidian *Timaeus*.[99] Michel Huglo has amply demonstrated the wide dissemination of this diagram within the first stage of the textual tradition of the *translato Calcidii*. Of the eighty-three manuscripts that conserve only the dedicatory epistle and the translation without the commentary, twenty-seven of them (an auspicious number), ranging from the eleventh through thirteenth centuries, contain such a diagram.[100] The diagram included in Darmstadt 1988 is an example of Huglo's category B, "la forme élaborée et glosée."[101] The outermost left and right branches of the diagram—explaining the scalar structure of the diatessaron (256 : 192) and diapente (384 : 256) respectively[102]—thus offer one answer to the twentieth question posed by the compiler of the *Quaestiones de musica*: "by what arrangement [or ratio] in a series of sounds are whole tones interwoven with semitones." Christian Meyer has deemed the Darmstadt *Quaestiones in musica* one of the "extremely rare examples of the presence of this Calcidian diagram in a musical context and, consequently, also the

[97] Steglich, *Quaestiones in musica*, 83: Qua ratione in sonorum serie toni cum semitoniis contexantur. [I]d apertius intueri poterimus, si prius, quae arithmetica medietas, quae geometrica, quaeque armonica sit, uideamus. Post proportiones, proportionalitates considerantur.

[98] Cf. *Scholica enchiriadis*: D: Quaeso, qua ratione vel ordine in sonorum serie toni cum semitioniis contexantur. M: Id apertius contueri poteris, si prius, quae arithmetica medietas, quae geometrica quaeque armonica sit, pandam. D: Pande rogo. M: Post proportiones proportionalitates considerantur (Hans Schmid, ed., *Musica et scolica enchiriadis una cum aliquibus tractatulis adiunctis* [Munich: Bayerische Akademie der Wissenschaften, 1981], 140).

[99] The diagram is edited in Steglich, *Quaestiones in musica*, 87; it is discussed (with facsimile and edition) in Christian Meyer, "L'âme du monde dans la rationalité musicale: Ou l'expérience sensible d'un ordre intelligible," in *Harmonia mundi: Musica mondana e musica celeste fra Antichità e Medioevo*, ed. Marta Cristiani, Cecilia Panti, and Graziano Perillo (Florence: SISMEL, Edizioni del Galluzzo, 2007), Ill. 4 and 74–75.

[100] Michel Huglo, "Recherches sur la tradition des diagrammes de Calcidius," *Scriptorium* 62 (2008), 185–230, especially the "Liste des manuscrits conservant le diagramme trilambdoïde" at 189.

[101] Ibid., 188: "les deux diagrammes VII [the first lambda diagram with an apex of 1] et VIII [the second lambda diagram with an apex of 6, incorporating the arithmetic and harmonic means] superposés (ou parfois inversés, le VIIe passant au dessus du VIIIe) restent groupés, mais le diagramme IX est refondu en sept demi-cercles chiffrés et annotés; trois demi-cercles sont inscrit sur la jambe gauche du lambda, avec l'inscription diatessaron et quatre demi-cercles s'inscrivent sur la jambe droit du lambda, avec l'inscription diapente. Un grand cercle englobe l'ensemble du diagramme."

[102] Both the text and the diagram are based, ultimately, on the series 192 : 256 : 288 : 384 (the thirty-second multiple of the basic series 6 : 8 : 9 : 12), filling in 192 : 256 (the diatessaron) with two tones and a semitone as 192 : 216 : 243 : 256; and likewise 256 : 384 (the diapente) with three tones and a semitone 256 : 288 : 324 : 364½ : 384.

presence of this Pythagorean-Platonic intellectual horizon among some music theorists during the early decades of the twelfth century."[103]

But this diagram is not so rare as Meyer suggests, and while Huglo has noted its presence in two Macrobian manuscripts (Baltimore, Walters Art Museum, W22, f. 66 and Munich, UB 8° 375, f. 42r), still more remains to be said. In the twelfth century, the diagram circulated well beyond the Calcidian *Timaeus*:[104] it is incorporated within the text of a twelfth-century copy of Macrobius (at *In Som. Scip.* 2.2.15; Cambridge, Trinity College, R.9.23, f. 50v, see figure 5.1); it features in several other glossed copies of Macrobius (e.g., Turin, Bibl. Naz. Universitaria, D.V.38, f. 50r;[105] El Escorial, Biblioteca del real monasterio de San Lorenzo S.III.5, 126r, etc.); it is appended to a late-twelfth or early-thirteenth-century compilation of (inter alia) glosses on Martianus's *De nuptiis* and Boethius's *Consolatio* (Zwettl, Stiftsbibliothek 313, f. 193v);[106] and, finally, it appears in a twelfth-century bifolium

103 Meyer, "L'âme du monde," 67.

104 This list is not exhaustive; doubtless, there are more.

105 Caiazzo, *Glosae Colonienses super Macrobium*, fig. 7.

106 For a description, see Haijo Jan Westra, "Martianus Capella: Addenda et Corrigenda to Volume II," in *Catalogus translationum et commentariorum: Mediaeval and Renaissance Latin Translations and Commentaries*, ed. Paul Oskar Kristeller and Ferdinand E. Cranz (Washington, DC: Catholic University Press, 1986), 6, 185–186; Joachim Rössl and Charlotte Ziegler, *Zisterzienserstift Zwettl: Katalog der Handschriften des Mittelalters 4: Codex 301–424* (Vienna and Munich: Schroll, 1997). It is accompanied by a descriptive gloss, which I have not found in any twelfth-century copy of the *Timaeus*, inaugurated by the Timaean lemma *natis itaque limitibus* (*Tim.* 36a = *Translatio Calcidii* 28.3). The gloss, which is partially copied on f. 192r (through *sint ita duo limites. modo*) and repeated in full on f. 192v, reads as follows: NATIS ITAQVE LIMITIBVS. In hac figura considera composicionem anime. Si monadem [monalem *a. corr.*] in uertice positam uidere desideras, uel si senarium in loco monadis positum disnoscere, utramque figuram inclusam uide. Si uero quomodo interualla tonis et semitoniis complentur agnoscere cupis, considera in capite figure cxcii positum in loco monadis uel senarii. Et ab illo numero, id est cxcii, inferius in uno latere debet poni duplus numerus, in alio triplus, sicut positi sunt in illis figuris in quibus unitas uel senarius sunt positi in uertice. Sed quia in ipsis paruis figuris satis ostensum est quomodo ipsa anima composita sit ex tribus duplis et ex tribus triplis, in hac uero tantum sufficiat considerare quomodo interualla compleantur tonis et semitoniis. Pone ergo ex cxcii in summitate, ut dictum est, et in illo loco in quo posusiti octonarium cum posuisti senarium in uertice, pone modo cclvi, et sint ita duo limites. Modo ad complenda interualla horum duorum limitum tonis et semitoniis, sic dispone. Post cxcii pone ccxvi, post ccxvi pone [c]ccxliiii, post ccxliii pone cclvi. Et sic inuenies consonantiam diatesseron, que noscitur ab extremis limitibus sibi epitrita racione respondentibus. Ducenti enim lvi continet totum cxcii et eius terciam partem, que est lxiv. Ideo est epitrita proportio. Fit autem diatesseron secundum epitritam proportionem. Constant autem duo toni et semitonii in interuallo huius consonancie, ad quos inueniendos in primo loco considera quomodo ccxvi habet se ad cxcii. Et inuenies quod habet se ad ipsum epogdoa proportione, quia contenet ipsum totum et eius octauam partem, id est xxiiii et ex hac proportione nascitur tonus. Ducenti autem xliii consideratus ad ccxvi continet ipsum totum et eius octauam partem, id est xxvii, et est epogdoa proportio, unde tonus. Ducenti enim lvi continet ccxliii et insuper tredecim, quod est minor quam octaua ⟨decima⟩ pars ducentorum xl trium, que octaua decima pars ccxl trium est tredecim et medietas unitatis. Est autem tredecim maior nona decima parte ccxliii, que est duodecim, deficientibus quatuor unitatibus in quatuor partibus ipsorum ducentorum et xl trium. Et ita ducenti lvi nec est sesqualiter nec sesquitercius nec sequioctauus ad ccxliii, et ita non est tonus, sed semitonium intelligitur.

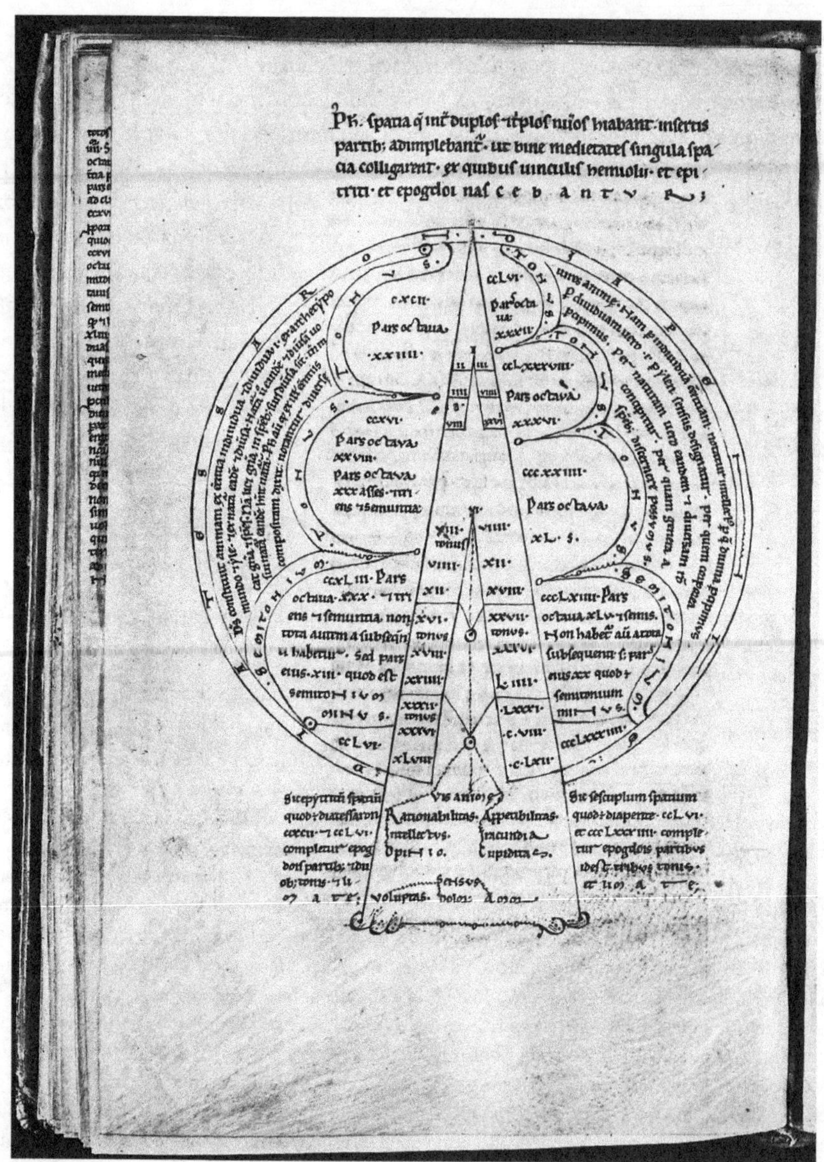

Figure 5.1 Twelfth-century "triple lambda diagram" incorporated into Macrobius, *In Som. Scip.* 2.2.15. Cambridge, Trinity College, Wren Library, MS R.9.23, f. 50v. Courtesy of the Master and Fellows of Trinity College Cambridge.

bound at the beginning of Oxford, Corpus Christi College, 283 (see figure 5.2),[107] where it accompanies a remarkable collection of texts that encompass arithmetic, music, and natural philosophy, including:

1. 2ra–b: a fragment of Isidore's *Etymologiae* on arithmetic;[108]
2. 2rb: a widely circulated gloss on Boethius's *De institutione arithmetica* 1.11;[109]
3. 2va–b: a brief tonary (complete with chant incipits notated with adiastematic neumes),[110] which is a hitherto unnoticed third witness to the *Primi toni differentia*, known from the mid-twelfth-century "Seligenstadt tonary" (Darmstadt, Universitäts- und Landesbibliothek, 3314/15, 9r–10v)[111] and the Kassel interpolations in the tonary of Theogerus of Metz (Kassel, Landesbibliothek und Murhardsche Bibliothek der Stadt Kassel, 4° Math 1, 28v–31v);[112]
4. 2vb: a short gloss on the elements drawn from William of Conches's *Philosophia* or *Glosae super Platonem*;[113]
5. 2vb: a definition of the diapente and diatessaron that recalls Guido's résumé of the monochord division at *Micrologus* 6.2–5;[114]

Ecce habes in predictorum epitritorum intervallis compleatis duos tonos et semitonium. Ad hunc modum, imple cetera interualla duplorum. Si tres duplos in hac maiori figura posueris, sicut in minoribus positi sunt, ad eundem modum facile implebuntur interualla triplorum in alio latere.

107 For a description, see Claude Lafleur, *Quatre introductions à la philosophie au XIIIe siècle: Textes critiques et étude historique* (Montreal: Institut d'études médiévales, 1988), 46–558, with corrections noted below.

108 Inc.: metiuntur, sed etiam alieno numero procreantur (*Etym.* 3.5.7); expl.: Ergo et dispares inter se atque diversi sunt, et singuli quique finiti sunt, et omnes infiniti sunt (*Etym.* 3.9.2). Lafleur (*Quatre introductions*, 49) deems this "Anonymous, Arithmétique acéphale d'une main du début du XIIIe siècle."

109 Inc.: In figura impariter paris numeri . . .; expl.: Similiter una medietas, id est cxii. This gloss is edited in Oosthout and Schilling, *Anicii Manlii Severini Boethii De institutione arithmetica*, 229. Lafleur (*Quatre introductions*, 49) does not recognize this as a separate text from the first fragment.

110 Inc.: Primi toni prima differentia duas habet initiales cantus sui litteras .D. et .F. S e u o u a e [= seculorum amen] Ecce nomen. Senex puerum. Colupna es F. Canite tuba. Speciosus. Aue maria. Appropinquabat. Misso hic. Biduo uiuens . . .; expl.: Quarta differentia [sc. octaui toni] unam habet initialem litteram .c. S e u o u a e Veniet fortior.

111 The "Seligenstadt tonary" is incomplete, including only the first four ecclesiastical modes. For an edition and commentary, see Michael Bernard, "The Seligenstadt Tonary," *Plainsong and Medieval Music* 13 (2004), 107–125. It is briefly mentioned in Michel Huglo, *Les tonaires: Inventaire, analyse, comparaison* (Paris: Société francais de musicologie, 1971), 257.

112 For an edition of the Kassel interpolations, see Fabian Lochner, "Dietger (Theogerus) of Metz and His Musica" (PhD diss., University of Notre Dame, 1995), 288–290.

113 Elementum, ut ait Constantinus in Pantegni, est simpla [al] et minima alicuius corporis particula. Simpla ad qualitatem, minima ad quantitatem. Cuius expositio talis est. Elementum est pars simpla, cuius non sunt contrariae qualitates. Minima, id est, quae est ita pars alicuius quod nichil est pars eiusdem. Vnde litterae dicuntur per simile elementa, quia ita sunt partes sillabae quod nichil est pars illarum. Elementa ergo sunt simplae et minimae particulae, quibus haec quatuor constant quae uidemus. Haec elementa numquam uidentur, sed ratione diuisionis intelliguntur. Cf. *Guillelmi Glos. sup. Tim.* 58.9–59.3; *Phil.* 1.21 (48D–49B).

114 Diapente currit ad fine⟨m⟩ monochordi [*add. sup. lin.*] tribus passibus ubicumque circinum apposueris, et fit sesqualtera proportio, ut tres ad duo. Dyapessaron [sic] currit ad finem monochordi

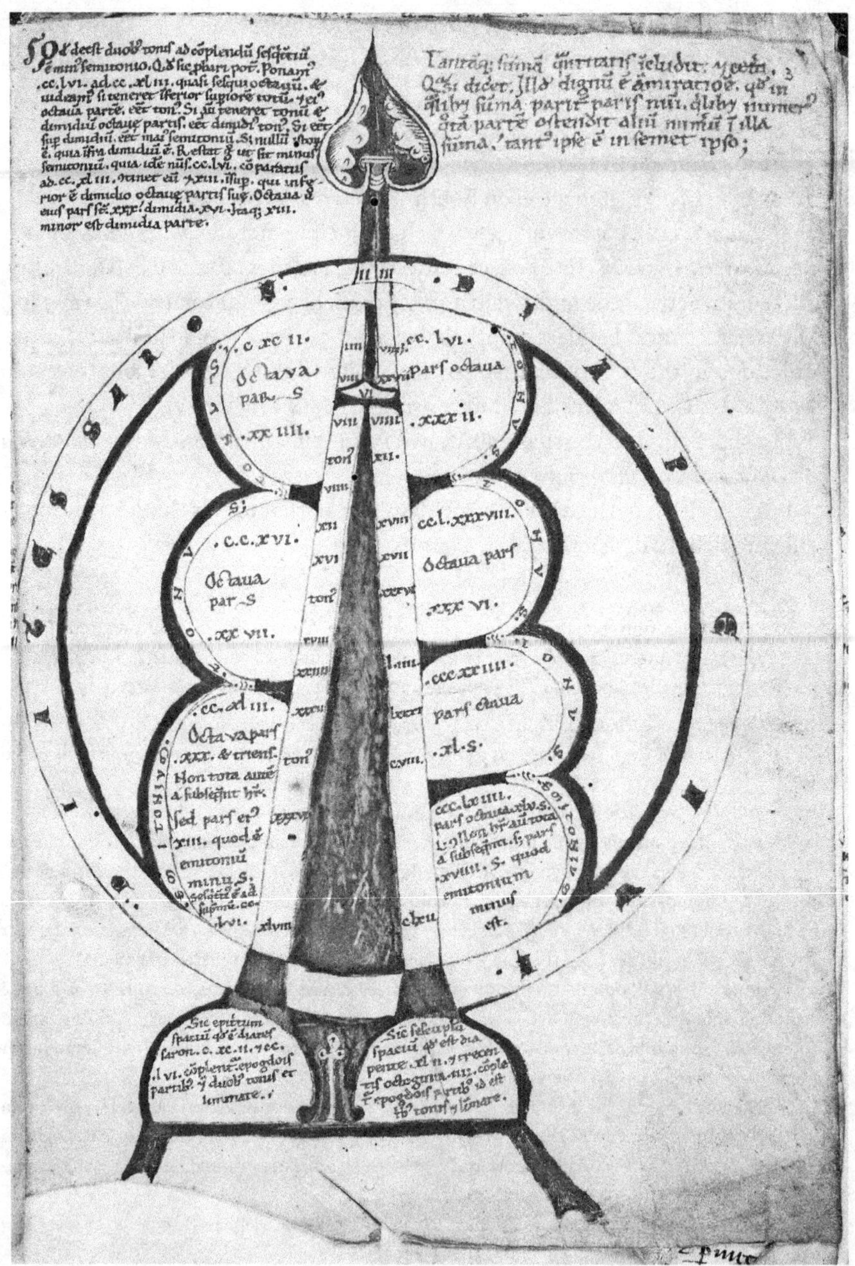

Figure 5.2 Twelfth-century "triple lambda diagram." Oxford, Corpus Christi College Library, MS 283, f. 3r. Courtesy of the CCC Library.

6. 2vb: a generic note on the arithmetic and harmonic means;[115]
7. 3r: the "triple lambda diagram," flanked on the left by the same note on the division of the tone that appears in the *Quaestiones* interpolation,[116] and on the right by a short gloss on Boethius's *Inst. ar.* 1.9 (18.15);[117]
8. 3va–b: a short text on the ratio of the minor semitone,[118] a longer text on the mathematical procedure for determining the proper ratio of the minor semitone, entitled "De Macrobio,"[119] and another brief note on the diatessaron and diapente.[120]

This diagram, originally taking shape among the pages of Calcidius but expanding into both the music-theoretical tradition and the twelfth-century philosophical tradition, is thus an icon of continuity between the two. The diagram is equally at home glossing a music-theoretical discussion of proportional theory, juxtaposed with a tonary representative of south German modal theory, and explaining Timaean and Macrobian discussions of the *anima mundi*. The twelfth-century philosophical tradition is, in a sense, an inversion of the music-theoretical tradition. Where music theorists were led through music theory to the Platonic division of the world soul, twelfth-century philosophers were drawn through the

quatuor passibus ubicumque circinum apposueris, et fit sesquitercia porportio, ut quatuor ad tres. Cf. Waesberghe, *Guidonis Aretini Micrologus*, 6.2–4 (114): Ut autem de divisione monochordi in paucis multa perstringam, semper diapason duobus ad finem passibus currit, diapente tribus, diatessaron quattuor, tonus vero novem, quae quanto passibus numerosiores tanto spatio breviores.

115 Arithmetica medietas in minoribus terminis maiores habet proportiones et in maioribus terminis minores habet propor[tio]tiones. Armonica uero medietas econtrario in maioribus terminis maiores habet proportiones et in minoribus terminis minores habet proportiones, ut viii ad iiii duplus et iiii ⟨ad⟩ iii sesquitertius et cetera.

116 Inc.: Quod deest duobus tonis ad complendum sesquitercium est minus semitonio [*recte* semitonium] . . .; expl.: Octaua uero eius pars sunt xxx [*recte* xxxii], dimidia xvi, itaque xiii minor est dimidia parte. For a transcription, see Alison M. Peden, "'De semitonio': Some Medieval Exercises in Arithmetic," *Studi medievali* 35 (1994), 400–401, and Meyer, "L'âme du monde," 74.

117 TANTAMQVE SVMMAM QVANTITATIS INCLVDIT, ETC. Quasi diceret: illud dignum est admiratione quod in qualibet summa pariter paris numeri, quilibet numerus quotam partem ostendit alium numerum in illa summa, tantus ipse est in semet ipso.

118 Inc.: Si uis uidere si ccxliii ad cclvi reddant semitonium . . .; expl.: istorum enim differentia est xiii, quod minus est quam x et vii. For a transcription, see Peden, "'De semitonio': Some Medieval Exercises in Arithmetic," 401.

119 Inc.: Liber dicit quod semitonium tam paruam [*In Som. Scip.* 2.1.22 (98.27–28)] . . .; expl.: et ita ad querendam habitudinem semitonii uenies. For a transcription and discussion of this and other related tracts, see Peden, "'De semitonio': Some Medieval Exercises in Arithmetic," 368–369. Peden, however, does not note that the same text on the semitone is found as a marginal gloss to Macrobius (*In Som. Scip.* 2.1.22) in Trinity College, Cambridge, R.9.23, f. 49r (immediately preceding the appearance of the triple lambda diagram).

120 Quemadmodum sesqualterum et sesquitertium arithmetice, ita musicae diapente et diatesseron considerantur. Sicut arithmetice [*add. sup. lin.*] enim in tribus ad duo sesqualtera, et in quatuor ad tria sesquitercia habetur proportio, eodem modo musice in tribus passibus ad duos dyapente, et in quatuor passibus ad tres perpenditur dyatessaron consonantia.

Platonic tradition to music theory, to (in the words of Macrobius) the "minute subtleties of whole tones and semitones" (*tonorum vel limmatum minuta subtilia*).[121] The Darmstadt compiler presents the Calcidian diagram as a philosophical gloss, drawn from outside the tradition, that reveals the Platonic orientation of semitone mathematics culled from the pages of the Carolingian *Scholica enchiriadis* (philosophy explains music theory). The twelfth-century philosophers, however, present the music-theoretical background as the primary explanatory grounds for understanding the musical orientation and semitonal implications of the Platonic division of the world soul (music theory explains philosophy).

Faced with the Platonic orientation of Boethius's *De institutione musica*, the anonymous St. Florian commentator was forced to deal with both traditions simultaneously. Accordingly, his discussion of the *anima mundi* is based upon a deep syncretism of the Calcidian *Timaeus*, Macrobius, and Martianus, as these authors had come to be understood through the commentary tradition. His comments are spurred by the mention of the *anima mundi* in Boethius's prooemium.[122] The St. Florian commentator first notes that where Boethius ought to speak about nature, he speaks instead about the *anima mundi*, as nature has its cause in its likeness.[123] The assimilation of *natura* and *anima mundi* has already begun. The *anima mundi*, as in William of Conches, is a *spiritus* infused throughout the *machina mundi* that imparts "motion" proper to each: some beings receive a vegetative force, some both vegetative and sensitive force, and a select few (namely humans) receive all three: the vegetative, sensitive, and rational forces.[124] The commentator then identifies the *anima mundi* with the *spiritus sanctus* (notably without qualification or indication that the position might be challenged by some), and this identification itself sets in motion a deeply synthetic chain of identifications: "it is the Holy Spirit, which is placed third in the golden chain and is called *endelichia* in Greek" (*haec est spiritus sanctus, quae in aurea catena tercia ponitur et greco vocabulo endelichie nuncupatur*).[125] The commentator has stepped, for the moment, outside of Boethius and has turned instead to Macrobius, where he would have found the Homeric golden chain, which begins from the highest god, from which comes mind (*nous*), and from mind in turn comes soul (*anima*) in the third position.[126] The identification of the world soul with *endelichia*, however, suggests that more than Macrobius is at work here, for Macrobius does not mention *endelichia* in this

121 *In Som. Scip.* 2.4.11 (109.6–7).

122 *Inst. mus.* 1.1 (180.4–5): non frusta a Platone dictum sit, mundi animam musica convenientia fuisse coniunctam.

123 *In inst. mus.* 28: ecce quod loquitur de anima mundi, cum de natura loqui deberet, nam natura ad similitudinem illius causata est.

124 *In inst. mus.* 28: Anima mundi est spiritus omni mundanae machinae infusus omnibus motum prestans, ita quod quibusdam etiam vegetationem, aliis cum vegetatione etiam sensualitatem, aliis cum vegetatione et sensualitate rationabilitatem.

125 Ibid.

126 Macrobius, *In Som. Scip.* 1.14.15 (58.2–13).

context.[127] The identification of *endelichia* with the world soul, rather, was a product of the Carolingian commentary tradition on Martianus, whose mythological allegory of the soul casts Psyche as the daughter of the Sun and Endelichia.[128] Both Eriugena and Remigius read Martianus through the lens of Calcidius and identified *endelechia* with the *anima mundi*,[129] and (likely through Remigius) the theory entered the twelfth-century commentary tradition. The appearance of *endelechia* in a commentary on Boethius's *De institutione musica* reveals that the commentator was approaching Boethius from the standpoint of the commentary tradition on both Martianus and Macrobius. The full passage reads as follows:[130]

> Haec est spiritus sanctus, quae in aurea catena tercia ponitur et greco vocabulo endelichie nuncupatur, de qua dicit Macrobius quod qua parte duo priora respicit, plenam eorum tenet similitudinem, sed inferiora respiciens paulatim degenerat et imminuitur; non tamen imminuitur, sed ideo imminui videtur, quia in quibusdam quasdam suas et non omnes exercet potentias, ita quod in quibusdam plures, in quibusdam pauciores, et ideo dicitur degenerare, quia cum in se perfectionem habet, suas infundendo potencias quibusdam plures, quibusdam pauciores imminui videtur, unde etiam Bachus dicitur a gygantibus membratim discerptus, sed post membris eius recollectis et in vanno [*scripsi*, Urano *Rausch*] positis postridie integer apparuit.
>
> This [sc. *anima mundi*] is the Holy Spirit, which is placed third in the golden chain; in Greek it is called *endelichia*. About this Macrobius says that in that part by which it beholds the two prior entities, it holds the full similitude of them, but insofar as it beholds the lower entities, it

127 Macrobius mentions the term only once, in his doxography of the soul (1.14.19): Aristoteles [dixit animam] ἐντελέχειαν.

128 *De nuptiis* 1.7 (4.10–13): voluit saltem Entelechiae ac Solis filiam postulare, quod speciosa quam maxime magnaque deorum sit educata cura; nam ipsi Ψυχῇ natali die dii ad convivium corrogati multa contulerant.

129 Cora E. Lutz, ed., *Iohannis Scotti Annotationes in Marcianum* (Cambridge, MA: The Mediaeval Academy of America, 1939), 10.16–24: Entelechia ut Calcidius in expositione Timei Platonis exponit perfecta aetas interpretatur. Aetas quippe adulta ἡλικία a Grecis dicitur. Entelechia vero quasi ἐντὸς ἡλικία, hoc est intima aetas. Generalem quippe mundi animam Entelechiam Plato nominat, ex qua speciales animae sive rationabiles sint sive racione carentes in singulas mundani corporis partes sole administrante, vel potius procreante, procedunt ut Platonici perhibent. Quorum sectam Martianus sequitur asserens Psichen, hoc est animam, Entelechie ac Solis esse filiam. Lutz, *Remigii Autissiodorensis Commentum in Martianum Capellam* 1:76.11–13: Endelychia secundum Calcidium perfecta aetas, secundum Aristotelem absoluta perfectio interpretatur. Plato tamen Endelychiam animam mundi dicit. Cf. Calcidius, *In Tim.* 222 (236.5–7). See Gerard Mathon, "Jean Scot Érigène, Chalcidius et le problème de l'âme universelle," in *L'Homme et son destin d'après les penseurs du Moyen Âge* (Louvain: Nauwelaerts, 1960), 361–375.

130 *In inst. mus.* 28.

> degenerates a bit and is lessened [*In Som. Scip.* 1.14.6–7 (56.9–13)]. It is not, however, actually lessened but only seems to be so for this reason: in certain things it exercises only some and not all of its powers such that in some it exercises more, in others, less. And hence it is said to degenerate, because although it has perfection within itself, by infusing more powers in some things and less powers in other things, it seems to be lessened. Whence Bacchus is said to have been torn apart, limb by limb, by the giants, but afterwards, with his limbs gathered together and placed in a winnowing-fan, he emerged the next day, whole.

One debt is clear: that to William of Conches, in particular to his interpretation of Bacchus in the *Glosae super Macrobium*, and at several points the similarities are *ad litteram*. Here, in his comments on Macrobius, is how William interprets Bacchus as an *integumentum* of the world soul:[131]

> Quia . . . uolunt philosophi quod anima mundi diuidatur per singula corpora, quamuis idem non operetur in eis . . ., et quia Bacus dicitur anima mundi, ideo de Bacho confingunt tale integumentum, quod in gigantomachia Bacus a gigantibus frustratim decerptus est et in uanno a diis positus in crastino rursus integer emersit . . ., quod nichil aliud est nisi, quod gigantes dicuntur humana corpora, quasi de terra genita, quae discerpunt animam; sed in uanno illa ponitur, quia uannus purgatio est leuium et grauium, similiter mors leuium et grauium, id est corporis et anime; sed quamuis per corpora nostra anima diuidatur, tamen tota integra reperitur.

> Because philosophers think that the world soul is divided throughout individual bodies, although it does not perform the same things within them . . . and because the world soul is called Bacchus, for this reason philosophers have confabulated such an *integumentum*: that in the battle of the giants, Bacchus was torn apart, limb by limb, by the giants and placed in the winnowing-fan by the gods. On the next day, he emerged whole. . . . This means nothing other than that the giants are called human bodies, as if born from the earth, which tear apart the soul, at least with respect to its power. But the soul is placed in a winnowing-fan, because the winnowing-fan is the purgation of the heavy and the light; similarly, death is the purgation of heavy and light, that is, of body and soul. But although the soul is divided among our bodies, nevertheless it is found whole and integral.

[131] *Glos. sup. Macr.*, comment. ad 1.12.12.

Peter Dronke has noted, rightly I think, that this passage suggests a polarity in the world soul, a polarity we have already encountered in other contexts: "it is both immanent and transcendent."[132] As both William and the St. Florian commentator observe, the world soul is differentially distributed among bodies through the different functions—vegetative, sensory, and rational—that it fulfills within each body (according to its need). Yet, it is still present, as a whole, in every life and limb, even though it exercises its powers differently in each. The presence of this integumental fable of Bacchus in what may seem an extraordinarily unrelated place, a commentary on Boethius's *De institutione musica*, highlights the very close connection between the St. Florian commentary and William's early works, in particular the commentary on Macrobius. Might not the St. Florian commentary be an echo of William's lost commentary on the *De institutione musica*? The question, I think, cannot be settled, but it is worth asking. At the very least, we should consider the possibility that the St. Florian commentator had access to and used the commentaries of William of Conches as a way of unpacking the Platonic references scattered throughout the *De institutione musica*.

A similar nexus of the *anima mundi, endelichia*, and the *spiritus sanctus* is found in an anonymous *Expositio super librum Martiani Capelle de nuptiis phylologie* copied into a late-fourteenth-century Florentine manuscript (Biblioteca Nazionale Centrale, Conv. Soppr. I.1.28). This commentary, too, has many striking points of overlap with the philosophy of William of Conches. So much so, in fact, that they led Dronke, the first to study the commentary, to suggest, albeit cautiously, that the redactor of the Florentine *Expositio*, perhaps a "disciple" of the Chartrian master, had quarried William's "lost commentary" on Martianus.[133] Dronke's caution was well founded, for the commentary upon which the Florentine text depends is still (partially) extant in a late-twelfth or early-thirteenth-century Cistercian manuscript, Zwettl, Stiftsbibliothek 313, fols. 142v–179v.[134] The Zwettl commentary is not by William of Conches, and the existence of William's presumed *Glosae super Martianum* (though it may yet be found) cannot be securely deduced from the Florentine *Expositio*.[135] The parallels with William's thought noted by Dronke,

132 Peter Dronke, *Fabula: Explorations into the Uses of Myth in Medieval Platonism* (Leiden: Brill, 1974), 24.

133 Dronke, *Fabula*, 179; Dronke, "William of Conches' Commentary on Martianus Capella," in *Études de civilisation médiévale (IXe–XII siècles). Mélanges offerts à Edmond-René Labande* (Poitiers: Centre d'Études Supérieures de Civilisation Médiévale, 1974), 232. Recent scholars have not been so circumspect; e.g., Claudio Leonardi subtitled a discussion of the Florentine glosses "The Interpretation of William of Conches" and deemed the author "Der Carnotenser" ("Der Kommentar des Johannes Scotus zu Martianus Capella im 12. Jahrhundert," in *Eriugena redivivus. Zur Wirkungsgeschichte seines Denkens im Mittelalter und im Übergang zur Neuzeit*, ed. Werner Beierwaltes, [Heidelberg: C. Winter, 1987], 77–88). In the *Glos. sup. Boet.* 5.p4.24–26, William alludes to his intention (at least) to comment on Martianus: *sed interim taceamus, quia super Martianum hoc exponemus*.

134 Zwettl 313 lacks both the accessus and the beginning of the commentary (entering at *De nuptiis* 1.3: Cum inter deos).

135 The accessus in Conv. Soppr. I.1.28 does not follow William's usual formula, nor does the Zwettl commentary evince any of William's stylistic trademarks (*continuatio, quandoquidem . . . ergo, uere . . .*

however, should not be discounted, for they reveal the influence of William's writings on the Martianus commentary tradition. The identification of the text in Zwettl 313, moreover, allows us to improve our understanding of a passage muddled by the Florentine scribe, which had puzzled Dronke: the anonymous commentator's discussion of *endelichia*:[136]

> Endelichia secundum Platonem interpretatur intima etas, secundum Aristotelem absoluta perfectio, quarum utraque ad animam mundi refertur. Ipsa enim intima etas dicitur secundum quam omnia uiuificantur et absoluta perfectio quoniam perfectione numerorum in Timeo [intimea *F*, intima *coni. Dronke*] compositionem sortita est [compositionem . . . est *Z*, compansatica (*uid.*) *F*, ⟨est⟩ compensatio *coni. Dronke*]. Hec est que omnibus prestat motum naturalem, secundum ⟨quam⟩ omnia uiuificata uegetantur, de qua Virgilius: "principio celum terras camposque uirentes [patentes *a. corr.*] lucentemque globum lune, titaniaque astra, spiritus intus alit." De quo Apostolus: "spiritus in quo sumus et in quo uiuimus." Quod quidam intelligunt de spiritu sancto, quia dei beneuolentia est que omnibus motum prestat et uitam. Aliqui dicunt hoc esse quemdam spiritum a deo creatum et per totius mundi partes distensum, secundum quem omnia administrantur. Sed aliquam creaturam tantam habere in rebus potentiam credere hereticum est. Huius tanquam maxime anime filie dicuntur minores anime. Vnde ex residuo eiusdem materie facte perhibentur a Platone. Quod bene conuenit spiritu sancto. Que enim est causa creationis humane anime nisi diuina beneuolentia?
>
> Endelichia according to Plato means "inner life"; according to Aristotle it means "absolute perfection." Both of these refer to the world soul. For the world soul is called "inner life" in accordance with which all things are vivified; it is called "absolute perfection" because in the *Timaeus* the world soul received its composition from the perfection of numbers. It is the world soul that grants natural motion to all things; in accordance with it, all things that have been vivified are quickened. Virgil says of the world soul: "In the beginning, heaven, earth, and the green fields, the moon's lucent globe and the stars of the Titans—all these are sustained by an inner spirit." About this spirit, the Apostle [says], "the spirit in which we exist, in which we live." Some understand this as the Holy Spirit, because it is God's benevolence that grants motion

nam, dicet aliquis . . . etc.). For more on this commentary, see Hicks, "Martianus Capella and the Liberal Arts," 322–324, with an edition and translation of the *accessus* at 324–328; on its relationship to the broader commentary tradition see Hicks, "Editing Medieval Commentaries on Martianus Capella."

[136] Florence, Conv. Soppr. I.1.28, 57r; Zwettl, Stiftsbib., 313, 145v.

> and life to all. Others say that it is a spirit created by God and extended through all the world's parts, in accordance with which all things are administered. But it is heretical to believe that some creature has such a great power over things. The lesser souls are called the daughters of this, as it were, greatest soul. This is why Plato said that they were created from the residue of the same substance. This accords well with the Holy Spirit. For what else is the cause of the human soul's creation if not divine benevolence?

Dronke's conjecture that the soul is perfect "because her inner balance lies in the perfection of numbers," (*quoniam perfectione numerorum intima ⟨est⟩ compensatio*)[137] can now be corrected in light of Zwettl's improved text: the soul is perfect "because in the *Timaeus* the world soul received its composition from the perfection of numbers" (*quoniam perfectione numerorum in Timeo compositionem sortita est*). The Timaean *psychogonia*, inflected by William of Conches's interpretation, remains the central point of reference throughout the gloss. The commentator's theologically inflected psychology (*que enim est causa creationis humane anime nisi diuina beneuolentia*), however, points us (perhaps unexpectedly) to Abelard.

The Peripatetic of Pallet (cf. John of Salisbury, *Metalogicon* 1.5) first approached the *anima mundi* through a philosophical back door. The issue arose in the *Dialectica* out of an unlikely context, namely the treatment of parts and wholes. Querying the division of a virtual whole into parts *secundum formam*, Abelard takes as a working example the division of the soul into its standard vegetative, sensitive, and rational powers (the *potentia uegetandi, sentiendi*, and *discernendi*) of which plants have only the first, animals the first and second, and humans alone all three. Abelard then raises the question: "But we must consider whether a division of this sort occurs more correctly with regard to the soul generally, or with regard to the world soul, which Plato thought to be singular and which others assert to be a species satisfied by a single individual (just like the Phoenix)."[138] After dealing with the first option in a conventionally Boethian manner, he returns to the world soul. "There are those," Abelard claims, "who accept this division of a virtual whole not with regard to the soul in general, but a singular soul, which Plato deemed the *anima mundi*."[139] He continues:[140]

137 Dronke, *Fabula*, 116.

138 *Dial.* 555.27–30: Sed utrum de anima generali siue de anima mundi, quam singularem Plato cogitauit quamque alii speciem contentam uno indiuiduo asserunt, sicut est Phenix, diuisio huiusmodi rectius fiat considerandum est.

139 *Dial.* 558.18–19: Sunt autem et qui hanc diuisionem uirtualis totius non de anima generali sed singulari, quam Animam mundi Plato uocauit, accipiunt.

140 *Dial.* 558.20–25.

> quam [sc. animam mundi] ipse ex Nou, idest Mente Diuina, natam [*scripsi*, nature *de Rijk*][141] asseruit et eamdem in omnibus simul esse corporibus fi⟨n⟩xit. Non tamen omnia animatione replevit, sed illa sola quorum mollior [est] natura ad animandum fuit idonea; cum enim eadem et in lapide tota simul et in animali credatur, in illo tamen pre duriti⟨a⟩ corporis suas exercere potentias non potuit, sed omnis anime uirtus in eo cessauit.
>
> He [sc. Plato] claimed that the world soul was born from Nous, i.e., the Divine Mind, and feigned that it was present within all bodies simultaneously. It did not, however, animate all things, but only those whose gentler natures were suited to animation. For although the same soul is believed to be wholly within stones and animals simultaneously, it was not able to exercise its powers in the former because of the hardness of their bodies, but every one of the soul's powers remained inactive in the stone.

The language of this passage, as well as Abelard's subsequent explanation of how some Catholics understood Plato's teaching on the world soul, reveals the source of Abelard's remarks. He is not working here solely from the *Timaeus*, but is reliant upon the account of Macrobius,[142] and presumably also knew the Macrobian commentary tradition, which Abelard seems to have in his sights in his critique:[143]

> Sunt autem nonnulli catholicorum qui allegorie nimis adherentes Sancte Trinitatis fidem in hac consideratione Platoni conantur ascribere, cum videlicet ex Summo Deo, quem tagaton appellant, Noun natam [natam *scripsi*, naturam *de Rijk*] intellexerunt quasi Filium ex Patre genitum, ex Nou vero animam mundi esse, quasi ex Filio Spiritum Sanctum procedere. Qui quidem Spiritus, cum totus ubique diffusus omnia contineat, quorumdam tamen fidelium cordibus per inhabitantem gratiam sua largitur charismata, que uiuificare dicitur suscitando in eas uirtutes; in quibusdam uero dona ipsius uacare uidentur, que sua digna habitatione non inuenit, cum tamen et [in] ipsis presentia eius non desit, sed uirtutum exercitium.
>
> There are, however, a few of the Catholic faith who, in their excessive adherence to allegory, try to ascribe to Plato faith in the Holy Trinity

[141] Cf. Macrobius, *In Som. Scip*. 1.2.14 (6.25–27): mentem, quem Graeci νοῦν appellant . . . ex summo natam et profectam deo. 1.2.16 (7.11): summus deus nataque ex eo mens.

[142] As pointed out in John Marenbon, "Life, Milieu, and Intellectual Contexts," in *The Cambridge Companion to Abelard*, ed. Jeffrey E. Brower and Kevin Guilfoy (Cambridge: Cambridge University Press, 2004), 37.

[143] *Dial*. 558.26–35.

with the following argument: they understand Nous to have been born from the Highest God (whom they call *tagaton*) [cf. Macrobius, *In Som. Scip.* 1.2.14 (6.23)], as the Son from the Father, but the world soul to have been born from Nous, as the Holy Spirit proceeds from the Son. This Spirit, since it is wholly diffused everywhere and contains all, bestows its spiritual gifts (*charismata*) in the hearts of some of the faithful through an in-residing grace, which it is said to vivify because it arouses virtues within them; in others, however, its gifts seem to be absent, as it does not find them to be worthy of its habitation, even though not its presence but only the exercise of its powers is lacking.

In his later theological works (the *Theologica "summi boni," Theologica christiana*, and *Theologica "scholarium"*), Abelard returns to the *anima mundi*, and he seems to have made a surprising about-face.[144] Employing language similar to that of those whom he had criticized as "excessively adhering to allegory," he now approves and promulgates the allegorical or integumental interpretation of the *anima mundi* as *spiritus sanctus*. It is, he now contends, a "beautiful allegory" (*pulchrum inuolucrum*), a beauty confirmed by an injection of euphonius musical arguments that were entirely absent from the *Dialectica*. Abelard still comes to the Platonic doctrine by way of Macrobius, and he offers in his theological triptych a sensitive reading of Macrobius (going well beyond the reading offered by William of Conches in his *Glosae super Macrobium*).[145] In the first book of his *Theologia "Summi boni,"* after citing the testimony of the prophets concerning the Trinity, he turns to the more controversial testimony of the (pagan) philosophers.[146] Following upon a brief discussion of "Mercurius" from the Hermetic tradition, he reaches his real target, the *maximus philosophorum*, Plato, "who, as testified by the Church Fathers, came closer to the Christian faith than any other pagan philosopher."[147] The Trinity discovered by Plato consists in the Macrobian Trinity denied in the *Dialectica*: highest God (the Father), the Mind born from God (the Son), and the

144 On the details, see Bezner, *Vela Veritatis: Hermeneutik, Wissen und Sprache in der Intellectual History des 12. Jahrhunderts*, 113–119; John Marenbon, "The Platonisms of Peter Abelard," in *Aristotelian Logic, Platonism, and the Context of Early Medieval Philosophy in the West* (Aldershot: Ashgate, 2000), 118–122; Marenbon, "Life, Milieu, and Intellectual Contexts," 35–38.

145 Ibid., 38: "Although he [sc. Abelard] and William think that Macrobius is talking about the Trinity, the lack of common ground between these remarks and William's commentary is striking. Even the point about the diversity of gifts of the Holy Spirit is changed and subsumed into a wider, more complex reading."

146 *TSum* 1.5.30 (295–297): Nunc autem post testimonia prophetarum de fide sancte trinitatis, libet etiam testimonia philosophorum supponere, quod ad unius dei intelligentiam ipsa philosophie ratio perduxit.

147 *TSum* 1.5.36 (348–351): Reuoluatur et ille maximus philosophorum Plato, qui testimonia sanctorum patrum pre ceteris gentium philosophis fidei christiane accedens, totius trinitatis summam post prophetas patenter edocuit.

(world) Soul that proceeds from Mind. This soul, Abelard now allows, is a Platonic expression of the Holy Spirit.[148] Here is Abelard's central claim:[149]

> Conferant humane anime corporibus nostris animalem uitam; conferat anima mundi, quam spiritum sanctum intellexit, ipsis animabus uitam spiritualem distributione suorum donorum, ut sint singule anime uita corporum, spiritus autem sanctus uita animarum, quas uirtutibus uegetando ad bonorum ⟨operum⟩ profectum promouet. Quodam itaque modo anime nostre corpora quedam spiritus sancti dicende sunt, quas ipse per aliquod gratie sue donum inhabitat et uirtutibus uiuificat. Sed et illud quod aiunt animam totam, singulis corporibus infusam, omnia uiuificare, atque animare que ad animandum idonea repperit, nulla ipsorum duritia uel ⟨densitatis⟩ natura impediente,[150] pulchrum est inuolucrum, quia caritas dei, quam spiritum sanctum diximus, cordibus humanis per fidei siue rationis donum primitus infusa, quaedam uiuificat, ad bonorum fructum operum nos promouendo ut uitam assequamur eternam, et in quibusdam ipse spiritus uacare dicitur, prauitatis eorum duritia repugnante.
>
> Human souls confer animal life upon our bodies. The world soul, which he [sc. Plato] understood to be the Holy Spirit, confers on souls themselves a spiritual life through the distribution of its gifts. In this way soul is the life of bodies, but the world soul the life of souls. By quickening souls with its powers, it urges them to the profit of good works. Thus our human souls could be called, in a manner of speaking, bodies for the Holy Spirit, as the Holy Spirit resides within them through the gift of its grace and vivifies them with its powers. But when it is said that the world soul is wholly diffused in individual bodies, that it vivifies all things, and that it animates everything it finds suitable to such animation (provided it is not impeded by their hardness or the density of their nature), this we must understand as a beautiful *inuolucrum*, because God's love, which we have called the Holy Spirit, when first infused in mens' hearts through the gift of faith or reason, vivifies some of us by urging us to the fruitfulness of good works; in others of us, however, the Spirit is said to be lacking, as the hardness of their depravity wars against the Spirit.

148 *TSum* 1.5.37 (361–364): De hac autem anima, si diligentius discutiuntur ea que dicuntur tam ab hoc philosopho quam a ceteris, nulli rei poterunt aptari, nisi spiritui sancto per pulcherrimam inuolucri figuram assignetur.

149 *TSum* 1.6.45–46 (473–488).

150 Cf. Macrobius, *In Som. Scip.* 1.14.14 (57.34–58.1): sed usum eius hebescere in animalibus corporis densitate.

In the first version of Abelard's Trinitarian theology, his comments on the musical implications of the world soul are brief.[151] In the later versions (*Theologia Christiana* and *Theologia "Scholarium"*) this same claim launches an impassioned encomium of the power of music and number, drawing largely on Boethius's *De institutione musica*:[152]

> Cuius etiam ut ineffabilem exprimerent benignitatis eius dulcedinem, totam ei musicarum consonantiarum adscribunt harmoniam, qua et ipsum iugiter resonare firmamentum et superiores mundi partes repleri perhibent. Nihil quippe est quod ita oblectet et nimia suauitate sui alliciat animos, sicut melodia. Nihil est ita pronum ad eos componendos et uel commouendos uel pacandos, ut iuxta illud primi capituli Boethianae Musicae scirent philosophi "quod nostrae tota animae corporisque compago musica coaptatione coniuncta sit," adeo quidem ut iracundias insaniasque melodia sedari et grauissimarum infirmitatum dolores curari animaduerterent atque efficerent.
>
> In order that they might express the ineffable sweetness of its goodness, they ascribe the entire harmony of musical consonances to it, with which, they claim, the firmament itself continually resounds, filling the higher parts of the universe. Indeed there is nothing else that delights and entices minds with its exceptional sweetness quite like melody, nothing else so well suited to composing, affecting, and pacifying minds. Philosophers know, in accord with the first chapter of Boethius's book on music, that "the entire union of our soul and body is conjoined by musical harmony," so much so, in fact, that philosophers note and bring into effect that anger and madness be sedated and the pains of extreme illness be cured by melody.

A similar emphasis on the theological aspects of the *anima mundi* is found in a mid-twelfth-century commentary on the Timaean *psychogonia* (*Tim.* 34b–36d). The text, transmitted in the third quire of Paris, Bibliothèque nationale, lat. 8624, is undoubtedly the most famous twelfth-century commentary that has been read (in full) by next to no one. For more than a century, its fame has rested upon less than one percent of its full text, a scant seven lines (of its 704 total) that

151 *TSum* 1.6.53–54 (538–548): Cui etiam philosophus totam uim et concordiam proportionalem numerorum tribuit, ut in diuinae gratiae bonitate uniuersarum rerum concordiam consistere doceat. Omnis quippe ordo naturae et concinna dispositio numerorum proportionibus uestigatur atque assignatur, et omnium perfectissimum exemplar numerus occurrit qui rebus congruit uniuersis. Quod quidem non latet qui philosophiae rimantur arcana. Hinc est etiam quod arithmetica, que tota circa proportiones numerorum consistit, mater est magistra ceterarum artium dicitur, quod uidelicet ex discretione numerorum ceterarum rerum uestigatio doctrinaque pendeat.

152 *TChr* 1.80 (1051–1062); *TSch* 1.136 (1577–1588).

present the comparison of a spider and its web to the soul and its body, which the commentator explicitly attributed to Heraclitus. Its author (christened Hisdosus Scholasticus in 1895 by his first documented modern reader, Alfred Gercke) has been well known to classicists since 1906, when Hermann Diels published these seven lines as Heraclitean fragment B67a in the second edition of his *Die Fragmente der Vorsokratiker*.[153]

The surprisingly widespread repute of Hisdosus Scholasticus in modern classical scholarship stands in stark contrast to the resolute silence of medieval sources on the identity of the commentator. The only evidence is internal to the commentary, as it is not cited by any other known text. In fact, the author is distinguishable from the most prolific medieval author, Anonymous, only because he happens to mention his own name in a discussion of *agnomen* (nickname) and *cognomen* (surname), occasioned by the names that Plato gave to the movements of the world soul at 36c4–7. On this passage, the heretofore anonymous commentator observes:

> Cognomen enim dicitur a cognatione datum, ut si quis aut proprio patris nomine uocetur, quomodo Tullius Marcus dictus est, aut etiam patris agnomine uel cognomine appelletur, quemadmodum ego, ne longe exempla petantur, appellor Hisdosus de patre meo.
>
> A cognomen is so-called because it is a name bestowed by cognation [sc. kinship], as when someone is called by his father's proper name (for instance, Tullius [Cicero] is called Marcus), or when someone is called by his father's agnomen or cognomen (for instance, to use an example close at hand, I am called Hisdosus from my father).

This name (in French, Hideux or Lehideux), as Édouard Jeauneau has pointed out, situates our author "en territoire francophone."[154] It is tempting to speculate with further precision, however, that the name would suggest northern France, for example, the Maison de Chambly (an hour's drive north of Paris), where in the twelfth century and after we find many members of the Hideux family (most of them named Pierre/Petrus), variously spelled in Latin Hisdeus, Hisdosus, and (tellingly) Hispidus, and thus perhaps roughly equivalent to the English surname Beard.[155]

[153] Alfred Gercke, while preparing his pioneering 1895 study of the *Überlieferung* of Seneca's *Naturales quaestiones* (*Seneca-Studien* [Leipzig: B. G. Teubner, 1895], 1–158), autopsied BnF, lat. 8624 and discovered the *Timaeus* commentary. He brought it to the attention of Max Pohlhenz, who subsequently transcribed and briefly discussed the now famous comparison (in a review of Hans von Arnem's *Stoicorum ueterum fragmenta* published in the August 1 issue of the 1903 *Berliner philologische Wochenschrift* [31/32], 971–972). It was Pohlhenz's text (not a new transcription) that Diels three years later printed among the Heraclitan fragments in the second edition of the *Die Fragmente der Vorsokratiker*.

[154] É. Jeauneau, ed., *Guillelmi de Conchis, Glosae super Platonem*, 333.

[155] M. J. Depoin, *La Maison de Chambly sous les Capétiens directs* (Paris: Imprimerie nationale, 1915): Cette branche apparaît à Chambly peu après l'avènement du comte Mathieu II. Lorsqu'en 1151,

It remains uncertain precisely when Hisdosus composed his commentary. He undoubtedly knew William of Conches's *Philosophia* (ca. 1125–1130), and there are numerous concordances with William's *Glosae super Platonem* (composed after the *Philosophia*), which would place the terminus post quem ca. 1140. The only concrete terminus ante quem is the date of the manuscript quire in which it is preserved, the late twelfth or early thirteenth century (see the introduction to Appendix 2). While the commentary could well have been written at any time during this period, the notable lack of any sources from the later twelfth century—including the Aristotelian *logica nova*, *De generatione et corruptione*, or *De anima*, all of which were available after 1150 and are utilized by later commentators—would suggest that the commentary is more likely to have been composed earlier in this span (ca. 1150) than later. This would well accord with the vivacity and immediacy with which Hisdosus engages his (unnamed) interlocutors.

Hisdosus's approach to the *Timaeus* reflects the teaching of twelfth-century schools,[156] and it is enticing to suppose that Hisdosus was a student of both Abelard and William of Conches. His commentary combines the theological emphases of Abelard's theological treatises with the mathematical, harmonic, and astronomical theories of William of Conches.[157] As Abelard does, Hisdosus reads Plato as a pagan prophet: "For Plato and a great chorus of philosophers said many things about the trinity of persons and the unity of the trinity (as testified by St. Augustine and other church fathers) that are congruent with [Christian] faith."[158] To support the identification of the *anima mundi* with the *spiritus sanctus*, Hisdosus supplies careful arguments (see Appendix 2.1) that have

son père lui abandonne le pouvoir en prenant le froc, l'auteur du lignage qui nous intéresse, Pierre Ier, n'est pas encore au nombre des chevaliers de l'assise de Beaumont, mais, en 1166, il prend rang parmi les conseillers du comte; depuis lors il en souscrit sans cesse les actes. Quelquefois il se nomme Pierre de Chambly; un jour Mathieu le qualifie "prepositus noster de Chambli"; le plus souvent on le voit gratifié d'un surnom sur le sens duquel on ne peut se méprendre, en face des trois formes sous lesquelles on le rend en latin: "Petrus Hisdosus, Petrus Hispidus, Petrus Horridus." Il semble bien, d'après ces équivalents, qu'il s'agisse d'un surnom physique, "hideux," dont la signification, dérivant du barbarisme "hispidosus," serait: "hirsute."

156 *De anima mundi Platonica*, 17r: Diuinitate, uniuersitatis conditrice, fauorem nobis praestante, infixa menti est sententia Timaeum (quantum ipsius a scolasticis nostris legitur, cum facilius et commodius fieri poterit) a nobis glosandum. 18r: De origine porro humanae animae diuersas a diuersis doctoribus prolatas fuisse sententias in scripturis aliorum uidimus et a meis magistris audiuimus, quas alias commodius deo fauente explicabimus.

157 For a brief discussion of the parallels between Hisdosus and William, see Édouard Jeauneau, *Guillelmi de Conchis Glosae super Platonem*, 331–337. Hisdosus seems also to have written a text on arithmetic. In a brief discussion of conjunct and disjunct proportions (arithmetic, geometric, and harmonic), he observes that it would be superfluous—given the context—to calculate a disjunct harmonic proportion. The *praeteritio*, however, gives him the opportunity to boast that he *could* do so, even though nearly everyone thinks it impossible, a position he has decisively refuted *in Arismetica*, presumably a commentary on Boethius's *De institutione arithmetica* (*De anima mundi Platonica* 20r: Dicunt tamen paene omnes eam non posse inueniri, quos in Arismetica euidentissime confutamus).

158 *De anima mundi Platonica*, 17r.

no parallel in William of Conches's commentaries but recapitulate (though not without a degree of originality) explanations offered by Abelard. For example, Hisdosus argues that such an identification does not entail the eternity of the world, as a critic might object,[159] for the name *anima mundi*—akin to *praeceptor* or *pater*—is a name granted ex officio, namely the function of vivifying everything that exists in the world. Therefore, the *spiritus sanctus* is eternally whatever it is, but it is not eternally the *anima mundi*, and thus the world is not necessarily eternal.[160] In the *Theologia "Summi boni,"* Abelard offers essentially the same argument to explain why the *anima mundi*, if it is an expression of the *spiritus sanctus*, has a beginning in time: "'Spirit' is the name of a nature, but 'soul' (*anima*) is the name of a function, which derives from 'animating'" (*"Spiritus" quippe nomen est naturae, "anima" uero officii, ab "animando" scilicet*).[161] In line with William of Conches, however, Hisdosus offers considerable detail on the harmonic construction of the world soul, and he structures his commentary in a manner that echoes William, noting, for instance, that any discussion of the world soul's division must address the following questions (see Appendix 2.2):

1. how the soul is said to have been divided by numbers;
2. how it is divided by seven numbers,
3. and by *these* seven numbers specifically;
4. how Plato placed unity at the beginning,
5. and the even and odd numbers that flow forth on either side;
6. how he calculated from even and odd the linear, planar, and cubic numbers;
7. and how he finished the division with the cubic numbers.

[159] The argument runs: (1) The *anima mundi* is the *spiritus sanctus*. (2) The *spiritus sanctus* is eternally whatever it is. (3) Thus the *anima mundi* is eternally whatever it is. (4) If *the anima mundi* is eternally the *anima mundi*, then the world is eternally animated by it. (5) If the world is eternally animated, then the world is eternal.

[160] The argument is reprised later in the commentary (18r): ORTVM ANIMAE. Hic uidetur uelle spiritum sanctum habere principium uel eum mundi animam non esse. Sed neutrum uerum est, quia Deum annuisse ortum animae non est aliud quam mundum istum habuisse principium uegetationis, quam Deus sua bonitate ei contulit. Ille creator uel summus spiritus dicitur anima quia animat omnia quae in mundo uita decorantur, quemadmodum creati spiritus angeli dicuntur tunc solum cum mittuntur. Anima namque et angelus nomina sunt officiorum non naturarum. Cf. Isidore, *Etym*. 7.5.2: Angelorum autem uocabulum officii nomen est, non naturae. Semper enim spiritus sunt, sed cum mittuntur, uocantur angeli.

[161] *TSum* 3.94 (1277–1281): Occurrit hoc loco illud determinandum quod Plato animam mundi incepisse uoluerit nec coaeternam esse deo et menti. Quod si diligenter consideretur, non est abhorrendum. Cum enim spiritum sanctum animam magis quam spiritum appellauerit quasi ab "animando," hoc est uiuificando nos donis suae gratiae per incrementa uirtutum, non semper anima, id est uiuificans, spiritus fuit, quia dum nondum creaturae essent quibus dona sua distribueret, nullam donorum distributionem exercebat. Sicut ergo spiritum sanctum, qui in se est omnino simplex, multiplicem tamen dicimus et septem spiritus appellamus secundum diuersitatem donorum, ita etiam philosophus eundem, qui ⟨in⟩ essentia propria aeternaliter subsistit incepisse quantum ad effecta sua uoluit,

Finally, when Hisdosus discusses the full sweep of the soul's division, including the *leimma* (the minor semitone), he (as William did) launches into a full-blown treatise on microtonal mathematics, proving how the ratio of the minor semitone can be determined, and he (as William did) employs a series of *regulae* as guideposts along the way (Appendix 2.3). But what is perhaps most striking about Hisdosus's commentary is that it makes almost no reference to the *musica caelestis*. It is mentioned only in passing, as an example of his claim that the massive *exagitatio* of the heavens cannot be perceived by the bodily senses, because the senses fail at both extremes, "which," he writes, "is clearly apparent in the case of celestial harmony (with respect to hearing) and in the case of atoms (with respect to sight)."[162] This is the only mention of the *musica caelestis* in Hisdosus's commentary, but in this way too Hisdosus reflects the larger pattern of thought in twelfth-century philosophical commentaries—for although the existence of the heavenly harmony is generally maintained across the century, its reality as an astronomical system gradually faded from view.

Musica caelestis

Two relatively well-known twelfth-century copies of Boethius's *De institutione musica* (Cambridge, University Library, Ii.3.12 and Cambridge, Trinity College, R.15.22, both originating from Christ Church, Canterbury)[163] present a curious amalgam of celestial harmony in an interpolated diagram (see figure 5.3) that

ex quibus eum animam magis quam spiritum appellauit. "Spiritus" quippe nomen est naturae, "anima" uero officii, ab "animando" scilicet. Cf. *TSch* 2.174 (2520–2533); *TChr* 4.145 (2287–2301).

162 *De anima mundi Platonica*, 22r: Constat inter omnes recte philosophantes tantam esse caeli exagitationem quod sensu corporeo percipi non potest. Ipse enim circa quaeque maxima et minima deficit, quod in caelesti armonia de auditu et atomis de uisu liquido apparet.

163 UL Ii.3.12 contains an incomplete catalogue of books from the Christ Church library (facsimile and transcription in Montague Rhodes James, *The Ancient Libraries of Canterbury and Dover* [Cambridge: Cambridge University Press, 1903], 3–12), one of which is a *Musica boetii*, keyed to the siglum EE, corresponding to Cambridge, Trinity College, R.15.22, a *Musica Boethii* from Christ Church, which bears on its first leaf the mark EE. UL Ii.3.12 also contains (f. 61v) a famous Romanesque illumination that depicts Boethius, in the upper left quadrant, flanked by Pythagoras, in the upper right, and in the lower half, Plato (left) debates with Nicomachus (right), each bearing in his hand a book inscribed MVSICA (on which see C. R. Dodwell, *The Canterbury School of Illumination, 1066–1200* [Cambridge: Cambridge University Press, 1954], 35ff.). Each of the three scenes is encircled by three descriptive (if flat-footed) leonine hexameters (wrongly transcribed in Margaret Gibson, "Illustrating Boethius: Carolingian and Romanesque Manuscripts," in *Medieval Manuscripts of the Latin Classics: Production and Use*, ed. Claudine A. Chavannes-Mazel and Margaret M. Smith [Los Altos Hills, CA: Anderson-Lovelace, 1996], 128): [Boethius:] Consul et eximiae scrutator phylosophyae / Vt uideat uocum discrimina per monochordum / Iudicat aure sonum percurrens indice neruuum. [Pythagoras:] Pythagoras physicus physicaeque latentis amicus / Pondera discernit trutinans et dissona spernit. / Pulsans aera probat quota quaeque proportio constat. [Plato and Nicomachus:] Edocet ipsorum summus Plato phylosophorum / Quomodo disparium paritas sonat una sonorum. / Obuiat instanti

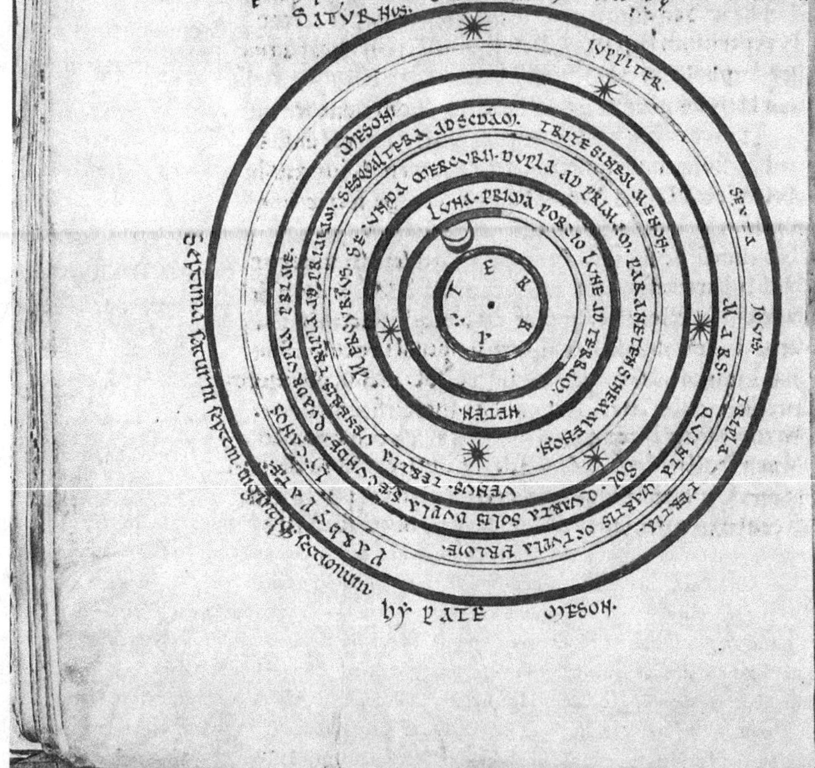

Figure 5.3 Twelfth-century planetary diagram incorporated in Boethius, *Inst. mus.* 1.27 ("Qui nerui quibus sideribus comparentur"). Cambridge, Trinity College, Wren Library, MS R.15.22, f. 23v. Courtesy of the Master and Fellows of Trinity College Cambridge.

ostensibly illustrates book 1, chapter 27, entitled "Which strings are comparable to which stars." The diagrams are identical in form, content, even color, suggesting either that they were copied from the same exemplar or that perhaps one was the exemplar for the other.[164] At 1.27, Boethius offers two "planetary scales": a seven-note scale (unattributed but based upon Nicomachus) descending from the *lunaris circulus* (sounding the *nete*) to Saturn (the *hypate meson*),[165] and an eight-note scale extrapolated from Cicero's *Somnium Scipionis* (5.1–2), ascending from the moon (*proslambanomenos*) to the highest heaven (*ultimum caelum*, the *mese*).[166] Both, however, follow the Chaldean planetary order, placing the sun in the middle (as opposed to the Egyptian order adopted by Plato, in which the sun orbits lower than Mercury and Venus).[167] The interpolated diagram depicts the planetary spheres as seven concentric circles, of which the first from the central earth, despite being inscribed with the customary lunar symbol (a crescent moon), is otherwise left blank. The planetary order thus begins with the moon in the second circle (bearing only a generic *stella*) and concludes with Saturn at the outermost periphery. The diagram describes within its planetary rings Boethius's first Nicomachean scale from *hypate meson* to *nete*: the moon is labeled *neten*, Mercury, *paratene sinemmenon*, etc.

Accompanying the diagram's planetary scale, however, is a numeric series that corresponds to a second, very different, formulation of celestial harmony: the

ratione Nichomacus illi. For a conspectus of both manuscripts, see Margaret Gibson and Lesley Smith, *Codices Boethiani: A Conspectus of Manuscripts of the Works of Boethius; I. Great Britain and the Republic of Ireland* (London: The Warburg Institute, 1995), nos. 6 (42) and 54 (84–85), respectively.

164 The second section (from the first half of the twelfth century) of the composite ms Bodleian, Selden Supra 25, also from Canterbury (St. Augustine's), includes a similar diagram at 1.27 (f. 57v), but it remains incomplete (i.e., eight blank concentric circles); on this manuscript, see *Codices Boethiani*, no. 201 (214–216).

165 *Inst. mus.* 1.27 (219.4–220.1): Illud tantum interim de superioribus tetrachordis addendum videtur, quod ab hypate meson usque ad neten quasi quoddam ordinis distinctionisque caelestis exemplar est. Namque hypate meson Saturno est adtributa, parhypate vero Ioviali circulo consimilis est. Lichanon meson Marti tradidere. Sol mesen obtinuit. Triten synemmenon Venus habet, paraneten synemmenon Mercurius regit. Nete autem lunaris circuli tenet exemplum. Cf. Nicomachus, *Harm.* 3 (241.3–242.18, with the translation and commentary in Barker, *Greek Musical Writings II*, 250–253) and *Excerpta ex Nicomacho* 3 (*Musici Scriptores Graeci*, 271.16–272.8), the planetary order of which (Moon, Mercury, Venus) corresponds more closely to Boethius's scale (as opposed to the Moon, Venus, Mercury order of *Harm.* 3). Cf. *Inst. mus.* 1.20 (206.10–14): Sed septimus nervus a Terpandro Lesbio adiunctus est secundum septem scilicet planetarum similitudinem. Inque his quae gravissima quidem erat, vocata est hypate quasi maior atque honorabilior, unde Iovem etiam hypaton vocant.

166 *Inst. mus.* 1.27 (220.12–25). On Boethius's solution to Cicero's "vague, ascending moon to firmament progression," see James Haar, "*Musica Mundana*: Variations on a Pythagorean Theme" (PhD diss., Harvard University, 1960), 178–181.

167 For a detailed discussion of the various planetary orders, see Georg Wissowa and Wilhelm Kroll, eds., *Paulys Realencyclopädie der classischen Altertumswissenschaft: Neue Bearbeitung* (Stuttgart: Alfred Druckenmüller, 1958), s.v. "hebdomas," VI. Die Planetenordnungen bei Babyloniern, Äegyptern, Griechen (vol. 7.2, 2561–2570).

"Timaean" system as formulated by Calcidius. Chapters 95 and 96 of Calcidius's commentary set forth the *positio planetum* as an intervallic series derived from the harmonic constitution of the *anima mundi*.[168] Calcidius (or his source, Adrastus) envisaged a Platonic cosmic harmony defined not by the identification of each sphere with a specific pitch within the gamut (as in Boethius), but rather by reckoning the successive intervals between the spheres, enumerated in the Egyptian order, in accord with the division of the world soul.[169] Thus the distance from the earth to the moon corresponds to the soul's first division, the single *portio*, whereas the outermost planet, Saturn, is twenty-seven times as far as the moon from the earth.[170] These planetary distances are visually described by an astronomical diagram that features eight concentric spheres—*terra* at the center, the *aplanes* at the outermost periphery—with the series 1 2 3 4 8 9 27 inscribed successively within each circle from the *circulus lunae* (1) to *circulus saturni* (27).[171] The outermost *aplanes*—although mentioned in the preceding chapter as part of the celestial

[168] Calcidius likely knew a planetary scale, because at *In Tim.* 72 (120.1–10) he translates ten lines of Hellenistic verse—sortitos celsis replicant anfractibus orbes, etc.; see Karl Buechner, *Fragmenta poetarum Latinorum epicorum et lyricorum praeter Ennium et Lucilium* (Leipzig: B. G. Teubner, 1982), 196–197 (no. 18)—dealing with the harmony of the planets (cf. Theon of Smyrna, *Exp.* 139.1–10). Calcidius, however, employs these verses within a discussion of the planetary order and thereby omits the subsequent sixteen lines (as given by Theon, *Exp.* 140.5–141.4), which present the planetary scale. On this poem and its scale, see Haar, "*Musica Mundana*," 104ff.

[169] *In Tim.* 95 (147.26–148.5). Cf. *In Tim.* 73 (120.11–13): Pythagoreum dogma est ratione harmonica constare mundum caelestiaque distantia congruis et consonis sibi inuicem interuallis impetu nimio et uelocitate raptatus edere sonos musicos (= Theon, *Exp.* 139.11–140.3). Macrobius, on the contrary, who explicitly attributes his position to Porphyry (*In Som. Scip.* 2.3.15 [107.1–2]: hanc Platonicorum persuasionem Porphyrius libris inseruit quibus Timaei obscuritatibus non nihil lucis infudit), maintains the linear model of the harmonic division and thus preserves the strict alternation of evens and odds (1 2 3 4 9 8 27), even though preserving this order comes at the cost of a nonsensical musical system, which sums to 46,656:1 or 15 octaves and a tritone. See *In Som. Scip.* 2.3.14 (106.21–31). Flamant argues that the celestial harmony of both Calcidius and Macrobius derives ultimately from Adrastus, but Macrobius reveals Porphyry's interventions, who "corrected Adrastus in order to respect the natural [even and odd] alteration of the linear diagram" (Jacques Flamant, *Macrobe et le Néo-Platonisme latin, à la fin du IVe siècle* [Leiden: Brill, 1977], 373).

[170] *In Tim.* 96 (148.12–19): Sectioni quoque partium ex quibus animam constituit positio planetum conueniens uidetur, cum unam ab uniuerso facit sumptam primitus portionem, id est minimam, a terra ad lunam; cuius duplicem secundam, id est quae inter lunam solemque interiacet, cuius triplam tertiam, scilicet Ueneris, quartam duplicem secundae, id est quadruplam primae, Mercurii, octuplam uero Martis, quae quinta sectio est, sextam triplam tertiae, id est regionem seu circulum Iouis, septem porro et uiginti partium Saturni nouissimam sectionem. This system is supposed by Thomas Heath to be an additive system because of Calcidius's specification that the second *portio* corresponds to *quae inter lunam solemque interiacet*, not *quae inter terram solemque interiacet* (Sir Thomas Heath, *Aristarchus of Samos: The Ancient Copernicus* [Oxford: Clarendon Press, 1913], 164). Such an interpretation, however, would do violence to the strict correspondence between the *positio planetum* and the division of the *anima mundi*. Elsewhere, Calcidius's language is more precise, e.g., *In Tim.* 73 (121.6–8): Plato etiam in hoc ipso Timaeo primam altitudinem a terra usque ad lunarem circulum, secundam usque ad solem liquido dimensus est.

[171] Waszink, *Timaeus a Calcidio translatus*, 149 (wrongly placed in chapter 97, as it illustrates chapter 96). This Calcidian diagram is not included in Bruce Eastwood and Gerd Graßhoff's handlist

harmony[172]—is left with no correspondence to the division of the *anima mundi*, and it is unclear how the fixed stars would fit within Calcidius's system.

Although the Calcidian and Boethian models of celestial harmony differ *toto caelo*, the Calcidian diagram, as well as the chapter it accompanies, likely inspired the interpolated diagram in the Christ Church manuscripts of the *De institutione musica* (and this would help to explain the "extra" circle in the Christ Church diagram, which does not include the *aplanes*). The text within the diagram reads as follows:

> terra
> luna . prima portio lunae ad terram . neten
> mercurius . secunda mercurii dupla ad primam . paranete sinemmenon
> uenus . tertia ueneris tripla ad primam, sesqualtera ad secundam . trite sinemmenon
> sol . quarta solis dupla secunde, quadrupla prime . meson
> mars . quinta martis, octupla prime . lychanos meson
> iuppiter . sexta iouis, tripla tertiae . parhypate
> saturnus . septima saturni septem uigintique sectionum . hypate meson

The scale is Boethian, the planetary distances are Calcidian,[173] and the combination of the two is, ultimately, nonsensical. The diagram describes an impossible cosmos. To my knowledge, the inclusion of this (modified) Calcidian diagram in Boethius's *De institutione musica* is unique to Canterbury sources; nonetheless, it neatly captures two primary themes of twelfth-century conceptions and applications of *musica mundana*: (1) an aggressive syncretism (sometimes to a fault), and (2) the centrality of the Timaean *anima mundi*.

But these were not the only scales that animated the twelfth-century cosmos. As Fronesis, the reluctant heroine of Alan de Lille's *Anticlaudianus*, begins her noetic ascent to the throne of Theology, first buffeted by the four winds within the dense air of the cosmos's lower strata, she eventually reaches the crystalline stillness of the first celestial sphere "where a more graceful breeze comforts all, where all is still and silent" (*quo gracior aura cuncta fovet, quo cuncta silent*). But the silence is not absolute:[174]

> hic rerum novitas, rerum decus, unica rerum
> forma, decor mundi visum demulcet euntis

of Calcidian diagrams: *Planetary Diagrams for Roman Astronomy in Medieval Europe, ca. 800–1500* (Philadelphia: American Philosophical Society, 2004).

[172] *In Tim.* 95 (148.9–11): Erit ergo animae aplanes ratio, planetes ut iracundia et cupiditas ceterique huius modi motus quorum concentu fit totius mundi uita modificata.

[173] Note, however, that the Calcidian planetary order—Luna, Sol, Venus, Mercurius—has been adjusted to match the Boethian scale, enumerated in the order Luna, Mercurius, Venus, Sol.

[174] *Anticl.* 4.345–355 (trans. Winthrop Wetherbee in *Alan of Lille: Literary Works* [Cambridge, MA: Harvard University Press, 2013], lightly modified).

virginis et cantus species nova debriat aurem,
sed parco tamen auditu sonituque minore
concipit illa sonum, certa tamen imbibit aure,
qualiter hic sonitus cithare celestis obesis
vocibus expirat, ubi lune sphera remisso
suspirat cantu, rauce sonat, immo sonando
pene silet, languetque sonans, nervique iacentis
inferius gerit illa vicem, cordamque minorem
reddit et in cithara sedem vix illa meretur.

Here the novelty and beauty of all things, the perfection of their form, the elegance of the cosmos charm the sight of the maiden as she passes, and a new sort of music intoxicates her ear; though she perceives the sound as barely audible and low in volume, she nonetheless drinks in with a ready ear how the sound of the celestial lyre issues forth in heavy tones. Here the Moon's sphere breathes out a languid song, sounds harsh, even falls nearly silent and grows faint as it resounds. It plays the role of a low-toned string, produces only a feeble note, and scarcely deserves to have a place in this music.

Fronesis has thus joined the rarefied company of those who have been in audience to the music of the spheres. As James Haar has rightly argued regarding this passage, despite Alan's adherence to the Platonic planetary order (with the sun in the second sphere), it is doubtless Martianus's celestial scale that echoes through Alan's depiction.[175] Alan, though, does not assign particular notes to the spheres, the sirens, and the muses heard by Fronesis in her celestial assent. To be sure, the twelfth century was not lacking in planetary scales. Honorius of Autun's *Imago mundi* forges two (conflicting) scales, one mapping the planets to the first eight notes in the Guidonian gamut and the second based on the Plinian planetary distances.[176] Honorius's scale is even found in glosses on Macrobius in the later twelfth century (although it is fundamentally at odds with the text it glosses).[177]

[175] Haar, "*Musica Mundana*," 293–296.

[176] *Imago mundi* 1.86: In terra namque si Gamma, in Luna A, in Mercurio B, in Venere C, in Sole D, in Marte E, in Iove F, in Saturno G ponitur, perfecto mensura musice invenitur. A terra usque ad firmamentum VII toni reperiuntur. A terra enim usque ad Lunam est tonus, a Luna usque ad Mercurium semitonium, a Mercurio usque ad Venerem semitonium, inde usque ad Solem tria semitonia, a Sole usque ad Martem tonus, inde ad Iovem semitonium, inde ad Saturnum semitonium, inde ad signiferum tria semitonia. Que simul iuncta VII tonos efficiunt. Tonus autem habet XVDCXXV milliaria, semitonium vero VIIDCCCXII milliaria et semissem. Cf. Pliny, *Naturalis historia* 2.19–20.

[177] E.g., London, British Library, Arundel 338, f. 139v (glossing Macrobius, *In som. Scip.* 2.2.1). The passage is commonly found in collections of short musico-mathematical texts, e.g., Paris, Bibliothèque nationale, lat. 7377C, 69v (= 47r according to a newer foliation), where it accompanies treatises on the *mensura fistularum*, the abacus, and Eratosthenes's geological calculations.

Similarly, as Susan Rankin has recently reminded us, numerous late-eleventh and early-twelfth-century manuscripts present us with diagrams, even poetry and music (e.g., the *Naturalis concordia uocum cum planetis*), that are designed to teach the elements of music alongside the constitution of the world.[178]

The presence of such diagrams and Honorian glosses notwithstanding, the commentators on the primary texts that developed the notion of celestial harmony—the *Timaeus*, Macrobius, and Martianus—are surprisingly silent about the particulars of this harmony, even while maintaining its existence. William of Conches, for instance, was generally content to note the potential discrepancy between the ancients on the exact formulation of the celestial harmony, contrasting Macrobius's ascending celestial progression (from the moon to the firmament) with Martianus, who offers the potential objection that "the firmament produces a low sound, the moon a high sound."[179] This may be surprising, since Martianus clearly agrees with Macrobius in positing an ascending scale from the moon to the firmament, witnessed in both the Apollonian grove (1.11) and the scalar ascent mounted by Philologia throughout book 2 of the *De nuptiis*. The Carolingian commentaries on Martianus, however, register the controversy of the planetary scale later referenced by William, and Eriugena's commentary (in both versions) argues for precisely the interpretation mentioned by William: that from the moon to Saturn is a *descending* scale, just the opposite of the scale presented in Martianus.[180] The St. Florian commentator jumbles the attribution of sundry scales: Plato is credited with the Nicomachean scale,[181] and

[178] Susan Rankin, "*Naturalis concordia vocum cum planetis*: Conceptualizing the Harmony of the Spheres in the Early Middle Ages," in *Citation and Authority in Medieval and Renaissance Musical Culture: Learning from the Learned*, ed. Suzannah Clark and Elizabeth Eva Leach (Woodbridge: Boydell, 2005), 3–19, discussing or mentioning Cambridge, Fitzwilliam Museum, MS McClean 52/II, f. 5v; Paris, Bibliothèque nationale, lat. 2389, f. 51v; and Paris, Bibliothèque nationale, lat. 7203, f. 2v–3r.

[179] *Glos. sup. Macr.*, comment. ad 2.4.10: Cum Macrobius dicat ex celeritate firmamenti acutum sonum effici, grauem uero ex tardo lunae motu, si opponatur de Martiano quod dicit firmamentum efficere grauem sonum, lunam acutum, quid Martianus intellexerit suo loco dicemus. Non enim hoc loco illud exponemus.

[180] On Eriugena's dynamic and synthetic cosmic harmony, see Mariken Teeuwen, *Harmony and the Music of the Spheres: The Ars musica in Ninth-Century Commentaries on Martianus Capella* (Leiden: Brill, 2002), 218–231; Gabriela Ilnitchi Currie, "*Concentum celi quis dormire faciet?* Eriugenian Cosmic Song and Carolingian Planetary Astronomy," in *Quomodo cantabimus canticum? Studies in Honor of Edward H. Roesner*, ed. David Butler Cannata et al. (Middleton, WI: American Institute of Musicology, 2008), 15–35.

[181] *In inst. mus.* 34: Plato enim et Socrates [*scripsit Rausch*, sc. *cod.*] dixerunt omnes planetas equaliter moveri, sed quosdam pro suorum circulorum brevitate tocius cursum perficere, ut Luna in mense perficeret cursum, quia brevissimum habet circulum; Sol et Mercurius et Venus in anno, Mars in duobus, Iupiter in XII, Saturnus in XXX, vel paulo plus vel paulo minus, et hi acutissimum sonum ponebant in Luna; sicut enim in cythara brevior corda acutiorem, longior autem graviorem sonum emittit, sic inter planetas Luna pro sui circuli brevitate acutiorem sonum emittit, ceteri autem quanto altiores sunt, tanto graviores faciunt; erat ergo gravissimus in firmamento.

Aristotle (!) is credited with the more usual ascending scale from the moon to the firmament.[182]

When William encountered Plato's description of the celestial motion as (in Calcidius's translation) a *chorea*,[183] he glosses it as a "circular dance performed with music." Thus the *chorea* subsumes the *musica caelestis*, whose existence is proven, William claims, by Macrobius. Even if the music accompanying the celestial dance exceeds the range of human hearing, we can yet perceive the motion of the dancers with our eyes.[184] When the text circles back again to the dance of the stars (*chorea stellarum*),[185] however, William observes that "to explain this dance would be to demonstrate which of the planets resounds with another planet in a diapente or some other consonance. But Plato omits to do so here."[186] Other twelfth-century writers followed suit and generally omitted detailed astronomical discussions of the music of the spheres.[187] Abelard, for instance, embraced the *musica caelestis* as an expression of the theological concord[188] conferred by the *spiritus sanctus*:[189]

> Bene itaque philosophi, immo Dominus per eos id forsitan ignorantes, tam ipsi animae mundi quam superioribus firmamenti partibus nimiam ac summam harmonicae modulationis suauitatem assignant, ut quanta pace, quanta fruantur corcordia, quam diligentius possent exprimerent, et quam concorditer cuncta in mundo diuina disponat bonitas; quam illi animam mundi, Veritas Spiritum Sanctum, ut dictum est, nominat. Quis enim, si diligenter attenderit, non animamduertat

[182] *In inst. mus.* 34: Aristoteles autem, qui magis et veritatem et probabilitatem in omnibus sequebatur, dixit quod acutior sonus in firmamento, gravissimus autem in Luna.

[183] *Tim.* 39b4; *Translatio Calcidii* 31.22.

[184] *Guillelmi Glos. sup. Tim.* 102.13–18: Chorea est circularis motus cum cantu. Sed cum octo sint quae in superioribus circulariter mouentur, scilicet firmamentum et planetae septem, sonum faciunt concordem ex motu suo, ut probat Macrobius. Sic ergo est in caelestibus quaedam chorea cuius motus potest oculis perpendi, sed sonus possibilitatem humanarum aurium excedit.

[185] *Tim.* 40c3; *Translatio Calcidii* 33.23.

[186] *Guillelmi Glos. sup. Tim.* 108.11–13: Persequi uero hanc choream est ostendere quis eorum cum alio reddat uel diapente uel aliam consonantiam: quod hic praetermittit Plato.

[187] There are exceptions. The *Glosae Colonienses super Macrobium* (as discussed by Alison Peden, though she wrongly attributes the theory to William of Conches) explains how planets with equal velocity can move at different speeds by distinguishing between "absolute and angular speed" (Peden, "Music in Medieval Commentaries on Macrobius," in *Musik – und die Geschichte der Philosophie und Naturwissenschaften im Mittelalter*, 156). See *Glos. Colonienses sup. Macr.*, comment. ad 2.1.3 (254.23–25): Nam quo sunt superiores, eo in circumvolvendo, celeriores; quo inferiores, eo segniores; et tamen eodem tempore omnes circumvolvuntur, ut patet in exteriore et interiore parte molendine. This argument was incorporated into the interpolated version of William's *Glosae super Macrobium*, Copenhagen, Det Kongelige Bibliotek, Gl. Kgl. Sammlung 1910 4°, f. 102r (whence Peden's ascription to William).

[188] Already noted by Haar, "*Musica Mundana*," 297: "The heavenly concert is here part of a Platonizing Christian theology. One suspects, however, that the literally-conceived 'sounding spheres' are yielding place to the theological metaphor."

[189] *TChr* 1.84 (1117–1132); *TSch* 1.141 (1660–1673).

quod de caelesti dixerunt harmonia quae in superioribus firmamenti partibus incessanter resonat, cum caelestes uidelicet spiritus ex assidua diuinae maiestatis uisione et summa inuicem concordia ligentur, et in eius quem conspiciunt laudem iugi et ineffabili exultatione illud decantent, quod iuxta Isaiam seraphim die ac nocte conclamare non cessant: Sanctus, sanctus, sanctus Dominus Deos sabaoth, etc.

Rightly, then, do philosophers (or rather, the Lord working through them in their state of ignorance) assign both to the world soul and to the upper parts of the firmament the exceedingly supreme sweetness of harmonic modulation, so that they might express, as diligently as they can, how great is the peace and concord enjoyed [by the world soul and firmament] and how concordantly divine goodness arranges everything within the universe. Philosophers call it the world soul; Truth, as we have already said, calls it the Holy Spirit. For who, given due diligence, would not notice what philosophers have said about this celestial harmony, which unceasingly resounds in the upper parts of the firmament, for the celestial spirits, in their perpetual vision of divine majesty, are both bound together in the utmost concord and, with ceaseless and ineffable exaltation in praise of him whom they behold, sing the same praises that, according to Isaiah, the seraphim never—day and night—cease to sing: *Sanctus, sanctus, sanctus, dominus deus sabaoth*?

In the commentary on Martianus ascribed to Bernard Silvestris, the music of the spheres becomes a celestial model of human ethics. As we may recall from Chapter 2, this commentary reordered the Boethian tripartition and elevated *musica humana* above *musica mundana*. This reshuffling has further implications, for the epistemological framework necessitates that the *musica caelestis*, so often cast as the pinnacle of musical understanding, be subordinated to the *musica humana*. He effects this subordination by developing an idiosyncratic and highly synthetic account of the music of the spheres. Bernard remains mute on most traditional topics pertaining to celestial harmony, offering no planetary scales, little in the way of celestial mechanics, and only a brief explication of its inaudibility in the sublunar realm.[190] But a curious etymological gloss on the Camenae, the Roman goddesses identified with the Greek muses, afforded him an opportunity to develop a *musica caelestis* in line with his epistemological framework. He begins

[190] *Comm. in Mart.* 3.76–84: CALLIOPEA optime vocis interpretatio est. Hec est autem armonia celestis, quam esse sic probant philosophi. Non possunt, ut aiunt, tanta corpora tam violento impetu silentio discurrere. Une necesse est quod incitatione eorum aer in sonum formetur. In celestibus nil expers moderamine. Quia ergo ibi est et sonus et concordia, est armonia. Set cur nostro se nequaquam audi-tui suggerat hec ratio? In omnibus sensibilibus modulo et mensura egent sensus humani. Visus enim, cum lucem intuetur, nimia luce fit hebes. Ergo et illius soni nimietatem capere noster ad hoc impar nequit auditus.

traditionally enough, following Remigius of Auxerre in deriving Camena from "to sing beautifully" (*canere amoene*): "The goddess Camena is so called because she sings beautifully in the heavenly harmony. For diversity and plurality produce every harmony of sounds. There is no harmony in identity."[191] A quick consonantal shuffle suggests a second etymology: "*Camena* as if *canema*, that is, singing to the soul" (*camena quasi canema, id est canens anime*).[192] For this fanciful etymology, the commentator gives two rationales. The first explains *canens anime* as the performance of music when the soul separates from the body, a reference (presumably) to funereal practices. The second and more speculative explanation posits the heaven's twin motions as a celestial song. The full passage reads as follows:[193]

> Vel "Camena" quasi "canema," id est canens anime. Dicitur enim quia animabus et aliis spiritibus in sua naturali regione cantus illos exhibet. Musicam enim credunt spiritibus gratam, unde in separatione anime a corpore tibias exercebant, quibus nostro tempore pulsus campanarum successit. Set melius quod anime in celestibus canit [canunt *Westra*] dum cursus planetarum et applanes iungat. Documentum enim in hoc habet anima cum videat in mundo meatum geminum: unum ab occidente in orientem, qui erraticus dicitur, quia ascendit et descendit; alium qui ab oriente in occidentem directus ad orientem refertur, qui rationabilis dicitur quia semper uniformis est. . . . Iterum anima videt in se quasi rationalem motum rationem, quasi erraticum sensualitatem; dumque nititur ratione sensualitatem cohibere, celestia imitatur. Diversitas itaque motus illos conferens anime canit, dum per eos omnia taliter instruit. Unde Plato deum inquit hominibus iccirco oculos dedisse, ut mentis et providentie circuitus qui fiunt in celo notantes, sue mentis motus erraticos corrigant.

191 *Comm. in Mart.* 3.261–263: Hec dea CAMENA dicitur quia amene canit in celi armonia. Diversitas et pluralitas sonorum armoniam omnem reddunt: nulla enim identitate armonia. Cf. Lutz, *Remigii Autissiodorensis Commentum in Martianum Capellam* 1:67. *Canens amoena* (or *amoene*) is a common etymology found in other twelfth-century commentaries, e.g., William of Conches, *Glos. sup. Boet.* 1.m1.41–42, and the anonymous Florentine commentary on Martianus (Florence, Bib. Naz., Conv. Soppr. I.1.28) discussed below.

192 *Comm. in Mart.* 3.263–264.

193 *Comm. in Mart.* 3.263–287. Cf. Calcidius, *In Tim.* 95 (148.9–10): Erit ergo animae aplanes ratio, planetes ut iracundia et cupiditas ceterique huius modi motus. Cf. *In inst. mus.* 28: Unde etiam philosophi duos ei motus assignaverunt: motum planeticum et motus firmamenti. Motus autem planeticus est ab occidente in orientem, motus firmamenti ab oriente in occidentem; tunc autem anima dicitur motu ferri planetico, quando eligendo malum nititur pervenire ad suum causatorem, et non potest, quia semper detruditur in hac terrena, sicut planetae a firmamento referuntur in occidentem; tunc autem dicitur uti motu firmamenti, quando fugiendo malum eligit bonum, tunc enim redit ad suum principium.

> Or "Camena," as if "Canema," is derived from *canens animae* (singing to the soul). For it is said that she reveals those songs to souls and other spirits in her natural region. For they believe that music is pleasing to spirits, whence at the separation of the soul from the body, they used to play *tibiae*; in our age, we have replaced this with the ringing of bells. But it is better that Camena sing to the soul in the heavens, when she joins together the courses of the planets and fixed stars. The soul has evidence of this, since it sees in the world a twin movement: one from the west to the east, which is called erratic because it ascends and descends; the other, which moves straight from the east to the west and then is carried back again to the east, is called rational because it is always uniform . . . Moreover, the soul sees in itself, like a rational motion, reason, and like an erratic motion, sensuality. When it struggles to suppress sensuality with reason, it imitates the heavens. Diversity, uniting these motions, sings to the soul, and in such a way teaches all things through these motions. Whence Plato says that God gave eyes to men for this reason, so that knowing the courses of the [divine] providence and mind that occur in the heavens, they might correct the erratic motions of their own mind.

Clear signposts (*dicitur* and the anonymous *credunt*) suggest that another source lurks behind this author's interpretation. That source, *ad sensum*, is likely Macrobius's *Commentarii in Somnium Scipionis*, 2.3.4–6 (104.18–105.5):

> Musas esse mundi cantum etiam Etrusci sciunt, qui eas Camenas quasi canenas a canendo dixerunt. ideo canere caelum etiam theologi comprobantes sonos musicos sacrificiis adhibuerunt, qui apud alios lyra vel cithara, apud non nullos tibiis aliisve musicis instrumentis fieri solebant. in ipsis quoque hymnis deorum per stropham et antistropham metra canoris versibus adhibebantur ut per stropham rectus orbis stelliferi motus, per antistropham diversus vagarum regressus praedicaretur, ex quibus duobus motibus primus in natura hymnus dicandus deo sumpsit exordium. mortuos quoque ad sepulturam prosequi oportere cum cantu, plurimarum gentium vel regionum instituta sanxerunt persuasione hac, qua post corpus animae ad originem dulcedinis musicae, id est ad caelum, redire credantur.
>
> The Etruscans too understood that the Muses indicated the song of the world, for they called the Muses "Camenae" from (by way of "Canenae") "canere" (to sing). For this reason, theologians too, since they approved the thesis that the heavens sing, used music during their sacrifices, which some performed with the lyre or cithara, others with the *tibia* or other instruments. In the hymns to the gods, too, the verses of the strophe and antistrophe used to be set to music, so that the strophe

> might represent the forward motion of the celestial sphere and the antistrophe the reverse motion of the planetary spheres; these two motions produced nature's first hymn in honor of the Supreme God. In funeral processions, too, the practices of diverse people have ordained that it was proper to have musical accompaniment, owing to the belief that souls after death return to the source of sweet music, that is, to the sky.

In this passage, which is occasioned by a similar etymological gloss, *Camenas quasi canenas a canendo*, Bernard would have found all the building blocks for his etymological rationale: *tibiae* and other instruments, the musicalized twin motions (*geminus motus*) of the heavens, and funeral music as a fitting accompaniment to departing souls. Inspired, perhaps, by Macrobius's comment that the heavens' twin motions comprise the first hymn to God, Bernard explicitly appeals to the *geminus motus* as the sole astronomical ground for the harmony of the spheres: its concordant diversity sings to the soul (*diversitas illos motus conferens anime canit*).[194] Moreover, this interpretation allows the commentator to connect the celestial symphony to Plato's famous *dictum* at *Timaeus* 47c that God gave us eyes with which to learn from the celestial choreography. Hence this gloss on Camena presents a remarkably synthetic view of celestial harmony: reading Martianus through a Boethian framework, Macrobius offered the commentator's rationale, and Plato provided his proof text. And this is not merely an ad hoc mélange; it is a strategic maneuver. By proceeding in this way, the author is able to align elegantly the celestial harmony with his own epistemological aim.

The Florentine commentary on Martianus, however, proceeds differently and glosses *Camena* as follows:[195]

> Filius [sc. Hymenaeus] Camenae est, id est iugabilis elementorum concordiae siue etiam caelestis armoniae. Vnde Camena dicitur quasi canens amena delectatione musicarum consonantiarum. Quemadmodum enim nouem sunt Musae (Camena est una ex octo earum facta), ita [est] in mundi compositione nouem sunt soni: unus in sphaera, septem in planetis, nonus autem in terra. Horum octo—scilicet sphaerae et septem planetarum—caelestem composuerunt concinentiam [*scripsi*,

[194] That the *geminus motus* underlies the celestial harmony, cf. Bernard's other reference to the twin motions, under the heading of *mundana musica in astris* (*Comm. in Mart.* 3.429–434): Aura est impetus concitatus—quod intelligimus esse geminum illum orbicularem motum—in quam philosophi animam mundi scissam astruunt. Dicit enim Boetius, a Platone et in hoc eruditus, quia mundi anima "cum secta, duos motum glomeravit in orbes." Unde et hoc loco motus ille aura mentis, id est anime mundi, dictus est.

[195] *Exp. in Mart.* (Florence, Bib. Naz. Centrale, Conv. Soppr. I.1.28, f. 50v).

> continentiam *F, Dronke*], ex cuius beneficio omnia mundi corpora proportionaliter conseruantur.[196]
>
> He [sc. Hymenaeus] is the son of Camena, i.e., the continuous concord of the elements or even the celestial harmony. Whence Camena is derived, as it were, from "singing beautiful things." For just as there are nine muses—for Camena is one made from eight of them—so too in the composition of the world there are nine sounds: one in fixed stars, seven in the planets, but the ninth on the earth. Eight of these, namely those of the fixed stars and the seven planets, compose the celestial harmony, from whose benefit the whole body of the world is proportionally conserved.

The sticking point here, of course, is the placement of that awkward ninth muse. The commentator is undoubtedly under the sway of Martianus, as filtered, perhaps, through the lens of Remigius's commentary.[197] *De nuptiis* 1.27–28 paints a vivid picture of the nine muses riding beautiful swans, each in her respective sphere, but the last muse, Thalia, is saddled with a balking swan that refuses to fly and thus remains earthbound.[198] Nonetheless, it is striking that the commentator enumerates *nine* distinct sounds and matches one of them to the earth, even if he qualifies the *caelestis concinentia* as arising from only eight of them. William of Conches knew better than to assign a pitch to the earth, and in his *Glosae super Macrobium* he follows (as we should expect) the Macrobian line, which had cast the ninth muse (Calliope) as the "harmony made from all of them" (*concinentia*

[196] The commentator reiterates the point later in the commentary (60v): Astrologi uero dicunt nouem musas nouem sonos, qui in celesti armonia notantur. Quorum septem in planetis septem constant, alii duo, unus in celesti spera quae aplanes dicitur, alter uero ex illis octo confectus, quem tota simul reddit armonia. Vel, ut alii dicunt, alter constituatur in terra ut accutissimus sonus sit in spera celesti, grauissimus sit in terra. Atque hoc rectius uidetur ut, sicut spere nouem, ita quaeque suum faciat sonum = (with minor discrepencies) Westra, *The Berlin Commentary*, 185. On medieval adaptations of Muses to the (harmony of the) spheres, see Marie-Thérèse d'Alverny, "Les Muses et les sphères célestes," in *Classical, Mediaeval, and Renaissance Studies in Honor of B. L. Ullman*, ed. Charles Henderson (Rome: Edizioni di Storia e Letteratura, 1964), 2.7–19; on the Muses in the Berlin commentary in particular, see Tanja Kupke, "Où sont les muses d'antan? Notes for a Study of the Muses in the Middle Ages," in *From Athens to Chartres: Neoplatonism and Medieval Thought: Studies in Honour of Édouard Jeauneau*, ed. Haijo J. Westra (Leiden: Brill, 1992), 421–436.

[197] Lutz, *Remigii Autissiodorensis Commentum in Martianum Capellam* 101.34–102.2: nouem ordines habere [sc. armonia caelestis] dinoscitur, scilicet propter septem planetas octavamque sphaeram caelestem atque ipsam terram quae totius consonantiae, informatis vocibus materiei, proportionem possidet. Cf. Honorius of Autun, *Imago mundi* 1.86: unde et philosophi viiii musas finxerunt quia a terra usque ad celum viiii consonantias deprehenderunt.

[198] *De nuptiis* 1.28 (13.8–10): sola vero, quod vector eius cycnus impatiens oneris atque etiam subvolandi alumna stagna petierat, Thalia derelicta in ipso florentis campi ubere residebat.

quae confit ex omnibus).[199] William glosses the Muses' appearance in Macrobius's text as follows:[200]

> per octo Musas designauit octo consonantias effectas ex motu firmamenti et planetarum, per nonam Musam designauit consonantiam quae conficitur ex octo aliis. . . . Theologi uolebant sic esse in caelo nouem Musas: septem planetarum, octauam firmamenti, nonam maximam.
>
> By the eight Muses, he indicated the eight consonances made from the motion of the firmament and the planets; by the ninth Muse, he indicated the consonance that is produced from the eight others. . . . Theologians were wont to say that there were nine muses in the heavens: seven pertaining to the planets, the eighth pertaining to the firmament, and the ninth being the great sum [of them all].

Here again, there is no mention of scales or notes, and no precise musical structure is brought to bear on the question.

In William's last cosmological work, the *Dragmaticon*, the heavens fall silent by omission; there is no mention of the music of the spheres, and the astronomy at work in the pages of the *Dragmaticon* is not exclusively the Platonic astronomy of William's *Glosae super Platonem* or the Macrobian astronomy of the *Glosae super Macrobium*. Rather, William turned instead to a work of Arabic cosmology with strongly Peripatetic slant, the *Liber de orbe* by Māshā'allāh (translated by Gerard of Cremona around the middle of the century), as Barbara Obrist has recently brought to light.[201] Although William does not accept Māshā'allāh's vigorous defense of the heavens' non-elemental constitution and "upholds with Plato against Aristotle the traditional Western, early medieval position of a fiery heaven,"[202] William's cosmos began to shift away from the Platonic, Macrobian, and Capellan models at work in his earlier commentaries and treatises. Hisdosus, too, undercut several key points in the basic Platonic cosmos by arguing vociferously against the thesis that the planets move contrary to the firmament, the very basis for the celestial harmony envisaged by Bernard Silvestris. Traditional arguments that the contrary motions could somehow temper or balance each other were brushed aside by Hisdosus: "We, however, in agreement with Helpericus and

[199] *In Som. Scip.* 2.3.1–2 (104.1–9): theologi quoque novem Musas octo sphaerarum musicos cantus et unam maximam concinentiam quae confit ex omnibus esse voluerunt. unde Hesiodus in Theogonia . . . ut ostenderet nonam esse et maximam quam conficit sonorum concors universitas, adiecit Καλλιόπη θ' ἣ δὴ προφερεστάτη ἐστὶν ἁπασέων.

[200] *Glos. sup. Macr.*, comment. ad 2.3.1–2.

[201] Barbara Obrist, "William of Conches, Māshā'Allāh, and Twelfth-Century Cosmology," *Archives d'histoire doctrinale et littéraire du Moyen Âge* 76 (2009), 29–87.

[202] Ibid., 32. See *Drag.* 3.5.

Aristotelian dogma, say that the planets are carried along from the rising [the east] to the setting [the west]."[203]

This shift away from the Platonic cosmos, and away from its variously formulated astronomical harmonies, dramatically plays out in an anonymous commentary on book 8 (astronomy) of Martianus's *De nuptiis* in British Library, Cotton Vespasian A.II, ff. 75v–122v, which directly challenges the reality of the *musica caelestis* on both acoustic and astronomical grounds. The commentary, included in the seventh section of this composite manuscript—a collection of *membra disiecta* from the twelfth through fourteenth centuries—was copied in England around the early thirteenth century, and the hand is similar to that of the manuscript's fifth section (ff. 27–40), which also focuses solely on astronomy (containing two works on the astrolabe by Rudolph of Bruges and Abraham ibn Ezra, and the latter's Book of the Foundations of the Astronomical Tables [incomplete]).[204] This Martianus commentary remains, to my knowledge, completely unstudied, and further work on late-twelfth and early-thirteenth-century astronomy will doubtless contribute to our understanding of music's role in the swiftly changing cosmological thought during the early stages of the "new Aristotelianism." My remarks here focus solely on the extended gloss that follows upon the lemma (as given in the text): *quo loco obliquitas solis, lunae ac siderum orbisque signiferi se circumducit* ("a region where the inclined path of the sun, moon, planets, and zodiac revolve").[205] An ensuing discussion of the various motions in the heavens[206] leads to the supposed consequence of such motions:[207]

> Aiunt enim quod quies et silentium circa idem subiectum indiuidue se comitantur. Motus uero et sonus proportionaliter in sua subiecta irrepunt. Vnde motus uelox et spissus, acumen, tardus et rarus grauitatem in uoce producit. Hanc autem proportionalitatem in inferioribus irrefragabiliter procedere conspiciunt. Vnde plerique coniectant quod cum sublimia proportionali sub uelocitate uelocissima sint, armoniam et acutissimam uociferationem intendunt. Vnde Boetius in musica: qui enim fieri potest, ut tam uelox celi machina tacito silentique cursu

[203] *De anima mundi Platonica*, 21v: Nos uero, Helperico et peripateticorum dogmati consentientes, dicimus ab ortu ad occasum ferri planetas. Hisdosus's arguments are directed primarily against William of Conches, *Phil.* 2.23 (65D–66C); *Drag.* 4.7.43–63.

[204] For a full description of the manuscript, see Marie-Thérèse d'Alverny, "Les 'Solutiones ad Chosroem' de Priscianus Lydus et Jean Scot," in *La transmission des textes philosophiques et scientifiques au Moyen Âge*, ed. Charles Burnett (Aldershot: Variorum, 1994), 150–151. On the astronomical texts in ff. 27–40, see Charles Burnett, *The Introduction of Arabic Learning into England* (London: British Library, 1997), 50–58.

[205] *De nuptiis* 8.814 (309.10–11).

[206] Cotton Vespasian A.II, 84vb: Sciendum itaque quod motuum alius directus, alius obliquus. Item alius naturalis, alius accidentalis. Item alius rationalis, alius irrationalis.

[207] Ibid., 85ra.

moueatur? Vnde et Cicero in sompnio Scipionis: Quis est qui complet aures meas tantus et tam dulcis sonus? Hinc plurimi persuasi profitentur materialem, consonantissimam, et perpetuam armoniam in sublimibus subsistere.

For they say that rest and silences indivisibly accompany each other within the same subject. Motion and sound, however, proportionally steal into their subjects. Whence a swift and frequent motion produces highness in pitch (*in uoce*), whereas a slow and infrequent motion produces lowness in pitch. They, moreover, observe that this proportionality inviolably proceeds in the terrestrial realm. Whence many conjecture that since the heavens are extremely swift in their proportional speed, they extend a harmony and most high-pitched sounds (*uociferatio*). For as Boethius says in his *De musica*: How could it happen that such a swift heavenly machine be moved in a mute and silent course? And Cicero too in his *Dream of Scipio*: What is that great and sweet sound that fills my ears? Many, persuaded by this, declare that a material, consonant, and perpetual harmony exists in the heavens.

The commentator's loaded language reveals his sympathies, which lie not with the proponents of celestial harmony but with its critics. He begins his summary of the proponents' rationale as follows: "Pursuing and exaggerating this view, they claim that it has been put forth not on the basis of the sense perception of mortal creatures, but from the argument of the philosophers (*ratio philosophorum*)."[208] The basic *ratio philosophorum* is simple: if there is motion in the heavens, then there must be sound.[209] The real burden of the proponents of the *musica caelestis* is to explain why we cannot hear it. The commentator lists the common arguments: we are deaf to the sound either because its intensity overwhelms the sense of hearing,[210] or because we do not know what it would sound like not to hear the sound, as we, in the terrestrial realm, are always already accustomed to it.[211] Unnamed others (*alii*), however, destroy this line of argument on acoustical grounds. Sounds, the reply goes, are proportional to the solidity of the objects that collide: collision of a solid body with air produces a minimal sound; collision with fire produces still less; and collision with the *quinta essentia* (the Aristotelian "fifth essence" of quintessence) produces no sound at all, because the quintessence has absolutely

208 Ibid.: Hanc etiam opinionem prosequentes et exaggerantes aiunt hanc existimationem non a sensu mortalium, sed a ratione philosophorum fuisse profectam.

209 Ibid.: Ratio autem haec est. Dicte siquidem armonie causam praedictam, scilicet motus uelocitatem et plurium motuum proportionalitatem, in sublimi praeiacere existimant. Et ob hoc ipsius causae effectum procedere non ambigendum esse decernunt.

210 Ibid., 85rb: Vehemens namque sonoritatis intensio auditum disssipat et hebetat, sicut et nimius splendor uisum. Solem namque directe intuentibus eius radii aciem retundunt et dissipant.

211 Ibid.: sicque accidit in cataduplis, in molendino, in ortu solis cotidiano.

no bodily mass or solidity.[212] There is thus no sound, and no music, in the heavenly quintessence.[213] We are now firmly in an Aristotelian cosmos, despite the fact that the very text upon which the commentator comments propounds the very view he is arguing against. Moreover, despite the clear Aristotelian slant to the text, there is no direct evidence that the commentator has read Aristotle's *De caelo* (in Gerard of Cremona's translation)—not only is there no appeal to the authority of Aristotle to refute and balance the "Platonic" opinions of Boethius and Cicero cited at the outset of the discussion, but there are no verbal echoes of Gerard's translation of the *De caelo* that would necessitate (or even suggest) a firsthand familiarity with the text.[214]

That the unnamed *alii* were in fact "Aristotelians" reading and thinking about the *De caelo* seems probable. What is important, however, is that the gradual silencing of the Platonic cosmos occurred in dialogue with the very Platonic texts that had grounded and guaranteed the material reality of the *musica caelestis*, and the *musica mundana* generally, for nearly a millennium. The quest to understand the *machina mundi* led ultimately to the unraveling of a materialized cosmic harmony. But it did not undo the epistemic attitude that had sustained the aspirational aurality in the first place. The music of the spheres did not disappear altogether, but it changed its tune considerably—so much so that it no longer would have been immediately recognizable to the twelfth-century readers of Plato, Calcidius, Macrobius, Martianus, and Boethius.[215]

212 Ibid.: Alii ratiocinatione a radice exscisa super extractionem diruunt et dissipant. Dicunt igitur, ad assignatam causam recidendam, non unius corporis motum sine alicuius soliditatis occursu sonum grauare, ut in collisione malleoli et tintinnabuli. Vnde soni soliditati collisorum proportionantur. Inde est quod, corpore quantumlibet solido ad aera non nichil soliditatis habentem colliso, minimam sonoritatem educit, et deinceps in igne mini[mi]orem, in quinta denique essentia, totius corpulentie et soliditas immuni, nullam.

213 Ibid.: Sicque motui sublimium sonum sonorumque consonantiam omnimodo denuntiant. Quo interempto tota sequens ratiocinatio dissoluitur.

214 For an edition of Gerard of Cremona's translation of *De caelo* 2.9, see Paul Hossfeld, ed., *Alberti Magni De caelo et mundo, Alberti Magni Opera omnia* 5.1 (Münster: Aschendorff, 1971), 162–165 (primus apparatus).

215 See, for instance, Cecilia Panti, "Robert Grosseteste's Theory of Sound," in *Musik – und die Geschichte der Philosophie und Naturwissenschaften im Mittelalter*, 3–18; Gilles Rico, "Music in the Arts Faculty of Paris in Thirteenth and Early Fourteenth Centuries"; Gilles Rico, "*Auctoritas cereum habet nasum*: Boethius, Aristotle, and the Music of the Spheres in the Thirteenth and Early Fourteenth Centuries," in *Citation and Authority in Medieval and Renaissance Musical Culture*, 20–28; Gabriela Ilnitchi, "*Musica mundana*, Aristotelian Natural Philosophy and Ptolemaic Astronomy."

Postlude

The Musical Aesthetics of a World So Composed

Without a doubt there is a world soul.

—Gilles Deleuze, forward to Éric Alliez, *Capital Times: Tales from the Conquest of Time*, xii.

For me the question is not whether disenchantment is a regrettable or a progressive historical development. It is, rather, whether the very characterization of the world as disenchanted ignores and then discourages affective attachment to that world.

—Jane Bennett, *The Enchantment of Modern Life*, 4

"The cosmos is an ordered collection of all created entities." We have come a long way from the introduction of this claim at the outset of this book, and we are now in a position to recognize that—as it was enacted, theorized, and realized in twelfth-century natural philosophy—it seeks not to describe a set of static objects of which the world is comprised and to which the world could be reduced. Rather, the claim articulates an ever-unfolding *process* of continual (re)harmonization in accord with a "preestablished harmony" that is discernible at every level of the macro- and microcosmic world. The ever-unfolding order plays within (in the language of Deleuze and Guattari) "a pure plane of immanence, univocality, composition, upon which everything is given, upon which unformed elements and materials dance" as they "enter into this or that individuated assemblage depending on their connections, their relations of movement."[1] It plays within the animated mechanism, or the enmattered vitalism, on the plane of *natura naturans* and *natura naturata* (Chapter 1), and the textualized and discursive aggregate of the known and the knowable in the encyclopedic divisions of philosophy (Chapter 2). It plays between the individual soul and the instrumentalized body (Chapter 3), between *artifex natura* and the sonic, material realities of the

[1] Gilles Deleuze and Félix Guattari, *A Thousand Plateaus: Capitalism and Schizophrenia*, trans. Brian Massumi (Minneapolis: University of Minnesota Press, 1987), 255.

human voice and its instrumental imitations (Chapter 4), and between the universal body, the *mundanum corpus*; the universal soul, *anima mundi*; and the sight unheard of the *musica caelestis* (Chapter 5). The material universe, this ordered collection of creation, realizes its unity in a collective melodic gesture, "such that all of Nature becomes an immense melody and flow of bodies," in the words of Deleuze, deliberately echoing Uexküll.[2] Despite Ronald Bogue's claim that "in virtually every regard, Deleuze and Guattari's treatment of music is the antithesis of the traditional, Platonic approach to the subject,"[3] their absorption and rescription of Uexküll's melodious *Umwelten* (in the vocabulary of milieus, refrains, and (de)territorialization) nonetheless inscribes them within the tradition of a musically animate cosmos: "the universe, the cosmos, is made of refrains; . . . the question is more what is not musical in human beings, and what already is musical in nature."[4] Bogue deems this constellation of concepts a grand "*natura musicans.*"[5] His (pseudo-)Latin neologism (*musicans*), however, simultaneously calls attention to and effectively effaces its historical pedigree.[6] In its *Nachleben* it can only be a dead metaphor.

But for twelfth-century natural philosophers, as well as for the heirs of Uexküll's melodious *Umwelten*, the harmony of the world is more than just a (dead) metaphor, more than just a harmony in name or (merely) analogy: it is harmony as life, in and through its very mode of existence. Maurice Merleau-Ponty, too, recognized the power of Uexküll's formulation: "'Every organism,' said Uexküll, 'is a melody that sings itself.' This is not to say that it knows this melody and attempts to realize it; it is only to say that it is a whole which is significant for a consciousness which knows it, not a thing which rests in itself."[7] Merleau-Ponty's musical metaphors, as Brett Buchanan has observed, encompass both the world and the organism's situatedness within the world.[8] "The world, in those of its sectors which realize a structure," Merleau-Ponty opines in good Uexküllian fashion, "is

[2] Gilles Deleuze, *The Fold: Leibniz and the Baroque*, trans. Tom Conley (London: Athlone Press, 1993), 135.

[3] Ronald Bogue, *Deleuze on Music, Painting, and the Arts* (New York: Routledge, 2003), 16.

[4] Deleuze and Guattari, *A Thousand Plateaus*, 309.

[5] Ibid., 75.

[6] Bogue would not have found *musico, musicare*—presumably meaning "to make music"—in any readily available ancient or medieval source, and I think it safe to say he was unaware of its two known attestations in Lambertus Ardensis and an anonymous life of S. Landelinus (Abbas). Aside from these, I know of no use before Nietzsche's pet phrase: *in rebus musicis et musicantibus*.

[7] Maurice Merleau-Ponty, *The Structure of Behavior*, trans. Alden Fischer (Pittsburgh: Duquesne University Press, 1983), 159. Cf. Merleau-Ponty, *La nature*, ed. Dominique Séglard (Paris 1995), 228: Quand nous inventons une mélodie, la mélodie se chante en nous beaucoup plus que nous ne la chantons; elle descend dans la gorge du chanteur, comme le dit Proust. De même que le peintre est frappé par un tableau qui n'est pas là, le corps est suspendu á ce qu'il chante, la mélodie s'incarne et trouve en lui une espèce de servant.

[8] Brett Buchanan, *Onto-Ethologies: The Animal Environments of Uexküll, Heidegger, Merleau-Ponty, and Deleuze* (Albany: SUNY Press, 2008), 115ff.

comparable to a symphony, and knowledge of the world is thus accessible by two paths: one can note the correspondence of the notes played at a same moment by the different instruments and the succession of those played by each one of them."[9] Elsewhere, however, Merleau-Ponty entertains and denies the possibility that the organism is a musical instrument played upon by the world; in fact the organism is a part of the larger worldly instrument, the *machina mundi* as the cosmologist might put it: "The organism cannot properly be compared to a keyboard on which the external stimuli would play and in which their proper form would be delineated for the simple reason that the organism contributes to the constitution of that form."[10] As Buchanan comments, "As opposed to a keyboard, which can be played only by external stimuli, organisms actively contribute to the melody itself. In other words, an organism is not a passive instrument that is excited and stimulated in a reactive manner but a form that sings itself."[11] In still other words: "Music *is* life; life *is* music. Empirical music-making on earth (the music we know historically, geographically, and socially) is one with the expressive living of all life, but is not essential for life to be musical."[12] With these words, Michael Gallope "sums up" Deleuze and Guattari's claims on a musical metaphysics. They would do equally for twelfth-century cosmology.

But this also entails that it is subject to the same critique: "the metaphysical philosophy of music comes with its own shortcomings. Most obviously, by simply affirming music to be one with life, it seems to say *hardly anything specific or interesting about music*. It eliminates the particular mediation of actual music, of any actual exemplars. It specifies little more than the generic musical components of rhythm, meter, and counterpoint."[13] This is a familiar complaint, made in widely disparate contexts. For instance, the famed eighteenth-century music historian Charles Burney, in an article on "Chinese Music" for Abraham Rees's *Cyclopaedia or Universal Dictionary of Arts, Sciences, and Literature*, claims to have been informed (by Père Amiot) that "the Chinese were probably the nation in the world that has best known harmony, and most universally observed its laws." But Burney presses his informant further, "what is this harmony?" The answer:

> "It is that which consists in the general accord of all things natural, moral, and political, including whatever constitutes religion and government; an accord of which the science of sound is only the representation and the image." So that the expressions concerning this divine

[9] Merleau-Ponty, *The Structure of Behavior*, 132.

[10] Ibid., 13.

[11] Buchanan, *Onto-Ethologies*, 124.

[12] Michael Gallope, "The Sound of Repeating Life: Ethics and Metaphysics in Deleuze's Philosophy of Music," in *Sounding the Virtual: Gilles Deleuze and the Theory and Philosophy of Music*, ed. Brian Hulse and Nick Nesbitt (Farnham: Ashgate Publishing Limited, 2010), 89.

[13] Ibid., 102 (emphasis in original).

> music, of which the learned missionary and the Abbé Roussier have laboured so much to explain the laws, are only allegorical and figurative! . . . we find that it was an allegorical music, as inaudible as that of the spheres.[14]

Lawrence Gushee, in a passage cited already in the prologue to this study, complains of the same, albeit in a more sober tone: "It would seem . . . from the situation in Chartres, that while Music's position in the liberal arts was strong, the texts used may rarely have had relevance to the practical concerns of standard plain-chant. The notorious (neo) Platonism of the intellectuals of Chartres must have something to do with this."[15] Frustratingly, maddeningly, liberatingly, the musical cosmos refuses to be concretized and pinned down.

Let me give one example of a tantalizing but still frustratingly elusory attempt, by the twelfth-century cosmologists themselves, to touch on "the practical concerns of standard plain-chant." The context is a single remark by Macrobius (at *In Som. Scip.* 2.3.5), who informs us that the ancients sang metrical hymns to the gods with "strophes and antistrophes" (*per stropham et antistropham*); the *stropha* indicated the regularity of the fixed stars, the *antistropha* the contrary wandering of the planets.[16] Numerous glossators and commentators took the bait and related Macrobius's "hymns to the gods" (despite that pesky plural) to the Christian liturgy. An anonymous twelfth-century gloss in London, British Library, Harley 2633 (45r) is one such instance:

> VT PER STROPHA. Stropha fit quando finito ⟨uersu⟩ replicamus responsorium a medio; anti⟨s⟩tropha dicitur contraria conuersio, quando responsorium non a medio sed a principio replicamus. Inde etiam dicitur antiphona quasi contrarius sonus, quia finito ⟨p⟩salmo a principio replicatur. Aliter: stropha est quando responsorium cantatur et uersus usque ad finem, antiphona uero quando resumimus regres⟨s⟩um. Et sic aplanos habet cantans stropham ab oriente in occidente⟨m⟩, alie septem stelle antistropham.[17]

[14] [Charles Burney], "Chinese Music" in Abraham Rees, with the assistance of eminent professional gentlemen, *The Cyclopædia, Or, Universal Dictionary of Arts, Sciences, and Literature*, 1st American Edition (Philadelphia: Samuel Bradford and Murray, Fairman and Co., [1805?–1825?]), vol. 8, s.v. "Chinese music" [unpaginated].

[15] Gushee, "Questions of Genre in Medieval Treatises on Music," 423.

[16] *In Som. Scip.* 2.3.5 (104.23–26): in ipsis quoque hymnis deorum per stropham et antistropham metra canoris versibus adhibebantur ut per stropham rectus orbis stelliferi motus, per antistropham diversus vagarum regressus praedicaretur.

[17] Cf. Oxford, Lincoln College Library, lat. 27, f. 148v (heavily trimmed): ⟨stro⟩pha est conuersio, ut quando conuer⟨sio⟩ de responsorio ad uer⟨sum⟩; antistropha ut quando iterum ⟨conuersio⟩ de uersu ad responsorium, ⟨uel ad⟩ totum uel ad partem. A similar explanation is offered in the *Glos. Colonienses sup. Macr.*, comment. ad 2.3.5 (261.1–7): STROPHON dicimus conversionem, quia dum sacrificia circuirent

AS THROUGH STROPHES. A "strophe" occurs when, upon completing the verse, we repeat the responsory from the middle; "antistrophe," meaning a "contrary conversion," [occurs] when we repeat the responsory not from the middle but from the beginning. Thence, too, is the term antiphon, meaning "contrary sound," because, upon completing the psalm, it is repeated from the beginning. In another way: a "strophe" is when the responsory and verse are sung through to the end; an "antiphon" is when we resume the repeat. So too the sphere of the fixed stars, as it sings, makes a strophe from rising [east] to setting [west], while the other seven stars complete the antistrophe.

A more intriguing variation on this gloss is found in an interpolated version of William of Conches's *Glosae super Macrobium* in Copenhagen, Det Kongelige Bibliotek, Gl. Kgl. Sammlung 1910 4°, f. 112r:

> Stropha dicitur simplex conuersio, et est stropha recta conuersio cantus quando fit sine organo. Antistropha est contraria conuersio quando organum cantui adhibetur, quia dum cantus extollitur, organum deprimitur et e conuerso. Vnde cantus ymnorum inuentus est per stropham et antistropham ad sonum firmamenti et planetarum qui contra celi conuersionem uoluuntur. Vnde quidam cantus solebant esse in eccelsia quos uocant strophas.
>
> "Strophe" means "simple conversion," and strophe is the straightforward conversion of a chant, when it is performed (*fit*) without *organum*. Antistrophe is a contrary conversion, when *organum* is added to a chant, because when the chant lifts on high, the *organum* (organal voice?) dips low, and vice versa. Whence hymns were invented throught the strophe and antistrophe in accordance with the sound of the firmament and the planets, which revolve in the opposite direction to the turning of the heavens. Whence some chants are generally used in church, which are called strophes.

There is not much to go on here. Since the tantalizing reference to *organum* occurs only in the interpolated version of William's commentary,[18] it is difficult to

naturali circuitu, strophan cantabant, per quam motum firmamenti designabant. Cum autem per eandem circuitionem reverterentur, ANTISTROPHAN cantabant id est contrarium strophae, ut per regressum motum planetarum significarent. Vel per "strophan" processum in cantu ut in responsorio; per "antistrophan" reciprocationem ut in antiphona post versum, inde dicitur antiphona quasi contrarius sonus, quia finito psalmo a principio replicatur. Similar glosses are found in other manuscripts, on which see Peden, "Music in Medieval Commentaries on Macrobius," 155.

[18] In the *uersio breuior* (*iuxta* Bamberg, Staatliche Bibl., Class. 40 [H.J.IV.21]) and *uersio longior* (*iuxta* Bibl. Apostolica Vaticana, Urb. lat. 1140) the gloss reads: PER STROPHAM ET ANTISTROPHAM. Stropha dicitur "simplex conuersio," antistropha "contra simplicem conuersionem." Vnde cantus hymnorum

localize the precise context of this remark. It seems highly probable that William (if these lines are by William) would have been familiar with the performance of *organum*, an a cappella polyphonic practice, as it resounded *in choro sanctae Mariae* (whether Notre Dame of Chartres or Notre Dame of Paris) in the early- to mid-twelfth century.[19] Of course, he may also be speaking of an organ, but this would be surprising, as there is very little evidence for the liturgical use of the organ, nor did either Notre Dame have an organ in the twelfth century.[20] Laconic as it is, this description of *organum* suggests a firsthand knowledge of such a performance practice, or at least a familiarity with its theoretical descriptions. The Macrobian commentator's emphasis on contrary motion—"when the chant lifts on high, the organal voice dips low, and vice versa" (*dum cantus extollitur, organum deprimitur et e conuerso*)—closely echoes, both *ad sensum* and *ad litteram*, the description of *diaphonia* in Johannes Affligemensis's *De musica:* "wherever there is an ascent in the original melody, there is at that point a descent in the organal part and vice versa" (*ubi in recta modulatione est elevatio, ibi in organica fiat depositio et e converso*).[21] But whether we can attribute this gloss directly to William of Conches, and where the author might have gained such knowledge (Chartres? Paris?), remain unknown and, it must be admitted, unknowable. The gloss is a one-off, and we have no more to go on.[22]

Such moments are few and far between, and even at their most specific, they "specify little more than the generic musical components of rhythm, meter, and

inuentus est per stropham et antistropham ad sonum firmamenti et planetarum qui contra caeli conuersionem uoluuntur. Vnde quidam cantus solebant esse in ecclesia quos uocabant strophas. On the interpolated commentary, see Helen Rodnite, "The Doctrine of the Trinity in Guillaume de Conches' Glosses on Macrobius: Texts and Studies" (PhD diss., Columbia University, 1972), 79–91, and Caiazzo, *Glosae Colonienses super Macrobium*, 67.

[19] William himself refers to "in choro sanctae Mariae" in his *Glosulae de Magno Prisciano, Versio prior* (Florence, Biblioteca Laurenziana, San Marco 310, 63vb). The twelfth-century performance of *organum* in both churches is documented, respectively, in the Chartrian *Ordo veridicus*, on which see Margot Fassler, *Gothic Song: Victorine Sequences and Augustinian Reform in Twelfth-Century Paris* (Cambridge: Cambridge University Press, 1993), 87–91, and the various *testimonia* assembled by Michel Huglo in "Les débuts de la polyphonie à Paris: Les premiers organa parisiens," *Forum Musicologicum: Basler Beiträge zur Musikgeschichte* 3 (1982), 93–163; see also Craig Wright, *Music and Ceremony at Notre Dame of Paris, 500–1150* (Cambridge: Cambridge University Press, 2008), 235–272.

[20] See Wright, *Music and Ceremony*, 143–144.

[21] Waesberghe, *Johannes Affligemenisis, De musica cum tonario*, 160.

[22] The more generic version of this gloss (*sine organo*) had a long afterlife, however. It found its way into the *Magnae Derivationes* by the twelfth-century Bolognese grammarian Huguccio of Pisa (ed. Enzo Cecchini and Guido Arbizzoni [Florence: SISMEL edizioni del Galluzzo, 2004], 1183–1184 [S 333]), through which it resurfaced later in the *Commentum Oxoniense in musicam Boethii* (ed. Matthias Hochadel, 40.7–14) and in Jacobus of Liège's *Speculum musice* (6.35) as part of his etymological discussion of the term *tropi*, one of the three received names (along with *toni* and *modi*) for the musical modes (Roger Bragard, ed., *Jacobi Leodiensis Speculum musicae* [[Rome]: American Institute of Musicology, 1955–1973], 3.5: 87).

counterpoint."[23] The cosmic refrain is resolutely irreducible to any singular sonic experience, even as it echoes, perpetually, in the ping of hammers in a blacksmith's forge and in the ringdown of colliding black holes 1.2 billion light-years away. We cannot point to a single score, to a single performance, to a single sounding reality. The celestial *chorea*, as William of Conches described it, is for us only a silent dance, a sight unheard. A musico-cosmological aesthetics, it would seem, must take seriously the claim that only Pythagoras could hear the music of the spheres. For us earthbound cosmologists, there is an acoustic chasm between the resolute silence of the *machina mundi* and its power to enchant us, to instill a sense of cosmic affect—the sense of wonder, love, and desire to hear the harmony of the world. This gap has nevertheless grounded the enduring legacy of cosmic music, which has continually changed its tune to harmonize with the prevailing musical aesthetics of its aspirational auditors. For the fourteenth-century mathematician Nicole Oresme, the beauty of the cosmos is manifest in an irrational, incommensurable geometry that shuns the arithmetical, commensurable periodicity of the repetitive structures that dominated the musical soundscape of the fourteenth century.[24] For Johannes Kepler, cosmic polyphony is (partially) manifest in the musical spirit of Orlando di Lasso;[25] for Leibniz, in "Baroque harmonies";[26] for Alfred Whitehead, in the "Beauty" of a Romantically tinged Victorian Classicism;[27] for Gilles Deleuze, in the "dissipation of tonality" and its opening into "polyphony of polyphonies" in the atonality of Boulez;[28] etc. The tune will continue to change, but the appeal to aesthetics remains a constant. The cosmologist is basically an aesthete, to echo Shaviro's discussion of Alfred Whitehead's aesthetics: "For Whitehead, the aim of the world—which is to say, the 'subjective aim' of every entity within the world, God included—is Beauty, rather than Goodness or Truth (and also rather than Nietzschean will-to-power, or Darwinian

[23] Gallope, "The Sound of Repeating Life," 102.

[24] "What song would please that is frequently or oft repeated? Would not such uniformity [and repetition] produce disgust? It surely would, for novelty is more delightful. A singer who is unable to vary musical sounds, which are infinitely variable, would no longer be thought best, but [would be taken for] a cuckoo. Now if all the celestial motions are commensurable, and if the world were eternal, the same, or similar, motions and effects would necessarily be repeated." Edward Grant, *Nicole Oresme and the Kinematics of Circular Motion: Tractatus de commensurabilitate vel incommensurabilitate motuum celi* (Madison: University of Wisconsin Press, 1971), 316–317.

[25] See Peter Pesic, "Earthly Music and Cosmic Harmony: Johannes Kepler's Interest in Practical Music, Especially Orlando di Lasso," *Journal of Seventeenth-Century Music* 11 (2005), http://www.sscm jscm.org/v11/no1/pesic.html.

[26] See Deleuze, *The Fold*, 121–137.

[27] See Steven Shaviro, *Without Criteria: Kant, Whitehead, Deleuze, and Aesthetics* (Cambridge, MA: MIT Press, 2009), 153: "Whitehead's own aesthetics of beauty and harmony, with its emphasis on 'subjective forms . . . severally and jointly interwoven in patterned contrasts' (1933/1967, 252), has an oddly retrograde, Victorian cast to it, and seems out of touch with the strenuous art of his modernist contemporaries and their successors."

[28] See Gallope, "The Sound of Repeating Life," 98–102.

self-replication). 'Any system of things which in any wide sense is beautiful is to that extent justified in its existence.'"[29]

The same is true, I argue, for the musical aesthetics of medieval cosmology. Let us return to Boethius's *musica mundana*:[30]

> Et primum ea, quae est mundana, in his maxime perspicienda est, quae in ipso caelo vel compage elementorum vel temporum varietate visuntur.
>
> First is *musica mundana*, which is especially evident in things observed in heaven itself, in the union of the elements, or in the variety of the seasons.

The first thing to be noted is the predominantly visual, not auditory, orientation of Boethius's description of *musica mundana*: it is a harmony that is above all observed (*perspicienda*), not heard (*audienda*), in things which are seen (*uisuntur*) in the heavens, the elements, and the seasons. A similar emphasis on the visibility of cosmic harmony inaugurates the *Consolatio philosophiae*. Lady Philosophy, stressing a "once"/"but now" (*quondam/nunc*) antithesis in her initial assessment of Boethius's ailment, frames her remarks in terms of the direction of the prisoner's gaze (*cernebat, uisebat, cernere*):[31]

> This man used once to wander free under open skies
> The paths of the heavens; used to gaze
> On rosy sunlight, and on the constellations
> Of the cold new moon,
> And on each star that on its wandering ways
> Turns through its changing circles—all such things
> He mastered and comprehended by number. . . .
> But now he lies
> His mind's light languishing,

[29] Shaviro, *Without Criteria*, 152 (quoting Whitehead, *Adventures of Ideas* [New York: The Free Press, 1933/1967]).

[30] *Inst. mus.* 1.2 (187.23–26).

[31] *Cons. phil.* 1.m2.6–12, 24–27: Hic quondam caelo liber aperto / suetus in aetherios ire meatus / cernebat rosei lumina solis, / uisebat gelidae sidera lunae / et quaecumque uagos stella recursus / exercet uarios flexa per orbes / comprensam numeris uictor habebat. / . . . / nunc iacet effeto lumine mentis / et pressus grauibus colla catenis / decliuemque gerens pondere uultum / cogitur, heu, stolidam cernere terram. Here I follow the translation of Tester in the Loeb Boethius. Cf. Joachim Gruber, *Kommentar zu Boethius, De consolatione philosophiae*, 2nd ed. (Berlin and New York: Walter de Gruyter, 2006), 82–83, who marshals numerous parallels to *mersa profundo mens*, including *Inst. ar.* 1.1 (11.66): oculum demersum.

Bowed with these heavy chains about his neck,
His eyes cast down beneath the weight of care,
Seeing nothing
But the dull, solid earth.

At *Cons. phil.* 1.m5, Boethius circles back again to the cosmic cycle of the heavens and the seasons, now in order to contrast the harmony of the heavens with the tyrannical disorder wrought by both *reges* and *fortuna*. As John Magee notes, however, Boethius's poetic evocation of the seasonal round[32] "is beautifully expressed, . . . but it is not philosophical."[33] The same could be said of the *descriptio caeli* that inaugurates the poem:[34]

O Maker of the circle of the stars,
Seated on your eternal throne,
Spinner of the whirling heavens,
Binding the constellations by your law. . .

It is enough for Boethius (at this point in the *Consolatio*, at least) to establish the simplicity and stability of divine governance in rhetorical terms, without any detailed appeal to the philosophical *ratio* which would necessarily underpin such a cosmology. The opening appeal to the *descriptio caeli et temporum* is but a setup for the prisoner's punchline:[35]

Look on this wretched earth,
Whoever you are who bind the world with law! . . .
Ruler, restrain their rushing waves and make the earth
Steady with that stability of law
By which you rule the vastness of the heavens!

Cosmic order and tyrannical disorder are, on at least one level, predominantly visual affairs.

David Chamberlain's influential article "Philosophy of Music in the *Consolatio* of Boethius" synthesizes the various expressions of *musica mundana* in the

[32] *Cons. phil.* 1.m5.18–24: Tua uis uarium temperat annum, / ut quas Boreae spiritus aufert / reuehat mites Zehyrus frondes, / quaeque Arcturus semina uidit / Sirius altas urat segetes: / nihil antiqua lege solutum / linquit propriae stationis opus.

[33] Magee, "Boethius' Anapestic Dimeters," 155–156.

[34] *Cons. phil.* 1.m5.1–4: O stelliferi conditor orbis, / qui perpetuo nixus solio / rapido caelum turbine uersas / legemque pati sidera cogis. . .

[35] *Cons. phil.* 1.m5.42–48: O iam miseras respice terras / quisquis rerum foedera nectis! / . . . / Rapidos, rector, comprime fluctus / et quo caelum regis immersum / firma stabiles foedere terras!

Consolatio, concluding that, although it does not "appear in the *Consolatio* by name," it nevertheless "permeates implicitly the imagery and thought of the work, and appears with the same major subdivisions as in the *De musica*, the musics [sic] of the stars, the elements, and the seasons."[36] To suggest as Chamberlain does, however, that Boethius would have countenanced a fourth species of music, "divine music" (*diuina musica*), is to succumb to the self-perpetuating logic of scholastic *divisiones* and to miss, ultimately, the message of Boethius's philosophical reply to the initial visualization of cosmic harmony in divine governance and the seemingly erratic disharmony wrought by *fortuna* and tyrants.[37] Magee's study of the four acatalectic anapestic dimeters—1.m5, 3.m2, 4.m6, and 5.m3, all of which chiastically circle the central themes of *musica mundana* (celestial, elemental, seasonal harmonies)[38]—reveals "Boethius' subtlest mode of poetic 'argument.'"[39] As Magee subtly argues, these metra gradually "mend the rift," break down the "flawed dichotomy" between the celestial and terrestrial domains, and offer a means of "making phenomenal particulars universal and intelligible, of coordinating them with the pattern."[40] This pattern (variously *series, modus, ordo*), which Chamberlain wants us to call *diuina musica*, already has a (Boethian) name, for in the discussion of *fatum et fortuna* in book 4, Boethius explains how it is, in fact, Divine Providence, in its worldly, temporal guise as Fate, that maintains both the balance of the cosmic cycle (which amounts to a *musica mundana*) and the actions and fortunes of men (*actus fortunasque hominum*):[41]

> Ea series caelum ac sidera movet, elementa in se invicem temperat et alterna commutatione transformat, eadem nascentia occidentiaque omnia per similes fetum seminumque renovat progressus. Haec actus etiam fortunasque hominum indissolubili causarum connexione constringit; quae cum ab immobilis providentiae proficiscatur exordiis,

[36] David Chamberlain, "Philosophy of Music in the *Consolatio* of Boethius," in *Boethius*, ed. Manfred Fuhrmann and Joachim Gruber (Darmstadt: Wissenschaftliche Buchgesellschaft, 1984), 386.

[37] Ibid., 401–402: "Going even farther beyond *De musica*, Boethius also embodies in the *Consolatio* a fourth species of music, *divina musica*, that which exists in God, and by which He first creates and thereafter maintains world music. . . . If Boethius had written his musical treatise later in his career, after rather than before the tractates and *Consolatio*, he might well have added this fourth species of his classification." Cf. Gersh, *Concord in Discourse*, 43: "such observations [on the development or extension of Boethius's tripartite division] take a form scarcely concealing that indwelling tendency to systematic proliferation present from the very beginning."

[38] See, in particular, Magee's commentary on 1.m5 and 4.m6 in "Boethius' Anapestic Dimeters," 155–162.

[39] Ibid., 168.

[40] Ibid., 160, 167–168.

[41] *Cons. phil.* 4.p6.18–21.

> ipsas quoque immutabiles esse necesse est. Ita enim res optime reguntur, si manens in divina mente simplicitas indeclinabilem causarum ordinem promat, hic vero ordo res mutabiles et alioquin temere fluituras propira incommutibilitate coerceat. Quo fit ut tametsi vobis, hunc ordinem minime considerare valentibus, confusa omnia perturbataque videantur, nihilo minus tamen suus modus ad bonum dirigens cuncta disponat.

> This chain [of fate] moves the heavens and the stars, proportionally mingles the elements with each other, transforms them in their alternating changes, and renews the cycle of generation and corruption through the similar progress of offspring and seeds. Moreover, it constrains the actions and fortunes of men by an insoluble connection of causes. Since this insoluble connection originates in unchangeable Providence, it is necessary that these causes be likewise unchangeable. For reality is best ruled when the simplicity that abides in the Divine Mind inaugurates an unvarying sequence of causes, but this sequence with its own immutability constrains mutable reality, which would otherwise randomly dissipate. So although all things may seem confused and perturbed to you, because you are entirely unable to grasp this sequence, all things nonetheless have their own pattern (*modus*), which orders and directs them toward the good.

Unchanging Divine Providence is thus the sole and single principle of changeable reality, both the cyclical patterning of the *musica mundana* and the eternal turn of the *rota fortunae*.[42] In his early quadrivial works, Boethius had given another name to this "simplicity that abides in the divine mind" (*manens in divina mente simplicitas*): arithmetic. The priority of arithmetic is not merely propaedeutic; it

[42] *Cons. phil.* 2.p1.19: Tu uero uoluentis rotae impetum retinere conaris? At, omnium mortalium stolidissime, si manere incipit fors esse desistit. At *Cons. phil.* 4.p6.13, Boethius goes so far as to suggest that the temporal realization of Fate, the unfolding of Divine Providence, may even be (or somehow be related to) the *anima mundi*, but the suggestion is made only in passing, as one in a long list of competing options that includes divine spirits, nature, the heavens, angels, and demons: Siue igitur famulantibus quibusdam prouidentiae diuinis spiritibus fatum exercetur seu anima seu tota inseruiente natura seu caelestibus siderum motibus seu angelica uirtute seu daemonum uaria sollertia seu aliquibus horum seu omnibus fatalis series texitur. On which list, see Gruber, *Kommentar*, 349–350. Cf. *In Perih.* II.231.11–232.10. Calcidius minimizes the relation between the *anima mundi* and *fatum*, arguing (*In Tim.* 144 [182.16–183.1]): At uero in substantia positum fatum mundi anima est tripertita in aplanem sphaeram inque eam, quae putatur erratica, et in sublunarem tertiam. See Jan Den Boeft, *Calcidius on Fate: His Doctrine and Sources* (Leiden: Brill, 1970), 9–13. At *In Tim.* 147 (184.22–185.2) Calcidius returns to the same theme: Ipsae uero leges quae dictae sunt fatum est idque diuina lex est mundi animae insinuata, salubre rerum omnium. Sic fatum quidem ex prouidentia est nec tamen ex fato prouidentia. As Martijn points out (*Proclus on Nature*, 34), Proclus rejects the identification of Fate and the world soul in his remarks on the Myth of Er (*In Remp.* II 357.7–27).

is the very exemplar in the divine mind from which the world was brought into being: "God, the creator of this worldly mass, held arithmetic first as exemplar of reasoning, and established all things according to its patterns by which everything, rationally formed through numbers of assigned order, found concord."[43] Thus the realization of the cosmic realm, the supremely ordered structure of the universe, proceeds from the (noetic) number that resides in the divine (or, perhaps, demiurgic) *paradeigma*.[44] A similar exemplarism, without the specification of arithmetic, characterizes the famous Timaean hymn that forms the cardinal point of the entire *Consolatio*:[45]

> from a heavenly pattern
> You draw out all things, and being yourself most beautiful,
> A beautiful world in your mind you bear, and forming it
> In the same likeness, bid it being perfect to complete itself in
> perfect parts.

In this poetic epitome of the *Timaeus* (cf. *Tim.* 29b2–d3), Boethius elliptically compresses the Timaean *psychogonia* and its concordant implications:[46]

> You, binding soul together in its threefold nature's midst,
> Soul that moves all things, then divide it into harmonious parts;
> Soul thus divided has its motions gathered
> Into two circles, moves to return into itself, and the Mind deep within
> Encircles, and makes the heaven turn, in likeness to itself.

It is as much the placement as it is the content of these lines that underscores their importance within the *Consolatio* and Boethius's philosophical outlook generally—as has often been remarked, they form the center point of the central metrum of the entire *Consolatio*.[47] These innermost lines thus explode outward, both intra- and intertextually. It is this cosmic exemplarism, which remained (as

[43] *Inst. ar.* 1.1 (12.76–79): hanc [sc. arithmeticam] ille huius mundanae molis conditor deus primam suae habuit ratiocinationis exemplar et ad hanc cuncta constituit, quaecunque fabricante ratione per numeros adsignati ordinis invenere concordiam.

[44] Cf. *Intr. ar.* 1.6.1 (12.1–12).

[45] *Cons. phil.* 3.m9.6–9: tu cuncta superno / ducis ab exemplo, pulchrum pulcherrimus ipse / mundum mente gerens similique in imagine formans / perfectasque iubens perfectum absoluere partes. See Gruber, *Kommentar*, 279–280.

[46] *Cons. phil.* 3.m9.13–17. Tu triplicis mediam naturae cuncta mouentem / conectens animam per consona membra resoluis / quae cum secta duos motum glomerauit in orbes, / in semet reditura meat mentemque profundam / circuit et simili conuertit imagine caelum. See Gruber, *Kommentar*, 281–282 for parallels with the *Timaeus* and Neoplatonic commentaries.

[47] Gruber, *Kommentar*, 22–24, with the fold-out table between 20 and 21; Magee, "Boethius' Anapestic Dimeters," 151, with further literature cited in n. 15.

we have seen) a primary theme in twelfth-century cosmology, that allows us to suggest one solution to the problem of the "aesthetics" of "scientific" medieval cosmology.

The aesthetics of science has been particularly contested ground since Thomas Kuhn's strong reintroduction of aesthetic criteria into the domain of the history of science in his 1957 study of the Copernican Revolution. Kuhn claims that the Copernican theory could not have toppled Ptolemy's theory on the grounds of either predictive accuracy or simplicity: "judged on purely practical grounds, Copernicus' new planetary system was a failure; it was neither more accurate nor significantly simpler than its Ptolemaic predecessors."[48] Rather, Kuhn argues that the Copernican theory gained subscribers on the strength of its *aesthetic* properties:

> Each argument cites an aspect of the appearances that can be explained by *either* the Ptolemaic *or* the Copernican system, and each then proceeds to point out how much more harmonious, coherent, and natural the Copernican explanation is. . . . New harmonies did not increase accuracy or simplicity. Therefore they could and did appeal primarily to that limited and perhaps irrational subgroup of mathematical astronomers whose Neoplatonic ear for mathematical harmonies could not be obstructed by page after page of complex mathematics leading finally to numerical predictions scarcely better than those they had known before.[49]

Although Kuhn tempered his appeal to aesthetic criteria in *The Structure of Scientific Revolutions* (1962) and *The Essential Tension* (1977), favoring instead a heuristic "fruitfulness" (a concession to his arch-critic Imre Lakatos), he nonetheless continued to smuggle in aesthetic appeals. The subsequent debate about the aesthetics of science has largely limited itself to the realm of "theory choice" and "paradigm shifts" (aka "scientific revolutions"). James W. McAllister, for instance, has recently offered "aesthetic induction" as a post-Kuhnian answer to the question of how we can assess the role of aesthetic factors in theory choice. On this view, aesthetic valuations dovetail on empirical valuations. McAllister explains "aesthetic induction" as follows. A given scientific community "perceives that some theories, which are to a notable degree visualizing (rather than abstract) theories, have been empirically successful, whereas others, which lend themselves to mechanistic analogies, have won little empirical success. Both visualization and tractability by mechanistic analogies are aesthetic properties of theories. In consequence of the empirical success of the visualizing theories, the property of

[48] Thomas Kuhn, *The Copernican Revolution: Planetary Astronomy in the Development of Western Thought* (Cambridge, MA: Harvard University Press, 1957), 171.

[49] Ibid., 181.

visualization will obtain an increased weighting in the aesthetic canon for theory evaluation that the community will hereafter apply."[50] Crucially, McAllister denies that aesthetic properties of theories are intrinsic to the theories themselves, and claims that they are instead projected onto the theory by a scientific community. Thus, the evaluative aesthetic canon employed by a given community is historically contingent and thereby evades any ahistorical claim that "beauty/simplicity entails truth," a view which has recently been rechristened a "Pythagorean metaphysics" by Mark Steiner and Sorin Bangu.[51] For McAllister's "aesthetic induction" to succeed, it makes no difference what aesthetic properties are initially projected; his inductive sorting procedure ensures that aesthetic factors with a higher degree of empirical valuation will win the day, at least until the next revolution in the community's "aesthetic canon."[52]

I want to close this study by reframing the question of intrinsic versus extrinsic aesthetic properties and advancing the view, already hinted at above, that for medieval cosmology the aesthetic properties of a theory are, and must be, deeply intrinsic to the relational properties of the phenomena, which encompass *both* the observed *and* the observer. The harmony is located not in its theoretical representation but somehow in the configuration of the phenomena themselves and the perspectives of their observers. Understood in this way, the aesthetics of medieval cosmology is not an inductive aesthetics of "theory-choice" but rather the very condition of possibility for theory itself.

Here, Steven Shaviro's imaginative "alternative world" of a philosophy after Whitehead can help; indeed, it exemplifies the very solution to the problem that I see at work in medieval cosmology. The watchword for Shaviro, as for Whitehead, is "Beauty," which arises as a *process* between perceiver and perceived, the aesthete and aestheticized. Shaviro's example is the orchid and the wasp, but it may as well be the cosmos and the *physicus*: Beauty does not inhere in an orchid, and neither is it a pure projection onto the orchid by a wasp; instead it comes about as a relation between the two or through an "aparallel evolution" of them.[53] Something similar happens to the *physicus* who encounters the cosmos. Each, in a way, is indifferent to the other, yet each is inextricably implicated in the constitution of the other (compare Friedrich Schelling's famous declaration at the outset of the *First Outline:* "To philosophise about nature is to create nature").[54] At root it is a problem of ground: *il n'y a pas de hors-musique* (with apologies to Derrida). There is no *punctum Archimedis* with which an external aesthetics could be leveraged, for

[50] James W. McAllister, *Beauty and Revolution in Science* (Ithaca: Cornell University Press, 1996), 78–79.

[51] Mark Steiner, *The Applicability of Mathematics as a Philosophical Problem* (Cambridge, MA: Harvard University Press, 1998); Sorin Bangu, "Pythagorean Heuristic in Physics," *Perspectives on Science* 14 (2006), 387–416.

[52] McAllister, *Beauty and Revolution* 85–86.

[53] Shaviro, *Without Criteria*, 2–4.

[54] Iain Hamilton Grant, *Philosophies of Nature after Schelling* (London: Continuum, 2006), 166.

the "pre-established harmony" of both microcosmic observer and macrocosmic observed is the same. Kepler states it most clearly and succinctly:

> God is the creator of all nature, and in this contrivance (*machinatio*) he took care for the future of humankind; accordingly this worldly theater was so ordered that there would appear in it appropriate signs by which the minds of humans, simulacra of God, would not only be induced to contemplate the divine works, from which they could judge the goodness of the Creator, but would also be helped to investigate them through and through.[55]

Kepler's God (like Plato's Demiurge, like Whitehead's God, like Boethius's *Rector*, etc.) is as aesthete who takes pleasure in the beauty of his creation: "Just as God the Creator has played, so He has taught Nature, His image, to play, and indeed to play the same as He has played before Her. . . . Accordingly, as God and Nature have played before, so must this playing after of the human mind be no foolish child's game, but a natural instinct implanted by God."[56] Heliocentric or geocentric, the aesthetic, as well as the epistemic, attitude it expresses is the same: "Providentially located in the cosmos, and mentally informed by the geometrical archetypes, we can rest assured that our aesthetic responses are reliable guides to the deepest truths about the fabric of the world."[57]

The musical aesthetics of medieval cosmology is the cosmos listening to itself. And the articulation of this theory is an act of "overhearing" that seeks to capture, if only mimetically, that self-reflexive experience. Moreover, recognizing the mimetic character of the musical aesthetics of theory versus the "real" intermaterial harmony of the cosmos (or the noetic harmony of its paradigm) underscores the difference, the *dis-analogy*, between theory and reality. To posit a musical aesthetics of medieval cosmology is to offer (paraphrasing Reviel Netz) an intellectually systematic correlate of the inexpressible and unheard—it is to literalize an epistemologically motivated analogy without losing its analogical force.[58] The real aesthetics of a "Pythagorean metaphysics" is not that the truth *is* beautiful but that it can be *perceived* (or can perceive itself) as beautiful. It

55 Johannes Kepler, *Astronomiae pars optica*, in *Gesammelte Werke*, ed. Max Caspar, Franz Hammer et al. (Munich: C. H. Beck, 1937–), vol. 2, 16.6–11; qtd. and trans. in Nick Jardine, "Kepler, God, and the Virtues of Copernican Hypotheses," in *Nouveau ciel, nouvelle terre: La révolution copernicienne dans l'Allemagne de la Réforme (1530–1630)*, ed. Miguel Ángel Granada and Édouard Mehl (Paris: Les Belles Lettres, 2009), 275.

56 Kepler, *Gesammelte Werke*, vol. 4, 246.23–24 and 32–38; qtd. and trans. in Jardine, "Kepler, God, and the Virtues of Copernican Hypotheses," 276.

57 Ibid.

58 "Thus proportion-statements are the most natural route to be taken by the Pythagoreans. Their project was to offer an intellectually systematic correlate of a mystery practice—as it were, to literalize metaphor without losing its metaphorical power" (Netz, "The Pythagoreans," 94).

bridges the gap between ontology and epistemology, a gap that has been filled, in different ways and to vastly different ends, by calculating, projecting, analogizing, even just bootstrapping an aestheticized *musica mundana*, even if—or for the very reason that—the music can never be heard. For to "really" compose the cosmic harmony, to replace the analogical *as* with the literal *is*, would be to force the non-identical into identity. And as every good Pythagorean knows, there is no harmony in identity.

Appendix 1

WILLIAM OF CONCHES, *GLOSULAE DE MAGNO PRISCIANO*

William of Conches's *Glosulae super Priscianum* survives in two primary recensions: (I) a *uersio prior*—Florence, Biblioteca Medicea Laurenziana, San Marco 310 (*M*)—probably composed in the early 1120s, which comments only upon *Priscianus maior* (i.e., *Institutiones*, books 1–16); and (II) a *uersio altera*—Paris, Bibliothèque nationale, lat. 15130 (*P*)—revised circa 1150 near the end of William's career (*quod iuuenes semiplenum scripsimus senes corrigimus*), which glosses both *Priscianus maior* (through the beginning of book 12) and *Priscianus minor*, also known as *De constructione* or *Liber constructionum* (i.e., books 17–18).[1] There exists a possible third redaction in the Laud collection at the Bodleian, Latin manuscript 67, which differs, sometimes considerably, from both *M* and *P*, but it is a short fragment of five folios that covers only *Institutiones* 2.12–21. Edited and translated below is the brief *tractatus de uoce* (glossing *Institutiones* 1.1.1–2) from the *uersio altera* (*P* 3va–5ra). The apparatus criticus registers every departure from *P*, as well as scribal corrections in *P*, except for minor orthographical variants, which are silently normalized (*calidus* for *callidus*, *oculos* for *occulos*, etc.). The apparatus also collates the partial transcription by Irène Rosier-Catach (*R-C* in the apparatus).[2]

William of Conches, *Glosulae de Magno Prisciano* (*Versio altera*), ad Prisc. 1.1.1–2 (*de uoce*)

PHILOSOPHI DIFFINIVNT. Priscianus tractat⟨ur⟩us de sillaba, littera, dictione, quia in diffinitione litterae facturus erat mentionem de uoce sic: "littera est

[1] On the manuscripts and the relations between the *uersio prior* and *uersio altera*, see Édouard Jeauneau, "Deux rédactions des gloses de Guillaume de Conches sur Priscien," in *Lectio Philosophorum*, 335–370.

[2] Rosier-Catach, "Le commentaire des *Glosulae* et des *Glosae* de Guillaume de Conches sur le chapitre *de voce* des *Institutiones Grammaticae* de Priscien," 135–144.

minima pars uocis compositae," ne uideretur ignotum per ignotius diffinire, uel ne interru⟨m⟩peretur suus tractatus quaerendo "quid est uox?" ante diffinit uocem, id est diffinitione ostendit cui conuenit esse uocem. Sed quoniam, cum sint quatuor species uocis, de una sola illarum in hoc opere intendit, diuisiuas differentias uocis enumerat. Deinde binas ad constructiones specierum generi omni uocum adiungit, ut separet illam speciem uocis de qua intendit ab illis de quibus non intendit. Ad ultimum ethimologiam huius nominis, quod est uox, ponit. Sed antequam litteram exponamus, aliquid de essentia uocis dicamus.

Natura igitur artifex hic constituit ut nichil sine calore ceteris qualitatibus dominante uiuere possit. Etsi enim quidam homines dicuntur frigidi, non ideo dicuntur quin plus habeant caloris quam frigiditatis, sed quia plus habent frigiditatis quam naturalis hominum complexio exigit. Vnde natura in medio humani corporis tria calidissima membra—scilicet cor, epar, cistam fellis—constituit. Sed quoniam proprium est caloris se et alia, nisi aliquid habeant quo temperetur, consumere, huic morbo natura remedium contulit attractione frigidi aeris cui membra ad hoc conuenientia, uidelicet pulmonem et alterias, deputauit. Sed quoniam nullus tam aequaliter potest aera attrahere quantum temperamentum exigeret, item aer attractus cito calescit, fuit necesse ut ille expelleretur et alius frigidus attraheretur. Cum igitur aperitur pulmo, aer subtrahitur. Sed ⟨cum⟩ concluditur, emittitur. Et sic opus spirandi et respirandi perficitur. Conti⟨n⟩git uero saepe quod aer qui emittitur naturalibus instrumentis in ore percutitur et in diuersas figuras formatur. Qui formatus, ab ore exiens, aera ori propinquum tangens, simili forma informat, et sic impellendo fit donec feriat aer sic formatus aures circumstantium. Qua percussione anima excitata quandam aeriam | 3vb | substantiam ad hoc deputatam per quosdam neruos ad aures emittit. Quae tangendo aera exteriorem simili forma imprimitur, cum qua uenit ad animam et in ea anima uoluntatem loquentis perpendit. Sic ostendit Boetius in Musica formari uocem per similitudinem lapidis proiecti in medium aquae stantis, qui facit breuissimum circulum, qui impellendo uicinam ⟨aquam⟩ facit laxiorem circulum, et ille alium, donec ad ripam peruenerit. Aer igitur qui sic est percussus ex percussione formatus est uox. Sed huic sententiae quaedam philosophicae rationes uidentur obuiare, quaedam garcionicae oblatrare. Philosophicas igitur ponentes et eis respondentes, garcionicas postponemus.

[6] separet *scripsi*, semper et *P* [9] calore *scripsi*, colore *P R-C* [10] non *scripsi cum R-C*, nam *P* [14] et *scripsi cum P*, quod *R-C* [16] alterias *pro* arterias [19] cum *suppleui cum R-C* [24] anima *scripsi*, aer *P*, autem *R-C* [26] anima *scripsi cum R-C*, animam *P* [29] uicinam *scripsi cum P*, intimum *R-C* [29] aquam *suppleui, forsan* undam *coniciendum* [31] philosophiae *a. corr. P* [32] oblatrare *scripsi cum P*, obla... *R-C* [33] postponemus *scripsi*, preponemus *P*

[4-5] de diuisiuis differentiis, uide Boethius, *Porphyrii Isagoge translatio*, "De differentia," et *In Isag.* II.255.4–256.16; 259.1–260.5. [27-30] Boethius, *Inst. mus.* 1.14 (200).

Dicit igitur Augustinus, "nullum corpus uno et eodem tempore totum potest esse in diuersis locis." Sed Boetius de uoce dicit, "et uox quidem una pariter replet auditum multorum." Si igitur uox est aer, et aer corpus, quomodo poterit stare quod ipsa sit in a⟨u⟩ribus diuersorum una et eadem? Huic sic respondent quidam quod eadem uox dicitur esse in auribus diuersorum non quia penitus eadem sit, sed quia consimilis ita quod nulla potest ibi perpendi differentia. Sed secundum istos non potest una et eadem uox bis dici. Quod non habent pro inconuenienti, cum Aristoteles ⟨dicat⟩: "dictum est et non potest amplius sumi," et Horatius: "et uolat emissum semel irreuocabile uerbum." Isti bene concedunt quod uox sit aer. Ideoque huiusmodi confingunt sententiam: neque aliquid euangelium nisi consimile. Non dicatur euangelium sensus uerborum.

Alii dicunt quod quemadmodum res quae uidetur non uenit ad oculos uidentium, sed radius exiens per oculos usque ad rem dirigitur, sic nec uox quae est aer percussus uenit usque ad aures sed anima per aures instrumentum audiendi, id est aeriam substantiam et substantialem, emittit usque ad os loquentium quae, formata forma quam reperit in aere percusso in ore, reuertitur ad animam. Et sic audit anima. Quemadmodum igitur dicitur "res ista facta est in oculis nostris," ita dicitur "uox ista est in auribus," quia auribus percipimus uocem istam. Non ergo ideo uerum quod idem corpus sit in diuersis locis.

Tertii dicunt quod infiniti aeres eadem forma informati sunt una et eadem uox, nec tamen idem corpus, quemadmodum infinitae dictiones sunt una pars orationis, nec tamen sunt una dictio. Ille ergo aer quem profero cum dico "homo" est eadem uox quae et ille aer quem alius profer⟨t⟩ dicendo "homo." Est igitur eadem uox in auribus diuersorum non tamen idem corpus, quia eadem uox est multa corpora ita quod unumquodque eorum.

Alii dicunt quod ille ultimus circulus aeris totus est una uox neque totus est in auribus diuersorum, sed pars in nostris auribus, pars in tuis. Sed tamen | 4ra | quia per partem illam possum totam formam uocis et significationem perpendere, dicitur tota in meis auribus uox esse. Sic igitur nullum corpus est in diuersis locis, et tamen eadem uox dicitur esse in auribus diuersorum. Illi qui dicunt quod eadem uox potest multotiens et a diuersis dici illi quod Aristoteles ⟨dicit⟩—"dictum est et non potest amplius sumi"—ita respondent Aristotelem non negasse quod dictum

[3] ar *a. corr. P* [4] et *scripsi cum P*, in *R-C* [8] cum Aristoteles ⟨dicat⟩ dictum est *scripsi*, cum ⟨ab⟩ Aristotele dictum est *R-C* [13] aer *scripsi*, ar *P* [16] reuersitur *a. corr. P* [18] percipimus *scripsi cum P*, percimus *R-C* [20] informati *scripsi cum R-C*, informata *P* [27] nostris *p. corr. P* [31] aristoteles *scripsi cum P*, ar *R-C* [32] respondent *scripsi*, responderet *P*

[1–2] *locum non inueni*; cf. Guillelmus de Conchis, *Drag.* 6.19.8: tunc unum corpus uno eodemque tempore totum in diuersis locis est, quod non posse esse Augustinus testatur. Abelardus, *Dial.* 70.19–20. [2–3] Boethius, *Cons. phil.* 2.p5.6: et uox quidem tota pariter multorum replet auditum. [8] Aristoteles, *Cat.* 5a33–35. [8–9] Horatius, *Epist.* 1.18.71. [17] Ps. 117:23; Matth. 21:42.

est posse iterum dici, sed iterum sumi, quia non potest digito demonstrari ubi et quomodo partes istius sunt sitae, quemadmodum in linea, superficie, et corpore. Illud uero Horatii—"uerbum uolat inreuocabile"—non quia non possit iter⟨um⟩ dici, sed quia postquam dictum est semel, non potest contingere non fuisse dictum. Neque potest homo illud ad uoluntatem suam ne audiatur tegere.

Iterum contra hanc sententiam uidetur Boetius esse, qui dicit "uox est percussio aeris," non "est aer." Sed ad hoc est facilis responsio, si ita exponatur: uox est percussio aeris, id est aer percussus. Iterum quod Macrobius dicit—ut sonus ⟨fiat⟩ esse necessaria corpora quae collidantur, et ita corpora collisa non sunt sonus sed efficiunt sonum, et ita aer collisus non est sonus, igitur nec uox—uerum est. Igitur ubicumque sonus efficitur, duo sunt corpora quae colliduntur, quorum neutrum uox est, tamen tertium, aer scilicet medius, qui est uox. Sed dicunt cum aer uirga percutitur quod sunt duo corpora quae concurrunt, quorum nullus est sonus. R⟨espondetur⟩ quod diuersi aeres sunt, id est aeris particulae. Est enim quaedam pars quae in illa percussione uirga sola tangitur, nec est sonus. Alia est quae et uirga et alia parte aeris percutitur, et illa est sonus.

Hae sunt philosophicae obiectiones contra sententiam quae dicit uocem esse aera. Pueriles uero istae: si uox est aer, ergo est calida et humida, quia est aer calidus et humidus. Et si aer qui emittitur post esum gariophili uel cinari uel cinnamomi redolet, ergo uox redolet. Similiter, si et foetet. Item, si pulex saliat per medium aeris qui emittitur, an saliat per medium uocis. Et si nomen meum est uox et omnis uox est corpus, ergo nomen meum est corpus. Sed huiusmodi nugatoria garcionibus relinquimus. Dedignatur enim sermo sobrius ista resoluere.

Secundum hos ergo qui retinent hanc sententiam, littera sic exponitur. PHILOSOPHI non grammatici—non enim pertinet ad grammaticos sed ad phisicos uocem diffinire—DIFINIVNT VOCEM, dicentes illam esse AEREM. Sed quia aer iste exterior est aer sed spis⟨s⟩us nec tamen est uox, addit: TENVISSIMVM. Cum enim sit tenuis, fit tenuior dum attrahitur; fit tenuissimus quia dicunt quidam philosophi | 4rb | ex hoc spisso aere homines non spirare sed tenuissimo et subtilissimo, qui ex superiori regione naturalibus instrumentis per poros huius spissi attrahitur, sed ex illo ex quo uiuunt uocem formatam. Sed quia hoc totum habet aer quem dormientes spiramus, addit: ICTVM. Determina: ictum naturalibus instrumentis, id est lingua, palato, dentibus, labiis, uel per se uel alio mediante. Et tunc

[2] partes *scripsi*, parte *P* [3] uero *scripsi cum P*, uersus *R-C* [6] iterum *scripsi cum P*, item *R-C* [7] *post* aeris *add.* id est aer percussus, *postea cancellatum P* [7] *post* hoc *add.* quod, *postea exp. P* [7] facilis *scripsi*, fascilis *P* [8] iterum *scripsi*, item *R-C* [8] fiat *scripsi*, ista *P* [13] ar *a. corr. P* [16] *post* quae *add.* est *P* [17] sententiam *scripsi cum R-C*, sententia *P* [20] foetet *P*, fitet *R-C* [23] dedignatur *scripsi cum R-C*, designatur *P* [26] uocem *bis repititur R-C* [27] ar *a. corr. P* [29] spirare *scripsi*, sprare *P* [30] qui *scripsi*, quod *P* [32] ictum *scripsi*, ictus *P*, a[ut] *R-C* [33] lingua *scripsi*, linga *P*

[6–7] Boethius, *In Perih.* II.4.18. [8–10] Macrobius, *In Som. Scip.* 2.1.5 (95–96).

nulla erit obiectio de aere percusso in ore digito uel ⟨de⟩ aere qui ab alio prius formato percutitur.

Sunt quidam qui propter praedictas obiectiones dicunt uocem non esse aera nec corpus, im⟨m⟩o quiddam quod in aere ipso auditu discern⟨i⟩tur, quemadmodum quiddam quod in aere odore discernitur. Qui tamen odor aer non est, sed in aere perpenditur. Similiter quiddam est quod in ipso aere auditu discernitur, sed quid sit illud—an qualitas, an quantitas—dissentiunt. Alii enim dicunt illud esse qualitatem, alii quantitatem. Tertii dicunt neutrum, nec aliquid de praedicamentalibus. Sed de hoc alias dicetur. Qui tenent hanc sententiam aiunt hanc diffinitionem datam esse per causam, uelut ista est: "dies est sol lucens super terram." Sed diffinitionis datae per causam haec est natura quod tota simul de diffinito ponitur, non tamen partes illius. Verum est enim quod dies est sol lucens super terram, non tamen dies est sol. Similiter uox est aer tenuissimus ictus, quia talis aer est causa uocis, nec tamen inde sequitur quod uox sit aer uel corpus.

VEL SVVM. Subiungit aliam diffinitionem uocis quae in hoc differt a priore, quod prior solis sonis qui ab animali proferuntur conuenit, sed ista omni sono quicumque sit ille. Continuatio: PHILOSOPHI dicunt VOCEM ESSE AEREM, ETC., uel dicunt uocem esse SENSIBILE, id est sensu corporeo esse perceptibile. Sed quia hoc habet omne corpus quod est sensibile, nec tamen est uox, addit: AVRIVM, ac si dicat: quod aure sentitur. Sed quia auris aliquando sentit frigus ⟨et⟩ calorem, quod est commune sensibile omnium membrorum, addit: SVVM, id est quod ita aure sentitur quod nullo alio instrumento. Vnde exponit: ID EST QVOD PROPRIE AVRIBVS ACCIDIT, ⟨id est⟩ conuenit.

ET EST PRIOR. Ostendit differentiam inter has duas diffinitiones, hanc scilicet quod prior substantialis, alia accidentalis. Et hoc est: PRIOR DIFFINITIO EST SVMPTA A SVBSTANTIA, id est constat ex substantialibus, scilicet ex genere et differentiis. Vel EST SVMPTA, id est incepta, A SVBSTANTIA, id est a genere (uere enim genus est substantia suae speciei). Secundum illos qui dicunt uocem non esse aera sic exponitur istud: PRIOR DIFFINITIO SUMPTA EST A SVBSTANTIA, id est a causa (causa enim quodammodo est substantia effectus in hoc quod confert illi esse). ALTERA diffinitio est sumpta A NOTIONE. Sed quia genus dicitur notio, ut ibi: "genus est notio ad plures differentias uel species pertinens," subiungit: QVAM notionem GRAECI VOCANT ENNOYAN (sola enim accidentalis notio ennoyan uocatur).

5 odore *scripsi*, ad ore *P R-C* 11 *post* simul *add.* est (et *R-C*) *P* 16 solis *scripsi cum P*, solum *R-C* 16 qui *scripsi*, quae *P R-C* 16 proferuntur *scripsi*, profertur *P R-C* 19 hoc *scripsi*, hic *P* 19 *post* habet *add.* animae, *postea exp. P* 23 accidit *om. R-C* 24 et est prior, *om. R-C*; prior *scripsi*, proprior *P* 24 ostendit *scripsi*, astra *(uid.) P, om. R-C* 24 differentiam *scripsi*, differentia *P R-C* 25 hoc *scripsi cum P*, hic *R-C* 25 prior *scripsi*, proprior *P* 28 speciei *scripsi cum P*, specie *R-C* 29 a *scripsi*, ab *P* 31 notio *scripsi*, nacio *P (hic et passim)* 33 uocant *P*, dicunt *iuxta editionem Hertzii* 33 ennoyan *scripsi*, annoyan *P (hic et passim)*

31–32 Cicero, *Topica* 31: genus est notio ad plures differentias pertinens.

| 4va | Vnde glosat: HOC EST assumpta AB ACCIDENTIBVS duobus, sensibile scilicet aurium et proprium. Vel ita: ALTERA diffinitio sumpta est A NOTIONE—sed ne uideretur talis descriptio contentibilis, commendat illam graeco nomine—QVAM, id est diffinitionem su⟨m⟩ptam a notione, GRAECI VOCANT ENNOYAN. Deinde glosat quid sonet "ennoyan": HOC EST AB ACCIDENTIBVS. Inde enim talis diffinitio dicitur "ennoyan," quod est sumpta ab accidente rei quae definitur.

ACCIDIT ENIM. Vere ista diffinitio sumpta est ab accidente, quia ab auditu. Idem enim est proprie aure sentiri et audiri. Et unde hoc "si ab auditu, ergo accidenti"? Quia AVDITVS ACCIDIT VOCI. Et nota quod auditus potest dici actio audiendi. Iste non accidit uoci, sed animali. Et ita accipitur cum dicitur "quinque sunt sensus corporis, uidelicet auditus, uisus, et cetera." Item dicitur auditus passio quae inest rei inde quod auditur. Ita hic accipitur, et iste accidit uoci. Est igitur sensus: AVDITVS, id est audiri, ACCIDIT VOCI. Sed quia contingit saepe uocem non audiri, cum omnis sonus hic dicatur uox, subdit: QVANTVM IN IPSA EST. Si enim non auditur, non remanet in ipsa, sed deest qui illam audiat.

VOCIS AVTEM. Data diffinitione uocis, illius diuisiuas ⟨differentias⟩ enumerat ut ex istis iunctis huic generi, quod est uox, quatuor species uocis continuet, ut separet illam speciem uocis de qua intendit ab illis de quibus non intendit. Continuatio: tales sunt uocis diffinitiones. Vocis uero sunt quatuor differentiae diuisiuae: ARTICVLATA, INARTICVLATA, LITTERATA, ILLITERATA. Et nota quod dicuntur diuisiuae differentiae non quia simul diuidant uocem, sed quia binae et binae sufficienter illam diuidunt. Omnis enim uox uel est articulata uel inarticulata. Similiter omnis est uel litterata uel illitterata. Sed quamuis binae quaelibet sufficienter uocem diuidant, non tamen species uocis perfecte constituunt. Et ideo non propter dictionem sed propter specierum constructionem quatuor differentias uocis apposuit.

ARTICVLATA. Diffinit articulatam uocem, id est diffinitione ostendit cui uoci esse articulatam conuenit. Etiam ethimologiam huius nominis "articulata" interserit. Et hoc est: illa uox articulata QVAE PROFERTVR. Sed quia hoc habet omnis uox, ad remotionem aliarum subdit: COARTATA. Quia coartare est et cogere et iungere, glosat: ID EST COPVLATA CVM ALIQVO SENSV MENTIS EIVS QVI LOQVITVR. Et est sensus: articulata est uox quae a loquente intentione significandi profertur. Sed INARTICVLATA EST illi (id est articulatae) CONTRARIA. Et determinat, id est QVAE PROFICISCITVR A NVLLO AFFECTV MENTIS, id est quae non profertur intentione significandi.

[1] ab *scripsi*, ad *P* [3] contentibilis *pro* contemptibilis [7] uere *scripsi cum P*, uoci *R-C* [10] iste non accidit *scripsi*, ista non accidunt *P*, ista non accidit *R-C* [17] continuet *scripsi*, continuat *P*, constituat *R-C* [19] uoces *a. corr. P* [19] diffinitiones *scripsi cum P*, diffinitionis *R-C* [28] etiam *scripsi cum P*, et iam *R-C* [31] id *P*, hoc *iuxta editionem Hertzii* [32] alquente *a. corr. P* [33] illi *scripsi cum R-C*, illa *P* [34] *post* quae *add.* non *P* [34] affectu *scripsi*, ff. *P*

Et attende quod de significatione uocis aliter Priscianus, aliter sentit Boetius. Dicit enim Boetius uocem esse significatiuam quae in audiente | 4vb | generat intellectum siue proferens causa significandi proferat illam siue non, unde dicit latratus canum ⟨iras⟩ significare. ⟨Priscianus uero dicit uocem esse significatiuam⟩ quae causa et intentione significandi profertur, etsi auditor non intelligat aliquid per illam. Quaeritur cur articulata et inarticulata sint diuisiuae differentiae uocis et constitutiuae specierum illius et ita substantiales, cum eadem uox possit esse et articulata et inarticulata et cum eadem uox modo profertur intentione significandi ⟨(et tunc est articulata), modo sine intentione significandi⟩ (et tunc est inarticulata). Contra hoc dicunt quidam in rebus hoc esse inconueniens, in nominibus non, ut una et eadem uox est nomen et uerbum, et significat cum tempore et sine tempore.

Alii dicunt quia uox, semel articulata et imposita ad significandum, nunquam postea est inarticulata. Illi sic exponunt diffinitionem: ARTICVLATA EST QVAE PROFERTVR, id est est pronuntiabilis, C⟨VM⟩ A⟨LIQVO⟩, ETC., INARTICVLATA quae non profertur, id est non est pronuntiabilis, CVM ALIQVO SENSV MENTIS. Ista igitur uox, etsi a rustico causa significandi non profertur, iuxta hoc tamen quod est apta significare articulata uocatur. Iterum attende quod Boetius in diffinitione interpretationis—ubi dicit "interpretatio est uox articulata aliquid significans per se"—aliter intellexit "articulata," id est ex articulis, scilicet ex litteris constans. Et tunc dicitur articulata ⟨ab⟩ articulo, sicque omnis uox quae constat ex litteris—siue significet siue non—dicitur articulata. Hic uero non dicitur articulata nisi sit significatiua et ab hoc homine prolata; solus enim homo mentem habet et loquitur. In hoc quod dicit "coartata" habes ethimologiam huius nominis "articulata," scilicet quod dicitur ab "arto, artas."

LITTERATA, ETC. Ostenso quid sit articulata et quid sit inarticulata uox, ostendit quid sit litterata et illiterata. Et hoc est: illa uox EST LITTERATA QVAE POTEST SCRIBI, id est figuris iam inuentis et usitatis repraesentari. Hic habemus Priscianum auctorem uocem posse scribi, quod tamen quidam gartiones negant. ILLITERATA est QVAE NON POTEST SCRIBI, id est figuris iam inuentis et usitatis repraesentari.

INVENIVNTVR. Demonstratis differentiis uocis subiungit qualiter ex eis coniunctis fiunt species uocis. Et notandum quod quotiens aliquod genus duobus

4 Priscianus uero—esse significatiuam *conieci* 5 quae *scripsi cum P*, quia *scripsit R-C* 5 et *scripsi cum P*, id est *R-C* 6 quaeritur *scripsi cum P*, quare *R-C* 6 cur *scripsi*, cum *P* 6 diuisiuae *scripsi*, diuersae *P* 9 et tunc—intentione significandi *conieci, om. P per homeoteleuton?* 15 c⟨um⟩ a⟨liquo⟩ *scripsi*, causa ⟨significandi⟩ *R-C* 18 iterum *scripsi cum P*, item *R-C* 21 sicque *scripsi cum P*, sic quod *R-C* 22 sit *bis repititur P* 23 mentem *scripsi cum R-C*, mente *P* 25 artas *scripsi cum P*, arto *R-C* 26 ostendit *scripsi cum P*, ostenditur *R-C* 32 *post* quod *add.* species, *postea exp. P*

2–4 Boethius, *In Perih.* II.54.24–26: Mutorum quoque animalium sunt quaedam uoces quae significent: ut canum latratus iras significat canum, alia uero mollior quaedam blandimenta designat.
19–20 Boethius, *In Perih.* II.6.4–5: interpretatio namque est uox articulata per se ipsam significans.

modis diuiditur per aliquas differentias, iuncta una differentia unius diuisionis cum differentia alterius, quaedam species illius generis perficitur, ut in hoc genere articulata et litterata unam speciem uocis perficiunt, articulata et illiterata secundam, et litterata et inarticulata tertiam, inarticulata et illiterata quartam. Nunquam uero differentiae eiusdem diuisionis eandem speciem constituunt; sunt etenim oppositae. Continuatio: Quandoquidem praedictae differentiae hoc genus, quod est uox, diuidunt, ergo illius species constituunt. Et hoc est: INVENIVNTVR QVAEDAM ARTICVLATAE et litteratae, deinde glosat, id est QVAE POSSVNT SCRIBI ET INTELLIGI. Sed inde quod possunt scribi, sunt litteratae, | 5ra | inde quod intelligi, articulatae, VT ista uox: ARMA VIRVMQVE CANO. Et est materiale impositum. Et hoc est prima species uocis. QVAEDAM inueniuntur QVAE NON POSSVNT SCRIBI et ita sunt illiteratae, tamen possunt intelligi et ita sunt articulatae. Et hoc est secunda species uocis, VT SIBILI HOMINVM. Latrones enim ad quendam affectum animi significandum sibi inuicem sibilant uel gemunt. Haec enim est commendatio exempli. ALIAE uoces SVNT, ⟨QVAE⟩, QVAMVIS SCRIBANTVR, id est sunt litteratae, TAMEN NICHIL significant, ⟨id est⟩ inarticulatae sunt. Et haec est tertia species uocis, ut COAX (uox ranae) et CRA (uox corui). Etsi enim augures in uoce corui aliquid perpendant—unde a ⟨Boetio⟩ significatiua uox naturaliter dicitur—tamen quia non profertur a coruo causa et intentione significandi, a Prisciano uox significatiua non dicitur. ALIAE SVNT INARTICVLATAE ET ILLITTERATAE, quae est quarta species uocis. Sunt igitur quatuor species uocis: articulata et litterata, articulata et illitterata, litterata et inarticulata, inarticulata et illiterata.

SCIRE, ETC. Ne aliquis putet quod praedictae differentiae praedictas species sine alio constituerent, dicit quod aduenientes huic generi, uoci, hoc faciunt. Continuatio: Non solum debemus scire quod hae differentiae constituunt has species uocis, AVTEM, id est sed, DEBEMVS SCIRE QVOD QVATVOR DIFFERENTIAE SVPERIORES, id est de quibus factus est sermo in superioribus, PERFICIVNT HAS QVATTVOR SPECIES VOCVM, non omnes singulas, sed BINAE AEQVE PER SINGVLAS, id est in constitutione singularum et non per se sed ACCIDENTES, id est aduenientes, HVIC GENERI VOCI. Sed ne aliquis putet "alicui uoci," addit: GENERALITER, id est aduenientes huic generi uoci has species constituunt.

"VOX" AVTEM. Post diffinitionem uocis et differentias et species, subiungit Priscianus huius nominis, quod est "uox," ethimologiam geminam. Quarum prior plus concordat cum uoce, minus cum significatione; posterior minus cum uoce,

[4] litterata *scripsi*, illiterata *P* [5] differentiae *scripsi cum P*, diffentie *R-C* [5] diuisionis *scripsi*, dictionis *P* [6] quandoquidem *scripsi cum P*, quando quidem *R-C* [8] quae *scripsi*, quod *P R-C* [11] species *scripsi*, specie *P* [12] tamen *scripsi cum R-C*, quando *P* [16] *post* tamen *add.* ⟨...⟩ *R-C* [18] a boetio *scripsi cum R-C*, alio *P* [28] aeque *P*, coeuntes *iuxta editionem Hertzii* [29] singularum *P*, singularium *R-C* [30] huic generi *non in editione Hertzii* [32] diffinitionem *scripsi cum P*, deffinitionem *R-C*

[10] Virgilius, *Aeneid.* 1.1.

plus cum significatione. Et est ethimologia, ut ait Cassiodorus, breuis oratio per certas significationes ostendens de quo nomine uel fonte uenerit illud de quo quaeritur nomen. Interpretatur tamen "origo nominis." Continuatio: VOX EST AER TENVISSIMVS, ETC. Sed dicitur "VOX" A VOCANDO non quia per omnem uocem aliquid uocemus, sed quia per quasdam. Sed ne uideretur mirum quod producta dictio a correpta deriuaretur, dicit per contrarium non esse mirum, cum correpta saepe deriuatur a producta, VT "DVX" A DVCENDO. Deinde subiungit ethimologiam sic: VEL uox dicitur APO TOY BOO, id est ab hoc uerbo "BOO"—et est APO ab, TOY articulus. Est igitur summa: "Vox" dicitur ab hoc uerbo BOO, BOAS, quod est "sono, -nas" (inde componitur "reboo, -as," id est "resono, -as") et fit inde mutata "b" in "u" consonantem et ultima "o" in "x." Haec ethimologia ad sensum plus pertinet. Quia enim omnis uox est sonus, merito a uerbo quod significat actum sonandi uox dicitur.

A translation of this text is available on the companion website.

2–3 de quo quaeritur *scripsi cum P*, ⟨**⟩ quare *R-C* 3 continuatio *om. R-C* 4 omnem *scripsi*, orationem *P R-C* 7 producta *scripsi*, praedicta *P R-C*

1–3 Cassiodorus, *Expositio Psalmorum* 1.1 (CCSL 97, 30): Etymologia est enim oratio breuis, per certas associationes ostendens ex quo nomine id, quod quaeritur, uenerit nomen.

Appendix 2

HISDOSUS, *DE ANIMA MUNDI PLATONICA*

Paris, Bibliothèque nationale, lat. 8624 (*olim* Colbertinus 3773; Regius 6116; Z. Z.a, as noted on f. 1r) is a composite manuscript of (in addition to the Timaean commentary) works by Symmachus, Seneca, and Apuleius in ten quires, drawn from at least four different manuscripts. Its contents and structure may be summarized as follows:

1. **Quires 1–2**, both quaternions, 25cm × 16cm, single column of 44 lines, writing above top line, simple initials alternating blue and red. **1r:** Incipiunt epistule Senece ⟨*man. rec.* Simachi⟩. Facis pro mutua diligentia—**16r:** ubi sedem sibi gratia diuinitatis extruxit. uale. = *Florilegium Symmachi epistolarum selectarum* (1.28, 31–34, 36–38, 43, etc.—3.45 [an incomplete but otherwise standard florilegium collection described by Seeck] + two final unidentified letters); *F*22 in Callu's edition.[1] **16r:** Lucii Annii Senece cordubensis de quatuor uirtutibus liber incipit. Quatuor uirtutum species multorum sapientium—**16v:** Continentiam uero si . . . [*cetera desunt*] = Martini episcopi Bracarensis *Formula uitae honestae*, assumed to be an epitome of a lost work by Seneca; from the tenth century on, this short text on Stoic ethics was commonly attributed to Seneca himself, as here.
2. **Quire 3**, quaternion, 25cm × 16cm, single column of 60 lines, writing above top line. **17r:** Diuinitate uniuersitatis—**22v:** non deberent dici planetae, sed planontae, id est errorem inserentes = Hisdosi Scholastici *De anima mundi Platonica*. The text is written in a late-twelfth or early-thirteenth-century late-Caroline, praegothica *textualis*, featuring a single compartment "a," occasional biting, and the uncrossed Tironian "et." It is not an autograph, as is clear from several occurrences of homeoteleuton, corrected by expunctuation. Moreover, several errors in the text (*semper amabilia* for *separabilia* and *quoniam* for *quae in*) are easily explained by misread or misplaced macrons. Though BnF, lat. 8624 (quire three) is the sole witness hitherto known for this text, at least one

[1] Otto Seeck, *Q. Aurelii Symmachi Quae supersunt* (Berlin: apud Weidmannos, 1883), xxviii–xxix; J. P. Callu, ed., *Symmaque: Lettres, Tome I (Livres I–I I)* (Paris: Les belles lettres, 1972).

other copy can be assumed. The commentary is followed by three related but independent fragments that fill the rest of the quire:

a. a long anonymous gloss (related to *Timaeus* 21e–24e) on the cyclical *inundationes* and *combustiones* of the world, touching upon the influence of the planets and the myths of Deucalion, Pyrrha, and Phaeton (**22v**: Invndatio alia generalis, alia spiritualis—**23v**: impossibile est generaliter contingere);
b. a second anonymous gloss on the birth of Erichthonius (**23r**: Legitur in libro qui minthologiarum [*sic*] inscribitur quod palladem de cerebro iouis natam uulcanus petiit—dixitque urbem athenas, quod interpretatur immortales); both of these glosses are related to explanations given by William of Conches (*Glosae super Platonem*, 24–30);
c. a short treatment of the *divisio philosophiae* (**23v**: Phylosophia aliter describitur secundum nominis ethimologiam, aliter secundum rei essentiam—**24v**: quod in fide trinitatis solidi esse debemus). This same treatise, entitled by its editor, Gilbert Dahan, the *Tractatus quidam de philosophia et partibus eius*, is found in BnF, lat. 6570, 57r–59r.[2] As in BnF, lat. 6570, this *divisio philosophiae* concludes with:
   i. a short gloss on the etymology of the terms *astronomia* and *astrologia* (**24v**: Astronomia est scientia speculandi motus planetarum ad cognoscendos effectus eorum—dicta astrologia quasi sermo de astris);
   ii. a *divisio terrae* (**24v**: Mundus distribuitur in grecos, latinos, barbaros—iuxta quam excedentia et excessa reperiuntur);
   iii. a discussion of *locutio et silentium* (**24v**: locutio et silentium quandoque cum quandoque fiunt sine ratione—melius autem dactalorinchite [sic] dicerentur); and
   iv. a short fragment concerning the ecclesiastic hierarchy according to Pseudo-Dionysius (**24v**: Ter ternae ter gerarchiae esse in ecclesia a dionisio dictae sunt—quod in fide trinitatis solidi esse debemus).

3. **Quires 4–8**, quaternions signed i–v in a contemporaneous hand (bottom verso at the close of each quire), 25cm × 16cm, single column of 44 lines, writing above top line, very similar in appearance to (1) above and probably from the same manuscript. **25r**: grandinem hoc modo fieri si tibi—**58r**: Quippe uernis. . . [*cetera desunt*] = Senecae *Naturales quaestiones* in the so-called *Grandinem* order, but lacking IVa.2.19 (*temporibus imbres*) to the end. BnF, lat. 8624 is siglum *H* (*olim Q*) in the *traditio textus* of the *Natural Questions*, and it is one of the ten primary manuscripts employed in the reconstruction of the archetype.[3] **58r**: Apuleii madaurensis platonis discipuli de deo socratis liber

[2] Cf. Fr. Alessio, "La filosofia e le *artes mechanicae* nel secolo XII," 156–157. The text has been partially transcribed from BnF, lat. 8624 by T. Gregory, *Platonismo medievale*, 123–124, n. 3. It has been edited in full from BnF, lat. 6570 in G. Dahan, "Une introduction à la philosophie au XIIe siècle," 155–193.

[3] Harry M. Hine, "The Manuscript Tradition of Seneca's *Natural Questions*," *Classical Quarterly* 30 (1980), 183–217; *Lucii Annaei Senecae Naturalium quaestionum libros recognouit* (Stuttgart: Teubner, 1996).

incipit. Qui me uoluisti dicere—**62r:** Ad lotofagos ascendit, nec remansit. Sirenas audiit, nec accessit. Explicit de deo sacratis [*sic*]. = Apulei Madaurensis *De deo Socratis*, complete. **62r:** Appuleii [*sic*] madaurensis platonis discipuli de platone et eius dogmate liber incipit. Platoni habitudo corporis cognomentum dedit—**64r:** quod teneras uisiones mollesque perturbet. Explicit de [de] platone et eius dogmate. Feliciter. = Apulei Madaurensis *De Platone et eius dogmate*, incomplete, lacking 1.15 (*pulmones loco*) to the end. BnF, lat. 8624 is siglum *A* in the *traditio textus* of the *De deo Socratis* and *De Platone*.[4] **64v:** blank.

4. **Quire 9**, quaternion, 17.6cm × 12cm, single column of 26 lines, writing above the top line, initials alternating red embellished with green and green embellished with red. **65r:** ni ergo tui miserear—**72v:** quid porro prodest paucos dies aut annos lu-. . . [*cetera desunt*] = Senecae *Epistulae ad Lucilium* 29.12–37.2. This quire was originally the sixth quire of a complete twelfth-century manuscript of letters 1–88, now dismembered and scattered among Vatican, Pal. lat. 1551, 1r–40v (original quires 1–5), BnF, lat. 8624, 65r–72v (original quire 6), and Vatican, Pal. lat. 1550 (original quires 7–17).[5]
5. **Quire 10**, a single bifolium, 22cm × 13.5cm, a single thin column of 37 (73r) and 38 (73v) lines, writing below the top line. **73r:** Incipit Ludus Senece de morte claudii Neronis. Quid actum sit in celo ante diem tercio idus—**73v** incomitatum dimittam. non oportet enim. . . [*cetera desunt*] = Senecae *Ludus de Morte Claudii* siue *Diui Claudii Apocolokyntosis* 1.1–3.4. **74:** blank. This final bifolium originally belonged to what is now BnF, lat. 8260, a manuscript copied for the library of Richard of Fournival (as no. 129 in his *Biblionomia*), which, as a note on the last flyleaf of BnF, lat. 8260 attests, had contained "Tragedie Senece et ludus eiusdem"; the last three words, "et ludus eiusdem," were later canceled and "detractus est" added. The final quire containing the *Ludus* was removed and its outer leaf (mysteriously) ended up bound with BnF, lat. 8624.

Precisely when these sundry parts were bound together is unknown. The core of the collection—certainly without the final two quires, but perhaps also without Hisdosus's third quire—was recorded as no. 596 in Pierre Dupuy's 1617 catalogue of manuscripts owned by Jacques Auguste de Thou (1553–1617): "Symmachi Epistolae. Senecae questiones naturales et alia. Apuleius de Deo Socratis 4°" (BnF, Coll. Dupuy 653, 31r). It subsequently appears in Dupuy's revised catalogue (org. 1622, rev. 1645) of the Bibliothèque du Roi as "1693. Symmachi Epistolae" (BnF, lat. 9352, f. 261r) and then in Nicolas Clément's 1682 catalogue as "6116. Symmachi Epistolae" (BnF, NAF 5402, f. 419r, with a concordance to 1693 in the earlier

4 C. Moreschini, ed., *Apuleius. De philosophia libri* (Stuttgart: Teubner, 1991).

5 J. Fohlen, "Manuscrits démembrés des *Epistulae ad Lucilium* de Sénèque," *Revue d'histoire des textes* 3 (1973), 241–245.

catalogue). De Thou's collection, which had since passed to his son, Jacques-Auguste II (d. 1677), was eventually sold to pay the family's debts; the majority of the library was purchased by Jean-Jacques Charron, but Jean-Baptiste Colbert (1619–1683) purchased the ancient manuscripts at the urging of his own librarian, Etienne Baluze. Accordingly, the manuscript reappears as no. 3773 in Baluze's first catalogue of the Colbert collection (BnF, Baluze 101, f. 68r): "Symmachi et Senecae quaedam." The description is too laconic to offer any certainty about its precise contents; however, in Beleuze's final catalogue of *codices Colbertini*, compiled shortly after Colbert's death and employed as the official inventory for the transfer of his library to the Bibliothèque royale (its final resting place) in 1732, the manuscript's current form is immediately recognizable in Baluze's more detailed description (BnF, NAF 5692, f. 339r):

> 3773 Epistolae [Senecae *del.*] Symmachi
> Senecae liber de quatuor uirtutibus
> Glossae in Timaeum Platonis
> Senecae quaestionum naturalium libri x
> Apuleii liber de deo Socratis
> Eiusdem liber de Platone et eius dogmate
> Quaedam epistolae Senecae
> Eiusdem ludus de morte Claudii Neronis

It would seem that the composite manuscript assumed its final form sometime between de Thou's 1617 catalogue and Colbert's last catalogue (after 1683). Whether Hisdosus's commentary was already among its contents in 1617, or was added at the same time as the Seneca fragments, cannot be determined. It remains possible, though, that the commentary traveled as an independent libellus prior to its inclusion in what is now BnF, lat. 8624.

In the following excerpts,[6] orthography has been silently normalized (except when reporting names and transliterations of Greek, in which case the original orthography of the manuscript is reported). The manuscript bears two levels of corrections, all of which have been recorded in the apparatus criticus: (1) corrections made in the course of writing by the original copyist (indicated with *post corr.* and *ante corr. P*) and (2) corrections made in slightly darker ink after the text had been copied but closely contemporaneous with the original hand (indicated with *P*[c]). The text has been collated with the short excerpts printed previously by Tullio Gregory (*T. Greg.* = *Platonismo medievale*, 124–132) and Edouard Jeauneau (*E. Jeaun.* = *Guillelmi de Conchis Glosae super Platonem*, Appendix I, 331–337). Lemmata (the quotations from the text being commented upon) are underlined in the manuscript and often heavily abbreviated; in the edition they are printed

[6] A full edition and study will be published in *Mediaeval Studies*.

in small capitals and their abbreviations silently expanded except where is there is ambiguity or a departure from Calcidius's text as edited by Waszink. An *apparatus fontium* provides *loci paralleli uel comparandi*.

2.1 Quid sit anima mundi

| 17r | Diuinitate, uniuersitatis conditrice, fauorem nobis praestante, infixa menti est sententia Timaeum (quantum ipsius a scolasticis nostris legitur, cum facilius et commodius fieri poterit) a nobis glosandum. In praesentiarum uero qualiter quod de anima mundi dicit Plato intelligamus, interuentu sociorum hunc sedule tradere curauimus. Postulamus igitur ut nemo lectorum in cachinni effusionem prorumpat, nemo auditorum liuoris linguam exacuat, si quandoque, in his quae dicturi sumus, patrem aut filium aut spiritum sanctum nominauerimus. Diligens lector potius adtendat quam difficile antiquorum scripta pura et inuiolata in posteros usque defluant. Plato namque et maximus philosophorum chorus multa de personarum trinitate et trinitatis unitate, ut testatur sanctus Augustinus et alii doctors ecclesiastici, fidei congrua dixerunt. Sed quia aliis uerbis philosophi gentilium utuntur, aliis moderni diuini cum de conditore uniuersitatis sermonem instituunt, aut refutantur ut futiles aut nichil de eo, a plerisque ut creditur, scientes abiciuntur, quasi non ille spiritus per os hominis, quamquam gentilis, qui asellae linguam resoluit loquendo uerba quae consueuit uox humana producere, ueritatem proferre dignetur. Sed haec hactenus, ne hunc tomum prolixitatis scriptor damnans utcumque constructum dissipet. Ille itaque uersus platonicus nobis glosandus occurrit, quo dicitur deus animam mundi in medietate locasse. Vbi haec mihi peruestiganda uidentur: quid sit mundi anima, quid medietas, quid sit deum animam mundi in eius medietate locasse.

Anima igitur mundi est ille creatoris amor aeternus quo cuncta creauit et creata concorditer regit ea concordia quae, si deficiat, statim mundi machinam dissoluat. Hunc amorem christianae religionis regulam sectantes theologi spiritum sanctum appellauerunt, ut quidam dicere uoluit, de homine ad deum uerba transferentes. Quemadmodum enim, inquit, in flatu hominis eius mens cognoscitur, utrum laetitia scilicet diffundatur an maerore angatur, ita per huius amoris uisionem peruenitur ad mentis diuinae cognitionem. Quod autem in flatu hominis et facie aut laetitia deprehendatur aut tristitia, non diffitetur Iuuenalis dicens,

[8] scripta *scripsi*, scriptura *P* [11] utuntur *con. T. Greg.*, utantur *P* [12] aut *scripsi*, et *P* [16] thomum *post corr. (-h- add. sup. lin.) P* [28] diffitetur *con. E. Jeaun.*, diffutetur *P*

[9–11] E.g., *Conf.* 7.9.14; cf. *De ciu. Dei* 8.5: "Nulli nobis [sc. Christianis] quam isti [sc. Platonici] propius accesserunt." [13–15] Num. 2:28–30. [18–20] *Tim.* 34b. [23–24] Vide infra, 278.12–17 (cum notis).

Deprehendas animi tormenta latentis in aegro
corpore deprehendas et gaudia, sumit utrumque
hunc habitum facies.

Sanctum uero appellauerunt illum spiritum antonomasice, id est excellenter. Ipse enim sanctorum sanctissimus est quippe qui sanctitatem ex se habens sui participatione ceteros cunctos bonos efficit. Alii denique amorem illum asserunt spiritum sanctum appellatum quia sancte spirat, id est procedit a patre et a filio. Iste enim spiritus est tertia trinitatis persona. Neque enim si pater est spiritus et sanctus, idcirco est spiritus sanctus. Similiter et de filio dicimus. Non enim quaecumque disiunctim praedicantur et coniunctim. Quare autem pater potentia, filius sapientia nuncupetur, suo loco plenius exponetur.

Alii denique diffiniunt animam mundi dicentes, mundi anima est uigor naturalis rebus insitus, quo quaedam tantum discernunt, ut angeli et spiritus alii. Aliae discernunt et sentiunt, ut rationalis natura humana. Aliae sentiunt sed non discernunt, ut bruta animalia. Aliae crescunt nec sentiunt, ut herbae et arbores quorum uita est uigor non anima. Aliae sunt nec crescunt, ut lapides. Ille naturalis uigor spiritus sanctus ab eisdem doctoribus dicitur. Haec sententia in nullo a priore discordat. Etsi uerba sint diuersa, idem est tamen sensus per omnia.

Quod mihi uidetur de mundi anima simpliciter pando, non omnibus aliorum sententiis praeiudicans. Quorum quidam dixerunt Platonem uoluisse mundum esse quoddam magnum animal, cuius animam dixerunt esse uitalem calorem a sole procedentem, qui per omnes mundi partes diffusus ipsum mundum uegetat. Alii dixerunt deum iecisse mundum istum quasi fundamentum et principium

[2] sumit *scripsi*, summit *P* [10] disiunctim *P*, disiuncti *T. Greg.* [10] coniunctim *P*, coniuncti *T. Greg.* [14] sentiunt *con. T. Greg.*, dissentiunt *P* [16] uigor *scripsi*, uiror *P* [18] idem *P*ᶜ, deest *P* [22] procedentem *P*ᶜ, procedente *P*

[1–3] Iuuenalis, *Sat.* 9.18–20; cf. (Ps.-?)Bernardus Silvestris, *Commentum super sex libros Aeneidos Virgilii*, ed. J. W. et E. F. Jones, 96, 15–17; Guillelmus de Conchis, *Glos. sup. Boet.*, 1.pr1.82–87. [4] Guillelmus de Conchis, *Phil.* 1.9 (45C): "Est autem proprie spiritus halitus, sed quia in spiritu et anhelitu saepe hominis uoluntas perpenditur (aliter anima spirat laetus, aliter iratus), divinam uoluntatem translatiue uocauerunt spiritum, sed antonomasice sanctum." Cf. Ioannes Saresberiensis, *Metalogicon* 2.16.16–17: "antonomasice, id est excellenter." [10–11] Cf. Guillelmus de Conchis, *Phil.* 1.5–9 (44D–45C); sed contra, *Drag.* 1.9. [12–17] Guillelmus de Conchis, *Glos. sup. Boet.* 3.m9.522–531: "Anima mundi est naturalis uigor quo quaedam res tantum habent moueri, quaedam crescere, quaedam sentire, quaedam discernere. Sed quid sit ille uigor naturalis quaeritur. Sed ut michi uidetur ille naturalis uigor est spiritus sanctus." *Phil.*, 1.15 (46D): "Alii dicunt animam mundi esse naturalem uigorem rebus insitum, quo quaedam uiuunt tantum, quaedam uiuunt et sentiunt, quaedam et sentient et discernunt." Vide T. Gregory, *Anima mundi*, 133ff. [20–23] Vide infra, 281.23–26 (cum notis). Cf. Augustinus, *Sermo* CCXLI: *In diebus Paschalibus, XII. De Resurrectione corporum, contra Gentiles*, cap. 7 (PL 38, 1137): "Sed nolo hinc diutius disputare, libros uestros lego: mundum istum animal dicitis, id est, coelum, terram, maria, omnia quae sunt ingentia corpora, immensa usquequaque elementa; totum hoc, uniuersumque corpus, quod ex his elementis omnibus constat, dicitis esse animal magnum, id est, habere animam suam, . . . quasi animam uniuersalem mundum regentem, et unum quoddam animal facientem."

omnium substantiarum, id est corporum et spirituum. Aiunt enim ex corpore mundi cuncta alia corpora fieri. Porro mundi animam ponunt quasi fontem quendam ceterarum animarum, quam uolunt esse quendam magnum spiritum per totum mundum diffusum, non audentes hunc dicere spiritum sanctum spiritum esse. Aliquantillum isti ueritati accedunt, sed nondum eam perfecte intuentur, suae ignorantiae culpam retorquentes in Platonem et Virgilium in philosophico more de anima mundi loquentes. Quomodo enim potuit manifestius expedire Virgilius quid mundi animam diceret, quam cum dixit,

> Principio caelum et terram camposque liquentes
> lucentemque globum lunae Tytaniaque astra
> spiritus intus alit, totosque infusa per artus
> mens molem agitat et magno se corpore miscet.
> [Inde hominum pecudumque genus uitaeque uolantum
> et quae marmoreo fert monstra sub aequore pontus]?

His uerbis manifestissime mundi animam spiritum Virgilius, ueritatis non inscius, nuncupauit. Vnde isti suam sententiam trahunt. Post haec nimirum inquit, "Inde hominum pecudumque genus uitaeque uolantum," quibus uersibus Virgilius intelligi uoluit spiritum sanctum, id est bonitatem diuinam, causam esse quare cuncta quae in mundo uita decorantur, anima uegetantur. Iste ⟨spiritus⟩ sanctus, quo omnia uegetari ait Virgilius, mundi anima a quibusdam philosophis est appellatus ea ratione, quod eo spiritu, id est creatoris bonitate, cuncta facta sunt. Quod uoluit dicere Lucanus in hoc uersu,

> Iupiter est quocumque uides quocumque moueris.

Et Virgilius hoc alio,

> A Ioue principium Musae, Iouis omnia plena.

[6] retorquentes *con. T. Greg.*, retorquentis *P* [6] Virgilium *con. T. Greg.*, Virgilio *P* [7] loquentes *con. T. Greg.*, loquentis *P* [8] quam *scripsi*, quod *P* [12] agitat P^c, agat *P* [13] uiteque *sup. lin.* P^c, interque *P* [17] uitaeque *scripsi*, .i.t.q. *P* [20] quo *scripsi*, quae *P* [23] quocumque . . . quocumque P^c, quodcumque . . . quodcumque *P*

[2–5] Bernardus Silvestris, *Comm. in Mart.* 8.991–994: "De anima mundi ueteres sensere philosophi quod, sicut mundanum corpus magnum est a quo omnia corpora prodeunt et in quod reducuntur, ita eius anima magnus quidam spiritus est a quo omnes animae ortum et in quem regressum habent." Macrobius, *In Som. Scip.* 1.6.20 (22.5): "aut mundi anima quae animarum omnium fons est." [9–14] Virgilius, *Aeneid* 6.724–729. Cf. Bernardus Silvestris, *Comm. in Mart.* 8.1008–1025; Macrobius, *In Som. Scip.* 1.14.14, etc. [23] Lucanus, *De bello ciuili* 9.580. [25] Virgilius, *Ecl.* 3.60. Cf. Macrobius, *In Som. Scip.* 1.17.14 (69.14).

Quod sola bonitate conditoris omnia facta sint, sic potest probari. Omnes causae quibus aliquid fit hae fere sunt: indigentia, coactionis necessitas, casus, benignitas. Creator igitur sibi usquequaque sufficiens nullo indigebat. Cogi uero ut contra uoluntatem quid faceret, quomodo potens omnia posset? Sed si casu mundus esset factus, aliquae causae mundum praecessissent, quarum concursus mundum operatus fuisset. Item si casu deus mundum fecisset, deo ignorante mundus prouenisset. Casus enim est inopinatus euentus rerum ex causis confluentibus sine intentione gerentium. Sola ergo conditoris bonitas fabricauit mundum et illius ornatum. Vnde ait Boetius,

> Quem non externae pepulerunt fingere causae
> materiae fluitantis opus uerum insita summi
> forma boni liuore carens.

Sunt qui animam mundi dicant esse quendam motum rebus a creatore insitum. Sed non intelligunt nec quid uelint dicere auditoribus intimare queunt. Fortasse aliquis quaeret: cum anima mundi sit spiritus sanctus, ⟨et spiritus sanctus⟩ sit ubique, estne anima mundi ubique? Quod si ubique est anima mundi, ergo in Socrate est anima mundi. Si igitur in Socrate mundi anima est, et Socratis est alia anima, ergo duae animae sunt in Socrate. Huic respondemus uerum esse mundi animam esse in Socrate et Socratis animam in eodem. Non tamen duae sunt in Socrate. Non enim est aliud animam mundi esse in Socrate quam Socratem habere hoc ex diuina bonitate quod ipse animatus est anima propria. Non ergo sequitur: si dei benignitas Socrati animam contulit, igitur duae animae sunt in Socrate. Item subiciet aliquis: si anima mundi est spiritus sanctus, et spiritus sanctus est ab aeterno quicquid ipse est, ergo anima mundi ab aeterno est quicquid ipsa est. Et si mundi anima ab aeterno est quicquid ipsa est, igitur mundi anima ab aeterno est mundi anima. Quod si mundi anima ab aeterno est mundi anima, igitur ab aeterno mundus est ea animatus. Sed si mundus ab aeterno est animatus, tunc mundus est ab aeterno. Nos uero hoc argumentum falsum esse dicimus: "si anima mundi uel spiritus sanctus est ab aeterno quicquid est uel anima mundi uel spiritus sanctus, ergo uel spiritus sanctus uel anima mundi ab aeterno est anima mundi." | 17v | Quomodo non sequitur, "si hic pater est quicquid ipse est antequam habuisset filium, ergo hic pater est ⟨pater⟩ antequam habuisset filium," sic non sequitur argumentatio. Quemadmodum enim pater est nomen habitudinis,

[4] quomodo *con. T. Greg.*, qualem *P* [8] bonitas *add. sup. lin. P*[c] [20] est *post corr.*, sed *ante corr. P*

[4–8] Guillelmus de Conchis, *Phil.* 1.5 (44B): "Si operatus esset casus mundum, aliquae causea praecessissent mundum, quarum concursus operaretur illum. Est enim casus inopinatus euentus ex causis confluentibus." Cf. Boethius, *Cons. phil.* 5.p1. [10–12] Boethius, *Cons. phil.* 3.m9.4–6. [15–18] Abelardus, *Dial.* 559.7–8. Guillelmus de Conchis, *Glos. sup. Boet.* 3.m9.545–546. *Phil.* 1.15 (46–47).

sic hoc uocabulum datum ex officio. Et quemadmodum hic praeceptor uel presbiter a pueritia sua ⟨est⟩ quicquid ipse est, non tamen hic praeceptor a pueritia sua est praeceptor nec hic presbiter a pueritia est presbiter, sic fateor quod spiritus sanctus ab aeterno ⟨est⟩ quicquid ipse est, non tamen ille spiritus est ab aeterno mundi anima. "Praeceptor" namque ex officio attribuitur. Et quomodo praeceptor dicitur aliquis eo quod praestet tortis uel etiam torquentibus, ita spiritus sanctus, id est dei bonitas, dicitur mundi anima ea ratione, quod conditoris bonitas cuncta quae in mundo uiuunt animat. Denique hoc uocabulum "quicquid" essentiam denotat, sed hoc nomen "praeceptor" uel "anima," officium, quomodo "pater," habitudinem. Quamobrem superius argumentum optime falsificatum est.

Dicto quid sit mundi anima, quid sit illius medietas incipiamus. Mundi ergo medietas illius communis participatio ⟨est⟩, medium autem solet dici commune. Mundi itaque animam in mundi medietate positam nichil aliud est quam uniuersitatem creaturam communiter diuina bonitate participare. Mundus enim dicitur omnium creaturarum collectio, et a parte designatur totum. Mundus namque dicitur superius elementum proprie ideo quod omnia ibi sint munda, pura, nitida, splendida. Dicitur etiam mundus iuxta illud Apostoli, mors intrauit in mundum per feminam, id est in uniuersum genus humanum. Vel aliter medietas dicitur proportionalitas, unde etiam dicitur in arismeticis quod alia medietas est arismetica, alia geometrica, alia armonica. In proportionalitate igitur locata est anima mundi, id est diuina bonitas ⟨ea⟩ quae in mundo sunt proportionaliter et concorditer creat et creata gubernat.

Alii autem dicunt quod mundi medietas est sol, quem cor totius mundi esse uolunt. Quemadmodum enim, inquiunt, anima hominis sedem et domicilium in corde habet, unde per membra corporis uires suas spargens in omnibus corporis membris tota sua membra uegetat, ita uitalis calor a sole procedens omnibus

[14] communiter *add. sup. lin. P*ᶜ, coiunt *P*

[1–10] Cf. Abelardus, *TSum* 3.94–99; *TChr* 4.145–147; *TSch* 2.174–176. [12] *Guillelmi Glos. sup. Tim.* 71.22: "Medium enim saepe pro communi accipitur." Cf. Augustinus, *Enarrationes in psalmos*, Ps. 103, Sermo 2.11. 12–13 (CCSL 40, 1497). Alanus de Insulis, *Dist.*, PL 210, 853C: "Medium sumitur pro communi." Manegoldus Lautenbachensis, *In psalmorum librum, Ps.* 73, PL 93, 880D: "Medium enim accipitur pro communi." [14–15] *Guillelmi Glos. sup. Tim.* 36.3. *Glos. sup. Boet.* 2.m8.13 and 3.m8.26–27. *Glos. sup. Macr.*, comment. ad 1.8.4: "Vt ait Apuleius, mundus est elementorum collectio cum ornatu eorumdem; et bene dicit 'ornatu,' quia aliter esset confusio." Ibid., 1.14.2: "Vniuersum quia uniuersa comprehendit: est enim ordinata collectio omnium creaturarum." Cf. Apuleius, *De mundo*, cap. 1 (initio): "Mundus est ornata ordinatio, dei munere, deorum recta custodia." [15–16] Calcidius, *In Tim.* 98 (151.3): "Caelum quoque usurpantes mundum omnem uocamus." Macrobius, *In Som. Scip.* 2.11.12 (129.24–25): "Mundus proprie caelum uocatur." [17–18] Cf. Rom. 5:12. [23–26] Macrobius, *In Som. Scip.* 1.20.6–7 (79). Calcidius, *In Tim.* 100 (151–152). Guillelmus de Conchis, *Glos. sup. Boet.* 3.m9.569–57. Remigius Autissiodorensis, *In Boethii Consolationem*, ed. E. T. Silk, *Saeculi noni auctoris in Boetii Consolationem Philosophiae commentarius*, 335–336. Anonymus, *Explanatiuncula in uersus 'O qui perpetua' Boetii*, 6 et 9, ed. É. Jeauneau, *Lectio philosophorum*, 324, 329. Anonymus, *In Timaeum Platonis*, ed. T. Schmid, *Classica et Mediaevalia. Revue danoise de philologie et d'histoire*, 10.2 (1949), 243. Vide supra, 278.20–23.

quae uiuunt uitam subministrat. Cui sententiae Eraclitus adquiescens optimam similitudinem dat de aranea ad animam, de tela araneae ad corpus. Sicut aranea, ait, stans in medio telae sentit quam cito musca aliquem filum suum corrumpit, itaque illuc celeriter currit, quasi de fili persectione dolens, sic hominis anima aliqua parte corporis laesa, illuc festine meat, quasi impatiens laesionis corporis, cui firme et proportionaliter iuncta est. Cum itaque mundi anima sit dei benignitas, medietas uero mundi proportionalitas seu communitas, non est aliud deum animam locasse in medietate quam creatorem sua bonitate cuncta quae in mundo uiuunt proportionaliter et concorditer animare.

2.2 Qualiter animam mundi diuisit

| 19r | DIVISIONEM INSTAVRANS HACTENVS, id est hoc modo uel usque ad summam hanc dixerat deum animam diuidisse per partes. Hic autem ostendit qualiter eam diuisit. Et est in hoc loco tertium integumentum, quod ut euidentissime aperiatur, haec a nobis discutienda sunt: qualiter per numeros anima diuisa dicatur, qualiter per septem et per hos septem, qualiter unitatem in principio posuit, qualiter pares et impares ab utroque latere diffluentes, qualiter a pari et impari lineares numeros apposuit et superficiales ⟨et solidos⟩, qualiter partitionem suam in solidos terminauit. Vnumquodque horum septem eo ordine quo annumerata sunt expedire temptemus.

Plato igitur uolens ostendere quod mundi anima, id est conditoris bonitas inenarrabilis, cuncta proportionaliter mouerit, dixit per numeros eam diuisam esse. In numeris enim solis aut in rebus eis subnectis proportio reperitur. Secundum numeros anima diuisa dicitur ut asseratur animae dignitas et potentiarum quas in rebus exercet. Numeri enim principio, id est unitate, nichil dignius est nec perfectius. Creator namque est ipsa unitas principalis. Denique nec numero illo aliqua creatura est excellentior. Numerus enim fuit exemplar in mente diuina. Vnde dictum est ad deum, "Omnia fecisti in numero et pondere et mensura." Iure igitur

8 medietate *scripsi*, medietatem *P* 10 instaurans *scripsi cum Calcidio*, in statu *P* 12 integumentum *P*ᶜ, *illeg. P* 17 *post* in solidos *add.* et solidos *P* 23 numeri *scripsi*, numerum *P*

1–6 Calcidius, *In Tim.* 220 (233.19–22). Diels-Kranz, *Die Fragmente der Vorsokratiker*, vol. I, Heraclitus, fr. 67a, 166. S. N. Mouraviev, *Héraclite d'Ephese: La tradition antique et médiévale* (Sankt Augustin: Academia Verlag, 1999), no. 238, T1209, 892. Cf. M. Markovich, *Heraclitus: Greek Text with a Short Commentary* (Merida, Venezuela: Los Andes University Press, 1967): "As I already suggested in *Phronesis*, 11 (1966), 26f., there is nothing from Heraclitus in the fragment." 17 Vnumquodque horum septem: id est, septem quaestiones, non septem numeri (et nota quod "qualiter per septem et per hos septem" continet duas quaestiones). 25 Boethius, *Inst. ar.* 1.1 (12.75–79): Haec [sc. arithmetica] enim cunctis prior est, non modo quod hanc ille huius mundanae molis conditor deus primam suae habuit ratiocinationis exemplar et ad hanc cuncta constituit, quaecumque fabricante ratione per numeros adsignati ordinis invenere concordiam." 26 Sap. 11:21.

Plato perfectionem et excellentiam uolens denotare uel asserere | 19v | ait creatorem eam per numeros diuisisse.

Partitionem uero istam usque septenarium numerum curauit Plato extendere ut per hoc innueret mundi animam spiritibus et corporibus essendi causam praebuisse. Ad spiritus enim ternarius, ad corpora uero refertur quaternarius, qui partes per aggregationem sunt septenarii. Sed septem sunt numeri a Platone in sectione appositi ut demonstraretur anima inuiolata esse et a nullo generata. Septenarius enim infra primum limitem, id est decadem, nec gignit quemquam numerum nec gignitur a quoquam. Vnde a mathematicis, ut testatur Macrobius, uirgo appellatus est. Aut propter aliud dici potest quod anima septies diuisa est, propter hoc scilicet ut ea ostenderetur perfecte omnia uiuificare. Nam cum sint septem partes, sex esse ibi interualla necesse est, sed senarius perfectus est numerus. Non enim partes illius aggregatae aut ipsum excedunt aut infra subsistunt. Omnis nimirum ille numerus perfectus esse dicitur cuius partes ei aequantur, superfluus uero cuius partes exsuperant, ut duodecim; imminutus autem cuius partes infra reperiuntur, ut octonarius. Qui haec plenius scire desiderat Arismeticam legat studiosissime ueterum lectioni utilissimam.

Verumtamen quomodo senarii partes ei aequantur incipiamus, illo praemisso quod partes in hoc loco per multiplicationem, non per aggregationem accipiendae sunt—porro numeri multiplicatio est unius numeri per alterum dimensio, aggregatio uero diuersorum nuermorum coniunctio. Sunt itaque senarii hae partes: ternarius qui est media pars, binarius qui est tertia pars, unitas quae est sexta pars. Sed tria et duo et unum sex reddit, nec exuberantes nec infra subsistentes. Septem ergo sunt partes ut per sex earum intercapedines perfectio inesse animae designaretur. Expedito cur anima a Platone per numeros diuisa dicatur et cur per septem, qualiter per hos septem aperiamus, prius oculis subiecta descriptione—ut in Platonibus solet ad euidentiam fieri—ut per eam quaedam quae iam dicta sunt et pluraque quae dicturi sumus tam oculis subiecta fidelibus quam per aurem intelligantur demissa [= first lambda diagram].

[15] cuius *add. sup. lin.* P^c [17] arismeticam P^c, arimeticam *P* [19] multiplicationem *scripsi*, multitudinem *P* [20] accipiendae P^c, accepiendae *P* [21] hae *scripsi*, heae *P* [26] septem *scripsi*, VI *P* [26] septem *scripsi*, VI *P*

[3–6] Cf. Hugo de Sancto Victore, *De scripturis et scriptoribus sacris praenotatiunculae*, 15 (De numeris mysticis sacrae Scripturae), PL 125, 22D: "Secundum multiplicationem numeri significant, ut duodenarius uniuersitatis signum est, quia ex ternario et quaternario inuicem multiplicatis perficitur; quoniam quaternarius corporalium, ternarius spiritualium forma est." [8–10] Macrobius, *In Som. Scip.* 1.6.11 (20.15–22). Cf. Calcidius, *In Tim.* 36 (85.14–18); Martianus Capella, *De nuptiis* 7.738 (267.3–6); *Bernardi Glos. sup. Tim.*, 5.136–139. [12–13] Calcidius, *In Tim.* 38 (87.15ff.); Macrobius, *In Som. Scip.* 1.6.12 (20.22–30). Martianus Capella, *De nuptiis* 8.736 (265). Boethius, *Inst. ar.* 1.19.43–51 (50). [13–16] Guillelmus de Conchis, *Glos. sup. Macr.*, comment. ad 1.6.12: "Superfluus dicitur numerus, cuius partes aggregatae reddunt maiorem summam ipso toto, sicut XII . . . Diminutus est ille, cuius partes aggregatae minorem summam reddunt ipso toto, ut VIII. [21–23] Macrobius, *In Som. Scip.* 1.6.12 (20.22–28). Calcidius, *In Tim.* 38 (87.17–19).

Per hos itaque numeros animae separatio facta est ut quod anima mundi secundum musicas consonantias proportionaliter cuncta moueat ostenderetur. Namque inter hos numeros sunt illae proportiones quae musicas consonantias resonant. Musicae autem consonantiae sunt quinque: diatessaron, diapente, diapason, ⟨diapason⟩ cai diapente, disdiapason. Tonus namque non est consonantia sed consonantiarum principium, cuius tamen effecta proportio inter hos numeros inueniri potest. Quomodo igitur in his numeris proportiones, quae musicas consonantias generant, inueniri queant, uideamus. Inter III itaque et IIII est epitrita proportio quae diatessaron facit. Sed ternarius ad duo hemiolia, id est ad sexqualteram proportionem, iungitur, haec diapente consonantiam resonat. Dupla uero proportione se habet ad binarium quaternarius uel ad eundem octonarius, haec autem proportio diapason generat. Nouenarius autem ternario et idem unitati tripla proportione copulatur, quae proportio parit diapason cai diapente. Denique inter octonarium et binarium uel quaternarium et unitatem est quadrupla proportio quae disdiapason efficit. Sed octonarius nouenario epogdoa proportione copulatur, ex qua tonus nascitur, qui tamen est principium consonantiarum non consonantia. Sed quoniam non omnes qui hoc opusculum legerint aut arismeticam nouerint aut cordetenus supradictarum proportionum dissertationes retinuerint, eas com⟨m⟩ode expediamus. Est igitur epitrita proportio, id est sexquitertia, quotiens numerus ad numerum comparatus continet eum totum et eius tertiam partem, ut quaternarius ad ternarium. Hemiolia uero cum numerus aliquis eum totum et eius mediam partem possidet. Dupla autem cum numerus alium bis infra se continet. Sed tripla cum unus in alio ter continetur, ut III: IX. Quadrupla uero cum numerus metitur alium quater, ut IIII: ⟨XVI⟩. Epogdoa, id est sexquioctaua, quotiens unus numerus continet alium et eius octauam partem, ut IX: VIII.

Reserato qualiter per numeros, qualiter per septem, qualiter per hos septem anima diuisa dicatur, qualiter primitus sumpta sit unitas enodemus. Est ergo et primo sumpta et in summo posita unitas, ut manifeste innueretur unum esse primum et summum principium omnium, a quo cuncta procedunt, tam corpora quam spiritus, tam mutabilia quam immutabilia, quae designant pares et impares ab utroque diffluentes. Pares ad corpora et mutabilia, impares autem ad spiritus et immutabilia referuntur.

[5] diapason cai diapente *scripsi*, c diapente *P*, cai diapente *P*[c]   [5] disdiapason *P*[c], diapason *P*; Macrobius, *In Som. Scip.* 2.1.24 (99.4–6).   [12] autem *scripsi*, aut *P*   [13] ternario *scripsi*, ternarius *P*   [15] dis- *add. sup. lin. P*   [21] hemiola *P*[c], hemolia *P*   [26] IX *post corr.*, X *ante corr.* *P*   [27] hos *P*[c], uos *P*   [31] quae *scripsi*, quam *P*

[7–17] Boethius, *Inst. mus.* 1.7 et 16 (194 et 201–203). Id., *Inst. ar.* 1.1 (13.100–113). Macrobius, *In Som. Scip.* 1.6.43–44 et 2.1.14–20 (26 et 97–99). Calcidius, *In Tim.* 35 et 46 (85 et 95–96).   [19–26] Macrobius, *In Som. Scip.* 2.1.15–20 (97–98). Cf. Boethius, *Inst. ar.* 1.24–27 (60–67). *Inst. mus.* 1.4 (191–192).

Aliter dicunt quidam unitatem esse sumptam in principio et postea pares et impares ut ostenderetur anima easdem potentias exercere in pueritia et omnem callem uitae usque ad annos discretionis simplici uia carpere. Tum uero quosdam bonae operationi insistere et desiderio aeternorum exaestuare, quod per impares manifeste designatur, alios autem mentis intentionem ad praua deflectere et temporalium et labentium cupiditate insatiabili feruere, quod per pares numeros intelligitur. Quae omnia uolens significare Pytagoras dixit in modum huius graecae litterae Y uitam humanam esse dispositam. Illa enim sic scribenda est ut ab uno illius pede duo rami prodeant. Alter quorum ad sinistrum uergens, ubi quasi a trunco exit, deorsumque tendens significat caduca appetentes et cum eis a quibus nec retineri uel quae retinere poterunt labentes. Alter uero ad dexteram surgens in principio strictus et in fine latus designat caelestis patriae proceres contemplationi caelestium collo inreflexo uacantes, ad uirtutum ardua indefesse contendentes, ut de uirtute in uirtutem gradientes deum deorum in Sion uidere mereantur. Ad dextrum consurgere ramum nec in sinistrum deflectere ostenditur Cornutus a Persio cum ad eum dicens, loquitur,

> Et tibi quae Samios deduxit littera ramos
> Surgentem dextro monstrauit limite callem.

Qui hanc secundam sententiam asserere conatur in errorem mihi relabi uidetur. Non enim hic de humana anima Plato tractat sed de mundana quam alicuius sorde uitii maculari nefas est dicere.

Quoniam dictum est qualiter animae sectio per numeros facta sit, qualiter per septem, qualiter per hos septem, qualiter unitas prima sumpta sit, qualiter post eam pares et impares ab eadem defluentes, qualiter lineares, superficiales, et solidi a pari et impari in sectione illa sint positi explicemus, quod ut colliquescat, primo paucis absoluamus qui sint lineares numeri, qui superficiales, qui solidi.

Omnis namque numerus per se consideratus linearis esse dicitur. Multiplicatus aut per se aut per alium, qui ex eo procreatur, superficialis nuncupatur, sed aut per se aut per alium aut partim per se partim per alium ter ducto numero soliditas numeri procreatur. Est ergo a pari binarius linearis numerus. Quaternarius uero superficialis nuncupatur, ex binario enim per se multiplicato surgit. Sed

2 omnem P^c, omnes *(?) P* 15 deflectere P^c, eflectere *(?) P* 16 ad *bis repetitur, postea expunctum* 18 limite *scripsi*, litera *P* 20 de mundana *scripsi*, md'ndana *P* 24 defluentes *post corr.*, diffluentes *ante corr. P* 24 et *scripsi*, qui *P* 27 linearis P^c, lineares *P*

---

14 Ps. 83:8. 17–18 Persius, *Sat.* 3.56–57. Cf. Isidorus, *Etym.* 1.3.6: "litteram Pythagoras Samius ad exemplum uitae humanae primus formauit; cuius uirgula subterior primam aetatem significat, incertam quippe et quae adhuc se nec uitiis nec uirtutibus dedit. Biuium autem, quod superest, ab adolescentia incipit: cuius dextra pars ardua est, sed ad beatam uitam tendens: sinistra facilior, sed ad labem interitumque deducens. De qua sic Persius ait . . ."

octonarius tres soliditatis dimensiones recipit, quippe qui conficitur ex binario ter ducto, quia bis bini bis sunt octo. Similiter ab impari ternarius linearis est numerus. Nouenarius est superficialis, ternarius enim bis ductus nouenarium producit—ter trium enim nouem sunt. Idem porro ternarius ter multiplicatus in XXVII numeri quantitatem accrescit—nam ter terni ter XXVII sunt. Lineares uero numeri tam a pari quam impari appositi sunt ad ostendendum quod anima mundi, id est summa opificis dei bonitas, in longum moueat tam caduca corpora quam non caduca; superficiales uero ut in latum; solidi quidem ut incomprehensibilis benignitas omnia corpora, scilicet ut sunt ea quae sunt infra lunam, et durabiliora, ut ea quae sunt in aplane, in spissum mouere crederetur.

Sciendum ⟨est⟩ numeros appellatos esse lineares uel superficiales uel solidos similitudine. Linea enim est longitudo sine latitudine, superficies uero latitudo sine spissitudine, soliditas autem crassitudo tres dimensiones obtinens: longitudinem, latitudinem, spissitudinem. Haec delibamus ne penitus ignorata huic caliginosae parti Platonis intelligentiae luculentum splendorem subripiant. Sed qui ea perfecte nosse desiderat, arismeticam non contemnat. In solidos autem haec partitio animae finita est ad demonstrandum quod [in] anima cuncta moueat solide, firme, indissolubiliter, uel ut ostenderetur nulla esse dimensio ultra soliditatem. Expeditis illis quae proposuimus, prout in anima nobis eloqui tribuit, ad litterae seriem explanandam accedamus.

2.3 Qualiter deus dicatur impleuisse interualla

NATIS ITAQVE LIMITIBVS. Hucusque ostendit Plato deum impleuisse interualla duplorum sexqualteris et sexquitertiis, quod qualiter intelligendum est pro posse nostro exposuimus. Hic autem dicit impleuisse deum interualla epitritorum omnium sexquioctauis et tonis, in quo haec consideranda sunt: qualiter deus dicatur impleuisse interualla illa, qualiter illius numeri sexquitertium inueniri queat, in quibus duos tonos et semitonium minus contineri dicit Plato, in quibus primis duo toni et semitonium minus inueniri possunt. Plato itaque considerans in omni sexquitertia proportione naturaliter contineri duas sexquioctauas proportiones etiam eam quae efficit minus semitonium, et omnem proprietatem cuiuslibet eiusdem dei benignitate esse collatam non ignorans ait deum impleuisse interualla sexquitertiorum epogdois et limate.

Illos uero numeros in quibus duos tonos continuos et lima ⟨contineri dicit Plato⟩ qui inuenire desiderat, hanc regulam artis arismeticae cordetenus retineat. Omnis multiplex numerus quoto loco distat ab unitate tot proportiones sui generis praecedit, id est duplex numerus tot sexqualteras proportiones praecedit

2 impari *scripsi*, impare *P* 15 *ante* intelligentiae *add.* ill, *postea expunctum* 27 duos *scripsi*, duobus *P*

quoto loco discedit ab unitate. Si enim primus duplus est, unam sexqualteram praecedit. Sed si in secundo loco ab unitate distat, duo. Si in tertio, tres. Similiter de triplis et quadruplis intelligite. Multiplex enim numerus dicitur qui alium uel bis uel ter uel quater uel quotienslibet continet. Sexqualterae autem proportiones dicuntur esse generis duplorum quia de duplis nascuntur sexqualterii, sexquitertiae generis triplorum quia de triplis sexquitertii procreantur. Similiter de quadruplis et sexquiquartis et aliis intelligite. Binarius ergo, quia primus duplus est, unum sexqualteram praecedit, id est in naturali numero, aut quoniam praecedit qui ad ipsum est sexqualter. Praecedit enim ternarium qui ad ipsum est sexqualter, ad quem nullus alius sexqualteram proportionem efficit. Binarius enim contra ternarium comparatus sexqualtera proportione tenetur. Qui ternarius, quia media parte caret, ad nullum sexqualter est. Sic et quaternarius, quia secundus duplus, duas sexqualteras proportiones praecedit. Praecedit enim senarium quem sequitur nouenarius, qui contra octonarium consideratus sexquioctauam proportionem reddit. Sexquioctauus enim numerus est ad numerum cum eum totum et eius octauam partem continet. Sed secundus octuplus duas sexquioctauas praecedit. Quia ergo primus non nisi unam praecedit sexquioctauam, de secundo inuestigemus utrum duos tonos et lima praeueniat.

Multiplicetur igitur octonarius per se ipsum. Sic octies octo LXIIII sunt. Superaddatur ergo LXIIII eius octaua pars. Surget LXXII. Octo enim LXIIII additi in LXXII excrescunt. Octaua uero pars LXXII, id est IX, eidem iuncta LXXXI reddunt. Sed horum ultimus, id est octoginta unum, non est epitritus ad priorem (id est ad LXIIII), quippe LXIIII, utpote carens parte tertia, ad nullum sexquitertia proportione comparatur. Oportet ergo hos numeros dimittere et alios sumere, quos per hanc facile quiuis reperiet regulam. Si aliquis numerus partem non habet quam uelles eum habere, per numerum a quo pars denominatur eum numerum, cuius partem uis esse, multiplica et ei quidem multiplicationi quae surget pars optata proueniet. Quia igitur LXIIII et LXXX unam sexquitertiam implere non possunt—quippe LXIIII parte tertia non tenetur—LXIIII ter multiplica,

4 proportiones *scripsi*, proportionis *P*   27 *post* multiplica *add.* et is qui ex illa multiplicatione procreabitur, *postea expunctum P*

286.35–287.3 Boethius, *Inst. mus.* 2.8 (234.26–235.1): "Unusquisque multiplex ab unitate scilicet computatus tot superparticulares habitudines praecedit suae scilicet in contrariam partem denominationis, quotus ipse ab unitate discesserit, hoc modo ut duplex sesqualiteras antecedat, triplex sesquitertias, quadruplex sesquiquartas, ac deinceps in hunc modum." Id., *Inst. ar.* 2.2 (97.14–18). Cf. Guillelmus de Conchis, *Glos. sup. Tim.* 85.12–14. Radulphus Laudunensis, *De semitonio*, ed. A. Peden "'De semitonio': Some Medieval Exercises in Arithmetic," 385. 3–4 Boethius, *Inst. mus.* 1.4 (191.11–13). 19–24 Boethius, *Inst. mus.* 2.28 (260–261); cf. Guillelmus de Conchis, *Glos. sup. Tim.* 85–86. 24–28 Guillelmus de Conchis, *Glos. sup. Tim.* 85.1–5: "Est alia regula artis arismeticae. Si in aliquibus numeris in aliqua proportione constitutis quaeramus partem quam non habeant, multiplicemus illos nomine partis quam quaerimus. Qui inde fient, in eadem erunt proportione et partem quam quaerimus optinebunt." Cf. Boethius, *Inst. mus.* 2.27 et 30 (261.13–17 et 264.23–26). Cf. *Glossa maior in Institutionem musicam Boetii* ad 2.28, vol. 2, 244: "utilis regula et generalis."

et is qui ex illa multiplicatione procreabitur tertiae partis sectionem non refugiet. Duc itaque ter LXIIII. Efficitur CXCII numerus. Partem tertiam habet necnon et octauam. Et addatur ei pars tertia. Inquiramus possintne inueniri duo toni et lima in hac epitrita proportione. Addatur itaque CXCII numero pars tertia sui, id est LXIIII. Et fiet CCLVI. Inter hos numeros duos tonos et lima—uera unitate nobis subueniente—poterimus inuenire hoc modo. Sumatur pars octaua CXCII, id est XXIIII, et ei addatur. Fiet CCXVI. Est igitur CCXVI ad CXCII sexquioctauus. Quod autem XXIIII sint VIII pars CXCII, sic colligite. Octies XX sunt CLX. Octies IIII, XXXII. Sed CLX et XXXII sunt CXCII. Est ergo CCXVI epogdous ad CXCII. Sed si octaua pars CCXVI ei apponatur, fiet CCXLIII. Pars uero octaua CCXVI est XXVII numerus. Est itaque CCXVI ad CXCII sexquioctauus, et ad CCXVI CCXLIII. Sed CCXLIII [et CXCLIII] et CXCII non possunt unam sexquitertiam proportionem facere, quoniam tantum deest illi impletioni quantum deest comparatione habita inter CCXLIII et CCLVI, id est tredecim unitates quae, si addantur CCXLIII numero, fiet CCLVI, qui numerus epitritus est ad CXCII. In hac igitur epitrita proportione duae sexquioctauae inueniri possunt, ea quoque quae lima, id est minus semitonium, restituit, quae hoc potest dici super XIII partiens ducentesimas quadragesimas tertias, CCLVI enim numerus continet CCXLIII et insuper tredecim unitates. Haec autem proportio quae minus semitonium facit maior est quam sexquidecima nona et minor quam sexquidecima octaua et ita cadit iter sexquidecimam nonam et sexquidecimam octauam.

Illa itaque differentia quae est inter CCXLIII et CCLVI facit lima, id est minus semitonium, quae lima dicitur quasi corruptum. Lima enim corruptio interpretatur. Vnde alimma incorruptum dicitur, quoddam unguentum quo corpus perfusum ab igne inuiolatum | 21r | seruatur. Hoc se perfudit Philologia aethereas sedes ascensura, ne ei sidereus ignis noceret et corpus adhuc mortale exureret. Sed maius semitonium apotome dicitur, id est supradecisionem. Apotome enim plus est quam media pars toni. Vnum semitonium dicitur quasi imperfectus tonus. Semitonium namque est pars composita ex "semus-ma-mum" quod est "imperfectus-ta-tum," non a "semis semissis" quod est medietas. Sed lima est toni

7 sexquioctauus *scripsi*, octuplus *P* 17 *fortasse* sic *pro* hoc *legendum?* 24 alimma *scripsi*, alimau *P* 24 unguentum *scripsi*, ungentum *P* 27 apotome *scripsi*, aphotome *P* 27 apotome *scripsi*, aphotome *P*

17–18 Cf. *Glossa maior in Institutionem musicam Boetii* ad 2.29, vol. 2, 260: "Vt sese CCLVI ad CCXLIII habent: CCLVI ad CCXLIII supertredecipartiens ducentessimas quadragesimas tertias est." Guillelmus de Conchis, *Glos. sup. Tim.* 86.2–3. 19–21 Boethius, *Inst. mus.* 2.29 (262.3–8). Guillelmus de Conchis, *Glos. sup Tim.* 86.4–7. 23–25 Remigius Autissiodorensis, *Comm. in Mart*, 46.15: "Limma Grece corruptio, alimma uero incorruptum siue incontaminatum sonat." Cf. Eriugena, *Annotationes in Martianum*, 46.16: "Limma corruptio, alimma incontaminatum. Per alimmata omnes intellige uirtutes quibus liberatur anima ab aeternis ardoribus." 25–26 Martianus Capella, *De nuptiis* 2.109–110. 27 Boethius, *Inst. mus.* 2.30 (263.21–22): "Reliqua igitur pars, quae maior est apotome nuncupatur a Graecis, a nobis uero potest decisio." 29–30 Boethius, *Inst. mus.* 1.16 (203.8–10): "Sed utraque semitonia nuncupantur, non quod omnino semitonia ex aequo sint media, sed quod semum dicit solet, quod ad integritatem usque non peruenit."

minor pars, cuius limatis partes dieses apellantur. Apotomis uero partes comata nuncupantur. Qui haec omnia ad plenum nosse desiderat, Musicam Boetii studiosissime legat.

Quia ista succincte auditoribus in quadruuio rudibus expedimus, ne penitus nescita obscuritati Timaei crassis tenebris obuolutae maiorem caliginem ingerant, non sit ergo fastidiosum non ignaris quadruuii si hic uerbosius euagati sumus quam eorum iam prouecta scientia exiget. Haec enim perscribimus introducendis, non perfectis. In his autem duobus numeris, CXCII ⟨et⟩ CCLVI, duo continui toni et lima reperiri possunt, quod uolens significare Plato posuit illos inter quos minus semitonium primo inueniri potest.

Fortasse aliquis dicat: Prior de duabus regulis datis superius ad inueniendos tonos duos continuos et lima nil utilitatis affert, quia secundum eam non extenduntur hic duae sexquioctauae, cum illa dicat, quoto loco distat ab unitate aliquis multiplex numerus, eum tot proportiones sui generis praecedere. Secundum illam regulam, inquam, non extenduntur, quod sic probari potest. CXCII nullo loco distat ab unitate, non enim in primo loco ab ea discedit. Imo octonarius est primus octuplus, secundus autem est LXIIII, tertius uero est CCCCCXII. Cum ergo nullo loco ab unitate discesserit iste octuplus, id est CXCII, quomodo ad eum inueniendum ista regula est utilis? Ad hoc respondemus regulam illam parum prodesse sine aliqua subsequente, sed per illas duas facile inueniri posse duos tonos et semitonium.

Vel aliter dicimus uerum esse quod nullo loco distat ab unitate CXCII octuplus numerus, sed a ternario et in secundo loco ab eodem distat. Ternario enim XXIIII numerus est octuplus. Octies enim tria XXIIII restituunt. Sed ad XXIIII CXCII octupla habitudine comparatur. Namque XXIIII numerus octies ductus in summam CXCII excrescit. Licet igitur a ternario in secundo loco distet CXCII numerus, nullo tamen ab unitate, ad duos tonos continuos inueniendos et lima ualde illa regula necessaria est. Quomodo enim "ab unitate" dicit, similiter intelligendum est de quolibet numero naturali unitatem sequente, ut sic intelligatur regula. Omnis multiplex numerus quoto loco distat ab unitate—et subintelligite uel a binario uel a ternario uel a quaternario et similiter a quolibet sequentium numerorum—tot proportiones sui generis praecedit. Nec sic intellecta haec regula alicubi fallit. Cum ergo a ternario CXCII numerus distet secundo loco, ad inueniendos tonos continuos et lima perutilis esse ostenditur superius data regula.

Quoniam expeditum est qualiter intelligendum sit quod Plato dicit deum impleuisse interualla epitritorum omnium epogdois et limate, qualiter inueniantur illi numeri, inter quos continentur duo toni et semitonium, et in quibus duo toni reperiantur et lima, ad litteram accedamus, prius tamen descriptione oculis

[1] apotomis *scripsi*, aphotonies *P* [2] nuncupantur *scripsi*, nuncupatur [3] Boethius, *Inst. mus.* 3.6 (277). [4] quadruuio *post corr.*, conuiuio *ante corr. P* [6] si hic uerbosius *scripsi*, sine his uerbosis *P* [9] uolens *post corr.*, uobis *ante corr. P* [17] CCCCCXII *scripsi*, CCCCCXXII *P*

subdita in qua duo toni et lima inter duos epitritos contineantur ut quaecumque dicta sunt de tonis et limate, in arca memoriae abscondita, nec obliuio demoliri nec inutilium curarum agmen possit surripere, et tantae rei subtilitas nequeat effugere.

A translation of this text is available on the companion website.

BIBLIOGRAPHY

Abbott, B. P., et al. "Observation of Gravitational Waves from a Binary Black Hole Merger." *Physical Review Letters* 116 (2016), 061102.

Albertson, David. *Mathematical Theologies: Nicholas of Cusa and the Legacy of Thierry of Chartres*. Oxford: Oxford University Press, 2014.

Alessio, Franco. "La filosofia e le *artes mechanicae* nel secolo XII." *Studi medievali* 6 (1965), 71–161.

Alliez, Éric. *Capital Times: Tales from the Conquest of Time*. Translated by Georges Van Den Abbeele. Theory out of Bounds 6. Minneapolis: University of Minnesota Press, 1996.

Badiou, Alain. *Being and Event*. Translated by Oliver Feltham. London: Continuum, 2005.

Baeumker, Clemens. *Der Platonismus im Mittelalter*. Munich: Verlag der K. B. Akademie der Wissenschaften, 1916.

Bakhouche, Béatrice. *Calcidius: Commentaire au Timée de Platon*. Paris: J. Vrin, 2011.

———. "Lectures médiévales de l'harmonie musicale de l'âme selon Platon (*Timée* 35b–36b): l'influence de Calcidius." *Revue de musicologie* 98 (2012), 339–362.

Balint, Bridget K. *Ordering Chaos: The Self and the Cosmos in Twelfth-Century Latin Prosimetrum*. Leiden: Brill, 2009.

Baltzly, Dirk, trans. *Proclus: Commentary on Plato's Timaeus*, Vol. 4: *Book 3, Part II: Proclus on the World Soul*. Cambridge: Cambridge University Press, 2009.

Bangu, Sorin. "Pythagorean Heuristic in Physics." *Perspectives on Science* 14 (2006), 387–416.

Barbera, André. "The Consonant Eleventh and the Expansion of the Musical Tetraktys: A Study of Ancient Pythagoreanism." *Journal of Music Theory* 28 (1984), 191–223.

———. *The Euclidean Division of the Canon: Greek and Latin Sources*. Greek and Latin Music Theory 8. Lincoln: University of Nebraska Press, 1991.

Barker, Andrew. "Aristotle on Perception and Ratios." *Phronesis* 26 (1981), 248–266.

———. *Greek Musical Writings*. Vol. 2, *Harmonic and Acoustic Theory*. Cambridge Readings in the Literature of Music. Cambridge: Cambridge University Press, 1989.

———. "Pythagorean Harmonics." In *A History of Pythagoreanism*, edited by Carl Huffman, 185–203. Cambridge: Cambridge University Press, 2014), 190.

———. *Scientific Method in Ptolemy's Harmonics*. Cambridge: Cambridge University Press, 2000.

———. *The Science of Harmonics in Classical Greece*. Cambridge: Cambridge University Press, 2007.

———. "Timaeus on Music and the Liver." In *Reason and Necessity: Essays on Plato's* Timaeus, edited by M. R. Wright, 85–99. London: Duckworth and the Classical Press of Wales, 2000.

Barnish, Samuel I. B. "Martianus Capella and Rome in the Late Fifth Century." *Hermes* 114 (1986), 98–111.

Bartusiak, Marcia. *Einstein's Unfinished Symphony: Listening to the Sounds of Space-Time*. Washington, DC: Joseph Henry Press, 2000.

Baur, Ludwig. *Dominicus Gundissalinus: De divisione philosophiae*. Beiträge zur Geschichte der Philosophie des Mittelalters 4.2–3. Münster: Aschendorff, 1903.

Beaujouan, Guy. "Réflexions sur les rapports entre théorie et pratique au Moyen Âge." In *The Cultural Context of Medieval Learning: Proceedings of the First International Colloquium on Philosophy, Science, and Theology in the Middle Ages—September 1973*, edited by John Emery Murdoch and Edith Dudley Sylla, 437–484. Boston Studies in the Philosophy of Science 26. Boston: D. Reidel, 1975.

———. "The Transformation of the Quadrivium." In *Renaissance and Renewal in the Twelfth Century*, edited by Robert L. Benson and Giles Constable, 463–487. Cambridge, MA: Harvard, 1982.

Bennett, Jane. *The Enchantment of Modern Life: Attachments, Crossings, and Ethics*. Princeton, NJ: Princeton University Press, 2001

———. *Vibrant Matter: A Political Ecology of Things*. Durham, NC: Duke University Press, 2010.

Bernard, Michael. "The Seligenstadt Tonary." *Plainsong and Medieval Music* 13 (2004), 107–125.

Bernhard, Michael, and Calvin Bower, eds. *Glossa maior in Institutionem musicam Boethii*. 4 vols. Munich: Bayerische Akademie der Wissenschaften, 1993–2011.

Bezner, Frank. *Vela Veritatis: Hermeneutik, Wissen und Sprache in der Intellectual History des 12. Jahrhunderts*. Studien und Texte zur Geistesgeschichte des Mittelalters 85. Leiden: Brill, 2005.

Boese, Helmut, ed. *Thomas Cantimpratensis: Liber de natura rerum*. Berlin: Walter de Gruyter, 1973.

Bogue, Ronald. *Deleuze on Music, Painting, and the Arts*. New York: Routledge, 2003.

Bossuat, Robert, ed. *Alain de Lille. Anticlaudianus: Texte critique, avec une introduction et des tables*. Paris: J. Vrin, 1955.

Bovey, Muriel. *Disciplinae cyclicae: L'organisation du savoir dans l'œuvre de Martianus Capella*. Polymnia 3. Trieste: Edizioni Università di Trieste, 2003.

Bower, Calvin. "Boethius and Nicomachus: An Essay Concerning the Sources of *De institutione musica*." *Vivarium* 16 (1978), 1–45.

———. *Fundamentals of Music: Anicius Manlius Severinus Boethius*. Edited by Claude V. Palisca. Music Theory in Translation. New Haven: Yale University Press, 1989.

Bragard, Roger, ed. *Jacobi Leodiensis Speculum musicae*. Corpus scriptorum de musica 3. [Rome]: American Institute of Musicology, 1955–1973.

Brandt, Samuel, ed. *Anicii Manlii Severini Boethii: In Isagogen Porphyrii commenta*. Corpus Scriptorum Ecclesiasticorum Latinorum 48. Vienna: F. Tempsky, 1906.

Brett, Philip. "Musicality, Essentialism, and the Closet." In *Queering the Pitch: The New Gay and Lesbian Musicology*, edited by Philip Brett, Elizabeth Wood, and Gary C. Thomas, 9–26. 2nd ed. New York and London: Routledge, 2006.

Brisson, Luc, ed. *Porphyre: Sentences*. 2 vols. Histoire des doctrines de l'antiquité classique 33. Paris: Librairie Philosophique J. Vrin, 2005.

Broadie, Sarah. *Nature and Divinity in Plato's* Timaeus. Cambridge: Cambridge University Press, 2011.

Buchanan, Brett. *Onto-Ethologies: The Animal Environments of Uexküll, Heidegger, Merleau-Ponty, and Deleuze*. Albany: SUNY Press, 2008.

Buechner, Karl, ed. *Fragmenta poetarum Latinorum epicorum et lyricorum praeter Ennium et Lucilium*. Bibliotheca scriptorum Graecorum et Romanorum Teubneriana. Leipzig: B. G. Teubner, 1982.

Burkhard, Karl, ed. *Nemesii episcopi Premnon physicon siue* ΠΕΡΙ ΦΥΣΕΩΣ ΑΝΘΡΩΠΟΥ *liber a N. Alfano archiepiscopo Salerni in Latinum translatus*. Bibliotheca scriptorum Graecorum et Romanorum Teubneriana. Leipzig: B. G. Teubner, 1917.

Burnet, John, ed. *Platonis Opera*. Scriptorum classicorum bibliotheca Oxoniensis. Oxford: Clarendon Press, 1900–1907.

Burnett, Charles. "Adelard, Ergaphalau, and the Science of the Stars." In *Magic and Divination in the Middle Ages: Texts and Techniques in the Islamic and Christian Worlds*, II, 133–145. Variorum Collected Studies Series 557. Aldershot: Ashgate, 1996.

———. "Adelard, Music, and the Quadrivium." In *Adelard of Bath: An English Scientist and Arabist of the Early Twelfth Century*, edited by Charles Burnett, 69–86. London: Warburg Institute, 1987.

———, ed. and trans. *Adelard of Bath, Conversations with His Nephew: On the Same and the Different, Questions on Natural Science and On Birds*. Cambridge: Cambridge University Press, 1998.

———. "The Chapter on the Spirits in the *Pantegni* of Constantine the African." In *Constantine the African and ʿAlī ibn al-ʿAbbās al-Maǧūsī: The* Pantegni *and Related Texts*, edited by Charles Burnett and Danielle Jacquart, 99–120. Studies in Ancient Medicine 10. Leiden: Brill, 1994.

———. *The Introduction of Arabic Learning into England*. Panizzi Lectures. London: British Library, 1997.

Burnett, Charles, Michael Fend, and Penelope Gouk, eds. *The Second Sense: Studies in Hearing and Musical Judgement from Antiquity to the Seventeenth Century*. Warburg Institute Surveys and Texts. London: University of London, 1991.

Burnett, Charles, and Danielle Jacquart, eds. *Constantine the African and ʿAlī ibn al-ʿAbbās al-Maǧūsī: The* Pantegni *and Related Texts*. Studies in Ancient Medicine 10. Leiden: Brill, 1994.

[Burney, Charles.] "Chinese Music." In Abraham Rees et al., *The Cyclopædia; or, Universal Dictionary of Arts, Sciences, and Literature*, vol. 8, s.v. "Chinese Music" [unpaginated]. 1st American ed. Philadelphia: Samuel Bradford and Murray, Fairman and Co. [1805?–1825?].

Busse, Adolf, ed. *Ammonii In Porphyrii Isagogen sive V voces*. Commentaria in Aristotelem Graeca 4.3. Berlin: Reimer, 1891.

Buttimer, Charles Henry, ed. *Hugonis de Sancto Victore Didascalicon de studio legendi: A Critical Text*. Studies in Medieval and Renaissance Latin 10. Washington, DC: Catholic University Press, 1939.

Buytaert, E. M., ed. *Petri Abaelardi Opera theologica II*. Corpus Christianorum. Continuatio Mediaevalis 12. Turnhout: Brepols, 1969.

Buytaert, E. M., and C. J. Mews, eds. *Petri Abaelardi Opera theologica III*. Corpus Christianorum. Continuatio Mediaevalis 13. Turnhout: Brepols, 1987.

Bynum, Caroline Walker. "Did the Twelfth Century Discover the Individual?" *Journal of Ecclesiastical History* 31 (1980), 1–17.

Caiazzo, Irène. "L'âme du monde: Un thème privilégié des auteurs chartrains au XIIe siècle." In *Le temps de Fulbert: Actes de l'Université d'été du 8 au 10 juillet 1996*, 79–89. Chartres: Société archéologique d'Eure-et-Loir, 1996.

———. "La discussione sull'*Anima mundi* nel secolo XII." *Studi filosofici* 16 (1993), 27–62.

———. "The Four Elements in the Work of William of Conches." In *Guillaume de Conches: Philosophie et science au XIIe siècle*, edited by Barbara Obrist and Irène Caiazzo, 3–66. Micrologus Library 42. Florence: SISMEL Edizioni del Galluzzo, 2011.

———. *Lectures médiévales de Macrobe: Les* Glosae Colonienses super Macrobium. Études de philosophie médiévale 83. Paris: J. Vrin, 2002.

———, ed. *Thierry of Chartres, The commentary on the* De arithmetica *of Boethius*. Studies and Texts 191. Toronto: Pontifical Institute of Mediaeval Studies, 2015.

Cameron, Alan. "The Date and Identity of Macrobius." *Journal of Roman Studies* 56 (1966), 25–38.

———. "Martianus and His First Editor." *Classical Philology* 81 (1986), 320–328.

Cameron, Margaret. "William of Champeaux and Early Twelfth-Century Dialectic." PhD diss., University of Toronto, 2005.

Cappuyns, Maïeul. "Le 'De imagine' de Grégoire de Nysse traduit par Jean Scot Érigène." *Recherches de théologie ancienne et médiévale* 32 (1965), 205–262.

Carpenter, Nan Cooke. *Music in the Medieval and Renaissance Universities*. Norman: University of Oklahoma Press, 1958.

Casini, Paolo. "Newton: The Classical Scholia." *History of Science* 22 (1984), 1–58.

Chamberlain, David. "Philosophy of Music in the *Consolatio* of Boethius." In *Boethius*, edited by Manfred Fuhrmann and Joachim Gruber, 377–403. Wege der Forschung 483. Darmstadt: Wissenschaftliche Buchgesellschaft, 1984.

Charlton, William. "Aristotle and the *Harmonia* Theory." In *Aristotle on Nature and Living Things: Philosophical and Historical Studies Presented to David M. Balme on his Seventieth Birthday*, edited by Allan Gotthelf, 131–150. Pittsburgh: Mathesis, 1985.

Chenu, M.-D. "Découverte de la nature et philosophie de l'homme à l'École de Chartres au XIIe siècle." *Cahiers d'histoire mondiale* 2 (1954), 313–325.

———. *Nature, Man, and Society in the Twelfth Century: Essays on New Theological Perspectives in the Latin West*. Translated by Jerome Taylor and Lester K. Little. Chicago: University of Chicago Press, 1968.

Cherniss, Harold, ed. and trans. *De animae procreatione in Timaeo*. Vol. 13.1 of *Plutarch: Moralia*. Loeb Classical Library. Cambridge, MA: Harvard University Press, 1976.

———. *The Platonism of Gregory of Nyssa*. University of California Publications in Classical Philology 11. Berkeley: University of California Press, 1934.

Chua, Daniel. "Vincenzo Galilei, Modernity and the Division of Nature." In *Music Theory and Natural Order from the Renaissance to the Early Twentieth Century*, edited by Suzannah Clark and Alexander Rehding, 17–29. Cambridge: Cambridge University Press, 2001.

Ciabattoni, Francesco. *Dante's Journey to Polyphony*. Toronto: University of Toronto Press, 2010.

Cimini, Amy. "Vibrating Colors and Silent Bodies: Music, Sound and Silence in Maurice Merleau-Ponty's Critique of Dualism." *Contemporary Music Review* 31 (2012), 353–370.

Clerval, Alexandre. *Les écoles de Chartres au Moyen Âge*. Paris: A. Picard et fils, 1895.

Cooper, John M. "The Psychology of Justice in Plato." *American Philosophical Quarterly* 14 (1977), 151–157.

Cornford, Francis MacDonald. *Plato's Cosmology: The* Timaeus *of Plato, Translated with a Running Commentary*. International Library of Psychology, Philosophy, and Scientific Method. London: Routledge, 1977.

Courcelle, Pierre. "Ambroise de Milan et Calcidius." In *Romanitas et Christianitas*, edited by W. den Boer, P. G. van der Nat, et al., 45–53. Amsterdam: North-Holland, 1973.

———. *Late Latin Writers and their Greek Sources*. Translated by Harry E. Wedeck. Cambridge, MA: Harvard University Press, 1969.

Creese, David E. *The Monochord in Ancient Greek Harmonic Science*. Cambridge: Cambridge University Press, 2010.

Cristante, Lucio. "*Spectaculo detinemur cum scripta intellegimus aut probamus*: Per un riesame della rappresentazione delle *Artes* in Marziano Capella." *Incontri triestini di filologia classica* 4 (2005), 375–390.

Currie, Gabriela Ilnitchi. "*Concentum celi quis dormire faciet?* Eriugenian Cosmic Song and Carolingian Planetary Astronomy." In *Quomodo cantabimus canticum? Studies in Honor of Edward H. Roesner*, edited by David Butler Cannata et al., 15–35. Middleton, WI: American Institute of Musicology, 2008.

Cusick, Suzanne. "Feminist Theory, Music Theory, and the Mind/Body Problem," *Perspectives of New Music* 32 (1994), 8–27.

Da Rios, Rosetta, ed. *Aristoxeni Elementa Harmonica*. Scriptores Graeci et Latini consilio Academiae Lynceorum editi. Rome: Typis publicae officinae polygraphicae, 1954.

Dahan, Gilbert. "Les classifications du savoir aux XIIe et XIIIe siècles." *L'enseignement philosophique* 40 (1990), 5–27.

———. "Une introduction à la philosophie au XIIe siècle: Le *Tractatus quidam de philosophia et partibus eius*." *Archives d'histoire doctrinale et littéraire du Moyen Âge* 49 (1982), 155–193.

Dales, Richard C. "A Twelfth-Century Concept of Natural Order." *Viator* 9 (1978), 179–192.

d'Alverny, Marie-Thérèse. "Alain de Lille et la *Theologia*." In *L'homme devant Dieu: Mélanges offerts au Père Henri de Lubac*, Vol. 2, 111–128. [Paris]: Aubier, 1964.

———. "Les Muses et les sphères célestes." In *Classical, Mediaeval and Renaissance Studies in Honor of B. L. Ullman*, edited by Charles Henderson, Vol. 2, 7–19. Rome: Edizioni di Storia e Letteratura, 1964.

———. "Les 'Solutiones ad Chosroem' de Priscianus Lydus et Jean Scot." In *La transmission des textes philosophiques et scientifiques au Moyen Âge*, edited by Charles Burnett, 145–160. Aldershot: Variorum, 1994.

Deleuze, Gilles. *The Fold: Leibniz and the Baroque*. Translated by Tom Conley. London: Athlone Press, 1993.

Deleuze, Gilles, and Félix Guattari. *A Thousand Plateaus: Capitalism and Schizophrenia*. Translated by Brian Massumi. Minneapolis: University of Minnesota Press, 1987.

De Rijk, L. M. *The Origin and Early Development of the Theory of Supposition*. Vol. 2.1 of *Logica Modernorum: A Contribution to the History of Early Terminist Logic*. Wijsgerige teksten en studies 16. Assen: Van Gorcum, 1967.

———, ed. *Petrus Abaelardus. Dialectica: First Complete Edition of the Parisian Manuscript.* Assen: Van Gorcum, rev. ed. 1970 [first published 1956].

Den Boeft, Jan. *Calcidius on Fate: His Doctrine and Sources.* Philosophia antiqua 18. Leiden: Brill, 1970.

Depuis, J., trans. *Théon de Smyrne philosophe platonicien: Exposition des connaissances mathématiques utiles pour la lecture de Platon.* Paris: Hachette, 1892.

Descartes, René. *Compendium musicae.* In *Oeuvres de Descartes*, vol. 10, edited by Charles Adam and Paul Tanery. Paris: Librarie Philosophique J. Vrin, 1973–1978.

Desmond, Karen. "*Sicut in grammatica*: Analogical Discourse in Chapter 15 of Guido's *Micrologus*." *Journal of Musicology* 16 (1998), 467–493.

Diehls, Ernst, ed. *Procli Diadochi in Platonis Timaeum commentaria.* 3 vols. Bibliotheca scriptorum Graecorum et Romanorum Teubneriana. Leipzig: B. G. Teubner, 1903–1906.

Diels, H., and W. Kranz. *Die Fragmente der Vorsokratiker.* 6th ed. Berlin: Weidmann, 1952.

Dillon, John, trans. *Alcinous: The Handbook of Platonism.* Oxford: Clarendon Press, 1993.

———. *The Middle Platonists: 80 b.c. to a.d. 220.* Rev. ed. Ithaca: Cornell University Press, 1996.

———. "Tampering with the *Timaeus*: Ideological Emendations in Plato, with Special Reference to the *Timaeus*." *American Journal of Philology* 110 (1989), 50–72.

Dodwell, C. R. *The Canterbury School of Illumination, 1066–1200.* Cambridge: Cambridge University Press, 1954.

Dörrie, Heinrich. *Porphyrios' "Symmikta Zetemata": Ihre Stellung in System und Geschichte des Neuplatonismus nebst einem Kommentar zu den Fragmenten.* Zetemata: Monographien zur Klassischen Altertumswissenschaft 20. Munich: Verlag C. H. Beck, 1959.

Doughton, Sandi. "Hearing the Music of the Universe: Hanford Helps Find Einstein's Gravitational Waves." *Seattle Times.* February 11, 2016.

Dronke, Peter, ed. *Bernardus Silvestris: Cosmographia.* Leiden: Brill, 1978.

———. *Fabula: Explorations into the Uses of Myth in Medieval Platonism.* Mittellateinische Studien und Texte 9. Leiden: Brill, 1974.

———. "Introduction." In *A History of Twelfth-Century Western Philosophy*, edited by Peter Dronke, 1–18. Cambridge: Cambridge University Press, 1988.

———. *The Spell of Calcidius: Platonic Concepts and Images in the Medieval West.* Millennio medievale 74. Florence: SISMEL, Edizioni del Galluzzo, 2008.

———. "William of Conches's Commentary on Martianus Capella." In *Études de civilisation médiévale (IXe–XIIe siècles): Mélanges offerts à Edmond-René Labande*, 223–235. Poitiers: Centre d'Études Supérieures de Civilisation Médiévale, 1974.

Düring, Ingemar. *Die Harmonielehre des Klaudios Ptolemaios.* Göteborgs Högskolas Årsskrift 36. Göteborg: Elanders Boktryckeri, 1930.

———. *Porphyrios Kommentar zur Harmonielehre des Ptolemaios.* Göteborgs Högskolas Årsskrift 38. Göteborg: Elanders Boktryckeri, 1932.

Dutton, Paul Edward, ed. *The* Glosae super Platonem *of Bernard of Chartres.* Studies and Texts 107. Toronto: Pontifical Institute of Mediaeval Studies, 1991.

———. "*Illustre ciuitatis et populi exemplum*: Plato's *Timaeus* and the Transmission from Calcidius to the End of the Twelfth Century of a Tripartite Scheme of Society." *Mediaeval Studies* 45 (1983), 79–119.

———. "The Materialization of Nature and of Quaternary Man in the Early Twelfth Century." In *Man and Nature in the Middle Ages*, edited by S. J. Ridyard and R. G. Benson, 137–156. Sewanee Medieval Studies. Sewanee, TN: University of the South Press, 1995.

———. "Medieval Approaches to Calcidius." In *Plato's "Timaeus" as Cultural Icon*, edited by Gretchen Reydams-Schils, 183–205. Notre Dame, IN: University of Notre Dame Press: 2003.

———. *The Mystery of the Missing Heresy Trial of William of Conches.* The Etienne Gilson Series 28. Toronto: Pontifical Institute of Mediaeval Studies, 2006.

———. "The Uncovering of the *Glosae super Platonem* of Bernard of Chartres." *Mediaeval Studies* 46 (1984), 192–221.

Dyer, Joseph. "The Place of *Musica* in Medieval Classifications of Knowledge." *Journal of Musicology* 24 (2007), 3–71.

Dyson, Frances. *The Tone of Our Times: Sound, Sense, Economy, and Ecology*. Cambridge, MA: MIT Press, 2014.

Eastwood, Bruce, and Gerd Graßhoff. *Planetary Diagrams for Roman Astronomy in Medieval Europe, ca. 800–1500*. Transactions of the American Philosophical Society 94.3. Philadelphia: American Philosophical Society, 2004.

Ebbesen, Sten. "Review of Dutton, *The Glosae super Platonem of Bernard of Chartres*." *Speculum* 71 (1996), 123–125.

Ebbesen, Sten, Karin Margareta Fredborg, and Lauge Nielsen. "*Compendium logicae Porretanum* ex codice Oxoniensi Collegii Corporis Christi 250: A Manual of Porretan Doctrine by a Pupil of Gilbert's." *Cahiers de l'Institut du Moyen-Âge grec et latin* 46 (1983), iii–xviii, 1–113.

Eggebrecht, Hans Heinrich. "Die Mehrstimmigkeitslehre von ihren Anfängen bis zum 12. Jahrhundert." In *Die mittelalterliche Lehre von der Mehrstimmigkeit*, edited by Thomas Ertelt and Frieder Zaminer, 9–87. Geschichte der Musiktheorie 5. Darmstadt: Wissenschaftliche Buchgesellschaft, 1984.

Eidsheim, Nina Sun. *Sensing Sound: Singing and Listening as Vibrational Practice*. Durham: Duke University Press, 2015.

Elferink, M. A. *La descente de l'âme d'après Macrobe*. Philosophia antiqua 16. Leiden: Brill, 1968.

Elford, Dorothy. "William of Conches." In *A History of Twelfth-Century Western Philosophy*, edited by Peter Dronke, 308–327. Cambridge: Cambridge University Press, 1988.

Erlmann, Veit. *Reason and Resonance: A History of Modern Aurality*. New York: Zone Books, 2010.

Evans, Michael. "The *Ysagoge in theologiam* and the Commentaries Attributed to Bernard Silvestris." *Journal of the Warburg and Courtauld Institutes* 54 (1991), 1–42.

Farmer, Henry George. *Al-Farabi's Arabic-Latin Writings on Music*. Collection of Oriental Writers on Music 2. New York: Hinrichsen Edition, 1965.

Fassler, Margot. *Gothic Song: Victorine Sequences and Augustinian Reform in Twelfth-Century Paris*. Cambridge Studies in Medieval and Renaissance Music. Cambridge: Cambridge University Press, 1993.

Feld, Stephen. "Acoustemology." In *Keywords in Sound*, edited by David Novak and Matt Sakakeeny, 12–21. Durham: Duke University Press, 2015.

Ferruolo, Stephen. *The Origins of the University: The Schools of Paris and Their Critics, 1100–1215*. Stanford, CA: Stanford University Press, 1985.

Festa, Nicolaus, and Ulrich Klein, eds. *Iamblichi De communi mathematica scientia liber*. Stuttgart: B. G. Teubner, 1975.

Festugière, André-Jean, trans. *Proclus: Commentaire sur le République*. 3 vols. Bibliothèque des textes philosophiques. Paris: J. Vrin, 1970.

Fidora, Alexander. *Die Wissenschaftstheorie des Dominicus Gundissalinus: Voraussetzungen und Konsequenzen des zweiten Anfangs der aristotelischen Philosophie im 12. Jahrhundert*. Wissenskultur und gesellschaftlicher Wandel 6. Berlin: Akademie Verlag, 2003.

Finamore, John F., and John M. Dillon. *Iamblichus* De anima: *Text, Translation, and Commentary*. Philosophia antiqua 92. Leiden: Brill, 2002.

Flamant, Jacques. *Macrobe et le Néo-Platonisme latin, à la fin du IVe siècle*. Études Préliminaires aux Religions Orientales dans l'Empire Romain 58. Leiden: Brill, 1977.

Flatten, Heinrich. *Die Philosophie des Wilhelms von Conches*. Koblenz: Görres-Druckerei, 1929.

Flint, Valerie. "Honorius Augustodunensis: *Imago mundi*." *Archives d'histoire doctrinale et littéraire du Moyen Âge* 49 (1982), 7–153.

Fontaine, Jacques. *Isidore de Séville et la culture classique dans l'Espagne wisigothique*. 2 vols. Paris: Études augustiniennes, 1959.

Foucault, Michel. *The Order of Things: An Archaeology of the Human Sciences*. London and New York: Routledge Classics, 2002.

Franklin-Brown, Mary. *Reading the World: Encyclopedic Writing in the Scholastic Age*. Chicago: University of Chicago Press, 2012.

Friedlein, Gottfried, ed. *Anicii Manlii Torquati Severini Boetii De institutione arithmetica, libri duo: De institutione musica, libri quinque*. Bibliotheca scriptorum Graecorum et Romanorum Teubneriana. Leipzig: B. G. Teubner, 1867.

Fuller, Sarah. "Early Polyphony." In *The New Oxford History of Music*, Vol. 2: *The Early Middle Ages to 1300*, 2nd ed., edited by Richard Crocker and David Hiley, 485–556. Oxford: Oxford University Press, 1990.

Gallop, David. *Plato: Phaedo*. Oxford: Clarendon Press, 1975.

Gallope, Michael. "The Sound of Repeating Life: Ethics and Metaphysics in Deleuze's Philosophy of Music." In *Sounding the Virtual: Gilles Deleuze and the Theory and Philosophy of Music*, edited by Brian Hulse and Nick Nesbitt, 77–102. Farnham: Ashgate, 2010.

Gerbert, Martin. *Scriptores ecclesiastici de musica*. 3 vols. St. Blaise, 1784.

Gercke, Alfred. *Seneca-Studien*. Leipzig: B. G. Teubner, 1895.

Gersh, Stephen. "Ancient Philosophy Becomes Medieval Philosophy." In *Cambridge History of Philosophy in Late Antiquity*, edited by Lloyd P. Gerson, 894–914. Cambridge: Cambridge University Press, 2010.

———. *Concord in Discourse: Harmonics and Semiotics in Late Classical and Early Medieval Platonism*. Approaches to Semiotics 125. Berlin and New York: Mouton de Gruyter, 1996.

———. *Middle Platonism and Neoplatonism: The Latin Tradition*. Publications in Medieval Studies 3. Notre Dame, IN: University of Notre Dame Press, 1986.

———. "(Pseudo?-) Bernard Silvestris and the Revival of Neo-Platonic Virgilian Exegesis." In *Sophies Maietores: Chercheurs de sagesse; Hommage à J. Pépin*, edited by Marie-Odile Goulet-Gazé, Goulven Madec, and Denis O'Brien, 573–593. Paris: Institut d'Études augustiniennes, 1992.

Geyer, Bernhard, ed. *Peter Abaelards Philosophische Schriften. I. Die Logica 'Ingredientibus'. 1. Die Glossen zu Porphyrius*. Beiträge zur Geschichte der Philosophie und Theologie des Mittelalters 21.1. Münster: Aschendorff, 1919.

———, ed. *Peter Abaelards Philosophische Schriften. I. Die Logica 'Ingredientibus'. 2. Die Glossen zu den Kategorien*. Beiträge zur Geschichte der Philosophie und Theologie des Mittelalters 21.2. Münster: Aschendorff, 1921.

Gibson, Margaret. "Illustrating Boethius: Carolingian and Romanesque Manuscripts." In *Medieval Manuscripts of the Latin Classics: Production and Use*, edited by Claudine A. Chavannes-Mazel and Margaret M. Smith, 119–129. Los Altos Hills, CA: Anderson-Lovelace, 1996.

Gibson, Margaret, and Lesley Smith. *Codices Boethiani: A Conspectus of Manuscripts of the Works of Boethius. I. Great Britain and the Republic of Ireland*. Warburg Institute Surveys and Texts 25. London: The Warburg Institute, 1995.

Gottschalk, H. B. "The *De Audibilibus* and Peripatetic Acoustics." *Hermes* 96 (1968), 435–460.

———. "Soul as Harmonia." *Phronesis* 16 (1971), 179–198.

Grant, Edward. *Nicole Oresme and the Kinematics of Circular Motion: Tractatus de commensurabilitate vel incommensurabilitate motuum celi*. Publications in Medieval Science 15. Madison: University of Wisconsin Press, 1971.

Grant, Iain Hamilton. *Philosophies of Nature after Schelling*. London: Continuum, 2006.

———. "'Philosophy Become Genetic': The Physics of the World Soul." In *The New Schelling*, edited by Judith Norman and Alistair Welchman, 128–150. London: Continuum, 2004.

Grabmann, Martin. *Handschriftliche Forschungen und Mitteilungen zum Schrifttum des Wilhelm von Conches und zu Bearbeitungen seiner naturwissenschaftlichen Werke*. Sitzungberichte der Bayerischen Akademie der Wissenschaften, Philosophische-historische Abteilung 10. Munich: Verlag der Bayrischen Akademie der Wissenschaften, 1935.

———. *Die Scholastische Methode von ihren ersten Anfängen in der Väterliteratur bis zum Beginn des 12. Jahrhunderts*. Vol. 1 of *Die Geschichte der Scholastischen Methode*. Freiburg im Breisgau: Herdersche Verlagshandlung, 1909.

Grebe, Sabine. "Gedanken zur Datierung von *De nuptiis Philologiae et Mercurii* des Martianus Capella." *Hermes* 128 (2000), 353–368.

Gregory, Tullio. *Anima mundi: La filosofia di Guglielmo di Conches e la scuola di Chartres*. Pubblicazioni dell'Istituto di Filosofia dell'Università di Roma 3. Florence: Sansoni, 1955.

———. "L'idea della natura nella scuola di Chartres." *Giornale critico della filosofia italiano* 4 (1952), 433–442.

———. "La nouvelle idée de nature et de savoir scientifique au XIIe siècle." In *The Cultural Context of Medieval Learning*, edited by J. E. Murdoch and E. D. Sylla, 193–218. Dordrecht and Boston: D. Reidel, 1975.

———. *Platonismo medievale: Studi e ricerche*. Studi storici 26–27. Rome: Istituto storico italiano per il Medio Evo, 1958.

Gruber, Joachim. *Kommentar zu Boethius, De consolatione philosophiae*. 2nd ed. Texte und Kommentare 9. Berlin and New York: Walter de Gruyter, 2006.

Guillaumin, Jean-Yves, ed. and trans. *Boèce: Institution arithmétique*. Paris: Belles lettres, 1995.

———. "Boethius's *De institutione arithmetica* and its Influence on Posterity." In *A Companion to Boethius in the Middle Ages*, edited by Noel H. Kaylor and Philip E. Phillips, 135–161. Leiden: Brill, 2012.

———, ed. and trans. *Martianus Capella: Les noces de Philologie et de Mercure: Livre VII, L'arithmétique*. Paris: Belles lettres, 2003.

Guillaumin, Jean-Yves, and Giovanni Gasparotto, eds. and trans. *Isidor: Étymologies, livre 3 (la mathématique)*. Auteurs latins du Moyen Âge. Paris: Belles lettres, 2009.

Gushee, Lawrence. "Questions of Genre in Medieval Treatises on Music." In *Gattungen der Musik in Einzeldarstellungen: Gedenkschrift Leo Schrade*, edited by Wulf Arlt, Ernst Lichtenhahn, and Hans Oesch, 365–433. Munich: Francke Verlag, 1973.

Haar, James. "*Musica Mundana*: Variations on a Pythagorean Theme." PhD diss., Harvard University, 1960.

Haas, Max. "Studien zur mittelalterlichen Musiklehre I: Eine Übersicht über die Musiklehre im Kontext der Philosophie des 13. und frühen 14. Jahrhunderts." In *Aktuelle Fragen der musikbezogenen Mittelalterforschung: Texte zu einem Basler Kolloquium des Jahres 1975*, edited by Hans Oesch and Wulf Arlt, 323–456. Forum Musicologicum 3. Winterthur: Amadeus, 1982.

Hackett, Jeremiah. "Roger Bacon on the Classification of the Sciences." In *Roger Bacon and the Sciences: Commemorative Essays*, edited by Jeremiah Hackett, 49–65. Studien und Texte zur Geistesgeschichte des Mittelalters 57. Leiden: Brill, 1997.

Hadot, Ilsetraut. *Arts libéraux et philosophie dans la pensée antique: Contribution à l'histoire de l'éducation et de la culture dans l'Antiquité*. 2nd ed. Textes et traditions 11. Paris: J. Vrin, 2005.

Hadot, Pierre. "Die Einteilung der Philosophie im Altertum." *Zeitschrift für Philosophische Forschung* 36 (1982), 422–444.

Halliwell, Stephen. "An Aristotelian Perspective on Plato's Dialogues." In *New Essays on Plato*, edited by F.-G. Herrmann, 189–211. Swansea: Classical Press of Wales, 2006.

Handschin, Jacques. "The 'Timaeus' Scale." *Musica Disciplina* 4 (1950), 3–42.

Häring, Nikolaus M. "Alan of Lille, *De planctu Naturae*." *Studi medievali* 19 (1978), 797–879.

———, ed. *Commentaries on Boethius by Gilbert of Poitiers*. Studies and Texts 13. Toronto: Pontifical Institute of Mediaeval Studies, 1966.

———, ed. *Commentaries on Boethius by Thierry of Chartres and his School*. Studies and Texts 20. Toronto: Pontifical Institute of Mediaeval Studies, 1971.

———. "Thierry of Chartres and Dominicus Gundissalinus." *Mediaeval Studies* 26 (1964), 271–286.

Hartmann, Wilfried, ed. *Manegold von Lautenbach: Liber contra Wolfelmum*. MGH Quellen zur Geistesgeschichte des Mittelalters 8. Weimar: Hermann Böhlaus Nachfolger, 1972.

Hayduck, Michael, ed. *Ioannis Philoponi in Aristotelis de anima libros commentaria*. Commentaria in Aristotelem Graeca 15. Berlin: Reimer, 1897.

Heath, Sir Thomas. *Aristarchus of Samos: The Ancient Copernicus*. Oxford: Clarendon Press, 1913.

Heilmann, Anja. *Boethius' Musiktheorie und das Quadrivium: Eine Einführung in den neuplatonischen Hintergrund von "De institutione musica."* Hypomnemata: Untersuchungen zur Antike und zu ihrem Nachleben 171. Göttingen: Vandenhoeck & Ruprecht, 2007.

Heller-Roazen, Daniel. *The Fifth Hammer: Pythagoras and the Disharmony of the World*. New York: Zone Books, 2011.

Henderson, John. *The Medieval World of Isidore of Seville: Truth from Words*. Cambridge: Cambridge University Press, 2007.

Heninger, S. K., Jr. *Touches of Sweet Harmony: Pythagorean Cosmology and Renaissance Poetics*. San Marino, CA: The Huntington Library, 1974.

Hentschel, Frank. *Sinnlichkeit und Vernunft in der mittelalterlichen Musiktheorie: Strategien der Konsonanzwertung und der Gegenstand der* musica sonora *um 1300*. Beiheft zum Archiv für Musikwissenschaft 47. Stuttgart: Franz Steiner Verlag, 2000.

Hentschel, Frank, and Martin Pickavé. "'Quaestiones mathematicales': Eine Textgattung der Pariser Artistenfakultät in frühen 14. Jahrhundert." In *Nach der Verurteilung von 1277: Philosophie und Theologie an der Universität von Paris im letzten Viertel des 13. Jahrhunderts*, edited by Jan A. Aertsen, Kent Emery, Jr., and Andreas Speer, 618–634. Berlin: Walter de Gruyter, 2001.

Hicks, Andrew. "Editing Medieval Commentaries on Martianus Capella." In *The Arts of Editing Medieval Greek and Latin: A Casebook*, edited by Elisabet Göransson, Gunilla Iversen, et al., 138–159. Studies and Texts 203. Toronto: Pontifical Institute for Mediaeval Studies, 2016.

———. "Martianus Capella and the Liberal Arts." In *The Oxford Handbook of Medieval Latin Literature*, edited by David Townsend and Ralph Hexter, 307–334. Oxford: Oxford University Press, 2012.

———. "*Musica speculativa* in the Cambridge Commentary on Martianus Capella's *De nuptiis*." *Journal of Medieval Latin* 18 (2008), 292–305.

———. "Pythagoras and Pythagoreanism in Late Antiquity and the Middle Ages." In *A History of Pythagoreanism*, edited by Carl Huffman, 416–434. Cambridge: Cambridge University Press, 2014.

———. "Re-interpreting an Arithmetical Error in Boethius's *De institutione musica*." *Music Theory and Analysis* 3 (2016), 1–26.

Hiller, Eduard, ed. *Theonis Smyrnaei philosophi Platonici Expositio rerum mathematicarum ad legendum Platonem utilium*. Bibliotheca scriptorum Graecorum et Romanorum Teubneriana. Leipzig: B. G. Teubner, 1878.

Hochadel, Matthias. *Commentum Oxoniense in musicam Boethii: Eine Quelle zur Musiktheorie an der spätmittelalterlichen Universität*. Veröffentlichungen der Musikhistorischen Kommission 16. Munich: Verlag der Bayerischen Akademie der Wissenschaften, 2002.

Hoche, Richard, ed. *Nicomachi Geraseni Pythagorei Introductionis arithmeticae libri duo*. Bibliotheca scriptorum Graecorum et Romanorum Teubneriana. Leipzig: B. G. Teubner, 1866.

Hoenig, Christina. "Εἰκὼς λόγος: Plato in Translation(s)." *Methodos* 13 (2013). Available online at http://methodos.revues.org/2994.

Holmberg, John, ed. *Das Moralium dogma philosophorum des Guillaume de Conches, lateinisch, altfranzösisch und mittelniederfränkisch*. Uppsala: Almqvist & Wiksell, 1929.

Holsinger, Bruce W. *Music, Body, and Desire in Medieval Culture: Hildegard of Bingen to Chaucer*. Figurae: Reading Medieval Culture. Stanford, CA: Stanford University Press, 2001.

Holtz, Louis. "Quelques aspects de la tradition et de la diffusion des *Institutiones*." In *Atti della settimana di studi su Flavio Magno Aurelio Cassiodoro (Cosenza-Squillace, 19–24 settembre 1983)*, edited by Sandro Leanza, 281–312. Soveria Mannelli: Rubbettino, 1986.

Honnefelder, Ludger. "The Concept of Nature in Medieval Metaphysics." In *Nature in Medieval Thought*, edited by C. Koyama, 75–93. Studien und Texte zur Geistegeschichte des Mittelalters 73. Leiden: Brill, 2000.

Horky, Phillip Sidney. *Plato and Pythagoreanism*. Oxford: Oxford University Press, 2013.

Hossfeld, Paul, ed. *Alberti Magni De caelo et mundo*. Alberti Magni Opera omnia 5.1. Münster: Aschendorff, 1971.

Huffman, Carl A. *Archytas of Tarentum: Pythagorean, Philosopher, and Mathematician King*. Cambridge: Cambridge University Press, 2005.

———. *Philolaus of Croton, Pythagorean and Presocratic: A Commentary on the Fragments and Testimonia with Interpretive Essays*. Cambridge: Cambridge University Press, 1993.

———. "The Pythagorean Conception of the Soul from Pythagoras to Philolaus." In *Body and Soul in Ancient Philosophy*, edited by Dorothea Frede and Burkhard Reis, 21–43. Berlin: Walter de Gruyter, 2009.

Huglo, Michel. "Abélard, poète et musicien." *Cahiers de civilisation médiévale* 22 (1979), 349–361.

———. "Les débuts de la polyphonie à Paris: Les premiers *organa* parisiens." *Forum Musicologicum: Basler Beiträge zur Musikgeschichte* 3 (1982), 93–163.

———. "Recherches sur la tradition des diagrammes de Calcidius." *Scriptorium* 62 (2008), 185–230.

———. *Les tonaires: Inventaire, analyse, comparaison*. Publications de la Société francais de musicologie: Troisième série 2. Paris: Société francais de musicologie, 1971.

Hunt, Richard W. "The Introductions to the 'artes' in the Twelfth Century." In *The History of Grammar in the Middle Ages: Collected Papers*, edited by G. L. Bursill-Hall, 117–144. Amsterdam: John Benjamins, 1980.

Hunt, Frederick Vinton. *Origins in Acoustics: The Science of Sound from Antiquity to the Age of Newton*. New Haven and London: Yale University Press, 1978.

Ilnitchi, Gabriela. "*Musica mundana*, Aristotelian Natural Philosophy and Ptolemaic Astronomy." *Early Music History* 21 (2002), 37–74.

Jacquart, Danielle. "Aristotelian Thought in Salerno." In *A History of Twelfth-Century Western Philosophy*, edited by Peter Dronke, 407–428. Cambridge: Cambridge University Press, 1988.

Jacquart, Danielle, and Agostino Paravicini Bagliani, eds. *La scuola medica Salernitana: Gli autori e i testi*. Florence: SISMEL, Edizioni del Galluzzo, 2007.

Jaeger, C. Stephen. *The Envy of Angels: Cathedral Schools and Social Ideals in Medieval Europe, 950–1200*. Philadelphia: University of Pennsylvania Press, 1994.

James, Montague Rhodes. *The Ancient Libraries of Canterbury and Dover*. Cambridge: Cambridge University Press, 1903.

Jan, Karl von, ed. *Musici scriptores graeci: Aristoteles, Euclides, Nicomachus, Bacchius, Gaudentius, Alypius, et melodiarum ueterum quidquid exstat*. Leipzig: B. G. Teubner, 1895.

Jardine, Nick. "Kepler, God, and the Virtues of Copernican Hypotheses." In *Nouveau ciel, nouvelle terre: La révolution copernicienne dans l'Allemagne de la Réforme (1530–1630)*, edited by Miguel Ángel Granada and Édouard Mehl, 269–281. Paris: Les Belles Lettres, 2009.

Jeauneau, Édouard, ed. *Guillelmi de Conchis Glosae super Platonem*. Corpus Christianorum. Continuatio Mediaevalis 203. Turnhout: Brepols, 2006.

———. *"Lectio philosophorum": Recherches sur l'École de Chartres*. Amsterdam: A. M. Hakkert, 1973.

———. "Macrobe, source de platonisme chartrain." In *"Lectio philosophorum": Recherches sur l'École de Chartres*, 279–300. Amsterdam: A. M. Hakkert, 1973.

———. *Rethinking the School of Chartres*. Translated by Claude Paul Desmarais. Rethinking the Middle Ages 3. Toronto: University of Toronto Press, 2009.

Jones, Julian Ward. "The So-Called Silvestris Commentary on the *Aeneid* and Two Other Interpretations." *Speculum* 64 (1989), 835–848.

Kane, Brian. *Sound Unseen: Acousmatic Sound in Theory and Practice*. Oxford: Oxford University Press, 2014.

King, Peter. "Metaphysics." In *The Cambridge Companion to Abelard*, edited by J. E. Brower and K. Guilfoy, 65–125. Cambridge: Cambridge University Press, 2004.

———."Why Isn't the Mind-Body Problem Medieval?" In *Forming the Mind*, edited by Henrik Lagerlund, 187–205. Dordrecht: Springer Verlag, 2007.

Klibansky, Raymond. *The Continuity of the Platonic Tradition during the Middle Ages: Outlines of a Corpus Platonicum Medii Aevi*. London: The Warburg Institute, 1939.

Kroll, Wilhelm, ed. *Procli Diadochi in Platonis Rem publicam commenarii*. 2 vols. Bibliotheca Scriptorum Graecorum et Romanorum Teubneriana. Leipzig: B. G. Teubner, 1899–1901.

Kuhn, Thomas. *The Copernican Revolution: Planetary Astronomy in the Development of Western Thought*. Cambridge, MA: Harvard University Press, 1957.

———. *The Essential Tension: Selected Studies in Scientific Tradition and Change*. Chicago: University of Chicago Press, 1977.

———. *The Structure of Scientific Revolutions*. Chicago: University of Chicago Press, 1962.

Kupke, Tanja. "Où sont les muses d'antan? Notes for a Study of the Muses in the Middle Ages." In From Athens to Chartres: *Neoplatonism and Medieval Thought; Studies in Honour of Edouard Jeauneau*, edited by Haijo J. Westra, 421–436. Leiden: Brill, 1992.

Lafleur, Claude. *Quatre introductions à la philosophie au XIIIe siècle: Textes critiques et étude historique*. Publications de l'Institut d'études médiévales 23. Montreal: Institut d'études médiévales, 1988.

Langton, Rae. "The Musical, the Magical, and the Mathematical Soul." In *History of the Mind-Body Problem*, edited by Tim Crane and Sarah A. Patterson, 13–33. London: Routledge, 2000.

Leach, Elizabeth Eva. *Sung Birds: Music, Nature, and Poetry in the Later Middle Ages*. Ithaca: Cornell University Press, 2007.

Lemoine, Michel, ed. *Guillelmus de Sancto Theodorico, De natura corporis et animae*. Auteurs Latins du Moyen Âge. Paris: Belles lettres, 1988.

Leonardi, Claudio. "Der Kommentar des Johannes Scotus zu Martianus Capella im 12. Jahrhundert." In *Eriugena redivivus. Zur Wirkungsgeschichte seines Denkens im Mittelalter und im Übergang zur Neuzeit*, edited by Werner Beierwaltes, 77–88. Abhandlungen der Heidelberger Akademie der Wissenschaften, Philosophisch-Historische Klasse, Jahrg. 1987, 1. Heidelberg: C. Winter, 1987.

———, ed. *Notae et glossae autographicae Ratherii Veronensis*. Corpus Christianorum. Continuatio Mediaevalis, 46A. Turnhout: Brepols, 1984.

———. "Raterio e Marziano Capella." *Italia Medioevale e Umanistica* 2 (1959), 73–102.

Lindsay, W. M., ed. *Isidori Hispalensis Episcopi Etymologiarum siue Originum libri xx*. Oxford: Clarendon Press, 1911.

Lochner, Fabian. "Dietger (Theogerus) of Metz and His *Musica*." PhD diss., University of Notre Dame, 1995.

Long, A. A. "The Harmonics of Stoic Virtue." In *Stoic Studies*, 202–223. Berkeley: University of California Press, 2001.

Long, A. A., and D. N. Sedley. *The Hellenistic Philosophers*. 2 vols. Cambridge: Cambridge University Press, 1987.

Lucentini, Paolo. "*Glosæ super Trismegistum*: Un commento medievale all'*Asclepius* ermetico." *Archives d'histoire doctrinale et littéraire du Moyen Âge* 62 (1995), 189–293.

Luscombe, David. "Nature in the Thought of Peter Abelard." In La*filosofia della natura nel medioevo*, 314–319. Milan: Società editrice Vita e pensiero, 1966.

Lutz, Cora E., ed. *Iohannis Scotti Annotationes in Marcianum*. Cambridge, MA: The Mediaeval Academy of America, 1939.

———, ed. *Remigii Autissiodorensis Commentum in Martianum Capellam*. 2 vols. Leiden: Brill, 1962–1965.

Lynch, Peter. *The Emergence of Numerical Weather Prediction: Richardson's Dream*. Cambridge: Cambridge University Press, 2014.

Magee, John. *Anicii Manlii Severini Boethii De divisione liber*. Philosophia Antiqua 77. Leiden: Brill, 1998.

———. "Boethius." In *Cambridge History of Philosophy in Late Antiquity*, ed., Lloyd P. Gerson, 788–812. Cambridge: Cambridge University Press, 2010.

———. "Boethius' Anapestic Dimeters (Acatalectic) with Regard to the Structure and Argument of the *Consolatio*." In *Boèce ou la chaîne des savoirs: Actes du Colloque international de la Fondation Singer-Polignac (Paris 8–12, juin 1999)*, edited by Alain Galonnier, 147–169. Philosophes Médiévaux 44. Louvain-la-Neuve: Peeters, 2003.

———. *Boethius on Signification and Mind*. Philosophia Antiqua 52. Leiden: Brill, 1989.

———. "On the Composition and Sources of Boethius' Second *Peri Hermeneias* Commentary." *Vivarium* 48 (2010), 7–54.

Mahdi, Muhsin. "Science, Philosophy, and Religion in Alfarabi's *Enumeration of the Sciences*." In *The Cultural Context of Medieval Learning: Proceedings of the First International Colloquium on Philosophy, Science, and Theology in the Middle Ages—September 1973*, edited by John Emery Murdoch and Edith Dudley Sylla, 113–147. Boston Studies in the Philosophy of Science 26. Boston: D. Reidel, 1975.

Maître, Claire. *La réforme cistercienne du plain-chant: Étude d'un traité théorique*. Cîteaux: Studia et Documenta 6. Brecht: Commentarii Cistercienses, 1995.

Mansfeld, Jaap. "Doxography and Dialectic: The *Sitz im Leben* of the 'Placita.'" In *Aufstieg und Niedergang der Römischen Welt*, edited by Wolfgang Hasse and Hildegard Temporini, 3056–3229. 36.4. Berlin: De Gruyter, 1990.

Marenbon, John. "Life, Milieu, and Intellectual Contexts." In *The Cambridge Companion to Abelard*, edited by Jeffrey E. Brower and Kevin Guilfoy, 13–44. Cambridge: Cambridge University Press, 2004.

———. *The Philosophy of Peter Abelard*. Cambridge: Cambridge University Press, 1997.

———. "The Platonisms of Peter Abelard." In *Aristotelian Logic, Platonism, and the Context of Early Medieval Philosophy in the West*, XII: 109–129. Aldershot: Ashgate, 2000.

Mariétan, Joseph. *Problème de la classification des sciences d'Aristote à St-Thomas*. Paris: Felix Alcan, 1901.

Martijn, Marije. *Proclus on Nature: Philosophy of Nature and Its Methods in Proclus' Commentary on Plato's* Timaeus. Philosophia antiqua 121. Leiden: Brill, 2010.

Mathon, Gerard. "Jean Scot Érigène, Chalcidius et le problème de l'âme universelle." In *L'Homme et son destin d'après les penseurs du Moyen Âge: Actes du premier congrès international de philosophie médiévale, Louvain-Bruxelles, 28 août–4 septembre 1958*, 361–375. Louvain: Nauwelaerts, 1960.

Maurach, Gregor, ed. *Wilhelm von Conches: Philosophia*. Pretoria: University of South Africa, 1980.

McAllister, James W. *Beauty and Revolution in Science*. Ithaca: Cornell University Press, 1996.

McCarthy, Thomas J. H. *Music, Scholasticism, and Reform: Salian Germany, 1024–1125*. Manchester Medieval Studies. Manchester and New York: Manchester University Press, 2009.

McDonough, Christopher J. "The Verse of Martianus Capella: Text, Translation, and Commentary on the Poetry in Books 1–V." PhD diss., University of Toronto, 1968.

McGinn, Bernard. *The Golden Chain: A Study in the Theological Anthropology of Isaac of Stella*. Cistercian Studies 15. Washington DC: Cistercian Publications, 1972.

McGuire, J. E., and P. M. Rattansi. "Newton and the 'Pipes of Pan.'" *Notes and Records of the Royal Society of London* 21 (1966), 108–143.

McKeon, Ralph. "Medicine and Philosophy in the Eleventh and Twelfth Centuries: The Problem of Elements." *The Thomist* 24 (1961), 211–256.

Meiser, Carol, ed. *Anicii Manlii Severini Boetii commentarii in librum Aristotelis* ΠΕΡΙ ΕΡΜΗΝΕΙΑΣ. Leipzig: B. G. Teubner, 1877 and 1880.

Mengozzi, Stefano. *The Renaissance Reform of Medieval Music Theory: Guido of Arezzo between Myth and History*. Cambridge: Cambridge University Press, 2010.

Merleau-Ponty, Maurice. *La nature: Notes, cours du Collège de France*, edited by Dominique Séglard. Paris: Editions du Seuil, 1995.

———. *The Structure of Behavior*. Translated by Alden Fischer. Pittsburgh: Duquesne University Press, 1983.

Meyer, Christian. "L'âme du monde dans la rationalité musicale: Ou l'expérience sensible d'un ordre intelligible." In *Harmonia mundi: Musica mondana e musica celeste fra Antichità e Medioevo; Atti del convegno internazionale di studi (Roma, 14–15 dicembre 2005)*, edited by Marta Cristiani, Cecilia Panti, and Graziano Perillo, 57–75. Micrologus' Library 19. Florence: SISMEL, Edizioni del Galluzzo, 2007.

———. trans. *Boèce: Traité de la musique*. Turnhout: Brepols, 2004.

Minio-Paluello, Lorenzo, ed. *Phaedo interprete Henrico Aristippo*. Corpus Platonicum Medii Aevi. London: The Warburg Institute, 1950.

———. *Twelfth-Century Logic: Texts and Studies I; Adam Balsamiensis Parvipontani Ars disserendi (Dialectica Alexandri)*. Rome: Edizioni di storia e letteratura, 1956.

Mirhady, David C. "Dicaearchus of Messana: The Sources, Text and Translation." In *Dicaearchus of Messana: Text, Translation, and Discussion*, edited by W. W. Fortenbaugh and E. Schütrumpf, 1–142. New Brunswick, NJ: Transaction, 2001.

Mitchell, David, and Sharon Snyder. *Narrative Prosthesis: Disability and the Dependencies of Discourse*. Ann Arbor: University of Michigan Press, 2000.

Modrak, Deborah K. *Aristotle: The Power of Perception*. Chicago: University of Chicago Press, 1987.

Moreschini, Claudi, ed. *Boethius: De consolatione philosophiae; Opuscula theologica*. Bibliotheca scriptorum Graecorum et Romanorum Teubneriana. Munich and Leipzig: K. G. Saur, 2005.

———, trans. *Calcidio: Commentario al "Timeo" di Platone; Testo latino a fronte*. Bompiani Il Pensiero Occidentale. Milan: Bompiani, 2003.

Morris, Colin. *The Discovery of the Individual 1050–1200*. New York: Harper, 1972.

Moseley, Roger. "Digital Analogies: The Keyboard as Field of Musical Play." *Journal of the American Musicological Society* 68 (2015), 151–228.

Mountain, W. J. *Sancti Aurelii Augustini De trinitate libri XV*. Corpus christianorum. Series Latina 50–50A. Turnhout: Brepols, 1968.

Mynors, R. A. B., ed. *Cassiodori Senatoris Institutiones divinarum et saecularium litterarum*. 2nd ed. Oxford: Clarendon Press, 1961.

Nauta, Lodi, ed. *Guillelmi de Conchis Glosae super Boetium*. Corpus Christianorum. Continuatio Mediaevalis 158. Turnhout: Brepols, 1999.

Nebeker, Frederik. *Calculating the Weather: Meteorology in the 20th Century*. San Diego: Academic Press, 1995.

Netz, Reviel. "The Pythagoreans." In *Mathematics and the Divine: A Historical Study*, edited by T. Koetsier and L. Bergmans, 77–97. Amsterdam: Elsevier, 2004.

Obrist, Barbara. "William of Conches, Māshā'Allāh, and Twelfth-Century Cosmology." *Archives d'histoire doctrinale et littéraire du Moyen Âge* 76 (2009), 29–87.

———. "Wind Diagrams and Medieval Cosmology." *Speculum* 72 (1997), 33–84.

O'Connell, Robert J. *St. Augustine's Early Theory of Man, A.D. 386–391*. Cambridge, MA: The Belknap Press of Harvard University Press, 1968.

O'Donnell, James J. *Cassiodorus*. Berkeley: University of California Press, 1979.

O'Meara, Dominic J. "The Concept of Nature in John Scottus Eriugena (*De divisione naturae* Book I)." *Vivarium* 19 (1981), 126–145.

———. "The Music of Philosophy in Late Antiquity." In *Philosophy and the Sciences in Antiquity*, edited by R. W. Sharples, 131–147. Keeling Series in Ancient Philosophy. Aldershot: Ashgate, 2005.

———. *Pythagoras Revived: Mathematics and Philosophy in Late Antiquity*. Oxford: Clarendon Press, 1989.

Oosthout, Henry, and Iohannes Schilling, eds. *Anicii Manlii Severini Boethii De arithmetica*. Corpus Christianorum. Series Latina, 94A. Turnhout: Brepols, 1999.

Otten, Willemien. "Nature, Body and Text in Early Medieval Theology: From Eriugena to Chartres." In *Divine Creation in Ancient, Medieval, and Early Modern Thought: Essays Presented to the Rev'd Dr. Robert D. Crouse*, edited by Michael Treschow, Willemien Otten, and Walter Hannam, 235–256. Studies in Intellectual History 151. Leiden: Brill, 2007.

———. *From Paradise to Paradigm: A Study of Twelfth-Century Humanism*. Leiden: Brill, 2004.

Pabst, Bernhard. *Atomtheorien des lateinischen Mittelalters*. Darmstadt: Wissenschaftliche Buchgesellschaft, 1994.

Palisca, Claude V., ed. *Hucbald, Guido, and John on Music: Three Medieval Treatises*. Translated by Warren Babb. Music Theory Translation Series 3. New Haven and London: Yale University Press, 1978.

Panti, Cecilia. "The First 'Questio' of ms Paris, B.N. lat. 7372: 'Utrum musica sit scientia.'" *Studi medievali* 33 (1992), 265–313.

———. "Robert Grosseteste's Theory of Sound." In *Musik – und die Geschichte der Philosophie und Naturwissenschaften im Mittelalter: Fragen zur Wechselwirkung von "musica" und "philosophia" im Mittelalter*, edited by Frank Hentschel, 3–18. Studien und Texte zur Geistesgeschichte des Mittelalters 62. Leiden: Brill, 1998.

Parent, Joseph-Marie. *La doctrine de la création dans l'École de Chartres*. Paris: J. Vrin, 1938.

Parkes, Malcolm B. "The Influence of the Concepts of *Ordinatio* and *Compilatio* on the Development of the Book." In *Medieval Learning and Literature: Essays Presented to Richard William Hunt*, edited by J. J. G. Alexander and M. T. Gibson, 115–141. Oxford: Clarendon, 1976.

Peden, Alison M. "'De semitonio': Some Medieval Exercises in Arithmetic." *Studi medievali* 35 (1994), 367–403.

———. "Music in Medieval Commentaries on Macrobius." In *Musik – und die Geschichte der Philosophie und Naturwissenschaften im Mittelalter: Fragen zur Wechselwirkung von "musica" und "philosophia" im Mittelalter*, edited by Frank Hentschel, 151–161. Studien und Texte zur Geistesgeschichte des Mittelalters 62. Leiden: Brill, 1998.

Pelosi, Francesco. *Plato on Music, Soul and Body*. Translated by Sophie Henderson. Cambridge: Cambridge University Press, 2010.

Pesic, Peter. "Earthly Music and Cosmic Harmony: Johannes Kepler's Interest in Practical Music, Especially Orlando di Lasso." *Journal of Seventeenth-Century Music* 11 (2005), http://www.sscm-jscm.org/v11/no1/pesic.html.

———. *Music and the Making of Modern Science*. Cambridge, MA: MIT Press, 2014.

Pietzsch, Gerhard. *Die Klassifikation der Musik von Boethius bis Ugolino von Orvieto*. Studien zur Geschichte der Musiktheorie in Mittelalter 1. Halle: M. Niemeyer, 1929.

Pisa, Uguccione da. *Derivationes*. Edited by Enzo Cecchini and Guido Arbizzoni. Florence: SISMEL Edizioni del Galluzzo, 2004.

Polansky, Ronald M. *Aristotle's* De anima. Cambridge: Cambridge University Press, 2007.

Préaux, Jean. "Les manuscrits principaux du *De nuptiis Philologiae et Mercurii* de Martianus Capella." In *Lettres latines du moyen-âge et de la renaissance*, edited by Guy Cambier, Carl Deroux, and Jean Préaux, 76–128. Collection Latomus 158. Brussels: Latomus, 1978.

———. "Securus Melior Felix, l'ultime Orator Urbis Romae." In *Corona gratiarum: miscellanea patristica, historica et liturgica Eligio Dekkers O.S.B. XII lustra complenti oblata*, 2: 101–121. 2 vols. Bruges: SintPietersabdij, 1975.

Prins, Jacomien. *Echoes of an Invisible World: Marsilio Ficino and Francesco Patrizi on Cosmic Order and Music Theory*. Brill's Studies in Intellectual History 234. Leiden: Brill, 2015.

Pronay, Andreas. *C. Marius Victorinus, Liber de definitionibus. Eine spätantike Theorie der Definition und des Definierens*. Frankfurt am Main: P. Lang, 1997.

Randel, Don Michael. "Al-Farabi and the Role of Arabic Music Theory in the Latin Middle Ages." *Journal of the American Musicological Society* 29 (1976), 173–188.

Rankin, Susan. "*Naturalis concordia vocum cum planetis*: Conceptualizing the Harmony of the Spheres in the Early Middle Ages." In *Citation and Authority in Medieval and Renaissance Musical Culture: Learning from the Learned*, edited by Suzannah Clark and Elizabeth Eva Leach, 3–19. Studies in Medieval and Renaissance Music 4. Woodbridge: Boydell, 2005.

Rausch, Alexander. "Der Boethius-Kommentar in der Handschrift St. Florian XI 282." *Studien zur Musikwissenschaft: Beihefte der Denkmäler der Tonkunst in Österreich* 48 (2002), 7–83.

Rees, D. A. "Bipartition of the Soul in the Early Academy." *Journal of Hellenic Studies* 77 (1957), 112–118.

Regen, Frank. "Zu Augustins Darstellung des Platonismus am Anfang des 8. Buches der *Ciuitas Dei*." In *Platonismus und Christentum: Festschrift für Heinrich Dörrie*, edited by Horst-Dieter Blume and Friedhelm Mann, 208–227. Münster: Verlag Aschendorff, 1983.

Reilly, Leo A., ed. *Petrus Helias, Summa super Priscianum*. 2 vols. Studies and Texts 113. Toronto: Pontifical Institute of Mediaeval Studies, 1993.

Reydams-Schils, Gretchen. "Calcidius." In *The Cambridge History of Philosophy in Late Antiquity*, edited by Lloyd P. Gerson, 498–508. Cambridge: Cambridge University Press, 2010.

———. "Calcidius on the Human and the World Soul and Middle-Platonist Psychology." *Apeiron* 39 (2006), 177–200.

———. "Meta-Discourse: Plato's *Timaeus* According to Calcidius." *Phronesis* 52 (2007), 301–327.

Richardson, Lewis Fry. *Weather Prediction by Numerical Process*. Cambridge: Cambridge University Press, 1922.

Rico, Gilles. "*Auctoritas cereum habet nasum*: Boethius, Aristotle, and the Music of the Spheres in the Thirteenth and Early Fourteenth Centuries." In *Citation and Authority in Medieval and Renaissance Musical Culture: Learning from the Learned*, edited by Suzannah Clark and Elizabeth Eva Leach, 20–28. Studies in Medieval and Renaissance Music 4. Woodbridge: Boydell, 2005.

———. "Music in the Arts Faculty of Paris in the Thirteenth and Early Fourteenth Centuries." PhD diss., Oxford University, 2005.

Riethmüller, Albrecht. "Probleme der spekulativen Musiktheorie im Mittelalter." In *Rezeption des antiken Fachs im Mittelalter*, edited by Frieder Zaminer, 163–201. Geschichte der Musiktheorie 3. Darmstadt: Wissenschaftliche Buchgesellschaft, 1990.

Rispoli, Gioia Maria. "La musica e le forme." In *La Musa dimenticata: Aspetti dell'esperienza musicale greca in età ellenistica; Convengo di studio Pisa, Scuola Normale Superiore 21–23 settembre 2006*, edited by Maria Chiara Martinelli, Francesco Pelosi, and Carlo Pernigotti, 101–139. Pisa: Edizioni della Normale, 2009.

Rodnite, Helen. "The Doctrine of the Trinity in Guillaume de Conches' Glosses on Macrobius: Texts and Studies." PhD diss., Columbia University, 1972.

Rodnite Lemay, Helen. "Science and Theology at Chartres: The Case of the Supracelestial Waters." *British Journal for the History of Science* 10 (1977), 226–236.

Rohloff, Ernst, ed. *Der Musiktraktat des Johannes de Grocheo nach den Quellen neu herausgegeben mit Übersetzung ins Deutsche und Revisionsbericht*. Media Latinitas musica 2. Leipzig: Komissionsverlag Gebrüder Reinecke, 1943.

Ronca, Italo, ed. *Guillelmi de Conchis Dragmaticon philosophiae*. Corpus Christianorum. Continuatio Mediaevalis 152. Turnhout: Brepols, 1997.

Ronca, Italo, and Matthew Curr, eds. *William of Conches: A Dialogue on Natural Philosophy*. Notre Dame Texts in Medieval Culture 2. Notre Dame, IN: University of Notre Dame Press, 1997.

Rosier-Catach, Irène. "Le commentaire des *Glosulae* et des *Glosae* de Guillaume de Conches sur le chapitre *De voce* des *Institutiones Grammaticae* de Priscien." *Cahiers de l'Institut du Moyen-Âge grec et latin* 63 (1993), 115–144.

———. "The *Glosulae in Priscianum* and Its Tradition." In *Flores grammaticae: Essays in Memory of Vivien Law*, 81–99. Henry Sweet Society Studies in the History of Linguistics 10. Münster: Nodus, 2005.

Rosolato, Guy. "La voix: Entre corps et langage." *Revue française de psychanalyse* 37 (1974), 75–94.

Rössl, Joachim, and Charlotte Ziegler. *Zisterzienserstift Zwettl: Katalog der Handschriften des Mittelalters 4: Codex 301–424*. Scriptorium Ordinis Cisterciensium Monasterii BMV in Zwettl 4. Vienna and Munich: Schroll, 1997.

Ruini, Cesarino, ed. *Ameri Practica artis musice*. Corpus scriptorum de musica 25. Neuhausen-Stuttgart: American Institute of Musicology, 1977.

Sachs, Klaus Jürgen. "Boethius and the Judgement of the Ears: A Hidden Challenge in Medieval and Renaissance Music Theory." In *The Second Sense: Studies in Hearing and Musical Judgement from Antiquity to the Seventeenth Century*, edited by Charles Burnett, Michael Fend, and Penelope Gouk, 169–198. Warburg Institute Surveys and Texts 22. London: The Warburg Institute, 1991.

Schmid, Hans, ed. *Musica et scolica enchiriadis una cum aliquibus tractatulis adiunctis*. Veröffentlichungen der Musikhistorischen Kommission 3. Munich: Bayerische Akademie der Wissenschaften, 1981.

Schrade, Leo. "Das propädeutische Ethos in der Musikanschauung des Boethius." *Zeitschrift für Geschichte der Erziehung und des Unterrichts* 20 (1930), 179–215.

Schrimpf, Gangolf. "Bernhard von Chartres, die Rezeption des 'Timaios' und die neue Sicht der Natur." In *Aufbruch—Wandel—Erneuerung: Beiträge zur "Renaissance" des 12. Jahrhunderts*, edited by Georg Wieland, 181–210. Stuttgart–Bad Cannstatt: Frommann-Holzboog, 1995.

Scruton, Roger. *The Aesthetics of Music*. New York: Oxford University Press, 1997.

Sedley, David. "The Dramatis Personae of Plato's *Phaedo*." In *Philosophical Dialogues: Plato, Hume, Wittgenstein*, edited by Timothy J. Smiley, 3–26. Proceedings of the British Academy 85. Oxford: Oxford University Press, 1995.

Shanzer, Danuta. "Augustine's Disciplines: *Silent diutius Musae Varronis*?" In *Augustine and the Disciplines: From Cassiciacum to Confessions*, edited by Karla Pollman and Mark Vessey, 69–112. Oxford: Oxford University Press, 2005.

———. "Felix Capella: *Minus sensus quam nominis pecudalis*." *Classical Philology* 81 (1986), 62–81.

———. *A Philosophical and Literary Commentary on Martianus Capella's* De Nuptiis Philologiae et Mercurii Book 1. University of California Publications. Classical Studies 32. Berkeley: University of California, 1986.

———. "Tatwine: An Independent Witness to the Text of Martianus Capella's *De Grammatica*?" *Rivista di filologia e d'istruzione classica* 112 (1984), 292–313.

Shaviro, Steven. *Without Criteria: Kant, Whitehead, Deleuze, and Aesthetics*. Cambridge, MA: MIT Press, 2009.

Silk, Edmund Taite, ed. *Saeculi noni auctoris in Boetii Consolationem philosophiae commentarius*. Papers and Monographs of the American Academy in Rome 9. Rome: American Academy in Rome, 1935.

Silverstein, Theodore. "*Elementatum*: Its Appearance Among the Twelfth-Century Cosmogonists." *Mediaeval Studies* 16 (1954), 156–162

———. "Guillaume de Conches and the Elements: *Homiomeria* and *Organica*." *Mediaeval Studies* 26 (1964), 363–367.

Smith, Andrew. *Porphyrii philosophi Fragmenta*. Bibliotheca scriptorum Graecorum et Romanorum Teubneriana. Stuttgart: Teubner, 1993.

Smits, E. R. "New Evidence for the Authorship of the Commentary on the First Six Books of Virgil's *Aeneid* Commonly Attributed to Bernardus Silvestris." In *Non nova, sed nove: Mélanges de civilisation médiévale dédiés à Willem Noomen*, edited by Martin Gosman and Jaap Van Os, 239–246. Mediaevalia Groningana 5. Groningen: Bouma's Boekhuis, 1984.

Sodano, Angelo Raffaele, ed. *Porphyrii In Platonis Timaeum commentariorum fragmenta*. Naples: s. n., 1964.

Somfai, Anna. "Calcidius' *Commentary* on Plato's *Timaeus* and Its Place in the Commentary Tradition: The Concept of *Analogia* in Text and Diagrams." In *Philosophy, Science and Exegesis in Greek, Arabic and Latin Commentaries*, Vol. 1, 203–220. 2 vols. Bulletin of the Institute of Classical Studies 83. London: Institute of Classical Studies, University of London, 2004.

Southern, Richard. *Medieval Humanism and Other Studies*. Oxford: Blackwell, 1970.

———. *Platonism, Scholastic Method and the School of Chartres, The Stenton Lecture 1978*. Reading: University of Reading Press, 1979.

———. *Scholastic Humanism and the Unification of Europe*. Vol. 1, *Foundations*. Oxford: Blackwell, 1995.

Speer, Andreas. "The Discovery of Nature: The Contributions of the Chartrians to Twelfth-Century Attempts to Found a *scientia naturalis*." *Traditio* 52 (1997), 135–151.

———. *Die entdeckte Natur: Untersuchungen zu Begründungsversuchen einer 'scientia naturalis' im 12. Jahrhundert*. Leiden: Brill, 1995.

———. "*Scientia quadruvii: Musica* in den 'Timaios'-Kommentaren des 12. Jahrhunderts." In *Musik – und die Geschichte der Philosophie und Naturwissenschaften im Mittelalter: Fragen zur Wechselwirkung von "musica" und "philosophia" im Mittelalter*, edited by Frank Hentschel, 99–123. Studien und Texte zur Geistesgeschichte des Mittelalters 62. Leiden: Brill, 1998.

Spitzer, Leo. *Classical and Christian Ideas of World Harmony: Prolegomena to an Interpretation of the Word 'Stimmung.'* Edited by Anna Granville Hatcher. Baltimore: Johns Hopkins Press, 1963.

Stahl, William Harris, trans. *Macrobius: Commentary on the Dream of Scipio*. Records of Civilization: Sources and Studies 48. New York: Columbia University Press, 1952.

Steege, Benjamin. "'The Nature of Harmony': A Translation and Commentary." In *The Oxford Handbook of Neo-Riemannian Music Theories*, edited by Edward Gollin and Alexander Rehding, 55–91. Oxford: Oxford University Press, 2011.

Steglich, Rudolf, ed. *Die* Quaestiones in musica: *Ein Choraltraktat des zentralen Mittelalters und ihr mutmasslicher Verfasser Rudolf von St. Trond (1070–1138)*. Leipzig: Breitkopf & Härtel, 1911.

Steiner, Mark. *The Applicability of Mathematics as a Philosophical Problem*. Cambridge, MA: Harvard University Press, 1998.

Stock, Brian. *Myth and Science in the Twelfth Century: A Study of Bernard Silvester*. Princeton: Princeton University Press, 1972.

Strunk, Oliver, ed. *Source Readings in Music History*. Rev. ed. New York: W. W. Norton, 1998.

Sullivan, Blair. "*Nota* and *notula*: Boethian Semantics and the Written Representation of Musical Sound in Carolingian Treatises." *Musica disciplina* 47 (1993), 71–97.

Switalski, B. Wladislaus. *Des Chalcidius Kommentar zu Plato's "Timaeus": Eine historisch-kritische Untersuchung*. Beiträge zur Geschichte der Philosophie des Mittelalters 3.6. Münster: Aschendorff, 1902.

Tanay, Dorit. *Noting Music, Marking Culture: The Intellectual Context of Rhythmic Notation, 1250–1400*. Musicological Studies and Documents 46. N.p.: American Institute of Musicology, 1999.

Tarán, Leonardo. "The Creation Myth in Plato's *Timaeus*." In *Collected Papers (1962–1999)*, 303–340. Leiden: Brill, 2001.

———. *Speusippus of Athens: A Critical Study with a Collection of the Related Texts and Commentary*. Philosophia antiqua 39. Leiden: Brill, 1981.

Tarlazzi, Caterina. "L'*Epistola de anima* di Isacco di Stella: Studio della tradizione ed edizione del testo." *Medioevo: Rivista di storia della filosofia medievale* 36 (2011), 167–278.

Tarrant, Harold, et al., trans. *Proclus: Commentary on Plato's Timaeus*. Cambridge: Cambridge University Press, 2007–.

———. *Thrasyllan Platonism*. Ithaca: Cornell University Press, 1993.

Taylor, A. E. *Plato. The Man and his Work*. 3rd ed., revised and expanded. London: Methuen, 1929.

Taylor, C. C. W. "The Arguments in the *Phaedo* Concerning the Thesis that the Soul Is a *Harmonia*." In *Essays on Plato's Psychology*, edited by Ellen Wagner, 51–67. Lanham: Lexington Books, 2001.

Teeuwen, Mariken. *Harmony and the Music of the Spheres: The Ars musica in Ninth-Century Commentaries on Martianus Capella*. Mittellateinische Studien und Texte 30. Leiden: Brill, 2002.

———. "The Study of Martianus Capella's *De nuptiis* in the Ninth Century." In *Learned Antiquity: Scholarship and Society in the Near East, the Greco-Roman World, and the Early Medieval West*, edited by Alasdair A. MacDonald, Michael W. Twomey, and Gerrit J. Reinik. Groningen Studies in Cultural Change 5. Leuven: Peeters, 2003.

———. "The Vocabulary of Martianus Capella Commentators of the Ninth Century: Some Observations." *Archivum Latinitatis Medii Aevi* 63 (2005), 71–81.

Towey, Alan. "Aristotle and Alexander on Hearing and Instantaneous Change: A Dilemma in Aristotle's Account of Hearing." In *The Second Sense: Studies in Hearing and Musical Judgement from Antiquity to the Seventeenth Century*, edited by Charles Burnett, Michael Fend, and Penelope Gouk, 7–18. Warburg Institute Surveys and Texts 22. London: The Warburg Institute, 1991.

Uexküll, Jakob von. *Bedeutungslehre*. Bios, Abhandlungen zur theoretischen Biologie und ihrer Geschichte sowie zur Philosophie der organischen Naturwissenschaften, Bd. 10. Leipzig: Verlag von J. A. Barth, 1940.

———. *A Foray into the Worlds of Animals and Humans, with A Theory of Meaning*. Translated by Joseph D. O'Neil. Posthumanities 12. Minneapolis: University of Minnesota Press, 2010.

———. "The New Concept of *Umwelt:* A Link between Science and the Humanities," trans. Gösta Brunow. *Semiotica* 134 (2001), 111–123.

———. *Theoretische Biologie*. Berlin: Verlag von Gebrüder Paetel, 1920.

Vassányi, Miklós. *Anima Mundi: The Rise of the World Soul Theory in Modern German Philosophy*. International Archives of the History of Ideas 202. Dordrecht: Springer, 2011.

Verdeyen, Paul, ed. *Guillelmi a Sancto Theodorico Opera omnia V: Opuscula adversus Petrum Abaelardum et de fide*. Corpus Christianorum. Continuatio Mediaevalis 89A. Turnhout: Brepols, 2007.

Vossen, Peter. "Über die Elementen-Syzygien." In *Liber floridus: Mittellateinische Studien; Paul Lehmann zum 65. Geburtstag am 13. Juli 1949*, edited by Bernhard Bischoff and Suso Brechter, 33–46. St. Ottilien: EOS Verlag der Erzabtei, 1950.

Waesberghe, Joseph Smits van, ed. *Adalboldi Episcopi Ultraiectensis Epistola cum tractatu de musica instrumentali humanaque ac mundana*. Divitiae Musicae Artis A.II. Buren: Knuf, 1981.

———, ed. *Guidonis Aretini Micrologus*. Corpus scriptorum de musica 4. [Rome]: American Institute of Musicology, 1955.

———, ed. *Johannes Affligemenisis, De musica cum tonario*. Corpus scriptorum de musica 1. [Rome]: American Institute of Musicology, 1950.

Wagner, Ellen. "Supervenience and the Thesis that the Soul Is a *Harmonia*." In *Essays on Plato's Psychology*, edited by Ellen Wagner, 69–88. Lanham: Lexington Books, 2001.

Waszink, J. H., ed. *Timaeus a Calcidio translatus commentarioque instructus*. 2nd ed. Plato Latinus 4. London: The Warburg Institute, 1975.

Watkins, Holly, and Melina Esse. "Down with Disembodiment; or, Musicology and the Material Turn." *Women and Music* 19 (2015), 160–168.

Weisheipl, James A. "Classification of the Sciences in Medieval Thought." *Mediaeval Studies* 27 (1965), 54–90.

———. "The Nature, Scope, and Classification of the Sciences." In *Science in the Middle Ages*, edited by David C. Lindberg, 461–482. Chicago: University of Chicago Press, 1978.

Westra, Haijo Jan. "Martianus Capella: Addenda et Corrigenda to Volume II." In *Catalogus translationum et commentariorum: Mediaeval and Renaissance Latin Translations and Commentaries*, edited by Paul Oskar Kristeller and Ferdinand E. Cranz, 6: 185–186. Washington, DC: Catholic University Press, 1986.

———, ed. *The Berlin Commentary on Martianus Capella's De nuptiis Philologiae et Mercurii*. Mittellateinische Studien und Texte 20. Leiden: Brill, 1994.

———, ed. *The Commentary on Martianus Capella's* De nuptiis Philologiae et Mercurii *Attributed to Bernardus Silvestris*. Studies and Texts 80. Toronto: Pontifical Institute of Mediaeval Studies, 1986.

Wetherbee, Winthrop. *Alan of Lille: Literary Works*. Dumbarton Oaks Medieval Library 22. Cambridge, MA: Harvard University Press, 2013.

———. "Philosophy, Cosmology, and the Twelfth-Century Renaissance." In *A History of Twelfth-Century Western Philosophy*, edited by P. Dronke, 21–53. Cambridge: Cambridge University Press, 1988.

———. *Platonism and Poetry in the Twelfth Century: The Literary Influence of the School of Chartres*. Princeton: Princeton University Press, 1972.

Whitney, Elspeth. *Paradise Restored: The Mechanical Arts from Antiquity through the Thirteenth Century*. Transactions of the American Philosophical Society 80.1. Philadelphia: American Philosophical Society, 1990.

Whittaker, John, ed. *Alcinoos: Enseignement des doctrines de Platon*. Translated by Pierre Louis. Paris: Belles lettres, 1990.

Williams, John R. "The Quest for the Author of the *Moralium dogma philosophorum*, 1931–1956." *Speculum* 32 (1957), 736–747.

Willis, James, ed. *Ambrosii Theodosii Macrobii Commentarii in Somnium Scipionis*. Bibliotheca scriptorum Graecorum et Romanorum Teubneriana. Leipzig: B. G. Teubner, 1963.

———, ed. *Martianus Capella*. Bibliotheca scriptorum Graecorum et Romanorum Teubneriana. Leipzig: B. G. Teubner, 1983.

van Winden, J. C. M. *Calcidius on Matter: His Doctrines and Sources: A Chapter in the History of Platonism*. Philosophia Antiqua 9. Leiden: Brill, 1959.

Wissowa, Georg, and Wilhelm Kroll, eds. *Paulys Realencyclopädie der classischen Altertumswissenschaft: Neue Bearbeitung*. Stuttgart: Alfred Druckenmüller, 1958.

Wittmann, Michael. *Vox atque sonus: Studien zur Rezeption der Aristotelischen Schrift "De anima" und ihre Bedeutung für die Musiktheorie*. Musikwissenschaftliche Studien 4. Pfaffenweiler: Centaurus-Verlagsgesellschaft, 1987.

Woerther, Frédérique. "Music and the Education of the Soul in Plato and Aristotle: Homoeopathy and the Formation of Character." *Classical Quarterly* 58 (2008), 89–103.

Wright, Craig. *Music and Ceremony at Notre Dame of Paris, 500–1150*. Cambridge Studies in Music. Cambridge: Cambridge University Press, 2008.

Wrobel, Johann, ed. *Platonis "Timaeus" intreprete Chalcidio cum eiusdem commentario*. Leipzig: B. G. Teubner, 1876.

Ziomkowski, Robert. *Manegold of Lautenbach: Liber contra Wolfelmum*. Dallas Medieval Texts and Translations 1. Paris and Leuven: Peeters, 2002.

INDEX